Lecture Notes in Computer Science 10568

Commenced Publication in 1973
Founding and Former Series Editors:
Gerhard Goos, Juris Hartmanis, and Jan van Leeuwen

More information about this series at http://www.springer.com/series/7412

Jie Zhou · Yunhong Wang
Zhenan Sun · Yong Xu
Linlin Shen · Jianjiang Feng
Shiguang Shan · Yu Qiao
Zhenhua Guo · Shiqi Yu (Eds.)

Biometric Recognition

12th Chinese Conference, CCBR 2017
Shenzhen, China, October 28–29, 2017
Proceedings

 Springer

Editors
Jie Zhou
Tsinghua University
Beijing
China

Yunhong Wang
Beihang University
Beijing
China

Zhenan Sun
Institute of Automation
Chinese Academy of Sciences
Beijing
China

Yong Xu
Harbin Institute of Technology (Shenzhen)
Shenzhen
China

Linlin Shen
Shenzhen University
Shenzhen
China

Jianjiang Feng
Tsinghua University
Beijing
China

Shiguang Shan
Institute of Computing Technology
Chinese Academy of Sciences
Beijing
China

Yu Qiao
Shenzhen Institute of Advanced Technology
Chinese Academy of Sciences
Shenzhen
China

Zhenhua Guo
Graduate School at Shenzhen
Tsinghua University
Shenzhen
China

Shiqi Yu
Shenzhen University
Shenzhen
China

ISSN 0302-9743   ISSN 1611-3349 (electronic)
Lecture Notes in Computer Science
ISBN 978-3-319-69922-6   ISBN 978-3-319-69923-3 (eBook)
https://doi.org/10.1007/978-3-319-69923-3

Library of Congress Control Number: 2017957549

LNCS Sublibrary: SL6 – Image Processing, Computer Vision, Pattern Recognition, and Graphics

Printed on acid-free paper

This Springer imprint is published by Springer Nature
The registered company is Springer International Publishing AG
The registered company address is: Gewerbestrasse 11, 6330 Cham, Switzerland

Preface

Security and privacy issues are topics of growing concern in the Internet era and as a result of the growing demand for anti-terrorism activity. This raises great interest in biometric technology, which provides substantial advantages over traditional password- or token-based solutions. Biometric recognition systems have been extensively deployed worldwide in law enforcement, government, and consumer applications. In China, thanks to the huge population using the Internet and smart phones and to the great investment of the government in security and privacy protection, the biometric market is rapidly growing and biometric research keeps attracting the attention of numerous scholars and practitioners. These researchers have been addressing various biometric problems, promoting diverse biometric techniques, and making significant contributions to the biometrics field. The Chinese Conference on Biometric Recognition (CCBR), an annual conference held in China, provides an excellent platform for biometric researchers to share their progress and advances in the development and applications of biometric theory, technology, and systems.

CCBR 2017 was held in Shenzhen during October 28–29, 2017, and was the 12th in the series that has been successfully held in Beijing, Hangzhou, Xi'an, Guangzhou, Jinan, Shenyang, Tianjin, and Chengdu since 2000. CCBR 2017 received 137 submissions, each of which was reviewed by at least three experts from the Program Committee. Based on the rigorous review comments, 15 papers (11%) were selected for oral presentation and 65 papers (47%) for poster presentation. These papers make up this volume of the CCBR 2017 conference proceedings covering a wide range of topics: face recognition and analysis; fingerprint, palm-print, and vascular biometrics; iris biometrics; gesture and gait; emerging biometrics; voice and speech; video surveillance; feature extraction and classification theory; and behavioral biometrics.

We would like to thank all the authors, reviewers, invited speakers, volunteers, and Organizing Committee members, without whom CCBR 2017 would not have been successful. We also wish to acknowledge the support of the Chinese Association for Artificial Intelligence, Institute of Automation of Chinese Academy of Sciences, Springer, Shenzhen University, Harbin Institute of Technology (Shenzhen), Pingan

Technology, ZKTeco Co., Ltd., IrisKing Co., Ltd., Taisau Co., Ltd. for sponsoring, and China Fortune Land Development Co., Ltd. this conference. Special thanks are due to Dan Chen and Hao Gui for their hard work in organizing the conference.

October 2017

Jie Zhou
Yunhong Wang
Zhenan Sun
Yong Xu
Linlin Shen
Jianjiang Feng
Shiguang Shan
Yu Qiao
Zhenhua Guo
Shiqi Yu

Organization

Advisory Committee

Anil K. Jain   Michigan State University, USA
Tieniu Tan   Institute of Automation, Chinese Academy of Sciences, China
David Zhang   The Hong Kong Polytechnic University, Hong Kong,
                        SAR China
Jingyu Yang   Nanjing University of Science and Technology, China
Xilin Chen   Institute of Computing Technology,
                        Chinese Academy of Sciences, China
Jianhuang Lai   Sun Yat-sen University, China

General Chairs

Jie Zhou   Tsinghua University, China
Yunhong Wang   Beihang University, China
Zhenan Sun   Institute of Automation, Chinese Academy of Sciences, China
Yong Xu   Harbin Institute of Technology (Shenzhen), China
Linlin Shen   Shenzhen University, China

Program Chairs

Jianjiang Feng   Tsinghua University, China
Shiguang Shan   Institute of Computing Technology,
                        Chinese Academy of Sciences, China
Yu Qiao   Shenzhen Institutes of Advanced Technology,
                        Chinese Academy of Sciences, China
Zhenhua Guo   Graduate School at Shenzhen, Tsinghua University, China
Shiqi Yu   Shenzhen University, China

Program Committee

Caikou Chen   Yangzhou University, China
Cunjian Chen   Canon Information Technology (Beijing), China
Fanglin Chen   National University of Defense Technology, China
Weihong Deng   Beijing University of Posts and Telecommunications, China
Yuchun Fang   Shanghai University, China
Keren Fu   Shanghai Jiao Tong University, China
Quanxue Gao   Xidian University, China
Shenghua Gao   ShanghaiTech University, China
Yongxin Ge   Chongqing University, China
Xun Gong   Southwest Jiaotong University, China

Zhe Guo	Northwestern Polytechnical University, China
Zhenhua Guo	Graduate School at Shenzhen, Tsinghua University, China
Hu Han	Institute of Computing Technology, Chinese Academy of Sciences, China
Zhenyu He	Harbin Institute of Technology (Shenzhen), China
Ran He	Institute of Automation, Chinese Academy of Sciences, China
Qingyang Hong	Xiamen University, China
Dewen Hu	National University of Defense Technology, China
Di Huang	Beihang University, China
Wei Jia	Hefei University of Technology, China
Xiaoyuan Jing	Wuhan University, China
Wenxiong Kang	South China University of Technology, China
Kurban Ubul	Xinjiang University, China
Zhihui Lai	Shenzhen University, China
Huibin Li	Xi'an Jiaotong University, China
Weijun Li	Institute of Semiconductors, Chinese Academy of Sciences, China
Wenxin Li	Peking University, China
Zhifeng Li	Shenzhen Institutes of Advanced Technology, Chinese Academy of Sciences, China
Dong Liang	Nanjing University of Aeronautics and Astronautics, China
Shengcai Liao	Institute of Automation, Chinese Academy of Sciences, China
Eryun Liu	Zhejiang University, China
Feng Liu	Shenzhen University, China
Heng Liu	Anhui University of Technology, China
Manhua Liu	Shanghai Jiao Tong University, China
Yiguang Liu	Sichuan University, China
Zhi Liu	Shandong University, China
Guangming Lu	Harbin Institute of Technology (Shenzhen), China
Jiwen Lu	Tsinghua University, China
Xiao Luan	Chongqing University of Posts and Telecommunications, China
Haifeng Sang	Shenyang University of Technology, China
Fumin Shen	University of Electronic Science and Technology of China, China
Kejun Wang	Harbin Engineering University, China
Yiding Wang	North China University of Technology, China
Yi Wang	Hong Kong Baptist University, Hong Kong, SAR China
Xiangqian Wu	Harbin Institute of Technology, China
Lifang Wu	Beijing University of Technology, China
Xiaohua Xie	Sun Yat-sen University, China
Yuli Xue	Beihang University, China
Haibin Yan	Beijing University of Posts and Telecommunications, China
Gongping Yang	Shandong University, China
Jinfeng Yang	Civil Aviation University of China, China
Jucheng Yang	Tianjin University of Science and Technology, China

Wankou Yang	Southeast University, China
Yingchun Yang	Zhejiang University, China
Yilong Yin	Shandong University, China
Weiqi Yuan	Shenyang University of Technology, China
Baochang Zhang	Beihang University, China
Lei Zhang	The Hong Kong Polytechnic University, Hong Kong, SAR China
Lin Zhang	Tongji University, China
Man Zhang	Institute of Automation, Chinese Academy of Sciences, China
Yongliang Zhang	Zhejiang University of Technology, China
Zhaoxiang Zhang	Institute of Automation, Chinese Academy of Sciences, China
Cairong Zhao	Tongji University, China
Qijun Zhao	Sichuan University, China
Weishi Zheng	Sun Yat-sen University, China
Xiuzhuang Zhou	Capital Normal University, China
En Zhu	National University of Defense Technology, China
Wangmeng Zuo	Harbin Institute of Technology, China

Organizing Committee Chair

Zhifeng Lai	Shenzhen University

Contents

Face

Fingerprint, Palm-Print and Vascular Biometrics

Emerging Biometrics

Voice and Speech

Video Surveillance

Feature Extraction and Classification Theory

Behavioral Biometrics

Face

Detecting Face with Densely Connected Face Proposal Network

Shifeng Zhang[1,2], Xiangyu Zhu[1,2], Zhen Lei[1,2(✉)], Hailin Shi[1,2],
Xiaobo Wang[1,2], and Stan Z. Li[1,2]

[1] CBSR & NLPR, Institute of Automation, Chinese Academy of Sciences,
Beijing, China
{shifeng.zhang,xiangyu.zhu,zlei,hailin.shi,xiaobo.wang,szli}@nlpr.ia.ac.cn
[2] University of Chinese Academy of Sciences, Beijing, China

Abstract. Accuracy and efficiency are two conflicting challenges for face detection, since effective models tend to be computationally prohibitive. To address these two conflicting challenges, our core idea is to shrink the input image and focus on detecting small faces. Specifically, we propose a novel face detector, dubbed the name Densely Connected Face Proposal Network (DCFPN), with high performance as well as real-time speed on the CPU devices. On the one hand, we subtly design a lightweight-but-powerful fully convolutional network with the consideration of efficiency and accuracy. On the other hand, we use the dense anchor strategy and propose a fair L1 loss function to handle small faces well. As a consequence, our method can detect faces at 30 FPS on a single 2.60 GHz CPU core and 250 FPS using a GPU for the VGA-resolution images. We achieve state-of-the-art performance on the AFW, PASCAL face and FDDB datasets.

Keywords: Face detection · Small face · Region proposal network

1 Introduction

Face detection is one of the fundamental problems in computer vision. With the great progress, face detection has been successfully applied in our daily life. However, there are still some tough challenges in the uncontrolled face detection problem. The challenges mainly come from two requirements for face detectors: (1) The large variation of facial changes requires face detectors to accurately address a complicated face and non-face classification problem; (2) The large search space of arbitrary face positions and sizes further imposes a time efficiency requirement. These two requirements are conflicting, since high-accuracy face detectors tend to be computationally expensive.

To meet these challenges, face detection has been studied mainly in two ways. One way is cascade based methods and it starts from the pioneering work [1]. After that, a number of improvements to the Viola-Jones face detector have been proposed in the past decade [2]. The other way is CNN [3] based methods

© Springer International Publishing AG 2017
J. Zhou et al. (Eds.): CCBR 2017, LNCS 10568, pp. 3–12, 2017.
https://doi.org/10.1007/978-3-319-69923-3_1

and some works based on R-CNN [4] have demonstrated the state-of-the-art performance on face detection tasks.

However, these two ways focus on different aspects. The former tends to great efficiency while the latter cares more about high accuracy. To perform well on both speed and accuracy, one natural idea is to combine the advantages of them. Therefore, cascade CNN based methods [5] are proposed that put features learned by CNN into cascade framework so as to boost the performance and keep efficient. However, there are two problems in cascaded CNN based methods: (1) Their speed is negatively related to the number of faces on the image. The speed would dramatically degrade as the number of faces increases; (2) The cascade based detectors optimize each component separately, making the training process extremely complicated and the final model sub-optimal.

Therefore, it is still one of the remaining open issues for practical face detectors to achieve real-time speed on CPU as well as maintain high performance. In this paper, we develop a state-of-the-art face detector with CPU real-time speed. Our core idea is to **shrink the input image and focus on detecting small faces**. Reducing high-resolution images into low-resolution images can significantly improve the detection speed, but it also results in smaller faces that need to pay more attention. Specifically, our DCFPN has a lightweight-but-powerful network with the consideration of efficiency and accuracy. Besides, we use the dense anchor strategy [6] and propose a fair L1 loss to handle small faces well. As a consequence, for VGA images to detect faces bigger than 40 pixels, the DCFPN can run at 30 FPS on a single CPU core and 250 FPS on a GPU card. For clarity, the main contributions of this work can be summarized as four-fold:

- We develop a novel face detector with real-time speed on the CPU devices;
- We design a lightweight-but-powerful fully convolution network for face detection;
- We propose a fair L1 loss and use dense anchor strategy to handle small faces well;
- We achieve state-of-the-art performance on common face detection benchmarks.

2   Related Work

Face detection approaches can be roughly divided into two different categories. One is based on hand-craft features, and the other one is built on CNN. This section briefly reviews them and refer more detailed survey to [2,7,8].

Hand-Craft Based Methods. The milestone work of Viola-Jones [1] proposes to use Haar feature, Adaboost learning and cascade inference for face detection. After that, many subsequent works focus on new local features [9,10], new boosting algorithms [11–13] and new cascade structures [14–16]. Besides the cascade framework, the deformable part model (DPM) [17] is introduced into face detection task by [18–22], which use supervised parts, more pose partition, better training or more efficient inference to achieve better performance.

CNN Based Methods. They show advantages in face detection recently. CCF [23] uses boosting on top of CNN features for face detection. Faceness [24] trains fully convolutional networks (FCN) to generate heat map of facial parts and then use the heat map to generate face proposals. CascadeCNN [5] uses six cascaded CNNs to efficiently reject backgrounds in three stages. STN [25] proposes a new Supervised Transformer Network and a ROI convolution for face detection. MTCNN [26] presents a multi-task cascaded CNNs based framework for joint face detection and alignment.

Generally, hand-craft based methods can achieve real-time speed on the CPU devices, but they are not accurate enough for the uncontrolled face detection problem. With learned feature and classifier directly from the image, CNN based methods can differentiate faces from highly cluttered backgrounds, while they are too time-consuming to reach real-time speed. Notably, our proposed DCFPN is able to achieve real-time speed on the CPU devices as well as maintain state-of-the-art detection performance.

3 Densely Connected Face Proposal Network

This section presents detail of DCFPN. It includes three key components: the lightweight-but-powerful architecture, the dense anchor strategy and the fair L1 loss.

3.1 Lightweight-But-Powerful Architecture

The architecture of DCFPN encourages feature reuse and leads to a substantial reduction of parameters. As illustrated in Fig. 1, the whole architecture consists of two parts.

Rapidly Digested Convolutional Layers (RDCL). It is designed for high efficiency via quickly reducing the image spatial size by 16 times with narrow but large kernels. On one side, face detection is a two classification problem

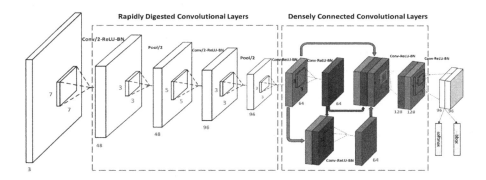

Fig. 1. The structure of DCFPN.

and does not require very wide network, hence the narrow kernels are powerful enough and can result in faster running speed, especially for CPU devices. On the other side, the large kernels are to alleviate the information loss brought by spatial size reducing.

Densely Connected Convolutional Layers (DCCL). Each layer in DCCL is directly connected to every other layer in a feed-forward fashion, and DCCL ends with two micro inception layers. There are two motivations. Firstly, the DCCL is designed to enrich the receptive field of the last convolutional layer that is used to predict the detection results. As listed in Table 1, the last convolutional layer of DCFPN has a large scope of receptive field from 75 to 235 pixels, which is consistent with our default anchors and is important for the network to learn visual patterns for different scales of faces. Secondly, the DCCL aims at combining coarse-to-fine information across deep CNN models to improve the recall rate and precision of detection. Since the information of the interest region is distributed over all levels of CNN with multiple level abstraction and they should be well organised.

To sum up, our lightweight-yet-powerful architecture consists of RDCL and DCCL. The former is designed to achieve real-time speed on the CPU devices. The latter aims at enriching the receptive fields and combining coarse-to-fine information across different layers to handle faces of various scales.

3.2   Dense Anchor Strategy

As listed in Table 1, we use 5 default anchors that are associated with the last convolutional layer. Hence, these 5 default anchors have the same tiling interval on the image (*i.e.*, 16 pixels). It is obviously that there is a tiling density imbalance problem. Comparing with large anchors (i.e., 64×64, 128×128 and 256×256), small anchors (i.e., 16×16 and 32×32) are too sparse, which results in low recall rate of small faces.

To improve the recall rate of small faces, we use the dense anchor strategy proposed by [6] for small anchor. Specifically, without this dense anchor strategy, there are 5 anchors for every center of the receptive filed (Fig. 2(a)). To densify one type of anchors, this strategy uniformly tiles several anchors around the center of one receptive field instead of only tiling one. As illustrated in Fig. 2(b) and (c), the sampling interval of 16×16 and 32×32 anchor are densified to 4 and 8 pixels, respectively. Consequently, for every center of the receptive filed, there are total 23 anchors (16 from 16×16 anchor, 4 from 32×32 anchor and 3 from the rest three anchors). This dense anchor strategy is crucial to detect small faces.

Table 1. The receptive field of the last convolutional layer and the default anchor of our DCFPN.

Receptive field	75×75, 107×107, 139×139, 171×171, 203×203, 235×235
Default anchor	16×16, 32×32, 64×64, 128×128, 256×256

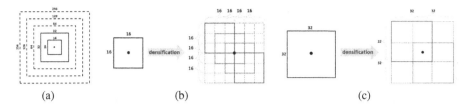

Fig. 2. Some illustrations of anchors. (a) 5 default anchors at a center of receptive filed. (b) 16 × 16 anchor densification. (c) 32 × 32 anchor densification. Best viewed in color.

3.3 Fair L1 Loss

Our model is jointly optimized by two loss functions, L_{cls} and L_{reg}, which compute errors of score and coordinate, respectively. We adopt a 2-class softmax loss for L_{cls}. As for L_{reg}, to locate small faces well, we propose the fair L1 loss that directly regresses the predicted box's relative center coordinate and its width and height as follows:

$$
\begin{aligned}
t_x &= x - x^a, & t_y &= y - y^a, & t_w &= w, & t_h &= h \\
t_x^* &= x^* - x^a, & t_y^* &= y^* - y^a, & t_w^* &= w^*, & t_h^* &= h^*
\end{aligned}
\tag{1}
$$

where x, y, w, and h denote the center coordinates and width and height. Variables x, x^a, and x^* are for the predicted box, anchor box, and GT box (likewise for y,w,h). The scale normalization is implemented to have scale-invariance loss value as follows:

$$
L_{reg}(t, t^*) = \sum_{j \in \{x,y,w,h\}} fair_{L_1}(t_j - t_j^*)
\tag{2}
$$

in which

$$
fair_{L_1}(z_j) = \begin{cases} |z_j| \ / \ gt_w & if \ j \in \{x, w\} \\ |z_j| \ / \ gt_h & otherwise \end{cases}
\tag{3}
$$

where gt_w and gt_h denote the GT box's width and height. It equally treats small and big face by directly regressing box's relative center coordinate and its width and height.

3.4 Training and Implementation Details

The DCFPN is trained end-to-end by the stochastic gradient descent (SGD) as follows:

Training Labels. Face detection is a face and non-face classification task, and a binary label (*i.e.,* the positive or negative label) need to be assigned to each anchor during the training stage. The positive anchor is defined by the following two conditions: (i) Matching each face to the anchor with the best jaccard overlap; (ii) Matching anchors to any face with jaccard overlap higher than a threshold (usually 0.5). Anchors that do not be matched by the two conditions are negative anchors.

Training Data. Our model is trained on 12880 images from the WIDER FACE [27] training set. To enrich the training dataset, each training image is sequentially processed by the color distortion, random cropping, scale transformation and horizontal flipping, eventually getting a 512×512 square sub-image from original image. The groundtruth bounding box is ignored if its center coordinate is located outside of the square sub-image. In the training process, each mini-batch is collected randomly from 48 images. For each mini-batch, all of the positive anchors and half of the negative anchors are used to train our model.

Implementation Details. We randomly initialize all layers by drawing weights from a zero-mean Gaussian distribution with standard deviation 0.01. We use 0.9 momentum and 0.0005 weight decay. The maximum number of iterations is 100 k, and the initial learning rate is set to 0.1 and multiplied by 0.1 every 20 k iterations. Our model is implemented in Caffe framework [28].

4   Experiments

In this section, we firstly analyze our model in an ablative way, then evaluate it on the common face detection benchmarks, finally introduce its runtime efficiency.

4.1   Model Analysis

We carry out extensive ablation experiments on the FDDB dataset to analyze our model. For all the experiments, we use the same settings, except for specified changes to the components. To better understand DCFPN, we ablate each component one after another to examine how each component affects the final performance. Firstly, we replace the fair L1 loss with smooth L1 loss. Meantime, the target of regression is the same as RPN. Secondly, we ablate the dense anchor strategy [6]. Finally, we take the place of DCCL with four convolutional layers, which all have 3×3 kernel size and whose output number are 64, 128, 192 and 256, respectively.

Some promising conclusions can be summed up according to the ablative results listed in Table 2. Firstly, the comparison between the first and second columns in Table 2 indicates that the fair L1 loss function effectively increases the mAP performance by 0.7%, owning to locating small faces well. Secondly, ablating the dense anchor strategy results in 0.8% decline, showing the importance of this strategy. Finally, the DCCL is used to enrich the receptive fields and combine coarse-to-fine information across different layers to handle faces of various scales. From the results listed in Table 2, we can observe that the mAP on FDDB is reduced from 93.7% to 93.2% after replacing the DCCL. The sharp decline (*i.e.*, 0.5%) demonstrates the effectiveness of the DCCL.

Table 2. Ablative results on FDDB. Accuracy means the true positive rate at 1000 false positives.

Component	DCFPN			
Designed architecture?	✓	✓	✓	
Dense anchor strategy [6]?	✓	✓		
Fair L1 loss?	✓			
Accuracy (mAP)	95.2	94.5	93.7	93.2

4.2   Evaluation on Benchmark

This section presents the face detection bechmarking using our proposed DCFPN approach. We compare our results with those of other leading methods.

AFW Database [22]. It contains 205 images with 473 labeled faces from Flickr. We evaluate our detector on this dataset and compare with well known research and commercial face detectors. Research detectors include [19, 21, 22, 24, 29]. Commercial detectors include Face.com, Face++ and Google Picasa. As can be observed from Fig. 3(a), our method outperforms strong all others by a large margin.

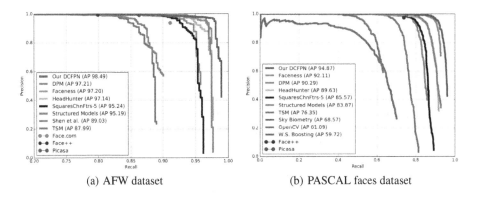

(a) AFW dataset   (b) PASCAL faces dataset

Fig. 3. Precision-recall curves.

PASCAL Face Database [21]. It consists of 851 images with 1335 labeled faces and is collected from the test set of PASCAL person layout dataset, which is a subset of PASCAL VOC. There are large face appearance and pose variations in this dataset. Note that this dataset is designed for person layout detection and head annotation is used as face annotation. The cases when the face is occluded are common. Figure 3(b) shows that our DCFPN method outperforms all other detectors.

FDDB Database [30]. It has 5, 171 faces in 2, 845 images taken from news articles on Yahoo websites. FDDB uses ellipse face annotations while our DCFPN outputs rectangle outputs. This inconsistency has a great impact to the continuous score. For a more fair comparison under the continuous score evaluation, we regress a transformation matrix according to the ellipse and rectangle annotations, and then transform our rectangle outputs to ellipse outputs. As shown in Fig. 4(a) and (b), our DCFPN performs better than all of the published face detection methods, demonstrating that DCFPN is able to robustly detect unconstrained faces.

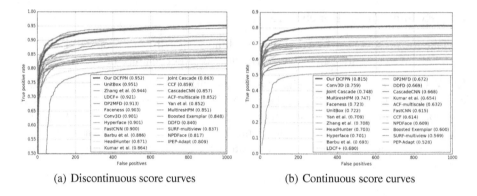

(a) Discontinuous score curves   (b) Continuous score curves

Fig. 4. Evaluation on the FDDB dataset.

4.3   Runtime Efficiency

CNN based methods have always been accused of their runtime efficiency. Recent CNN algorithms are getting faster on high-end GPUs. However, in most practical applications, especially CPU based applications, they are not fast enough.

Our DCFPN is efficient and accurate enough to meet practical requirements. Specifically, due to the great ability to detect small faces, the proposed DCFPN can shrink the test images by a few times and detect small faces, so as to reach real-time speed as well as maintain high performance. This means that faces can be efficiently detected by shrinking the test image and detecting smaller ones. With this advantage, our method can detect faces bigger than 40 pixels at 30 FPS on a 2.60 GHz CPU for the VGA-resolution images. Besides, our method with only 3.2 M parameter can directly run on a GPU card at 250 FPS for the VGA-resolution images.

5   Conclusion

In this paper, we propose a novel face detector with real-time speed on the CPU devices as well as high performance. On the one hand, our DCFPN has a lightweight-but-powerful framework that can well incorporate CNN features from different sizes of receptive field at multiple levels of abstraction. On the other hand, we use the dense anchor strategy and propose the fair L1 loss function to handle small faces well. The state-of-the-art performance on three challenge datasets shows its ability to detect faces in the uncontrolled environment. The proposed detector is very fast, achieving 30 FPS to detect faces bigger than 40 pixels on CPU and can be accelerated to 250 FPS on GPU for the VGA-resolution images.

Acknowledgments. This work was supported by the National Key Research and Development Plan (Grant No. 2016YFC0801002).

References

1. Viola, P., Jones, M.J.: Robust real-time face detection. IJCV **57**(2), 137–154 (2004)
2. Zhang, C., Zhang, Z.: A survey of recent advances in face detection. Technical report (2010)
3. Lecun, Y., Bengio, Y.: Convolutional networks for images, speech, and time-series. In: The Handbook of Brain Theory and Neural Networks (1995)
4. Girshick, R., Donahue, J., Darrell, T., Malik, J.: Rich feature hierarchies for accurate object detection and semantic segmentation. In: CVPR (2014)
5. Li, H., Lin, Z., Shen, X., Brandt, J., Hua, G.: A convolutional neural network cascade for face detection. In: CVPR (2015)
6. Zhang, S., Zhu, X., Lei, Z., Shi, H., Wang, X., Li, S.Z.: FaceBoxes: a CPU real-time face detector with high accuracy. In: IJCB (2017)
7. Yang, M.H., Kriegman, D.J., Ahuja, N.: Detecting faces in images: a survey. PAMI **24**(1), 34–58 (2002)
8. Zafeiriou, S., Zhang, C., Zhang, Z.: A survey on face detection in the wild: past, present and future. Comput. Vis. Image Underst. **138**, 1–24 (2015)
9. Yang, B., Yan, J., Lei, Z., Li, S.Z.: Aggregate channel features for multi-view face detection. In: IJCB (2014)
10. Zhang, L., Chu, R., Xiang, S., Liao, S., Li, S.Z.: Face detection based on multi-block LBP representation. In: Lee, S.-W., Li, S.Z. (eds.) ICB 2007. LNCS, vol. 4642, pp. 11–18. Springer, Heidelberg (2007). doi:10.1007/978-3-540-74549-5_2
11. Huang, C., Ai, H., Li, Y., Lao, S.: High-performance rotation invariant multiview face detection. PAMI **29**(4), 671–686 (2007)
12. Jones, M., Viola, P.: Fast multi-view face detection. In: MERL (2003)
13. Zhang, C., Platt, J.C., Viola, P.A.: Multiple instance boosting for object detection. In: NIPS (2005)
14. Bourdev, L., Brandt, J.: Robust object detection via soft cascade. In: CVPR (2005)
15. Li, S.Z., Zhu, L., Zhang, Z.Q., Blake, A., Zhang, H.J., Shum, H.: Statistical learning of multi-view face detection. In: Heyden, A., Sparr, G., Nielsen, M., Johansen, P. (eds.) ECCV 2002. LNCS, vol. 2353, pp. 67–81. Springer, Heidelberg (2002). doi:10.1007/3-540-47979-1_5
16. Xiao, R., Zhu, L., Zhang, H.J.: Boosting chain learning for object detection. In: ICCV (2003)
17. Felzenszwalb, P.F., Girshick, R.B., McAllester, D., Ramanan, D.: Object detection with discriminatively trained part-based models. PAMI **32**(9), 1627–1645 (2010)

18. Ghiasi, G., Fowlkes, C.C.: Occlusion coherence: detecting and localizing occluded faces. arXiv preprint arXiv:1506.08347 (2015)
19. Mathias, M., Benenson, R., Pedersoli, M., Gool, L.: Face detection without bells and whistles. In: Fleet, D., Pajdla, T., Schiele, B., Tuytelaars, T. (eds.) ECCV 2014. LNCS, vol. 8692, pp. 720–735. Springer, Cham (2014). doi:10.1007/978-3-319-10593-2_47
20. Yan, J., Lei, Z., Wen, L., Li, S.Z.: The fastest deformable part model for object detection. In: CVPR (2014)
21. Yan, J., Zhang, X., Lei, Z., Li, S.Z.: Face detection by structural models. Image Vis. Comput. **32**(10), 790–799 (2014)
22. Zhu, X., Ramanan, D.: Face detection, pose estimation, and landmark localization in the wild. In: CVPR (2012)
23. Yang, B., Yan, J., Lei, Z., Li, S.Z.: Convolutional channel features. In: ICCV (2015)
24. Yang, S., Luo, P., Loy, C.C., Tang, X.: From facial parts responses to face detection: a deep learning approach. In: ICCV (2015)
25. Chen, D., Hua, G., Wen, F., Sun, J.: Supervised transformer network for efficient face detection. In: Leibe, B., Matas, J., Sebe, N., Welling, M. (eds.) ECCV 2016. LNCS, vol. 9909, pp. 122–138. Springer, Cham (2016). doi:10.1007/978-3-319-46454-1_8
26. Zhang, K., Zhang, Z., Li, Z., Qiao, Y.: Joint face detection and alignment using multi-task cascaded convolutional networks. arXiv preprint arXiv:1604.02878 (2016)
27. Yang, S., Luo, P., Loy, C., Tang, X.: Wider face: a face detection benchmark. In: CVPR (2016)
28. Jia, Y., Shelhamer, E., Donahue, J., Karayev, S., Long, J., Girshick, R., Guadarrama, S., Darrell, T.: Caffe: convolutional architecture for fast feature embedding. In: ACM MM (2014)
29. Shen, X., Lin, Z., Brandt, J., Wu, Y.: Detecting and aligning faces by image retrieval. In: CVPR (2013)
30. Jain, V., Learned-Miller, E.G.: Fddb: a benchmark for face detection in unconstrained settings. UMass Amherst Report (2010)

Deep Transformation Learning for Depression Diagnosis from Facial Images

Yajun Kang, Xiao Jiang, Ye Yin, Yuanyuan Shang, and Xiuzhuang Zhou[(✉)]

College of Information Engineering, Capital Normal University, Beijing 100048, China
{Yajun.Kang,Xiao.Jiang,Ye.Yin,Xiuzhuang.Zhou}@cnu.edu.cn

Abstract. As a severe emotional disorder, depression seriously affects people's thoughts, behavior, feeling, sense of well-being and daily life. With the increasing number of depression patients, it has aroused the attention of researchers in this field. An effective and reliable machine learning based system has been expected to facilitate automated depression diagnose. This paper presents a novel deep transformation learning (DTL) method for visual-based depression recognition. Different from most existing depression recognition methods, our DTL trains a deep neural network that learns a set of hierarchical nonlinear transformations to project original input features into a new feature subspace, so as to capture the non-linear manifold of depression data. Extensive experiments are conducted on the AVEC2014 dataset and the results demonstrate that our method is highly competitive to several state-of-the-art methods for automated prediction of the severity of depression.

Keywords: Automated depression diagnosis · Facial analysis · Deep transformation learning · Deep neural network

1 Introduction

In recent years, mental health problems have been gained more and more attention from all walks of life.Major depression disorder (MDD), also known as mood disorders, is a serious threat to people's mental health in all age groups [1]. Depressed people may feel sad, helpless, anxious, empty, worried, loss of appetite, irritable, or restless, severe depression patients could even lead to suicide [2]. Although depression seriously hampers people's normal life and work, it can be cured by drugs, psychotherapy, physical therapy or other treatment methods [3]. Currently, the diagnosis of depression depends mainly on experienced clinical experts, but because of the increase in depression patients, the early stage diagnosis of depression patients and follow-up treatment can be constrained. It is therefore desirable to provide an objective assessment and rapid automatic diagnosis machine-based system, which can bring timely treatment to depressed people.

Most of the existing methods for automated depression diagnosis are based on either visual information [4–6] or audio cue [7–9]. Visual and vocal features are

© Springer International Publishing AG 2017
J. Zhou et al. (Eds.): CCBR 2017, LNCS 10568, pp. 13–22, 2017.
https://doi.org/10.1007/978-3-319-69923-3_2

indispensable in depression recognition, since depressed people tend to behave disorderly in facial expressions, gestures, language, etc. [10]. Previous studies indicated that facial expression plays a primary role in representing emotional states of human being. Some researchers attempt to extract facial features from static face images to describe expressions, e.g. [11]. However, these features are incompetency for some subtle expressions, such as anger and disgust, so people gradually turn their focus to facial expressions in video data because they convey richer information than images. In this paper, we focus on video-based nonverbal behavior around facial region for diagnosis of depression. We first extract facial features from videos by a pre-trained convolutionary neural network (CNN) [12]. Then, a set of hierarchical nonlinear transformations are learned by deep trans-formation learning (DTL) to project these features into a new feature subspace for better prediction of the depression. The basic idea of our method is illus-trated in Fig. 1. Experimental results on the AVEC2014 dataset [13] demon-strate that our method achieves better performance than several state-of-the-art visual-based methods for depression recognition.

The rest part of the paper is organized as follows: Sect. 2 briefly reviews related work. Section 3 provides a detailed description of the proposed method. In Section 4, we present and discuss the experimental results on the AVEC2014 dataset. Section 5 concludes the paper.

2   Related Work

Face analysis technology has become a popular topic and been applied in many fields in recent years, such as facial expression recognition [14], face verification [15] and so on. Facial features have also been proved to be effective for diagnosis of depression. In this paper, we mainly consider visual-based nonverbal behavior for depression recognition.

Most existing methods estimate the score of depression from facial region by two steps: feature extraction and regression. The goal of feature extraction is to get a representation robust to irrelevant factors. Regression methods are used to predict the score of depression, such as support vector regression (SVR) [16], partial least squares (PLS) [17] and canonical correlation analysis (CCA) [18]. In [19], the authors extract visual information from voice and silence segments separately, and built depression recognition models by using affective dimen-sions. Finally, these features were fed into a SVR for prediction. In the video based approach from [10], the authors focused on three features, Local Binary Patterns (LBP), Edge Orientation Histogram (EOH) and Local Phase Quan-tization (LPQ). Motion History Histograms (MHH) is then applied to capture the dynamic movement of the features. Finally, PLS and linear regression are applied to predict the depression score. In [20], the author extracted two differ-ent features, LGBP_TOP and LPQ features from the inner facial region that correspond to eyes and mouth area. Then the Canonical Correlation Analysis (CCA) is applied on the feature vectors and the two features are combined to generate the final regression results. In [21], Wen et al. extracted dynamic feature descriptor LPQ from Three Orthogonal Planes (LPQ_TOP) in facial region sub-volumes, and adopted sparse coding and MFA to further improve the accuracy for depression diagnosis.

While encouraged recognition performance has been achieved by previous methods, automated depression diagnosis remains open so far. Different from previous methods, our proposed DTL method can capture non-linear manifold of depression data in an efficient way, and the experimental results demonstrated the efficacy of our approach for the automated diagnosis of depression from facial images.

3   Proposed Approach

In this section, we will elaborate the DTL algorithm for visual-based depression recognition. The structure of the proposed DTL network is shown in Fig. 1.

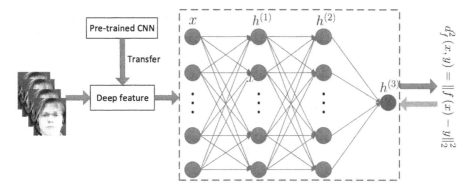

Fig. 1. The framework of proposed DTL method for depression diagnosis. For a given video, we extract face features by a pre-trained CNN model. Then they are mapped into the new feature subspace as $h^{(1)}$ and $h^{(2)}$ by using deep transformation learning (DTL). The output of the last layer of DTL is used to determine the score of depression.

3.1   DTL

As shown in Fig. 1, DTL employs a deep neural network to learn the nonlinear transformations where the back propagation algorithm is used to train the model. Assume the network has $M+1$ layers, and there are d_m units in the mth layer, where $m = 1, 2, ..., M$. Given a face feature vector $x \in R^{d_0}$ (extracted by a pre-trained CNN), the output of the first layer is $h^{(1)} = s\left(W^{(1)}x + b^{(1)}\right) \in R^{d_1}$, where $W^{(1)} \in R^{d_1 \times d_0}$ is a weight matrix in the first layer, $b^{(1)} \in R^{d_1}$ is a bias vector, and $s(\cdot)$ represents a nonlinear activation function, e.g., the $tanh$ or $sigmoid$ function. The output of the first layer $h^{(1)}$ is used as the input of the second layer. Similarly, the output of the second layer is $h^{(2)} = s\left(W^{(1)}h^{(1)} + b^{(2)}\right) \in R^{d_1}$, the output of the mth layer is $h^{(m)} = s\left(W^{(m)}h^{(m-1)} + b^{(m)}\right) \in R^{d_m}$, and the output of the last layer can be computed as:

$$f(x) = h^{(M)} = s\left(W^{(M)}h^{(M-1)} + b^{(M)}\right) \in R^{d_M} \tag{1}$$

where the mapping $f : R^{d_o} \mapsto R^{d_M}$ is a parametrized nonlinear function determined by the parameters $W^{(m)}$ and $b^{(m)}$, $m = 1, 2, ..., M$. Given a face feature x, they can be finally represented as $f(x) = h^{(M-1)}$. At the top level, $f(x) = h^{(M)}$ represents the score of depression, and the regression loss is defined by the distance between it and the label y, which can be computed as the squared Euclidean distance:

$$d_f^2(x, y) = (f(x) - y)^2 \tag{2}$$

In this setting, our DTL is formulated as the following optimization problem:

$$\arg\min_f J = \frac{1}{2}g(d_f^2(x,y)) + \frac{\lambda}{2}\sum_{m=1}^{M}(\left\|W^{(m)}\right\|_F^2 + \left\|b^{(m)}\right\|_2^2) \tag{3}$$

where $g(z) = \frac{1}{\beta}\log\left(1 + \exp(\beta z)\right)$ is logistic loss function, $\|A\|_F$ and λ are Frobenius norm of the matrix A, and regularization parameter, respectively. To solve the optimization problem in Eq. (3), we use the stochastic gradient descent (SGD) to obtain the network parameters $\left\{W^{(m)}, b^{(m)}\right\}$, $m = 1, 2, ..., M$. The gradient of the objective function J can be computed as follows:

$$\frac{\partial J}{\partial W^{(m)}} = \Delta^{(m)}h^{(m-1)} + \lambda W^{(m)} \tag{4}$$

$$\frac{\partial J}{\partial b^{(m)}} = \Delta^{(m)} + \lambda b^{(m)} \tag{5}$$

where $h^{(0)} = x$. For $m = 1, 2, ..., M-1$ we have the following updating equations:

$$\Delta^{(M)} = g'(c)\left(h^{(M)} - y\right) \odot s'\left(z^{(M)}\right) \tag{6}$$

$$\Delta^{(m)} = W^{(m+1)^T}\Delta^{(m+1)} \odot s'\left(z^{(m)}\right) \tag{7}$$

where the operation $\odot$ denotes the element-wise multiplication, c and $z^{(m)}$ are defined as follows:

$$c \triangleq d_f^2(x, y) \tag{8}$$

$$z^{(m)} \triangleq W^{(m)}h^{(m-1)} + b^{(m)} \tag{9}$$

Finally, $W^{(m)}$ and $b^{(m)}$ can be updated by using the following stochastic gradient descent algorithm until convergence:

$$W^{(m)} = W^{(m)} - \mu\frac{\partial J}{\partial W^{(m)}} \tag{10}$$

$$b^{(m)} = b^{(m)} - \mu\frac{\partial J}{\partial b^{(m)}} \tag{11}$$

where μ is the learning rate. Algorithm 1 summarizes the detailed procedure of the proposed DTL method.

Algorithm 1. DTL

Input: Training set: $X = \{x_1, x_2, \cdots x_n\}$ with n videos, where $x_i = \{x_{i1}, x_{i2}, \cdots, x_{il}\}$ with l frames; number of network layers $M + 1$; learning rate μ; iteration number I_t; regularization parameter λ; label $L = \{y_1, y_2, \cdots, y_n\}$.

Output: Weights and biases: $\left\{ W^{(m)}, b^{(m)} \right\}_{m=1}^{M}$

//Initialization:

Initialize $\left\{ W^{(m)}, b^{(m)} \right\}_{m=1}^{M}$

//Optimization by back prorogation:

for $t = 1, 2, ..., I_t$ **do**

    for $i = 1, 2, ..., nl$ **do**

        Randomly select a sample in X to obtain a frame x.

        //Forward propagation

        for $m = 1, 2, ..., M$ **do**

            Do forward propagation to get $h^{(m)}$.

        end

        //Computing gradient

        for $m = M, M - 1, ..., 1$ **do**

            Obtain gradient by back propagation according to Eqs.(4) and (5).

        end

        //Model updating

        for $m = 1, 2, ..., M$ **do**

            Update $W^{(m)}$ and $b^{(m)}$ according to Eqs.(10) and (11).

        end

    end

end

Return: $\left\{ W^{(m)}, b^{(m)} \right\}_{m=1}^{M}$

---

4   Experiments

4.1   AVEC2014 Depression Database

The proposed approach is evaluated on the AVEC2014 depression database [13]. There are 300 video clips (ranging in duration from 6 s to 4 min 8 s) from 292 subjects that performed a human-computer interaction task. These videos in the database was recorded by a webcam and microphone. There is only one person in each clip. The average age of the subjects is 31.5 years old, with a range of 18 to 63 years. In the AVEC2014 depression sub-challenge, there are 150 video clips which are split into three partitions: training, development, and test, with 50 videos in each dataset. Some examples of video frames in AVEC2014 depression database are shown in Fig. 2.

4.2   Experimental Setting

For the AVEC2014 dataset, we sample 50 frames for each video clip with an interval of 10 frames due to large amount of video frames. There are totally about

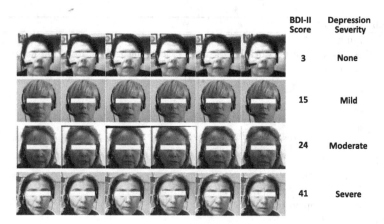

	BDI-II Score	Depression Severity
	3	None
	15	Mild
	24	Moderate
	41	Severe

Fig. 2. Sampled video frames with depression score (BDI-II) and its severity categories from the AVEC2014 depression dataset.

7500 video frames extracted from the AVEC2014 dataset in our experiment. Then, face detection and feature extraction are performed for these video frames by a face recognition toolkit (SeetaFace) [22]. Specifically, each face region is cropped into 256×256 to extract LBP and LPQ face features.

As a deep learning component of SeetaFace toolkit, VIPLFaceNet [22] contains seven convolution layers and two fully connected layers. The output of the VIPLFaceNet FC2 layer (2048-dimensional) is used as the feature input to our DTL. For DTL, we train a deep neural network with four layers ($M = 3$), and the learning rate μ, regularization parameter λ and sharpness parameter β are empirically set to 0.005, 10^{-10}, 13, respectively. $W^{(m)}$ and $b^{(m)}$ are initialized as identity matrix and a zero vector, respectively. The *tanh* function is adopted as the activation function.

4.3   Results and Analysis

Comparison with Pervious Methods. For a fair comparison, we compare our approach with five previous visual-based depression recognition methods on the AVEC2014 dataset. One of the main differences between our approach and previous works is that we combine the deep transformation learning and regression prediction in a unified framework. Note that the support vector regression (SVR), partial least square (PLS) and canonical correlation analysis (CCA) regression are used in [10,19,20], respectively. Different from the above mentioned method, our DTL trains a deep neural network that learns a set of hierarchical nonlinear transformations to project original input features into one new feature subspace, so as to capture non-linear manifold of depression data. From Table 1 we can see that our approach achieves better performance on the dataset.

Table 1. Comparison of different recognition methods on the AVEC2014 dataset.

Method	RMSE	MAE
Baseline [13]	10.86	8.86
Espinosa et al. [19]	11.91	9.35
Jan et al. [10]	10.50	8.44
Kaya et al. [20]	9.97	7.96
Zhu et al. [23]	10.36	7.82
Proposed	**9.43**	**7.74**

Effectiveness of DTL. We conduct two different experiments to demonstrate the effectiveness of DTL. In the first experiment, three DTL-based methods with different features input (LBP, LPQ, and SeetaFace) are compared. The results are summarized in Table 2. From Table 2 we can see that SeetaFace feature transferred from CNN achieves the best recognition performance in comparison with the other local features (LBP and LPQ). Specifically, SeetaFace achieves an average RMSE of 9.43 and MAE of 7.74. In the second experiment, three different depression recognition methods using the same deep feature input (SeetaFace) are compared: SeetaFace+SVR, SeetaFace + PCA + SVR, and SeetaFace + DTL. The comparison result of different methods are listed in Table 3. Again, we can see that SeetaFace + DTL achieves the best recognition performance in the experiment. These results show the effectiveness of the proposed DTL for depression recognition.

Table 2. Comparison of DTL with different features on the AVEC2014 dataset.

Method	RMSE	MAE
LPQ + DTL	11.35	9.41
LBP + DTL	12.06	9.27
SeetaFace + DTL	**9.43**	**7.74**

Table 3. Comparison of different recognition methods with deep feature (SeetaFace) on the AVEC2014 dataset.

Feature	Methods	RMSE	MAE
SeetaFace	SVR	9.64	8.33
SeetaFace	PCA + SVR	10.39	8.69
SeetaFace	DTL	9.43	7.74

Parameters Analysis. There are several import parameters in our DTL methods: the number of network layers $M+1$, the learning rate μ, and the regularization parameter λ. We investigate how these parameters affect the performance of DTL in the experiment. Fig. 3(a) presents the depression MAE/RMSE versus different number of network layers on the AVEC2014 dataset. We can see that the best performance of DTL can be achieved when the number of network layers is set to 4. Also, we investigate how the regularization parameter λ affects the recognition performance of DTL. From Fig. 3(b) we can see that the best performance of DTL is achieved when λ is set as 10^{-10}. Finally, we investigate how the learning rate μ affect the performance of DTL. From Fig. 4(a) we can see that the loss function converges faster when the learning rate is set to 0.005. Moreover, we can also see from Fig. 4(b) that the best recognition result can be achieved when using this learning rate.

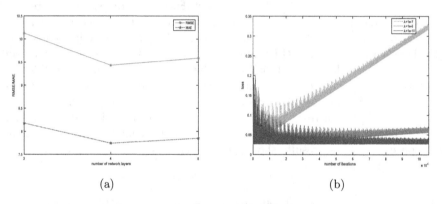

(a)   (b)

Fig. 3. (a) The depression MAE/RMSE versus different number of network layers on the AVEC2014 dataset; (b) The loss versus number of iterations with different regularization parameter λ on the AVEC2014 dataset.

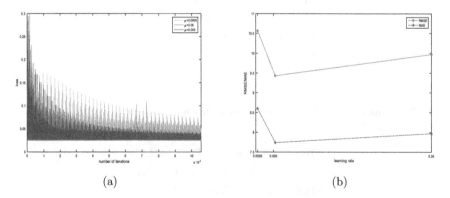

(a)   (b)

Fig. 4. (a) The loss versus number of iterations with different learning rates on the AVEC2014 dataset; (b) The depression MAE/RMSE versus different learning rates on the AVEC2014 dataset.

5   Conclusion

In this paper, we have presented a new DTL method for depression recognition. DTL trains a deep neural network that learns a set of hierarchical nonlinear transformations to project original input features into a new feature subspace, so as to capture the non-linear manifold of depression data. Extensive experiments on the AVEC2014 dataset demonstrated that our method is highly competitive to several state-of-the-art methods for prediction of the severity of depression. In this paper, we only use the visual-based face appearance cue for depression recognition. However, facial dynamic features (e.g., optical flow) can also be effective for improved recognition performance, as reported [23]. In future work, we will investigate multimodal features (e.g., facial appearance, dynamic features and audio cues) for more effective depression recognition.

Acknowledgement. This work is supported by the National Natural Science Foundation of China under grant No. 61373090, the Beijing Great Scholars Program under grant No. CIT&TCD20170322, and the Youth Innovative Research Team of Capital Normal University.

References

1. Belmaker, R.H., Agam, G.: Major depressive disorder. N. Engl. J. Med. **358**(1), 55–68 (2008)
2. Kessler, R.C., Berglund, P., Demler, O., Jin, R., Koretz, D., Merikangas, K.R., Rush, A.J., Walters, E.E., Wang, P.S.: The epidemiology of major depressive disorder: results from the national comorbidity survey replication (NCS-R). Jama **289**(23), 3095–3105 (2003)
3. Pincus, H.A., Pettit, A.R.: The societal costs of chronic major depression. J. Clin. Psychiatry **62**, 5–9 (2000)
4. Jones, I.H., Pansa, M.: Some nonverbal aspects of depression and schizophrenia occurring during the interview. J. Nerv. Mental Dis. **167**(7), 402–409 (1979)
5. Fisch, H.-U., Frey, S., Hirsbrunner, H.-P.: Analyzing nonverbal behavior in depression. J. Abnorm. Psychol. **92**(3), 307 (1983)
6. Ellgring, H.: Non-verbal Communication in Depression. Cambridge University Press, Cambridge (2007)
7. Yang, Y., Fairbairn, C., Cohn, J.F.: Detecting depression severity from vocal prosody. IEEE Trans. Affect. Comput. **4**(2), 142–150 (2013)
8. Balsters, M.J.H., Krahmer, E.J., Swerts, M.G.J., Vingerhoets, A.J.J.M.: Verbal and nonverbal correlates for depression: a review. Curr. Psychiatry Rev. **8**(3), 227–234 (2012)
9. Joshi, J., Goecke, R., Alghowinem, S., Dhall, A., Wagner, M., Epps, J., Parker, G., Breakspear, M.: Multimodal assistive technologies for depression diagnosis and monitoring. J. Multimodal User Interfaces **7**(3), 217–228 (2013)
10. Jan, A., Meng, H., Gaus, Y.F.A., Zhang, F., Turabzadeh, S.: Automatic depression scale prediction using facial expression dynamics and regression. In: Proceedings of the 4th International Workshop on Audio/Visual Emotion Challenge, pp. 73–80. ACM (2014)

11. Shan, C., Gong, S., McOwan, P.W.: Facial expression recognition based on local binary patterns: a comprehensive study. Image Vis. Comput. **27**(6), 803–816 (2009)
12. Li, H., Lin, Z., Shen, X., Brandt, J., Hua, G.: A convolutional neural network cascade for face detection. In: Proceedings of the IEEE Conference on Computer Vision and Pattern Recognition, pp. 5325–5334 (2015)
13. Valstar, M., Schuller, B., Smith, K., Almaev, T., Eyben, F., Krajewski, J., Cowie, R., Pantic, M.: AVEC 2014: 3D dimensional affect and depression recognition challenge. In: Proceedings of the 4th International Workshop on Audio/Visual Emotion Challenge, pp. 3–10. ACM (2014)
14. Almaev, T.R., Valstar, M.F.: Local Gabor binary patterns from three orthogonal planes for automatic facial expression recognition. In: 2013 Humaine Association Conference on Affective Computing and Intelligent Interaction (ACII), pp. 356–361. IEEE (2013)
15. Junlin, H., Jiwen, L., Tan, Y.-P.: Discriminative deep metric learning for face verification in the wild. In: Proceedings of the IEEE Conference on Computer Vision and Pattern Recognition, pp. 1875–1882 (2014)
16. Basak, D., Pal, S., Patranabis, D.C.: Support vector regression. Neural Inf. Process.-Lett. Rev. **11**(10), 203–224 (2007)
17. Geladi, P., Kowalski, B.R.: Partial least-squares regression: a tutorial. Anal. Chim. Acta **185**, 1–17 (1986)
18. Hardoon, D.R., Szedmak, S., Shawe-Taylor, J.: Canonical correlation analysis: an overview with application to learning methods. Neural Comput. **16**(12), 2639–2664 (2004)
19. Espinosa, H.P., Escalante, H.J., Villaseñor-Pineda, L., Gómez, M.M., Pinto-Avedaño, D., Reyez-Meza, V.: Fusing affective dimensions and audio-visual features from segmented video for depression recognition: INAOE-BUAP's participation at AVEC'14 challenge. In: Proceedings of the 4th International Workshop on Audio/Visual Emotion Challenge, pp. 49–55. ACM (2014)
20. Kaya, H., Çilli, F., Salah, A.A.: Ensemble CCA for continuous emotion prediction. In: Proceedings of the 4th International Workshop on Audio/Visual Emotion Challenge, pp. 19–26. ACM (2014)
21. Wen, L., Li, X., Guo, G., Zhu, Y.: Automated depression diagnosis based on facial dynamic analysis and sparse coding. IEEE Trans. Inf. Forensics Secur. **10**(7), 1432–1441 (2015)
22. Liu, X., Kan, M., Wanglong, W., Shan, S., Chen, X.: VIPLFaceNet: an open source deep face recognition SDK. arXiv preprint arXiv:1609.03892 (2016)
23. Zhu, Y., Shang, Y., Shao, Z., Guo, G.: Automated depression diagnosis based on deep networks to encode facial appearance and dynamics. IEEE Trans. Affect. Comput. (2017)

Comparison and Fusion of Multiple Types of Features for Image-Based Facial Beauty Prediction

Fangmei Chen[1]([✉]), David Zhang[2], Cunrui Wang[3], and Xiaodong Duan[3]

[1] Information and Communication Engineering Department,
Dalian Minzu University, Dalian 116600, China
cfm@dlnu.edu.cn
[2] Biometrics Research Centre and the Department of Computing,
The Hong Kong Polytechnic University, Kowloon, Hong Kong
[3] Computer Science and Engineering Department,
Dalian Minzu University, Dalian 116600, China

Abstract. Facial beauty prediction is an emerging research topic that has many potential applications. Existing works adopt features either suggested by putative rules or borrowed from other face analysis tasks, without an optimization procedure. In this paper, we make a comprehensive comparison of different types of features in terms of facial beauty prediction accuracy, including the rule-based features, global features, and local descriptors. Each type of feature is optimized by dimensionality reduction and feature selection. Then, we investigate the optimal fusion strategy of multiple types of features. The results show that the fusion of AAM, LBP, and PCANet features obtains the best performance, which can serve as a competitive baseline for further studies.

Keywords: Facial beauty · Feature extraction · Fusion

1 Introduction

Image-based facial beauty prediction has many potential applications such as aesthetic surgery planning, cosmetic recommendation, photo retouching, entertainment, etc. The core of facial beauty prediction is discovering the relationship between low-level visual features and high-level perceived attractiveness.

Two categories of features have been adopted in existing works. One includes putative rules, most of which are defined in the form of some ideal ratio. Computational models of facial beauty have been built with those putative ratio features [1–3]. It is found that only a small subset of ratio features is important for facial beauty prediction [2]. Another category of features is inspired from face recognition studies, e.g., shape parameters, eigenface, Gabor filter responses [4], local binary patterns (LBP) [5], etc. Researchers often combine multiple types of facial features to build regression models of facial beauty. For example, Eisenthal et al. [6] combine geometric features, hair color, and skin smoothness into the

© Springer International Publishing AG 2017
J. Zhou et al. (Eds.): CCBR 2017, LNCS 10568, pp. 23–30, 2017.
https://doi.org/10.1007/978-3-319-69923-3_3

regression model. Nguyen et al. [7] concatenate LBP, Gabor filter responses, color moment, shape context, and shape parameters as a feature vector and apply PCA to reduce the dimensionality. Gray et al. [8] design a multi-scale feature model by local filters and down-sampling. Although so many features have been used for facial beauty prediction, few works compare the discriminative power of different types of features and investigate the optimal fusion strategy.

In this paper, we make a comprehensive study on comparison and fusion of features for facial beauty prediction. Besides the features used in previous works, AAM parameters [9] and PCANet features [10] are also employed. Firstly, different types of features are compared in terms of facial beauty prediction performance. Secondly, dimensionality reduction and feature selection techniques are performed to optimize each type of feature. Thirdly, we investigate the optimal fusion strategy of multiple types of features to further improve the performance. The model built by the optimal fusion strategy can serve as a competitive benchmark for further studies.

2   Feature Extraction

Most putative rules on facial beauty are defined as ratios. We review the relevant studies and provide a concise summary in our previous work [18]. There are 26 putative ratio rules, including the neoclassical and golden ratio rules [1,2]. 98 landmarks are extracted (see Fig. 1), which are distributed on the major facial organs. Given the landmarks, it is convenient to calculate the ratios.

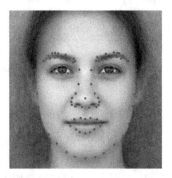

Fig. 1. The layout of 98 landmarks on a face image.

For global features, shape parameters, eigenface, and AAM features are considered. First, the shape, texture, and appearance models are learned on a training face image set. Then, each input face image can be represented by a vector of model parameters. The x- and y- coordinates of the 98 landmarks are concatenated to form a vector that represents the geometry of the face, i.e., $[x_1, x_2, \ldots, x_{98}, y_1, y_2, \ldots, y_{98}]^T$. Given the landmark vectors, shape features can be obtained by Procrustes superimposition [11]. Then, PCA is performed on the shape vectors to reduce the dimensionality to 50, which keeps 97.3% of the total energy. The 50-dimensional component scores are called shape parameters. Eigenface [12] is a method of texture representation. A face image is represented by a vector of pixel values. Suppose the training data are $I_1, \ldots, I_n$, the mean vector μ is subtracted from I_i, and a data matrix $X = [I_1 - \mu, \ldots, I_n - \mu]$ is constructed. The eigenvectors of $X^T X$ are called eigenfaces. AAM [9] parameterizes and combines the shape and the texture of a face. We keep the first 100 dimensions, which explains 97% of the appearance variations.

Local descriptors are also considered. Gabor filters encode facial shape and texture information over a range of spatial scales. Following [4], we use five scales and eight orientations. Other parameters are set as $k_{max} = \pi$, $f = \sqrt{2}$, and $\sigma = 2\pi$. LBP operator encodes every pixel of an image with an 8-bit binary number by thresholding the neighborhood of the pixel with the center pixel value. The histogram of the labels is used as a texture descriptor. In our implementation, the face images are cropped and resized into 128×128 and divided into 7×7 local regions. Then the $\text{LBP}_{8,2}^{u2}$ operator [5] is applied to each region. PCANet is a simple deep learning network proposed by [10]. It has three components: cascaded PCA filtering, binary hashing, and block-wise histogram, as shown in Fig. 2. For each input image, the output of the first layer filtering is L_1 images, which are inputs for the second layer. Each of the L_1 input images has L_2 outputs, which are binarized and converted to a single integer-valued image by

$$I^{(3)} = \sum_{l=1}^{L_2} 2^{l-1} I_l^{(2)}. \tag{1}$$

The pixel value of $I^{(3)}$ is in the range $[0, 2^{L_2} - 1]$. The L_1 images in layer three are divided into 64 blocks of size 16×16. The histograms of the blocks are cascaded to obtain the final feature vector. In our implementation, $k_1 = k_2 = 7$, $L_1 = L_2 = 8$.

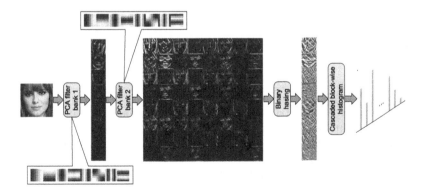

Fig. 2. Illustration of PCANet feature extraction.

3   Feature Selection

Because the number of training data is often limited, removing the irrelevant and redundant variables will alleviate the curse of dimensionality. We adopt the lasso [13] method for feature selection for its good performance and moderate computational cost. The objective function of the lasso is

$$\hat{\beta}^{Lasso} = \underset{\beta}{\operatorname{argmin}}\{\frac{1}{2}\|y - X\beta\|_2^2 + \lambda\|\beta\|_1\}, \tag{2}$$

where X is the input data matrix, y is the beauty score vector, and λ is the regularization parameter. The l_1 penalty will promote sparse solutions. To solve the entire lasso path, we use SpaSM, a toolbox for sparse statistical modeling [14]. The variables are then sorted according to the path.

Given the sorted variables, a nested sequence of models can be obtained. To decide the optimal number of variables to keep, we train models with increasing number of sorted variables. The first k variables are selected if none of the larger feature subsets can increase the prediction accuracy significantly, which is determined by two-sample t-tests.

4   Optimal Fusion Strategy

In this section, we investigate the combinations of multiple types of features to further increase the facial beauty prediction accuracy. Seven types of features are introduced in Sect. 2. Hence, there are totally 127 combinations, which can be represented by $Comb = [C_1, C_2, \ldots, C_{127}]$, where $C_1 = \{1\}$, $C_2 = \{1, 2\}, \ldots, C_{127} = \{1, 2, 3, 4, 5, 6, 7\}$. They are evaluated by score level fusion performance. The outputs of the seven models are denoted by $y_1, \ldots, y_7$. For the combination C_k, the score level fusion result is

$$\hat{y} = \sum_{i \in C_k} w_i^{(k)} y_i. \tag{3}$$

The weight vector $w^{(k)}$ can be obtained by solving the least squares problem

$$w^{(k)} = \underset{w}{\operatorname{argmin}} \|y - Y^{(k)} w\|, \tag{4}$$

where $Y^{(k)}$ is a $n \times |C_k|$ matrix including n entries of model outputs selected by C_k, and y is human-rated beauty scores. The correlation between the predicted scores $\hat{y}$ and human rated scores y is used to evaluate the prediction performance, i.e.,

$$r_{y,\hat{y}} = \frac{cov(y, \hat{y})}{\sigma_y \sigma_{\hat{y}}} = \frac{E[(y - \mu_y)(\hat{y} - \mu_{\hat{y}})]}{\sigma_y \sigma_{\hat{y}}}. \tag{5}$$

The optimal fusion strategy is the least complex model with the most competitive performance.

5   Experiments

5.1   Data Set and Preprocessing

The experiments are based on the database built by [15], which includes 390 celebrity face images of Miss Universe, Miss World, movie stars, and super models collected from the web and 409 common face images. The beauty scores are given. Active shape model (ASM) [16] is used to detect the landmarks, and we develop a tool for manual adjustment to further improve the precision of landmark positions. To extract eigenface, Gabor, LBP, and PCANet features, the images are cropped with a squared bounding box and resize the cropped image into 128×128.

5.2   Comparison of Features

The features are compared in terms of facial beauty prediction performance, which is measured by the correlation between predicted beauty scores and human-rated scores. Three statistical regression methods were applied to build the computational models: K-nearest neighbor (KNN), linear regression (LR), and support vector regression (SVR) [17]. In KNN regression, the parameter k was optimized by search. The SVR method used RBF kernels, and the parameters were obtained by grid search. As the original Gabor, LBP, and PCANet features are high-dimensional, PCA was performed to reduce the dimension to 100, which is the same with the eigenface and AAM features. We randomly selected 90% of the data for training and the remaining 10% were used for testing. The procedures were run 100 times. Figure 3 shows the average prediction accuracies of the three methods with different types of features. We can see that PCANet achieves the highest accuracy, followed by AAM. Among the three regression methods, SVR achieves the best performance consistently.

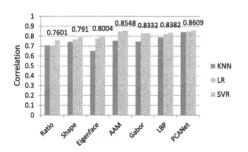

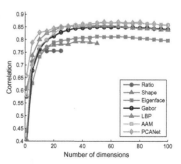

Fig. 3. Comparison of regression methods in terms of facial beauty prediction accuracy.

Fig. 4.   Prediction performance with increasing number of selected feature dimensions.

5.3   Feature Selection Results

A series of models were trained with increasing number of features ordered by the lasso method. The models were built with SVR method, as suggested by Sect. 5.2. The results are plotted in Fig. 4. We can see that at first the performances of all types of features increase rapidly, and after selecting about 20% of the total features, the performance curves become flat. Hence, there are irrelative or redundant variables. The numbers of selected features are determined by multiple two-sample t tests with significance level $\alpha = 0.05$. For most of the cases, about a half of features are discarded. However, the performances of the selected features are even slightly better than those of the original features.

5.4   Optimal Fusion Strategy

In this part, we investigated the optimal fusion strategy of multiple types of features. For 7 types of features, there are 127 different combinations. In order to obtain the combination weights defined in (4), we need to construct the single-type-feature output matrix Y. We randomly selected 90% of the faces to train 7 models corresponding to the 7 types of features. The models predicted beauty scores of the remaining 99 faces, so that there were 99×7 scores. Repeating this procedure for 10 times, we obtained a matrix of size 990×7, which served as the matrix Y. Then, by solving (4), we got the combination weights. The final scores are weighted sum of the outputs of the n models. We run 10-fold cross validation and the average performances of different fusion strategies are plotted in Fig. 5. The optimal strategy is the most parsimonious one with competitive prediction accuracy, as marked in Fig. 5. Table 1 shows the optimal combinations constrained by the number of feature types. We can see that the fusion of PCANet, LBP, and AAM can significantly improve the prediction performance, and adding more types of features cannot increase the performance significantly.

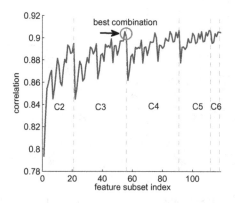

Fig. 5. Prediction performance of different feature combinations. For example, C2 means all combinations of two feature types, which has $C_7^2 = 21$ subsets.

Table 1. Optimal combinations and score level fusion results

No. of types	Optimal combination	Performance
1	PCANet	0.8708
2	PCANet+LBP	0.8947
3	PCANet+LBP+AAM	0.9056
4	PCANet+LBP+AAM+Gabor	0.9067

5.5   Comparison with Other Works

Our method was compared with those proposed by other works. As facial beauty prediction is still an emerging topic, there is no public database for comparison. We implemented the methods of other works on our database. As shown in Table 2, three methods are compared. [2] build a linear model with ratio features. [8] train a convolutional neural network for facial beauty prediction. [7] cascade shape, Gabor, LBP, and color moment features into a high-dimensional vector and performs PCA to reduce the feature dimension to 350. We did not include the color moment feature, because the images were collected from many sources, and the various illumination conditions distort the true face colors. For each method, 10-fold cross-validation was performed and the average prediction accuracy is shown in Table 2. The results show that our method is much better than other methods.

Table 2. Comparison with other works

Work	Feature	#Dimension	Method	Performance
[2]	Ratios	23	LR	0.6958
[8]	convNet	-	Neural network	0.7512
[7]	Shape+Gabor+LBP	350	SVR	0.8185
Our	AAM+LBP+PCANet	151	SVR+fusion	**0.9056**

6   Conclusion

In this paper, we give a comprehensive study on feature design and fusion strategy for facial beauty prediction. Ratio, shape, eigenface, AAM, Gabor, LBP, and PCANet features are compared in terms of facial beauty prediction accuracy. It is found that feature selection can promote the prediction performance. For feature selection, the lasso method performs better than filter and sequential wrapper methods. Then the optimal fusion strategy of multiple types of features is investigated. The results show that the best single-type feature is PCANet, and the optimal feature combination is PCANet, LBP, and AAM. By score level fusion, the final model achieves a correlation of 0.9056 between predicted scores and human rated scores, which is much better than existing methods.

References

1. Gunes, H., Piccardi, M.: Assessing facial beauty through proportion analysis by image processing and supervised learning. Int. J. Hum. Comput. Stud. **64**(12), 1184–1199 (2006)
2. Schmid, K., Marx, D., Samal, A.: Computation of a face attractiveness index based on neoclassical canons, symmetry, and golden ratios. Pattern Recogn. **41**(8), 2710–2717 (2008)
3. Fan, J., Chau, K.P., Wan, X., Zhai, L., Lau, E.: Prediction of facial attractiveness from facial proportions. Pattern Recogn. **45**(6), 2326–2334 (2012)
4. Liu, C., Wechsler, H.: Gabor feature based classification using the enhanced fisher linear discriminant model for face recognition. IEEE Trans. Image Process. **11**(4), 467–476 (2002)
5. Ahonen, T., Hadid, A., Pietikainen, M.: Face description with local binary patterns: application to face recognition. IEEE Trans. Pattern Anal. Mach. Intell. **28**(12), 2037–2041 (2006)
6. Eisenthal, Y., Dror, G., Ruppin, E.: Facial attractiveness: beauty and the machine. Neural Comput. **18**(1), 119–142 (2006)
7. Nguyen, T.V., Liu, S., Ni, B., Tan, J., Rui, Y., Yan, S.: Towards decrypting attractiveness via multi-modality cues. ACM Trans. Multimedia Comput. Commun. Appl. **9**(4), 28 (2013)
8. Gray, D., Yu, K., Xu, W., Gong, Y.: Predicting facial beauty without landmarks. In: Daniilidis, K., Maragos, P., Paragios, N. (eds.) ECCV 2010. LNCS, vol. 6316, pp. 434–447. Springer, Heidelberg (2010). doi:10.1007/978-3-642-15567-3_32
9. Cootes, T.F., Edwards, G.J., Taylor, C.J.: Active appearance models. IEEE Trans. Pattern Anal. Mach. Intell. **23**(6), 681–685 (2001)
10. Chan, T.H., Jia, K., Gao, S., Lu, J., Zeng, Z., Ma, Y.: PCANet: A Simple Deep Learning Baseline for Image Classification? arXiv:1404.3606 (2014)
11. Dryden, I.L., Mardia, K.V.: Statistical Shape Analysis. Wiley, Hoboken (1998)
12. Sirovich, L., Kirby, M.: Low-dimensional procedure for the characterization of human faces. JOSA A **4**(3), 519–524 (1987)
13. Hastie, T., Tibshirani, R., Friedman, J.: The Elements of Statistical Learning. SSS. Springer, New York (2009). doi:10.1007/978-0-387-84858-7
14. Sjöstrand, K., Ersbøll, B.: SpaSM: A MATLAB Toolbox for Sparse Statistical Modeling, October 2015. http://www2.imm.dtu.dk/projects/spasm/
15. Chen, F., Xu, Y., Zhang, D.: A new hypothesis on facial beauty perception. ACM Trans. Appl. Percept. **11**(2), 1–20 (2014)
16. Cootes, T.F., Taylor, C.J., Cooper, D.H., Graham, J.: Active shape models-their training and application. Comput. Vis. Image Underst. **61**(1), 38–59 (1995)
17. Vapnik, V.: The Nature of Statistical Learning Theory. Springer, New York (1995). doi:10.1007/978-1-4757-2440-0
18. Chen, F., Zhang, D.: Evaluation of the putative ratio rules for facial beauty indexing. In: 2014 International Conference on Medical Biometrics, pp. 181–188. IEEE Press, New York (2014)

Deep Embedding for Face Recognition in Public Video Surveillance

Guan Wang[1,2] [iD], Yu Sun[2] [iD], Ke Geng[3](✉) [iD], Shengguang Li[1] [iD],
and Wenjing Chen[4] [iD]

[1] First Research Institute of the Ministry of Public Security of PRC,
Beijing 100048, China
[2] School of Information Science and Technology, Beijing Forestry University,
Beijing 100083, China
[3] School of Electronic and Information Engineering, Beihang University,
Beijing 100191, China
gengk@avic.com
[4] School of New Media, Beijing Institute of Graphic Communication,
Beijing 102600, China

Abstract. Face recognition is essential to the surveillance-based crime investigation. The recognition accuracy on benchmark datasets has been boosted by deep learning, while there is still large gap between academic research and practical application. This work aims to identify few suspects from the crowd in real time for public video surveillance, which is a large-scale open-set classification task. The task specific face dataset is built from security surveillance cameras in Beijng subway. The state-of-the-art deep convolutional networks are trained end-to-end by triplet supervisory signal to embed faces into 128-dimension feature spaces. The Euclid distances in the embedding space directly correspond to face similarity, which enables real time large scale recognition in embedded system. Experiments demonstrate a $98.92\% \pm 0.005$ pair-wise verification accuracy, which indicates the automatic learned features are highly discriminative and generalize well to new identities. This method outperforms other state-of-the-art methods on the suspects identification task, which fills the application gap in public video surveillance.

Keywords: Face recognition · Convolutional neural networks · Public video surveillance · Triplet loss

1 Introduction

Face recognition has been studied extensively for decades due to its practical applications. The key challenge of face recognition is to develop effective feature representations for reducing intra-personal variations while enlarging inter-personal

---

Guan Wang and Yu Sun contributed equally to this work.

© Springer International Publishing AG 2017
J. Zhou et al. (Eds.): CCBR 2017, LNCS 10568, pp. 31–39, 2017.
https://doi.org/10.1007/978-3-319-69923-3_4

differences. Recently, deep learning has achieved great success on vision community [1–3], significantly improving the state-of-the-art in classification problems.

The face recognition accuracy on the *de-facto* benchmark Labeled Faces in the Wild (LFW) [4] dataset has been boosted rapidly. The DeepFace [5] uses an ensemble of deep convolutional neural networks (CNNs) trained on 4 million 3D aligned face images spanning 4000 unique identities. It employs the Siamese network architecture to minimize the distance between congruous pairs of faces and maximize the distance between incongruous pairs. The DeepFace is then extended by the DeepID series methods [6–9]. Compared to DeepFace, the DeepID methods only uses 2D affine face alignment. The DeepID1 [6] incorporates multiple CNNs to learn more discriminative features at different face patches. The Deep ID2 [7] employs a Bayesian learning framework to train a metric, multi-task learning using joint identification-verification supervisory signal. The Deep ID2+ [8] updates the CNN architectures with fully connected branches after each convolution layers to generate more joint supervisory signal. The Deep ID3 [9] uses very deep networks inspired by the VGGnet [1] and GoogLeNet [2]. More recently, the Facenet [10] directly embeds faces into compact vectors using CNNs end-to-end trained with triplet distance loss. The Facenet currently achieves state-of-the-art performance in LFW and YouTube Faces DB [11]. The open source project OpenFace [12] is developed based on triplet loss for real-time face recognition. The model achieved competitive accuracy on the LFW benchmark with a small training dataset. The Ministry of Public Security of the People's Republic of China sponsors the skynet project, which deploys surveillance cameras in stations, airports, streets, *etc.* for public security. But the surveillance-based crime investigation heavily depends on human labor. Despite significant recent advances, implementing face recognition in public video surveillance presents serious challenges to current approaches. Models trained on web images of celebrities suffer from low accuracy in practical surveillance scenarios.

To bridge between the literature and the industry, this work employs the deep embedding method for suspects identification in public video surveillance. The modified Inception-ResNet-v2 models are trained on the public surveillance images. The triplet loss is employed as supervisory signal to extract discriminative features. The experiment results demonstrate that the proposed method offers higher accuracy and validation rate with lower false accept value than OpenFace in surveillance scenarios.

2   Materials and Methods

2.1   Task Specification and Face Dataset

The images are captured by public surveillance cameras in Beijing subway. Four cameras are set up at both sides of the subway security check sensor gate, with two cameras on each side. When a person walks through the sensor gate, four images are captured simultaneously by cameras fixed at different angles of the gate, as indicated in Fig. 1a. Figure 1b shows the position of two cameras at one side of the gate. The other two cameras are located at the same position on the other side. The typical 4 images of one identity are shown in Fig. 1c.

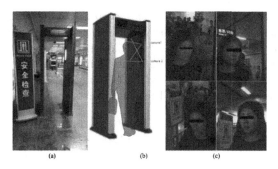

(a)   (b)   (c)

Fig. 1. (a) The face checkpoint at Beijing subway. (b) Position of the two cameras at one side of the gate. (c) Typical images of one identity captured simultaneously by 4 cameras.

The LFW is the *de-facto* testbed for face verification, which contains 13,233 images of 5,750 celebrities [1]. The LFW faces are web images of all human races captured at uncontrolled condition. Compared with LFW, our dataset manifests unique characters: faces are captured at relatively controlled condition, with fixed focal length under indoor illumination from almost the same distance. After human elimination of disqualified images, our dataset includes 1,806 Chinese citizens, ranging from teenage students, adults to aged people. What's more, the images captured in subway suffer from low illumination and high ISO noise.

Following the LFW's unrestricted with labeled outside data evaluation protocol [13], we constructed two test sets. The first test set is a balanced one like LFW, consisting of 1055 congruous face pairs and 1055 incongruous face pairs. The pairs are split into 5 folds. The balanced test set aims to assess the threshold deciding whether a pair is congruous or not, and evaluate the performance of the trained model using the benchmark same as LFW. The second test set is an imbalanced one that contains 6000 pairs. The 6000 pairs are split into 10 folds. All the identities in test set are held out from training. The other identities are left in the training set without pair labels, *i.e.* only labeled by an ID number. Compared with the LFW test set, there are two differences: First, the congruous pairs only account for 1% in the imbalanced test set. In each fold, only one person is the suspect and constitutes 6 congruous pairs. The other 594 pairs are incongruous pairs of the suspect with the other 594 identities. The incongruous pairs are used as varieties of distractors. Second, all images except the ones of the suspects are used only once in each fold. The imbalanced test set aims to evaluate the performance of the model for recognizing few suspects from the crowd. Thus the task is an open set classification problem, which demands that recognition model could generalize to massive identities beyond the training set.

2.2   Deep Embedding with Triplet Loss

Most CNNs use a softmax classification layer at training stage and then take an intermediate bottleneck layer as the representation at test stage, while the indirect bottleneck representation could not generalize to new faces. What's more, the parameters in the classification layer increase exponentially with identities in the training set. To circumvent the above problems, deep embedding trained by triplet loss is employed in our task. The Euclid distance in the embedding space directly corresponds to face similarity. A triplet consists of three face images of two identities: an anchor image x^a, a positive image x^p of the same identity, and a negative image x^n of another identity. The deep CNN followed by L2 normalization embeds each image x into a 128 dimensional hypersphere. The triplet loss is defined as:

$$L = \sum_{i=1}^{N} \left[\left\| f(x_i^a) - f(x_i^p) \right\|_2^2 - \left\| f(x_i^a) - f(x_i^n) \right\|_2^2 + \alpha \right], \tag{1}$$

where $f(x)$ is the output embedding of the model, and N is the mini-bath size. As shown in Fig. 2, the training aims to separate the positive pair from the negative by a distance margin α for any triplet.

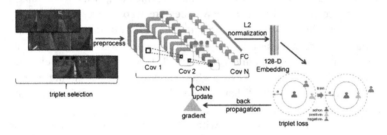

Fig. 2. End to end deep embedding training with triplet loss

As shown in Fig. 2, a deep CNN followed by L2 normalization is directly trained to output a compact embedding supervised by a triplet loss. The triplet loss is minimized by back propagation at training stage. To convergence the training algorithm in feasible time on our dataset, the selected triplets are which violate the margin α as the top of Fig. 2 indicates. For a certain anchor, the hard positive x^p which $\mathrm{argmax}_{x^p}(\left\| f(x^a) - f(x^p) \right\|_2^2)$ and the hard negative x^n that $\mathrm{argmin}_{x^n}(\left\| f(x^a) - f(x^n) \right\|_2^2)$ should be selected from the training set. Our dataset contains massive identities, while each identity has 4 images at most. So we choose the hard positives across all intra-identity images, while select the hard negatives within a random subset. Each mini-batch of triplets is generated online by the latest network checkpoint. To tradeoff between training efficiency and mini-batch coverage, the hard negatives in one mini-batch are searched in the range of 600 identities.

3 Experiments

3.1 Data Preprocessing

Both the training and test set are detected and aligned by Multi-task CNN (MTCNN) [14]. The original MTCNN select all faces in one image. But each image captured by the public video surveillance often includes more than one person, and the largest face are often far from the image center. So the MTCNN is revised in this paper to ignore the face position and only select the largest face. And then aligned with 5 face landmarks (two eyes, nose and mouth corners) by affine transformation. The faces in the training set are resized to 182×182 resolution with a maximal margin of 22 pixels. Before fed into CNNs, the aligned faces are randomly cropped to 160×160 resolution, randomly flipped and then normalized to standard distribution. The faces in test set are directly resized to 160×160 resolution and normalized to standard distribution.

3.2 Models Architecture

The Inception-ResNet-v2 [15] network is employed for feature extraction, which achieves a state-of-the-art in terms of accuracy on the ILSVRC image classification benchmark [16]. The network combines two most recent ideas, the inception blocks and the residual connections. The model uses three types of inception blocks, inception-a, inception-b, and inception-c. Residual connections allow shortcuts in the model and enable deeper neural networks, which also significantly simplify the inception blocks by reducing parallel towers. We modify the model by stacking different number of inception blocks. Three modified versions of the Inception-ResNet-v2 model are evaluated systemically in this work. For each version, the number of the three types of inception blocks are 1-2-1, 5-10-5 and 10-20-10, respectively. The final softmax layer for close set classification is replaced with a L2-normalization layer for deep embeddings.

Both the MTCNN and the modified Inception-ResNet-v2 models are implemented in the open source deep learning framework TensorFlow 1.0 [17] with TF-Slim library. All the experiments are conducted on an Ubuntu 16.04 Linux server with an Intel i7-6700 CPU with 64 GB memory and one NVIDIA TitanX GPU with 12 GB memory.

3.3 Training Algorithm

Deep neural networks are trained aiming to minimize the triplet loss function L, *i.e.* finding the value of parameters W that minimizes the loss. We use the Adagrad algorithm [18] where W is updated iteratively as:

$$W- = lr * \frac{g}{\sqrt{\sum g^2 + \varepsilon}}, \qquad (2)$$

where lr is the learning rate, g is the gradient in each iteration and ε is a small value of 10^{-6}.

All the models are trained for 80 epochs or qualified triplets are exhausted. We use an initial learning rate of 0.1, multiplying it by 0.1 every 35 epochs. To avoid model collapse, *i.e.* $f(x) = 0$, we initiate the distance margin value $\alpha = 0$ and increase α progressively. As training progresses, the difficulty of triplets increases accordingly.

3.4   Evaluation Protocol

The method is evaluated on the face verification task. Given a pair of face images (x_i, x_j) of identities (i, j), a squared L2 distance threshold d is used to determine the pair is same or different. The set of true accept TA(d) and false accept FA(d) is define as:

$$\text{TA}(d) = \left\{ (i,j) \in P_{same}, \text{ with } \left\| f(x_i) - f(x_j) \right\|_2^2 \leq d \right\}, \tag{3}$$

$$\text{FA}(d) = \left\{ (i,j) \in P_{diff}, \text{ with } \left\| f(x_i) - f(x_j) \right\|_2^2 \leq d \right\}, \tag{4}$$

where P_{same} denotes the congruous pairs and P_{diff} denotes the incongruous pairs. The validation rate VAL(d), the false accept rate FAR(d) and verification accuracy ACC (d) are defined as:

$$\text{VAL}(d) = \frac{TA(d)}{P_{same}}, \quad \text{FAR}(d) = \frac{FA(d)}{P_{diff}}, \quad \text{ACC}(d) = \frac{TA(d) + P_{diff} - FA(d)}{P_{same} + P_{diff}}. \tag{5}$$

3.5   Threshold Learning

The squared L2 distance threshold d is important to the performance of the method. The threshold is estimated using the method in [19], *i.e.* it is learned separately on each fold to maximize the accuracy on the test pairs. As the second test set is highly imbalanced, 5 thresholds are learned on the 5 folds of the first test set, and then the average of the learned thresholds is used on the second test set.

4   Results and Discussion

We use the ACC value on the balanced test set for the comparison of results of the three models. All the three models, 1-2-1, 5-10-5 and 10-20-10, obtain similar high performance, with an accuracy of 92.94%, 93.27% and 94.36% respectively. It is noted that the accuracy slightly improves with the increase of model depth, and the best performance is achieved by the 10-20-10 model. We compare our best model with OpenFace on the two test sets and report the results in Table 1. The Receiver Operating Characteristic (ROC) curves are plotted in Fig. 3. From the results we have the following observations. First, the proposed model improves the accuracy of OpenFace model by a wide margin of 34.74% and 18.77% on the balanced and imbalanced test set, respectively. The ACC of 94.36% ± 0.01 and 98.92% ± 0.005 are achieved on the two test sets, respectively. The excellent performance indicates that our model is robust to the low quality of the images. But the OpenFace model trained on web images cannot generalize well. Second, the VAL value on the imbalanced test set of our model is 98.33% ± 0.05, *i.e.* only one pair images of one suspect is not recognized. Last, a low FAR is obtained by our model, with only 3.77% ± 0.01 and 1.08% ± 0.005 on

Table 1. Comparison with the OpenFace model

Test set	Method	VAL	FAR	ACC
Balanced	OpenFace	70.24% ± 0.08	50.73% ± 0.09	59.62% ± 0.04
	Proposed method	92.48% ± 0.02	3.77% ± 0.01	94.36% ± 0.01
Imbalanced	OpenFace	38.33% ± 0.29	19.43% ± 0.08	80.15% ± 0.08
	Proposed method	98.33% ± 0.05	1.08% ± 0.005	98.92% ± 0.005

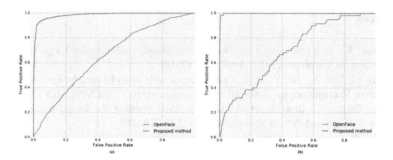

Fig. 3. The ROC curves on the (a) balanced and (b) imbalanced test set

the balanced and imbalanced test set, respectively. The varieties of distractors have very limited influence on our model.

Though OpenFace is developed for mobile applications, the model has not been implemented on any embedded system. Our trained models are deployed to the Jetson TX2 embedded system. The time taken on the device to process 100 pairs of images for the 1-2-1, 5-10-5 and 10-20-10 models are 13.75, 22.36 and 65.10 s respectively, with the accuracy consistent with that on the x86 workstation. Thus the face recognition can be conducted offline in real time at a low electrical power. The model with the best trade-off between accuracy and time cost could be selected according to practical application scenarios.

5 Conclusion

In this work, the first Chinese citizen face image dataset is built from public surveillance cameras in Beijng subway. The modified Inception-ResNet-v2 deep learning models are trained end-to-end by triplet supervisory signal to embed faces into 128-dimension feature spaces. The trained models are deployed to the Jetson TX2 embedded system for real time offline identification. The classification accuracy of 94.36% ± 0.01 and 98.92% ± 0.005 are achieved on the balanced and imbalanced test set, respectively. With the threshold learned from the balanced test set, a VAL of 98.33% ± 0.05 with 1.08% ± 0.005 FAR is achieved on the imbalanced test set. The experiments demonstrate that the automatic learned features are highly discriminative and generalize well to new identities. The proposed model is capable of identifying suspects from crowd in real time for public video surveillance, which bridges the gap between academic research and practical application.

Acknowledgment. The authors thank Shiwei Zhao and Li Li at First Research Institute of the Public Security Ministry for images collection. This work was supported by the Fundamental Research Funds for the Central Universities: 2017JC02. Yu Sun and Guan Wang contributed equally to this work.

References

1. Simonyan, K., Zisserman, A.: Very Deep Convolutional Networks for Large-Scale Image Recognition. arXiv preprint arXiv:1409.1556 (2014)
2. Szegedy, C., Liu, W., Jia, Y., et al.: Going deeper with convolutions. In: Computer Vision and Pattern Recognition, pp. 1–9 (2015). https://doi.org/10.1109/CVPR.2015.7298594
3. He, K., Zhang, X., Ren, S., et al.: Deep residual learning for image recognition. In: Computer Vision and Pattern Recognition, pp. 770–778 (2015)
4. Huang, G.B., Ramesh, M., Berg, T., et al.: Labeled faces in the wild: a database for studying face recognition in unconstrained environments. University of Massachusetts, Amherst (2007)
5. Taigman, Y., Yang, M., Ranzato, M., et al.: DeepFace: closing the gap to human-level performance in face verification. In: Computer Vision and Pattern Recognition, pp. 1701–1708 (2014). https://doi.org/10.1109/CVPR.2014.220
6. Sun, Y., Wang, X., Tang, X.: Deep learning face representation from predicting 10,000 classes. In: Computer Vision and Pattern Recognition, pp. 1891–1898 (2014). https://doi.org/10.1109/CVPR.2014.244
7. Sun, Y., Chen, Y., Wang, X., et al.: Deep learning face representation by joint identification-verification. In: Neural Information Processing Systems, pp. 1988–1996 (2014)
8. Sun, Y., Wang, X., Tang, X.: Deeply learned face representations are sparse, selective, and robust. In: Computer Vision and Pattern Recognition, pp. 2892–2900 (2015). https://doi.org/10.1109/CVPR.2015.7298907
9. Sun, Y., Liang, D., Wang, X., et al.: DeepID3: face recognition with very deep neural networks. arXiv preprint arXiv:1502.00873 (2015)
10. Schroff, F., Kalenichenko, D., Philbin, J.: FaceNet: a unified embedding for face recognition and clustering. In: Computer Vision and Pattern Recognition, pp. 815–823 (2015). https://doi.org/10.1109/CVPR.2015.7298682
11. Wolf, L., Hassner, T., Maoz, I.: Face recognition in unconstrained videos with matched background similarity. In: Computer Vision and Pattern Recognition, pp. 529–534 (2011). https://doi.org/10.1109/CVPR.2011.5995566
12. Amos, B., Ludwiczuk, B., Satyanarayanan, M.: OpenFace: a general-purpose face recognition library with mobile applications. Carnegie Mellon University (2016)
13. Huang, G.B., Learned-miller, E.: Labeled faces in the wild: updates and new reporting procedures. University of Massachusetts, Amherst (2014)
14. Zhang, K., Zhang, Z., Li, Z., et al.: Joint face detection and alignment using multi-task cascaded convolutional networks. IEEE J. Solid-State Circuits **23**, 1161–1173 (2016). doi:10.1109/LSP.2016.2603342
15. Szegedy, C., Ioffe, S., Vanhoucke, V., et al.: Inception-v4, Inception-ResNet and the Impact of Residual Connections on Learning. arXiv preprint arXiv:1602.07261 (2016)

16. Russakovsky, O., Deng, J., Su, H., et al.: Imagenet large scale visual recognition challenge. Int. J. Comput. Vis. **115**, 211–252 (2015). doi:10.1007/s11263-015-0816-y
17. Abadi, M., Agarwal, A., Barham, P., et al.: TensorFlow: Large-Scale Machine Learning on Heterogeneous Distributed Systems (2016)
18. Duchi, J.C., Hazan, E., Singer, Y.: Adaptive subgradient methods for online learning and stochastic optimization. J. Mach. Learn. Res. **12**, 2121–2159 (2011)
19. Parkhi, O.M., Vedaldi, A., Zisserman, A.: Deep face recognition. In: British Machine Vision Conference (2015). https://doi.org/10.5244/C.29.41

Random Feature Discriminant for Linear Representation Based Robust Face Recognition

Jian-Xun Mi[1,2], Xiangbin Ma[1(✉)], Qiankun Fu[1], Chaowei Zhao[1], and Can Long[1]

[1] College of Computer Science and Technology,
Chongqing University of Posts and Telecommunications, Chongqing, China
mijianxun@gmail.com, xiangbinma42@gmail.com, fqiankun@gmail.com,
2014211694@stu.cqupt.edu.cn, 935353776@qq.com
[2] Key Laboratory of Machine Intelligence and Advanced Computing,
Ministry of Education, Sun Yat-sen University, Guangzhou, China

Abstract. The linear representation based classification methods include two independent steps: representation and decision. First, the query image is represented as a linear combination of training samples. Then the classification decision is made by evaluating which class leads to the minimum class-wise representation error. However, these two steps have different goals. The representation step prefers accuracy while the decision step requires discrimination. Thus precisely representing the query image does not always benefit the decision process. In this paper, we propose a novel linear representation based classifier which no longer separates representation from decision. We repeatedly construct linear representation based classification models with randomly selected features. Then the best model is selected by using the representation discriminant criterion (RDC) which evaluates the discrimination of a representation model. We conduct extensive experiments on public benchmark databases to verify the efficacy of the proposed method.

Keywords: Face recognition · RANSAC · Linear representation · Feature selection

1 Introduction

Face recognition (FR) has been extensively studied for decades due to its wide applications, such as access control and video surveillance. Although many breakthroughs have been made, it is still one of the most challenging problems in computer vision and pattern recognition. Born with the curse of dimensionality, FR is not an easy task theoretically. Face images usually are in high dimension and sufficient amount of training images is not always available in many scenarios. Furthermore, face images are sensitive to uncontrolled factors including illumination, pixel corruption, and expression and so on. This makes it more tough to fulfill the requirement of real life FR applications. Therefore more efficient and robust FR methods are still desired.

© Springer International Publishing AG 2017
J. Zhou et al. (Eds.): CCBR 2017, LNCS 10568, pp. 40–47, 2017.
https://doi.org/10.1007/978-3-319-69923-3_5

During the past decades, many methods for FR have been proposed. Eigenface [1] and Fisherface [2] are classic and widely used for FR. LBP operator [3] and gradientface [4] are insensitive to lighting changes and capable of dealing with various illumination. Based on extracted face features, many classifiers can be employed to determine which class the query image belongs to, such as NN, NS, SVM and boosting. Recently, the deep learning based methods have achieved amazing performance in face recognition (identification and validation), such as FaceNet [5], DeepFace [6] and DeepID [7].

According to the linear subspace assumption, a test sample can be represented as a linear combination of other samples from the same class. Under this assumption many linear representation based FR methods have been proposed. Linear Regression Classification (LRC) [8] casts FR to a linear regression problem. It reconstructs a query sample by a linear combination of gallery images from each class. Then classification decision is made by checking which class yields the minimum reconstruction residual. It is not hard to realize that LRC is equivalent to a NS classifier. Usually face images from different subjects share some similarities. Therefore using samples of other subjects can alleviate the shortage of training samples and represent the query image more accurately. Collaborative Representation (CR) based methods recover a query image by images from all classes and then identify it by checking class-wise representation residuals. Typical CR based methods include Sparse Representation based Classification (SRC) [9], CR based Classification with Regularized Least Square (CRC-RLS) [10] and their variants. SRC approximates a query image with a small number of images in the gallery, which is guaranteed by employing a ℓ_1-norm regularization. CRC-RLS gains a competitive result with significant less complexity than SRC by using a ℓ_2-norm regularization. But SRC still shows more robustness in the case of occlusion. Many variants and developments of these two methods have been proposed. ASRC [11] can automatically balance ℓ_1- and ℓ_2-norm regularization according to the correlation of training data. Structured SRC methods [12] incorporate the label information of training data and promote group level sparsity. LCRC-SS [13] makes full use of similarity between images and takes local similarity subspace as projective space rather than the global space.

A representation-and-decision schema can be easily noticed from linear representation based FR methods mentioned above. They first recovery the query image with some constrain as accurate as possible and then make classification decision by checking class-wise representation errors. But these two steps are separated from each other and have inconsistent goals. The regression process tries to approximate the test image as accuracy as possible, while the classification aims to group the testing sample into one class. The precise recovery could lead to a misclassification when the test image is polluted by strong noise. The discrimination is weak when some images of different subjects are very similar to each other. So the accurate reconstruction of the query image dose not always help identification. To address this issue, we propose a method which combines the representation and decision together. The proposed method generates multiple linear representation based classification models by employing a RANSAC-like feature selection paradigm. The classification decision is made by the most discriminative model. In order to find this model, we evaluate each model with Representation Discriminant Criteria (RDC) that is the ratio of the minimum representation error and second smallest one. The major contributions of this work are as follows.

(1) We innovatively employ a RANSAC-like paradigm for feature selection. The RANSAC algorithm is usually used for estimating model parameters from a set of observed data that contains outliers. We utilize its outlier-removal ability to prune the features affected by noise.
(2) Instead of classifying by residual, we propose RDC to measure the discrimination of a linear representation based classification model. By using RDC, we can obtain a representation that benefits classification.
(3) We propose a representation based FR method which makes the representation step and decision step more consistent. Our extensive experiments demonstrate that our method produces more stable and robust classification results.

2   Random Sample Consensus

RANdom SAmple Consensus or RANSAC [14] is widely used for model parameters estimation. It is capable of finding the correct model from heavily contaminated observed data. Since being proposed, RANSAC has become a fundamental tool in the computer vision and image processing community.

Conventional smoothing techniques use as much data as possible to obtain an initial model and then attempt to eliminate invalid data. RANSAC, however, follows an opposite philosophy. It uses as small initial dataset as feasible and enlarge this set with consensus when possible. The generic RANSAC algorithm repeats two steps iteratively. In the first step, a minimal subset of data, called tentative set, is randomly picked from the observed dataset. A model and its corresponding parameters are computed using the tentative set. In the second step, all elements of observed dataset are checked with the obtained model. The set of elements fitting the model within a error threshold is called consensus set of this model. After enough iterations have been conducted, we choose the model with the largest consensus set as the final model. It is theoretical guaranteed that the underlying model can be found with a probability of p as long as the times of iteration k satisfies Eq. (1).

$$k = \frac{\log(1 - p)}{\log(1 - w^n)} \tag{1}$$

In Eq. (1) w denotes the inlier ratio of observed data and n is the number of data points required for fitting a model. This result indicates that RANSAC suffers from time consumption when the inlier ratio is low. If there is a problem-related rationale for selecting points to form the tentative sets, we should use a deterministic selection process instead of the random one. A developed version of RANSAC, Progressive Sample Consensus PROSAC [15] achieves significant time savings by taking advantage of the ordering structure of observed dataset.

3   Our Method

In this section, we firstly introduce a RANSAC-like feature selecting strategy. Then we provide more details on applying it to FR with CRC-RLS method.

3.1   Random Feature Discriminant

According to the linear subspace assumption, the representation of a given sample produces a very small residual on its identity class and large residuals on other classes. Therefore the classification decision can be made by comparing residuals on different classes, i.e., the query sample belongs to the class yielding the smallest residual. The effect of noise may invalidate the linear subspace assumption of data, which weakens the linear representation based classifiers. In this paper, we assume the effect of noise is local, that means noise only destroys partial features of the data and the remaining features are unaffected or only slightly affected. Partial occlusion and local illumination are typical cases of this kind of noise. Good classification results can be achieved by using the unaffected features because the linear subspace assumption still holds on subspace determined by these features. So we transform the classification problem into a feature selection problem, that is, to find a feature set that is not affected by noise.

Due to the unpredictability of noise, we use a RANSAC-like approach to handle with feature selection. Specifically, we randomly select a feature subset to construct a classification model and evaluate the classification results with RDC. We define the RDC value as $r_{\#1}/r_{\#2}$ where $r_{\#1}$ and $r_{\#2}$ stand for the minimal and the second minimal class-wise representation residual respectively. This metrics measures the capacity of a model grouping the testing sample into one class and separating it from others. After enough models have be generated, the final decision is made by the model which yields the minimum RDC value.

Obviously it's very time-consuming to generate a satisfying model by a random way, especially when the data are in high dimension. Inspired by PROSAC, we assign a score to each pixel to guide the pixel selection precess. We compute the difference between the query image and the average image of all training samples. Pixel that has a small difference with the average is more likely to be unaffected. We evaluate each pixel by using a quality function

$$q(e) = 1 - \frac{1}{1 + \exp\left\{-a(e - c)\right\}} \tag{2}$$

where e is a pixel-wise difference and (a, c) is the parameter of sigmoid function. We use the value of $q(\cdot)$ as the probability that a pixel is noise-free. By introducing this probability, we decrease the randomness of feature selection process and achieve significant time savings.

3.2   Face Recognition with Random Feature Discriminant

Considering we have a training set $A \in \mathbb{R}^{m \times n}$ containing training samples in its columns and a query image $y \in \mathbb{R}^{m \times 1}$. Firstly, we compute the difference between the query image and the average image, that is $e = [e_1, \ldots, e_m]^T = y - \bar{y}$. We view the value of $q(|e_i|)$ as the probability that the i-th pixel is not affected by noise. Then, we semi-randomly pick out m' pixels from the training images and the test image by evaluating the $q(\cdot)$ function to each pixel. This is equivalent to extract corresponding rows from A and y. We define a set $W = \{w_i\}_{i=1}^{m'}$ as the row indices of picked rows. The linear sub-model still holds on the extracted rows:

$$Wy = WAx \tag{3}$$

where $W \in \mathbb{R}^{m \times m}$ contains 1s in its w_i-th diagonal elements and 0s in other places. Next the partial data are fed into the CRC-RLS model:

$$\hat{x} = \arg \min_{x} \|Wy - WAx\|_2^2 + \lambda \|x\|_2^2. \tag{4}$$

The solution is obtained by

$$\hat{x} = (A^T WA + \lambda I)^{-1} A^T Wy. \tag{5}$$

A predicted label is given by comparing the class-wise reconstruction error:

$$\text{label}(y) = \arg \min_{i} \|Wy - WA_i x_i\|_2^2 \tag{6}$$

where A_i and x_i are the matrix of training samples from i-th class and the corresponding coefficient vector, respectively. We repeatedly generate models via above steps until it reaches the maximal iteration times which can be estimated by Eq. (1) or manually specified. At last we select the model with the minimum RDC value to make final classification decision.

4   Experimental Results

In this section, we conduct experiments on public face databases to demonstrate the performance of the proposed method by comparing it with LRC, CRC-RLS and SRC. No feature extraction is adopted and we directly use the raw pixel value for classification. All the images used in experiments are converted to gray scale and resized to the order of 50×40 pixels. In all experiments, we manually set the maximum iteration times as 10.

(1) AR database: The AR database [16] consists of over 4000 color images from 126 individuals. There are 26 photos taken for each subject in two sessions with variations of facial expressions, illumination and disguise. In this experiments, we select a subset of 50 male and 50 female subjects from the database. We follow three commonly used evaluation protocols for experiments on this database. Evaluation Protocol 1 (EP1) takes the first seven images of each subject from

Session 1 for training and the corresponding seven image from Session 2 for testing. For EP2, we select 800 non-occluded face images with facial expressions from both sessions for training and the 600 images with sunglasses for testing. EP3 uses the same training set of EP2 and the 600 images with scarves for testing. The parameter setting is $(\lambda, a, c) = (0.01, 40, 0.5)$ for EP1, $(0.001, 30, 0.1)$ for EP2 and $(0.001, 50, 0.2)$ for EP3. The comparison of competing methods is shown in Table 1. Our method obtains promising results on EP1 and EP3, and is still satisfying on EP2.

Table 1. Recognition accuracy (%) on the AR database

Evaluation protocol	Method	Recognition rate
EP1	CRC-RLS	94.1
	SRC	93.3
	LRC	76.1
	Ours	97.2
EP2	CRC-RLS	51.3
	SRC	87.0
	LRC	39.2
	Ours	84.1
EP3	CRC-RLS	63.7
	SRC	59.5
	LRC	10.2
	Ours	88.0

(2) ORL database: The ORL or AT&T database [17] contains 400 gray scale images of 40 individuals. It incorporates wide variations including facial gestures, rotation, wearing of scale and glasses. In this experiment, we take first t ($t = 1, 2, 3, 4, 5$) image(s) of each subject for training and the remaining for testing. We fix $(\lambda, a, c) = (0.1, 10, 0.1)$ for all experimental settings. The mean recognition rate is taken as the final result for our method. The experimental results under different t values are listed in Table 2. The experimental result shows that our method achieves similar accuracy to CRC-RLS and is outperformed by SRC. This suggests that our method is more sensitive to facial gestures and rotation than SRC.

(3) Extended Yale B database: Extended Yale B database [18,19] contains 2414 frontal face images from 38 subjects which were captured under controlled lighting conditions. We divide the dataset into five subsets according to the damage cased by lighting. From subset 1 to subset 5, the extent of image corruption increases. We use subset 1 as training set and other four as test sets. The classification results are listed in Table 3. We can see that our method shows more robustness to lighting changes than other methods.

Table 2. Recognition accuracy (%) on the ORL database

Method	$t = 1$	$t = 2$	$t = 3$	$t = 4$	$t = 5$
CRC-RLS	71.4	84.4	89.3	90.4	93.5
SRC	73.3	86.6	90.0	92.0	92.5
LRC	67.5	80.0	85.0	86.7	91.5
Ours	70.3	83.8	89.3	89.6	93.5

Table 3. Recognition accuracy (%) on the Extended Yale B Database

Method	subset 2	subset 3	subset 4	subset 5
CRC-RLS	100	100	74.2	26.0
SRC	100	100	67.9	22.9
LRC	100	100	88.7	42.4
Ours	100	100	94.1	52.3

5 Conclusion

In this paper, we proposed a novel robust representation based classifier for FR which combines representation and decision together. The proposed method is extensively evaluated on public face databases with several experimental protocols. Specially the challenges of occlusion and illumination are addressed. The experimental results shows that our method outperforms competing methods on aligned database. On unaligned database it obtains better result when we use enough training samples. We defined RDC to measure model discrimination which bridges the gap between representation and decision in conventional representation based classifiers. Even though we employed CRC-RLS for classifying in this paper, other classifiers can be adopted such as SRC and ASRC. The RFD can be used alone as a feature selection method. Our future directions include the robustness issue related to pose variation and misalignment.

Acknowledgments. This work was supported partially by Foundation of Key Laboratory of Machine Intelligence and Advanced Computing of the Ministry of Education. And partially this research is funded by Scientific and Technological Research Program of Chongqing Municipal Education Commission under Grant Nos. KJ1500402 and KJ1500417.

References

1. Turk, M.A., Pentland, A.P.: Face recognition using eigenfaces. In: Proceedings of IEEE Computer Society Conference on Computer Vision and Pattern Recognition, CVPR 1991, pp. 586–591. IEEE (1991)

2. Belhumeur, P.N., Hespanha, J.P., Kriegman, D.: Eigenfaces vs. fisherfaces: recognition using class specific linear projection. IEEE Trans. Pattern Anal. Mach. Intell. **19**(7), 711–720 (1997)

3. Ahonen, T., Hadid, A., Pietikainen, M.: Face description with local binary patterns: application to face recognition. IEEE Trans. Pattern Anal. Mach. Intell. **28**(12), 2037–2041 (2006)

4. Zhang, T., Tang, Y.Y., Fang, B., Shang, Z., Liu, X.: Face recognition under varying illumination using gradientfaces. IEEE Trans. Image Process. **18**(11), 2599–2606 (2009)

5. Schroff, F., Kalenichenko, D., Philbin, J.: Facenet: a unified embedding for face recognition and clustering. In: Proceedings of the IEEE Conference on Computer Vision and Pattern Recognition, pp. 815–823 (2015)

6. Taigman, Y., Yang, M., Ranzato, M., Wolf, L.: Deepface: closing the gap to human-level performance in face verification. In: Proceedings of the IEEE Conference on Computer Vision and Pattern Recognition, pp. 1701–1708 (2014)

7. Sun, Y., Wang, X., Tang, X.: Deeply learned face representations are sparse, selective, and robust. In: Proceedings of the IEEE Conference on Computer Vision and Pattern Recognition, pp. 2892–2900 (2015)

8. Naseem, I., Togneri, R., Bennamoun, M.: Linear regression for face recognition. IEEE Trans. Pattern Anal. Mach. Intell. **32**(11), 2106–2112 (2010)

9. Wright, J., Yang, A.Y., Ganesh, A., Sastry, S., Ma, Y.: Robust face recognition via sparse representation. IEEE Trans. Pattern Anal. Mach. Intell. **31**(2), 210–227 (2009)

10. Zhang, L., Yang, M., Feng, X.: Sparse representation or collaborative representation: which helps face recognition? In: 2011 IEEE International Conference on Computer Vision (ICCV), pp. 471–478. IEEE (2011)

11. Wang, J., Lu, C., Wang, M., Li, P., Yan, S., Hu, X.: Robust face recognition via adaptive sparse representation. IEEE Trans. Syst. Man Cybern. **44**(12), 2368–2378 (2014)

12. Tang, X., Feng, G., Cai, J.: Weighted group sparse representation for undersampled face recognition. Neurocomputing **145**, 402–415 (2014)

13. Gao, R., Yang, W., Sun, X., Li, H., Liao, Q.: Locally collaborative representation in similar subspace for face recognition. Biometric Recognition. LNCS, vol. 9428, pp. 88–95. Springer, Cham (2015). doi:10.1007/978-3-319-25417-3_11

14. Fischler, M.A., Bolles, R.C.: Random sample consensus: a paradigm for model fitting with applications to image analysis and automated cartography. Commun. ACM **24**(6), 381–395 (1981)

15. Chum, O., Matas, J.: Matching with PROSAC-progressive sample consensus. In: IEEE Computer Society Conference on Computer Vision and Pattern Recognition, CVPR 2005, vol. 1, pp. 220–226. IEEE (2005)

16. Martinez, A., Benavente, R.: The AR face database. CVC Technical report, no. 24 (1998)

17. Samaria, F., Harter, A.: Parameterisation of a stochastic model for human face identification (1994)

18. Georghiades, A.S., Belhumeur, P.N., Kriegman, D.J.: From few to many: illumination cone models for face recognition under variable lighting and pose. IEEE Trans. Pattern Anal. Mach. Intell. **23**(6), 643–660 (2001)

19. Lee, K.C., Ho, J., Kriegman, D.J.: Acquiring linear subspaces for face recognition under variable lighting. IEEE Trans. Pattern Anal. Mach. Intell. **27**(5), 684–698 (2005)

Adv-Kin: An Adversarial Convolutional Network for Kinship Verification

Qingyan Duan[1], Lei Zhang[1(✉)], and Wei Jia[2]

[1] College of Communication Engineering, Chongqing University,
No. 174 Shazheng Street, Shapingba District, Chongqing 400044, China
{qyduan,leizhang}@cqu.edu.cn
[2] School of Computer and Information, Hefei University of Technology,
No. 193 Tunxi Road, Baohe District, Hefei 230009, China
china.jiawei@139.com

Abstract. Kinship verification in the wild is an interesting and challenging problem, which aims to determine whether two unconstrained facial images are from the same family. Most previous methods for kinship verification can be divided as low-level hand-crafted features based shallow methods and kin data trained generic convolutional neural network (CNN) based deep methods. Nevertheless, these general methods cannot well mining the potential information implied in kin-relation data. Inspired by MMD and GAN, Adv-Kin method is proposed in this paper. The discrimination of deep features can be improved by introducing MMD loss (ML) to minimize the distribution difference between parents domain and children domain. In addition, we propose the adversarial loss (AL) that can further improve the robustness of CNN model. Extensive experiments on the benchmark KinFaceW-I, KinFaceW-II, Cornell KinFace and UB KinFace show promising results over many state-of-the-art methods.

Keywords: Kinship verification · Convolutional neural networks · Maximum mean discrepancy · Adversarial loss

1 Introduction

Human face carries with lots of individual information, and most human characteristics such as identity, age, gender, emotion etc. can be distinguished by facial images. Facial analysis has been widely studied in computer vision. Face verification aims to verify whether the two facial images belong to the same person [1]. Biologists find that human facial appearance is an important cue for genetic similarity measurement. The purpose of kinship verification is to recognize whether the two persons are from the same family. It has many potential applications, such as missing children searching and social media mining, etc. [2]. In this work, the parent-child based kinship is studied, such as father-daughter, father-son, mother-daughter and mother-son. Some facial image pairs with kinship and

© Springer International Publishing AG 2017
J. Zhou et al. (Eds.): CCBR 2017, LNCS 10568, pp. 48–57, 2017.
https://doi.org/10.1007/978-3-319-69923-3_6

Fig. 1. Some positive (with kinship relation) and negative pairs (no kinship relation) from KinFaceW-I, KinFaceW-II, Cornell KinFace and UB KinFace, respectively. The first two rows are positive pairs and the last two rows are negative pairs. The kinship relation types from left to right are: father-daughter, father-son, mother-daughter and mother-son, respectively.

no kinship have been shown in Fig. 1, from which the difficulty of kin-relation discovery is shown.

There are many algorithms proposed for kinship verification. Most of these works follow the technical routine from hand-crafted low-level feature extraction to large-margin metric learning. A representative work can be referred to as [2], in which a neighborhood repulsed metric learning (NRML) was proposed by learning a projection based metric with large margin and achieved excellent performance on kinship verification. Also, the hand-crafted features (e.g. LBP, HOG) are often used for general face analysis. However, this kinship verification algorithm strongly depends on the choice of metric learning, not the kin-relation specific features. As a result, the implicit and abstract kinship information cannot be adequately represented [3].

Deep learning, proposed by Hinton and Salakhutdinov [4], has become the most popular machine learning algorithm for discovering discriminative intermediate and high-level representations in a hierarchical manner [5]. In particular, convolutional neural networks have recently been shown to achieve great success in various computer vision tasks, such as face recognition [1,6], object recognition, etc. Recently, convolutional neural networks (CNNs) have also been used for kinship verification [3,7]. Although these works greatly promote kinship verification, they adopted a conventional CNN architecture. The loss functions are normally connected on the last fully-connected layer, but the distribution difference between the different input domains is not considered. The accuracy of kinship verification will be affected by this distribution difference. Maximum mean discrepancy (MMD) can be used to solve this problem, motivated by this fact,

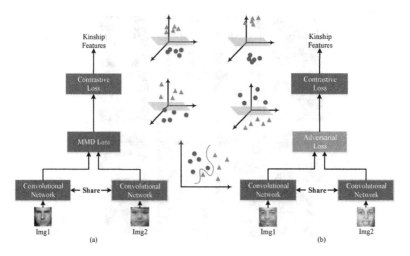

Fig. 2. Pipeline of our proposed approach. Circle denotes kinship pair, triangle denotes no-kinship pair.

a MMD based loss is proposed in this paper. In addition, inspired by generative adversarial net (GAN), an adversarial loss is proposed to further improve the robustness and avoid overfitting. The pipeline of the proposed Adv-Kin methods is shown in Fig. 2.

The key contributions of this work are threefold.

– We propose a new loss function (called MMD loss) to solve the problem of distribution difference in high-level features. With the joint supervision of the MMD based loss and the contrastive loss, the highly discriminative features can be obtained.
– In order to further improve the robustness of CNN model, inspired by GAN, an adversarial loss is proposed in this paper. The discrimination and robustness of deep features can be further enhanced by the game between the contrastive loss and the adversarial loss.
– Experimental comparisons with shallow and deep learning methods demonstrate that our methods outperform many state-of-the-art methods, and the gap of human-machine performance is further narrowed.

2   Related Work

In this section, we review two closely related topics with this paper: kinship verification and deep convolutional networks.

2.1   Kinship Verification

Kinship verification via facial image analysis is a challenging problem in computer vision. Existing feature representation approaches for kin-relation data include histogram of gradient (HOG) [8], scale-invariant feature transform (SIFT) [2], and local binary pattern (LBP) [2]. Some algorithms aim to learn an effective metric or model for distinguishing whether two face images are with kinship relation, such as neighborhood repulsed metric learning (NRML) [2], prototype-based discriminative feature learning (PDFL) [9], transfer subspace learning [10,11], support vector machine (SVM) [9], large margin multi-metric learning [12], ensemble similarity learning (ESL) [13]. Those previous works have achieved great progress over the challenging kinship verification. However, the common shortcoming is that the extracted image features are general representation of faces and lack of structural kin-relation meaning.

2.2 Deep Convolutional Networks

Deep learning has shown its effectiveness in face recognition. CNN is an end-to-end supervised learning methods from pixel based images to the high-level semantic. The features from the bottom to top in the network architecture can be identified from low-level and high-level image representation. Several popular CNN models are summarized as follows. MTCNN [14] used the candidate CNNs to detect facial landmarks. A Deepface [15] was proposed to solve 3D-align issue. FaceNet [1] constructed a triplet-loss model to improve the face verification accuracy. Recently, the center-loss model proposed in [6] aims to obtain within-class separable features. GAN [16] is a hot framework with generative and discriminative model via an adversarial process. SMCNN [3] achieved the kin-relation verification through a similarity metric based cost function. Although these algorithms achieved surprisingly good performance for computer vision, the progress of kinship verification is still insufficient.

3 Adv-Kin Method

3.1 The Contrastive Loss

In order to obtain kinship specific features, a siamese CNN that contains 4 convolutional layers is adopted. Each convolutional layer is followed by a max pooling layer. The input is a pair of 64×64 RGB kinship images. There are two fully-connected layers, and the discriminative deep features are drawn from the last fully-connected layer. For clarity, the CNN model with contrastive loss is termed as the baseline. The details of the baseline model are described in Table 1.

Table 1. Baseline configuration.

Conv1	Pool1	Conv2	Pool2	Conv3	Pool3	Conv4	FC
conv11-6	max-2	conv21-16	max-2	conv31-30	max-2	conv4-60	FC1-128
conv12-6		conv22-16		conv32-30			FC2-80

In baseline model, contrastive loss is acted as a supervisory signal. Let x_n^1, x_n^2 are the nth features of left and right kinship images, respectively. The contrastive loss function is presented as follows.

$$L_C = \frac{1}{2N} \sum_{n=1}^{N} (y_n d^2 + (1 - y_n) \max(margin - d, 0)^2) \qquad (1)$$

where N denotes the batch size, $d = ||x_n^1 - x_n^2||_2$ is the Euclidean distance between x_n^1 and x_n^2, and y_n denotes the label of the nth pair of kinship samples. The label is 1 if there is a kinship relation between two persons, otherwise 0. $margin$ is an adjustable parameter, which can control the maximal distance of negative pair.

Hence, it is concluded that the aim of contrastive loss is to train a model by pulling the positive pair as close as possible, while repulsing the negative pair as far as possible, simultaneously. In generic CNN model, contrastive loss normally acts on the last fully-connected layer only, but the distribution difference between the two fully-connected layers is not considered. The discrimination of deep features cannot be further improved under the influence of this distribution difference.

3.2 MMD Based Adversarial Loss

MMD is a straight-forward test statistic to calculate the difference between distribution embeddings. It can be used to minimize the distribution difference between different domains on the domain adaptive issue [17]. Let $\hbar$ be the reproducing kernel Hilbert space (RKHS). Given two distributions s and t, which are mapped to a reproducing kernel Hilbert space by using function $\phi(\cdot)$. The MMD between s and t is defined as

$$\text{MMD}^2(s, t) = \sup_{||\phi||_\hbar \leq 1} ||E_{\mathbf{x}^s \sim s}[\phi(\mathbf{x}^s)] - E_{\mathbf{x}^t \sim t}[\phi(\mathbf{x}^t)]||_\hbar^2 \qquad (2)$$

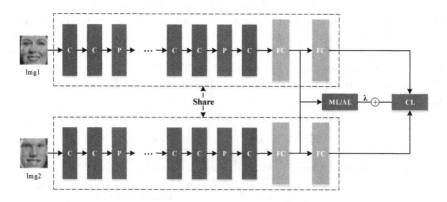

Fig. 3. The proposed Adv-Kin architecture.

where $E_{\mathbf{x}^s \sim s}[\phi(\cdot)]$ denotes the expectation with regard to the distribution s, and $||\phi||_\hbar \leq 1$ defines a set of functions in the unit ball of a RKHS $\hbar$. The most important property is that, we have MMD $(s,t) = 0$ if and only if $s = t$.

Inspired by MMD and GAN, we propose the Adv-Kin method, as shown in Fig. 3. The input of our CNN model is a pair of face images, one comes from parents, and the other from children. Thus, the distribution difference exists between parents domain and children domain. In order to minimize this difference, inspired by MMD, a MMD based loss is proposed as

$$L_M = \frac{1}{2N} \sum_{n=1}^{N} (y_n ||\phi(\mathbf{x}_n^1) - \phi(\mathbf{x}_n^2)||_\hbar^2 - (1 - y_n)||\phi(\mathbf{x}_n^1) - \phi(\mathbf{x}_n^2)||_\hbar^2) \quad (3)$$

However, some indirect approaches are also used to optimize the property of a system or a network. For example, robustness can be improved by introducing the additive interference. This thought is also applied to the CNN model, the performance of GAN has been improved just by the adversarial process between generative model and discriminative model [16]. Inspired by GAN, in order to further improve the discrimination and robustness of deep features, the adversarial loss is proposed as

$$L_A = -\frac{1}{2N} \sum_{n=1}^{N} (y_n ||\phi(\mathbf{x}_n^1) - \phi(\mathbf{x}_n^2)||_\hbar^2 - (1 - y_n)||\phi(\mathbf{x}_n^1) - \phi(\mathbf{x}_n^2)||_\hbar^2) \quad (4)$$

We adopt the joint supervision of contrastive loss and adversarial loss to train the CNN model for kin-relation features learning, as formulated in Eq. (5).

$$\begin{aligned} L &= L_C + \lambda L_A \\ &= \frac{1}{2N} \sum_{n=1}^{N} (y_n d^2 + (1 - y_n) \max(margin - d, 0)^2 \\ &\quad + \lambda (1 - 2y_n)(||\phi(\mathbf{x}_n^1) - \phi(\mathbf{x}_n^2)||_\hbar^2) \end{aligned} \quad (5)$$

where λ is a scalar used for balancing the two functions. The contrastive loss can be considered as a special case of this joint supervision, if λ is set to 0. Effected by game between adversarial loss and contrastive loss like Eq. (5), the robustness of deep features layer can be further improved.

By comparing MMD loss with adversarial loss, the only difference is the minus sign. So only the optimizion of adversarial loss is explained as follows.

In Eq. (4), $\phi(\cdot)$ denotes the feature map associated with the kernel map $k(\mathbf{x}_n^1, \mathbf{x}_n^2) = \langle \phi(\mathbf{x}_n^1), \phi(\mathbf{x}_n^2) \rangle$. Thus, the Eq. (4) can be rewritten as

$$L_A = \frac{1}{2N} \sum_{n=1}^{N} (1 - 2y_n)(k(\mathbf{x}_n^1, \mathbf{x}_n^1) + k(\mathbf{x}_n^2, \mathbf{x}_n^2) - 2k(\mathbf{x}_n^1, \mathbf{x}_n^2)) \quad (6)$$

Here, we adopt the Gaussian kernel function to optimize the proposed loss. The gradients of L_A with respect to $\mathbf{x}_n^1$ and $\mathbf{x}_n^2$ are computed respectively as:

$$\frac{\partial L_A}{\partial \mathbf{x}_n^1} = \frac{1}{N\sigma^2}(1 - 2y_n)\exp(-\frac{||\mathbf{x}_n^1 - \mathbf{x}_n^2||_2^2}{2\sigma^2})(\mathbf{x}_n^1 - \mathbf{x}_n^2) \qquad (7)$$

$$\frac{\partial L_A}{\partial \mathbf{x}_n^2} = \frac{1}{N\sigma^2}(1 - 2y_n)\exp(-\frac{||\mathbf{x}_n^1 - \mathbf{x}_n^2||_2^2}{2\sigma^2})(\mathbf{x}_n^2 - \mathbf{x}_n^1) \qquad (8)$$

4   Experiments

In this section, in order to demonstrate the effectiveness of our proposed approach, four benchmark kinship datasets are used.

4.1   Datasets

In experiments, KinFace data (4K) is considered, which includes four publicly available datasets, such as KinFaceW-I, KinFaceW-II [2], Cornell KinFace [8] and UB KinFace [18].

- Both KinFaceW-I and KinFaceW-II include four different types of kin relationships: father-son (F-S), father-daughter (F-D), mother-son (M-S) and mother-daughter (M-D). KinFaceW-I consists of 156, 134, 116, and 127 pairs, respectively. KinFaceW-II consists of 250 pairs for each relationship.
- Cornell KinFace contains totally 150 parent-child pairs.
- UB KinFace contains 200 triplets and each triplet is structured by child, young parent and old parent.

4.2   Experimental Setup

In experiments, the proposed models are trained on KinFace via 5-fold cross validation, and finally NRML metric [2] is used for kinship verification. The mini-batch stochastic gradient descent (SGD) based error back propagation algorithm is used for training, with an initial learning rate of 10^{-2}. The batch size is 151 images, and the *margin* of contrastive loss is set as 1.

We have compared Adv-Kin method with four state-of-the-art methods in kinship verification, including two shallow learning methods such as MNRML [2] and MPDFL [9], and two deep learning methods such as SMCNN [3] and DKV [7]. Additionally, the performance comparison with human score [9] is also analyzed. Notably, for all algorithms, 5-fold cross-validation is used by following the standard setting.

4.3   Comparison with Previous Methods

The verification results of the proposed MMD Loss (i.e. ML) and Adversarial Loss (i.e. AL) on four benchmark kinship datasets have been shown in Table 2. Specifically, from the results listed in Table 2, we can observe that:

- The proposed Adv-Kin methods consistently outperform state-of-the art face verification methods, i.e. MNRML and MPDFL based on feature ensemble and metric learning. The effectiveness of high-level kin-relation semantic discovery is demonstrated.
- The proposed Adv-Kin methods also outperform the deep learning based face verification methods, i.e. SMCNN and DKV which are modeled under the generic loss.
- By comparing our method with human knowledge on the KinFaceW-I and KinFaceW-II, the results show that our methods achieve even better performance than human.
- By comparing ML with AL, we get that AL based Adv-Kin shows superiority to ML based Adv-Kin. Thus it can be seen that the robustness of deep features can be further improved by introducing adversarial characteristic.
- For UB dataset, the accuracy of our methods is lower than MNRML and MPDFL. The reason may be that UB datasets consists of triplet samples, the contrastive loss may not distinguish the positive samples and negative samples in this dataset. However, the result of Adv-Kin methods are better than contrastive loss based baseline, it means that our methods still work in UB data.

Table 2. Accuracy of different methods. ML and AL denote the Adv-Kin method with MMD loss and adversarial loss, respectively.

Methods	KinFaceW-I					KinFaceW-II					UB			Cor
	F-S	F-D	M-S	M-D	Mean	F-S	F-D	M-S	M-D	Mean	0-1	0-2	Mean	-
Human A	62.0	60.0	68.0	72.0	65.6	63.0	63.0	71.0	75.0	70.9	-	-	-	-
Human B	68.0	66.5	74.0	75.0	70.9	72.0	72.5	77.0	80.0	75.4	-	-	-	-
MNRML	72.5	66.5	66.2	72.0	69.6	76.9	74.3	77.4	77.6	76.5	67.3	66.8	67.1	71.6
MPDFL	73.5	67.5	66.1	73.1	70.1	77.3	74.7	77.8	78.0	77.0	**67.5**	**67.0**	**67.3**	71.9
SMCNN	75.0	75.0	68.7	72.2	72.7	75.0	79.0	78.0	85.0	79.3	-	-	-	-
DKV	71.8	62.7	66.4	66.6	66.9	73.4	68.2	71.0	72.8	71.3	-	-	-	-
Baseline	74.7	**77.6**	72.4	81.1	76.5	85.8	85.8	84	83.8	84.5	58.3	60.0	59.2	76.2
ML	**77.3**	74.6	**78.0**	83.6	78.4	85.8	84.6	86.6	**88.0**	86.3	59.8	61.0	60.4	78.3
AL	76.9	77.3	75.8	**85.9**	**80.0**	**86.2**	**86.2**	**87.4**	87.0	**86.9**	60.3	63.8	62.1	**79.6**

4.4 Parameter Analysis

The parameter σ^2 is first to be investigated. Table 3 shows the accuracy of ML and AL versus different bandwidth σ^2. It can be seen that ML and AL based Adv-Kin can obtain the best classification performance when σ^2 is 0.5 and 1.0, respectively. We can also observe that the proposed methods demonstrate a stable recognition performance with different bandwidth σ^2.

After fixing σ^2, we also evaluate the performance with different loss weight λ. Table 4 shows the accuracy of ML and AL versus different loss weight λ. We can see that ML and AL based Adv-Kin can obtain the best classification performance when λ is set as 2.0 and 0.2, respectively.

Table 3. Accuracy of ML and AL with different bandwidth σ^2.

Methods	σ^2	KinFaceW-I					KinFaceW-II				
		F-S	F-D	M-S	M-D	Mean	F-S	F-D	M-S	M-D	Mean
ML	0.5	**77.3**	74.6	**78.0**	**83.6**	**78.4**	**85.8**	**84.6**	**86.6**	**88.0**	**86.3**
ML	1.0	75.0	**76.9**	73.7	83.5	77.3	84.4	84.0	85.4	87.0	85.2
ML	2.0	75.4	76.8	75.9	82.3	77.6	84.8	83.2	85.2	**88.0**	85.2
AL	0.5	**75.3**	74.3	75.4	79.5	76.1	85.2	82.6	84.0	86.8	84.7
AL	1.0	74.4	**76.9**	75.9	**85.0**	**78.1**	**87.4**	85.0	**86.8**	**87.0**	**86.6**
AL	2.0	74.7	74.3	**77.1**	81.4	76.9	85.8	**85.4**	83.4	**87.0**	85.4

Table 4. Accuracy of ML and AL with different loss weight λ.

Methods	λ	KinFaceW-I					KinFaceW-II				
		F-S	F-D	M-S	M-D	Mean	F-S	F-D	M-S	M-D	Mean
ML	0.2	76.0	73.9	73.6	80.7	76.1	83.8	83.8	82.6	83.4	83.4
ML	1.0	75.0	**76.5**	75.0	81.9	77.1	84.0	83.8	**87.0**	86.2	85.3
ML	2.0	**77.3**	74.6	**78.0**	**83.6**	**78.4**	**85.8**	**84.6**	86.6	**88.0**	**86.3**
AL	0.2	**76.9**	**77.3**	**75.8**	**85.9**	**80.0**	85.2	85.4	**88.6**	**88.0**	86.8
AL	1.0	76.3	**77.3**	74.6	84.6	78.2	**86.2**	**86.2**	87.4	87.0	**86.9**
AL	2.0	74.4	76.9	75.9	85.0	78.1	**87.4**	85.0	86.8	87.0	86.6

5 Conclusion

In this paper, we propose two loss functions as supervisory signals for kinship verification, which is motivated by the MMD and GAN. The performance of CNN model for kinship verification can be improved by using of the MMD loss to minimize the distribution difference between parents domain and children domain. In order to improve the discrimination and robustness of deep features, inspired by GAN, the adversarial loss is proposed. Extensive experiments on the benchmark KinFaceW-I, KinFaceW-II, Cornell KinFace and UB KinFace show the promising results compared to many state-of-the-art methods. In future, the combined deep learning and metric learning will be studied.

Acknowledgements. This work was supported by the National Science Fund of China under Grants (61771079, 61401048) and the Fundamental Research Funds for the Central Universities (No. 106112017CDJQJ168819).

References

1. Schroff, F., Kalenichenko, D., Philbin, J.: Facenet: a unified embedding for face recognition and clustering. In: Proceedings of the IEEE Conference on Computer Vision and Pattern Recognition, pp. 815–823 (2015)

2. Lu, J., Zhou, X., Tan, Y.P., Shang, Y., Zhou, J.: Neighborhood repulsed metric learning for kinship verification. Proc. IEEE Trans. Pattern Anal. Mach. Intell. **36**(2), 331–345 (2014)

3. Li, L., Feng, X., Wu, X., Xia, Z., Hadid, A.: Kinship verification from faces via similarity metric based convolutional neural network. In: Campilho, A., Karray, F. (eds.) ICIAR 2016. LNCS, vol. 9730, pp. 539–548. Springer, Cham (2016). doi:10. 1007/978-3-319-41501-7_60

4. Hinton, G.E., Salakhutdinov, R.R.: Reducing the dimensionality of data with neural networks. Science **313**(5786), 504–507 (2006)

5. Glorot, X., Bordes, A., Bengio, Y.: Domain adaptation for large-scale sentiment classification: a deep learning approach. In: Proceedings of the 28th International Conference on Machine Learning, pp. 513–520 (2011)

6. Wen, Y., Zhang, K., Li, Z., Qiao, Y.: A discriminative feature learning approach for deep face recognition. In: Computers & Operations Research, pp. 11–26 (2016)

7. Wang, M., Li, Z., Shu, X., Wang, J.: Deep kinship verification. In: Proceedings of the IEEE International Workshop on Multimedia Signal Processing, pp. 1–6 (2015)

8. Fang, R., Tang, K.D., Snavely, N., Chen, T.: Towards computational models of kinship verification. In: Proceedings of the 17th IEEE International Conference on Image Processing, pp. 1577–1580 (2010)

9. Yan, H., Lu, J., Zhou, X.: Prototype-based discriminative feature learning for kinship verification. IEEE Trans. Cybern. **45**(11), 2535–2545 (2015)

10. Shao, M., Xia, S., Fu, Y.: Genealogical face recognition based on UB KinFace database. In: Proceedings of the IEEE Computer Society Conference on Computer Vision and Pattern Recognition Workshops, pp. 60–65 (2011)

11. Xia, S., Shao, M., Fu, Y.: Kinship verification through transfer learning. In: Proceedings of the International Joint Conference on Artificial Intelligence, pp. 2534–2544 (2011)

12. Hu, J., Lu, J., Yuan, J., Tan, Y.-P.: Large margin multi-metric learning for face and kinship verification in the wild. In: Cremers, D., Reid, I., Saito, H., Yang, M.-H. (eds.) ACCV 2014. LNCS, vol. 9005, pp. 252–267. Springer, Cham (2015). doi:10.1007/978-3-319-16811-1_17

13. Zhou, X., Shang, Y., Yan, H., Guo, G.: Ensemble similarity learning for kinship verification from facial images in the wild. Inf. Fusion **32**, 40–48 (2016)

14. Zhang, K., Zhang, Z., Li, Z., Qiao, Y.: Joint face detection and alignment using multitask cascaded convolutional networks. IEEE Sig. Process. Lett. **2**(10), 1499–1503 (2016)

15. Taigman, Y., Yang, M., Ranzato, M., Wolf, L.: Deepface: closing the gap to human-level performance in face verification. In: Proceedings of the IEEE Conference on Computer Vision and Pattern Recognition, pp. 1701–1708 (2014)

16. Goodfellow, I., Pouget-Abadie, J., Mirza, M., Xu, B., Warde-Farley, D., Ozair, S., Aaron, C., Bengio, Y.: Generative adversarial nets. In: Advances in Neural Information Processing Systems, pp. 2672–2680 (2014)

17. Long, M., Cao, Y., Wang, J., Jordan, M.: Learning transferable features with deep adaptation networks. In: Proceedings of the International Conference on Machine Learning, pp. 97–105 (2015)

18. Xia, S., Shao, M., Fu, Y.: Kinship verification through transfer learning. In: Proceedings of the International Joint Conference on Artificial Intelligence, pp. 2539–2544 (2011)

Max-Feature-Map Based Light Convolutional Embedding Networks for Face Verification

Zhou Yang[1], Meng Jian[1], Bingkun Bao[2,3(✉)], and Lifang Wu[1]

[1] Faculty of Information Technology, Beijing University of Technology,
Beijing, China
yangzhoufrank@yeah.net, jianmeng648@163.com,
lfwu@bjut.edu.cn
[2] Nanjing Jingjunhai Network Ltd., Nanjing, Jiangsu, China
bingkunbao@gmail.com
[3] National Laboratory of Pattern Recognition, Institute of Automation,
Chinese Academy of Sciences, Beijing, China

Abstract. The powerful image feature extraction ability of convolutional neural network makes it possible to achieve great success in the field of face recognition. However, this category of models tend to be deep and paralleled which is not capable to be applied in real-time face recognition tasks. In order to improve its feasibility, we propose a max-feature-map activation based fully convolutional structure to extract face features with higher speed and less computational cost. The learned model has a great potential on embedding in the hardware devices due to its high recognition performance and small storage space. Experimental results demonstrate that the proposed model is *63* times smaller in comparison with the famous VGG model. At the same time, *96.80%* verification accuracy is achieved for a single network on LFW benchmark.

Keywords: Face verification · Convolutional neural network · Feature extraction

1 Introduction

With the development of computer vision techniques and advanced hardware support, convolutional neural network (CNN) gradually becomes one of the most widely used and successful face recognition and verification algorithms in recent years. CNN construction is initially employed to solve the multiclass classification problem [1] and achieves great success. With further investigation on this structure, other functions are also developed, for instance, object detection [2], natural language processing [3, 4], face recognition [5–7] and so on.

For the face verification task, since the working principle of convnet is more similar to the characteristics of biological neural network, numerous breakthroughs are made on various challenging recognition tasks. On LFW [19] benchmark, the results of CNN based algorithms [7] outperform human performance [8, 9] on the face verification tasks. CNN is capable of learning robust feature of human faces even the images are filled with noise or disturbance like pose variation, background chaos, illumination and so on.

© Springer International Publishing AG 2017
J. Zhou et al. (Eds.): CCBR 2017, LNCS 10568, pp. 58–65, 2017.
https://doi.org/10.1007/978-3-319-69923-3_7

The deep model is able to capture the tiny but discriminative characteristic of human face which is tough for human eyes to recognize. However, many existing CNN based recognition algorithms depend on complex data pre-processing method [5] or deep network [10] with numerous connection parameters and parallel computing. Thus, for the real-time supervision system, current CNN based algorithms require to transmit captured data to the server which cannot meet the need of real-time recognition tasks. Also, some methods [6, 11] simultaneously utilize both verification and identification supervisory signals to train the deep model. However, the trade-off between identification and verification loss is hard to set.

Light CNN [12–14] utilized Max-Feature-Map (MFM) activation to get a compact and informative feature expression from competitive relationship between two feature maps. This ingenious design reduces the parameters to some degree in the network. The idea of MFM operation solves the problem of key message lost during the first layers caused by ReLU activation. However, the information in the fully connected layer still exists data redundancy which may reduce the availability of real-time deployment of the algorithm. Fully Convolutional Networks (FCN) [15] discards non-convolution portion in CNN and trains a network with only stacked convolutional layers. As an extension of traditional CNN structure, the idea of fully convolutional arrangement also has a great potential in classification field. However, to our knowledge, few of people and organizations try to transplant this idea in face verification and identification tasks.

In this work, we deeply analyze the data distribution and propagation in the network and then combine MFM operation with fully convolutional layer structure and then build a deep learning framework, denoted as Improved Light CNN. The contributions of the proposed Improved Light CNN for face verification task are summarized as follows.

- The MFM operation, which plays the role of activation in the proposed network, produces compact representation and sparse connection. The proposed model employs convolutional structure instead of fully-connected structure to alleviate data redundancy in feature representation. Both MFM and convolutional embedding make the model occupy relatively small disk space with low computational burden.

- Due to the powerful feature selection ability of our network, a low dimension vector (256-d) is capable enough to represent discriminative face characteristics. Such low dimensional data advances the efficiency of information processing and analysis in the later steps. Hence the superiority of less computational burden gives our model a great potential and probability for embedding in real-time applications.

The paper is organized as follows. In Sect. 2, we describe the architecture of Improved Light CNN network and detailed information of each layer. The performance on LFW benchmark and the computational efficiency of the proposed model are presented in Sect. 3. Finally, we briefly conclude this work in Sect. 4.

2   Network Architecture

In this section, we firstly introduce the overall architecture of Improved Light CNN framework and then discuss the principle and feasibility of feature extraction from a convolutional layer.

2.1   The Improved Light CNN Framework

The configuration and detailed parameters of Improved Light CNN network are outlined in Table 1. The network consists of 6 convolutional layers, 4 max-pooling layers and MFM activations. Also, we utilize 1×1 kernel size convolutional layers as network in network architecture [10] which can introduce nonlinear to the network and improve feature extraction ability of the model. MFM function, adopted as activation in our network, is an efficient and convenient feature selection tool. The working principle of MFM operation can be shown via Fig. 1. Since MFM operation brings the competition relationship into network, informative nodes are able to be kept during forward

Table 1. Architecture of the proposed Improved Light CNN. In the left column of the table, the layer names refer to the layers in the network built in Caffe framework. Conv refers to convolutional layer, MFM denotes as MFM activation and Pool refers to pooling layer.

Layer name	Filter size	Output size	Parameters
Conv1	$6 \times 6/2, 2$	$64 \times 64 \times 96$	3.4K
MFM1	-	$64 \times 64 \times 48$	-
Pool1	$2 \times 2/2$	$32 \times 32 \times 48$	-
Conv1a	$1 \times 1/1$	$32 \times 32 \times 96$	4.6K
MFM1a	-	$32 \times 32 \times 48$	-
Conv2	$3 \times 3/1, 1$	$32 \times 32 \times 192$	82K
MFM2	-	$32 \times 32 \times 96$	-
Pool2	$2 \times 2/2$	$16 \times 16 \times 96$	-
Conv2a	$1 \times 1/1$	$16 \times 16 \times 192$	18K
MFM2a	-	$16 \times 16 \times 96$	-
Conv3	$3 \times 3/1, 1$	$16 \times 16 \times 384$	331K
MFM3	-	$16 \times 16 \times 192$	-
Pool3	$2 \times 2/2$	$8 \times 8 \times 192$	-
Conv3a	$1 \times 1/1$	$8 \times 8 \times 384$	73K
MFM3a	-	$8 \times 8 \times 192$	-
Conv4	$3 \times 3/1, 1$	$8 \times 8 \times 256$	442K
MFM4	-	$8 \times 8 \times 128$	-
Conv4a	$1 \times 1/1$	$8 \times 8 \times 256$	32K
MFM4a	-	$8 \times 8 \times 128$	-
Conv5	$3 \times 3/1$	$8 \times 8 \times 256$	131K
MFM5	-	$8 \times 8 \times 128$	-
Pool4	$2 \times 2/2$	$4 \times 4 \times 128$	-
Conv-fc	$4 \times 4/1$	512	1048K
MFM-Conv	-	256	-
Total	-	-	2165K

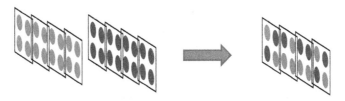

Fig. 1. Illustration of MFM operation. The result values from MFM operation are the max ones between the neural nodes in the corresponding positions. The calculated feature map after MFM operation contains the activated neuron from previous feature maps.

propagation. At the same time, convolutional layer can do the similar job as the fully connected layer as long as expanding the kernel size to cover the whole feature map.

Given a convolutional layer which outputs 2 N feature maps. Denoting by W and H as the width and the height of the feature and by z_{ij}^{l+N} as the neural nodes in the feature maps, where N = {1, ..., 2 N}, $1 \leq l \leq N$, $1 \leq i \leq H$, $1 \leq j \leq W$. The MFM operation can be represented as

$$\hat{z}_{ij}^{l} = max\left(z_{ij}^{l}, z_{ij}^{l+N}\right) \qquad (1)$$

2.2 Face Feature Extraction from Convolutional Layer

Traditional CNN based face verification models often extract face feature vectors from the fully-connected layer. However, in this case, data redundancy may be caused to some extent because the majority of learned parameters are in the fully-connected layer.

When the verification algorithm is embedded on mobile devices, too much computational pressure may lead to unexpected error which may degrade the user experience.

In order to alleviate the computational burden and enhance the practicability in real-time applications, we propose a new method of applying MFM operation as network activation and replace the fully-connected layer in traditional CNN by a convolutional layer. The core of convolutional layer is local connection while the fully-connected layer is global connection. When we expand the kernel size in a convolutional layer until covering the whole input image, it can be approximately regarded as fully-connected construction. Both of the above two structures utilize dot product to compute neuron output. A 512-dimensional column feature vector will be generated after each global kernel convolution as shown in Fig. 2. The feature representations will be further compressed and simplified by MFM activation to a 256-dimensional face representation.

Pool4 Output   Conv-fc   Feature Vector

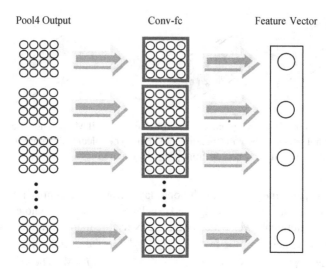

Fig. 2. Conv-fc layer process the feature map generated from Pool4 layer by convolutional layer with global information kernel. The output is 512-D column feature vectors.

3   Experiments

In this section, we firstly introduce the CASIA-Webface database [11] and the training methodology of Improved Light CNN network. Then we briefly present the face image pre-processing method. Finally, we evaluate our model on LFW standard testing benchmark and compare the results as well as compute efficiency with other deep learning model.

3.1   Face Image Pre-processing

CASIA-Webface, one of the biggest public face image databases, is chosen to train our Improved Light CNN network. The database contains 493,456 images from 10,575 various identities. The images are all randomly collected from Internet which can guarantee the generalization ability of learned model. The size of the original images in the database are all 250×250, which contains some noises including complex backgrounds and face pose variations. To ensure efficiently feature learning of the model, we pre-process the original image to eliminate the interference caused by pose variation to a great extent. We follow the pre-process idea in [14]. After image alignment, the distance between eyes center and mouth center and the distance of eyes center to the top of the image are both fixed into 48 pixels. This operation makes it possible to effectively solve the problem of angled face recognition tasks.

3.2   Training Methodology

We utilize the open source deep learning framework Caffe [16] to train the Improved Light CNN model. For the partition of training set and validation set, we randomly select one image from every identity in the database as the validation part and treat the remaining as training resources. Moreover, the TITAN X GPU is equipped to train the model.

In data layer, we use crop operation to resize the input aligned image from 144×144 to 128×128. Also, we apply the mirror function to expand the training data which can alleviate the phenomenon of network overfitting. For the specific settings of hyper parameters, we set the initial learning rate to 1e-3 and gradually reduce to 1e-6 by step policy. The dropout ratio after MFM-Conv layer is set to 0.6. The momentum parameter is set to 0.9 and we use Xavier initialization policy in convolutional layer. Besides, because the network may face the problem of loss convergence the gradient explosion, we firstly set the learning rate in all the convolutional layer except the last one to 0 and the back propagation will only make effects on the last convolutional layer to train the classifier. When observing the network loss converges steadily, we recover the learning rate policy in each convolutional layer.

3.3   Results on the LFW Benchmark

We followed the standard unsupervised testing protocol on challenging LFW benchmark. There is no identities overlap between LFW dataset and CASIA-Webface dataset, which means all the images in the LFW is unacquainted to our model. Totally 6,000 face pairs which contains 3,000 positive pairs and 3,000 negative pairs are officially given for verification test. The testing images follows the same pre-processing method and are cropped into 128×128. Then we straightly extract the 256-D feature vectors from two images in one pair and compute their cosine similarity. The equal error rate (EER) obtained by ROC curve is applied to represent the performance of our model.

As shown in Table 2, our model achieves 96.80% accuracy on LFW database under unsupervised protocol. We do not try to build and test multi network models, because our model aims at real-time applications. The proposed Improved Light CNN drops slightly on accuracy compared with the original version of Light CNN which is mainly because we try to optimize the verification speed and storage place of the model thus it is acceptable to sacrifice part of the verification accuracy for further practicability of the model.

Table 2. Single network performance comparison with other method on LFW under unsupervised verification protocol.

Method	Networks	Accuracy	Protocol
LBPNet [17]	1	94.04%	Unsupervised
DeepFace [5]	1	95.92%	Unsupervised
DeepID2 [6]	1	95.43%	Unsupervised
Webface [11]	1	96.13%	Unsupervised
Webface + PCA [11]	1	96.30%	Unsupervised
Light CNN A [14]	1	97.77%	Unsupervised
Light CNN B [14]	1	98.13%	Unsupervised
Improved Light CNN	**1**	**96.80%**	**Unsupervised**

3.4   Performance on Computational Cost and Storage Space

The success of a feature extractor model cannot be reflected purely on its recognition performance. The computational efficiency and running burden ought to be considered at the same time. We make a specific comparison on model working efficiency between our model and other released deep learning frameworks including DeepFace, VGG, CenterLoss, Light CNN A and Light CNN B.

To prove the ability of fast face verification, we compare our model with DeepFace, VGG, Light CNN A and Light CNN B on computing efficiency. From Table 3, it is obvious that our model has a superiority on data processing speed and model storage cost. The results also demonstrate that the substitutability of fully connected layer by global kernel convolutional layer in classification tasks and feature extractions. Due to the small size, fast verification ability and less learning parameter, our model is able to make contribution to real-time identification and verification tasks.

Table 3. The model working cost compared with other method on parameters, feature dimension, operation time per image and storage space. The data is tested on a single Intel Xeon e3 CPU.

Model	Parameters	Feature dimension	Times (per image)	Storage space
DeepFace	120,000K	4096	198 ms	-
VGG [10]	27,749K	4096	455 ms	553 MB
CenterLoss [18]	19,596K	1024	140 ms	-
Light CNN A	3,961K	256	68 ms	26 MB
Light CNN B	5,556K	256	65 ms	32.8 MB
Improved Light CNN	2,165K	256	29 ms	8.7 MB

4   Conclusion

In this paper, we proposed a deep learning framework Improved Light CNN for efficiently face verification tasks. The network applies MFM activation to screen informative neural node and provide a compact data distribution for forward propagation. Fully convolutional structure is utilized to further reduce the data redundancy. A low dimensional feature representation is extracted from the model and achieves 96.60% on LFW verification task. Both small occupied space and optimized parameters make it more promising for embedding on smart devices and real-time supervision systems.

Acknowledgment. This work was supported in part by the National Natural Science Foundation of China under Grant 61572503, Beijing Natural Science Foundation Grant 4152053.

References

1. He, K., Zhang, X., Ren, S., Sun, J.: Delving deep into rectifiers: surpassing human-level performance on imagenet classification. CoRR, pp. 1026–1034 (2015)

2. Redmon, J., Divvala, S., Girshick, R., Farhadi, A.: You only look once: unified, real-time object detection. CoRR, pp. 779–788 (2016)
3. Nguyen, T.H., Grishman, R.: Relation extraction: perspective from convolutional neural networks. In: The Workshop on Vector Space Modeling for Natural Language Processing, pp. 39–48 (2015)
4. Zhang, Y., Wallace, B.: A sensitivity analysis of (and practitioners' guide to) convolutional neural networks for sentence classification. Comput. Sci. (2015)
5. Taigman, Y., Yang, M., Ranzato, M., Wolf, L.: DeepFace: closing the gap to human-level performance in face verification. In: IEEE Computer Vision and Pattern Recognition, pp. 1701–1708 (2014)
6. Sun, Y., Wang, X., Tang, X.: Deep learning face representation by joint identification-verification. Adv. Neural. Inf. Process. Syst. **27**, 1988–1996 (2015). MIT Press
7. Schroff, F., Kalenichenko, D., Philbin, J.: FaceNet: a unified embedding for face recognition and clustering. In: IEEE Conference on Computer Vision and Pattern Recognition, pp. 815–823 (2015)
8. Kumar, N., Berg, A.C., Belhumeur, P.N., Nayar, S.K.: Attribute and simile classifiers for face verification. In: IEEE International Conference on Computer Vision, pp. 365–372 (2010)
9. Kumar, N., Berg, A.C., Belhumeur, P.N., Nayar, S.K.: Describable visual attributes for face verification and image search. IEEE Trans. Pattern Anal. Mach. Intell. **33**, 1962–1977 (2011)
10. Simonyan, K., Zisserman, A.: Very deep convolutional networks for large-scale image recognition. Comput. Sci. (2014)
11. Yi, D., Lei, Z., Liao, S., Li, S.Z.: Learning face representation from scratch. Comput. Sci. (2014)
12. Wu, X.: Learning robust deep face representation. Comput. Sci. (2015)
13. Wu, X., He, R., Sun, Z.: A lightened CNN for deep face representation. Comput. Sci. (2015)
14. Wu, X., He, R., Sun, Z., Tan, T.: A light CNN for deep face representation with noisy labels. Comput. Sci. (2016)
15. Long, J., Shelhamer, E., Darrell, T.: Fully convolutional networks for semantic segmentation. In: IEEE Computer Vision and Pattern Recognition, pp. 3431–3440 (2015)
16. Jia, Y., Shelhamer, E., Donnahue, J., Karayev, S., Long, J., Girshick, R.B., Guadarrama, S., Darrell, T.: Caffe: convolutional architecture for fast feature embedding. In: ACM International Conference on Multimedia, pp. 675–678 (2014)
17. Xi, M., Chen, L., Polajnar, D., Tong, W.: Local binary pattern network: a deep learning approach for face recognition. In: IEEE International Conference on Image Processing (2016)
18. Wen, Y., Zhang, K., Li, Z., Qiao, Y.: A discriminative feature learning approach for deep face recognition. In: Leibe, B., Matas, J., Sebe, N., Welling, M. (eds.) ECCV 2016. LNCS, vol. 9911, pp. 499–515. Springer, Cham (2016). doi:10.1007/978-3-319-46478-7_31
19. Huang, G.B., Mattar, M., Berg, T., Learned-Miller, E.: Labeled faces in the wild: a database for studying face recognition in unconstrained environments. Month (2008)

Three Dimensional Face Recognition via Surface Harmonic Mapping and Deep Learning

Xiaofan Wei[1], Huibin Li[1(✉)], and Xianfeng David Gu[2]

[1] School of Mathematics and Statistics, Xi'an Jiaotong University, Xi'an, China
stoppable911222@stu.xjtu.edu.cn, huibinli@xjtu.edu.cn
[2] Department of Computer Science and Department of Mathematics,
State University of New York at Stony Brook, New York, USA
gu@cs.stonybrook.edu

Abstract. In this paper, we propose a general 3D face recognition framework by combining the idea of surface harmonic mapping and deep learning. In particular, given a 3D face scan, we first run the pre-processing pipeline and detect three main facial landmarks (i.e., nose tip and two inner eye corners). Then, harmonic mapping is employed to map the 3D coordinates and differential geometry quantities (e.g., normal vectors, curvatures) of each 3D face scan to a 2D unit disc domain, generating a group of 2D harmonic shape images (HSI). The 2D rotation of the harmonic shape images are removed by using the three detected landmarks. All these pose normalized harmonic shape images are fed into a pre-trained deep convolutional neural network (DCNN) to generate their deep representations. Finally, sparse representation classifier with score-level fusion is used for face similarity measurement and the final decision. The advantage of our method is twofold: *(i) it is a general framework and can be easily extended to other surface mapping and deep learning algorithms. (ii) it is registration-free and only needs three landmarks.* The effectiveness of the proposed framework was demonstrated on the BU-3DFE database, and reporting a rank-one recognition rate of 89.38% on the whole database.

Keywords: 3D face recognition · Surface harmonic mapping · Deep learning

1 Introduction

With the fast development of 3D scanning techniques, 3D face recognition has witnessed great success in the past decade. 3D face scans, capturing the full 3D geometry and shape information of human faces, more and more likely to play an irreplaceable effect for some core parts of face recognition system such as large-pose face alignment [1,2], anti-spoofing of extraordinary attack [3], and heterogeneous 3D or 2D-3D multi-modal face recognition [4].

Although traditional methods for 2D face recognition have achieve some progress [5–7], deep learning, particularly the DCNN based approaches have

© Springer International Publishing AG 2017
J. Zhou et al. (Eds.): CCBR 2017, LNCS 10568, pp. 66–76, 2017.
https://doi.org/10.1007/978-3-319-69923-3_8

achieved great breakthrough for 2D face detection, alignment and recognition [8–12]. There is no doubt that this success benefited from the availability of millions of 2D face images of different subjects for deep network training. For example, the Facenet proposed by Google [10] was trained by using 200 million images of eight million unique identities. However, deep learning is still far from exploited for 3D face recognition. Obviously, one of the main reason is that there is not enough 3D face scans publicly available, which can be used to train an end-to-end deep model for 3D face recognition. Another key bottleneck is the inherent difficult of running CNN on non-Euclidean surface manifolds. Fortunately, surface planar parameterization, which can build the one-to-one correspondence between 3D surface and its 2D parameter domain with geometry and shape preserving, opens a door of implementing DCNN on surface manifolds. Readers are strongly suggested to refer to [13,14] as two successful examples of applying deep learning on surfaces based on surface parameterization algorithms.

Following the same spirit of [13,14], in this paper, we propose to combine the idea of surface harmonic mapping and deep learning, and developing a general 3D face recognition framework. Notice that other surface mapping algorithms, such as conformal mapping [15] and area-preserving mapping [16] can also be used. Due to the limitation of enough training 3D face scans, we propose to use a pre-trained deep face CNN to extract the deep features of different harmonic shape images. The main pipeline of the proposed framework is shown in Fig. 1.

In the past decade, 3D face recognition methods have received widely attention [17,18] and a large number of approaches have been proposed. According to [19], these methods can be classified into three categories: (1) *Expression deformation modeling based approaches*, which generally assume that facial surfaces are non-rigid and deformable surfaces, and the deformation behaviors are modeled by statistical shape analysis. (2) *Intrinsic surface-distance based approaches*,

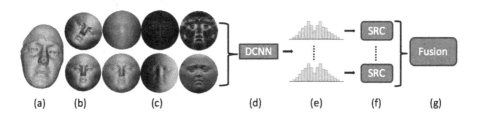

(a)   (b)   (c)   (d)   (e)   (f)   (g)

Fig. 1. Overview of the proposed approach. Given a 3D face scan with three automatically detected facial landmarks (i.e., nose tip and two inner eye corners) (a), we first run surface harmonic mapping algorithm, and generate the original harmonic map (i.e., harmonic depth image) and its rotation normalized map (b), from which, different harmonic shape images (c), including harmonic depth image, harmonic curvedness image, harmonic shape index image, and three harmonic normal component images can be generated. Then, each type of these harmonic shape images are fed into a pre-trained deep convolutional neural network (DCNN) (d), respectively, to generate their deep representations (e). Finally, sparse representation classifier is used for face similarity measurement (f) and score-level fusion (g) is used for the final decision.

which usually assume that facial surfaces are compact, connected, and zero-genus manifolds embedded in 2D Euclidean space. (3) *Local region or local feature based approaches*, which conduct 3D face recognition by matching some rigid regions, local texture descriptors or local shape descriptors. To overview all of those algorithms is out the scope of this paper, here we only review some very related works in the following.

There are already some works which use surface mapping for 3D face recognition, the idea of using harmonic mapping for 3D face surface matching was originally introduced in [20], in which the concept of harmonic shape images was firstly proposed. Pan *et al.* [21] proposed a 3D face recognition algorithm based on depth images of surface mapping. In particular, they used a conformal parametrization algorithm to minimize the harmonic energy, and the surface distortion is measured by considering the tradeoff between angle-preserving mapping and area-preserving mapping. Face recognition is conducted by performing the eigenface on the mapped depth images. Experiments was carried out on the FRGC v1.0 dataset which contains 276 individuals and totally 943 face models. An identification rate of 95% was reported. Wang *et al.* [15] proposed a general framework of using conformal geometry for 3D shape matching, recognition and stitching. Specifically, the least squares conformal maps was used for 3D face recognition. Although a recognition rate of 97.3% was reported, the face database used for evaluation only contains 100 3D face scans of 10 subjects. Szeptycki *et al.* [22] proposed a conformal mapping-based 3D face recognition. Their conformal mapping was computed by using the holomorphic one-forms. Then the Möbius transformation was used to "compress" facial expression sensitive regions, and $(2D)^2PCA$ was used to extract features from the 2D shape index maps. Finally, nearest neighbor classifier was used for face matching. A recognition rate of 86.43% was reported on 62 subjects randomly selected from the FRGC v2.0 dataset. This method was further extended by using only the eyes and nose part of the face for face recognition [23]. Experiment tests on a subset (231 subjects) of the FRGC v2.0 dataset show approximately 80% rank-one recognition rate. Recently, Echeagaray-Patron [24] proposed to use spectral conformal parameterization and curvature analysis for 3D facial recognition. Their method was tested on the scans of 30 subjects of the CASIA database and 30 subjects of the Gavab database. Han *et al.* [25] proposed to use conformal representation, i.e., conformal factor images and mean curvature images, for 3D face recognition. Linear Discriminant Analysis (LDA) was applied for feature extraction and the nearest neighbor classifier was applied for face matching. From the above discussions, we can see that surface mapping based 3D face recognition algorithms are still far from to be explored. All most all of the existing algorithms were evaluated on a small datasets and resulting in not competitive recognition scores.

2 Surface Harmonic Mapping

2.1 Surface Harmonic Mapping: Smooth Case

Suppose $\mathcal{S}$ is a smooth, topological disc surface embedding in Euclidean space $\mathbb{R}^3$ with induced Euclidean measure g. A harmonic function $f : \mathcal{S} \rightarrow \mathcal{D} \subset \mathbb{R}^2$ is defined as the minimizer of the following harmonic energy:

$$\min_f E(f) = \int_{\mathcal{S}} |\nabla_g(f)|^2 d\mathcal{A}. \tag{1}$$

A harmonic function satisfies the Laplace equation

$$\triangle_g f = 0, \tag{2}$$

with Dirichlet boundary condition

$$f|_{\partial \mathcal{S}} = h, \tag{3}$$

where $\partial \mathcal{S}$ denotes the boundary of $\mathcal{S}$, and h is a given function. Suppose we choose an isothermal coordinate system (u, v), then the Riemannian metric is represented as

$$g = e^{2\lambda(u,v)}(du^2 + dv^2), \tag{4}$$

and the Laplace-Beltrami operator is

$$\triangle_g = e^{-2\lambda(u,v)}\left(\frac{\partial^2}{\partial u^2}, \frac{\partial^2}{\partial v^2}\right). \tag{5}$$

Surface harmonic mapping is very useful for various applications, since it gives a diffeomrophism mapping from 3D surfaces and 2D domains under some appropriate conditions. According to Rado's theorem [26], suppose $f : \mathcal{S} \rightarrow \mathcal{D}$ is a surface harmonic mapping, $\mathcal{D}$ is a planar convex domain. If the restriction of the map on the boundary is a homeomorphism, then the interior mapping is also a diffeomorphism (i.e., a bijective and smooth mapping).

2.2 Surface Harmonic Mapping: Discrete Case

Now suppose that $\mathcal{M}$ is a discrete, topological disc triangulation mesh. A piecewise linear function $f : \mathcal{M} \rightarrow \mathcal{D} \subset \mathbb{R}^2$ defined as:

$$f(p) = \lambda_i f(v_i) + \lambda_j f(v_j) + \lambda_k f(v_k), \tag{6}$$

where $p = \lambda_i v_i + \lambda_j v_j + \lambda_k v_k$ is a point inside a triangle $[v_i, v_j, v_k]$, and $(\lambda_i, \lambda_j, \lambda_k)$ satisfy $\lambda_i + \lambda_j + \lambda_k = 1$, which are the *barycentric coordinates* of p. By direct computation, it is easy to show that the harmonic energy of function f can be written as

$$E(f) = \sum_{[v_i, v_j] \in M} w_{ij}(f(v_i) - f(v_j))^2, \tag{7}$$

where w_{ij} is the well-known *cotangent weight* on edge $[v_i, v_j]$, and defined as

$$w_{ij} = \begin{cases} \frac{1}{2}(cot\theta_k + cot\theta_l), & [v_i, v_j] \notin \partial M \\ \frac{1}{2}cot\theta_k, & [v_i, v_j] \in \partial M. \end{cases} \tag{8}$$

where θ_k is the corner angle in $[v_i, v_j, v_k]$ at vertex v_k, and θ_l is the corner angle in $[v_j, v_i, v_l]$ at vertex v_l. Then the discrete Laplace equation becomes:

$$E(f) = \sum_{[v_i, v_j] \in M} w_{ij}(f(v_i) - f(v_j)) = 0, \forall v_i \notin \partial M. \tag{9}$$

This is a linear equation system. In practice, we first uniformly map all the boundary vertices to an unit circle. Then, all edge weights w_{ij} are computed. For each interior vertex, we construct its discrete Laplace equation as (9) by using its surrounding vertices and solving the linear system. In this paper, we use the Harmonic Mapper[1] developed by David Gu to compute the surface harmonic mapping for all 3D face scans.

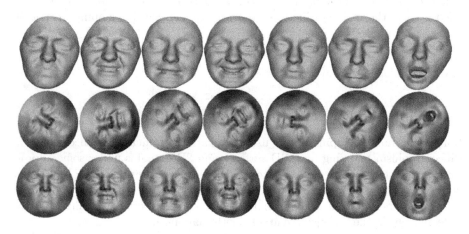

Fig. 2. Illustration of surface harmonic mapping: for each column, from top to bottom: original 3D face scan, its harmonic map, and rotation normalized harmonic map. And for each row, from left to right are different facial expressions: angry, disgust, fear, happiness, neutral, sadness and surprise.

3   Deep Representations of Harmonic Shape Images

Since the ordering of boundary vertices may different from one face scan to another, the harmonic maps may have different rotations as shown in the second

---

[1] http://www3.cs.stonybrook.edu/~gu/tutorial/HarmonicMap.html.

row of Fig. 2. In this paper, we use the mapped 2D planar coordinates of two inner eye corners to estimated a 2D rotation matrix:

$$\begin{pmatrix} cos\theta & -sin\theta \\ sin\theta & cos\theta \end{pmatrix}$$

for rotation normalization, where θ is the angle between the horizontal line and the segment connecting the two inner eye corners. The rotation normalized harmonic maps are shown in the bottom row of Fig. 2.

3.1   Harmonic Shape Images

Once we get the normalized surface harmonic map, different surface differential quantities can also be mapped to 2D domain. In this paper, we propose to transfer the surface coordinates, normals, and curvatures to 2D domain and generate different harmonic shape images for a given 3D face scan. For surface normal estimation, we first estimate the normal vector of each triangle according to the cross production of the edge vectors. Then, the normal vector at each vertex can be computed by averaging the normal vectors of its surrounding faces. According to Goldfeather and Interrante [27], the principal curvatures can be computed by fitting a cubic-order surface patch:

$$z(x, y) = \frac{A}{2}x^2 + Bxy + \frac{C}{2}y^2 + Dx^3 + Ex^2y + Fxy^2 + Gy^3 \qquad (10)$$

and its normal vectors $(z_x(x, y), z_y(x, y), -1)$ using both the 3D coordinates and the normal vectors of the associated local neighbor vertices (two-ring). The maximum principal curvatures κ_1 and the minimum principal curvatures κ_2 at a given vertex can be computed as the eigenvalues of the *Weingarten* matrix. Then the shape index values and the curvedness at each vertex can be estimated as

$$Shapeindex = \frac{1}{2} - \frac{1}{\pi}arctan(\frac{\kappa_1 + \kappa_2}{\kappa_1 - \kappa_2}) \qquad (11)$$

and

$$Curvedness = \sqrt{\kappa_1{}^2 + \kappa_2{}^2} \qquad (12)$$

All these differential quantities are transferred to a rotation normalized 2D disc domain according to the harmonic surface mapping. This give us a group of harmonic shape images, including harmonic depth image (HSI_g), harmonic shape index image (HSI_s), harmonic curvedness image (HSI_c), and three harmonic normal component images: HSI_{n_x}, HSI_{n_y}, and HSI_{n_z} (see Fig. 3).

3.2   Deep Representations of Harmonic Shape Images

To comprehensively highlight the harmonic shape images, in this paper, we use the "vgg deep face net" for deep feature extraction. This net was trained for 2D face recognition by using 982,803 face images of 2,622 identities [8]. It comprises

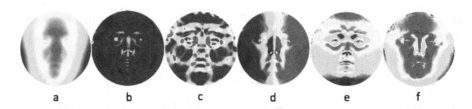

Fig. 3. Harmonic Shape Images (HSI) in color: from left to right, harmonic depth image (HSI$_g$), harmonic curvedness image (HSI$_c$), harmonic shape index image (HSI$_s$), and three harmonic normal component images: HSI$_{n_x}$, HSI$_{n_y}$, and HSI$_{n_z}$. (Color figure online)

16 learnable weight layers, 13 of which are convolutional layers and followed by 3 fully connected (FC) layers [28]. Each weight layer contains a linear operator followed by one or more non-linearities such as ReLU and max pooling. The input to this deep network is a color face image of size $214 \times 214 \times 3$. The outputs of the first two FC layers are 4,096 dimensional and the last FC layer has either 2,622 or 1,024 dimensions, depending on the face identification and verification tasks, respectively.

Given a harmonic shape image $I \in \mathbb{R}^{214 \times 214 \times 3}$ and a DCNN with L layers $\varphi_L \circ \cdots \circ \varphi_1$. The output of each layer $x_l = \varphi_l \circ \cdots \circ \varphi_1(x)$ can be seen as a descriptor tensor $x_l \in \mathbb{R}^{W_l \times H_l \times N_l}$, where W_l and H_l are the width and height of the tensor and N_l is the number of filters. If all φ_l are convolutional layers, this descriptor tensor can preserve the facial spatial information. The deep representation of harmonic shape image is generated by simply resize the descriptor tensor as a feature vector and then normalized to be unit norm. Note that considering the trade-off between feature dimension and generalization ability, we only use the activations of the last convolutional layer (i.e., *conv5-3* of the vgg deep face net) to generate the deep representations of different harmonic shape images, and denoted as DHSI$_g$, DHSI$_s$, DHSI$_c$, DHSI$_{n_x}$, DHSI$_{n_y}$, and DHSI$_{n_z}$.

4   Sparse Representation-Based Classifier

Sparse Representation-based classifier (SRC) is originally proposed for robust 2D face recognition [29] and then extended to 3D face recognition [30]. Given a gallery set with N 3D face scans, each of which belongs to one subject, we define the dictionary of sparse representation model as $D \doteq [d_1, d_2, \ldots, d_N]$. Then for any probe y we have

$$y = Dx + \varepsilon. \tag{13}$$

Sparse coefficient x in Eq. (13) can be solved by the following l_0 minimization problem:

$$\min \|y - Dx\|_2^2 \text{ s.t. } \|x\|_0 \leq L. \tag{14}$$

where L measures the sparsity of the representation coefficient. Assume $\hat{x}$ is the minimizer of problem (14), then the index of minimal reconstruction error vector:

$$r_i(\boldsymbol{y}) = \|\boldsymbol{y} - \boldsymbol{D}\delta_i(\hat{\boldsymbol{x}})\|_2^2, i = 1, 2, \ldots, N \tag{15}$$

delivers the identity of the probe $\boldsymbol{y}$, where δ_i is a characteristic function which selects the coefficient associated with the i-th gallery. In this paper, $\boldsymbol{d_i}$ and $\boldsymbol{y}$ are the deep features extracted from different harmonic shape images.

5   Experimental Results

5.1   Database and Experimental Protocol

In this paper, we use the BU-3DFE database [31] to evaluate the effectiveness of the proposed approach. This database contains 100 subjects (56 female and 44 male) with different ages, and with a variety of ethnic ancestries. For each subject, 24 samples with six prototypic expressions (happiness, disgust, fear, angry, surprise and sadness) of four intensity levels in addition to a neutral one are included. In our experiments, the single neutral sample of each subject is used as gallery, and the scans with different types of expressions are used as probe samples, respectively.

5.2   Effectiveness of the Deep Representations

To show the effectiveness of deep representations, we compare it with the widely used local texture descriptor: Multi-scale Local Binary Patterns (MS-LBP) for the same harmonic shape images and the same sparse representation-based classifier. All the parameters for MS-LBP are the same as the ones used in [30]. From Table 1, we can find that there existing considerable complementarity for different LBP encoding scales, and different harmonic shape images, especially for the three different harmonic normal component images. Moreover, deep representations of harmonic shape images (DHSI) always performs better than MS-LBP for all harmonic shape images except the harmonic curvedness map. Finally, the fusion of the three different harmonic normal component images and the harmonic shape index image, i.e., $DHSI_{s+n_{xyz}}$, achieves the best rank-one recognition rate of 89.38%. Fusing of harmonic depth image and harmonic curvedness image both drops the performance.

5.3   Comparison with the State-of-the-Art

In Table 2, we compare our approach with two state-of-the-art 3D face recognition methods for different facial expression subsets and the whole dataset. From the table, we can see that our approach are more robust to facial expression variations than [32,33]. In particular, our approach achieves rank-one scores of 92.0% and 95.8% for fear and sadness expressions, which outperform about 10% and 10.8%, respectively than [32]. Furthermore, it will be very interest if we can compare our results with the very related surface mapping based methods mentioned in the introduction such as [15,21,22,24,25]. However, due to the difficulties of reproducing these methods and variations in experimental protocols (most of these methods only used a small dataset or a small subset of a standard dataset like FRGC v2.0), conducting fair comparisons are difficult.

Table 1. Rank-one recognition rates on the whole BU-3DFE database.

	$LBP_{Q(1,8)}$	$LBP_{Q(2,16)}$	$LBP_{Q(3,24)}$	MS-LBP	DCNN
$DHSI_{n_x}$	61.29%	60.54%	54.54%	69.83%	**72.42%**
$DHSI_{n_y}$	66.38%	64.33%	54.54%	71.21%	**82.79%**
$DHSI_{n_z}$	65.04%	61.88%	57.25%	72.21%	**75.96%**
$DHSI_{n_{xyz}}$	72.83%	73.29%	73.25%	79.33%	**87.04%**
$DHSI_{s+n_{xyz}}$	75.04%	77.33%	78.92%	82.17%	**80.38%**
$DHSI_{g+s+n_{xyz}}$	73.75%	77.21%	78.58%	81.50%	**85.42%**
All	74.83%	79.33%	80.96%	83.21%	**83.83%**

Table 2. Comparison with the state-of-the-art for different facial expressions.

Approaches	Happy	Surprise	Fear	Sadness	Anger	Disgust	All
Hajati *et al.* [32]	86.0%	84.0%	82.0%	85.0%	93.0%	79.0%	84.83%
Emambakhsh *et al.* [33]	88.5%	91.0%	89.8%	92.3%	90.1%	81.8%	88.90%
Our approach ($DHSI_{s+n_{xyz}}$)	**88.8%**	83.0%	**92.0%**	**95.8%**	**93.5%**	**83.3%**	**89.38%**

6   Conclusion

In this paper, we proposed a general 3D face recognition framework by combing the idea of differential geometry and deep learning. In particular, surface harmonic mapping is employed to generate different harmonic shape images. Then, the vgg deep face net is used to extract the deep representations of different harmonic shape images. And finally, sparse representation classifier is used for face similarity measurement, and score-level fusion for the final decision. Experimental results carried out on the BU-3DFE dataset demonstrated the effectiveness of different DHSI, and their robustness to expression variations. The proposed framework opens a window of using deep learning for 3D face recognition. In the future, we will compare the performance of the proposed framework with different surface mapping algorithms. Furthermore, we will consider to collect more 3D face scans and train a deep face net to further improve the performance of the proposed framework.

Acknowledgement. This work was supported in part by the NSFC under grant 11401464, Chinese Postdoctoral Science Foundation under grant 2014M560785, and International Exchange Foundation of China NSFC and United Kingdom RS under grant 61711530242.

References

1. Zhu, X., Lei, Z., Liu, X., Shi, H., Li, S.Z.: Face alignment across large poses: a 3D solution. In: IEEE Conference on Computer Vision and Pattern Recognition, pp. 146–155 (2016)

2. Jourabloo, A., Liu, X.: Large-pose face alignment via CNN-based dense 3D model fitting. In: IEEE Conference on Computer Vision and Pattern Recognition, pp. 4188–4196 (2016)
3. Tang, Y., Chen, L.: 3D facial geometric attributes based anti-spoofing approach against mask attacks. In: IEEE Conference on Face and Gesture, pp. 1–8 (2017)
4. Zhang, J., Huang, D., Wang, Y., Sun, J.: Lock3DFace: a large-scale database of low-cost Kinect 3D faces. In: International Conference on Biometrics, pp. 1–8 (2016)
5. Shen, F., Shen, C., van den Hengel, A., Tang, Z.: Approximate least trimmed sum of squares fitting and applications in image analysis. IEEE Trans. Image Process. **22**(5), 1836–1847 (2013)
6. Shen, F., Yang, Y., Zhou, X., Shen, H.T.: Face identification with second-order pooling in single-layer networks. Neurocomputing **187**, 11–18 (2015)
7. Shen, F., Shen, C., Zhou, X., Yang, Y., Shen, H.T.: Face image classification by pooling raw features. Pattern Recogn. **54**, 94–103 (2016)
8. Parkhi, O.M., Vedaldi, A., Zisserman, A.: Deep face recognition. In: Proceedings of the British Machine Vision Conference, pp. 41.1–41.12 (2015)
9. Yi, D., Lei, Z., Liao, S., Li, S.Z.: Learning face representation from scratch. Computing Research Repository abs/1411.7923 (2014)
10. Schroff, F., Kalenichenko, D., Philbin, J.: Facenet: a unified embedding for face recognition and clustering. In: IEEE Conference on Computer Vision and Pattern Recognition, pp. 815–823 (2015)
11. Sun, Y., Wang, X., Tang, X.: Deep learning face representation from predicting 10,000 classes. In: IEEE Conference on Computer Vision and Pattern Recognition, pp. 1891–1898 (2014)
12. Taigman, Y., Yang, M., Ranzato, M., Wolf, L.: Deepface: closing the gap to human-level performance in face verification. In: IEEE Conference on Computer Vision and Pattern Recognition, pp. 1701–1708 (2014)
13. Sinha, A., Bai, J., Ramani, K.: Deep learning 3D shape surfaces using geometry images. In: Leibe, B., Matas, J., Sebe, N., Welling, M. (eds.) ECCV 2016. LNCS, vol. 9910, pp. 223–240. Springer, Cham (2016). doi:10.1007/978-3-319-46466-4_14
14. Maron, H., Galun, M., Aigerman, N., Trope, M., Dym, N., Yumer, E., Kim, V., Lipman, Y.: Convolutional neural networks on surfaces via seamless toric covers. ACM Trans. Graph. **36**, 1–10 (2017)
15. Wang, S., Wang, Y., Jin, M., Gu, X.D., Samaras, D.: Conformal geometry and its applications on 3D shape matching, recognition, and stitching. IEEE Trans. Pattern Anal. Mach. Intell. **29**(7), 1209–1220 (2007)
16. Su, Z., Wang, Y., Shi, R., Zeng, W., Sun, J., Luo, F., Gu, X.: Optimal mass transport for shape matching and comparison. IEEE Trans. Pattern Anal. Mach. Intell. **37**(11), 2246–2259 (2015)
17. Bowyer, K.W., Chang, K., Flynn, P.: A survey of approaches and challenges in 3D and multi-modal 3D + 2D face recognition. Comput. Vis. Image Underst. **101**, 1–15 (2006)
18. Smeets, D., Claes, P., Hermans, J., Vandermeulen, D., Suetens, P.: A comparative study of 3-D face recognition under expression variations. IEEE Trans. Syst. Man Cybern. Part C **42**(5), 710–727 (2012)
19. Drira, H., Amor, B.B., Srivastava, A., Daoudi, M., Slama, R.: 3D face recognition under expressions, occlusions, and pose variations. IEEE Trans. Pattern Anal. Mach. Intell. **35**(9), 2270–2283 (2013)
20. Zhang, D., Hebert, M.: Harmonic maps and their applications in surface matching. In: IEEE Computer Society Conference on Computer Vision and Pattern Recognition, vol. 2, p. 530 (1999)

21. Pan, G., Han, S., Wu, Z., Wang, Y.: 3D face recognition using mapped depth images. In: IEEE Computer Society Conference on Computer Vision and Pattern Recognition, p. 175 (2005)
22. Szeptycki, P., Ardabilian, M., Chen, L.: A coarse-to-fine curvature analysis-based rotation invariant 3D face landmarking. In: International Conference on Biometrics: Theory, Applications and Systems, pp. 3206–3211 (2009)
23. Szeptycki, P., Ardabilian, M., Chen, L., Zeng, W., Gu, D., Samaras, D.: Partial face biometry using shape decomposition on 2D conformal maps of faces. In: 20th International Conference on Pattern Recognition, pp. 1505–1508 (2010)
24. Echeagaray-Patron, B.A., Miramontes-Jaramillo, D., Kober, V.: Conformal parameterization and curvature analysis for 3D facial recognition. In: International Conference on Computational Science and Computational Intelligence, pp. 843–844 (2015)
25. Junhui, H., Fang, C., Ding, X., Sun, J., Gu, X.: 3D face recognition via conformal representation. In: Proceedings of SPIE - The International Society for Optical Engineering, vol. 9013 (2014)
26. Schoen, R., Yau, S.T.: Lectures on Harmonic Maps. International Press, Inc., Boston (1997)
27. Goldfeather, J., Interrante, V.: A novel cubic-order algorithm for approximating principal direction vectors. ACM Trans. Graph. **23**(1), 45–63 (2004)
28. Simonyan, K., Zisserman, A.: Very deep convolutional networks for large-scale image recognition. In: International Conference on Learning Representations (2015)
29. Wright, J., Yang, A.Y., Ganesh, A., Sastry, S.S., Ma, Y.: Robust face recognition via sparse representation. IEEE Trans. Pattern Anal. Mach. Intell. **31**(2), 210–227 (2009)
30. Li, H., Huang, D., Morvan, J., Chen, L., Wang, Y.: Expression-robust 3D face recognition via weighted sparse representation of multi-scale and multi-component local normal patterns. Neurocomputing **133**, 179–193 (2014)
31. Yin, L., Wei, X., Sun, Y., Wang, J., Rosato, M.J.: A 3D facial expression database for facial behavior research. In: 7th International Conference on Automatic Face and Gesture Recognition, pp. 211–216 (2006)
32. Hajati, F., Raiea, A.A., Gao, Y.: 2.5 D face recognition using patch geodesic moments. Pattern Recogn. **45**, 969–982 (2012)
33. Emambakhsh, M., Evans, A.: Nasal patches and curves for expression-robust 3D face recognition. IEEE Trans. Pattern Anal. Mach. Intell. **39**(5), 995–1007 (2017)

2D-3D Heterogeneous Face Recognition Based on Deep Canonical Correlation Analysis

Shupeng Wang[1], Di Huang[1(✉)], Yunhong Wang[1], and Yuanyan Tang[2]

[1] IRIP Lab, School of Computer Science and Engineering, Beihang University,
Beijing 100191, China
{wangshupeng,dhuang,yhwang}@buaa.edu.cn
[2] Faculty of Science and Technology, University of Macao, Macao, China
yytang@umac.mo

Abstract. As one of the major branches in Face Recognition (FR), 2D-3D Heterogeneous FR (HFR), where face comparison is made across the texture and shape modalities, has become more important due to its scientific challenges and application potentials. In this paper, we propose a novel and effective approach, which adapts the Deep Canonical Correlation Analysis (Deep CCA) network to such an issue. Two solutions are presented to speed up the training process and improve the recognition accuracy so that Deep CCA better fits the problem of matching different types of face images. Thanks to the deep structure, the proposed approach hierarchically learns the mapping between 2D and 3D face clues and shows distinct superiority to the previous hand-crafted feature based techniques. Experiments are carried out on the FRGC v2.0 database, and the results achieved clearly demonstrate its competency.

Keywords: 2D-3D Face Recognition · Deep learning · Canonical Correlation Analysis

1 Introduction

Face Recognition (FR) is one of the most popular topics in the domain of computer vision and pattern recognition. As one of the major branches in FR, 2D-3D Heterogeneous FR (HFR) has received increasing attention due to its scientific challenges and application potentials. Traditional scenarios of 2D-2D or 3D-3D FR that demand gallery and probe data in the same modality, i.e. 2D texture, 3D shape, etc., or even require data captured by the same type of sensing devices. In contrast to them, 2D-3D HFR matches face images in the 2D texture and 3D shape modality respectively, and aims to provide a solution to FR when different views of faces are available. It has become more useful as various 2D, 3D, and RGB-D sensors are emerging, and plays a critical role in retrieving faces across data for biometric, forensic, or entertainment systems.

In 2D-3D HFR, the key issue is to find the mapping between facial texture and shape, where sub-space learning techniques are commonly exploited. For

© Springer International Publishing AG 2017
J. Zhou et al. (Eds.): CCBR 2017, LNCS 10568, pp. 77–85, 2017.
https://doi.org/10.1007/978-3-319-69923-3_9

example, Canonical Correlation Analysis (CCA), one of the most widely used methods, has achieved promising performance. CCA or its kernel vision, denoted as KCCA, assumes that there is a pair of linear or non-linear combinations which are able to maximize correlation between two groups of variables in the projected space. However, current methods are highly dependent on the way of facial representation which generally needs certain specialized skills on hand-crafted feature extraction, particularly when it is expected to be robust to typical changes in expression, illumination, pose, etc. It is also the reason that existing 2D-3D HFR methods take much effort to handle these factors in preprocessing.

Recently, the advent of deep learning allows computers to automatically learn facial representation from raw data. Such presentation proves powerful in describing characteristics conveyed and thus dominates many detection and classification tasks, involving the signals of audio, image, video, text, etc. Moreover, it is more reliable to the aforementioned problems than the hand-crafted ones. Meanwhile, to better correlate different modalities, Andrew et al. extended original CCA to Deep CCA [1]. They propagate gradient of correlation with respect to the input to optimize the neural network, and effectively enforce the correlation between different views. Even though the original Multi-Layer Perception (MLP) based Deep CCA works well on the MNIST dataset, it is not adequate to model 2D-3D HFR, which is much more complex than digit classification.

In this paper, we propose a novel approach to 2D-3D HFR, making use of Deep CCA to learn the mapping between texture and shape clues. Different from [1], we present a new architecture which embeds Convolutional Neural Network (CNN) for facial representation in both the modalities. Besides, we present two solutions to make this approach more suitable for the given issue. Specifically, we employ Stochastic Gradient Descent (SGD) [2] to alleviate the high computational cost caused by this large-scale network model and vast amounts of data in the training phase. In addition, we introduce an innovative network construction, called global average pooling, to improve the performance since it is more native to convolution by enforcing correspondences between feature maps and categories. We evaluate the proposed approach on the FRGC v2.0 database, and the experimental result is superior to the best ones so far reported, indicating its effectiveness.

2   Related Work

To the best of our knowledge, Riccio and Dugelay [3] made the first attempt on matching 2D and 3D faces, and they introduced geometric invariants calculated according to several pre-defined landmarks in both the face modalities. They reached promising results on a small dataset since the features are intrinsic and remain stable in heterogeneous data, but the method has to locate the fiducial points on 2D and 3D face data, which brought in another difficulty.

Rama et al. [4] employed Partial Principal Component Analysis (P^{2}CA) to extract features of a low dimensionality. Cylindrical texture images of whole faces supposed to provide 3D cues are regarded as gallery samples and ordinary

2D face images as the ones in the probe set. However, the claimed 3D data offer texture information without any shape clue. Moreover, they only consider pose variations in the yaw direction, much easier than the real case.

Yang et al. [5] exploited CCA and KCCA to compute the mapping between 2D and 3D face images, where the patch based representation strategy was used to increase the robustness of heterogeneous mappings. Good accuracies were delivered; nevertheless, pixel based features are sensitive to lighting changes that often occur in real cases.

Huang et al. [6,7] regarded textured 3D face models as galleries and 2D face images as probes, and thus divided the matching process into 2D-2D FR and 2D-3D FR, whose similarity scores were combined for decision making. In their 2D-3D channel, they incorporated LBP facial features [17] into CCA to improve the performance in the presence of lighting changes. Subsequently, they replaced LBP features with a biologically inspired feature, namely Oriented Gradient Maps (OGMs) [8], as the representation of both 2D texture and 3D range images, to further enhance their previous version. This approach reports state of the art performance on a comprehensive dataset, but it requires sophisticated preprocessing on illumination and pose variations.

Toderici et al. [9] located several key landmarks on 2D facial images in different poses by a generic 3D face model, and then roughly aligned them to a frontal 3D model for matching where bidirectional relighting was employed for normalization illumination. Zhang et al. [10] presented a 3D assisted face recognition framework. It first estimated the pose of a given 2D probe face and then rotated the textured 3D face models in the gallery set to the same viewpoint. FR was finally conducted between the projected 2D gallery faces and the probe one. They showed another similar framework later, where random forest was used to estimate the head pose and localize key facial points and shape-based 3D morphable model was applied for pose correction. However, these methods actually adopt 3D models to enhance 2D-2D FR in better handling the hard issues, and do not perform 2D-3D HFR.

Although great progress has been achieved in 2D-3D HFR as the increasing performance shows, the conventional methods basically make use of hand-crafted features, which leaves space for following improvement. Additionally, the results depend on some complicated and specific preprocessing steps especially to the 2D channel, making these methods still have a distance from practice. Compared with them, the proposed method adopts a Deep CNN framework, which hierarchically builds 2D and 3D facial representations, from which more robust heterogeneous mappings are learned.

3   Deep CCA Based 2D-3D HFR

3.1   Canonical Correlation Analysis

The goal of CCA is to find pairs of projection vectors that maximize the total correlation between two types of variables. Its objective function is given as follows:

$$(a, b) = \underset{a,b}{\operatorname{argmax}} \, corr(a^T X, b^T Y) \tag{1}$$

where $X \in R^{d_x \times m}$, $Y \in R^{d_y \times m}$ represent data from two different views respectively. d_x and d_y denote their dimensionalities, and m is the data size. (a, b) means a single pair of linear projection vector.

Define the covariance of X, Y as Σ_{xx}, Σ_{yy}, and the cross covariance as Σ_{xy}. The objective function can be rewritten as:

$$(a, b) = \underset{a,b}{\operatorname{argmax}} \, \frac{a^T \Sigma_{xy} b}{\sqrt{a^T \Sigma_{xx} a b^T \Sigma_{yy} b}} \tag{2}$$

Since (2) does not depend on the scaling of a and b, and the projection vectors in different directions are orthogonal to each other. We combine top-k projection vectors into the columns of projection matrices $A = [a_1, a_2, \ldots, a_k]$ and $B = [b_1, b_2, \ldots, b_k]$, and the objective can be adapted as:

$$(A, B) = \underset{A,B}{\max} \, tr(A^T \Sigma_{xy} B)$$
$$subject \ to : A^T \Sigma_{xx} A = B^T \Sigma_{yy} B = I \tag{3}$$

We use the method [11] for solution. Let $T = \Sigma_{xx}^{-\frac{1}{2}} \Sigma_{xy} \Sigma_{yy}^{-\frac{1}{2}}$, and U^k, V^k be the first k left- and right-vectors of T. The projection matrices A, B are achieved as $A = \Sigma_{xx}^{-\frac{1}{2}} U^k$, and $B = \Sigma_{yy}^{-\frac{1}{2}} V^k$. If $k = d_x = d_y$, the total correlation can be expressed as the matrix trace norm of T:

$$corr(X, Y) = \|T\|_{tr} = tr(\sqrt{T^T T}) \tag{4}$$

With projection matrices, both modalities are projected to a common subspace, where they can be compared more easily.

3.2   Deep CCA

Unlike traditional CCA that establishes the mapping between hand-crafted features of different modalities, Deep CCA incorporates the neural network framework into CCA, which can generate learning based representation from raw data. In [1], Andrew et al. employed MLP based neural network as the feature learning model to compute representations of data. Although nonlinear features can be obtained by passing given data across each layer in MLP, such a representation is not sufficiently effective and efficient for diverse images in the real world. Considering the reputed ability of CNN in describing images, different from the Deep CCA method in [1], we propose to integrate the CNN structure in CCA, delivering a new Deep CCA architecture for 2D-3D HFR.

The overview of the proposed Deep CCA based 2D-3D HFR is illustrated in Fig. 1. The network framework in Deep CCA is roughly similar to the CNN configuration D provided in [12]. The ConvNet is comprised by five sequences of convolutional layers: two 64-dims, two 128-dims, three 256-dims, three 512-dims, and three 512-dims. ReLU is used as the activation function. A Local Response

Normalization (LRN) layer is added after each convolutional layer. The size of all the receptive fields is 3×3 and the stride in all the layers is 1. A max pooling layer is inserted between each pair of sequences. The difference from the network construction provided in [12] lies in that the global pooling layer [13] (see Sect. 3.4 for more details) is used instead of the fully connected layer.

After CNN, we extract the couple output of different networks as facial representations of 2D texture and 3D range images and compute the total correlation according to CCA. The gradient of the correlation with respect to parameters (W, b) in the network is then propagated down.

3.3   Efficiency Optimization in Training

Note that Andrew et al. [1] exploited the full batch algorithm in the training step. In Deep CCA, the objective depends on the covariances of two views. Taking all data as a whole maximally makes use of the covariance information. However, the full batch algorithm consumes a significant amount of hardware resources and incurs very high computational cost as optimizing a deep network, especially with a large training set. On the other side, Wang et al. [2] brought the Stochastic Gradient Descent (SGD) algorithm into the Deep CCA model, assuming that the information of covariances can be sufficiently estimated with a mini-batch which is large enough and the gradient is thus adequate for training.

Inspired by this fact, to make sure that the covariance matrices are positive definite in practice. The regularizer are added and the definitions are given as follows:

$$\Sigma_{xx} = \frac{1}{m-1}\bar{X}\bar{X}^T + \lambda_x I$$

$$\Sigma_{yy} = \frac{1}{m-1}\bar{Y}\bar{Y}^T + \lambda_y I \tag{5}$$

$$\Sigma_{xy} = \frac{1}{m-1}\bar{X}\bar{Y}^T$$

where $\bar{X}, \bar{Y}$ are the centers of X, Y and λ_x, λ_y are regularization constants.

As shown in (4), the total correlation is the sum of all the singular values of T. As an alternative solution of (4), we have $corr(X,Y) = \sum_i^k \sigma_i(T)$, where $\sigma_i(T), i = 1, 2, \ldots, k$ are the k largest singular values. Let $T = U^k D V^{k^T}$ be the rank-k Singular Value Decomposition (SVD) of T, and we obtain the gradient of the correlation with respect of X as:

$$\frac{\partial \sum_i^k \sigma_i(T)}{\partial X} = \frac{1}{m-1}(2\Delta_{xx}\bar{X} + \Delta_{xy}\bar{Y}) \tag{6}$$

where $\Delta_{xx} = -\frac{1}{2}\Sigma_{xx}^{-\frac{1}{2}}U^k D U^{k^T}\Sigma_{xx}^{-\frac{1}{2}}, \Delta_{xy} = \Sigma_{xx}^{-\frac{1}{2}}U^k V^{k^T}\Sigma_{yy}^{-\frac{1}{2}}$
Similarly, the correlation gradient with respect of Y is:

$$\frac{\partial \sum_i^k \sigma_i(T)}{\partial Y} = \frac{1}{m-1}(2\Delta_{yy}\bar{Y} + \Delta_{yx}\bar{X}) \tag{7}$$

where $\Delta_{yy} = -\frac{1}{2}\Sigma_{yy}^{-\frac{1}{2}}V^k D V^{k^T}\Sigma_{yy}^{-\frac{1}{2}}, \Delta_{yx} = \Sigma_{yy}^{-\frac{1}{2}}V^k U^{k^T}\Sigma_{xx}^{-\frac{1}{2}}$.

Gradients of correlation in two different views are propagated down along the networks respectively.

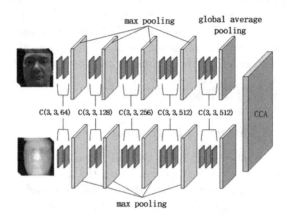

Fig. 1. Overview of the proposed Deep CCA based 2D-3D HFR method, where $C(m, n, k)$ denotes the convolutional layer with an m-by-n receptive field and k channels.

3.4   Global Average Pooling

In traditional CNN, as a feature extractor, the convolutional layer amplifies discriminant information of the input data and minimizes the interference of irrelevant variations. The feature map of the last convolutional layer is frequently vectorized as the input of fully connected layers. The fully connected layers are used as a part of the classifier to maximize the classification performance. In Deep CCA, the matching result is critically dependent on the correlativity between the features of different modalities from the same subject.

Global average pooling has the advantage over the fully connected layer, since it is more native to the convolution structure by enforcing correspondences between feature maps and categories [13]. Considering such a property, we employ global average pooling instead of the fully connected layers. Global average pooling takes the mean of each feature map at the last convolutional layer and the resulting vector is treated as the final feature of the network, which is then fed into CCA. Actually, it performs average pooling at the full scale. In this way, we directly enforce correspondences between 2D or 3D facial features and their correlation. Additionally, compared to fully connected layers, global average pooling avoids overfitting, because there is no parameter to optimize.

4   Experiments

For validation, we carry out experiments in the entire FRGC v2.0 dataset [14], which is the most famous and comprehensive in evaluating 2D-2D, 3D-3D, and

2D-3D FR approaches. It consists of 4007 textured 3D face models of 466 subjects, containing large changes in facial expression and illumination and moderate variations in head pose. The face texture and range images separately extracted from 3D models are resized to 224×224 pixels as the input. We take the last 366 subjects according to the order of ID in filename that have 2964 images for each view as training data to fine-tune CNN. The range images of the first 3D models of the remaining 100 subjects compose the gallery set, and the texture images of the rest 3D models of the 100 subjects (943 images) are used as probes. At last, the cosine distance is exploited to measure the similarity between heterogeneous face images in the latent space for matching. There are two major experiments: one is to show the comparison with the state of the arts, and the other is to highlight the contribution of global average pooling.

4.1 Comparison with State of the Arts

The structure of CNN is described in Sect. 3. The batch size of Deep CCA is set to 32. The Labeled Faces in the Wild (LFW) dataset [15] is used to pre-train the CNNs in the two modalities, and the training data from FRGC v2.0 are used for fine-tuning. The proposed method is compared with pixel feature based CCA [6] and OGM feature based CCA [16] under the same experiment setting. The original texture (depicted in gray-scale images) and range faces are adopted in comparison. Meanwhile, to highlight the robustness of the proposed method to pose variations, we also show the result of [16] achieved after pose correction. It should be noted that the best parameters in [16] are used in our case.

Table 1. Comparison of 2D-3D HFR on FRGC v2.0.

2D-3D HFR methods	Accuracy
Original Faces + PCA [6]	0.5970
Original OGMs + PCA [16]	0.7232
Aligned OGMs + PCA [16]	0.9385
Deep CCA based method	**0.9650**

The results of the proposed method and the counterparts are shown in Table 1. From this table we can see that the hand-crafted feature based methods highly require the preprocessing quality, as the result of OGM after face alignment is up to 93.85%, 20 points more than the one of original faces. It is worth noting that the proposed Deep CCA based 2D-3D HFR method reaches the best performance, 96.50%, with original image. Unlike the traditional methods that require pre-processing techniques to normalize facial images, the deep network does not make use of any additional processes to raw data, which demonstrates its robustness in representing face images of different modalities.

4.2   Contribution of Global Average Pooling

To study the effect of global average pooling, we replace the global average pooling layer with the regular fully connected layers, and remain the other parts of the model unchanged. We set the number of fully connected layers the same as that of the output of global average pooling (512 dimension). Both models are tested on the FRGC v2.0 dataset, and the protocol is identical to the one in Sect. 4.1. In order to maximize the advantage of CNN, we use the original RGB images rather than the gray-scale ones in the previous experiment. The accuracies are displayed in Table 2.

Table 2. Comparison of CNNs with the fully connected layer and the global average pooling layer on FRGC v2.0.

Methods	Accuracy
CNN with fully connected layer	0.9555
CNN with global average pooling layer	**0.9756**

As shown in Table 2, global average pooling layer reports better performance (97.56%) than fully connected layer does (95.55%). We can also see that the results of both two methods with Deep CCA are superior to the ones of the conventional methods (listed in the first three rows in Table 1). Moreover, in contrast to gray images, the RGB images convey more discriminative information of face, which contributes to HFR.

5   Conclusion

In this paper, we introduce a 2D-3D HFR approach based on Deep CCA, which incorporates CNN into CCA, thus learning the mapping between hierarchically learned features of different modalities. In order to optimize the efficiency in training the large-scale network, we adopt the SGD algorithm in the Deep CCA model. Meanwhile, we exploit global average pooling layer to improve performance and robustness of the proposed method. We compare our approach with the competing methods in the FRGC v2.0 dataset, and the experimental result of 2D-3D HFR achieved is up to 97.56%, which demonstrates the effectiveness of the proposed method.

Acknowledgement. This work was partly supported by the Hong Kong, Macao, and Taiwan Science and Technology Cooperation Program of China (Grant No. L2015TGA9004 and 008/2014/AMJ) and the National Natural Science Foundation of China (No. 61673033).

References

1. Andrew, G., Arora, R., Bilmes, J., Livescu, K.: Deep canonical correlation analysis. In: ICML, pp. 1247–1255 (2013)
2. Wang, W., Arora, R., Livescu, K., Bilmes, J.A.: Unsupervised learning of acoustic features via deep canonical correlation analysis. In: IEEE ICASSP, pp. 4590–4594 (2015)
3. Riccio, D., Dugelay, J.-L.: Asymmetric 3D/2D processing: a novel approach for face recognition. In: Roli, F., Vitulano, S. (eds.) ICIAP 2005. LNCS, vol. 3617, pp. 986–993. Springer, Heidelberg (2005). doi:10.1007/11553595_121
4. Rama, A., Tarres, F., Onofrio, D., Tubaro, S.: Mixed 2D-3D information for pose estimation and face recognition. In: IEEE ICASSP, p. II (2006)
5. Yang, W., Yi, D., Lei, Z., Sang, J., Li, S.Z.: 2D-3D face matching using CCA. In: IEEE FG, pp. 1–6 (2008)
6. Huang, D., Ardabilian, M., Wang, Y., Chen, L.: Asymmetric 3D/2D face recognition based on LBP facial representation and canonical correlation analysis. In: IEEE ICIP, pp. 3325–3328 (2009)
7. Huang, D., Ardabilian, M., Wang, Y., Chen, L.: Automatic asymmetric 3D-2D face recognition. In: IEEE/IAPR ICPR (2010)
8. Huang, D., Soltana, W.B., Ardabilian, M., Wang, Y., Chen, L.: Textured 3D face recognition using biological vision-based facial representation and optimized weighted sum fusion. In: IEEE CVPR Workshop (2011)
9. Toderici, G., Passalis, G., Zafeiriou, S., Tzimiropoulos, G.: Bidirectional relighting for 3D-Aided 2D face recognition. In: IEEE CVPR, pp. 2721–2728 (2010)
10. Zhang, W., Huang, D., Wang, Y., Chen, L.: 3D aided face recognition across pose variations. In: Zheng, W.-S., Sun, Z., Wang, Y., Chen, X., Yuen, P.C., Lai, J. (eds.) CCBR 2012. LNCS, vol. 7701, pp. 58–66. Springer, Heidelberg (2012). doi:10.1007/978-3-642-35136-5_8
11. Mardia, K.V., Kent, J.T., Bibby, J.M.: Multivariate Analysis (Probability and Mathematical Statistics). Academic Press, San Diego (1980)
12. Simonyan, K., Zisserman, A.: Very deep convolutional networks for large-scale image recognition. In: ICLR (2015)
13. Lin, M., Chen, Q., Yan, S.: Network in network. In: ICLR (2014)
14. Phillips, P.J., Flynn, P.J., Scruggs, T., Bowyer, K.W., Chang, J., Hoffman, K., Marques, J., Min, J., Worek, W.: Overview of the face recognition grand challenge. In: IEEE CVPR, pp. 947–954 (2005)
15. Huang, G.B., Ramesh, M., Berg, T., Erik, L.M.: Labeled faces in the wild: a database for studying face recognition in unconstrained environments. Technical report (2007)
16. Huang, D., Ardabilian, M., Wang, Y., Chen, L.: Oriented gradient maps based automatic asymmetric 3D-2D face recognition. In: IEEE ICB, pp. 125–131 (2012)
17. Huang, D., Shan, C., Ardabilian, M., Wang, Y., Chen, L.: Local binary patterns and its application to facial image analysis: a survey. IEEE T-SMCC **41**(6), 765–781 (2011)

Age Estimation by Refining Label Distribution in Deep CNN

Wanxia Shen, Li Sun$^{(\boxtimes)}$, Song Qiu, and Qingli Li

Shanghai Key Laboratory of Multidimensional Information Processing,
East China Normal University, Shanghai, China
sunli@ee.ecnu.edu.cn

Abstract. This paper proposes an age estimation algorithm by refining the label distribution in a deep learning framework. There are two tasks during the training period of our algorithm. The first one finds the optimal parameters of supervised deep CNN by given the label distribution of the training sample as the ground truth, while the second one estimates the variances of label distribution to fit the output of the CNN. These two tasks are performed alternatively and both of them are treated as the supervised learning tasks. The AlexNet and ResNet-50 architectures are adopted as the classifiers and the Gaussian form of the label distribution is assumed. Experiments show that the accuracy of age estimation can be improved by refining label distribution.

Keywords: Age estimation · Label distribution · CNN

1 Introduction

Facial image analysis has been an active research topic. Specifically, face recognition has been used in different types of computer vision system such as identity verification, surveillance monitoring and human-computer interaction. An amount of information can be provided by human face, and among these characteristics, age is one of the most useful. Therefore, age estimation attracts researchers' attention for its practical applications. Generally speaking, age estimation methods can be divided into three categories: multi-classification method [3,14,16], regression method [2,7,25] and hybrid method [7].

Although a great many methods have been proposed to tackle age estimation problem as mentioned above, age estimation is still an challenging task for following reasons. First, it is hard to obtain the data with ground truths like other vision tasks. The real age of one person in a given picture depends on the dates of both birth and photo acquisition. So it is difficult to get abundant data labeled with the real ages. Second, as is shown in Fig. 1, there are two facts: A. the facial appearance of the same person changes rapidly at both

W. Shen—This work was supported in part by the National Natural Science Foundation of China under Project 61302125, 61671376 and in part by Natural Science Foundation of Shanghai under Project 17ZR1408500.

© Springer International Publishing AG 2017
J. Zhou et al. (Eds.): CCBR 2017, LNCS 10568, pp. 86–96, 2017.
https://doi.org/10.1007/978-3-319-69923-3_10

young and old age, but it is relative stable at mid-age. B. People under the same age may have large differences on facial appearances. Thus, it is difficult to find reliable features for age estimation. To tackle this issue, label distribution learning (LDL) is particularly useful. In [4], they apply the LDL in age estimation task. They provide two types of solutions for LDL, which are Improved Iterative Scaling(IIS-LDL) and Conditional Probability Neural Network (CPNN). In CPNN, the classic background propagation is adopted to update the weight parameters in the neural network. Later, they propose an advanced version of LDL by fitting the parameter of label distribution under the assumption of the Gaussian form in [6]. And they use non-linear programming method for optimization. As CNN continuously achieves good results in both face detection and recognition, researchers begin to pay attention to its application in age estimation task. Yang [27] presents a CNN-based method. In their work, a two stream CNN architecture is proposed. VGGFace architecture is used to learn age distribution by Huo [13]. In [23], Tan proposes a soft softmax regression function and apply CNN to age estimation.

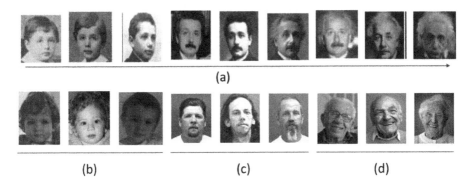

Fig. 1. (a) Facial images of Albert Einstein in different age stages; (b) three different people at 1 years old; (c) three different people at 40 years old; (d) three different people at 100 years old.

CNN for age estimation with the help of the label distribution has already been considered in [13,23,27] mentioned above, but they just use label distributions generated by fixed parameters instead of using automatically learned variables to produce label distributions. The works in [6,12] both adapt the variance of the label distribution, but they don't use back propagation (BP) in neural network. In this paper, we emphasize that the parameters of label distributions are essential and should be learned from training data directly rather than given fixed values. And we propose to estimate the label distribution parameters by BP in CNN framework. The AlexNet [15] and ResNet-50 [11] are selected to carry out our experiments respectively. Three types of loss function, AS-KL divergence, S-KL divergence and softmax, are used to confirm our method on MORPH 2 and FG-NET. The main contributions of our work are that the CNN is chose to fit the variances of label distributions to get adapted label distribution for each age and our model is end to end.

2   The Proposed Method

The flowchart of the proposed method is shown in Fig. 2. There are two tasks. The blue dashed box in Fig. 2 shows the process of training CNN. The red dashed box in Fig. 2 indicates the procedure of refining m_{l_z} ($l_z \in [0, 99]$). m_{l_z} is the parameter of Gaussian label distribution at chronological age l_z and it which is the reciprocal of the variance σ^2 in the Gaussian distribution formula. The parameters of all ages comprise a set $\mathbf{M}$, namely $m_{l_z} \in \mathbf{M}$. The dashed narrow indicates the BP process of the task with the same color. An outer loop is used to control two tasks working alternatively. In this section, details of the two tasks are described.

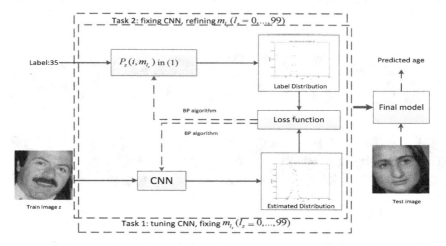

Fig. 2. The flowchart of our proposed method. Label distribution is generated by the parameter m_α. Estimated distribution is the output of the CNN. (Color figure online)

The softmax function is applied remarkably in the field of classification with CNN. However, age estimation is not a simple classification problem because age is continuous. So a label distribution is taken as the aging information of a facial image $\mathbf{z}$ rather than only the chronological age $l_{\mathbf{z}}$. Following the works [4,6,23], we label a facial image $\mathbf{z}$ by a discrete Gaussian distribution function centered at the chronological age $l_{\mathbf{z}}$ and use (1) to represent the degree of l_i corresponding to the chronological age $l_{\mathbf{z}}$. Besides, in the label distribution the description degree of $l_{\mathbf{z}}$ is the highest and the description degrees decrease from $l_{\mathbf{z}}$ to its both sides gradually.

$$P_{\mathbf{z}}(i, m_{l_{\mathbf{z}}}) = \frac{e^{-m_{l_{\mathbf{z}}}(i-l_{\mathbf{z}})^2}}{\sum_j e^{-m_{l_{\mathbf{z}}}(j-l_{\mathbf{z}})^2}} \tag{1}$$

where $\mathbf{z}$ is the input image; i is an age value and $i = 0, 1, \ldots, k$, and k is 99; $P_\mathbf{z}(i, m_{l_\mathbf{z}}) \in [0, 1]$, $\sum_i P_\mathbf{z}(i, m_{l_\mathbf{z}}) = 1$.

2.1 Training CNN

We regard the age estimation problem as a deep classification problem followed by AS-KL and S-KL divergence refinement. CNN is chose as the classifier. The AlexNet [15] is a classical CNN, that is why we choose AlexNet. It has 5 convolution layers. And in the interest of seeing whether deeper CNN can get better results, we also select ResNet-50 [11] which has 50 convolution layers to verify our algorithm. We change the number of the outputs of the last full-connected layer of those two CNN architectures to 100 to satisfy the age range 0–99 in our work. This task aims to learn the parameters of CNN model through the label distributions given by $\mathbf{M}$. And just the parameters of the CNN are trained. BP algorithm is opted to optimize the CNN.

$$Loss_{AS-KL} = \sum_i P_\mathbf{z}(i, m_{l_\mathbf{z}}) \log \frac{P_\mathbf{z}(i, m_{l_\mathbf{z}})}{f(z_i)} \tag{2}$$

$$Loss_{S-KL} = \sum_i (f(z_i) \log \frac{f(z_i)}{P_\mathbf{z}(i, m_{l_\mathbf{z}})} + P_\mathbf{z}(i, m_{l_\mathbf{z}}) \log \frac{P_\mathbf{z}(i, m_{l_\mathbf{z}})}{f(z_i)}) \tag{3}$$

where $f(z_i) = \frac{e^{z_i}}{\sum_j e^{z_j}}$ is the output of the softmax layer.

2.2 Refining M

During the process of refining $\mathbf{M}$, the label distribution is needed to be automatically learned from the distribution of the output of the CNN. Therefore, the parameters of the CNN are immobilized and only refine $\mathbf{M}$. Because one people has different speeds of facial age speeding during different age stages, we group the train part of one certain data-set by ages and refine each value of $\mathbf{M}$ according to the chronological age $l_\mathbf{z}$ respectively. BP algorithm is also used to fit $\mathbf{M}$. According to the principle of BP algorithm, the derived formulas of $Loss_{AS-KL}$ and $Loss_{S-KL}$ are shown as (4) and (5).

$$\frac{\partial Loss_{AS-KL}}{\partial m_{l_\mathbf{z}}} = \sum_i \{P_\mathbf{z}(i, m_{l_\mathbf{z}})[\frac{\sum_j [e^{\phi(j)}(j - l_\mathbf{z})^2]}{\sum_j e^{\phi(j)}} - (i - l_\mathbf{z})^2][1 + \log \frac{P_\mathbf{z}(i, m_{l_\mathbf{z}})}{f(z_i)}]\} \tag{4}$$

$$\frac{\partial Loss_{S-KL}}{\partial m_{l_\mathbf{z}}} = \sum_i \{P_\mathbf{z}(i, m_{l_\mathbf{z}})[\frac{\sum_j [e^{\phi(j)}(j - l_\mathbf{z})^2]}{\sum_j e^{\phi(j)}} - (i - l_\mathbf{z})^2][1 + \log \frac{P_\mathbf{z}(i, m_{l_\mathbf{z}})}{f(z_i)} - \frac{f(z_i)}{P_\mathbf{z}(i, m_{l_\mathbf{z}})}]\} \tag{5}$$

where $\phi(j) = -m_{l_\mathbf{z}}(j - l_\mathbf{z})^2$, so $P_\mathbf{z}(i, m_{l_\mathbf{z}}) = \frac{e^{\phi(i)}}{\sum_j e^{\phi(i)}}$.

3   Experiments

The results of our experiments will be presented in this section. We firstly introduce the data-sets that we used and settings of our experiments. Then we report the evaluation results on MORPH 2 and FG-NET separately. For the purpose of quantitative evaluation, we compute the average of the mean absolute errors (MAE). Following [20], MAE is computed between the ground truth value and the predicted value which is gained by $\sum_{i=0}^{k} f_i l_i$, where f_i is the predicted probability of the corresponding age label l_i. Last, a discussion about the results will conclude this section. And the models in this work can be accessed through the link: https://github.com/Ella0102/Age-estimation-with-the-CNN.git.

3.1   Data-Sets

We employ 3 different data-sets in total in this paper, which are shown in Fig. 3. IMDB-WIKI [20] data-set is only used to finetune the CNN, which means using this data-set firstly to finetune the CNN to make it learn facial information before using training data-sets. And MORPH 2 [19] and FG-NET [18] data-sets are applied to evaluate our method respectively.

(a) IMDB   (b) WIKI

(c) MORPH   (d) FG-NET

Fig. 3. Examples of data-sets we used.

IMDB-WIKI is the largest public available data-set for age estimation of people in the wild environment. It contains 523,051 labeled facial images in total. MORPH 2 contains 55,000 face images, whose age ranges from 16 to 77. The facial images in this data-set are recorded under uneven distribution of gender and also from different races. Following [23,28], we randomly divide MORPH 2 data-set into three non-overlapped subsets S1, S2 and S3 by two rules: (1) Male:Female = 3; (2) White:Black = 1. FG-NET includes 1002 greyscale and colorful facial images in total. This data-set consists of 82 groups and its age ranges from 0 to 69. For the purpose of evaluation on FG-NET, we use leave-one-person-out (LOPO) cross validation test method like the works [1,2,7,21,25]. And we report the average performance over the 82 groups.

As Fig. 3 shows that some faces of the data-sets used in this work are captured in the wild. And age information is only related to the face, so the Coc-DPM algorithm [17] is selected to detect the faces from facial images and then crop them for both training and testing in this work. In order to improve the robustness of our algorithm to face poses, we do not align the facial images for both training and testing.

3.2 Settings

For refining $\mathbf{M}$, each value of $\mathbf{M}$ is initialized to 0.125 for MORPH 2 because most facial ages of this data-set are mid-age and the facial age appearance changing speed of mid-age is relatively slower than other age stages. As the facial ages of FG-NET are mostly in young stage during which facial age appearance changes relatively faster, each value of $\mathbf{M}$ is initialized to 0.5. The max number of iterations of this process is assigned 2 and the learning rate is assigned 0.001.

For training CNN, the base learning rate of CNN is set to 0.001 for AS-KL divergence and 0.0001 for S-KL divergence. The max number of iterations is set to 18000 for MORPH 2, 600 for FG-NET when using AlexNet framework and 10000 for MORPH 2, 600 for FG-NET with ResNet-50 architecture. To get a mild start for training, we use AlexNet model that is trained on ImageNet for image classification and ResNet-50 model file provided by Kaiming He as the pre-trained models for AlexNet and ResNet-50 respectively.

3.3 Results of Age Estimation

Evaluation on the MORPH 2 Data-Set. Table 1 shows the results of our experiments on MORPH 2. We get the best result, a MAE of 3.02, with AS-KL loss function by finetuning with IMDB-WIKI when use the ResNet-50. And the comparison of our method with other methods which use MORPH 2 by the same way is listed in the left column of Table 2. We can see our result is better than others. In [21], Rothe uses this data-set by the way different from ours and they get a MAE of 2.68. Although there is no direct comparability with ours, we still report it here.

Evaluation on the FG-NET Data-Set. For the fact that FG-NET is a small data-set which is not enough to train a deep CNN, finetuning with IMDB-WIKI before using this data-set can make up for the deficiency and works better than just finetuning with this data-set, as shown in Table 3. We get our best result, a MAE of 3.12, by using the AS-KL divergence and the ResNet-50 architecture. The right column of Table 2 shows the comparison of our method with other methods on this data-set. As we can see, our best result is a little lower than the work [21].

Table 1. Results of our method on MORPH 2.

Refining **m** or not	CNN	Method	Train set	Test set	MAE	Arv.MAE
Not refining **m**	AlexNet	Softmax	S1	$S2 + S3$	3.58	3.60
			S2	$S1 + S3$	3.62	
		S-KL	S1	$S2 + S3$	3.27	3.28
			S2	$S1 + S3$	3.29	
		AS-KL	S1	$S2 + S3$	3.27	3.29
			S2	$S1 + S3$	3.31	
		Softmax with finetuned	S1	$S2 + S3$	3.24	3.21
			S2	$S1 + S3$	3.18	
		S-KL with finetuned	S1	$S2 + S3$	3.11	3.15
			S2	$S1 + S3$	3.14	
		AS-KL with finetuned	S1	$S2 + S3$	3.09	3.10
			S2	$S1 + S3$	3.11	
	ResNet-50	AS-KL	S1	$S2 + S3$	3.08	3.07
			S2	$S1 + S3$	3.06	
		AS-KL with finetuned	S1	$S2 + S3$	3.04	3.07
			S2	$S1 + S3$	3.09	
Refining **m**	AlexNet	S-KL	S1	$S2 + S3$	3.25	3.25
			S2	$S1 + S3$	3.25	
		AS-KL	S1	$S2 + S3$	3.19	3.20
			S2	$S1 + S3$	3.20	
		S-KL with finetuned	S1	$S2 + S3$	3.09	3.10
			S2	$S1 + S3$	3.11	
		AS-KL with finetuned	S1	$S2 + S3$	3.08	3.09
			S2	$S1 + S3$	3.10	
	ResNet	AS-KL	S1	$S2 + S3$	3.02	**3.02**
			S2	$S1 + S3$	3.02	
		AS-KL with finetuned	S1	$S2 + S3$	3.02	**3.02**
			S2	$S1 + S3$	3.02	

3.4   Discussion

Refining M Analysis. Each value of **M** is initialized to the same value for one data-set because we want to confirm that whether refining **M** with our method works. As can be seen from Fig. 4, the horizontal axis is age and the vertical axis is the value of m_{l_z}. Since the data of some ages is not available in either MORPH 2 or FG-NET, we can see from Fig. 4 that the values in **M** corresponding to these ages are unchanged and remain at the initial values. For the number of facial images of MORPH 2 after 60 years old is few, from Fig. 4(a) and (b) we can see that m_{l_z} becomes smaller mostly after 60 years old which means that σ^2 of the Gaussian distribution formula becomes larger. The results authenticates

Table 2. Comparison of age estimation algorithms.

MORPH 2					FG-NET	
Method	Train set	Test set	MAE	Avg.MAE	Method	MAE
BIF+CCA [9]	S1	$S2 + S3$	5.39	5.37	AGES [5]	6.77
	S2	$S1 + S3$	5.35			
BIF+LSVM [9]	S1	$S2 + S3$	5.06	5.09	SVR [7]	5.66
	S2	$S1 + S3$	5.12			
BIF+KSVM [9]	S1	$S2 + S3$	4.89	4.91	[22]	5.01
	S2	$S1 + S3$	4.92			
CNN [26]	S1	$S2 + S3$	4.64	4.60	OHRank [1]	4.85
	S2	$S1 + S3$	4.55			
BIF+PLS [8]	S1	$S2 + S3$	4.58	4.56	MTWGP [29]	4.83
	S2	$S1 + S3$	4.54			
BIF+rCCA [9]	S1	$S2 + S3$	4.43	4.42	DIF [10]	4.80
	S2	$S1 + S3$	4.40			
BIF+KPLS [8]	S1	$S2 + S3$	4.07	4.04	Human workers [10]	4.70
	S2	$S1 + S3$	4.01			
BIF+KCCA [9]	S1	$S2 + S3$	4.00	3.98	CA-SVR [2]	4.67
	S2	$S1 + S3$	3.95			
Multi-scale CNN [28]	S1	$S2 + S3$	3.72	3.63	DLA [24]	4.26
	S2	$S1 + S3$	3.54			
[23]	S1	$S2 + S3$	3.14	3.03	DEX [21]	3.09
	S2	$S1 + S3$	2.92			
Our method	S1	$S2 + S3$	3.02	3.02	our method	3.12
	S2	$S1 + S3$	3.02			

Table 3. Results of our method on FG-NET.

CNN	Method	MAE (not refining **m**)	MAE (refining **m**)
AlexNet	S-KL	5.47	4.44
	AS-KL	5.48	4.84
	S-KL with finetuned	3.66	3.25
	AS-KL with finetuned	3.68	3.22
ResNet-50	AS-KL	4.68	3.62
	AS-KL with finetuned	3.57	**3.12**

that when the amount of data of one age class is small, the data of its adjacent age classes can be used. And we can see the final refined $m_{l_\mathbf{z}}$ at age $l_\mathbf{z} \in [0, 99]$ of FG-NET from Fig. 4(c). When $l_\mathbf{z} < 20$ and $l_\mathbf{z} > 60$, $m_{l_\mathbf{z}}$ is smaller than which

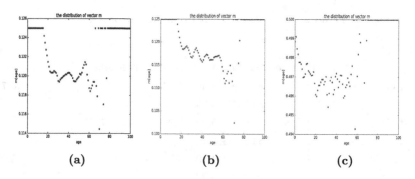

Fig. 4. (a) Final refined **M** of MORPH 2; S1 train; (b) final refined **M** of MORPH 2; S2 train; (c) final refined **M** of FG-NET.

when $l_{\mathbf{z}} \in [20, 60]$. The result confirms the fact that facial aging speed is faster during young and old age than that during mid-age.

Comparison of AleNet and ResNET-50 Based on Our Results. Tables 1 and 3 display that the results of ResNet-50 are better than that of AlexNet. Our experiments prove deeper CNN works better with our method.

4   Conclusion

In this paper we present an age estimation algorithm by refining the label distribution in a deep learning framework. We choose AlexNet [15] and ResNet-50 [11] as the classifiers and the Gaussian form of the label distribution is assumed. We use the CNN to refine the variances of label distributions to fit the output of the classifier. And the results of our experiments verify that refining **M** can get better results. With fitting **M**, we get a MAE of 3.02 on MORPH 2 which is better than the state of the art in the case of our test way of MORPH 2.

References

1. Chang, K.Y., Chen, C.S., Hung, Y.P.: Ordinal hyperplanes ranker with cost sensitivities for age estimation. In: Computer Vision and Pattern Recognition, pp. 585–592 (2011)
2. Chen, K., Gong, S., Xiang, T., Chen, C.L.: Cumulative attribute space for age and crowd density estimation. In: IEEE Conference on Computer Vision and Pattern Recognition, pp. 2467–2474 (2013)
3. Lanitis, A., Draganova, C., Christodoulou, C.: Comparing different classifiers for automatic age estimation. IEEE Trans. Syst. Man Cybern. Part B Cybern. **34**(1), 621–628 (2004). A Publication of the IEEE Systems Man & Cybernetics Society
4. Geng, X., Yin, C., Zhou, Z.H.: Facial age estimation by learning from label distributions. IEEE Trans. Pattern Anal. Mach. Intell. **35**(10), 2401–2412 (2013)

5. Geng, X., Zhou, Z.H., Smithmiles, K.: Automatic age estimation based on facial aging patterns. IEEE Trans. Pattern Anal. Mach. Intell. **29**(12), 2234–2240 (2007)
6. Geng, X., Wang, Q., Xia, Y.: Facial age estimation by adaptive label distribution learning. pp. 4465–4470 (2014)
7. Guo, G., Fu, Y., Dyer, C.R., Huang, T.S.: Image-based human age estimation by manifold learning and locally adjusted robust regression. IEEE Trans. Image Process. **17**(7), 1178–1188 (2008)
8. Guo, G., Mu, G.: Simultaneous dimensionality reduction and human age estimation via kernel partial least squares regression. In: IEEE Conference on Computer Vision and Pattern Recognition, CVPR 2011, 20–25 June, pp. 657–664. Colorado Springs, CO, USA (2011)
9. Guo, G., Mu, G.: Joint estimation of age, gender and ethnicity: CCA vs.PLS. In: IEEE International Conference and Workshops on Automatic Face and Gesture Recognition, pp. 1–6 (2013)
10. Han, H., Otto, C., Liu, X., Jain, A.K.: Demographic estimation from face images: human vs. machine performance. IEEE Trans. Pattern Anal. Mach. Intell. **37**(6), 1148–1161 (2015)
11. He, K., Zhang, X., Ren, S., Sun, J.: Deep residual learning for image recognition. arXiv preprint (2015). arXiv:1512.03385
12. Hou, P., Geng, X., Huo, Z.W., Lv, J.Q.: Semi-supervised adaptive label distribution learning for facial age estimation. In: 31st AAAI Conference on Artificial Intelligence (2017)
13. Huo, Z.W., Yang, X., Xing, C., Zhou, Y., Hou, P., Lv, J.Q., Geng, X.: Deep age distribution learning for apparent age estimation. In: Proceedings of IEEE Conference on Computer Vision and Pattern Recognition Workshops, pp. 17–24 (2016)
14. Guo, G., Mu, G.: Human age estimation: what is the influence across race and gender?. In: Computer Vision and Pattern Recognition Workshops, pp. 71–78 (2010)
15. Krizhevsky, A., Sutskever, I., Hinton, G.E.: Imagenet classification with deep convolutional neural networks. In: International Conference on Neural Information Processing Systems, pp. 1097–1105 (2012)
16. Zhou, H., Miller, P., Zhang, J.: Age classification using Radon transform and entropy based scaling SVM. In: BMVC (2011)
17. Mathias, M., Benenson, R., Pedersoli, M., Gool, L.: Face detection without bells and whistles. In: Fleet, D., Pajdla, T., Schiele, B., Tuytelaars, T. (eds.) ECCV 2014. LNCS, vol. 8692, pp. 720–735. Springer, Cham (2014). doi:10.1007/978-3-319-10593-2_47
18. Panis, G., Lanitis, A., Tsapatsoulis, N., Cootes, T.F.: An overview of research on facial aging using the FG-NET aging database. IET Biometr. **5**(2), 37–46 (2015)
19. Rawls, A.W.: Morph: development and optimization of a longitudinal age progression database. In: Joint Cost 2101 and 2102 International Conference on Biometric ID Management and Multimodal Communication, pp. 17–24 (2009)
20. Rothe, R., Timofte, R., Gool, L.V.: Dex: deep expectation of apparent age from a single image. In: IEEE International Conference on Computer Vision Workshop, pp. 252–257 (2016)
21. Rothe, R., Timofte, R., Van Gool, L.: Deep expectation of real and apparent age from a single image without facial landmarks. Int. J. Comput. Vis. 1–14 (2016). https://doi.org/10.1007/s11263-016-0940-3
22. Rothe, R., Timofte, R., Gool, L.V.: Some like it hot - visual guidance for preference prediction. In: Conference on Computer Vision and Pattern Recognition, pp. 5553–5561 (2016)

23. Tan, Z., Zhou, S., Wan, J., Lei, Z., Li, S.Z.: Age estimation based on a single network with soft softmax of aging modeling. In: Lai, S.-H., Lepetit, V., Nishino, K., Sato, Y. (eds.) ACCV 2016. LNCS, vol. 10113, pp. 203–216. Springer, Cham (2017). doi:10.1007/978-3-319-54187-7_14

24. Wang, X., Guo, R., Kambhamettu, C.: Deeply-learned feature for age estimation. In: Applications of Computer Vision, pp. 534–541 (2015)

25. Yan, S., Wang, H., Tang, X., Huang, T.S.: Learning auto-structured regressor from uncertain nonnegative labels. In: IEEE International Conference on Computer Vision, ICCV 2007, Rio De Janeiro, Brazil, pp. 1–8, October 2007

26. Yang, M., Zhu, S., Lv, F., Yu, K.: Correspondence driven adaptation for human profile recognition. In: Computer Vision and Pattern Recognition, pp. 505–512 (2011)

27. Yang, X., Gao, B.B., Xing, C., Huo, Z.W., Wei, X.S., Zhou, Y., et al.: Deep label distribution learning for apparent age estimation. In: IEEE International Conference on Computer Vision Workshop, pp. 344–350 (2015)

28. Yi, D., Lei, Z., Li, S.Z.: Age estimation by multi-scale convolutional network. In: Cremers, D., Reid, I., Saito, H., Yang, M.-H. (eds.) ACCV 2014. LNCS, vol. 9005, pp. 144–158. Springer, Cham (2015). doi:10.1007/978-3-319-16811-1_10

29. Zhang, Y., Yeung, D.Y.: Multi-task warped Gaussian process for personalized age estimation. In: Computer Vision and Pattern Recognition, pp. 2622–2629 (2010)

Face Recognition via Heuristic Deep Active Learning

Ya Li[1], Keze Wang[2], Lin Nie[2], and Qing Wang[2(✉)]

[1] Guangzhou University, Guangzhou 510006, China
liya@gzhu.edu.cn
[2] Sun Yat-sen University, Guangzhou 510006, China
wangkeze@alumni.sysu.edu.cn, nie.lin@foxmail.com,
wangq79@mail.sysu.edu.cn

Abstract. Recent successes on face recognition tasks require a large number of annotated samples for training models. However, the sample-labeling process is slow and expensive. An effective approach to reduce the annotation effort is active learning (AL). However, the traditional AL methods are limited by the hand-craft features and the small-scale datasets. In this paper, we propose a novel deep active learning framework combining the optimal feature representation of deep convolutional neural network (CNN) and labeling-cost saving of AL, which jointly learns feature and recognition model from unlabeled samples with minimal annotation cost. The model is initialized by a relative small number of labeled samples, and strengthened gradually by adding much more complementary samples for retraining in a progressive way. Our method takes both high-uncertainty samples and the high-confidence samples into consideration for the stability of model. Specifically, the high-confidence samples are selected in a self-paced learning way, and they are double verified by the prior knowledge for more reliable. These high-confidence samples are labeled by estimated class directly, and our framework jointly learns features and recognition model by combining AL with deep CNN, so we name our approach as heuristic deep active learning (HDAL). We apply HDAL on face recognition task, it achieves our goal of "minimizing the annotation cost while avoiding the performance degradation", and the experimental results on Cross-Age Celebrity Dataset (CACD) show that the HDAL outperforms other state-of-the-art approaches in both recognition accuracy and annotation cost.

Keywords: Active learning · Deep CNN · Self-paced learning · Face recognition

1 Introduction

With the growth of mobile phones and social networks, it is fairly easy to obtain facial images. The demands of developing intelligent systems with face recognition technology are increasing accordingly. Traditional approaches handle this problem by supervised learning. However, it is a slow and expensive process to label these images

© Springer International Publishing AG 2017
J. Zhou et al. (Eds.): CCBR 2017, LNCS 10568, pp. 97–107, 2017.
https://doi.org/10.1007/978-3-319-69923-3_11

for preparing a good labeled training dataset. An effective approach to reduce the annotation effort is active learning (AL), which helps learner to select the most informative samples and obtains a high recognition performance.

The basic principle of AL methods is to progressively select and annotate the most informative unlabeled samples, and boost the current model by them in an incremental way. The sample selection criteria are extremely important in AL. Specifically, the high-uncertainty samples, together with other criteria like density and diversity of categories distribution under current model, are generally treated as the informative candidates for model retraining. However, the existing AL approaches all neglect the role of high-certainty samples. The recently proposed self-paced learning (SPL) algorithm [1, 2] demonstrates the important role of high-certainty samples. The SPL presents the training data in an easy to difficult order [3, 4], which imitates the learning process of humans. An easy sample in SPL is the one with high prediction confidence by current model. It is interesting that the AL and SPL actually select samples in the opposite criteria. We want to investigate the possibility of making them complementary to each other.

On the other hand, the existing AL approaches are limited by hand-craft features and small-scale datasets. As well known, the learned features and joint architectures of deep learning methods have made dramatic progress on many vision tasks, especially the deep convolutional neural network (CNN) methods. But a deep CNN model requires many more labeled samples than shallow structure. Those learned features by CNN are updated all the time with the classifier's upgrading, and traditional AL methods can't provide sufficient samples for CNN fine-tuning and make it difficult to obtain the optimal feature representation. Using a batch of high-confidence samples in a self-paced way can bridge the gap of deep CNN and AL well. We think that these high-confidence samples play an important role in the stability of the model, and adding them into training set will reduce the annotation effort further. However, it will result in the deviation problem if assigning the estimated labels as supervised information directly because of the low reliability of the initial model. Therefore, we must take certain measures to ensure the prediction accuracy.

In this paper, we propose a useful framework combining the deep CNN and AL in a self-paced fashion. The framework jointly learns features and recognition model from unlabeled samples with minimal annotation cost. Unlike the existing AL methods only selecting the high uncertainty samples, our method also takes the high-confidence samples as complementary samples for better stability and robustness of model. We employ the dynamic confidence threshold on the sample selecting stage. With the model's performance improving, the samples selection threshold decreases correspondingly. Specifically, considering that the initial model is unreliable and tends to deviate by outliers, we take the prior knowledge into consideration. The high-confidence samples are further ranked by the distance to labeled samples. More close to samples of same identity, more reliable. Those samples both with high-confidence and high distance rank are labeled by predicted category, we called the labels as pseudo labels, and we name our approach as heuristic deep active learning (HDAL). By using softmax output as category probability, the AL method can be easily combined with deep CNN. Our HDAL approach handles both manually annotated and pseudo-labeled samples simultaneously.

There are two contributions of this work: (1) we propose a useful framework combining the AL with CNN, which makes it is possible in the large-scale scenarios by using pseudo-labeled samples for the upgrading of model; (2) we applies the novel framework into face recognition task, and the experiments on Cross-Age Celebrity Dataset (CACD) [5] show that our approach outperforms other methods in both recognition accuracy and annotation cost.

2 Related Work

The samples selection criteria are extremely important for AL. One of the most common strategies is the uncertainty sampling. Lewis et al. [6] selected uncertainty samples by category probability with probabilistic classifier. A more general method is using entropy to realize uncertainty sampling. Joshi et al. pointed out in multi-class cases, the entropy values were heavily influenced by probability values of unimportant classes, and they proposed a Best-versus-Second-Best (BvSB) approach to address this problem in [7], which took the difference between top two high estimated probability values as uncertainty measure. There are many methods using Query-by-committee (QBC) [8, 9], which select samples those have high classification variance. SVM-margin based method [10] took the samples closer to decision boundary as high uncertainty samples.

Many works incorporate density of unlabeled samples into AL [11–13]. Settles and Craven [11] weighted an unlabeled sample by its average similarity to other unlabeled samples. Compared with cosine similarity used in [11], the work [12] used mutual information density and the work [13] used clustering-based density information.

Moreover, there are some researches [13–15] take the samples diversity into consideration for class balance. Brinker [14] considered the angles between the induced classification hyperplanes, where each newly chosen sample corresponded to a hyperplane which maximizes the minimum angle to previous hyperplanes. Elhamifar et al. [15] captured the distribution of samples with low confidence scores. Demir and Bruzzone [13] selected the samples at center of K-means clusters for diversity.

The methods mentioned above all ignore the "from easy to complex" learning process of human. The inspiration of SPL can be explained in analogous to human cognitive process. Bengio et al. [1] initialized the conceptual learning paradigm as curriculum learning (CL), the key in which is to find a ranking function that assigns learning priorities to training samples. Kumar et al. [2] designed a new formulation for adjusting the predetermined curriculum by the feedback about the learner, named SPL. Jiang et al. formulated SPL as a concise optimization problem [3], and further discovered the missing link between CL and SPL [4].

3 Our Approach

In this section, we illustrate how our HDAL model works. Suppose we have a face image set containing n images of m persons, the label of image x_i is person ID j, that is, $y_i = j, j \in \{1, \ldots, m\}$. Let the labeled sample set is $\mathcal{L}$, unlabeled sample set is $\mathcal{U}$, and the current classification model is $\mathcal{M}$. The HDAL for face recognition is formulated as follows:

$$\min_{\theta} -\frac{1}{n} [\sum_{i=1}^{n} \sum_{j=1}^{m} 1\{y_i = j\} p(y_i = j \mid x_i; \theta)], \tag{1}$$

where θ is the network parameters of the CNN, $1\{\cdot\}$ is indicator function, and $p(y_i = j \mid x_i; \theta)$ is the softmax output of CNN, which represents the probability of estimating x_i as j class.

3.1   CNN Classification Model

We use CNN classification model for retraining, which contains 8 layers, the front 5 layers are convolution-pooling layers, next 2 layers are fully-connected layers and the last one is softmax output layer. Figure 1 shows the overall network architecture. Neurons in two fully-connected layers are dropped out by 50%.

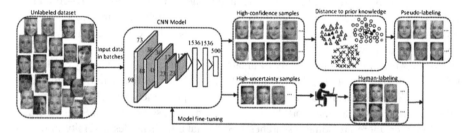

Fig. 1. Illustration of our propose HDAL framework.

Our HDAL has 3 main stages: (1) Initialization. For each class we randomly select a small number of unlabeled samples and manually annotate them as training samples to initialize the CNN. (2) Complementary samples selection. We first rank all unlabeled samples by the current CNN model: for high-confidence samples, we further calculate their distances to prior knowledge and keep samples with low distance, then assign their pseudo-labels directly using estimated labels; for high-uncertainty samples, we deliver them to human annotator. (3) CNN fine-tuning. All labeled complementary samples are put into CNN for retraining. The complementary samples selecting and CNN fine-tuning are executed alternatively until the model converged.

3.2   Sample Selection Criteria

High-Uncertainty Sample Selection

We extend the common uncertainty sampling criteria to select top-K uncertainty samples instead of only one in an iteration considering the convergence rate of large-scale database. We introduce three common active learning criteria, which are based on the probability of a sample class.

(1) Least confidence (LC). It selects the top-K samples, which are ranked by the most likely class probability in descending order. Suppose y^* is the most likely class label for sample x^*. LC can be formulated as:

$$x^* = \underset{x \in U, \text{topK}}{\operatorname{argmax}}(1 - p(y^* \mid x; M)), \tag{2}$$

(2) Best vs second-best (BvSB). Suppose y_1^* and y_2^* are the first and the second likely class label of x^*. The smaller difference of top two classes probabilities, the much more uncertain the category.

$$x^* = \underset{x \in U, \text{topK}}{\operatorname{argmax}} -(p(y_1^* \mid x; M) - p(y_2^* \mid x; M)). \tag{3}$$

(3) Entropy measure (EN). Entropy is often used as an uncertainty measure in informatics. The larger sample entropy, the much more uncertain the category.

$$x^* = \underset{x \in U, \text{topK}}{\operatorname{argmax}} -\sum_i p(y_i^* \mid x; M) log p(y_i^* \mid x; M). \tag{4}$$

High-Confidence Sample Selection
The high-confidence samples with their pseudo-labels are used for retraining directly. To ensure the reliability of pseudo-labels, high-confidence and distance to prior knowledge are taken into account jointly. We employ a dynamic confidence threshold δ, which is decreased in decay rate β with iteration step t. Feeding the training data in an easy to complex order, it imitates the learning process of human like SPL. Denote the high-confidence candidates set as $\mathcal{H}'$, it is formulated as:

$$\mathcal{H}' = \{x^* \mid p(y^* \mid x; M) > \delta\}$$
$$\delta = \delta - \beta t. \tag{5}$$

Suppose the predicted label of a selected sample x^* is p, $p=1, 2, \ldots, m$. Then we compute the distance between x^* and samples centroid of same identity P, and the distance between x^* and samples centroid of different identities $\bar{P}$. The lower difference of above two distances means that the more reliable of the predicted label. We rank the difference values of all the selected samples and use them for double verification. We further select top-k high-confidence samples $\mathcal{H}$ and assign them the pseudo-labels. The distance to prior knowledge criterion can be formulated as:

$$\mathcal{H} = \{x^* \mid \underset{x \in H', \text{topk}}{\operatorname{argmin}}[(x_p^* - P) - (x_p^* - \bar{P})]\}, \tag{6}$$

The recognition model can be retrained after adding these new labeled samples, which include the high-uncertainty samples U_c annotated by human annotator and the high-confidence samples $\mathcal{H}$ with pseudo-labels. The whole HDAL algorithm is shown in Algorithm 1.

Algorithm 1 The Whole HDAL Algorithm

Input: labeled set $\mathcal{L}$, unlabeled set $\mathcal{U}$, initialized model $\mathcal{M}$

Output: the face recognition model $\mathcal{M}$

1: for $t = 1$ to T do /* T is the maximum iteration */

2: $\mathcal{M} = \text{train}(\mathcal{L}, \mathcal{M})$; /* model fine-tuning, see Algorithm 2 for detail */

3: $P = \text{test}(\mathcal{U}, \mathcal{M})$; /* using $\mathcal{M}$ to estimate the class probability of $\mathcal{U}$ */

4: $[U_c, \mathcal{H}] = \text{select}(\mathcal{U}, P, \text{strategy})$; /* select high-uncertainty samples U_c by Eq.(2)-Eq.(4) and select high-confidence samples $\mathcal{H}$ by Eq.(5)-Eq.(6) */

5: $\text{query}(U_c)$; /* resort to annotator */

6: $\text{pseudoLabel}(\mathcal{H})$; /* assign the pseudo-labels */

7: $\mathcal{L} = \mathcal{L} + H + U_c$; /* update $\mathcal{L}$ */

8: end for

3.3 Parameter Optimization

Adding the complementary samples into the labeled sample set $\mathcal{L}$, we fine-tuning the CNN model iteratively. Suppose the number of samples in $\mathcal{L}$ is increased to N, the cost function of our HDAL is rewritten as follows:

$$J(\theta) = -\frac{1}{N}[\sum_{i=1}^{N}\sum_{j=1}^{m} 1\{y_i^* = j\}p(y_i^* = j \mid x_i^*; \theta)], \tag{7}$$

where $p(y_i^* = j \mid x_i^*; \theta) = \frac{e^{\theta_j^T x_i^*}}{\sum_{l=1}^{m} e^{\theta_l^T x_i^*}}$.

There is no closed-form solution for θ, we therefore resort to gradient descent algorithm and employ the standard back propagation to update the CNN's parameters θ. The partial derivative of the network parameters θ is:

$$\frac{\partial J(\theta)}{\partial \theta_j} = -\frac{1}{N}\sum_{i=1}^{N} x_i^*(1\{y_i^* = j\} - p(y_i^* = j \mid x_i^*; \theta)). \tag{8}$$

Then update θ_j by Eq. (9) on each iteration.

$$\theta_j = \theta_j - \alpha\frac{\partial J(\theta)}{\partial \theta_j} \quad j = 1, 2, \ldots, m. \tag{9}$$

The fine-tuning of CNN model is realized in Algorithm 2.

Algorithm 2 CNN Model Fine-tuning Algorithm

Input:

    labeled training set X, initial parameters θ, and learning rate α

Output:

    network parameters θ

1: for $s = 1$ to S do /* S is the maximum iteration */

2:    $P = test(X, \theta)$; /* estimate the class probability of X */

3:    $G = -\dfrac{1}{N} \times X \times (1 - P^s)$; /*compute gradient by Eq.(8) */

4:    $\theta = \theta - \alpha G$; /* update parameters by Eq.(9) */

5: end for

---

4 Experiments

We present experimental results for the proposed HDAL on face recognition task using CACD[1] database [5]. The CACD database is a large-scale database released in 2014, which contains more than 160,000 images of 2,000 celebrities. There are only 200 celebrities' images are manually checked originally, and we extend the number to 580. Among them, the images of 80 individuals are utilized for pre-training of feature presentation, and the rest 500 persons' images are used to perform the HDAL approach. The 10% images with their labels are used to initialize the CNN model, and the rest 90% images are performed a five-folder cross-validation.

Our CNN model is constructed based on Caffe [16], the initial parameters are set by Gaussian distribution $\mathcal{N}(0, 0.01)$, and the learning rates of all the layers are set as 0.01. The experiments are executed on a PC with Nvidia Titan X GPU. We first detect the faces using the method proposed in paper [17] and resize the faces to 150×200. In each iteration, the number of high-uncertainty samples K is set as 1000; the selection threshold of high-confidence samples δ are set as 0.98, and the reduced rate of threshold β is set as 0.0033.

First a baseline experiment is conducted, which train the CNN model with 80% labeled images and test the rest 20% images. The recognition rate of baseline method is 92%, which can be considered as the best performance of CNN model can reach.

Then we verify the effectiveness of the high-confidence samples selection criterion by a set of experiments. According to different high-uncertainty samples selection

---

[1] http://bcsiriuschen.github.io/CARC/.

strategies, our approach further is named as HDAL_LC, HDAL_BvSB and HDAL_EN. For the traditional AL method without using the high-confidence samples, we name them as DAL_LC, DAL_BvSB and DAL_EN. Figure 2 illustrates the performance comparison between our heuristic selection strategy and traditional active learning strategies. The subfigures (a)–(c) demonstrate different high-uncertainty sampling criteria: (a) is LC, (b) is BvBS, and (c) is EN. To achieve 85% recognition accuracy, the labeled training samples required for HDAL_LC, HDAL_BvBS, HDAL_EN are 28.7%, 28.2% and 26.8% respectively, while for DAL_LC, DAL_BvBS, DAL_EN are 34.4%, 36% and 37%. When the 50% training samples are labeled, the recognition accuracies of HDAL_LC, HDAL_BvBS, HDAL_EN are 90%, 90% and 90.5% respectively, while for DAL_LC, DAL_BvBS, DAL_EN are 88.8%, 88.4% and 87.9%. To reach the baseline recognition accuracy 92%, HDAL_LC, HDAL_BvBS and HDAL_EN require 67%, 67.6% and 68% labeled training samples respectively. We can see that the performance of our HDAL is much better than the DAL.

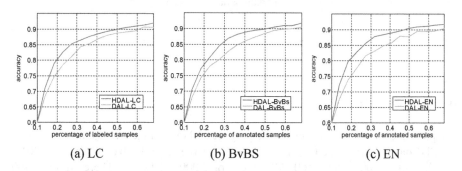

(a) LC   (b) BvBS   (c) EN

Fig. 2. The comparison of recognition accuracies between HDAL and DAL.

We further evaluate the contributions comes from different components of HDAL. First using SPL and AL standalone respectively and then using their combination. For AL method, we tried the random and entropy-based selection strategies, which are denoted as RAND and DAL. RAND points to randomly selecting the samples to be labeled by annotator. Figure 3 illustrates the accuracies obtained by using SPL, AL and HDAL. The accuracies of SPL, RAND, DAL and HDAL are 71.4%, 78.2%, 82.5%, and 86.9% respectively, when the percentage of labeled samples is 30%. AL can resort annotator for the informative samples labeling, so RAND and DAL are both better than SPL. RAND and DAL gain 6.8% and 11.1% accuracy improvement over SPL. The combination of SPL and DAL, that is HDAL, can automatically exploit the majority of the high-confidence samples, and further achieves 4.4% accuracy improvement over DAL.

At last we compare our HDAL with other active learning methods, such as TCAL [13], CPAL [15], and RAND. CPAL annotates samples in each step based on prediction uncertainty and sample diversity. And TCAL takes uncertainty, diversity and density into account jointly; it outperforms other state-of-the-art methods. We re-implement CPAL and TCAL by using our CNN model without last softmax output layer as feature representation for fair comparison. RAND method is randomly selecting the samples to be labeled for CNN fine-tuning. The performance of RAND can be regarded as the worst performance in active learning methods. The comparison results are shown in Fig. 4. Our HDAL model outperforms the competing methods in accuracy when the same amount labeled samples. When the 50% training samples are labeled, the recognition accuracy of TCAL, CPAL and RAND are 87.5%, 87.9% and 84.9% respectively. On the other hand, our HDAL reduces the annotation effort compared to other method. To achieve 85% recognition accuracy, TCAL, CPAL and RAND requires 39.5%, 40.8% and 49.8% labeled samples respectively, while HDAL only requires 26.8%. Our HDAL shows the better performance than the TCAL and CPAL on both accuracy and labeling cost.

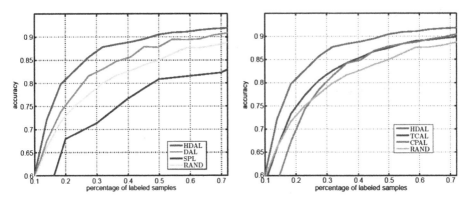

Fig. 3. Accuracies of different components with labeled samples increasing.   **Fig. 4.** The comparison with other state-of-the-art methods.

From above experiments, one can see that our HDAL is better than other methods in both recognition accuracy and annotation cost. We think that the good performance of HDAL stems from the better discrimination by CNN model and the better robustness by jointly considering high-confidence samples and high-uncertainty samples.

5 Conclusion

In this paper, we propose a novel heuristic deep active learning approach and apply it in face recognition task. Our HDAL framework combining AL with deep CNN jointly learns features and recognition model from unlabeled samples with minimal annotation cost. We take the high-confidence samples as complementary samples for better stability and robustness of model compared with the traditional AL methods, which only take the high-uncertainty samples into consideration. Specifically, the high-confidence samples are selected in a self-paced learning way, and they are double verified by the prior knowledge for more reliable. By using softmax output as category probability, HDAL combines the deep CNN with AL successfully. The better discrimination of CNN model and the better robustness of jointly considering high-confidence samples and high-uncertainty samples make it outperform other state-of-the-art methods. In future, we plan to apply our HDAL approach on more challenging and general object recognition task. We also plan to generalize our framework into other vision tasks.

Acknowledgments. This research is supported by the Research Project of Guangzhou Municipal Universities (No. 1201620302), National Undergraduate Scientific and Technological Innovation Project (No. 201711078017), the Science and Technology Planning Project of Guangdong Province (Nos. 2015B010128009, 2013B010406005). The authors would like to thank the reviewers for their comments and suggestions.

References

1. Bengio, Y., Louradour, J., Collobert, R., Weston, J.: Curriculum learning. In: ICML, pp. 41–48. ACM (2009)
2. Kumar, M.P., Packer, B., Koller, D.: Self-paced learning for latent variable models. In: NIPS, pp. 1189–1197 (2010)
3. Jiang, L., Meng, D., Mitamura, T., Hauptmann, A.G.: Easy samples first: self-paced reranking for zero-example multimedia search. In: MM, pp. 547–556. ACM (2014)
4. Jiang, L., Meng, D., Zhao, Q., Shan, S., Hauptmann, A.G.: Selfpaced curriculum learning. In: AAAI, pp. 2694–2700. AAAI Press (2015)
5. Chen, B.-C., Chen, C.-S., Hsu, W.H.: Cross-age reference coding for age-invariant face recognition and retrieval. In: Fleet, D., Pajdla, T., Schiele, B., Tuytelaars, T. (eds.) ECCV 2014. LNCS, vol. 8694, pp. 768–783. Springer, Cham (2014). doi:10.1007/978-3-319-10599-4_49
6. Lewis, D.D.: A sequential algorithm for training text classifiers: corrigendum and additional data. In: ACM SIGIR Forum, pp. 13–19. ACM (1995)
7. Joshi, A.J., Porikli, F., Papanikolopoulos, N.: Multi-class active learning for image classification. In: CVPR, pp. 2372–2379. IEEE (2009)
8. Freund, Y., Seung, H.S., Shamir, E., Tishby, N.: Selective sampling using the query by committee algorithm. Mach. Learn. 133–168 (1997)
9. McCallumzy, A.K., Nigamy, K.: Employing em and pool-based active learning for text classification. In: ICML, pp. 359–367. Citeseer (1998)
10. Tong, S., Koller, D.: Support vector machine active learning with applications to text classification. J. Mach. Learn. Res. 45–66 (2002)
11. Settles, B., Craven, M.: An analysis of active learning strategies for sequence labeling tasks. In: Empirical Methods in Natural Language Processing, pp. 1070–1079. Association for Computational Linguistics (2008)
12. Li, X., Guo, Y.: Adaptive active learning for image classification. In: CVPR, pp. 859–866. IEEE (2013)
13. Demir, B., Bruzzone, L.: A novel active learning method in relevance feedback for content-based remote sensing image retrieval. IEEE Trans. Geosci. Remote Sens. 2323–2334 (2015)
14. Brinker, K.: Incorporating diversity in active learning with support vector machines. In: ICML, pp. 59–66 (2003)

15. Elhamifar, E., Sapiro, G., Yang, A., Sasrty, S.S.: A convex optimization framework for active learning. In: ICCV, pp. 209–216 (2013)
16. Jia, Y., Shelhamer, E., Donahue, J., Karayev, S., Long, J., Girshick, R., Guadarrama, S., Darrell, T.: Caffe: convolutional architecture for fast feature embedding. In: MM, pp. 675–678. ACM (2014)
17. Sun, Y., Wang, X., Tang, X.: Deep convolutional network cascade for facial point detection. In: CVPR, pp. 3476–3483. IEEE (2013)

One-Snapshot Face Anti-spoofing Using a Light Field Camera

Xiaohua Xie[1,2,3], Yan Gao[1,2,3], Wei-Shi Zheng[1,2,3], Jianhuang Lai[1,2,3(✉)], and Junyong Zhu[1,2,3]

[1] School of Data and Computer Science, Sun Yat-sen University, Guangzhou, China
[2] Guangdong Key Laboratory of Information Security Technology, Sun Yat-sen University, Guangzhou, China
[3] Key Laboratory of Machine Intelligence and Advanced Computing, Ministry of Education, Sun Yat-sen University, Guangzhou, China
{xiexiaoh6,zhwshi,stsljh,zhujuny5}@mail.sysu.edu.cn, gaoy47@mail2.sysu.edu.cn

Abstract. Face recognition is an increasingly popular technology for user authentication. However, face recognition is susceptible to spoofing attacks. Therefore, a reliable way to detect malicious attacks is crucial to the robustness of the face recognition system. This paper describes a new approach to utilizing light field camera for defending spoofing face attacks, like (warped) printed 2D facial photos and high-definition tablet images. The light field camera is a sensor that can record the directions as well as the colors of incident rays. Needing only one snapshot, multiple refocused images can be generated. In the proposed method, three kinds of features extracted from a pair of refocused images are extracted to discriminate fake faces and real faces. To verify the performance, we build a light field photograph databases and conduct experiments. Experimental results reveal that the employed features can achieve remarkable anti-spoofing accuracy under different types of spoofing attacks.

Keywords: Face liveness detection · Light field · Fake face · Face recognition

1 Introduction

Due to the prominent features of face for human identification, face recognition technologies have been widely applied to security systems in order to make those systems more convenient and stronger. However, the face spoofing behaviors that use fake faces to cheat security systems have occurred. Spoofing attacks upon face recognition systems involve presenting artificial facial replicas of authorized users to falsely infer their presence in order to bypass the biometric security measures. The spoofing faces include the 2D printed photos, digital images displayed on screen, video replay, 3D masks, and so on. In this case, technological defense against spoofing attacks is needed to develop.

© Springer International Publishing AG 2017
J. Zhou et al. (Eds.): CCBR 2017, LNCS 10568, pp. 108–117, 2017.
https://doi.org/10.1007/978-3-319-69923-3_12

In order to improve the security measures of face recognition systems against deliberate spoof attacks, face liveness detection has received significant recent attention from researchers. Face liveness detection is a process to judge whether an input face is directly captured from a human or not. Many related works have been reviewed in [1,2]. Many of existing methods focus on extracting discriminant texture descriptors or frequency components from still images, or motion cues and 3D information from videos to distinguish fake faces from actual ones.

To make defense systems stronger, researchers have also considered using other sensors rather than the visual camera. The RGB-D camera, structured light system, thermal and near infrared sensors are some representative examples. In this paper, a novel method is proposed for detecting spoofing faces with a special sensor, light field camera.

The light field camera was developed by Lippmann in 1908 and evolved by Adelson and Wang [3] in 1990s. Unlike the conventional camera that outputs an image by summing all the lights falling into each pixel, in a single snapshot, the light field camera can record the direction as well as the color with the intensity of incident rays. Specifically, a microlens array is embedded in front of the photosensor to separates the light, so that the direction and the intensity of each split light are recorded in pixels of the photosensor. These capabilities enable digital image refocusing and surface depth reconstruction. Recently, portable light field cameras such as Lytro[1] [4] and Raytrix [5] are available in the market, and a camera array module that takes light field photographs in a mobile phone has been developed [6]. As a result, the light field camera is being applied in various research fields, such as 3D surface reconstruction [7], face recognition [8], and iris recognition [9].

Kim et al. [10] analyze the raw light field photograph microscopically and apply it to detect spoofing faces. Unlike Kim et al.'s method emphasizing on raw light field data, we utilize the refocusing effect of light field camera to discriminate fake faces from real ones. Specifically, for each input face (real or fake), we samples its 4D light field using a Lytro camera, and further obtain two images with different focuses. Based on these two images, three kinds of features are extracted and used for face liveness detection. Our algorithm framework is partially inspired by Kim et al.'s method [11,12]. The main difference is that their system works on a hand-held digital camera or a webcam using multiple exposures. Specially, Kim et al.'s method on hand-held digital camera requires a manual selection of focusing plane during photographing stage, which is not practicable for a face anti-spoofing system. As a comparison, our method only needs a single photographic exposure, which can be used in an automatic mode. Furthermore, we investigate one more feature, i.e., the intensity entropy, which is effective in detecting warped printed faces. Actually, detecting the warped printed faces is very challenging since they can simulate the main 3D shape of human faces.

---

[1] Available online: https://www.lytro.com/.

To evaluate our method, we have collected a databases using the light field camera. Experimental results tell the merits of using light field camera in face liveness detection.

2 Preliminaries

2.1 Brief Introduction to Light Field Camera

The light field camera is a sensor that can record information from incident light rays. The information of the light field contains not only the intensity and color, but also the directions of the light rays. In this paper, we use the Lytro camera [4] which is the first consumer light field camera. The Lytro camera samples the 4D light field on its sensor in a single photographic exposure. This is achieved by inserting a microlens array between the sensor and main lens, forming a simplified plenoptic camera. Each microlens measures not just the total amount of light deposited at that location, but rather the full 4D light field measuring the amount of light traveling along each ray that intersects the sensor. By resorting the measured rays of light to where they would have terminated in slightly different, synthetic cameras, the sharp photographs focused at different depths can be computed. In the macrophotography regime, the synthetic photographs from a range of different viewpoints can be also computed. Due to this properties, light field photograph can be conveniently used to deduce the 3D shapes of scene.

2.2 Acquisition of Refocused Images

After taking photographs, the original 4D light field data (in LFP format) from the camera can be imported into a computer, and light field photographs can be further exported from the light field. We use the Light Field Toolbox [13] for the decoding, colour correction, and visualization of light field photographs. For Lytro camera, the angular resolution and spatial resolution of light field photograph are 9×9 and 380×380, respectively. For refocusing, Ng et al. [4] reveal that the traditional shifting and summing the sub-aperture images works well in most cases. Specifically, sub-aperture images are made by reordering incident rays in the raw light field photograph. Each sub-aperture image is composed of the pixels of same position selected from each microlens image. More interpretations can be referred from [4,10]. For attaining better image quality for the refocusing images, the higher-order quadrature techniques such as supersampling with a quadrilinear reconstruction filter can be used. In practice, we also use the Light Field Toolbox for getting refocusing images. Specifically, there is a parameter α for controlling the refocusing.

We try to select two images so that the focal plane of the first image lies on the nose tip, and that of the second image lies on the ears. Even then, there is little visual difference between the two refocused images (see Fig. 2). However, we will show that the refocused images from real face still have differences in specific feature space.

3 Proposed Methodology

3.1 Overview

The most significant difference between real and fake faces is whether the 3D information exists or not. When performing refocusing on a real face, the generated photographs may hold changing in sharpness with respect to different facial components. Instead, there is little difference in clarity on different facial components of a fake face, regardless of the focus. We emphasize this characteristic and utilize the refocusing effect of light field camera to discriminate real faces from fake faces.

For the face to be recognized, the system takes a photographs by the light field camera in a single exposure, then two specific images relevant to different focus depths can be acquired. Based on this image pair, the variations of focus are computed by considering information entropy, focus feature, and power histogram feature. Afterwards, the spoofing faces can be detected according to the focus variations. The flowchart of the proposed face liveness detection method is shown in Fig. 1. The technical details of our method are introduced as follows.

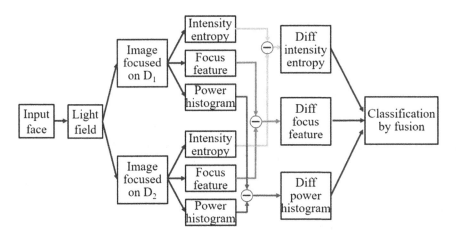

Fig. 1. Flowchart of the proposed face liveness detection method.

3.2 Features Extraction for Face Liveness Detection

As mentioned above, the focus variations of refocused photographs can be used to distinguish the real faces from spoofing ones. We adopt three kinds of image features to represent the degrees of focusing, further to compute the variation of focus. The employed features including intensity entropy, modified Laplacian (LAPM), and power histogram, are related to spacial and frequency analysis, respectively. Specially, the usage of latter two are followed Kim's work [11,12].

Intensity Entropy. Intensity Entropy (IE) is a statistical form of features that represent the amount of information contained in the aggregate feature of the intensity distribution in an image. We find that it can partially reflect the degree of focusing of an image. Let p_i represent the proportion of the pixels with the gray value of i in an grayscale image I with gray range $[1\,255]$, then the unary intensity entropy of I is defined as:

$$IE = \sum_{i=0}^{255} p_i \log p_i. \tag{1}$$

Denote the intensity entropies of two images of an face with different focuses as IE and IE', respectively. Then the difference in intensity entropies, $Diff_I E = IE - IE'$, is used as a feature for liveness detection.

Focus Feature. The modified Laplacian (LAPM) [14,15] is also employed to calculate the focus measure. Specifically, the LAPM is presented as the sum of transformed Laplacian filters. For a 2D image I, the LAPM can be calculated by Eq. 2

$$LAFM(i,j) = \sum_{(x,y)\in\Omega(i,j)} \triangle_L^2 I(x,y) \cdot t$$

$$\triangle_L^2 I(x,y) = |\frac{\partial^2 I}{\partial x^2}| + |\frac{\partial^2 I}{\partial y^2}| \tag{2}$$

$$t = \begin{cases} 1 & LAPM(x,y) \geq T \\ 0 & otherwise \end{cases}$$

where $\Omega(i,j)$ means neighbourhood of (i,j) and T is an empirical threshold. Since the focusing regions look sharper and correspond to higher LAPM values than the out-of-focus ones, the LAPM is related to the degrees of focusing.

Examples of the LAPMs calculated on different focusing images are shown in Fig. 2. In the figure, the refocused images as well as corresponding LAPMs from real face, screen face, and printed face, respectively, are shown. For LAPM maps, bright pixels represent high values of LAPM. Through human eyes, it is difficult to examine the difference between two images under different focusing, regardless of real face or fake face. However, for the image pair from real face, their LAPMs are obviously discriminant from each other (attention on the red lines), while the LAPM pair from fack face have little differences.

Consequently, the LAPM variations between two refocused images can be used to discriminant the real face from fake face. For an input face, denote $LAPM_1$ and $LAPM_2$ as the focus measures of two images focusing on different depth $D1$ and $D2$, respectively. The final focus feature can be calculated according to following steps:

(1) Compute the difference of FM, i.e., $Diff_{FM} = LAPM_1 - LAPM_2$;
(2) Accumulate all of the $Diff_{FM}$ in the same column, i.e., $Diff_{FM}^p(i) = \sum_j Diff_{FM}(i,j)$;

(3) Fit the single-dimension representation of $Diff_{FM}^p$ using a quadratic equation, $y = ax^2 + bx + c$.

Then, the coefficients $[a, b, c]$ are exploited as a feature for classification.

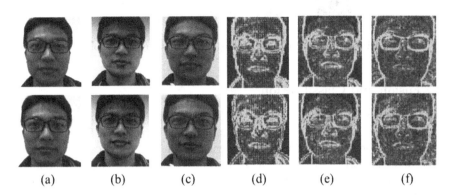

(a)   (b)   (c)   (d)   (e)   (f)

Fig. 2. Refocused images as well as corresponding LAPM maps. (a), (b), and (c) are the images from an actual face, screen face, and printed face, respectively, focused on different depth planes. (d), (e), and (f) are LAPM maps corresponding to (a), (b), and (c), respectively. The instances in the first row correspond to a deeper focus while the instances the second row correspond to a shallower focus. (Color figure online)

Power Histogram Feature. The refocusing variations can be also detected by frequency information. In our method, the power histogram feature is employed. The process of extracting the power histogram feature P for an image is as follows.

(1) Divide I radially into K subregions, $\{S_k\}_{k=1}^K$, as shown in Fig. 3;
(2) Perform center-shifted FFT for each subregion;
(3) For each subregion $S_k, k = 1, K$, divide the frequency spectrum into C circles $\{C_k^c\}_{c=1}^{c=C}$ by allowing it to be superimposed;
(4) Compute the percentage of power within each circular region C_k^c by $Perc_k^c = \frac{\sum_{(u,v) \in C_k^c} P(u,v)}{\sum_{(u,v) \in S_k} P(u,v)}$, where $P(u,v) = real(u,v)^2 + imag(u,v)^2$ with $real(u,v)$ and $imag(u,v)$ as the real and imaginary parts of the frequency component, respectively.
(5) Concatenate K histograms by $PH = [PH_1, \cdots, PH_K]$, where $PH_k = [Perc_k^1, \cdots, Perc_k^C]$.

Figure 3 illustrates the process of extracting the power histogram feature for an image. With real faces, power histograms vary depending on different focused images. However, those of fake faces do not vary. For two images of an input face with different focuses, I and I', denote their power histogram features as PH and PH', respectively. Then the difference in the power histograms, $Diff_{PH} = PH - PH'$, is used as a feature for liveness detection. In our experiment, we set $K = 2$ and $C = 7$, respectively.

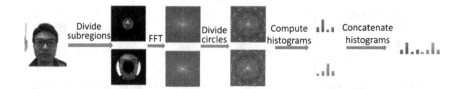

Fig. 3. Flowchart of power histogram feature extraction.

3.3 Fusion and Classification

Both feature-level and decision-level fusion algorithms can be employed in our issue. In the experiment, we will investigate using three usual fusion method, respectively. The first one simply concatenates different features into a feature vector (namely feature fusion). The second one trains three classifiers relevant to three kinds of features, respectively, and then counts up their classification scores with weights (namely weighted fusion). The third one also trains three classifiers relevant to three kinds of features, respectively, but votes for the final decision by three classifiers (namely vote fusion). Specifically, the SVM classifier is used in our experiment.

4   Experiment

4.1 Experimental Dataset

To evaluate our proposed method, we have built a light field face database for liveness detection by ourselves. The database includes three kinds of fake faces, i.e., normally printed face (NP), warped printed face (WP), and HD tablet face (HD). The printed face photos are taken by SLR camera (Canon EOS 60D) under constrained indoor light and white background, with a shooting distance of 30 cm, and printed on A4 white paper with a color printer. The printed photos bent over the face are used as another kind of attack, which to a certain extent, can simulate three-dimensional information of face. The HD tablet face refers displaying a face in the high-resolution color LCD. The resolution of LCD is 1280 by 1024 pixels. All real faces as well as fake faces are photographed using a Lytro light field camera to form the database. To enrich the database by considering the shooting distance, each object (real face or fake face) is photographed by three kind of shooting distances (30 cm, 45 cm, 60 cm). Finally, the database contains 57 subjects, 684 light field photos, resulting in 1,368 refocusing images. Figure 4 shows samples of databases.

4.2 Experimental Setting

For each attack pattern, we randomly select 20% real faces and fake faces to train the classifier, and use the rest samples for testing. The average classification accuracy over 50 times cross validation is used as the final result. For each

Fig. 4. Samples of databases. The real face, normally printed face (NP), warped printed face (WP), and HD tablet face (HD) are displayed from left to right, respectively.

original light field data, we get two images at different re-focusing depths. We use the following parameter settings at different shooting distances: setting re-focus parameter to −0.2 and 0.2, respectively, in 30 cm; setting the re-focus parameter to 0 and 0.2, respectively, in 45 cm; setting the re-focus parameter to 0.1 and 0.3, respectively, in 60 cm. For the SVM classifier, the radial basis function is selected.

4.3   Experimental Results and Analysis

The experimental results are shown in Table 1. With respect to our method, different features seem to be good at determining different kinds of attacks. For example, the intensity entropy gets high accuracy rate in detecting the warped printed faces, but gets relatively low accuracy rate in detecting the normally printed face and HD tablet faces. On the contrary, the focusing feature has a better recognition effect on the normally printed face and the HD tablet faces than on the warped printed faces. The power histogram seems not prejudiced against the attack patterns, but can not attain the best performance for any kind of attack mode.

The method using multiple features generally get better result than the one using only one kind of feature, but it is not always. Feature fusion method

Table 1. The accuracy rate (%) of different methods in different spoofing attack

	Printed faces			Warped printed face			HD tablet face		
	30 cm	45 cm	60 cm	30 cm	45 cm	60 cm	30 cm	45 cm	60 cm
Intensity entropy	75.3	70.5	62.3	**99.5**	92.6	81.0	61.2	64.0	63.5
Focus feature	94.3	81.5	71.0	81.5	91.8	82.8	87.8	80.4	68.2
Power histogram	92.0	80.3	71.7	87.8	87.0	81.6	84.7	**80.5**	**78.1**
Feature fusion	**98.6**	**89.3**	**84.5**	97.3	92.4	85.9	**90.9**	82.3	75.3
Weighted fusion	95.2	83.6	76.4	96.4	**95.0**	**90.1**	85.3	80.4	75.8
Vote fusion	95.2	83.6	76.4	96.4	**95.0**	**90.1**	85.3	80.4	75.8

works better than other fusion manners. Furthermore, with the increase of photographing distance, the classification accuracies on three kinds of fake faces are all reduced.

The experimental results reveal that the employed features in this paper is effect in face anti-spoofing using a light field camera. In practice, we should take feature selection as well as fusion manner into account according to the way of attack.

5   Conclusion

We come up with a new approach to utilizing light field camera for face liveness detection in this paper. Without taking image sequences, we can capture the change of the face appearance under refocusing, which can be use to detect fake faces and real faces. Three kinds of features are employed. For evaluating our proposed method, we collected a light field database with normal print, warped print and HD tablet attacks. Experiments reveal that different features are skilled at determining different kinds of spoofing attacks. Nowadays, the light field camera attracts engineers attentions. Besides refocusing technology, there are many factors to apply the light field photograph to face liveness detection and other visual tasks.

Acknowledgment. We would like to thank Ms. Yun Lei and Mr. Xiya Jia who have made important contributions to this project. This project is supported by the Natural Science Foundation of China (No. 61672544), Guangdong Natural Science Foundation (No. 2015A030311047), Guangzhou Project (No. 201604046018), Fundamental Research Funds for the Central Universities (No. 161gpy41), Shenzhen Innovation Program (No. JCYJ20150401145529008), and Tip-top Scientific and Technical Innovative Youth Talents of Guangdong special support program (No. 2016TQ03X263).

References

1. Kahm, O., Damer, N.: 2D face liveness detection: an overview. In: BIOSIG, pp. 1–12. IEEE (2012)
2. Parveen, S., Ahmad, S.M.S., Hanafi, M., Azizun, W.: Face anti-spoofing methods. Curr. Sci. **108**(8), 1491–1500 (2015)
3. Adelson, E.H., Wang, J.Y.: Single lens stereo with a plenoptic camera. IEEE TPAMI **14**(2), 99–106 (1992)
4. Ng, R., Levoy, M., Brédif, M., Duval, G., Horowitz, M., Hanrahan, P.: Light field photography with a hand-held plenoptic camera. CSTR **2**(11), 1–11 (2005)
5. Perwass, C., Wietzke, L.: Single lens 3D-camera with extended depth-of-field. In: HVEI, vol. 17, p. 829108 (2012)
6. Venkataraman, K., Lelescu, D., Duparré, J., McMahon, A., Molina, G., Chatterjee, P., Mullis, R., Nayar, S.: PICAM: an ultra-thin high performance monolithic camera array. ACM TOG **32**(6), 166 (2013)
7. Bishop, T.E., Favaro, P.: The light field camera: extended depth of field, aliasing, and superresolution. IEEE TPAMI **34**(5), 972–986 (2012)

8. Raghavendra, R., Yang, B., Raja, K.B., Busch, C.: A new perspective–face recognition with light-field camera. In: ICB, pp. 1–8. IEEE (2013)
9. Raghavendra, R., Raja, K.B., Yang, B., Busch, C.: Combining iris and periocular recognition using light field camera. In: ACPR, pp. 155–159. IEEE (2013)
10. Kim, S., Ban, Y., Lee, S.: Face liveness detection using a light field camera. Sensors **14**(12), 22471–22499 (2014)
11. Kim, S., Yu, S., Kim, K., Ban, Y., Lee, S.: Face liveness detection using variable focusing. In: ICB, pp. 1–6. IEEE (2013)
12. Kim, S., Ban, Y., Lee, S.: Face liveness detection using defocus. Sensors **15**(1), 1537–1563 (2015)
13. Dansereau, D.G., Pizarro, O., Williams, S.B.: Decoding, calibration and rectification for lenselet-based plenoptic cameras. In: CVPR, pp. 1027–1034 (2013)
14. Nayar, S.K., Nakagawa, Y.: Shape from focus. IEEE TPAMI **16**(8), 824–831 (1994)
15. Pertuz, S., Puig, D., Garcia, M.A.: Analysis of focus measure operators for shape-from-focus. Pattern Recogn. **46**(5), 1415–1432 (2013)

Content-Independent Face Presentation Attack Detection with Directional Local Binary Pattern

Le Qin[1], Le-Bing Zhang[1], Fei Peng[1(✉)], and Min Long[2]

[1] College of Computer Science and Electronic Engineering, Hunan University,
Changsha 410082, China
{qinle,zhanglebing}@hnu.edu.cn, eepengf@gmail.com
[2] College of Computer and Communication Engineering,
Changsha University of Science and Technology, Changsha 410014, China
caslongm@gmail.com

Abstract. Aiming to counter photo attack and video attack in face recognition (FR) systems, a content-independent face presentation attack detection scheme based on directional local binary pattern (DLBP) is proposed. In order to minimize the influences of the image content, DLBP is proposed to investigate the noise characteristics of the facial image. By using directional difference filtering, the discrepancies between the real face and the facial artefact in terms of the consistency of adjacent pixels are effectively exploited. With the DLBP feature, the detection is accomplished by using a Softmax classifier. Experiments are done with four public benchmark databases, and the results indicate its effectiveness both in intra-database and cross-database testing.

Keywords: Face presentation attack detection · Content-independent · Noise component · Directional local binary pattern

1 Introduction

As one of the most important identity authentication mechanisms, biometric identification has been widely used in entry access systems, criminal investigations, and in high-security inspection equipment. Among them, face recognition (FR) has attracted extensive attention due to its high security, good stability, and ease of use [1]. However, images or videos containing a target's face can be easily acquired from online social networks nowadays. If they are misused by malicious attackers, it is possible to launch presentation attack (also known as spoofing attack) on FR systems [2].

The existing face presentation attack detection (abbreviated as PAD, also known as spoofing detection or liveness detection [3]) methods can be classified into sensor-based methods and feature-based methods. Sensor-based methods [4, 5] can improve the security of FR systems by using additional equipment, but they increase cost and complexity of applications. Feature-based methods are mainly focused on motion analysis or texture analysis of original face images. Static texture features [6–10], dynamic texture features [11, 12], image quality features [13], motion information [14],

© Springer International Publishing AG 2017
J. Zhou et al. (Eds.): CCBR 2017, LNCS 10568, pp. 118–126, 2017.
https://doi.org/10.1007/978-3-319-69923-3_13

and hybrid features [15–18] are generally extracted, used as an input of a classifier to determine the liveness. Nevertheless, these clues are sensitive to the contents of the facial image, and cannot be well generalized under different detection scenarios. To exploit the noise signatures of the facial video, Pinto et al. proposed a face PAD method based on visual rhythms [19]. The residual noise is first extracted by individual frames, and their Fourier spectrum are computed. After that, the detection features are extracted from the visual rhythms by calculating local binary pattern (LBP), gray level co-occurrence matrix, and histogram of oriented gradient. However, the residual noise is still inevitable contaminated by the image contents.

To counter photo attack and video attack in FR systems and to address the above problems, directional local binary pattern (DLBP) is proposed to investigate the noise characteristics of facial images. This investigation is based on the fact that artefacts in a photo or video are recaptured by a device while real faces are originally captured images. Recaptured images tend to be more seriously distorted by the reproduction process, and thus additional noise components are introduced. As known to us, there exists inherent discrepancies between the recaptured images and the originally captured images in terms of noise components. On the basis of these properties, it is reasonable to assume that the real faces and the artefacts can be identified by different noise features. DLBP takes advantage of the directional difference filter [20, 21], and it can capture the essential distinction between the real face and the artefact.

The contributions of this paper are:

(1) In order to minimize the influence of image content, DLBP is proposed to extract the noise characteristics of facial image, the rationale and the motivation are explained.
(2) Based on the DLBP, a novel face PAD method is proposed, and it can achieve stable performance across four public benchmark databases.

2 Directional Local Binary Pattern

2.1 Motivation

The motivation of the proposed scheme is that there exists inherent noise discrepancies between the real faces and the artefacts (photo attacks and video attacks) considering from the originally captured images and the recaptured images. As the real face images belong to the originally captured images, they have strong consistency between adjacent pixels. This property means that the intensities of adjacent pixels are very close, and the difference between adjacent pixels is approximately independent of the pixel itself [20, 21]. In contrast, the facial artefacts can be viewed as a type of recaptured images to a certain extent, which are inevitably affected by the print block effects or video noises in the recapture procedure. This progress directly imposes on the consistency of the adjacent pixels. Therefore, in order to characterize the facial discrepancies between the real faces and the facial artefacts, DLBP is proposed to capture the noise features.

Figure 1 illustrates the examples of the real faces and the facial artefacts in RGB color space (a), R channel in RGB color space (b), and the difference filtered image with the corresponding direction $\{\rightarrow, \uparrow, \nearrow, \searrow\}$ in the R channel (c–f), respectively. It can be found that the facial texture of the artefact is more complex than that of the real one. This is mainly because the strong consistency of adjacent pixels in the real facial image. After directional difference filtering, the correlated image contents are removed, and only the edges of the real face are retained. While for the facial artefact, the consistency of adjacent pixels is deteriorated by various noises. Therefore, the impacts of noise interference are amplified by the directional difference filtering, so the facial texture of artefact is more complex than that of the real one.

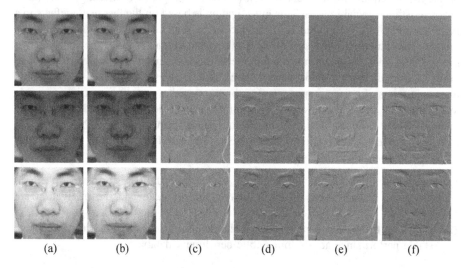

(a)   (b)   (c)   (d)   (e)   (f)

Fig. 1. Examples of images after directional difference filter. From top to bottom: real face, print attack, and video attack. From the left to the right: (a) RGB images. (b) R channel of RGB images. (c) R channel images after horizontal directional difference filter. (d) R channel images after vertical directional difference filter. (e) R channel images after main diagonal directional difference filter. (f) R channel images after anti-diagonal directional difference filter. (Color figure online)

2.2   Construction of DLBP

For an image I, directional difference filters [20, 21] are performed to get the corresponding directional difference matrix M. Four directional quantities are denoted by superscripts $\{\rightarrow, \uparrow, \nearrow, \searrow\}$, respectively. The feature of each direction is first calculated independently, and finally they are concatenated to form the DLBP feature. For example, the directional difference matrix after difference filtering in horizontal direction (left-to-right) is defined as:

$$M^{\rightarrow}(x,y) = I(x,y) - I(x,y+1), \tag{1}$$

where $I(x, y) \in \{0, 1, 2,..., 255\}$, and x, y represent the row and the column of I, respectively. For a given pixel (x, y) of M, its DLBP can be obtained by calculating the LBP [22] with the corresponding pixel in the directional difference matrix M, and it is defined as:

$$DLBP_{P,R}^{U2}(x,y) = \begin{cases} \sum_{i=0}^{P-1} s(M_i - M_c)2^i, & \text{if} \quad U \leq 2, \\ P(P-1) + 3, & \text{otherwise}, \end{cases} \tag{2}$$

$$s(x) = \begin{cases} 1, & x \geq 0 \\ 0, & x < 0 \end{cases}, \tag{3}$$

where P and R represent the pixel number in the neighborhood and the neighborhood radius, M_c and M_i represent the intensities of the central pixel and the neighborhood pixels, respectively. U is the transition time of '0' and '1' (such as '01' or '10') in DLBP coding mode. The construction of DLBP feature is illustrated in Fig. 2.

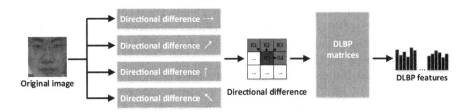

Fig. 2. Construction of directional local binary pattern feature.

3 The Proposed Face Presentation Attack Detection Scheme

On the basis of the different noise characteristics between the real face and the facial artefact, a face PAD scheme based on DLBP is proposed in this paper (see Fig. 3). For an input frame (image), the face area is detected and normalized to a facial image with a fixed size to decrease the computational complexity and to avoid the influence of different size of the input frame. After that, noise characteristics are extracted by calculating the proposed DLBP, which are used to characterize the degradation of the artefact. Finally, these features are fed to a Softmax classifier [23], and the output predicted label determines the liveness. Given the requirements of real-time detection in FR scenarios, only the first 25 frames of each video (about 1 s) in the test set are selected for testing, and the predicted label of the given video is determined by the average decision score of these 25 frames.

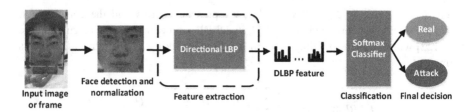

Fig. 3. Framework of the proposed face presentation attack detection scheme.

4   Experimental Results

4.1   Experimental Setup

Experiments are made with four public benchmark databases, and they are Replay-Attack database [24], CASIA face anti-spoofing database (CASIA FASD) [25], MSU mobile face spoofing database (MSU MFSD) [13], and Replay-Mobile database [26]. For fair comparison, all experiments are strictly performed with the original protocol. The details of the databases and the evaluation measures such as equal error rate (EER), half total error rate (HTER), attack presentation classification error rate (APCER), bona fide presentation classification error rate (BPCER), and average classification error rate (ACER) can be found in [13, 24–26].

In face detection and normalization, eyes locations provided by [13] are used for MSU MFSD, CASIA FASD, and Replay-Attack databases. As no public eye location data are provided in Replay-Mobile database, Face++ SDK [27] is used for eyes localization in this database. To maintain comparability with the previous works, the face image is resized to 64×64 before feature extraction. For DLBP, the pixel number in the neighborhood and the neighborhood radius are set as $P = 8$ and $R = 1$, and uniform pattern ($U <= 2$) is utilized. Inspired by [6], DLBP features are extracted from HSV and YCbCr color spaces to exploit color information of facial image.

4.2   Performance Comparison with LBP Variants

Experiments are conducted to compare the performances of the existing LBP variants with the proposed DLBP. For fair comparison, the LBP variants are extended to multi-channel version with HSV and YCbCr color spaces, and only features with single scale are used for comparison. The results are listed in Table 1, and DLBP can achieve stable detection performance across five protocols.

4.3   Performance Comparison

Experiments have been conducted to compare the performances of the existing face PAD methods with the proposed scheme, and the results of intra-database testing are listed in Tables 2 and 3, respectively. The proposed method outperforms the existing methods with MSU MFSD and Replay-Mobile databases, and also achieves competitive results with CASIA FASD and Replay-Attack databases. However, the EER

Table 1. Performance comparison of DLBP and existing LBP variants with Replay-Mobile database. The results are reported for each protocol: MP – *mattescreen-photo*, MV – *mattescreen-video*, PF – *print-fixed*, PH – *print-hand*, and GT – *Grandtest*.

Method	Test BPCER (%) at APCER = 0.01					
	MP	MV	PF	PH	GT	Mean
LBP [22]	12.73	12.73	16.36	2.73	22.73	13.46
CoALBP [28]	3.64	0.00	19.09	0.00	24.55	9.46
PRICoLBP [29]	1.82	0.00	1.82	0.00	27.27	6.18
OC-LBP [30]	26.36	14.55	22.73	0.91	36.36	20.18
DCP [31]	1.82	9.09	23.64	0.91	10.91	9.27
DLBP (proposed)	6.36	2.73	9.09	0.00	9.09	**5.45**

Table 2. Performance comparison of intra-database testing with Replay-Mobile database using frame based evaluation. The results are reported for each protocol: MP – *mattescreen-photo*, MV – *mattescreen-video*, PF – *print-fixed*, PH – *print-hand*, and GT – *Grandtest*.

Method	Test HTER (%)					Test ACER (%)
	MP	MV	PF	PH	GT	
IQM [26]	7.70	13.64	4.22	5.43	7.80	13.64
Gabor [26]	8.64	9.53	9.40	8.99	9.13	9.53
DLBP (proposed)	2.18	2.88	3.62	0.55	4.74	**5.04**

Table 3. Performance comparison of intra-database testing with MSU MFSD, CASIA FASD, and Replay-Attack databases, respectively.

Method	MSU MFSD	CASIA FASD	Replay-Attack
	Test EER (%)	Test EER (%)	Test HTER (%)
Frame based evaluation			
IDA [13]	8.58	N/A	7.41
GIF + IQA [7]	N/A	18.70	**1.31**
Pulse + LBP-ms-color [15]	7.50	N/A	N/A
LBP + GS-LBP [10]	7.87	**3.05**	3.31
DLBP (proposed)	**6.13**	10.23	6.08
Video based evaluation			
LBP-TOP [11]	N/A	10.00	7.60
Noise signatures [19]	N/A	N/A	14.27
Spectral cubes [14]	N/A	14.00	2.75
Color LBP [6]	N/A	6.20	2.90
LDP-TOP [12]	6.54	8.94	**1.75**
LBP + GS-LBP [10]	8.54	**2.53**	3.13
DLBP (proposed)	**3.33**	4.44	4.88

increases with CASIA FASD under frame based evaluation, and this is due to the presence of additional camera noises in low quality samples.

The performance comparison of the cross-database testing [32] is shown in Table 4. The results indicate that the proposed method can achieve stable performance even in cross-database testing.

Table 4. Performance comparison of cross-database testing with MSU MFSD, CASIA FASD, and Replay-Attack databases in terms of mean HTER (%).

Trained on	Replay-Attack		CASIA FASD		MSU MFSD	
Tested on	CASIA FASD	MSU MFSD	Replay-Attack	MSU MFSD	Replay-Attack	CASIA FASD
LBP-TOP [32]	60.67	N/A	49.81	N/A	N/A	N/A
Spectral cubes [14]	50.00	N/A	34.38	N/A	N/A	N/A
Color LBP [6]	**35.40**	32.90	37.90	21.00	**44.80**	45.70
LBP + GS-LBP [10]	40.26	36.07	48.36	**18.57**	45.31	40.59
DLBP (proposed)	46.62	**31.08**	**21.63**	26.26	48.84	**40.20**

To analyze the processing time, the evaluation is implemented in a PC with a configuration of 2.90 GHz CPU and 16 GB RAM without parallel processing, the average processing time for the test set of MSU MFSD is 1.277 s per video, which indicate the potential application in real time detection.

5   Conclusions

A content-independent face PAD method based on DLBP is proposed in this paper (The implementation is available on https://github.com/pp21/DLBP-for-Face-PAD). The detection exploits the advantage that DLBP can extract the noise characteristics of facial image, and the influences of image content are minimized. Experiments have been done with four public benchmark databases, and the results demonstrate the stable performance of the proposed PAD scheme both in intra-database and cross-database testing. The future work will focus on the improvements of sampling and quantization strategies of the proposed DLBP by using feature driven approaches.

Acknowledgments. This work was supported in part by project supported by National Natural Science Foundation of China (Grant Nos. 61572182, 61370225), and project supported by Hunan Provincial Natural Science Foundation of China (Grant No. 15JJ2007).

The authors would like to thank Idiap research institute, Institute of Automation, Chinese Academy of Sciences (CASIA), and Michigan State University for providing the benchmark databases. The authors would also like to thank Zi-Xing Lin and Xiang Zhang for their kind proofreading of this manuscript.

References

1. Ramachandra, R., Busch, C.: Presentation attack detection methods for face recognition systems: a comprehensive survey. ACM Comput. Surv. **50**(1), 8 (2017)
2. Li, Y., Li, Y., Xu, K., Yan, Q., Deng, R.: Empirical study of face authentication systems under OSNFD attacks. IEEE Trans. Dependable Secur. Comput. (2016, in Press). doi:10. 1109/TDSC.2016.2550459
3. Information Technology—Biometric Presentation Attack Detection—Part 1: Framework, ISO/IEC JTC1 SC37 Biometrics, ISO/IEC Standard WD 30107-1 (2015)
4. Lin, Q., Li, W., Ning, X., Dong, X., Chen, P.: Liveness detection using texture and 3D structure analysis. In: You, Z., Zhou, J., Wang, Y., Sun, Z., Shan, S., Zheng, W., Feng, J., Zhao, Q. (eds.) CCBR 2016. LNCS, vol. 9967, pp. 637–645. Springer, Cham (2016). doi:10. 1007/978-3-319-46654-5_70
5. Biggio, B., Fumera, G., Marcialis, G.L., Roli, F.: Statistical meta-analysis of presentation attacks for secure multibiometric systems. IEEE Trans. Pattern Anal. Mach. Intell. **39**(3), 561–575 (2017)
6. Boulkenafet, Z., Komulainen, J., Hadid, A.: Face anti-spoofing based on color texture analysis. In: IEEE ICIP, pp. 2636–2640 (2015)
7. Peng, F., Qin, L., Long, M.: POSTER: non-intrusive face spoofing detection based on guided filtering and image quality analysis. In: Deng, R., Weng, J., Ren, K., Yegneswaran, V. (eds.) SecureComm 2016. LNICSSITE, vol. 198, pp. 774–777. Springer, Cham (2017). doi:10. 1007/978-3-319-59608-2_49
8. Manjani, I., Tariyal, S., Vatsa, M., Singh, R., Majumdar, A.: Detecting silicone mask based presentation attack via deep dictionary learning. IEEE Trans. Inf. Forensics Secur. **12**(7), 1713–1723 (2017)
9. Boulkenafet, Z., Komulainen, J., Hadid, A.: Face anti-spoofing using speeded-up robust features and fisher vector encoding. IEEE Signal Process. Lett. **24**(2), 141–145 (2017)
10. Peng, F., Qin, L., Long, M.: Face presentation attack detection using guided scale texture. Multimedia Tools Appl. (2017, in Press). doi:10.1007/s11042-017-4780-0
11. de Freitas Pereira, T., Komulainen, J., Anjos, A., De Martino, J.M., Hadid, A., Pietikäinen, M., Marcel, S.: Face liveness detection using dynamic texture. EURASIP J. Image Video Process. **2014**(1), 1–15 (2014)
12. Phan, Q.T., Dang-Nguyen, D.T., Boato, G., De Natale, F.G.: Face spoofing detection using LDP-TOP. In: IEEE ICIP, pp. 404–408 (2016)
13. Wen, D., Han, H., Jain, A.K.: Face spoof detection with image distortion analysis. IEEE Trans. Inf. Forensics Secur. **10**(4), 746–761 (2015)
14. Pinto, A., Pedrini, H., Robson Schwartz, W., Rocha, A.: Face spoofing detection through visual codebooks of spectral temporal cubes. IEEE Trans. Image Process. **24**(12), 4726–4740 (2015)
15. Li, X., Komulainen, J., Zhao, G., Yuen, P.C., Pietikäinen, M.: Generalized face anti-spoofing by detecting pulse from face videos. In: IEEE ICPR, pp. 4244–4249 (2016)
16. Yang, D., Lai, J., Mei, L.: Deep representations based on sparse auto-encoder networks for face spoofing detection. In: CCBR, pp. 620–627 (2016)
17. Wu, L., Xu, Y., Xu, X., Qi, W., Jian, M.: A face liveness detection scheme to combining static and dynamic features. In: You, Z., Zhou, J., Wang, Y., Sun, Z., Shan, S., Zheng, W., Feng, J., Zhao, Q. (eds.) CCBR 2016. LNCS, vol. 9967, pp. 628–636. Springer, Cham (2016). doi:10.1007/978-3-319-46654-5_69

18. Patel, K., Han, H., Jain, A.K.: Cross-database face antispoofing with robust feature representation. In: You, Z., Zhou, J., Wang, Y., Sun, Z., Shan, S., Zheng, W., Feng, J., Zhao, Q. (eds.) CCBR 2016. LNCS, vol. 9967, pp. 611–619. Springer, Cham (2016). doi:10. 1007/978-3-319-46654-5_67

19. Pinto, A., Schwartz, W.R., Pedrini, H., de Rezende Rocha, A.: Using visual rhythms for detecting video-based facial spoof attacks. IEEE Trans. Inf. Forensics Secur. 10(5), 1025–1038 (2015)

20. Pevny, T., Bas, P., Fridrich, J.: Steganalysis by subtractive pixel adjacency matrix. IEEE Trans. Inf. Forensics Secur. 5(2), 215–224 (2010)

21. He, Z., Lu, W., Sun, W., Huang, J.: Digital image splicing detection based on Markov features in DCT and DWT domain. Pattern Recogn. 45(12), 4292–4299 (2012)

22. Ojala, T., Pietikäinen, M., Mäenpää, T.: Multiresolution gray-scale and rotation invariant texture classification with local binary patterns. IEEE Trans. Pattern Anal. Mach. Intell. 24(7), 971–987 (2002)

23. Anzai, Y.: Pattern Recognition and Machine Learning. Elsevier, Amsterdam (2012)

24. Chingovska, I., Anjos, A., Marcel, S.: On the effectiveness of local binary patterns in face anti-spoofing. In: IEEE BIOSIG, pp. 1–7 (2012)

25. Zhang, Z., Yan, J., Liu, S., Lei, Z., Yi, D., Li, S.Z.: A face antispoofing database with diverse attacks. In: IAPR ICB, pp. 26–31 (2012)

26. Costa-Pazo, A., Bhattacharjee, S., Vazquez-Fernandez, E., Marcel, S.: The REPLAY-MOBILE face presentation-attack database. In: IEEE BIOSIG, pp. 1–7 (2016)

27. Face++ SDK. https://www.faceplusplus.com.cn/face-detection/

28. Nosaka, R., Ohkawa, Y., Fukui, K.: Feature extraction based on co-occurrence of adjacent local binary patterns. In: Ho, Y.-S. (ed.) PSIVT 2011 Part II. LNCS, vol. 7088, pp. 82–91. Springer, Heidelberg (2011). doi:10.1007/978-3-642-25346-1_8

29. Qi, X., Xiao, R., Li, C.G., Qiao, Y., Guo, J., Tang, X.: Pairwise rotation invariant co-occurrence local binary pattern. IEEE Trans. Pattern Anal. Mach. Intell. 36(11), 2199–2213 (2014)

30. Zhu, C., Bichot, C.E., Chen, L.: Image region description using orthogonal combination of local binary patterns enhanced with color information. Pattern Recogn. 46(7), 1949–1963 (2013)

31. Ding, C., Choi, J., Tao, D., Davis, L.S.: Multi-directional multi-level dual-cross patterns for robust face recognition. IEEE Trans. Pattern Anal. Mach. Intell. 38(3), 518–531 (2016)

32. de Freitas Pereira, T., Anjos, A., De Martino, J.M., Marcel, S.: Can face anti-spoofing countermeasures work in a real world scenario? In: IEEE ICB, pp. 1–8 (2013)

Matching Depth to RGB for Boosting Face Verification

Han Liu, Feixiang He, Qijun Zhao[✉], and Xiangdong Fei

National Key Laboratory of Fundamental Science on Synthetic Vision,
College of Computer Science, Sichuan University, Chengdu, China
qjzhao@scu.edu.cn

Abstract. Low cost RGB-D sensors like Kinect and RealSense enable easy acquisition of both RGB (i.e., texture) and depth images of human faces. Many methods have been proposed to improve the RGB-to-RGB face matcher by fusing it with the Depth-to-Depth face matcher. Yet, few efforts have been devoted to the matching between RGB and Depth face images. In this paper, we propose two deep convolutional neural network (DCNN) based approaches to Depth-to-RGB face recognition, and compare their performance in terms of face verification accuracy. We further combine the Depth-to-RGB matcher with the RGB-to-RGB matcher via score-level fusion. Evaluation experiments on two databases demonstrate that matching depth to RGB does boost face verification accuracy.

Keywords: RGB-D · Deep learning · Score fusion · Face recognition

1 Introduction

In the past decade, face recognition achieved great progress thanks to the recent advances in deep neural networks. The latest works, such as [1–4], not only outperform traditional hand-crafted feature based face recognition, but are also at the brink of human level accuracy. Most of existing approaches rely on texture face images. As a result, they still suffer from serious performance degradation when pose, illumination and expression variations occur to the texture face images in uncontrolled scenarios.

Depth information is believed to be more robust to pose and illumination variations, and provide useful cues for facial expressions. Thanks to the availability of low cost RGB-D sensors (e.g., Kinect and RealSense), increasing research efforts have been denoted to exploring depth information for face recognition [6,7,12]. While most existing RGB-D based face recognition methods conduct RGB-to-RGB and Depth-to-Depth face matching separately, little attention has been paid to Depth-to-RGB face matching, which is demanded in some real-world applications. One example is when a user claims his/her identity in front of a RGB-D sensor using the identity (ID) card that contains his/her 2D face image. See Fig. 1. The deployment of RGB-D sensors at the verification phase

© Springer International Publishing AG 2017
J. Zhou et al. (Eds.): CCBR 2017, LNCS 10568, pp. 127–134, 2017.
https://doi.org/10.1007/978-3-319-69923-3_14

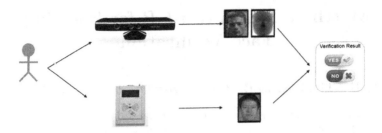

Fig. 1. An example RGB-D vs. RGB based face verification scenario: a user claims his/her identity in front of a RGB-D sensor using the identity (ID) card that contains his/her 2D face image.

can not only enhance the robustness of the face recognition system to spoofing attacks, but also boost the face recognition accuracy if the depth information is effectively utilized for face matching.

In this paper, we propose two different approaches to matching depth to RGB face images, i.e., image-mixing and image-fusion. Both approaches are implemented based on deep convolutional neural networks (DCNNs). The image-mixing approach mixes the RGB and Depth face images into a single training data set and trains a DCNN that takes either RGB or depth face images as input. The image-fusion approach first combines a pair of RGB and Depth face images into a single multi-channel image, and then trains a DCNN to classify such a multi-channel image into either genuine or imposter class with 'genuine' indicating that the source RGB and Depth face images are of the same subject and 'imposter' indicating different subjects. To show the effectiveness of Depth-to-RGB face matching in boosting face recognition accuracy, we further fuse the Depth-to-RGB and RGB-to-RGB face matchers at score level. Evaluation experiments have been conducted on two databases with a state-of-the-art RGB-to-RGB face matcher as baseline. The experimental results demonstrate the benefit of Depth-to-RGB face matching to face verification.

The rest of the paper is organized as follows. In Sect. 2, we discuss the existing RGB-D based face recognition methods and an asymmetric scenario considered in our work. The details of matching Depth-to-RGB face images as well as combining the RGB-to-RGB and Depth-to-RGB matchers are presented in Sect. 3. Evaluation experiments are then reported in Sect. 4. Finally, Sect. 5 concludes the paper.

2   Related Work

Existing RGB-D based face recognition methods mostly assume that RGB-D face data are captured at both enrollment and recognition stages. They usually utilize the depth information in two different ways. The first way is to match the probe Depth face image with the enrolled Depth face image, and combine the result with the matching result of probe and enrolled RGB face images [12].

A variety of feature representations have been applied to both RGB and Depth face images, including handcrafted features (e.g., LBP features [8], eigenface features [9]) and learning-based features (e.g., extracted features based on CNN [22]). Based on these features, various classifiers have been employed, such as Cosine distance metric [23], Joint Bayesian [2], SVM [12]. The second way is to render new face images at different pose angles from the RGB-D face data to enlarge the gallery database such that faces can be effectively recognized in a larger range of pose angles [11]. Unlike these existing RGB-D based face recognition methods, we in this paper consider an asymmetric scenario in which RGB-D face data need to be matched to RGB face images. Matching RGB-D face data to RGB face images, particularly matching Depth to RGB (i.e., Texture) face images, is essentially a heterogeneous face recognition problem. However, to the best knowledge of the authors, no research work on the problem of matching Depth to Texture has been published in the face recognition literature.

A number of RGB-D face databases (e.g., Lock3DFace [19]) are available in the public domain. However, all these RGB-D face databases are constructed for research on RGB-D to RGB-D face recognition. In this paper, we will choose from these public databases the RGB components captured in one session as gallery, and the RGB-D data captured in other sessions as probe to evaluate the RGB-D to RGB face recognition performance.

3   Proposed Methods

In this section, we first introduce in detail the proposed image-mixing and image-fusion approaches to matching Depth-to-RGB face images, and then present a score-fusion based RGB-D vs. RGB face verification method.

3.1   Image-Mixing Approach

Our proposed methods are based on a state-of-the-art deep neural network for face recognition, specifically, LightCNN [14]. LightCNN was initially designed for extracting facial features from RGB face images. It can achieve comparable face recognition accuracy with other complex networks by using a significantly smaller set of parameters. Therefore, we employ it as the baseline in our experiments. In order to enable LightCNN to extract discriminative features from both RGB and Depth face images, the image-mixing approach simply mixes the RGB and Depth face images to form a single training set. This training set is then used to finetune the original LightCNN. See Fig. 2(a).

Once the LightCNN is finetuned by the mixed training set of RGB and Depth face images, it can be used to extract features from RGB or Depth face images by exporting the output of the FC_1 layer. Based on the extracted features, the Cosine distance metric [21] is used to measure the similarity between a pair of RGB and Depth face images.

3.2   Image-Fusion Approach

In the above image-mixing approach, we neither revise the structure of LightCNN, nor change its loss function. In this section, we propose another approach, namely image-fusion approach. This approach differs from the image-mixing approach mainly in two aspects. First, pairs of RGB and Depth face images are fused across channels, resulting in multi-channel face images, which are used as the input to the network in the image-fusion approach. See Fig. 2(b). Before the fusion, the pixel values in depth images are normalized via min-max normalization to the same range as the pixel values in RGB images. Second, the LightCNN is adapted for verification, rather than identification, in the image-fusion approach. To this end, the adapted LightCNN performs a two-class classification on the input multi-channel face image, i.e., whether the source pair of RGB and Depth face images are from the same subject (genuine class) or two different subjects (imposter class). It outputs a probability for each of the two classes, and assigns the input data into the class corresponding to the larger probability. Obviously, the image-mixing approach aims to seek for unified feature representations that are suitable for both RGB and Depth face images. In contrast, the image-fusion approach fulfills an end-to-end face verification through explicitly exploring the correlation between the RGB and Depth face images.

3.3   RGB-D vs. RGB Based Face Verification

In the scenario of RGB-D vs. RGB based face verification, we propose to conduct RGB-to-RGB face matching by using a conventional 2D face matcher, and mean-

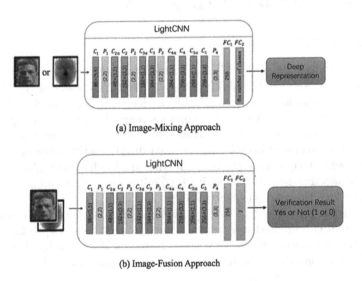

(a) Image-Mixing Approach

(b) Image-Fusion Approach

Fig. 2. Matching Depth to RGB face images, (a) is Image-Mixing Approach, (b) is Image-Fusion Approach. Note that RGB images are converted to gray images.

while perform Depth-to-RGB face matching by using the methods presented in the past two sections. The matching results of the RGB-to-RGB and Depth-to-RGB face matchers are combined at the score level with a weighted sum fusion rule:

$$s = \lambda_1 s_r + \lambda_2 s_d \tag{1}$$

where s_r is the score of RGB-to-RGB face matching, s_d is the score of Depth-to-RGB face matching, λ_1 is the weight given to RGB-to-RGB matching, λ_2 is the weight of Depth-to-RGB matching, and s is the combined score employing the two models for the final verification.

Note that the similarity score output by the image-mixing approach is defined by the classifier (i.e., Cosine distance based nearest neighbor classifier in this paper) over the extracted features, and the similarity score output by the image-fusion approach is defined as the probability of the genuine class.

4   Experiments

4.1   Databases

Lock3DFace [19], a public RGB-D face database, is used in our experiments. In order to simulate the proposed scenario, we choose the neutral frontal RGB images as gallery set, and the remained RGB-D images as probe set which contain pose, illumination and expression variations.

The gallery RGB face images and the probe RGB-D face data in the above database is acquired by using the same devices in the lab. Therefore, we construct a private database by ourselves in real-world applications. We use the RealSense scanner mounted on a gate at the entrance of a railway station. When a subject passes through the gate, he/she is asked to stand in front of the gate and have his/her RGB-D face data collected. We finally acquire 100 RGB-D face images for each of 2,293 subjects. We call this database as Realistic RGB-D face database (in short, Realistic-RGB-D).

Following LightCNN training protocol, all face images are converted to grayscale and resized to 144×144 based on the face rectangle detected by MTCNN. Afterwards, RGB face images are divided by 255 while Depth maps are divided by its maximum distance, both of which are normalized to $[0, 1]$. Due to deep learning is robust to translation and scale but not to rotation, we rotate two eye points to be horizontal according to the 5 facial points detected by [20], which can overcome the pose variations in roll angle. The training data sets are further enlarged by applying various tricks, including random cropping, mirroring and scale jittering.

4.2   Evaluation Protocol

To train the proposed Depth-to-RGB face matchers, we choose a subset from both Lock3DFace and Realistic-RGB-D as training data. Specifically, the training set contains 450 subjects and the left 50 subjects are used for testing on

Lock3DFace while 2,164 subjects are used for training and 129 subjects for testing on Realistic-RGB-D.

In order to avoid imbalanced data and overfitting, the training of the image-fusion based Depth-to-RGB face matcher requires that one half of the image pairs are genuine and the other half of the image pairs are impostor, produced by randomly pairing images of different subjects. For testing, we randomly form 1,500 genuine pairs and 1,500 imposter pairs for Lock3DFace which mainly contains expression and pose variations, and 1,040 genuine pairs and 1,040 imposter pairs for Realistic-RGB-D, which mainly contains pose and illumination variations.

4.3   Results

Table 1 shows the accuracy of the proposed two approaches in terms of the percentage of correctly recognized testing image pairs. Note that for the image-mixing approach, a similarity threshold is required to determine whether an image pair is genuine or imposter. Here, we choose the threshold that maximizes the accuracy. As can be seen, the image-fusion approach performs better than the image-mixing approach on both of the two databases. This proves the importance of exploring the correlation between the depth and texture (i.e., RGB) information of faces, which is useful for boosting face recognition accuracy.

Table 1. Face verification accuracy of the proposed Depth-to-RGB matchers on Realistic-RGB-D and Lock3DFace databases.

Test set	Method	Accuracy
Realistic-RGB-D	Image-Mixing	79.3%
	Image-Fusion	86.7%
Lock3DFace	Image-Mixing	79%
	Image-Fusion	87.4%

To evaluate the contribution of depth information to existing RGB-based face matchers, we combine our proposed Depth-to-RGB face matchers with the baseline RGB-to-RGB LightCNN matcher via score level weight sum fusion (refer to Sect. 3.3). Table 2 lists the obtained recognition accuracy (i.e., True Positive Rate or TPR when False Positive Rate or FPR is 1% or 0.1%) on the Realistic-RGB-D and Lock3DFace databases. From these results, we can clearly see that the proposed image-fusion approach, compared with the image-mixing approach, makes a larger improvement thanks to its more effective utilization of the depth information.

Table 2. Face verification accuracy of the baseline LightCNN matcher and its fusion with the proposed Depth-to-RGB matcher on Realistic-RGB-D and Lock3DFace databases.

Test set	Method	TPR@FPR = 1%	TPR@FPR = 0.1%
Realistic-RGB-D	LightCNN	97.8%	94.5%
	Image-Mixing + LightCNN	98%	95.7%
	Image-Fusion + LightCNN	98.4%	96.2%
Lock3DFace	LightCNN	95.5%	91%
	Image-Mixing + LightCNN	95.6%	91.2%
	Image-Fusion + LightCNN	96%	92.3%

5   Conclusions

In this paper, we have proposed two methods, referred to as image-mixing and image-fusion approaches, to solve the problem of matching Depth to RGB face images. Image-fusion approach proves to be more effective than image-mixing approach. This indicates the advantage of exploring the correlation between Depth and RGB face images in boosting face recognition accuracy. Furthermore, depth maps, as a complementary type of information, improve the verification accuracy of state-of-the-art face recognition methods, as shown in the experiments on two databases. The two approaches proposed in this paper essentially perform on the image data level. In the future, we are going to collect ID photos as our gallery to complete our experiments. Furthermore, we will tackle the Depth-to-RGB face matching problem from a feature transform perspective.

Acknowledgments. This work is supported by National Key Research and Development Program of China (2017YFB0802303, 2016YFC0801100) and the National Key Scientific Instrument and Equipment Development Projects of China (2013YQ49087904).

References

1. Sun, Y., Wang, X., Tang, X.: Deep learning face representation from predicting 10,000 classes. In: IEEE Conference on Computer Vision and Pattern Recognition, pp. 1891–1898 (2014)
2. Sun, Y., Wang, X., Tang, X.: Deeply learned face representations are sparse, selective, and robust. In: IEEE Conference on Computer Vision and Pattern Recognition, pp. 2892–2900 (2015)
3. Taigman, Y., Yang, M., Ranzato, M.A., Wolf, L.: Deepface: closing the gap to human-level performance in face verification. In: IEEE Conference on Computer Vision and Pattern Recognition, pp. 1701–1708 (2014)
4. Wen, Y., Zhang, K., Li, Z., Qiao, Y.: A discriminative feature learning approach for deep face recognition. In: European Conference on Computer Vision, pp. 499–515 (2016)

5. Lin, C.P., Wang, C.Y., Chen, H.R., Chu, W.C., Chen, M.Y.: RealSense: directional interaction for proximate mobile sharing using built-in orientation sensors. In: 21st ACM International Conference on Multimedia, pp. 777–780 (2013)

6. Li, W., Li, X., Goldberg, M., Zhu, Z.: Face recognition by 3D registration for the visually impaired using a RGB-D sensor. In: European Conference on Computer Vision, pp. 763–777 (2014)

7. Hayat, M., Bennamoun, M., El-Sallam, A.A.: An RGB based image set classification for robust face recognition from Kinect data. Neurocomputing **171**, 889–900 (2016)

8. Ahonen, T., Hadid, A., Pietikainen, M.: Face description with local binary patterns: application to face recognition. IEEE Trans. Pattern Anal. Mach. Intell. **28**(12), 2037–2041 (2006)

9. Turk, M., Pentland, A.: Eigenfaces for recognition. J. Cogn. Neurosci. **3**(1), 71–86 (1991)

10. Goswami, G., Vatsa, M., Singh, R.: RGB-D face recognition with texture and attribute features. IEEE Trans. Inf. Forensics Secur. **9**(10), 1629–1640 (2014)

11. Ciaccio, C., Wen, L., Guo, G.: Face recognition robust to head pose changes based on the RGB-D sensor. In: 6th International Conference on Biometrics: Theory, Applications and Systems (BTAS), pp. 1–6 (2013)

12. Lee, Y., Chen, J., Tseng, C.W., Lai, S.H.: Accurate and robust face recognition from RGB-D images with a deep learning approach. In: British Machine Vision Conference (2016)

13. Sarfraz, M.S., Stiefelhagen, R.: Deep perceptual mapping for thermal to visible face recognition (2015). arXiv preprint arXiv:1507.02879

14. Wu, X., He, R., Sun, Z., Tan, T.: A light CNN for deep face representation with noisy labels (2016). arXiv preprint arXiv:1511.02683v2

15. Goodfellow, I.J., Warde-Farley, D., Mirza, M., Courville, A., Bengio, Y.: Maxout networks (2013). arXiv preprint arXiv:1302.4389

16. Lin, M., Chen, Q., Yan, S.: Network in network (2013). arXiv preprint arXiv:1312.4400

17. Chopra, S., Hadsell, R., LeCun, Y.: Learning a similarity metric discriminatively, with application to face verification. In: IEEE Conference on Computer Vision and Pattern Recognition, pp. 539–546 (2005)

18. Bloch, I.: Information combination operators for data fusion: a comparative review with classification. IEEE Trans. Syst. Man Cybern.-Part A: Syst. Hum. **26**(1), 52–67 (1996)

19. Zhang, J., Huang, D., Wang, Y., Sun, J.: Lock3DFace: a large-scale database of low-cost Kinect 3D faces. In: International Conference on Biometrics (ICB), pp. 1–8 (2016)

20. Zhang, K., Zhang, Z., Li, Z., Qiao, Y.: Joint face detection and alignment using multitask cascaded convolutional networks. IEEE Sig. Process. Lett. **23**(10), 1499–1503 (2016)

21. Nguyen, H., Bai, L.: Cosine similarity metric learning for face verification. In: Asian Conference on Computer Vision, pp. 709–720 (2010)

22. Goodfellow, I., Bengio, Y., Courville, A.: Deep Learning. MIT Press, Cambridge (2016)

23. Sun, Y., Chen, Y., Wang, X., Tang, X.: Deep learning face representation by joint identification-verification. In: Advances in Neural Information Processing Systems, pp. 1988–1996 (2014)

Deeply Learned Pore-Scale Facial Features

Xiaodong Wang[1], Yuwei Liang[1], Xianxian Zeng[1], Dong Li[1(✉)], and Wei Jia[2]

[1] School of Automation, Guangdong University of Technology, Guangzhou, China
dong.li@gdut.edu.cn
[2] School of Computer and Information, Hefei University of Technology, Hefei, China

Abstract. Pore-scale facial features consist of pores, fine wrinkles, and hair, which commonly appear in the whole face region. Similar to iris features and fingerprint features, pore-scale facial features are one of the biometric features that can distinguish human identities. Most of the local features of biometric depend on hand-crafted design. However, such hand-crafted features rely heavily on human experience and are usually composed of complicated operations, costing a great deal of time. This paper introduces a novel pore-scale facial features - Deeply Learned Pore-scale Facial Features (DLPFF). We use Convolutional Neural Networks (CNNs) to learn discriminant representations of pore-scale facial features. Experiments show that our deep network based method outperforms the state-of-the-art methods on the Bosphorus database.

Keywords: Pore-scale facial feature · Face recognition · Feature descriptors · Deep learning

1 Introduction

Local feature plays an important role in many computer-vision applications. For example, 3D face reconstruction, face matching and so on, are depended on local features to establish correct correspondences between two faces with different viewpoints.

Over past few decades, the best performance relied on carefully hand-crafted features [1–5]. Particularly, a feature transform method specifically designed for extracting pore-scale facial features has been proposed, named as Pore Scale Invariant Transform (PSIFT) and has shown outstanding performance in terms of face matching. This method is adapted from SIFT, to extract the characteristics of pore-scale facial features. The relative-position information about the neighboring keypoints is constructed from an expanded region containing 8×8 sub-regions, each of which represents a histogram of 8 orientation bins. Thus a 512-element PSIFT descriptor contains rich information about the local area centered on the corresponding keypoint. However, applications based on PSIFT suffer from the sophisticated operations of its hand-crafted extraction process.

D. Li—This work was partially supported by National Natural Science Foundation of China: 61503084 and Natural Science Foundation of Guangdong Province, China: 2016A03031034.

© Springer International Publishing AG 2017
J. Zhou et al. (Eds.): CCBR 2017, LNCS 10568, pp. 135–144, 2017.
https://doi.org/10.1007/978-3-319-69923-3_15

In recent years, methods based on deep learning [6–9] have started to out-perform shallow methods in many areas of computer-vision. Learned Invariant Feature Transform (LIFT) [10] is proposed to use a deep network architecture which implements the full feature point handling pipeline, that is, detection, orientation estimation, and feature description. Nevertheless, LIFT is trained by general dataset (Piccadilly, Roman-Forum) [15], it can not detect and extract the pore-scale facial feature to achieve satisfactory performance. Inspiring from the architecture of LIFT, we establish a framework to represent the pore-scale feature using deep learning. Our framework can extract pore-scale facial features and achieve robust representations. Extensive experiments on the Bosphorus database [13] show that our method can get a better performance than the state-of-the-art methods.

Our framework is depicted by Fig. 1. It consists of the detector (DET) and the descriptor (DESC). The framework is similar to LIFT, but without orientation estimator, because most of the keypoints of the pore scale facial features do not have a coherent orientation. The detector is based on PSIFT [12], while the descriptor is based on Convolutional Neural Networks (CNNs) and imitate recent ones [9]. We utilize PSIFT to detect the locations of keypoints which determine the patches input descriptor.

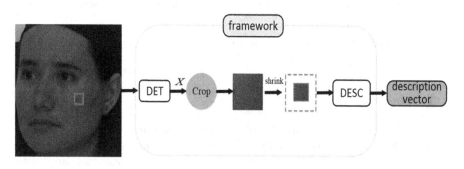

Fig. 1. Our pore-scale facial features extraction framework. Our framework consists of two major components: the detector (DET) and the descriptor (DESC).

There is a pore datasets [16] that can be used to train the descriptors. The pore dataset has 80,236 unique points, each with 4 corresponding pore patches Fig. 2(e) shows some examples.

We build a Siamese network to train our descriptor using the patches extracted by Pore-SIFT (PSIFT) [12]. To learn the descriptor in an effective manner we deal with the vast potential pairs with stochastic sampling of the training set and an aggressive mining strategy for patches that are hard to classify. Therefore, we detect the keypoints with PSIFT and made use of the powerful deep learning technique for extracting pore-scale facial features, called Deeply Learned Pore-scale Facial Features (DLPFF). In the next section, we present our method in detail and show that it outperforms the traditional methods.

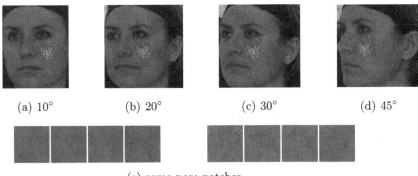

(a) 10°   (b) 20°   (c) 30°   (d) 45°

(e) some pore patches

Fig. 2. (a–d) are different poses images of the same subject. The red points are the keypoints of the skin region, and the green points are the matched keypoints of all the 4 different poses. (e) show some pore patches (Color figure online)

2   Method

In this section, we first introduce the creation of our large-scale pore-to-pore matching dataset, and then we describe the descriptor and the training procedure in detail. Finally, the detector based on PSIFT is specified.

2.1   Constructing the Training Dataset

A pore-to-pore correspondences dataset [16] is used to train the pore scale feature descriptor.

To achieve invariance we need images that capture views of the same subject from different perspectives. We thus turned to Bosphorus database [13]. We find the matched pore scale keypoints of the same subject from different perspectives, which relies of PSIFT features. We use 105 face-region pairs cropped from 420 face images, which were captured at 10°, 20°, 30° and 45° to the right of the frontal view. Then a 3D face model is used to fitting the face of the images, and to constrain the keypoints matching. Finally, we establish a pore-to-pore correspondences dataset with 80236×4 patches. Some examples are shown in Fig. 2.

We extract grayscale training patches according to the scale σ of the point, for both feature and non-feature point image regions. Patches **p** are extract from a $24\sigma \times 24\sigma$ support region at these locations, and standardized into $S \times S$ pixels where $S = 64$. Finally, we normalize the patches with the grayscale mean and standard deviation of the entire training set.

2.2   Descriptor

The descriptor is constructed with three convolutional neural layers, each of which is followed by a hyperbolic tangent unit, l_2 pooling and local subtractive normalization. The Descriptor can be formulated as:

$$\mathbf{d} = \mathbf{h}_\rho(\mathbf{p}) \tag{1}$$

where $\mathbf{h}(.)$ denotes the Descriptor CNN, ρ are its parameters, and $\mathbf{p}$ is the 64×64 image patch.

We propose to learn the descriptors with a Siamese network [14], where a nonlinear mapping is represented by a CNN. The Siamese network will be optimized for pairs of corresponding or non-corresponding patches. The input to each branch is an image patch $\mathbf{p}$ with the size of 64×64. Through the Descriptor CNN $\mathbf{h}_\rho$, a 128-element vector $\mathbf{d}$ is returned as the feature descriptor. The structure of the Descriptor is depicted in Fig. 3.

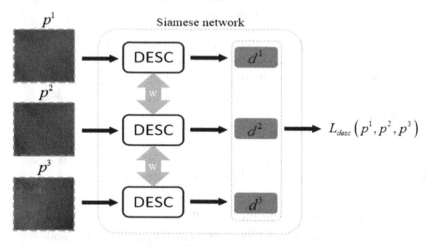

Fig. 3. Detailed structure of the Descriptor CNN.

The Descriptor can be divided into three parts, each with the same components and unique settings: a single convolutional layer, a hyperbolic tangent unit, an l_2 pooling operation and a local subtractive normalization operation (Table 1).

In order to improve the repeatability and distinctiveness of pore-scale facial features, we build a three-branch Siamese architecture to train the Descriptor, taking triplets of image patches $(\mathbf{p}^1, \mathbf{p}^2, \mathbf{p}^3)$ as input, in which $\mathbf{p}^1$ and $\mathbf{p}^2$ correspond to the same feature point while $\mathbf{p}^1$ and $\mathbf{p}^3$ correspond to different ones.

The parameters of the Descriptor network are updated via back-propagation by minimizing the loss function for the Descriptor, which can be formalized as:

$$L_{desc}(p^k, p^l) = \begin{cases} \|h(p^k) - h(p^l)\|_2 & k \text{ and } l \text{ are positive pairs} \\ max(0, 4 - \|h(p^k) - h(p^l)\|_2) & k \text{ and } l \text{ are negative pairs} \end{cases} \tag{2}$$

For positive pairs, $h(p^k)$ and $h(p^l)$ should be as close as possible, so that $L_{desc}(p^k, p^l) = \|h(p^k) - h(p^l)\|_2$ should be minimized, while for negative pairs, the difference between $h(p^k)$ and $h(p^l)$ should be as large as possible, leading to smaller value of L_{desc}.

Table 1. Layer settings of the three-layer network.

Layer	1	2	3
Input size	64×64	29×29	8×8
Convolution			
Kernel size	$32 \times 7 \times 7$	$64 \times 6 \times 6$	$128 \times 5 \times 5$
Conv. stride	1	1	1
Nonlinearity	Tanh	Tanh	Tanh
Pooling			
Pooling size	2×2	3×3	4×4
Pooling stride	2	3	4
Local subtractive normalization			
Subtractive Norm	5×5	5×5	5×5
Norm. stride	1	1	1

2.3   Learning Descriptor

Let us consider a pore dataset with m unique 3D patch indices, each with $c_i = 4$ corresponding pore patches. Then, the number of matching pore patches, P (positives) and the number of non-matching pore patches, N (negatives) is:

$$P = \sum_{i=1}^{m} \frac{c_i(c_i - 1)}{2} \quad and \quad N = \sum_{i=1}^{m} c_i(mc_i - c_i) \tag{3}$$

Our goal is to optimize the network parameters from our pore datasets that contain 320,944 patches and 80,236 unique 3D patch indices. Since both P and N are very large, we resort to SGD, using random batch of our training set to train our descriptor network. For positives we randomly sample a batch of 3D point indices from the set $\{p_1, \ldots, p_m\}$. For each chosen 3D index p_i we randomly pick two 2D patches with corresponding 3D point indices and randomly choose one 2D patches with another 3D point indices. These three kind of patches form triplet to input the Descriptor network.

During training, we initialize the parameters of Descriptor CNN from the DeepDesc [9]. As hard mining during training was shown in DeepDesc to be critical for descriptor performance, we also use hard mining to train our model. Use this method, we forward K_f sample pairs but only back-propagate the K_b pairs with the highest training loss, where $r = K_f/K_b = 8$ is the mining ratio. Here, the batch size is set to 1024, momentum to 0.9, The initial learning rate is set to 0.001 and decreases by a factor of 10 every 8,00 batches (56,00 batches in total). We back-propagate the network with 128 positive pairs and 128 negative pairs, mining each separately.

2.4   Detector

Pore-scale facial features, such as pores and fine wrinkles, are darker than their surroundings in a skin region. Therefore, PSIFT apply the DoG detector for keypoint detection on multi-scales, which is shown as follow.

$$D(x, y, \sigma) = L(x, y, k\sigma) - L(x, y, \sigma) = (G(x, y, k\sigma) - G(x, y, \sigma)) * I(x, y), \quad (4)$$

where the scale space of an image $L(x, y, \sigma)$ is the convolution of the image I(x,y) and the Gaussian kernel

$$G(x, y, \sigma) = \frac{1}{2\pi\sigma^2} exp(\frac{-(x^2 + y^2)}{2\sigma^2}), \quad (5)$$

PSIFT construct the DoG in octaves, which have the σ doubled in the scale space. Li [12] find that the PSIFT detector only need the maxima of the DoG to locate the darker keypoints in face regions, and the example is shown in Fig. 4(c). Besides, a blob-shaped pore-scale keypoint is a small, darker point due to its small concavity, where incident light is likely blocked, so PSIFT model the blob-shaped skin pores using a Gaussian function, as follow:

$$pore(x, y, \sigma) = 1 - 2\pi\sigma^2 G(x, y, \sigma). \quad (6)$$

where σ is the scale of the pore model. Then, the DoG response of a pore, denoted as D_{pore}, can be computed as follows:

$$D_{pore}(x, y, \sigma_1, \sigma_2) = [G(x, y, k\sigma_1) - G(x, y, \sigma_1)] * pore(x, y, \sigma_2), \quad (7)$$

and the pore-scale keypoints is the maxima of the D_{pore}.

Fig. 4. (a) Four face images with different skin conditions from the Bosphorus face database, (b) local skin-texture images, (c) the DoG of the local skin-texture image.

2.5   Runtime Pipeline

The runtime pipeline is shown in Fig. 5. During runtime, the Detector and the Descriptor are decoupled and used separately.

First, we run the Detector over the full image to obtain keypoint location proposals. Next, we extract 128×128 image patches on the full image, each with a keypoint at the center. These image patches will be scaled down to half of its size, to be 64×64, which serve as the input to the Descriptor.

The Descriptor takes these patches as input, and returns 128-dimension feature vectors for the corresponding feature point. During the test, if we want to get a 512-dimension feature vectors, just simply change the last Pooling layer size to 2×2, and we can get a more distinct descriptor.

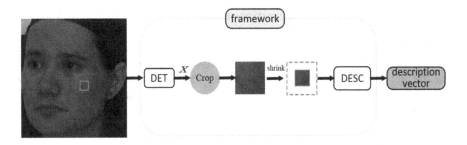

Fig. 5. The full pipeline at run-time.

3 Experimental Validation

In this section, experiments were conducted using the Bosphorus database [13]. The face images in this database were captured unsynchronized and from different views. The subjects were filmed at different angles by rotating the chair

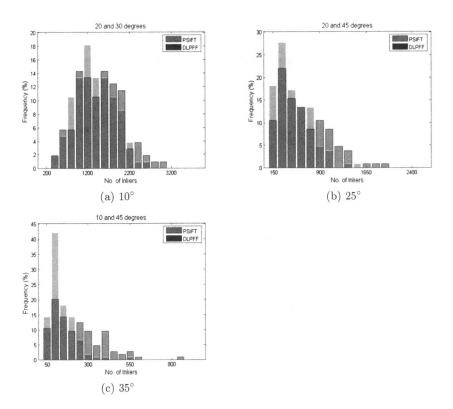

Fig. 6. Distributions of the number of inliers for all 105 subjects in the Bosphorus database using PSIFT and LDAPSIFT: (a) 10° (images at 20° and 30°); (b) 25° (images at 20° and 45°); (c) 35° (images at 10° and 45°).

they were sitting in to align with stripes placed on the floor indicating the corresponding angles. All 105 subjects in the Bosphorus database were used to evaluate the performance of our method under different skin conditions. In our experiment, the distance threshold used in RANSAC [17] is set at 0.0001, considering the fact that the images are unsynchronized and that the facial appearances are non-rigid. Particularly, rather than the matching experiment in PSIFT uses twice RANSAC, DLPFF only use one RANSAC. Figure 6 shows the frequency of subjects with respect to the different numbers of inliers detected for three sets of image pairs with different combinations of poses (20° and 30°, 20° and 45°, and 10° and 45° poses) based on PSIFT and DLPFF.

We also compare the median in three sets of image pairs between PSIFT and DLPFF. DLPFF and PSIFT matching results for those pairs of faces with the median number of inliers of all 105 subjects for three pose variations: 10° pose difference, DLPFF 1494 inliers detected while PSIFT 1317 inliers detected; 25° pose difference, DLPFF 546 inliers detected while PSIFT 430 inliers detected; 35° pose difference, DLPFF 213 inliers detected while PSIFT 116 inliers detected. Figure 7 shows three samples of the matching results based on DLPFF, with the median number of inliers detected with respect to the three pose combinations, and with an image resolution of 700×600.

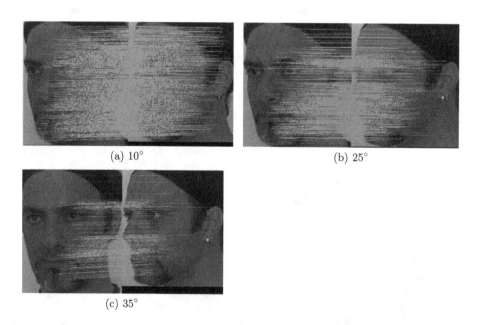

(a) 10°   (b) 25°

(c) 35°

Fig. 7. DLPFF matching results for those pairs of faces with the median number of inliers of all 105 subjects for three pose variations: (a) 10° pose difference, 1494 inliers detected; (b) 25° pose difference, 546 inliers detected; (c) 35° pose difference, 213 inliers detected.

4 Conclusion

We propose a framework that can extract pore-scale facial features and achieve robust representations together. Our framework detects the keypoints with PSIFT and use Convolutional Neural Networks (CNNs) to learn discriminant representations of pore-scale facial features. Our experimental results demonstrate that our integrated approach outperforms the state-of-the-art method. To further improve performance, we will look into strategies that how to train the network as a whole and then propose a better detector and descriptor.

References

1. Lowe, D.G.: Distinctive image features from scale-invariant keypoints. Int. J. Comput. Vis. **60**, 91C–110 (2004)
2. Bay, H., Tuytelaars, T., Van Gool, L.: SURF: speeded up robust features. In: Leonardis, A., Bischof, H., Pinz, A. (eds.) ECCV 2006. LNCS, vol. 3951, pp. 404–417. Springer, Heidelberg (2006). doi:10.1007/11744023_32
3. Tola, E., Lepetit, V., Fua, P.: A fast local descriptor for dense matching. In: CVPR, pp. 1–8 (2008)
4. Rublee, E., Rabaud, V., Konolidge, K., Bradski, G.: ORB: an efficient alternative to SIFT or SURF. In: ICCV, pp. 2564–2571 (2011)
5. Mainali, P., Lafruit, G., Tack, K., Van Gool, L., Lauwereins, R.: Derivative-based scale invariant image feature detector with error resilience. TIP **23**(5), 2380–2391 (2014)
6. Han, X., Leung, T., Jia, Y., Sukthankar, R., Berg, A.C.: MatchNet: unifying feature and metric learning for patch-based matching. In: CVPR, pp. 3279–3286 (2015)
7. Zagoruyko, S., Komodakis, N.: Learning to compare image patches via convolutional neural networks. In: CVPR, pp. 4353–4361 (2015)
8. Yi, K., Verdie, Y., Lepetit, V., Fua, P.: Learning to assign orientations to feature points. In: CVPR, pp. 107–116 (2016)
9. Simo-Serra, E., Trulls, E., Ferraz, L., Kokkinos, I., Fua, P., Moreno-Noguer, F.: Discriminative learning of deep convolutional feature point descriptors. In: ICCV, pp. 118–126 (2015)
10. Yi, K.M., Trulls, E., Lepetit, V., Fua, P.: LIFT: learned invariant feature transform. In: Leibe, B., Matas, J., Sebe, N., Welling, M. (eds.) ECCV 2016. LNCS, vol. 9910, pp. 467–483. Springer, Cham (2016). doi:10.1007/978-3-319-46466-4_28
11. Chapelle, O., Wu, M.: Gradient descent optimization of smoothed information retrieval metrics. Inf. Retr. **13**(3), 216–235 (2009)
12. Li, D., Lam, K.M.: Design and learn distinctive features from pore-scale facial keypoints. Pattern Recogn. **48**(3), 732–745 (2015)
13. Savran, A., Alyüz, N., Dibeklioğlu, H., Çeliktutan, O., Gökberk, B., Sankur, B., Akarun, L.: Bosphorus database for 3D face analysis. In: Schouten, B., Juul, N.C., Drygajlo, A., Tistarelli, M. (eds.) BioID 2008. LNCS, vol. 5372, pp. 47–56. Springer, Heidelberg (2008). doi:10.1007/978-3-540-89991-4_6
14. Bromley, J., Guyon, I., Lecun, Y., Sckinger, E., Shah, R.: Signature verification using a Siamese time delay neural network. In: NIPS (1994)
15. Wilson, K., Snavely, N.: Robust global translations with 1DSfM. In: Fleet, D., Pajdla, T., Schiele, B., Tuytelaars, T. (eds.) ECCV 2014. LNCS, vol. 8691, pp. 61–75. Springer, Cham (2014). doi:10.1007/978-3-319-10578-9_5

16. Zeng, X., Li, D., Zhang, Y., Lam, K.M.: Pore-scale facial features matching under 3D morphable model constraint. In: CCCV (2017)
17. Fischler, M.A., Bolles, R.C.: Random sample consensus: a paradigm for model fitting with applications to image analysis and automated cartography. Commun. ACM **24**(6), 381–395 (1981)

Synthesis and Recognition of Internet Celebrity Face Based on Deep Learning

Jiancan Zhou, Guohang Zeng, Jia He, Xi Jia, and Linlin Shen[✉]

College of Computer Science and Software Engineering,
Shenzhen University, Shenzhen, China
llshen@szu.edu.cn

Abstract. The similarity among Internet Celebrity Faces brings a big challenge to the recognition and verification of faces. To study this problem, more than 20,000 Internet Celebrity Face pictures are collected from the Internet. We utilize these faces to train the Variational Auto-Encoder (VAE) to synthesize the fake Internet Celebrity Faces and compare the faces with real samples. Results show that the performance of the deep network in Internet Celebrity Face greatly decreases. 20 pairs of the same or different Internet Celebrity Faces are selected to test the human's ability to recognize Internet Celebrity Faces by question-naire. The comparison with the VGG deep network shows that the deep learning algorithm performs much better than human in terms of recognition accuracy.

Keywords: Internet Celebrity · Face recognition · VAE · Statistical analysis

1 Introduction

The traditional face recognition method usually use local features like Local Binary encoding [1], Gabor features [2], and global features like PCA [3] and LDA [4]. Since the winning of AlexNet [5] in ILSVRC-2012 competition, deep learning algorithms have been widely used in face recognition. DeepFace [6] trained with four million face images, from Facebook, utilized a local-connected Convolution Neural Network (CNN) structure and achieved 97.35% accuracy in the LFW [7] dataset. DeepID1 [8] reached 97.45% accuracy by extracting multiple face image patches and connecting the feature map of the convolution layer and the pool layer. FaceNet [9] trained a 22-layer deep convolution network with 200 million face images, and used Triplet Loss as a loss function for optimizing, resulting in 99.63% accuracy in LFW.

In addition to supervised learning approaches like CNN [10, 11], unsupervised learning methods like GAN [11] and VAE [12], have also recently attracted lots of attentions and been applied for Face Synthesis. For example, Gauthier [13] utilized specific face attributes as a condition to synthesize faces with Generative Adversarial Network. Dong et al. [14] used two unsupervised learning phases to transfer from

J. Zhou—The work is supported by the National Natural Science Foundation of China (61672357) and Shenzhen Science Foundation (JCYJ20160422144110140).

© Springer International Publishing AG 2017
J. Zhou et al. (Eds.): CCBR 2017, LNCS 10568, pp. 145–153, 2017.
https://doi.org/10.1007/978-3-319-69923-3_16

image to image. They first set the real image as input with Encoder, and then took the output of the encoder as the input of the Conditional Generative Adversarial Network. Hou et al. [15] treated the pre-trained VGG model as a regularization item to supervise the training process of VAE, and classified the extracted features in the CelebA [16] database to improve its effectiveness.

Internet Celebrity is the person who received much attention on the Internet. To make them attractive, their faces are usually modified by plastic surgery, make-up and beautified by software like photoshop. As a result, these faces look very similar. The main features of the Internet Celebrity face are listed as follows:

(1) Face shape: awl face and pointed chin;
(2) Mouth: small mouth, smile lips, and toot lips;
(3) Nose: straight nose;
(4) Eyes: big eyes, double-edged eyelids, cosmetic contact lenses, and fake eyelashes;
(5) Eyebrows: flat, thick, and straight eyebrows;
(6) Forehead: high forehead;

The similarity among Internet Celebrity faces raise big challenges to current face recognition system, as it's very difficult for the algorithm to distinguish them. Figure 1 shows several examples of Internet Celebrity faces, which is very difficult to be distinguished. In this figure, (a), (c) and (d), (e) are from the same person respectively.

   (a)   (b)   (c)   (d)   (e)   (f)

Fig. 1. Example of Internet Celebrity faces

In recent years, with the rapid development of the medical cosmetic industry, the rise of micro-surgery, and the popularity of photo-editing apps, people are able to modify their appearance. This brings challenges to face identification and face verification at the same time.

Meanwhile, the Internet Celebrity face recognition brings a new research direction to face recognition research community. Improving the recognition accuracy of the algorithm for the Internet Celebrity face, helps to improve the ability to identify similar face images. Moreover, it enhances the robustness of face recognition algorithm, and expands the application of face recognition technology in real life. It is therefore important to study the Internet Celebrity face recognition problem.

2   Face Recognition and Synthesis Based on Deep Learning

2.1   Face Recognition Based on VGG

In this paper, VGGFace [17] is utilized as the recognition algorithm for experiments, which is widely used in face recognition. The network is a 16-layer convolution network model trained with 2.6 million face images, which achieved an accuracy of 98.95% on the LFW dataset.

In the previous study [17], the authors compared a variety of learning methods on the LFW database, and the results are shown in Table 1. One can see that the VGGFace trained using the smallest number of images achieved competitive accuracy.

Table 1. Comparison of different methods on LFW

Method	Training images	Networks	Accuracy
Fisher Vector face	–	–	93.10%
DeepFace (Facebook)	4M	3	97.35%
DeepFace Fusion (Facebook)	500M	5	98.37%
DeepID-2,3	–	200	99.47%
FaceNet (Google)	200M	1	98.87%
FaceNet+Alignment (Google)	200M	1	99.63%
VGGFace	2.6M	1	98.95%

2.2   Face Synthesis Based on VAE

The reconstruction error of the VAE model is based on the MSD of each pixel, which is very sensitive to variations like translation. To solve this problem, the DFC-VAE model is used in this paper. The overall framework of the model is shown in Fig. 2.

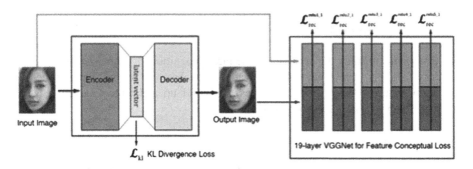

Fig. 2. DFC-VAE model

The DFC-VAE model utilizes the feature perceptual loss to measure the difference between two images. The perceptual loss of image features is defined as the error calculated from the features extracted from the convolution layer of the composite image and real image in VGG-19 model [18].

We select the VGG-19 model as a perceived feature loss for the reason that VGG-19 is a deep convolution network model which can learn the hierarchical expression of the image and is trained on the ImageNet database. The rich natural scene images in ImageNet database make the model learn numerous features.

We utilize the open-source deep learning library Torch for the DFC-VAE training. At the beginning of the model training, the composite image is vague, as shown in Fig. 3(a). After nearly half of the entire database were input to the network for training, the face become relatively clear, and the mouth and lipstick color start to appear. As the training continues, as shown in Fig. 3(b), the generated faces become more and more clear.

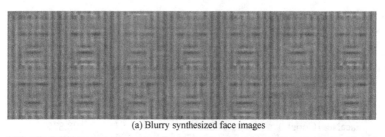

(a) Blurry synthesized face images

(b) Clearly synthesized face images

Fig. 3. Visualization of DFC-VAE training process

3   ICFace Database

This paper aims to study the accuracy of the face recognition algorithm on the Internet Celebrity face. As there is no publicly available database for testing, we collected a number of Internet Celebrity face images and build up a database named ICFace (Internet Celebrity Face) for experiments.

3.1   Data Collection

We tried to collect images with Internet Celebrity faces from the Internet. We wrote a simple crawler program to crawl the Internet Celebrity face images on the Internet through the homepage/images tagged with the keywords of "Internet Celebrity", "self-snapshot" and "beauty". After running the crawler program on three personal computers for one day, we collected about 400,000 images.

3.2   Data Cleansing

Given the collected data, there are a lot of duplications in the database. They are different in filename, but the size and content information are exactly the same. This is because we only used the tag information when we crawled the image. Although the URL is completely different, they linked to the same picture. In order to screen out these duplicate image files, we follow the idea of dictionary coding to determine whether an image C and the next image C+1 are the same picture. After cleaning, 34,846 images remained.

After removing a large number of duplicate images, we used the MTCNN method [19] for face detection. Images with no face detected were removed as well. Finally, 23,200 images remained in the database. The number of ICFace images in the database were listed in Table 2. Figure 4 shows five example faces in the ICFace database, where (a), (e) and (b), (d) are from the same person respectively.

Table 2. The number of images in the ICFace collection process

Step	Number
Data collection	400,000
File check	34,846
Face detection	23,220

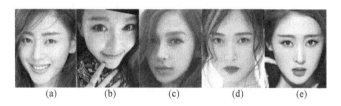

(a)   (b)   (c)   (d)   (e)

Fig. 4. Five example images in ICFace

3.3   Internet Celebrity Face Synthesis

After training the DFC-VAE model using the 23,220 Internet Celebrity face images, we can input the real Internet Celebrity face to the network and get synthesized face images. 32 synthesized face images are randomly selected and shown in Fig. 5.

4   Experimental Results

4.1   VGG Recognition Performance

We firstly test the VGG model on Internet Celebrity faces. 800 pairs of real face samples from the same person in the ICFace database, and another 800 pairs of face images consisting of both real and synthesized 'fake' faces were selected for testing. Table 3 shows the recognition accuracy of VGGFace in ICFace and LFW respectively.

Fig. 5. Face images synthesized by DFC-VAE

Table 3. The performance of VGGFace in different databases

Database	Number of pairs	Accuracy
ICFace	1600	65.7%
LFW	6000	98.75%

One can observe from Table 3 that the performance of VGGFace on the ICFace database is significantly lower than that on LFW database. When the face images are from different internet celebrities, the images generated by our VAE model is also confusing.

4.2   Comparison Between Human and Deep Learning Model

For testing the difference between deep network VGG model and human in recognition ability on the Internet Celebrity face, 20 pairs of Internet Celebrity face images are randomly selected from the same and different people from the ICFace database, and 241 people are invited for testing. Figure 6 shows an example of the pair. We use online questionnaire to collect the answers by 241 volunteers. Statistics results were presented in the next section.

Fig. 6. An example of the testing faces

From Fig. 7, we can clearly see the difference of recognition ability at different ages. People with ages 18 to 23 have the highest accuracy, which is followed by that of 24 to 29 group. And people with over 30-year-old may have difficulty in recognizing the Internet Celebrity face.

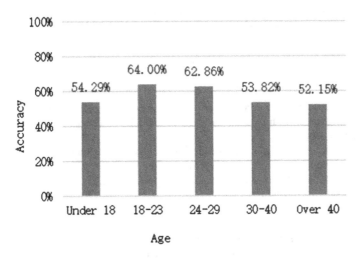

Fig. 7. The variation of accuracy with age

This result is also in line with our expectations. As Internet Celebrity face is produced with the development of the Internet and mobile Internet, young people have better ability to recognize them.

4.3   Comparison with Deep Learning Algorithm

20 pairs of Internet Celebrity face images are used to test the trained VGG deep network model. The accuracy of the recognition is shown in Table 4. The experimental results show that the accuracy of the deep learning algorithm for the Internet Celebrity face recognition problem is much higher than that of human beings.

Table 4. Comparison of human and deep learning for Internet Celebrity face recognition

	Accuracy
Human	56.0%
VGG	80.0%

5   Conclusion

The problem of Internet Celebrity face recognition arises as the Internet become more popular in people's daily life. This paper studies this problem by setting up a Internet Celebrity face database. We train the DFC-VAE model on the ICFace database to generate a number of 'false' Internet Celebrity face images and use them to test face recognition algorithms.

Through the study on the comparison of human and recognition algorithms, we find that human do not perform well on ICFace. Gender, age and other factors have a certain impact on the ability. The face recognition algorithms, which perform well on the general face database, perform much worse on the Internet Celebrity face. More works are expected to study this problem.

References

1. Ojala, T., Pietikainen, M., Maenpaa, T.: Multiresolution gray-scale and rotation invariant texture classification with local binary patterns. IEEE Trans. Pattern Anal. Mach. Intell. **24** (7), 971–987 (2002)
2. Liu, C., Wechsler, H.: A gabor feature classifier for face recognition. In: Proceedings of the IEEE International Conference on Computer Vision, vol. 2, pp. 270–275 (2001)
3. Wold, S., Esbensen, K., Geladi, P.: Principal component analysis. Chemometr. Intell. Lab. Syst. **2**(1–3), 37–52 (1987)
4. Blei, D.M., Ng, A.Y., Jordan, M.I.: Latent dirichlet allocation. J. Mach. Learn. Res. 993–1022 (2003)
5. Krizhevsky, A., Sutskever, I., Hinton, G.E.: Imagenet classification with deep convolutional neural networks. In: Advances in Neural Information Processing Systems, pp. 1097–1105 (2012)
6. Taigman, Y., Yang, M., Ranzato, M., Wolf, L.: Closing the gap to human-level performance in face verification. In: Proceedings of the IEEE Conference on Computer Vision and Pattern Recognition, pp. 1701–1708 (2014)
7. Huang, G.B., Mattar, M., Berg, T., Learned-Miller, E.: Labeled faces in the wild: a database for studying face recognition in unconstrained environments. In: Workshop on Faces in 'Real-Life' Images: Detection, Alignment, and Recognition (2008)
8. Sun, Y., Wang, X., Tang, X.: Deep learning face representation from predicting 10,000 classes. In: Proceedings of the IEEE Conference on Computer Vision and Pattern Recognition, pp. 1891–1898 (2014)
9. Schroff, F., Kalenichenko, D., Philbin, J.: Facenet: a unified embedding for face recognition and clustering. In: Proceedings of the IEEE Conference on Computer Vision and Pattern Recognition, pp. 815–823 (2015)
10. LeCun, Y., Bottou, L., Bengio, Y., Haffner, P.: Gradient-based learning applied to document recognition. Proc. IEEE **86**(11), 2278–2324 (1998)
11. Goodfellow, I., Pouget-Abadie, J., Mirza, M., Xu, B., Warde-Farley, D., Ozair, S., Courville, A., Bengio, Y.: Generative adversarial nets. In: Advances in Neural Information Processing Systems, pp. 2672–2680 (2014)
12. Kingma, D.P., Welling, M.: Auto-encoding variational bayes (2013). arXiv preprint arXiv: 1312.6114
13. Gauthier, J.: Conditional generative adversarial nets for convolutional face generation. Class Project for Stanford CS231N: Convolutional Neural Networks for Visual Recognition, Winter Semester, vol. 5, p. 2 (2014)
14. Dong, H., Neekhara, P., Wu, C., Guo, Y.: Unsupervised image-to-image translation with generative adversarial networks (2017). arXiv preprint arXiv:1701.02676

15. Hou, X., Shen, L., Sun, K., Qiu, G.: Deep feature consistent variational autoencoder. In: 2017 IEEE Winter Conference on Applications of Computer Vision (WACV), pp. 1133–1141 (2017)
16. Liu, Z., Luo, P., Wang, X., Tang, X.: Deep learning face attributes in the wild. In: Proceedings of the IEEE International Conference on Computer Vision, pp. 3730–3738 (2015)
17. Parkhi, O.M., Vedaldi, A., Zisserman, A.: Deep face recognition. In: BMVC, vol. 1, no. 3, p. 6 (2015)
18. Simonyan, K., Zisserman, A.: Very deep convolutional networks for large-scale image recognition (2014). arXiv preprint arXiv:1409.1556
19. Zhang, K., Zhang, Z., Li, Z., Qiao, Y.: Joint face detection and alignment using multitask cascaded convolutional networks. IEEE Sig. Process. Lett. 23(10), 1499–1503 (2016)

Face Detection with Better Representation Using a Multi-region WR-Inception Network Model

Lianping Yang, Yuanyuan Li, Xu Duan, and Xiangde Zhang[✉]

College of Sciences, Northeastern University, Shenyang 110819, China
{yanglp, zhangxiangde}@mail.neu.edu.cn,
liyuanyuanmath@163.com, duanxumath@163.com

Abstract. This paper proposes a multi-region WR-Inception network model for face detection based on the Faster RCNN framework. Firstly, we utilize multi-region features to obtain better face representation and introduce block loss to enable our model to be robust to occluded faces. Then we adopt WR-Inception network with shallower and wider layers as our base feature extractor. Finally, we apply a new pre-training strategy to learn representation more suitable for face detection, and exploit soft-nms for the post processing. Specially, experimental results show that our method achieves recall rate of 85.1% on FDDB dataset.

Keywords: A multi-region WR-Inception model · Face detection · Block loss · New pre-training strategy

1 Introduction

Face detection is a classical problem in computer vision, which has been widely studied over the past few decades. However, due to large variations in pose, blur, occlusion and illumination condition, face detection is still confronted with some challenges. Recently, Faster RCNN [1] and its improvement have been demonstrated impressive performance on object detection. Jiang and Learned-Miller [2] just trained a Faster RCNN model and achieved the state-of-the-art performance on FDDB benchmark [3]. Besides, Xiaomi [4] exploited the idea of hard negative mining and iteratively update the Faster RCNN based face detector, and also achieved prominent success. Instead of adding some tricks of training based on Faster RCNN for face detection, this paper proposed a multi-region WR-Inception network model for face detection based on the Faster RCNN framework. Firstly, we utilized multi-region features in Sect. 2.1 to obtain better face representation, and introduced block loss in Sect. 2.2 to enable our model to be robust to occluded faces. Then we adopted WR-Inception network [5] with shallower and wider layers as our base feature extractor. Finally, we applied a new pre-training strategy to learn representation more suitable for face detection, and exploited soft-nms for the post processing. Specially, experimental results show that our method can not only cope with faces with small scale and pose variations, but also handle occlusion and blur.

© Springer International Publishing AG 2017
J. Zhou et al. (Eds.): CCBR 2017, LNCS 10568, pp. 154–161, 2017.
https://doi.org/10.1007/978-3-319-69923-3_17

The rest of this paper is organized as follows: Sect. 2 describes our face detector in details. Experimental settings and results are presented in Sect. 3. And conclusions of our paper are drawn in Sect. 4.

2   The Proposed Method

Compared with hand-crafted design pipeline of traditional computer vision approaches, deep learning methods could automatically extract better features from data, and achieve the state-of-the-art performance in many computer vision tasks. One of the lessons learned from this is that feature matters a lot in computer vision. And based on this, better face representation of our method is obtained from two aspects: (1) multi-region features and block loss (2) adoption of WR-Inception network and concatenation of features. The following will discuss the procedure in details.

2.1   Multi-region Feature Extractor

For face detection, face representation should capture not only whole appearance of a face but distinct appearance of different face parts and contextual appearance. And we believe that such rich representation would help face detector to improve performance under complex conditions. In order to achieve this, we proposed a multi-region model including six regions, each of which focused on a different part of a face to collect discriminative face representations. We will describe six regions in Fig. 1.

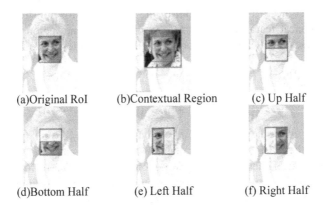

(a)Original RoI   (b)Contextual Region   (c) Up Half

(d)Bottom Half   (e) Left Half   (f) Right Half

Fig. 1. Illustration of six regions used in our model (Red rectangles represent the original RoI, and green rectangles represent the regions proposed in this paper) (Color figure online)

Details and roles of six regions above are described as follows:

(1) Original RoI: it is obtained by RPN network in Faster RCNN framework. And it could guide model to capture the whole appearance information of the whole face.

(2) Contextual region: it is obtained by scaling the original RoI by factor of 2. And it could guide model to capture the contextual appearance information that surrounds a face, which aims to make the representation more robust to small faces.

(3) Half part regions: they are up/bottom/left/right half parts of the original RoI. They could guide model to capture the appearance information of each half part of a face, which aims to make the representation more robust to faces with occlusion.

Features consisted by six regions above combine local information with contextual information to gain richer face representation. And experimental results in Sect. 3 show that it helps our method to achieve good performance on face detection under unconstrained conditions.

2.2 Block Loss in Our Face Detector

Due to information loss by occlusion, problem of partially occluded faces is still challenging in detection. And detection of a partially occluded face heavily relies on positive response of its certain parts. Therefore, inspired by Opitz et al. [6] we regard (c)(d)(e)(f) in Fig. 1 as four blocks, which would produce positive response for a face. And margin of each block is set to 0.5, which weights the discrimination of the block to the whole RoI. Block loss is defined in function (1).

$$L_{blocks} = \sum_{i=1}^{4} (0.5 \cdot y - \frac{1}{1+e^{-z_i}}) \tag{1}$$

where z_i is output of our model corresponding to block i. $y_j \in \{0, 1\}$ denotes the class label of the RoI (whether it contains any face or not).

Due to negative responses of certain blocks corresponding to less discriminative face parts, we also need to utilize output of the whole RoI for holistic classification. Therefore, we concat features of region (a) (original RoI) and region (b) (contextual region) for holistic classification. And our final classification loss is defined as follows:

$$L_c = L_{whole} + \eta L_{blocks}$$
$$= (y - \frac{1}{1+e^{-z}}) + \eta \sum_{i=1}^{4} (0.5 \cdot y - (\frac{1}{1+e^{-z_i}})) \tag{2}$$

where η weights the block classifiers vs. the holistic classifier and is set to 1. Compared with direct division of the RoIs in [6], we adopted four blocks to form more block classifiers and help our model to pay more attention on less discriminative blocks. Experiments in Sect. 3 show that this strategy helps our model to be robust to faces with occlusion.

2.3 Our Whole Model

For feature extraction network, we adopted WR-Inception-12 [5] with shallower and wider layers, which captured objects in various sizes on the same feature map based on a residual inception structure. Meanwhile, we concatenated features of conv3_2 and conv4_4 for multi-scale representation.

After feature extraction and obtaining RoIs by RPN network, we can get two $7 \times 7 \times 384$-dimensional feature maps corresponding to (a) and (b) in Fig. 1 for every RoI, and we shared the weights between region (a)(b) and other four regions (c)(d)(e)(f) on account of runtime and memory. And finally we fed them into our model as follows (Fig. 2):

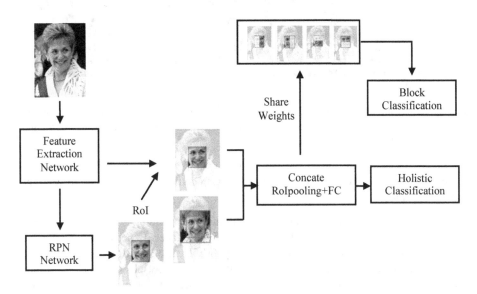

Fig. 2. Our multi-region model with WR-Inception network as feature extraction network

3 Experiments

3.1 Experimental Settings

New Pre-training Strategy. Due to millions of parameters of network, it is common for detection task to carry out pretraining on large-scale image classification data and then to finetune on detection datasets. However, difference between classification task and detection task leads to less effective pretraining. For classification task, which recognizes the object within an image, learned features would be robust to change on location and size of the object. However, detection task not only recognizes the object within an image but also locate where the object is, which requires learned features to be sensitive to change on location and size of the object. Therefore, for pretraining of our network, we replaced image classification data with face recognition database after alignment to focus on better face representation.

We choose casia webface database [7] which contains 10,575 subjects and 494,414 images for the pretraining. Ratio of training set and validation set is 9:1. And all faces without alignment were cropped and resized into 100×100 as input of our network. And in training process, we adopted SGD with a batch size of 32 and momentum of

0.9. The learning rate was initially set to 0.01. And our model performed 1M iterations. And effect of new pre-training strategy is shown in Fig. 3.

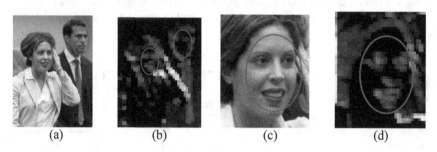

    (a)   (b)   (c)   (d)

Fig. 3. Illustration of effect of new pre-training strategy ((a) is an image from FDDB dataset, and (c) is cropped from (a). (b) and (d) are corresponding visualization of feature maps of (a) and (c) after our feature extraction network)

As shown in Fig. 3, model pretrained on our new pre-training strategy is able to represent face with different size and location, which could help our detector to get tight box for the face.

Finetuning Strategy. Our model was finetuning with training set of WIDER face dataset [8], which contains 12,880 images and 159,424 faces. Experimental settings of fine-tuning were set as follows: (1) Restricting fg/ bg ratio for RPN. The number of negative samples is no more than 1.5 times of the number of positive ones to further mitigate data imbalance; (2) New scales for WIDER face dataset. We used 4 scales (64, 128, 256, 512) for WIDER face dataset, leading to $k = 12$ anchors at each location. Then we re-scaled the images such that their shorter side is 600 pixels, and limited the maximum side to 1000 pixels. Our face detector was trained for 60 k iterations with a base learning rate of 0.0001 which is reduced by 10 times for every 20 k iterations.

3.2   Experimental Results

Test stage. We took FDDB [3] dataset as test sets. FDDB dataset, which has in total 5,171 faces with occlusions, difficult poses, and various scene in 2,845 images, is released with rich annotation and a standard performance evaluation scheme for face detection. We adopted soft-nms [9] for the post processing. And comparisons of experimental results are conducted on FDDB dataset.

Analysis of Experimental Results. Firstly, we compared the performance of our model with and without multi-region features and block loss on FDDB dataset in Table 1.

Table 1. Comparison of performance of our model with and without multi-region features and block loss on FDDB dataset

Model	Recall rate (%)	False positive
Our	83.0%	1700
Our+multi-region features+block loss	85.1%	1700

Table 1 illustrates that multi-region features and block loss lead to richer representation of images and it outperforms the model without adding them.

Then we compared the performance of our model with other state-of-the-art face detectors on FDDB dataset. In particular, we compared recall rate of our method with XZJY [10], PEP-Adapt [11], Face++ [12], and DDFD [13] in Table 2. True positive rate-False positive curve is shown in Fig. 4.

Table 2. Comparison of performance of our model with other state-of-the-art face detectors on FDDB dataset

Model	Recall rate(%)	False positive
XZJY	80.0%	1700
PEP-Adapt	81.8%	1700
Face++	84.5%	1700
DDFD	84.6%	1700
Our+multi-region features+block loss	**85.1%**	1700

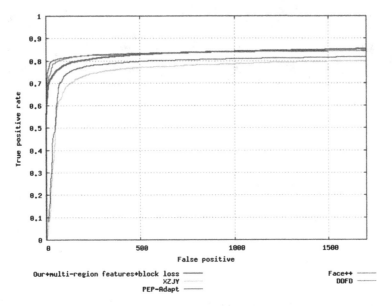

Fig. 4. Comparison of performance of our model with other state-of-the-art face detectors

Some detection results are shown in Fig. 5.

Table 2 and Fig. 4 illustrate our method illustrate that our method outperforms other state-of-the-art face detectors and achieves great improvements of face detection under unconstrained conditions. Detection results in Fig. 5 show that our method can not only cope with faces with small scale and pose variations, but also handle occlusion and blur.

Fig. 5. Some detection results of our face detector on FDDB dataset

4   Conclusion

This paper proposed a multi-region WR-Inception network model for face detection based on the Faster RCNN framework. Specially, we adopted multi-region features, block loss, WR-Inception network and new pre-training strategy to obtain better face representation, which helped our face detector to be robust to faces with small scales, heavy occlusion, blur and other complex situations. Experimental results show that our method achieves recall rate of 85.1% on FDDB dataset.

Conflict of Interests
The authors declare that there is no conflict of interests regarding the publication of this paper.

Acknowledgment. This work is supported by the Fundamental Research Funds for the Central Universities (Grant No. N160504007) and supported by the National Natural Science Foundation of China (Grant No. 31301086).

References

1. Ren, S., He, K., Girshick, R., et al.: Faster R-CNN: towards real-time object detection with region proposal networks. IEEE Trans. Pattern Anal. Mach. Intell. **39**(6), 1137–1149 (2015)
2. Jiang, H., Learned-Miller, E.: Face detection with the faster R-CNN. arXiv preprint arXiv: 1606.03473 (2016)
3. Jain, V., Learned-Miller, E.: Fddb: a benchmark for face detection in unconstrained settings. UMass Amherst Technical report (2010)
4. Wan, S., Chen, Z., Zhang, T., et al.: Bootstrapping Face Detection with Hard Negative Examples. arXiv preprint arXiv:1608.02236 (2016)
5. Lee, Y., Kim, H., Park, E., et al.: Wide-Residual-Inception Networks for Real-time Object Detection. arXiv preprint arXiv:1702.01243 (2017)
6. Opitz, M., Waltner, G., Poier, G., Possegger, H., Bischof, H.: Grid loss: detecting occluded faces. In: Leibe, B., Matas, J., Sebe, N., Welling, M. (eds.) ECCV 2016. LNCS, vol. 9907, pp. 386–402. Springer, Cham (2016). doi:10.1007/978-3-319-46487-9_24
7. Yi, D., Lei, Z., Liao, S., et al.: Learning face representation from scratch. arXiv preprint arXiv:1411.7923 (2014)
8. Yang, S., Luo, P., Loy, C.C., et al.: Wider face: a face detection benchmark. In: 2016 IEEE Conference on Computer Vision and Pattern Recognition, pp. 5525–5533. IEEE Press, United States (2016)
9. Bodla, N., Singh, B., Chellappa, R., et al.: Improving Object Detection with One Line of Code. arXiv preprint arXiv:1704.04503 (2017)
10. Shen, X., Lin, Z., Brandt, J., et al.: Detecting and aligning faces by image retrieval. In: 2013 IEEE Conference on Computer Vision and Pattern Recognition, pp. 3460–3467. IEEE Press, United States (2013)
11. Li, H., Hua, G., Lin, Z., et al.: Probabilistic elastic part model for unsupervised face detector adaptation. In: 2013 IEEE International Conference on Computer Vision and Pattern Recognition, pp. 793–800. IEEE Press, United States (2013)
12. Face++. https://www.faceplusplus.com/
13. Farfade, S.S., Saberian, M.J., Li, L.J.: Multi-view face detection using deep convolutional neural networks. In: Proceedings of the 5th ACM on International Conference on Multimedia Retrieval, pp. 643–650. ACM, China (2015)

Coarse and Fine: A New Method for Gender Classification in the Wild

Qianbo Jiang, Li Shao, Zhengxi Liu, and Qijun Zhao[✉]

National Key Laboratory of Fundamental Science on Synthetic Vision,
College of Computer Science, Sichuan University, Chengdu, China
qjzhao@scu.edu.cn

Abstract. As one of the most important soft biometrics, gender has substantial applications in various areas such as demography and human-computer interaction. Successful gender estimation of face images taken under real-world also contributes to improving the face identification results in the wild. However, most existing gender classification methods estimate gender under well controlled environment, which limits its implementation in real-world applications. In this paper, we propose a new network architecture to combine the coarse appearance features with delicate facial features for gender estimation task. We call this method "coarse and fine" to give a harsh description of the gender estimation process. Trained on the large scale uncontrolled CelebA dataset without any alignment, the proposed network tries to learn how to estimate gender of real-world face images. Cross-database experiments on LFWA and CASIA-WebFace dataset show the superiority of our proposed method.

Keywords: Coarse and fine · Gender classification · Convolutional neural networks

1 Introduction

Gender, age and race are important soft biometric traits, which have many applications in face recognition and social media. Unlike most of other soft biometrics, the gender of a person can be seen stable, which benefits a lot when conducting face recognition or verification tasks for the reason that with the gender information of a face image, the search scope in the face database can be halved down (if the number of male and female face images in the database are equal) or even more. In addition to the face recognition applications, gender is also a kind of valuable demography information of an individual or statistics about a population.

With numerous applications, automatic estimation of gender from face images has received an increasing attention in recent years and many gender classification algorithms have been proposed [1–7]. Unfortunately, most of these algorithms are designed to estimate the gender of face images taken under experimental environment, and are thus not suitable for the real-world conditions.

© Springer International Publishing AG 2017
J. Zhou et al. (Eds.): CCBR 2017, LNCS 10568, pp. 162–171, 2017.
https://doi.org/10.1007/978-3-319-69923-3_18

With the popularization of smart phones, more and more face images are taken by mobile phones, under uncontrolled environment. As a result, the gender classification algorithms are expected to process the real-world data obtained from uncontrolled environment, such as airports, customs and stadiums, with varying conditions such as facial occlusions, illumination changes and facial expressions.

In this paper, we propose a new method to estimate the gender of face images taken under real-world environment. From the perspective of how human beings judge the gender of a person, we find that we usually combine coarse appearance features with delicate facial features for the gender estimation task. As for the coarse appearance features, we usually focus on the hair: if a person has long hair, we tend to classify the person as a female, and vice versa. With a coarse impression about the person, we then analyse the delicate facial features carefully to obtain the final judgement: if the facial features are exactly the female facial features, along with the coarse impression, we think the face belongs to a woman, and if the facial features are much more similar to the male facial features such as goatee and mustache, despite the person has long hair we think it is a man. Inspired by the above observation, in this work, we train two networks at the same time, one for coarse appearance features, especially for the hair information, and another for the delicate facial features that are dominant in gender classification, then the learned features of these two networks are concatenated to estimate the gender of input faces, we call this method "coarse and fine". The architecture of our proposed network is shown in Fig. 1. Cross-database experiments on LFWA and CASIA-WebFace show the superiority of our proposed method.

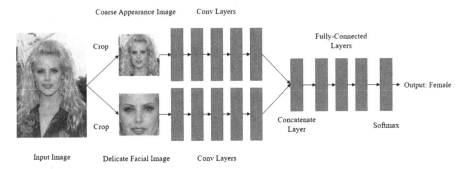

Fig. 1. Our "coarse and fine" network architecture for gender classification. We feed this network with a cropped facial image and corresponding appearance image which contains the contextual information about hair. This network combines the coarse features extracted from cropped appearance images with delicate features extracted from cropped facial images for gender estimation task.

The remainder of the paper is structured as follows. The relevant literature is reviewed in Sect. 2. In Sect. 3, our "coarse and fine" architecture is introduced in detail. Section 4 describes our cross-database experimental validation and comparison with other gender classification algorithms. Section 5 concludes the paper with discussion on future work.

2 Related Work

Traditional approaches for gender recognition that are based on hand-crafted features can be grouped into either global [1–3] or local [4–6]. In [7], Perez et al. tried to combine these two kinds of features for gender estimation task and obtained satisfactory performance. O'Toole et al. [8] showed that depth information can be helpful in this binary classification task. Most of these aforementioned methods were tested on the highly controlled FERET dataset [9], in which images are taken under experimental conditions and almost all the images are exactly frontal. Shan [10] employed the Local Binary Patterns (LBP) and achieved good performance on some frontal or near frontal face images in the LFW dataset [11], a challenging benchmark initially designed for face recognition. For more details about the traditional works, we refer our readers to [12,13].

The implementation of neural networks for gender classification task dates back to 1990s, when shallow neural networks [1,14,15] were used and obtained state-of-the-art results at that time. However, the shallow structure of the early neural networks heavily constrained their performance and applicability. With the great success of AlexNet [16] in ImageNet Recognition Challenge, neural networks regained researchers' attention. In the following years, various deep neural networks are successfully applied to a variety of visual recognition tasks including gender classification. Verma and Vig [17] showed that CNN is more robust and performs much better than previous classifiers like SVM and Random Forest etc. Inspired by the dropout technique in training phase, Eidinger et al. [18] trained a SVM with random dropout of some features and achieved promising results on their relatively small Adience dataset. In [19], Levi and Hassner showed that by learning representations through the use of deep convolutional neural networks, a significant increase in performance can be obtained on the gender estimation task. Instead of training on entire images, Mansanet et al. [20] trained with local patches and reported better accuracies than holistic image based networks of similar depth.

3 Proposed Method

In this section, we first describe the proposed method and point out the main difference between our method with other gender classification algorithms, then we introduce the network architecture in detail and the pipeline of this network will be discussed later.

3.1 Method Overview

At a high level, we feed two images cropped from the input image (one is the delicate facial image and another is the coarse appearance image containing contextual information) into a neural network, and the network successively outputs the gender of the input face image. Unlike other gender classification methods, we train our network with the face images taken under uncontrolled environment without any face alignment or other extra operations, because we find that trained with aligned images we get worse gender classification performance than that trained with "wild" images without alignment operations, as for this phenomenon we think that most of the existing face alignment algorithms cannot work well in the wild conditions and the misaligned training data may damage the accuracy of gender classification. Therefore we choose to train our network end-to-end without face alignment and the network are forced to learn features that robust to wild conditions. As a result, the network are skilled to estimate the gender of faces taken under real-world environment.

3.2   Network Architecture

The network architecture, as shown in Fig. 1, is composed of two 5-convolutional layers, and the feature maps are then concatenated to feed into three fully connected layers, followed by a softmax layer to obtain the final possibilities of different gender results. In this model, we feed paired delicate facial images and coarse appearance images which contain contextual information about hair into a sequence of convolutional layers, note that the delicate facial images and coarse appearance images are cropped from the same input image, which guarantees the correspondence of these two input images. The output of these convolutional layers is a set of features that capture a high-level representation of the inputs.

The outputs of these convolutional layers are then concatenated by a concatenate layer to feed through a number of fully connected layers. The role of the fully connected layers is to combine the coarse gender information extracted from coarse appearance images with the delicate gender information extracted from delicate facial images for gender estimation task.

In more detail, the convolutional layers in our model are taken from the first five convolutional layers of the AlexNet architecture [16]. We concatenate the output of these convolutional layers (i.e. the pool5 features) into a single vector. This vector is input into three fully connected layers, among which the first and second layer contain 4096 nodes, the third layer contains 2 nodes representing the output gender labels. Finally, we connect the last fully connected layer to a softmax layer to predict the possibilities of different gender results. To describe the proposed method better, we pick up a name called "coarse and fine" for this new gender classification method.

3.3   Training

Before network training, a face detection algorithm is used for detecting faces in the input images, based on these detected faces, another two face images are cropped, namely the delicate facial images and corresponding coarse appearance images. As long as a face is detected, we can obtain the width and height of the detected face, as well as the coordinate of the center point, which are denoted by w, h and (x, y) respectively. The delicate facial images are exactly the detected faces cropped from the input images, and the paired coarse appearance images are k times larger than the detected faces, note that the delicate facial images and coarse appearance images are cropped based on the center point of the detected faces. In detail, if we have obtained the center point (x, y) of a detected face, extend with $w/2$ horizontally and $h/2$ vertically we can get the delicate facial image, while extend with $k \times w/2$ horizontally and $k \times h/2$ vertically we can get the coarse appearance image, then the cropped delicate facial images and coarse appearance images are resized to the same scale as the inputs of the network. We use these paired images to train our network as described in Sect. 3.2. During test time, these paired two crops are fed into the network to estimate the gender of input faces.

4   Experimental Results

4.1   Databases for Training and Testing

We train our network with the CelebFaces Attributes Dataset (CelebA) [21], which contains 202,599 face images from 10,177 identities (41.68% males and 59.32% females). CelebA is a large scale face attributes dataset designed as the training and testing dataset for the task of face attribute recognition, face detection, and landmark localization. Images in this dataset cover large pose variations, illumination changes, facial expressions and heavy occlusions. Some examples are shown in Fig. 2. Using these challenging images without any alignment for training, we try to simulate the real-world conditions. As a result, the network has to learn how to estimate the gender of a face taken under uncontrolled environment.

Fig. 2. Images in CelebA dataset cover large pose variations, illumination changes, facial expressions and heavy occlusions. We use images in this dataset without any alignment for training, for the purpose that forcing the network to learn the capability of classifying gender of a face taken under uncontrolled environment.

To evaluate the effectiveness of the proposed method, two large scale uncontrolled datasets, namely LFWA and CASIA-WebFace, are used. LFWA dataset is a richly labeled version of the popular Labeled Faces in the Wild (LFW) database [11], which is originally designed for face recognition tasks. It contains 10,236 male images and 2,997 female images. The dataset has 40 facial attributes labels (including gender) for each image and covers a large range of pose variation and background clutter, some example images are shown in Fig. 3.

Fig. 3. Challenging examples in LFWA dataset.

CASIA-WebFace dataset [22] is a large scale dataset containing 494,414 images from 10,575 subjects. Images in this dataset cover heavy occlusions, large pose variations and illumination changes, as shown in Fig. 4. Considering the fact that each person in CASIA-WebFace dataset has many pictures, we randomly select 50,000 images from this dataset to test our network, among which 28,263 images are males and 21,737 images belong to females.

Fig. 4. Challenging examples in CASIA-WebFace dataset.

4.2   Experimental Setup

We use MTCNN [23] to detect faces and then crop delicate facial images and coarse appearance images as described in Sect. 3.3. MTCNN performs well in face detection, it successfully detected 202,027 faces in the total 202,599 images. The width and height of the cropped facial images are kept the same (i.e. $w = h$), as for coarse appearance images, factor k is set to 2.5 to contain enough contextual information. The cropped delicate facial images and coarse appearance images are resize to 227×227 pixels as the inputs of the network. We split the training set into 90% for learning the weights and 10% for validation during the training phase. The learning rate for all layers except the last layer is set to 0.001. To better learn the capacity for gender estimation, we set the learning rate for the last layer to 0.01. We train with a moment of 0.9 and a weight decay of 0.0005. The learning rate is reduced every 10 passes through the entire data by a factor of 10.

4.3 Results

In this Section, we demonstrate and discuss the recognition results of our proposed method. We conduct contrast experiment with the network that trained without using "coarse and fine" strategy, namely the simple version network which is composed of five convolutional layers and three fully-connected layers only (i.e. AlexNet [16]). We train the simple version network with delicate facial images and coarse appearance images respectively to analyse the effectiveness of the "coarse and fine" strategy. LANet [21] and LDNN [20] method are also included for more comparison, the gender recognition results are shown in Table 1. Note that in Liu's work [21], two networks are trained: LNet is trained for locating the face regions and ANet is trained for attributes prediction. Unlike Liu's work, we don't have to crop a set of overlapping patches to cope with the misalignment of face regions, we train our network without alignment or any post-procedure to offset the misalignment. The utilization of coarse appearance features and delicate facial features at the same time is another major difference between our proposed method and the LANet method. By comparing with the state-of-the-art LANet and LDNN methods, we indicate the superiority of our proposed method.

Table 1. Recognition accuracy of our proposed method on two large scale uncontrolled datasets is compared with that trained on AlexNet using different crops. The state-of-the-art LANet and LDNN methods are also included for comparison.

	LFWA	CASIA-WebFace
AlexNet [16] + facial	95.18%	97.83%
AlexNet [16] + appearance	95.69%	98.06%
LANet [21]	94.02%	97.36%
LDNN [20]	96.25%	98.32%
Proposed method	**96.38%**	**98.68%**

As shown in Table 1, the performance of the simple version network without "coarse and fine" strategy (i.e. AlexNet) is worse than our proposed method which combines the coarse contextual information with the delicate facial information to estimate gender of input faces. The AlexNet trained on coarse appearance images performs better than that trained on delicate facial images proves our conjecture that the contextual information including hair contributes to improving gender recognition accuracy. Experimental results on LFWA and CASIA-WebFace dataset indicate our proposed method outperforms the state-of-the-art LANet and LDNN method.

For more comparison, we trained our network with aligned images from CelebA dataset. To better distinguish these two networks trained with different training data, we denote the one trained with aligned face images as "Aligned-Network". Classification results of the "Aligned-Network" and proposed method on the aligned LFWA and CASIA-WebFace dataset are shown in Table 2.

From Table 2, we can see that the classification accuracies of "Aligned-Network" on the aligned LFWA and CASIA-WebFace dataset are 94.48% and 96.35% respectively, lower than our proposed method by a large margin. Note that classification accuracies of our proposed method on the original LFWA and CASIA-WebFace dataset (96.38% and 98.68% respectively) are lower than that on aligned LFWA and CASIA-WebFace (97.99% and 98.78% respectively), but higher than "Aligned-Network" on the aligned datasets (94.48% and 96.35% respectively). In a more concise way, we say that

$Acc(Aligned\text{-}Network + aligned\ datasets) < Acc(Proposed\ Method + wild\ datasets)$
$< Acc(Proposed\ Method + aligned\ datasets),$

Table 2. Recognition accuracy of "Aligned-Network" and proposed method on aligned LFWA and CASIA-WebFace dataset.

	Aligned LFWA	Aligned CASIA-WebFace
Aligned-network	94.48%	96.35%
Proposed method	**97.99%**	**98.78%**

where $Acc(.)$ is the gender recognition accuracy and "*wild datasets*" refers to the original LFWA and CASIA-WebFace dataset. The objective fact that most of the existing face alignment algorithms can not work well in the wild conditions (such as large pose variations, extremely lighting conditions and exaggerate facial expressions) may responsible for this phenomenon. On one hand, training on the unreliable aligned data may damage the accuracy of gender estimation, while training on images taken under wild conditions without face alignment in an end-to-end way will eventually force the network to learn how to estimate the gender of real-world face images; on the other hand, using the aligned data for testing is helpful in improving gender recognition accuracy.

5   Conclusion

In this paper, we proposed a new network architecture to combine the coarse contextual information with delicate facial information to estimate gender of real-world face images. Experiments indicate that coarse contextual information containing hair contributes to improving the gender recognition accuracy, however more coarse contextual information means less subtle facial information which is dominant in gender estimation. In our work, we combine these two important information together, namely the "coarse and fine" strategy for gender estimation task. Trained on the large scale uncontrolled CelebA dataset without any alignment, the proposed network tries to learn how to estimate gender of face images taken under real-world environment. Cross-database experiments on LFWA and CASIA-WebFace show the superiority of our proposed "coarse and fine" method. Since the straightforward feature concatenation strategy is applied in this work and better gender recognition accuracy has been achieved, we believe that if dynamic weight assignment is applied in the feature concatenation, even better result can be obtained. In the future, we will concatenate these two features in dynamic weight assignment way to further improve the gender classification accuracy.

Acknowledgments. This work is supported by National Key Research and Development Program of China (2017YFB0802303, 2016YFC0801100) and the National Key Scientific Instrument and Equipment Development Projects of China (2013YQ49087904).

References

1. Gutta, S., Wechsler, H.: Gender and ethnic classification of human faces using hybrid classifiers. In: Proceedings of the International Joint Conference on Neural Networks, pp. 4084–4089 (1999)
2. Jain, A., Huang, J., Fang, S.: Gender identification using frontal facial images. In: Proceedings of the IEEE International Conference on Multimedia and Expo, p. 4 (2005)
3. Baluja, S., Rowley, H.: Boosting sex identification performance. Int. J. Comput. Vis. **71**(1), 111–119 (2007)
4. Benabdelkader, C., Griffin, P.: A local region-based approach to gender classification from face images. In: Proceedings of the IEEE Computer Society Conference on Computer Vision and Pattern Recognition, p. 52 (2005)
5. Toews, M., Arbel, T.: Detection, localization, and sex classification of faces from arbitrary viewpoints and under occlusion. IEEE Trans. Pattern Anal. Mach. Intell. **31**(9), 1567–1581 (2009)
6. Ullah, I., Hussain, M., Muhammad, G., Aboalsamh, H.: Gender recognition from face images with local WLD descriptor. In: Proceedings of the International Conference on Systems, Signals and Image Processing, pp. 417–420 (2013)
7. Perez, C., Tapia, J., Estvez, P., Held, C.: Gender classification from face images using mutual information and feature fusion. Int. J. Optomechatronics **6**(1), 92–119 (2012)
8. O'Toole, A., Vetter, T., Troje, N., Blthoff, H.: Sex classification is better with three-dimensional head structure than with image intensity information. Perception **26**(1), 75–84 (1997)
9. Phillips, P.J., Wechsler, H., Huang, J., Rauss, P.J.: The FERET database and evaluation procedure for face-recognition algorithms. Image Vis. Comput. **16**(5), 295–306 (1998)
10. Shan, C.: Learning local binary patterns for gender classification on real-world face images. Pattern Recogn. Lett. **33**(4), 431–437 (2012)
11. Huang, G.B., Mattar, M., Berg, T., Learned-Miller, E.: Labeled faces in the wild: a database for studying face recognition in unconstrained environments. Technical report 07–49, University of Massachusetts (2007)
12. Makinen, E., Raisamo, R.: Evaluation of gender classification methods with automatically detected and aligned faces. IEEE Trans. Pattern Anal. Mach. Intell. **30**(3), 541–547 (2008)
13. Reid, D.A., Samangooei, S., Chen, C., Nixon, M.S., Ross, A.: Soft biometrics for surveillance: an overview. Mach. Learn.: Theory Appl. 327–352 (2013). Elsevier

14. Golomb, B.A., Lawrence, D.T., Sejnowski, T.J.: SEXNET: a neural network identifies sex from human faces. NIPS **1**, 2 (1990)

15. Poggio, B., Brunelli, R., Poggio, T.: HyberBF networks for gender classification. In: NIPS, vol. 2 (1990)

16. Krizhevsky, A., Sutskever, I., Hinton, G.E.: Imagenet classification with deep convolutional neural networks. In: Proceedings of the Advances in Neural Information Processing Systems, pp. 1097–1105 (2012)

17. Verma, A., Vig, L.: Using convolutional neural networks to discover cogntively validated features for gender classification. In: Proceedings of the International Conference on Soft Computing and Machine Intelligence, pp. 33–37 (2014)

18. Eidinger, E., Enbar, R., Hassner, T.: Age and gender estimation of unfiltered faces. IEEE Trans. Inf. Forensics Secur. **9**(12), 2170–2179 (2014)

19. Levi, G., Hassner, T.: Age and gender classification using convolutional neural networks. In: Proceedings of the IEEE Conference on Computer Vision and Pattern Recognition Workshops, pp. 34–42 (2015)

20. Mansanet, J., Albiol, A., Paredes, R.: Local deep neural networks for gender recognition. Pattern Recogn. Lett. **70**, 80–86 (2016)

21. Liu, Z., Luo, P., Wang, X., Tang, X.: Deep learning face attributes in the wild. In: Proceedings of the IEEE International Conference on Computer Vision, pp. 3730–3738 (2015)

22. Yi, D., Lei, Z., Liao, S., Li, S.Z.: Learning face representation from scratch. arXiv preprint arXiv:1411.7923 (2014)

23. Zhang, K., Zhang, Z., Li, Z., Qiao, Y.: Joint face detection and alignment using multitask cascaded convolutional networks. IEEE Sig. Process. Lett. **23**(10), 1499–1503 (2016)

Joint Collaborative Representation with Deep Feature for Image-Set Face Recognition

Hui Li[1] and Meng Yang[1,2(✉)]

[1] College of Computer Science and Software Engineering,
Shenzhen University, Shenzhen, China
lihui2016@email.szu.edu.cn, yang.meng@szu.edu.cn
[2] School of Data and Computer Science,
Sun Yat-sen University, Guangzhou, China

Abstract. With the progress and development of mobile camera and video surveillance, it becomes more efficiently to collect multiple face images for each query. Face recognition based on image set has attracted more and more attention in the community of computer vision and the application of biometrics. In this paper, instead of using handcraft features, we proposed to utilize the deep feature (e.g., convolutional neural network feature) in the application of image-set face recognition. In order to fully explore the discrimination of original query samples and the query virtual nearest point, we proposed a novel joint collaborative representation with a newly designed class-level similarity constraint on the coding coefficients. An alternative solving algorithm is proposed to solve the proposed model. Two experiments were conducted on the YouTube Face database and a new image-set database established based on Labeled Faced in the Wild (LFW). The result of experiments show that our approach has more advantages than previous image-set face recognition approaches.

Keywords: Joint collaborative representation · Image-set face recognition · Deep feature

1 Introduction

Face recognition (FR) has been an active research topic in the fields of computer vision and biometrics in recent years [1–3]. In particular, face recognition based on image set is a highly active area. Compared with the traditional face recognition based single query [4], face recognition based on image sets can handle more serious challenging due to that many images exist in the query set. Face recognition based on image sets has a wide range of applications, such as human-computer interaction, video surveillance and other unconstrained application scenarios.

Although face recognition based image sets are expected to give better performance than the single query image based methods due to more information about face provided [5–7] in the image set. It is still a huge challenge to face recognition based on image-set. Because these images are captured in monitor and less controlled/uncontrolled

J. Zhou et al. (Eds.): CCBR 2017, LNCS 10568, pp. 172–182, 2017.
https://doi.org/10.1007/978-3-319-69923-3_19

environments. The temporal relationship between the images of the collection may not necessarily exist. The classification accuracy is still not satisfactory due to these factors.

Generally speaking, image-set face recognition can be categorized as parametric model-based [9–11] or non-parametric sample-based. The parametric method of face recognition is too dependent on the relationship between each frame of the training data, which may be useless when dealing with some disordered image sets or video without temporal information. Furthermore, the parametric model-based methods are difficult to estimate the parameter of the problem. On the one hand, there are many linear subspace-based non-parametric methods, e.g., the Discriminant Canonical Correlations (DCC) [14] and Mutual Subspace Method (MSM) [12], which, however, cannot well handle face recognition with variations. And then the Template Deep Reconstruction Model (TDRM) [22] which can automatically learn the underlying geometric structure was proposed. The TDRM can discover the complex geometric surface on the images.

Recently, the sparse representation of the method has attracted the attention of the researchers in the field of face recognition. The closest distance of the sparse approximated nearest points (SANP) [5] selected from each gallery and query set (one point in each hull) is also proposed for image-set face recognition. The final measurement of SANP is defined as the distance between the two nearest points in the gallery set and the query set. Following SANP, Yang et al. [6] proposed a new method that is regularized nearest points (RNP) to improve previous methods. RNP established each image set as a regularized affine Hull. The two image sets of similarity are measured by the regularized nearest points in this model. Then Wu et al. [7] propose method named the collaboratively regularized nearest points (CRNP) by searching all regularized nearest points in the framework of collaborative representation. Although SANP [5], RNP [6], and CRNP [7] have realized promising performance, there are many representation and undefined variable in SANP. RNP ignored the collaboration and competition between nearest points and other classes. In addition, the previous face feature in image-set FR is not as powerful as deep feature, and representation based methods only use the virtual nearest point in the query set but ignore the original query samples.

In order to solve the previous problems, we proposed a novel model of joint collaborative representation with deep feature (JCR-DF). In JCR-DF, the powerful deep feature is utilized in our methods. More important, we proposed a joint collaborative representation model for image-set FR. The virtual nearest point in the query set and the original query samples are collaboratively represented on the gallery set, with their coefficient class-level similar. The proposed class-level similarity constraint can make joint use of all the information of query set. Experiments are conducted on YouTube Faces database and LFW database to show the advantage of our proposed method.

Our main contributions are summarized as follows three-fold

1. We attempt to find how to effectively combine spare presentation with deep learning in image sets classification tasks. In our method, it is more discriminative to deep convolution feature.

2. We proposed a novel joint collaborative representation model, which can effectively use the virtual nearest points and the original query samples for the recognition.
3. Compared to past frameworks, our framework show more advantages in increasing accuracy based image set of face recognition.

The rest of this paper is illustrated as follows. In Sect. 2 we briefly introduce related work. In Sect. 3 we describe our classifier model. Section 4 conduct experiments to verify our model and Sect. 5 concludes the paper.

2 Brief Review of Related Works

Sparse representation is one of the hotspots in machine learning and computer vision in recent years. Many sparse representation based image-set face recognition are proposed. Among these methods, SANP [5] and CRNP [7] are two representative ones, which are briefly reviewed as follows.

2.1 SANP

According to the previous work where each image set is modeled as an affine hull. Recently, Hu et al. [5] propose an effective way to deal with face recognition based on image sets named spare approximated nearest points (SANP). The method of SANP combine the affine hull representation and spare representation. There are two goals being proposed for SANP. Firstly, SANP minimize the affine-hull regularize distance between two point image sets.

$$F_{v_i, v_j} = \left\| (\mu_i + U_i v_i) - \left(\mu_j + U_j v_j \right) \right\|_F^2 \tag{1}$$

where the sample mean of the k-th class data is μ_k. After Eq. (1) minimized, $\mu_i + U_i v_i$ and $\mu_j + U_j v_j$ are called the nearest points between the i-th and j-th classes. The coding coefficients are v_i and v_j.

In addition, each of the two nearest points should be sparely represented by the original data matrix is the second objective of SANP.

$$G_{v_i, \alpha} + \lambda_1 \|\alpha\|_1 = \left\| (\mu_i + U_i v_i) - X_i \alpha \right\|_F^2 + \lambda_1 \|\alpha\|_1$$
$$Q_{v_i, \beta} + \lambda_1 \|\beta\|_1 = \left\| (\mu_i + U_i v_i) - X_i \beta \right\|_F^2 + \lambda_2 \|\beta\|_1 \tag{2}$$

$\lambda 1$ and $\lambda 2$ are parameters that adjust the sparse effect constraint in Eq. (2). According to the above description, the final module of SANP is

$$\left(\hat{v}_i, \hat{v}_j, \hat{\alpha}, \hat{\beta} \right) = \min_{v_i, v_j, \alpha, \beta} \left(F_{v_i, v_j} + \gamma \left(G_{v_i, \alpha} + Q_{v_j, \beta} \right) + \lambda_1 \|\alpha\|_1 + \lambda_2 \|\beta\|_1 \right) \tag{3}$$

SANP set two parameters λ_1 and λ_2 to adjust the effect of spare constraint. The find classification of SANP is conducted to search which class has the minimal between-set distance.

2.2 CRNP

Collaboratively regularized nearest points (CRNP) [7] is also method based on representation. The shortage that ignores the collaboration and competition of different classes is overcomed in CRNP

$$\min_{\alpha,\beta}\|X\alpha - Y\beta\|_2^2 + \lambda_1\|\alpha\|_2^2 + \lambda_2\|\beta\|_2^2 \, s.t. \sum_k\sum_k \alpha_{i,k} = 1, \sum_k \beta_k = 1 \qquad (4)$$

The method of CRNP performs collaborative representation and compute the coding coefficients of all gallery set simultaneously. The method of CRNP use l_2-norm instead of l_1-normsimilar to the work of CRC (Collaborative Representation for Classification) [17]. CRNP calculated the between-set distance as

$$e_i = \left(\|X_i\|_* + \|Y_i\|_*\right).\|X_i\alpha^i - Y\beta\|_2^2 / \|\alpha^i\|_2^2 \qquad (5)$$

Which considers the class-specific reconstruction error, coding coefficients and the representation ability of each gallery set.

3 Our Classifier Model

In the past years, deep learning has made a great success in face recognition such as face recognition and verification and image classification. Specially, Convolutional neural networks have achieved great advantage on computer vision community. More and more researchers improve neural network by adding more supervision signals to enhance the discrimination of convolutional networks feature learned. Spare representation, as one of the hotspots in machine learning and computer vision, is an effective representation-based classifiers, which has shown promising results in face recognition based on image set. Motivated by the success of spare representation and deep convolution features in face recognition, we integrate deep feature and sparse representation based classification for image-set face recognition.

3.1 Deep Feature Extraction for Image Set

For image set, we simply extract the deep CNN feature for each image in the image set. We use CAISA database to train convolutional neural networks [13] under the framework of caffe. All faces in the picture have been cropped and aligned. Then these image will be resized to 112×96. We put all data labeled into network for training. We stop training until the network converges well enough. After the training network complete, we can get the model of caffe to extract deep CNN feature on YouTube Faces and LFW database. In the following sections of our paper, we denote the deep feature of the query set and the deep feature of the gallery set by Y and X, respectively, where $X = [X_1, X_2,..., X_c]$, $Y = [y_1, y_2, ..., y_N]$.

3.2 Joint Collaborative Representation

Conventional sparse representation based image-set face recognition, e.g., SANP [5], RNP [6], CRNP [7], and JRNP [4], only measure the distance of the virtual nearest point in the query set to the gallery set, while ignore the direct utility of original query samples, which also contains much discrimination. In order to fully use the discrimination of all query samples, we proposed a novel joint collaborative representation model for image-set face recognition:

$$
\min_{\alpha,\beta} \left\{ \begin{array}{l} \|Y\beta - X\alpha\|_2^2 + \lambda_1\|\alpha\|_2^2 + \lambda_2\|\beta\|_2^2 + \gamma\|P(\alpha - \alpha_m)\|_2^2 \\ + \sum_{j=1}^{N} \left\{ \|y_j - X\alpha_j\|_2^2 + \lambda_1\|\alpha_j\|_2^2 + \gamma\|P(\alpha_j - \alpha_m)\|_2^2 \right\} \end{array} \right\} \quad \text{s.t.} \ \sum_k \beta_k = 1, \ \alpha \geq 0, \ \alpha_j \geq 0
$$

$$(6)$$

where the constraint of $\sum_k \beta_k = 1$ is to avoid the trivial solution, and the regularization of $\alpha > 0$ and $\alpha_j > 0$ is to make the representation more meaningful is a predefined matrix, which compute the class-level coefficients. For instance, if there are two gallery set with 3 gallery sample per subject, then P is defined as [1 1 1 0 0 0; 1 1 1 0 0 0]. It can be observed that $P\alpha > 0$ generate the sum of coefficients associated to different gallery subjects.

This model contains three parts: the virtual nearest point representation, the real sample representation, and the class-level joint representation. The term $\|Y\beta - X\alpha\|_2^2$ refers to the representation of the query virtual nearest point on the gallery set. The term $\sum_{j=1}^{N} \left\{ \|y_j - X\alpha_j\|_2^2 \right\}$ is used to indicate the real sample representation. The term $\|P(\alpha - \alpha_m)\|_2^2$ and $\|P(\alpha_j - \alpha_m)\|_2^2$ refer to the class-level joint representation.

3.3 Optimization of Joint Collaborative Representation

By relaxing the constraint, the proposed model can changes to

$$
\min_{\alpha,\beta} \left\{ \begin{array}{l} \|Y\beta - X\alpha\|_2^2 + \lambda_1\|\alpha\|_2^2 + \lambda_2\|\beta\|_2^2 + \gamma\|P(\alpha - \alpha_m)\|_2^2 + \eta\|1 - 1^T\beta\|_2^2 \\ + \sum_{j=1}^{N} \left\{ \|y_j - X\alpha_j\|_2^2 + \lambda_1\|\alpha_j\|_2^2 + \gamma\|P(\alpha_j - \alpha_m)\|_2^2 \right\} \end{array} \right\} \quad \text{s.t.} \ \alpha \geq 0, \ \alpha_j \geq 0
$$

$$(7)$$

The proposed model of Eq. (7) can be solved by alternatively updating the coding coefficient α_m, β, α_j and α. The detailed optimization procedure is as follows.

Initialization
We initialize $\beta = 1^T/N$; and then initialize the α and α_j by optimize the following model

$$
\min_{\alpha} \left\{ \begin{array}{l} \|Y\beta - X\alpha\|_2^2 + \lambda_1\|\alpha\|_2^2 \\ + \sum_{j=1}^{N} \left\{ \|y_j - X\alpha_j\|_2^2 + \lambda_1\|\alpha_j\|_2^2 \right\} \end{array} \right\} \quad \text{s.t.} \ \alpha \geq 0, \ \alpha_j \geq 0 \qquad (8)
$$

Alternative updating α_m

$$\min_{\alpha_m}\left\{\gamma\|P(\alpha - \alpha_m)\|_2^2 + \sum_{j=1}^{N}\left\{\gamma\|P(\alpha_j - \alpha_m)\|_2^2\right\}\right\} \quad (9)$$

It has an analytical solution, which is

$$\alpha_m = (1 + N)^{-1}\left(\alpha + \sum_{j=1}^{N}\alpha_j\right). \quad (10)$$

Alternative updating α_j and α.
Let $y = Y\beta$, the proposed model changes to

$$\min_{\alpha,\beta}\left\{\begin{array}{l}\|y - X\alpha\|_2^2 + \lambda_1\|\alpha\|_2^2 + \gamma\|P(\alpha - \alpha_m)\|_2^2 \\ + \sum_{j=1}^{N}\left\{\|y_j - X\alpha_j\|_2^2 + \lambda_1\|\alpha_j\|_2^2 + \gamma\|P(\alpha_j - \alpha_m)\|_2^2\right\}\end{array}\right\} \text{ s.t. } \alpha \geq 0, \ \alpha_j \geq 0 \quad (11)$$

It can see that the optimization of α has a similar procedure to that of α_j in the initialization step and the step of updating α and α_j. Take the optimization of α as an example, the optimization of solving α changes to

$$\min_{\alpha}\|y - X\alpha\|_2^2 + \lambda_1\|\alpha\|_2^2 + \gamma\|P(\alpha - \alpha_m)\|_2^2 \text{ s.t. } \alpha \geq 0 \quad (12)$$

Which can be iteratively solved. Let α^t denote the value of α in the t iteration, then α can be iteratively solved by

$$\begin{array}{l}\alpha^{(t+1/2)} = \alpha^{t-1} - \eta\partial f(\alpha^{t-1})/\partial\alpha^{t-1} \\ \alpha^t = \max(\alpha^{t-1}, 0)\end{array} \quad (13)$$

where $f(\alpha) = \left\{\|Y\beta - X\alpha\|_2^2 + \lambda_1\|\alpha\|_2^2 + \gamma\|P(\alpha - \alpha_m)\|_2^2\right.$.

Alternative updating β
The original joint collaborative representation model changes to

$$\min_{\beta}\|Y\beta - X\alpha\|_2^2 + \lambda_2\|\beta\|_2^2 + \eta\|1 - 1^T\beta\|_2^2 \quad (14)$$

Which can be analytically solved, and the solution is

$$\beta = \left(\begin{bmatrix} Y \\ \sqrt{\eta}1^T \end{bmatrix}^T \begin{bmatrix} Y \\ \sqrt{\eta}1^T \end{bmatrix} + \lambda_2 I\right)^{-1} \begin{bmatrix} Y \\ \sqrt{\eta}1^T \end{bmatrix}^T \begin{bmatrix} X\alpha \\ \sqrt{\eta}1 \end{bmatrix} \quad (15)$$

3.4   Classification of Joint Collaborative Representation

After several alternative updating α, α_j, β and α_m, the optimization of the joint collaborative representation will converge locally since each alternative updating will reduce the objective value of the proposed model. With the solution of the coding coefficient, the class-specific representation error of the query image set to the i-th class gallery set is computed as

$$e_i = \left(\|Y\|_* + \|X_i\|_* \right) \left(\|Y\beta - X_i\alpha^i\|_2^2 \Big/ \|\alpha^i\|_2^2 + \|Y - X_i[\alpha_1^i\ \alpha_2^i\ \cdots\ \alpha_N^i]\|_2^2 \Big/ \|[\alpha_1^i\ \alpha_2^i\ \cdots\ \alpha_N^i]\|_F^2 \right)$$

(16)

The $\|Y\beta - X_i\alpha^i\|_2^2 \big/ \|\alpha^i\|_2^2$ term aims to calculate reconstruction error from a query set and all gallery set. The term $\|Y - X_i[\alpha_1^i\ \alpha_2^i\ \cdots\ \alpha_N^i]\|_2^2 \big/ \|[\alpha_1^i\ \alpha_2^i\ \cdots\ \alpha_N^i]\|_F^2$ aims to calculate error from each sample in query set and all gallery set according to each class of labels. Through these two terms, we minimize the error e_i, and find the class with the minial e_i as the identity of the query set.

4   Experiments

4.1   Experiments Setup

We conduct experiments on benchmark image-set face database to demonstrate the effectiveness of CRNP [7], RNP [6], SANP [7], GJRNP and our own classifier (JCR-DF), furthermore, we use the method of AHISD [18] on Labeled Faced in the Wild (LFW). In our paper, we evaluate our approach on a large database: YouTube Faces and database established by ourselves based on LFW. Since all database are video, we need image to train convolutional neural networks. So we intercepted each frame of the video with a face image. After we obtain these image set, all images were resized to 112×96. It is convenient for training neural networks.

All the experiments are running on Matlab2014. We extract the depth feature on the Linux operating system with the framework of caffe. The dimension of all depth features is set to 512. There are some regularization parameters In JCR-DF. λ_1 and λ_2 in Eq. (7) control the l_2-norm regularization of coding coefficients for α, β and α_j. γ in Eq. (7) is the step of gradient for calculate α and α_j. η in Eq. (13) is constraint about the sum of β. In all the experiments, λ_1, λ_2, γ are all set to 0.001. And we fix $\eta = 0.01$.

4.2   Experiments on YouTube Faces

YouTube Face is a large database that contains nearly 1600 different objects for more than 3000 videos. We select one of the 100 objects, including 200 videos due to Matlab memory of limitations. We set up three kinds of experiments with the frame number 50, 75 and 100 for You Tube Faces. We selected each class set of the first video as the training set, with the remaining image sets belong to the class as testing set. In some special conditions, some pictures don't detect the face so that we don't extract the deep

Fig. 1. Some example frames of YouTube Faces dataset

feature due to the limitations of face detection technology. We chose to remove these frames to avoid the impact of the experimental results. Some example frames with occlusion, pose and expression variations of this dataset are shown in Fig. 1

The experimental results of all competing methods with deep feature and with LBP feature are listed in Table 1. From Table 1, we can observe that the previous methods that don't use deep feature such as CRNP-LBP, RNP-LBP and SANP-LBP, achieve very low recognition rate. SANP-LBP achieve 8% and 10%.The method of CRNP-LBP reach 18%, 19% and 19%. RNP-LBP attain 6%, 8% and 9% when frames are set to 50, 75 and 100. In a word, these methods don't achieve good results due to without deep feature.

Table 1. Identification rates on YouTube Faces database of all competing methods.

Method	50 frame	75 frame	100 frame
RNP [6]	57%	65%	64%
RNP-LBP	6%	8%	9%
CRNP [7]	79%	80%	80%
CRNP-LBP	18%	19%	19%
SANP [5]	75%	76%	76%
SANP-LBP	8%	10%	10%
GJRNP [4]	79%	80%	81%
GJRNP-LBP	19%	20%	20%
JCR-DF	**83%**	**82%**	**82%**

We can find also out the superiority of our method compared to other methods. In particular, compared to RNP, the improvements are 26%, 17% and 18% when frame is 50, 75 and 100. Similarly our method are obviously better than the other methods. CRNP and GJRANP use all gallery image set to collaboratively represent the query set closest point. So these two methods overcome the small scale sample problem, making better performance than RNP. Compared with the previous method, our classifier achieve higher accuracy rate, which is 83% on YouTube Faces.

4.3   Experiments on LFW

We construct the image-set database from LFW by selecting the subjects with more than 10 face images. Then we divide the images of each subject into several image sets, of which each has about 5 face images. The constructed LFW-based image set database contains 865 image sets of 158 different subjects. We select a subset of 100 subjects, including 626 videos to conduct experiment. There are about 15 to 20 image in per class of subject about LFW. The only difference is that the number of pictures in each video is five images. Because LFW database pictures are not as much as YouTube Faces. We choose the first video of each class as the training set, the rest as the test set. Some example frames with expression variations of this dataset are shown in Fig. 2.

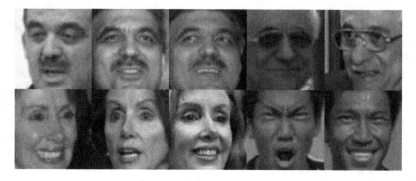

Fig. 2. Some example frames of LFW

Face recognition based on image set is quite difficulty than single sample face recognition due to uncontrolled scenes. However, our method has reached a very high result than other compared methods from above Table 2. This shows that our classification framework, i.e., the joint use of original query sample and the virtual nearest query point, has a better effect. According to the results shown in the table, compared to RNP, SRNP and AHISD, the improvements of our method are 14.07%, 12.99% and 14.45%. We can find our method making better performance in the term of dealing with LFW database established by us.

Table 2. Identification rates on LFW database by using deep convolutional feature

Methods	Deep convolution feature
RNP [6]	71.10%
CRNP [7]	82.88%
GJRNP [4]	82.69%
SANP [5]	70.72%
AHISD [18]	72.81%
JCR-DF	**85.17%**

5 Conclusion

In this paper, we proposed a novel joint collaborative representation model with deep feature for image-set face recognition. The deep feature of face image has much more discrimination than previous handcraft features. And our proposed joint collaborative representation model can more effectively use the original query samples. Two experiments on YouTube Face datasets and LFW datasets are conducted. The experimental results clearly show the advantage of our proposed method.

Acknowledgment. This work is partially supported by the National Natural Science Foundation for Young Scientists of China (no. 61402289), and National Science Foundation of Guang-dong Province (no. 2014A030313558).

References

1. Huang, Z.H., Li, W.J., Shang, J., Wang, J., Zhang, T.: Non-uniform patch based face recognition via 2D-DWT. Image Vis. Comput. **37**(5), 12–19 (2015)
2. Liu, H.D., Yang, M., Gao, Y., Cui, C.Y.: Local histogram specification for face recognition under varying lighting condictions. Image Vis. Comput. **32**(5), 335–347 (2014)
3. Moeini, A., Moeini, H., Faez, K.: Unrestricted pose-invariant face recognition by sparse dictionary matrix. Image Vis. Comput. **36**(4), 9–22 (2015)
4. Yang, M., Liu, W., Shen, L.: Joint regularized nearest points for image set based face recognition. In: IEEE International Conference and Workshops on Automatic Face and Gesture Recognition, pp. 1–7. IEEE (2015)
5. Hu, Y.Q., Mian, A.S., Owens, R.: Face recognition using sparse approximated nearest points between image sets. IEEE Trans. Pattern Anal. Mach. Intell. **34**(10), 1992–2004 (2012)
6. Yang, M., Zhu, P.F., Van Gool, L., Zhang, L.: Face recognition based on regularized nearest points between image sets. In: Proceedings of FG (2013)
7. Wu, Y., Minoh, M., Mukunoki, M.: Collaboratively regularized nearest points, In: Proceedings of BMVC, (2013)
8. Herrmann, C., Willersinn, D., Beyerer, J.: Low-Resolution Convolutional Neural Networks for Video Face Recognition. In: AVSS (2016)
9. Lee, K.C., Ho, J., Yang, M.H., Kriegman, D.: Video-base face recognition using probabilistic appearance manifolds. In: Proceedings of CVPR (2003)
10. Arandjelovic, O., Shakhnarovich, G., Fisher, J., Cipolla, R., Darrel, T.: Face recognition with image sets using manifold density divergence. In: Proceedings of CVPR (2005)
11. Shakhnarovich, G., Fisher, J.W., Darrell, T.: Face recognition from long-term observations. In: Heyden, A., Sparr, G., Nielsen, M., Johansen, P. (eds.) ECCV 2002. LNCS, vol. 2352, pp. 851–865. Springer, Heidelberg (2002). doi:10.1007/3-540-47977-5_56
12. Yamaguchi, O., Fukui, K., Maeda, K.-i.: Face recognition using temporal image sequence. In: Proceedings of FG (1998)
13. Wen, Y., Zhang, K., Li, Z., Qiao, Y.: A discriminative feature learning approach for deep face recognition. In: Leibe, B., Matas, J., Sebe, N., Welling, M. (eds.) ECCV 2016. LNCS, vol. 9911, pp. 499–515. Springer, Cham (2016). doi:10.1007/978-3-319-46478-7_31
14. Kim, T.K., Arandjelovic, O., Cipolla, R.: Discriminative learning and recognition of image set classes using canonical correlations. IEEE Trans. Pattern Anal. Mach. Intell. **29**(6), 1005–1018 (2007)

182 H. Li and M. Yang

15. Wright, J., Yang, A.Y., Ganesh, A., Sastry, S.S., Ma, Y.: Robust face recognition via sparse representation. IEEE Trans. Pattern Anal. Mach. Intell. **31**(2), 21–227 (2009)
16. Shah, S.A.A., Bennamoun, M., Boussaid, F.: Iterative deep learning for image set based face and object recognition. Neurocomputing **174**, 866–874 (2016)
17. Zhang, L., Yang, M., Feng, X.C.: Sparse representation or collaborative representation: which helps face recognition? In: Proceedings of ICCV (2011)
18. Cevikalp, H., Triggs, B.: Face recognition based on image sets. In: Proceedings of CVPR (2010)
19. Fumin, S., Chunhua, S., Zhou, X., Yang, Y., Shen, H.T.: Face image classification by pooling raw features. Pattern Recogn. **54**(6), 94–103 (2016)
20. Shen, F., Shen, C., van den Hengel, A., Tang, Z.: Approximate least trimmed sum of squares fitting and applications in image analysis. IEEE Trans. Image Process. **22**(5), 1836–1847 (2013)
21. Shen, F., Yang, Y., Zhou, X., Liu, X., Shao, J.: Face identification with second-order pooling in single-layer networks. Neurocomputing **187**, 11–18 (2016)
22. Hayat, M., Bennamoun, M., An, S.: Deep reconstruction models for image set classification. IEEE Trans. Pattern Anal. Mach. Intell. **37**(4), 713–727 (2015)

Multi-task Deep Face Recognition

Jirui Yuan[1($\boxtimes$)], Wenya Ma[2], Pengfei Zhu[2], and Karen Egiazarian[1]

[1] Tampere University of Technology, Tampere, Finland
`jirui.yuan@student.tut.fi, karen.egiazarian@tut.fi`
[2] School of Computer Science and Technology, Tianjin University, Tianjin, China
`{wyma,zhupengfei}@tju.edu.cn`

Abstract. In recent years, deep learning has become one of the most representative and effective techniques in face recognition. Due to the high expense of labelling data, it is costly to collect a large-scale face dataset with accurate label information. For the tasks without sufficient data, deep models cannot be well trained. Generally, parameters of deep models are usually initialized with a pre-trained model, and then fine-tuned on a small dataset of specific task. However, by straightforward fine-tuning, the final model usually does not generalize well. In this paper, we propose a multi-task deep learning (MTDL) method for face recognition. The superiority of the proposed multi-task method is demonstrated by experiments on LFW and CCFD.

Keywords: Deep learning · Multi-task · Face recognition · Convolution neural network

1 Introduction

Deep learning has achieved great performances in face recognition because it can capture the face variations by learning hierarchical high-level representation. The recognition accuracy has exceeded 99.00% on the challenging benchmark LFW [1] dataset such as DeepID3 [2] achieves 99.53% and FaceNet [3] achieves 99.63%. A few latest results that break the record have been continuously reported recently. Deep convolutional neural network has become the most representative and effective technology for face recognition in the wild.

In many computer vision tasks, we only have a dataset with small sample size. Whereas, a deep learning model cannot be well trained without sufficient training data because of parameters explosion in deep neural networks. One possible solution is to train a model directly on the dataset with small sample size. This approach is simple enough but it is difficult for the model to obtain a satisfactory result. The better solution is to utilize the large-scale dataset to train a deep model, and the model can handle a specific task called task A. We can utilize the pre-trained model to fulfil task B which is a task related with task A by fine-tuning. Fine-tuning methods can utilize the relationship between the two datasets, but sometimes they can not avoid overfitting.

© Springer International Publishing AG 2017
J. Zhou et al. (Eds.): CCBR 2017, LNCS 10568, pp. 183–190, 2017.
https://doi.org/10.1007/978-3-319-69923-3_20

Multi-task Learning (MTL) is an inductive transfer mechanism whose principle goal is to improve generalization performance. Generally, it jointly learns the parameters of multiple related tasks simultaneously by pursuing a shared presentation [4]. MTL works because it effectively increases the sample size by implicit data augmentation [5]. Additionally, by learning common representation for multiple tasks, the effect of noise in each task can be compressed. By capturing the similarity among different tasks, MTL can also avoid over-fitting on a specific task to some extent. MTL has already been used in multiple tasks including face recognition network DeepId2 [6], object detection network Faster R-CNN [7], fine-grained vehicle classification network [8], facial landmarks detection and attributes classification network TCDCN [5].

Motivated by multi-task learning, we propose a multi-task deep learning method for face recognition by using multiple face datasets. We consider learning on multiple datasets as a multi-task learning problem. First, we pre-train a model on a large-scale dataset and consider it as an initial task. Then for other specific tasks, we initialize parameters with the pre-trained model, and then fine-tune on the multiple datasets that consist of the large-scale dataset and the limited dataset of the specific tasks. The hidden layers are shared by all datasets while task-specific output layers are leaned for each dataset. This method makes full use of both the large-scale dataset with small sample size. In this way, the final model can get better performance than straightforward fine-tuning. Furthermore, the accuracy on the initial task can be maintained. Meanwhile, the pre-trained model can be migrated conveniently to other tasks with limited data and reduce time consumption of model training. Experiments on LFW and CCFD validate the effectiveness of the proposed multi-task deep learning model for face recognition.

The rest of this paper is organized as follows: Sect. 2 presents the multi-task deep learning framework. Section 3 introduces multi-task deep face recognition with different face datasets. Section 4 conducts experiments. Section 5 comes to the conclusion.

2   Multi-task Learning Model

In this section, we introduce the multi-task deep learning model.

2.1   Task Loss

Figure 1 shows the structure of the multi-task deep learning method. For face recognition, we train a deep model by using multiple face datasets. Here, each dataset is considered as an individual task. Assume that there are two datasets, i.e., one large-scale dataset and one limited dataset with small sample size. An accurate model can be pre-trained on the large-scale dataset. To utilize the relation between two datasets and avoid overfitting, both datasets are combined as the input layer and share the common representation, i.e., the hidden layers. Finally the data are split and dataset-specific fully connected layers are designed.

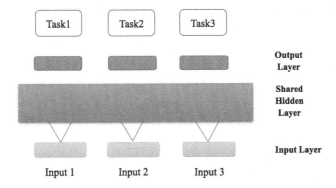

Fig. 1. Deep network for multi-task deep learning. Different inputs mean the different tasks of data. Task 1, Task 2 and Task 3 represent the loss function for each task. The proposed multi-task deep learning model learns shared hidden layers while tasks-specific output layers.

Assume that there are two related tasks that they are all classification tasks. Task A has C_A series and task B has C_B series. In Caffe [9], for each mini-batch, the loss function of task A is:

$$L_A = \frac{-1}{N_A} \sum_{n=1}^{N_A} \log(\hat{p}_{nl_n}), \quad l_n \in [0, 1, \ldots, C_A - 1], \tag{1}$$

where N_A is the images number in one mini-batch and $\hat{p}_{nl_n} = \frac{e^{x_n l_n}}{\sum_{c=0}^{C_A-1} e^{x_n c}}$.
Thus, the loss of two tasks is given as follow:

$$L_A = \frac{-1}{N_A} \sum_{n=1}^{N_A} \log(\frac{e^{x_n l_n}}{\sum_{c=0}^{C_A-1} e^{x_n c}}), \quad l_n \in [0, 1, \ldots, C_A - 1], \tag{2}$$

$$L_B = \frac{-1}{N_B} \sum_{n=1}^{N_B} \log(\frac{e^{x_n l_n}}{\sum_{c=0}^{C_B-1} e^{x_n c}}), \quad l_n \in [0, 1, \ldots, C_B - 1], \tag{3}$$

2.2 Back Propagation

As shown in Fig. 1, each task calculates its own loss. Whereas, during back propagation, all gradients will be added to update the parameters of the deep model. When learning a task, multi-task deep learning method can obtain the knowledge of other tasks with shared representation. Multiple tasks in parallel training share features learned from other different tasks, which is the main idea of multi-task learning. By adding all gradients to execute the back propagation, it makes sure that parameters in the deep convolutional neural network update with the right trend for model training of different tasks.

3   Multi-task Deep Learning for Face Recognition

In this section, we firstly introduce the basis of multi-task deep learning method based on multiple datasets and then introduce how to utilize multi-task deep learning method to train models. Figure 2 shows the overview of our approach.

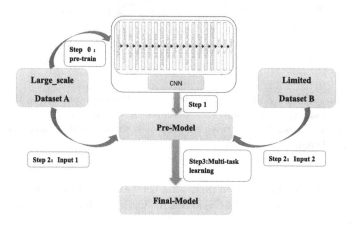

Fig. 2. Overview of our approach.

3.1   Pre-train Model

Our approach is based on fine-tuning method. In our approach, there is a large-scale dataset called D_A corresponding to task T_A. Firstly, we need find or construct a deep convolution neural network to train a deep model for T_A with D_A. This model has excellent accuracy on the T_A and then it will be used as pre-trained model to fine-tune with multiple dataset in the next steps. The model is the basis of our approach.

3.2   Multi-task Deep Learning for Multiple Datasets

In our approach, after pre-trained model was generated, it is time to carry on multi-task deep learning for multiple datasets. First, there are two datasets D_A for task T_A, D_B for task T_B. We need unit them as the input data used for model training. We unit multiple data in axis n as shown in Fig. 3. Then the combined data is used to train our convolution neural network. Note that we don not unit labels of multiple datasets.

The united data is splitted before classification. Here, data is splitted after the penultimate full connected layer. Generally, the penultimate fully connected layer carry on feature representation and the last fully connected layer do the classification work. Then every task calculate their own loss. The structure of

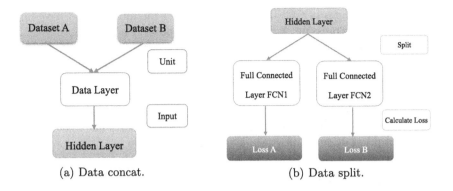

(a) Data concat.   (b) Data split.

Fig. 3. Data concat and data split in our approach.

data split is shown in Fig. 3. In order to be consistent, data split at the axis of n. We only operate on the sample space and their labels is fixed.

In our approach, multiple tasks should be relevant. Multiple tasks share the convolution layers and some fully connected layers including feature representation layer in our next experiments. But in other real-world tasks, maybe we can only share convolution layers while learning task-specific fully-connected layers like deep relationship networks [10].

4   Experiments

In this section, we evaluate our approach on the real-world datasets. We conduct experiments to examine the multi-task deep learning method when we have a large-scale face dataset and a limited dataset. In our experiments, we use MS dataset to train a model and then utilize MS dataset and CCFD dataset for multi-task learning. In next subsections, we introduce datasets, settings and conclusions of our experiments.

4.1   Datasets

We investigate our approach on three datasets: MS dataset, CCFD dataset and LFW dataset.

MS: MS dataset is a subset of large-scale noisy dataset of real-world called MS-Celeb-1M [11]. After artificially marked, MS dataset is clean enough. MS dataset has 3,095,536 real-world facial images of 41,857 identities. It is a large-scale dataset that contains large variations in age, pose and so on.

CCFD: CCFD (Chinese Celebrity Face Dataset) is a large-scale real-world face dataset collected by VIPL. This dataset consists of 263,696 images of 1,001 subjects, with two subsets for training and testing. The training set contains 171,792 images of 701 subjects and the testing set contains 91,904 images of 301 subjects. Facial images in CCFD are collected from the internet and have large variations in age, expression, light, occlusion and pose.

In our approach, in order to ensure the consistency of the experiments, all the face images are normalized to 256 × 256 and five facial points are aligned. In addition, for face recognition, the detection tasks of European & American and Chinese are two different tasks because of the difference between human race. The faces in MS dataset are almost from European and American, and the identities in CCFD dataset are all Chinese. The two datasets meet the demand of our assumption of our multi-task deep learning method.

4.2   CNN and Settings

In our experiments, we use Resnet-VIPL as convolution neural network to train deep model. Resnet-VIPL evolves from Resnet [12] and it consists of 82 convolutional layers and 2 fully connected layers. It has less calculations compared to Resnet-101 but also has a satisfactory accuracy in experiments.

The platform of our experiments is Caffe. SGD is utilized to train the Resnet-VIPL. In all the experiments, we set The learning rate is decreased according to the polynomial policy with *gamma* value equals to 0.5. The base learning rate of direct learning is 0.05 and the base learning rate of multi-task deep learning method while fine-tuning is 0.008. In addition, the dimension of face features is 1,024. The input ratio for each batch among different datasets is the same.

4.3   Results and Analysis

In this section, we will introduce the testing protocols then show and analysis results in our experiments.

The testing set of CCFD contains 91,904 images of 301 subjects and then it was divided into two parts named Target set and Query set. We chose 50% images from every identity in CCFD testing set randomly as Query set and the rest images are as Target set. We evaluate accuracy according to similarity matrix Sim, where $Sim(i, j)$ represents the similarity of the i-th image in Query set and the j-th image in Target set. By calculating verification rate under different false acceptance rates, we can judge the performance of a model. In our experiments, the accuracy of CCFD testing rate is the verification rate when false acceptance rate equals to 0.1%.

Table 1. The accuracy on LFW.

Deep method	Dataset of pre-train	Learning method	Accuracy
Resnet-VIPL	MS	None	**99.23%**
Resnet-VIPL	MS	Fine-tune	98.38%
Resnet-VIPL	MS	Multi-task	**99.13%**

Table 2. The accuracy on CCFD.

Deep method	Dataset of pre-train	Learning method	Accuracy
Resnet-VIPL	MS	None	64.28%
Resnet-VIPL	MS	Fine-tune	69.46%
Resnet-VIPL	MS	Multi-task	**71.88%**

Table 1 shows that the pre-trained model has the best performance than straightforward fine-tuning and multi-task learning. From the results, it is obvious that the learning method with straightforward fine-tuning drops a lot in the accuracy of LFW. At the same time, the accuracy drops a little with the multi-task method. It shows that multi-task deep learning method has a better performance than straightforward fine-tuning. Table 2 shows the accuracy on CCFD of pre-trained model with different learning methods. We can find that multi-task deep learning gets the best performance. Although with fine-tuning method the accuracy on CCFD improves 5.18% compared to pre-trained model, multi-task deep learning method improves 7.6%. The results show the advantages of multi-task deep learning method on both tasks.

Table 3. The accuracy on LFW and CCFD with different learning methods compared to the pre-trained model.

Deep method	Learning method	Accuracy on LFW	Accuracy on CCFD
Resnet-VIPL	None	-	-
Resnet-VIPL	Fine-tune	−0.85%	+5.18%
Resnet-VIPL	Multi-task	**−0.10%**	**+7.60%**

According to the comparison in Table 3, it is obvious that multi-task deep learning method has the best performance on both tasks. First, the accuracy of fine-tuning directly is less than the accuracy of multi-task deep learning method on LFW and CCFD test datasets. Second, although the accuracy on LFW of our approach is less than without fine-tuning, the gap is so small and the accuracy on CCFD of approach is much higher than without fine-tuning. In total, experiments prove that our approach is easy to transfer and it achieves the best results compared to methods without fine-tuning and straightforward fine-tuning. By combining multi-task deep learning and fine-tuning method, our method makes full use of minute large-scale dataset that we can obtain and we also can get a satisfactory model works on both tasks in good performance.

5   Conclusions

In this paper, we proposed a MTDL method for face recognition. Datasets with diverse properties are considered as different tasks. MTDL firstly pre-trains a deep model on a large-scale face dataset. Then by combining multiple face datasets as the input of the deep model, MTDL shares the same hidden layers while learns task-specific fully-connected layers for different datasets. Experiments on LFW and CCFD datasets show that MTDL generalizes well on different face databases and achieves better performance than the straightforward fine-tuning strategy.

Acknowledgements. This work was supported by the National Program on Key Basic Research Project under Grant 2013CB329304, the National Natural Science Foundation of China under Grants 61502332, 61432011, 61222210.

References

1. Huang, G.B., Mattar, M., Berg, T., Learned-Miller, E., et al.: Labeled faces in the wild: a database forstudying face recognition in unconstrained environments. In: Workshop on Faces in Real-Life Images: Detection, Alignment, and Recognition (2008)
2. Sun, Y., Liang, D., Wang, X., Tang, X.: Deepid3: face recognition with very deep neural networks. arXiv preprint arXiv:1502.00873 (2015)
3. Schroff, F., Kalenichenko, D., Philbin, J.: Facenet: a unified embedding for face recognition and clustering. In: Computer Vision and Pattern Recognition (CVPR), pp. 815–823 (2015)
4. Caruana, R.: Multitask learning. In: Thrun, S., Pratt, L. (eds.) Learning to Learn, pp. 95–133. Springer, Heidelberg (1998). doi:10.1007/978-1-4615-5529-2_5
5. Zhang, Z., Luo, P., Loy, C.C., Tang, X.: Facial landmark detection by deep multi-task learning. In: Fleet, D., Pajdla, T., Schiele, B., Tuytelaars, T. (eds.) ECCV 2014. LNCS, vol. 8694, pp. 94–108. Springer, Cham (2014). doi:10.1007/978-3-319-10599-4_7
6. Sun, Y., Chen, Y., Wang, X., Tang, X.: Deep learning face representation by joint identification-verification. In: Advances in Neural Information Processing Systems (NIPS), pp. 1988–1996 (2014)
7. Ren, S., He, K., Girshick, R., Sun, J.: Faster R-CNN: towards real-time object detection with region proposal networks. In: Advances in Neural Information Processing Systems, pp. 91–99 (2015)
8. Zhang, X., Zhou, F., Lin, Y., Zhang, S.: Embedding label structures for fine-grained feature representation. In: Proceedings of the IEEE Conference on Computer Vision and Pattern Recognition, pp. 1114–1123 (2016)
9. Jia, Y., Shelhamer, E., Donahue, J., Karayev, S., Long, J., Girshick, R., Guadarrama, S., Darrell, T.: Caffe: convolutional architecture for fast feature embedding. In: Proceedings of the 22nd ACM International Conference on Multimedia, pp. 675–678. ACM (2014)
10. Long, M., Wang, J.: Learning multiple tasks with deep relationship networks. arXiv preprint arXiv:1506.02117 (2015)
11. Guo, Y., Zhang, L., Hu, Y., He, X., Gao, J.: MS-Celeb-1M: A dataset and benchmark for large scale face recognition. In: European Conference on Computer Vision, Springer (2016)
12. He, K., Zhang, X., Ren, S., Sun, J.: Deep residual learning for image recognition. arXiv preprint arXiv:1512.03385 (2015)

Enhancing 3D Facial Expression Recognition by Exaggerating Geometry Characteristics

Weijian Li[1], Yunhong Wang[1], Huibin Li[2], and Di Huang[1(✉)]

[1] IRIP Lab, School of Computer Science and Engineering,
Beihang University, Beijing 100191, China
{liweijian,yhwang,dhuang}@buaa.edu.cn
[2] School of Mathematics and Statistics, Xi'an Jiaotong University,
Xi'an 710049, China
huibinli@mail.xjtu.edu.cn

Abstract. This paper studies exaggerated facial shapes in addition to original facial shapes to assist 3D Facial Expression Recognition (FER). We propose a Poisson equation based approach to exaggerate facial shape characteristics to highlight expression clues that are latent in original facial surfaces but useful for recognizing expressions. To validate this idea, we exploit two off-the-shelf descriptors that reach state of the art performance in 3D FER, namely Geometric Scattering Representation (GSR) and Multi-Scale Local Normal Patterns (MS-LNPs) for expression-related feature extraction, and adopt early fusion to combine the credits of the original surface and the enhanced one, followed by the SVMs and Multiple Kernel Learning (MKL) classifiers. The accuracy gain of two features achieved on BU-3DFE is 0.8% and 1.3% respectively. Such results show that the exaggerated faces are complementary to the original faces in discriminating different facial expressions in the 3D domain.

Keywords: Facial Expression Recognition · 3D facial expression exaggeration · Feature fusion

1 Introduction

In daily life, we communicate emotions with each other not only through language, but also by facial expressions, and the latter has become one of the most natural and prominent approaches. In computer vision and human-machine interaction, it has always been an ideal objective to facilitate artificial intelligence techniques in understanding human facial expressions. Until now, FER has involved in many applications, including psychology, games, children education, etc.

During the past few decades, the researchers have focused on 2D FER and put forward various effective methods. However, due to illumination and head pose changes, FER remains a rather challenging and unsolved problem. In recent years, with the technique innovation of high resolution 3D imaging equipments,

© Springer International Publishing AG 2017
J. Zhou et al. (Eds.): CCBR 2017, LNCS 10568, pp. 191–200, 2017.
https://doi.org/10.1007/978-3-319-69923-3_21

3D FER has been greatly developed. Theoretically, 3D data provide accurate geometric information that is more directly related to facial expressions, and they are also reputed to possess invariance to lighting variations and simplicity in pose correction.

Existing studies on 3D FER can be roughly divided into two categories: model-based methods and feature-based methods. Model-based methods usually adopt some optimization algorithms to fit the 3D face template to a test sample, and use the parameters obtained to predict its expression label. For example, in [1], an elastically deformable model approach was used to establish the correspondence for a set of faces, and bilinear models were constructed and fitted to a probe face. Finally, maximum-likelihood was used for expression classification. Gong et al. [2] proposed Expressional Shape Component (ESC) and basic Facial Shape Component (BFSC) to describe facial expressions, BFSC represents the facial structure information and shape while ESC contains variations of shape caused by facial expressions, then an SVM classifier was adopted to predict the expression label. Zhao et al. [3] introduced Statistical Facial Feature Model (SFAM) for automatically landmarking, and shape and texture features were then extracted from the face regions around 19 points for 3D FER. Zhen et al. [4,5] proposed Muscular Movement Model (MMM), which utilized vertex-to-vertex correspondence to segment input 3D face scans into several pre-defined areas, and the decision was made by SVM on a set of fundamental geometry features.

Feature-based approaches concentrate on extracting expression sensitive features from facial regions centered at fiducial landmarks. [6,7] proposed to adopt landmark distances to discriminate 3D FER. [8] introduced the Local Shape Analysis (LSA) based FER which represented the regions or patches from facial surfaces by making use of sets of closed curves; then a Riemannian framework was used to extract features. [9] proposed to adopt an Annotated Face Model (AFM) to fit a 3D face scan and Normal Map and Curvature Map were then computed, projection pursuit techniques were finally adopted to select features. [10,11] proposed to adopt the Histogram of Oriented Gradients (HOG) algorithm to extract features of Differential Mean Curvature Maps (DMCMs) of a 3D face. SIFT was adopted in [12] to extract features of depth images according to a set of facial landmarks. MS-LNPs proposed in [13] can be seen as the extension and application on 3D FER of the well-known LBP operator. Geometric Scattering Representation (GSR) introduced in [14,15] was adopted to extract features of Normal Map and Shape Index Map. [16] proposed Graph Laplacian Features (GLF) which was calculated on the decomposition of the geometry in the spatial frequency components relevant to natural characteristics of the surface.

Nowadays, although most of the 3D FER approaches differ in the manner of extracting facial features, they still start from original faces. In this case, some expressions are too subtle to recognize. To the best of our knowledge, few attempts study the preprocessing step of 3D face data. In fact, as stated in [17], humans tend to better recognize exaggerated faces than regular ones, and [18] claims that an exaggerated and caricatured face could be more recognizable than a normal image.

Inspired by the facts above, in this paper, we aim to take the advantage of exaggerated facial features and regard the 3D face as two components, i.e. the original surface and the exaggerated one to enhance 3D FER. Specifically, we firstly employ the Poisson equation based exaggeration method to highlight facial expressions. Subsequently, we extract features from the original faces and their exaggerated ones. Furthermore, we adopt an early fusion scheme to combine the credits of the two components.

To evaluate the proposed method, we conduct experiments on the BU-3DFE database [19]. Two off-the-shelf approaches that reach state of the art performance in 3D FER are investigated, where Geometric Scattering Representation (GSR) [14] and Multi-Scale Local Normal Patterns (MS-LNPs) [13] are used for expression-related feature extraction respectively, and SVMs are exploited for decision making. The accuracies of the GSR and MS-LNP method are improved by 0.8% and 1.3% on BU-3DFE, and those scores indicate that the exaggerated faces are effective in complementing the original faces in discriminating 3D facial expressions.

2   The Proposed Method

Since the key idea of the proposed method is to verify the effectiveness of facial expression exaggeration for 3D FER, we first give a detailed introduction on the exaggeration method, then shortly list the following feature extraction and classification methods used for label prediction.

2.1   Exaggeration of 3D Face Scans Based on Poisson Equation

In [20], the gradient-based surface deformation algorithm can deform the shape of a given surface S locally and arbitrarily by changing its gradient field according to the following poisson equation:

$$\Delta f = \mathbf{div} w \quad s.t. \quad f|_{\partial \Omega} = f^*|_{\partial \Omega} \tag{1}$$

where f is the coordinate-functions of the deformed surface $\tilde{S}$, f^* is the Dirichlet boundary function, $\partial \Omega$ denotes the boundary of S, and $w = (w_x, w_y, w_z)$ denotes the gradient vector field of S. $\Delta = \frac{\partial^2}{\partial x^2} + \frac{\partial^2}{\partial y^2} + \frac{\partial^2}{\partial z^2}$ is the Laplacian operator. $\mathbf{div} w = \frac{\partial w_x}{\partial x} + \frac{\partial w_y}{\partial y} + \frac{\partial w_z}{\partial z}$ is divergence of the w. As a common formula in differential geometry, Eq. (1) means that the Laplacian operator of the deformed surface $\tilde{S}$ equals to the divergence of the vector field of the original surface S. Now assume that S is a discrete triangle mesh surface with n vertexes, then its Laplacian operator can be described as:

$$\Delta f = \begin{bmatrix} w_{11} & \cdots & w_{1n} \\ \vdots & \ddots & \vdots \\ w_{n1} & \cdots & w_{nn} \end{bmatrix} \cdot \begin{bmatrix} p_1 \\ \vdots \\ p_n \end{bmatrix} \tag{2}$$

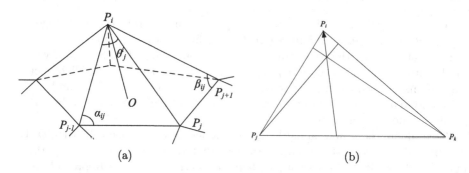

Fig. 1. Illustration of the Laplacian and gradient operators defined on a triangle mesh.

where $w_{ij} = \sum_{p_j \in N(p_i)}^{N} \frac{1}{2} (\cot \alpha_{ij} + \cot \beta_{ij})$ if $i = j$, and $w_{ij} = -\cot \alpha_{ij} - \cot \beta_{ij}$ if $i \neq j$, as shown in Fig. 1(a). In order to calculate the gradient vector field of a discrete surface, suppose g is a piecewise linear function defined on the triangle mesh as follows,

$$\nabla g(p) = g_i \cdot \nabla \varphi_i + g_j \cdot \nabla \varphi_j + g_k \cdot \nabla \varphi_k \tag{3}$$

where $\varphi_i + \varphi_j + \varphi_k = 1$, and $\varphi_i = 1$ at p_i, $\varphi_i = 0$ at p_j and p_k (as shown in Fig. 2-b). Then the gradient can be formulated as:

$$w = \nabla g(p) = (g_j - g_i) \frac{(p_i - p_k)^{\perp}}{2A_{p_i p_j p_k}} + (g_k - g_i) \frac{(p_j - p_i)^{\perp}}{2A_{p_i p_j p_k}} \tag{4}$$

where $\perp$ stands for the counterclockwise 90 rotation operator, and $A_{p_i p_j p_k}$ denotes the area of $\triangle p_i p_j p_k$. Therefore for an arbitrary point on the face, we have:

$$\mathbf{div} w(p_i) = \sum_{T_k \in N(p_i)} \nabla g_{ik} \cdot w \cdot A_k \tag{5}$$

where T_k denotes the triangles within one-ring of point p_i and A_k denotes the area of T_k.

According to the above equations, we can deform a triangle-meshed 3D face scan by changing its gradient field ∇g_{ik}. In particular, Sela et al. [21] propose to deform a discrete surface by scaling the given gradient field based on the above Poisson equation. The scale can be controlled by $|K|$, which is the simplest isometry invariant differential quantity, making the deformation invariant to pose and gesture variations. In this paper, we use the following Gauss-Bonnet formula [22] to calculate the Gaussian curvature. That is,

$$K(p_i) = \frac{1}{A_i} \left(2\pi - \sum_{j \in N(i)} \theta_j^i \right) \tag{6}$$

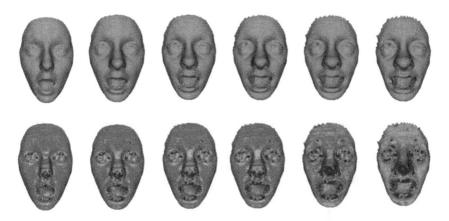

Fig. 2. Illustration of exaggerated face scans of a surprise expression (the most left one) with different γ values (from left to right 0.1, 0.15, 0.2, 0.25, 0.3). The bottom row shows the absolute Gaussian curvatures of the face scans of the first row, where green color denotes smaller values and red for larger ones. (Color figure online)

where A_i is Voronoi area of the vertex p_i, and θ_j^i are the incident angles of p_i. Then the final Poisson equation can be adjusted as:

$$\Delta f\left(\tilde{S}\right) = \mathbf{div}\left(\left|K\left(p\right)\right|^{\gamma} \bigtriangledown g\left(S\right)\right) \tag{7}$$

where the parameter $\gamma \in [0, 1]$ is used to control the degree of facial surface deformation (i.e., exaggeration). A sequence of exaggerated 3D faces with different γ for a given 3D face scan with the surprise expression are shown in Fig. 3. We can see that the degree of expression exaggeration increases for larger γ. However, severe exaggeration with a large γ probably damages the expression-related surface structures and is not useful in FER.

2.2 Facial Expression Feature Extraction and Classification

To verify the effectiveness of facial surface exaggeration for 3D FER, we employ two kinds of state-of-the-art 3D geometric expression features, namely Geometric Scattering Representation (GSR) [14] and Multi-Scale Local Normal Patterns (MS-LNPs) [13] as shown in Fig. 4. GSR extracts the scattering transform information from both Normal Map (NOM) and Shape Index Map (SIM), as shown in Fig. 3. NOM is regarded as the 1st-order differential geometry quantity, which captures the shape information along with x, y, and z directions. SIM, which is quantized by two principal curvatures, is considered as the 2nd-order differential geometry quantity, capturing the local shape bending information of a surface. Compared to SIFT [12] and HOG [10], GSR transform highlights the high frequency information, corresponding to facial deformations caused by expression changes. As in [14], GSR with M = 2 is used on geometric maps including NOMx,

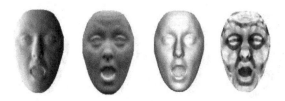

Fig. 3. Illustration of geometric maps of a 3D face scan (from left to right: NOMx, NOMy, NOMz, and SIM).

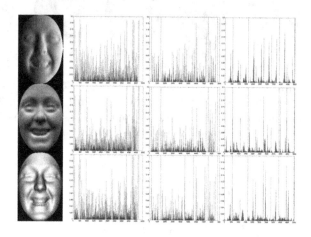

Fig. 4. Images of NOMx, NOMy, NOMz and their features extracted from three scales: Q1,8, Q2,16 and Q3,24 (columns from left to right).

NOMy, NOMz, and SIM generated from both original and the exaggerated 3D face scans. Similarly, the same parameters of MS-LNPs in [13] are used.

When used for 3D FER, we find that the Poisson equation based facial expression exaggeration is a global procedure, which means that it cannot partially exaggerate facial geometry characteristics. To keep the expression related information of the original 3D face scan, we propose to use a feature level fusion scheme to combine the expression features extracted from both the original and exaggerated 3D face, i.e., concatenating the feature vectors.

For expression classification, the multi-class SVM with sum rule based score level fusion (as in [14]) is adopted for different kinds of geometric maps. For MS-LNPs, we make use of the Multiple Kernel Learning (MKL) classifier as in [13] to combine the contributions of different encoding scales and various normal components for final expression prediction.

3   Experimental Results

To evaluate the proposed method, we carry out extensive experiments on the BU-3DFE database. We describe the database, protocol, and results in the following.

3.1   Database

The BU-3DFE dataset [19] is one of the most popular benchmarks for validating 3D FER methods. It totally contains 2500 3D faces, 100 persons (56 females and 44 males). For each subject, there are 24 expressive samples (4 intensities of 6 expressions: anger (AN), disgust (DI), fear (FE), happiness (HA), sadness (SA), and surprise (SU)) as well as a neutral one.

3.2   Protocol

The parameter γ significantly influences the exaggeration extent as shown in Fig. 3, and we tune its value by cross-validation NOMx, NOMy, NOMz, and SIM with the size of 160×120 pixels are calculated from an input face scan. M is set to 2 for each map and SVMs are adopted in GSR, while local patch sizes of 8×8, 20×16 and 40×32, and SimpleMKL with the Chi-square distance [13] are applied in MS-LNPs.

For fair comparison, we conduct 3D FER experiments following the common experimental protocol. Fixed 60 persons are selected during the whole experiment, while the two highest intensities of each expression are employed classification. 10-fold cross-validation is used for training and testing. As a result, 60 persons are divided into 10 subsets. In one turn, 1 subset (6 persons with 72 faces) is selected as the test set and 9 subsets (54 persons with 648 faces) are selected as the train set. This experiment is repeated 100 rounds to deliver a stable average recognition accuracy.

3.3   Results

The results in Table 1 show that our method has improved the performance in terms of each single attribute map compared to [14]. When $\gamma = 0.2$, the accuracies of NOMx, NOMy, NOMz, and SIM are 1.7%–3.3% better than the ones in [14]. The final average accuracy of our method is 0.8% higher than that in [14]. Such facts indicate the effectiveness of the exaggerated faces in 3D FER. We can see from Table 1, with the increase of γ, the final accuracy improves, and when γ continuously becomes larger than 0.2, the accuracy starts to descend. The main reason probably lies in when exaggeration exceeds certain extent, the face loses intrinsic information. Therefore, an appropriate extent of exaggeration is essential.

Table 2 displays the similar conclusion by using another descriptor MS-LNPs [13]. With the increase of γ, the final accuracy improves, and when $\gamma = 0.2$, the final average accuracy of our method is 1.3% higher than the result in [13].

Table 3 gives the result comparison with the state of the art ones, and our method achieves an average recognition of 85.6% on the BU-3DFE dataset, and our method outperforms the best ones reported in the literature. In addition, the exaggeration step only consumes 0.8 s on a 3D face model.

Table 1. Average expression recognition accuracies of GSR [14] that makes use of the original surfaces (os) combined with exaggerated surface (es) of different extents for each single attribute map and their score-level fusion

Faces	NOMx	NOMy	NOMz	SIM	NOM+SIM
os [14]	76.30%	79.80%	78.20%	78.22%	84.80%
os + es ($\gamma = 0.10$)	78.25%	82.43%	80.03%	80.96%	84.61%
os + es ($\gamma = 0.15$)	79.10%	83.30%	80.48%	80.61%	85.26%
os + es ($\gamma = 0.20$)	**79.64%**	**82.88%**	**80.67%**	**79.98%**	**85.60%**
os + es ($\gamma = 0.25$)	80.29%	82.76%	79.71%	79.08%	84.55%
os + es ($\gamma = 0.30$)	79.39%	83.23%	79.85%	77.87%	84.28%

Table 2. Average expression recognition accuracies of MS-LNPs [13] that makes use of the original surfaces (os) combined with the exaggerated surface (es) of different extents

Face	MS-LNPs
os [13]	80.90%
os + es ($\gamma = 0.10$)	81.81%
os + es ($\gamma = 0.15$)	82.14%
os + es($\gamma = 0.20$)	**82.20%**
os + es ($\gamma = 0.25$)	82.11%
os+ es ($\gamma = 0.30$)	81.22%

Table 3. Comparison between the proposed method and the state-of-the-art ones.

Method	Automatic	Accuracy
2006 Wang et al. [23]	No	61.79%
2007 Soyel et al. [6]	No	67.52%
2008 Tang et al. [7]	No	74.51%
2009 Gong et al. [2]	Yes	76.22%
2011 Li et al. [24]	No	82.01%
2013 Lemaire et al. [10]	Yes	76.61%
2015 Yang et al. [14]	Yes	84.80%
2015 Li et al. [25]	Yes	84.87%
2016 Zhen et al. [4]	Yes	84.50%
Our approach	Yes	**85.60%**

4   Conclusion

This paper proposes to exaggerate 3D faces before recognizing its expressions. The exaggeration method is conducted based on the Poisson equation and early fusion for better discriminating different expressions. Furthermore, we control the degree of exaggeration by adjusting the value of γ, and experiments are carried out to find the optimal effect of the information of the exaggerated faces. Experimental results on BU-3DFE show that our method using GSR outperforms the primary method and the state-of-the-art ones. Meanwhile, our method demonstrates the adaptability on the MS-LNP descriptor in FER. Both the facts illustrate that the exaggerated faces assist original ones in 3D FER by supplementing additional discriminative information.

Acknowledgement. This work is partly supported by the National Natural Science Foundation of China (No. 61673033); the Research Program of State Key Laboratory of Software Development Environment (SKLSDE-2017ZX-07); and Microsoft Research Asia Collaborative Program (FY17-RES-THEME-033).

References

1. Mpiperis, I., Malassiotis, S., Strintzis, M.G.: Bilinear models for 3D face and facial expression recognition. IEEE TIFS **3**(3), 498–511 (2008)
2. Gong, B., Wang, Y., Liu, J., Tang, X.: Automatic facial expression recognition on a single 3D face by exploring shape deformation. In: MM, pp. 569–572. ACM (2009)
3. Zhao, X., Huang, D., Dellandrea, E., Chen, L.: Automatic 3D facial expression recognition based on a Bayesian belief net and a statistical facial feature model. In: ICIP, pp. 3724–3727. IEEE (2010)
4. Zhen, Q., Huang, D., Wang, Y., Chen, L.: Muscular movement model-based automatic 3D/4D facial expression recognition. IEEE TMM **18**(7), 1438–1450 (2016)
5. Zhen, Q., Huang, D., Wang, Y., Chen, L.: Muscular movement model based automatic 3D facial expression recognition. In: He, X., Luo, S., Tao, D., Xu, C., Yang, J., Hasan, M.A. (eds.) MMM 2015. LNCS, vol. 8935, pp. 522–533. Springer, Cham (2015). doi:10.1007/978-3-319-14445-0_45
6. Soyel, H., Demirel, H.: Facial expression recognition using 3D facial feature distances. In: Kamel, M., Campilho, A. (eds.) ICIAR 2007. LNCS, vol. 4633, pp. 831–838. Springer, Heidelberg (2007). doi:10.1007/978-3-540-74260-9_74
7. Tang, H., Huang, T.S.: 3D facial expression recognition based on automatically selected features. In: CVPR Workshops, pp. 1–8. IEEE (2008)
8. Maalej, A., Ben Amor, B., Daoudi, M., Srivastava, A., Berretti, S.: Local 3D shape analysis for facial expression recognition. In: CVPR, pp. 4129–4132. IEEE (2010)
9. Ocegueda, O., Fang, T., Shah, S.K., Kakadiaris, I.A.: Expressive maps for 3D facial expression recognition. In: ICCV Workshops, pp. 1270–1275. IEEE (2011)
10. Lemaire, P., Ben Amor, B., Ardabilian, M., Chen, L., Daoudi, M.: Fully automatic 3D facial expression recognition using a region-based approach. In: ACM Workshop on HGB, pp. 53–58. ACM (2011)
11. Li, H., Ding, H., Huang, D., Wang, Y., Zhao, X., Morvan, J.M., Chen, L.: An efficient multimodal 2D + 3D feature-based approach to automatic facial expression recognition. In: CVIU, vol. 140, no. SCIA, pp. 83–92 (2015)
12. Berretti, S., Del Bimbo, A., Pala, P., Ben Amor, B., Daoudi, M.: A set of selected sift features for 3D facial expression recognition. In: ICPR, pp. 4125–4128. IEEE (2010)

13. Li, H., Chen, L., Huang, D., Wang, Y., Morvan, J.M.: 3D facial expression recognition via multiple kernel learning of multi-scale local normal patterns. In: ICPR, pp. 2577–2580. IEEE (2012)
14. Yang, X., Huang, D., Wang, Y., Chen, L.: Automatic 3D facial expression recognition using geometric scattering representation. In: FG, vol. 1, pp. 1–6. IEEE (2015)
15. Yao, Q., Huang, D., Yang, X., Wang, Y., Chen, L.: Texture and geometry scattering representation based facial expression recognition in 2D+3D videos. In: ACM TOMMCAP (2017)
16. Derkach, D., Sukno, F.M.: Local shape spectrum analysis for 3D facial expression recognition. In: arXiv preprint arXiv:1705.06900 (2017)
17. Mauro, R., Kubovy, M.: Caricature and face recognition. Memory Cogn. **20**(4), 433–440 (1992)
18. Valentine, T., Valentine, P.T.: Face-space models of face recognition. J. Math. Psychol. 83–113 (2001)
19. Yin, L., Wei, X., Sun, Y., Wang, J., Rosato, M.J.: A 3D facial expression database for facial behavior research. In: FG, pp. 211–216. IEEE (2006)
20. Zhou, K., Yu, Y.: Mesh editing with poisson-based gradient field manipulation. ACM TOG **3**, 641–648 (2004)
21. Sela, M., Aflalo, Y., Kimmel, R.: Computational caricaturization of surfaces. CVIU **141**, 1–17 (2015)
22. Meyer, M., Desbrun, M., Schröder, P., Barr, A.H.: Discrete differential-geometry operators for triangulated 2-manifolds. Vis. Math. **3**(2), 52–58 (2002)
23. Wang, J., Yin, L., Wei, X., Sun, Y.: 3D facial expression recognition based on primitive surface feature distribution. In: CVPR, vol. 2, pp. 1399–1406. IEEE (2006)
24. Li, H., Morvan, J.-M., Chen, L.: 3D facial expression recognition based on histograms of surface differential quantities. In: Blanc-Talon, J., Kleihorst, R., Philips, W., Popescu, D., Scheunders, P. (eds.) ACIVS 2011. LNCS, vol. 6915, pp. 483–494. Springer, Heidelberg (2011). doi:10.1007/978-3-642-23687-7_44
25. Li, H., Sun, J., Wang, D., Xu, Z., Chen, L.: Deep representation of facial geometric and photometric attributes for automatic 3D facial expression recognition. In: arXiv preprint arXiv:1511.03015 (2015)

Fingerprint, Palm-Print and Vascular Biometrics

Dorsal Hand Vein Recognition Based on Improved Bag of Visual Words Model

Yiding Wang and Shan Dong[(⊠)]

North China University of Technology, Beijing, China
shan_dong1992@163.com

Abstract. At present, the Bag of Visual Words (BoVW) model has been successfully applied to Image Retrieval and Object Recognition. However, how to build a visual dictionary with high efficiency and low redundancy is still a key issue. Therefore, in this paper, we proposed an improved BoVW model to study the dorsal hand vein recognition problem. Specifically, when constructing a visual dictionary, we first use K-means++ to obtain some clustering center points for each image category, and each center point represents a visual word. Secondly, we combine all the categories of words into a visual dictionary. Finally, we use the mutual information method to eliminate redundancy between words to optimize the visual dictionary. The proposed method was tested on image databases collected under weak constraints, and the results show that the improved model has good robustness, low computational complexity, and the expression of each image category is more prominent, so it can get better performance.

Keywords: Dorsal hand vein recognition · K-means++ · BoVW · Mutual information · Weak constraint

1 Introduction

In recent years, dorsal vein recognition technology has emerged from a variety of biometrics, due to its uniqueness, long-term stability and difficult to forge reasons. And the hand vein recognition technology has made great progress, but it is mainly under strong constraint condition, such as need controlled environment and user cooperation, so the actual application is affected by many factors. Therefore, how to improve the recognition accuracy under weak constraints is an urgent problem to be solved.

In addition, most of the existing image algorithms are identified by extracting the underlying features such as SIFT, LOG or LBP [1, 2], and these ignored the spatial correlation between the image patches. Now, the BoVW model has been successfully applied to Image Retrieval and Object Recognition. It implements the selection and combination of the underlying features to represent more abstract and complex high-level features. And the high-level features can be used to discover the inherent distributed of the data [3]. However, how to build a visual dictionary with high efficiently and low redundancy is still a key issue.

The traditional BoVW model regards the features extracted from all image categories as a whole to use K-means clustering method when constructing a visual dictionary. However, for a large number of high-complexity feature data, the K-means is

© Springer International Publishing AG 2017
J. Zhou et al. (Eds.): CCBR 2017, LNCS 10568, pp. 203–212, 2017.
https://doi.org/10.1007/978-3-319-69923-3_22

used to randomly initialize all clustering center points, which results in a slower convergence and poor robustness of the visual dictionary. Therefore, in this paper, we proposed an improved BoVW model to study the dorsal hand vein recognition problem under the weak constraint condition.

2 The Principle of the Traditional BoVW Model

The BoVW model was first used in the field of Natural Language Processing and Information Retrieval. But now it has been widely used in the field of Computer Vision [4]. The model framework is shown in Fig. 1.

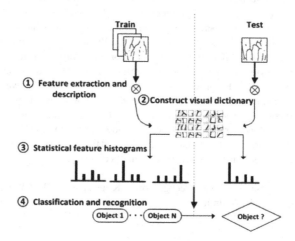

Fig. 1. BoVW model framework

According to Fig. 1, when the traditional BoVW model is used for hand vein identification, the process can be divided into the following four steps:

① Feature extraction and description:
   The main task is to extract the representative local features from images which can reflect the detail information. Scale Invariant Feature Transform (SIFT) can effectively resist the challenges of rotation, scale and perspective, so this paper uses Dense SIFT method to sample the image evenly. The implementation step of the process is to set a fixed size grid in advance, and then slide the grid at a specific step in the region of interest. And each grid is defined as a patch. In each patch will calculate a 128-dimensional SIFT feature vector. However, the differences in grid size will produce different feature expressions and affect the final recognition rate. Therefore, we discuss three different patch sizes in the latter phase of hand vein recognition experiments.
② Construct visual dictionary:
   The K-means clustering is carried out by extracting the features from all the training images through step 1, and these clustering center points will form our

visual dictionary. The traditional BoVW model constructs the visual dictionary process as shown [5] in Fig. 2.

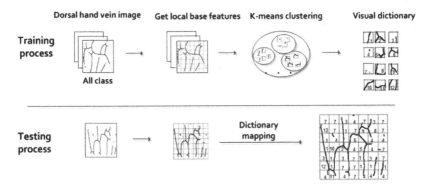

Fig. 2. Construct a visual dictionary

③ Statistical feature histograms:
These training images are mapped onto the visual dictionary dimension to generate the corresponding vector histogram to obtain the BoVW model representation of the image. Since the BoVW model ignores the spatial position information of the image, this paper adopts the weighted Spatial Pyramid Matching model (SPM) [6] method. The image is divided into three levels, and the histogram features are counted from each grid in each level, then each grid assigns a different weight. Now, the histogram features of each grid are weighted together to form the final eigenvector. The frame is shown in Fig. 3.

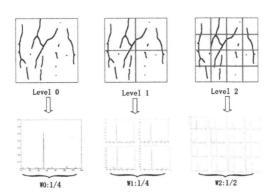

Fig. 3. SPM model

④ Classification and recognition:
Support Vector Machine (SVM) is a very promising classification technology [7], so this paper uses LIBSVM [8] to implement it. It contains cross validation

capabilities, and various kernel functions that can be used to handle multiple classification problems.

However, when the traditional BoVW model is applied to the hand vein recognition, the following unavoidable shortcomings will arise in the construction of this dictionary, which will seriously affect the final recognition accuracy:

(1) For a large number of high-complexity feature data, the K-means algorithm is used to randomly initialize all clustering center points, which will result in a long iteration and easy convergence to a locally optimal value. So it will eventually affect the robustness of the visual dictionary;

(2) Since the number of visual words needs to be artificially given, it is easy to set the K value too large or too small. This can lead to redundancy between words or reduced discernment between words.

Therefore, in this paper, we propose an improved BoVW model to study the dorsal hand vein recognition problem.

3   Dorsal Hand Vein Recognition Based on Improved BoVW Model

Now the above shortcomings were improved in this paper, the specific process as follows: first we use K-means++ algorithm to get some clustering center points from each image category and each of centers represents a visual word. Then adopt the method of Combine Categories Visual Vocabulary (CCVV) [9] to put all categories of visual words together to form a visual dictionary. Finally, we use mutual information to measure the correlation between two words, and remove the redundancy to optimize the visual dictionary. The hand vein recognition framework based on the improved BoVW model is shown in Fig. 4.

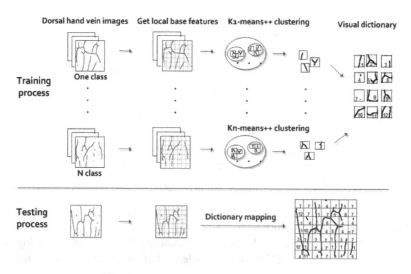

Fig. 4. Improved BoVW model framework

3.1   Combine Category Visual Vocabulary Method Based on K-Means++

In this paper, we propose a CCVV [9] method based on K-means++ to form a visual dictionary. In other words, each category will be clustered separately to obtain the visual words, and then all words are combined together to form a visual dictionary. K-means algorithm has the advantages of simple calculation, easy implementation, and quick calculation. The K-means++ algorithm inherits the above advantages and improves the selection method of K initial center points. The selection strategy is to make the distance between points as large as possible, but also to eliminate the impact of noise. The process is as follows:

(1) A point is selected randomly from the input data as the first clustering center point;
(2) We calculates the distance D(x) between each point of the dataset and his nearest cluster center point;
(3) Then we select a new point as a new cluster center, the selection principle is: D (x) larger points, the probability of being selected as the center is larger;
(4) Repeat (2) and (3) until k number of initial cluster center points are selected;
(5) Run standard k-means algorithm.

There is still no formal way to calculate the number of cluster center points for each category. So, we take different size of visual dictionary (K) for experiments, and select the K value with better recognition rate. Given the K value, we can compute the number of visual words (K_i) in each category. The definition K_i as follows:

$$K_i = K * \frac{F_i}{F_{All}} \qquad (1)$$

In formula (1), F_i represents the number of features extracted from the i-th image category; F_{All} represents the number of features extracted from all image categories. So we can summarize the mathematical expressions of K and K_i as follows:

$$K = K_1 + K_2 + \ldots + K_N \qquad (2)$$

Compared with the traditional model, this method has obvious advantages in constructing visual dictionary as follows:

Using K-means++ algorithm to select K initial center points can speed up the convergence rate and generate a robust visual dictionary; The CCVV algorithm based on K-means++ reduces the space complexity and time complexity, as shown in Table 1 [9]. This F is represents the number of features, R is represents the number of iterations. And the visual words obtained from a category will highlight the performance of the image in this category.

Table 1. Comparison of complexity

	CCVV model	Traditional model
Time complexity	$O(K_i * F_i * R)$	$O(K * F * R)$
Space complexity	$O(K_i * F_i)$	$O(K * F)$

3.2   Using Mutual Information to Optimize Visual Dictionary

Mutual information is a useful measurement method in Information Theory, and it is also a method to measure the statistical correlation between two random variables [10]. It is assumed that the joint distribution of the two random variables X,Y is P(x, y), and the marginal distribution is P(x), P(y), and the Mutual Information I(X; Y) is the relative entropy of the joint distribution P(x, y) and the product distribution P(x) P(y). I (X; Y) is defined as follows:

$$I(X; Y) = \sum_{x \in X} \sum_{y \in Y} P(x, y) \log \frac{P(x, y)}{P(x)P(y)} \tag{3}$$

The size of the visual dictionary needs to be given artificially then select the K value with better recognition rate, but the whole process is time-consuming and inefficient. Therefore, in this paper, we propose to use the MI method to optimize the visual dictionary. For example, two visual words have large mutual information, and then we will remove one of the words to reduce redundancy. So the final retained words constitute a visual dictionary.

Due to the similarity of the dorsal hand vein structure patches, we set the threshold of MI to be larger. We set the threshold to 0.7, if the MI between two words is greater than 0.7, we considered that the correlation is relatively large and one of them is retained to reduce the similarity between words. When the size of K in the range of 120–260, the corresponding need to eliminate the number of words, as shown in Fig. 5.

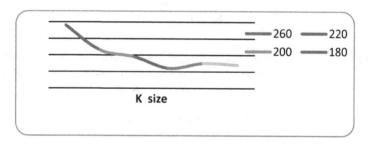

Fig. 5. The relationship between the number of words removed and K value

It can be seen that when K is 260, the maximum number to be removed is 48. However, when K is between 120 and 200 the number need to be removed is still around 25. This is due to the fact that the high similarity of the hand vein structure between different people. But we can get a reasonable range of K values and improve the computational efficiency.

4   Results and Analysis of Experiment

The dorsal vein image library used in this article was collected by Professor Wang Yiding's team under weak constraints. The experimental data consist of three image databases. Each database contains 42 people and each person collected ten left hand vein images. As the left and right hand vein structure is different, so only take single hand vein image to study. We will select a database of 420 images as a training set, and select another database of 420 images as a test set, a total of 840 images.

4.1 Image Preprocessing

Under the condition of weak constraint, The hand vein images collected by the three devices are different, such as size, illumination, rotation and so on. So it is necessary to carry out the pretreatment operation, which mainly includes filter handle, grayscale normalization, two-value segmentation, refine, intercept ROI [11], ultimately get the average image size of 380 * 380. The results of the preprocessing in the three databases are shown in Fig. 6.

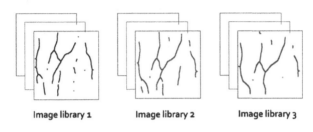

Image library 1   Image library 2   Image library 3

Fig. 6. Three databases for the same person's image preprocessing results

4.2 Statistical Results

In the feature extraction stage, different sizes of image patch will produce different feature expressions and affect the final recognition rate. So, in our experience, we choose three sizes of patches, that is, 18 * 18, 25 * 25, 30 * 30, and the size of the sliding step is always ten. And the selected visual dictionary K ranges from 100–240. Using the first library as the training set and the second library as the test set, the recognition rate of the improved BoVW model and the traditional model under different parameters are shown in Fig. 7.

In Fig. 7 the red and the blue curves represent the recognition rate when using the improved BoVW model and the traditional model. It can be seen that the recognition performance is closely related to each parameter. And compared with the traditional model when the patch size is 25 and the K size is 200, the proposed method can achieve the highest recognition rate 85.9524%.

4.3 Analysis and Demonstration

As can be seen from Fig. 7, the recognition rate of the proposed method is slightly lower than traditional model when the patch size is 18 * 18 or 30 * 30. That's because when the patch size is too small, the image will contain a large number of background patches and the similarity between patches is high. Therefore, it is possible to produce the opposite effect when optimizing the visual dictionary, such as curve oscillation and

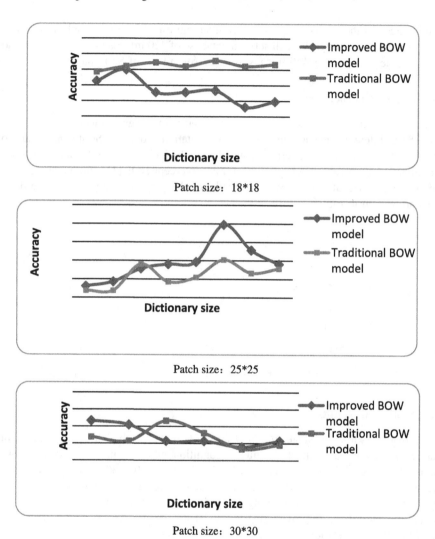

Patch size: 18*18

Patch size: 25*25

Patch size: 30*30

Fig. 7. The effect of different parameters on the recognition rate

low recognition rate. Traditional models also have similar problems in the identification process. And when the patch size is too large, the number of features can be reduced and the image can't be described in a comprehensive way, so the false recognition rate is increased. Although the trend of the two curves is similar, the computational efficiency is better than the traditional method. When the K is 200 and the patch size is 25 * 25, we compared the time spend by improved BoVW model and by traditional model in the construction of visual dictionary. The result is shown in Table 2.

The above two sizes of the patch are not able to achieve the desired performance, while when the patch size is 25 * 25, the recognition rate has been improved on the basis of the previous, but the size of the visual dictionary also restricts the final results. In

Table 2. Comparison of the time used to build the visual vocabulary

	Improved BoVW model	Traditional BoVW model
Total vocabulary	200	200
Total time consumed(s)	86.3043	184.3375

Fig. 7, it can be seen that our proposed method has a more stable recognition performance, but when K reaches a certain value the curve has a downward trend. Although the MT method is used to remove the more relevant words, there is still some redundancy when K is too large. Due to the high similarity between images and the MI has a certain threshold. In the traditional model, the initial K center values are randomly selected in the clustering process, and there are some words probably with large correlation in the visual dictionary. So, the curve fluctuates greatly, and the recognition rate is not high. In Fig. 7 we can see that the recognition rate of the improved model is not always better than the traditional model, on the one hand the result is affected by the number of samples, on the other hand the similarity between the images is high and it is also affected by various parameters, but in general the recognition rate is still within the acceptable range.

Now, we compared results after using different algorithms across different databases. The results are shown in Table 3. It can be seen that the accuracy and speed of the improved BoVW model are obviously higher than that of the traditional BoVW model and other feature extraction methods. In addition, the recognition rate is higher when the first database was regarded as training set and the second database was test set. So, we consider that the quality of the images collected by the first and second devices is better under weak constraints.

Table 3. Statistical results of different algorithms for different databases

Algorithms	1–2	1–3	2–3
Improved BoVW model	85.952%	64.76%	71.67%
Traditional BoVW mode	84.04%	63.54%	70.19%
Deep Learning [12]	71.38%	78.24%	75.32%
GDRKG [13]	69.08%	66.32%	68.93%
SIFT	49%	48.5%	46%

5   Conclusion

In this paper, an improved BoVW model is proposed to apply the dorsal vein recognition under weak constraints. The key step is to use K-means++ algorithm to get K_i visual words from each image category, and combined all words together to form a visual dictionary, then we use mutual information method to optimize the visual dictionary. Compare with other open common identification algorithms, the proposed algorithm further improves the recognition rate and significantly reduces the time and space complexity. But, the size of the visual dictionary plays a very important role in the whole process, there is still no formal way to calculate it, so in the late how to find an efficient algorithm to calculate the dictionary size will be the focus problem of the study.

Acknowledgment. This work was supported by the National Natural Science Fund Committee of China (NSFC no. 61673021).

References

1. Wang, Y., Liu, T., Jiang, J., Zhang, Z., Zhou, S.: Hand vein recognition using local SIFT feature analysis. J. Opto-electron. Laser **20**(5), 681–684 (2009)
2. Bu, W., Wub, X., Gaob, E.: Hand vein recognition based on orientation of LBP. Proc. of SPIE **8371**(83711), 1–12 (2012)
3. Lin, K.-H., Lam, K.-M., Siu, W.C.: Spatially eigen-weighted Hausdorff distances for human face recognition. Pattern Recogn. **36**(8), 1827–1834 (2003)
4. Ren, Y., Bugeau, A., Benois-Pineau, J.: Bag-of-bags of words—irregular graph pyramids vs spatial pyramid matching for image retrieval. In: IPTA, pp. 247–252 (2014)
5. Dong, L.M., Yang, G.P., Yin, Y.L., Liu, F., Xi, X.M.: Finger vein verification based on a personalized best patches map. In: 2014 IEEE International Joint Conference on Biometrics (IJCB), p. 8. IEEE (2014)
6. Lazebnik, S., Schmid, C., Ponce, J.: Beyond bags of features: spatial pyramid matching for recognizing natural scene categories. In: CVPR (2006)
7. Hsu, C.W., Lin, C.J.: A comparison of methods for multiclass support vector machines. IEEE Trans. on Neural Netw. **13**(2), 415–425 (2002)
8. Chang, C.-C., Lin, C.-J.: LIBSVM: a library for support vector machines. http://www.csie.ntu.edu.tw/cjlin/libsvm
9. Zhang, J., Luo, L.: Combined category visual vocabulary: a new approach to visual vocabulary construction. In: Proceedings of the 4th International Congress on Image and Signal Processing, pp. 15–17, October 2011
10. Guo, L.J., Zhao, J.Y., Zhang, R.: A novel method to construct visual vocabulary based on maximization of mutual information. In: Proceedings of International Conference on Artificial Intelligence and Computation Intelligence, no. 2, pp. 123–127 (2009)
11. Wang, J., Li, D., Li, M., Lin, Y.: Research on the extraction to the region of interest area in palmprint. In: 2012 24th Chinese Control and Decision Conference (CCDC),Taiyuan, China, pp. 3714–3718, May 2012
12. Zhang, R., Huang, D., Wang, Y., et al.: Improving feature based dorsal hand vein recognition through random keypoint generation and fine-grained matching. In: Proceedings of International Conference on Biometrics, [S.1], pp. 326–333. IEEE Press (2015)
13. Hinton, G., Osindero, S., Teh, Y.: A fast learning algorithm for deep belief nets. Neural Comput. **18**(7), 1527–1554 (2006)

Local Orientation Binary Pattern
with Use for Palmprint Recognition

Lunke Fei[1(✉)], Yong Xu[2], Shaohua Teng[1], Wei Zhang[1], Wenliang Tang[3],
and Xiaozhao Fang[1]

[1] School of Computer Science and Technology, Guangdong University of Technology,
Guangzhou, China
flksxm@126.com, xzhfang168@126.com, {shteng,weizhang}@gdut.edu.cn
[2] Shenzhen Graduate School, Harbin Institute of Technology, Shenzhen, China
yongxu@ymail.com
[3] School of Software, East China Jiaotong University, Nanchang, China
twlecjtu@163.com

Abstract. In this paper, we extensively exploit the discriminative orientation features of palmprint, including the principal orientation and corresponding orientation confidence, and further propose a local orientation binary pattern (LOBP) for palmprint recognition. Different from the existing binary based representation methods, the LOBP method first captures the principal orientation consistency by comparing the center point with the neighbor sets, and then captures the confidence variations by thresholding the center confidence with neighborhoods so as to obtain orientation binary pattern (OBP) and confidence binary pattern (CBP), respectively. Furthermore, the block-wise statistics of OBP and CBP are concentrated to generate a novel descriptor, namely LOBP, of palmprint. Experiment results on different types of palmprint databases demonstrate the effectiveness of the proposed method.

Keywords: Biometric · Palmprint recognition · Orientation binary pattern · Confidence binary pattern

1 Introduction

As one of relative new and emerging biometric traits, palmprint contains not only the line based features but also the ridge and minutiae points [1–3], which are considered to be immutable and unique to an individual. Therefore, palmprint has been corroborated to have the merits of high distinctiveness, and palmprint based personal authentication has a wide range of civilian, commercial and forensic applications [3].

In past decades, many methods were proposed for low-resolution palmprint recognition. The existing methods of palmprint recognition can be roughly grouped into four categories, including line-based methods, orientation-based methods, subspace-based methods and representation-based methods. The representative work of the line-based methods is generally based on the principal

© Springer International Publishing AG 2017
J. Zhou et al. (Eds.): CCBR 2017, LNCS 10568, pp. 213–220, 2017.
https://doi.org/10.1007/978-3-319-69923-3_23

lines and wrinkles of palmprint [4]. However, the performance of the line-based methods is not very good for the line features of a palmprint are relatively limited. Therefore, the orientation-based methods are developed. Typically, Zhang et al. [5] designed a palmcode method by extracting and coding a certain orientation feature of palmprint. Later, a large number of orientation based coding methods are proposed. The representative methods include the competitive code [6], ordinal code [7], half orientation code (HOC) [8], and discriminative robust competitive code (DRCC) [9] methods. In addition, subspace and representation based classification methods can also be used for palmprint recognition. To sum up, the orientation-based methods are the most popular and competitive in the family of palmprint recognition methods [10].

Recently, the study of local texture representation is very active, and various local texture descriptors have been proposed for image processing. Among them, local binary pattern (LBP) [11] is one of the most powerful one due to its high efficiency and low computation complexity. Extensive works [12] have demonstrated that the LBP based methods are able to achieve reliable performance for image-based recognition. Inspired by that, LBP has begun to use for palmprint recognition [13]. Nevertheless, these methods generally extract LBP on the raw data without extensively considering the characteristics of palmprint. In this paper, we propose a local orientation binary pattern (LOBP) for palmprint recognition. A novel orientation binary pattern is proposed to represent the principal orientation consistency, and a new a confidence binary pattern is designed to describe the changes of the orientation confidence. Further, the block-wise statistical values of OBP and CBP are effectively combined to form a LOBP descriptor. Extensive experiments on three benchmark palmprint databases validate the effectiveness of the proposed method.

The remainder of this paper is organized as follows. Section 2 proposes a local orientation binary pattern for palmprint representation and recognition. Section 3 evaluates the proposed method and presents the experimental results. Section 4 offers the conclusion this paper.

2 Local Orientation Binary Pattern

In this section, we propose a local orientation binary pattern for palmprint representation and recognition.

2.1 Principal Orientation and Orientation Confidence of Palmprint

The basic principle of orientation feature extraction is using a group of line detectors with different orientations to detect the principal orientation of palmprint. Typically, the Gabor filter is one of the most powerful tool for palmprint orientation detection, which has the following general form:

$$G(x, y, \theta, \mu, \sigma, \beta) = \frac{1}{2\pi\sigma\beta} exp[-\pi(\frac{x^2}{\sigma^2} + \frac{y^2}{\beta^2})] exp(i2\pi\mu(xcos\theta + ysin\theta)), \quad (1)$$

where $i = \sqrt{-1}$, μ is the radial frequency in radians per unit length, σ and β are the standard deviations of the elliptical Gaussian along the x and y axis, respectively. According to the experiences of [5], the optimal parameters in Eq. (1) are set as $\mu = 0.0916$, $\sigma = \beta = 5.6179$, and the sizes of the Gabor filter, that is the ranges of x and y, are defined as 35×35. θ defines the orientation of the Gabor function. In this paper, six different orientations, that is $(j-1)\pi/6(j = 1, 2, ..., 6)$, are used so as to define six templates. In palmprint principal orientation extraction, the real parts of the Gabor filters are convolved with a palmprint:

$$c_j(x, y) = G_j^r \otimes (255 - I(x, y)), \tag{2}$$

where G_j^r represents the real part of the Gabor filter with the orientation of $(j-1)\pi/6$, "$\otimes$" is the convolution operator, I represents an input palmprint image, and c is the corresponding convolved result between the Gabor templates and the input palmprint. Based the convolved results, the principal orientation of palmprint can be obtained as follows:

$$o(x, y) = arg \max_j c_j(x, y). \tag{3}$$

Intuitively, the convolved results on the principal orientation essentially reflects the significance and stability of the orientation. Therefore, we treat the maximum convolved result, that is $c_{o(x,y)}(x, y)$, as the confidence of the principal orientation, which can be obtained as:

$$c_o(x, y) = c_{o(x,y)}(x, y) = arg \max_c c_j(x, y). \tag{4}$$

2.2 LOBP

It is seen that $o(x, y)$ and $c_o(x, y)$ essentially reflect the orientation features of a palmprint. In other words, $o(x, y)$ represents the principal direction, and the corresponding $c_o(x, y)$ reflects the confidence of the principal direction. Therefore, we propose to encode and combine both the principal orientation and the orientation confidence for palmprint representation and recognition.

Given a line of a palmprint, the points along the line within a small local region generally have similar principal orientation, which is the orientation of the line. By contrast, the other points within the local region are not on this line, which possibly leads to different principal orientations. Therefore, the relationship of the principal orientations within a small patch essentially reflects the orientation change trend. The relationship of the principal orientation within a local neighbor area can be represented as follows.

$$OBP = \sum_{i=1}^{8} e(o_i, o_c)2^i, \tag{5}$$

where o_c is the principal orientation of a central pixel, and o_i denotes the principal orientation of the neighbor pixels. In this paper, the neighbor region is empirically defined as the (8,1) neighbor sets [11], that is, the central point is compared with the most nearest eight points. $e(u, v)$ is 1 when u equals to v, and 0 otherwise.

The maximum convolved results on the principal orientation, that is $c_o(x, y)$, essentially represent the confidence of the principal orientation. The difference of c_o within a (8,1) neighboring patch can capture the orientation confidence variances, which can represented as:

$$CBP = \sum_{i=1}^{8} s(c_{o,i} - c_{o,c}) 2^i, \tag{6}$$

where $c_{o,c}$ and $c_{o,i}$ denotes the orientation confidence of a central pixel and corresponding neighboring point, respectively. $s(u)$ is 1 when $u > 0$, and 0 otherwise. Unlike conventional LBP, CBP is based on the convolved results, which should be more stable and robust than using the raw data.

Since $o(x, y)$ and $c_o(x, y)$ carry highly correlated information, OBP should be combined with CBP. In general, different areas of a palmprint usually have different line and texture feature so as to carry different orientation features. Therefore, we propose to use block-wise statistics of the OBP and CBP to form a global palmprint descriptor. Specifically, given a palmprint image, we uniformly divided it into a set of non-overlapping blocks, the sizes of which are empirically set to 16 × 16 pixels. For each block, the principal orientation and corresponding confidence are respectively extracted so as to obtain the OBP and CBP maps, and further to compute the histograms of OBP and CBP, respectively. After that, we concentrate the block-wise OBP based histogram and CBP based histogram to obtain a global histogram of the palmprint, which is named as the local orientation binary pattern (LOBP). Figure 1 shows the framework of our proposed LOBP method.

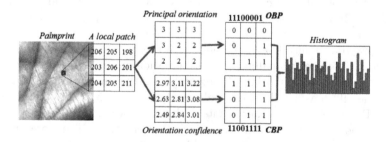

Fig. 1. The basic idea of the LOBP method.

2.3   LOBP Based Palmprint Matching

Given two compared palmprint images, the LOBP based descriptors of them are first calculated. Then, the simple and effective Chi-square distance is employed to determine the similarity of them as follows.

$$\chi^2(P,Q) = \sum_{i=1}^{N_m} \frac{(p_i - q_i)^2}{p_i + q_i}, \tag{7}$$

where P and Q denote two LOBP descriptors of two palmprint images, and p_i and q_i are the value of P and Q at the $i - th$ bin, respectively.

3 Experiments

In this section, we evaluate the effectiveness of the LOBP method on three widely used palmprint databases.

3.1 Palmprint Databases

The PolyU palmprint database contains 7,752 palmprint images, which were captured from 193 different individuals, and a palm provided about 20 samples. The PolyU database is available at "http://www4.comp.polyu.edu.hk/~biometrics/".

The multispectral palmprint database includes four palmprint databases, including the Red, Green, Blue, and NIR palmprint databases. Each database consists of 6,000 samples corresponding to 250 individuals for both the left and right palms, and each palm provides 12 palmprint images. In this study, we adopt the Green spectral palmprint database, referred as M_Green database, to conduct the experiment. The M_Green database can be downloaded at "http://www.comp.polyu.edu.hk/~biometrics/".

The IITD palmprint database consists of 2,601 palmprint images corresponding to 230 subjects with 460 palms, each of which provided 5 to 6 samples. The IITD database is available at "http://www4.comp.polyu.edu.hk/~csajaykr/IITD/".

3.2 Palmprint Verification

Palmprint verification [5] is a procedure of one-to-one palmprint matching, which answers the question that whether a query palmprint is from the same palm of a gallery palmprint. A palmprint matching is called as a genuine match when the query palmprint is from the same palm as the gallery palmprint; otherwise, the comparison is considered as an impostor match. In other words, a genuine match is an intra-class comparison and an impostor match represents an inter-class comparison.

In palmprint verification experiments, a palmprint image in a database will be matched with all other samples using the LOBP method. Then, we calculate the False Acceptance Rate (FAR) and Genuine Acceptance Rate (GAR), and further draw the ROC curve. Moreover, the conventional state-of-the-art methods, including the competitive code [6], ordinal code [7], BOCV [14], E-BOCV [15], HOC [8] and DRCC [9] methods, are also implemented to compare the proposed LOBP method. The ROC curves drawn based on different methods are

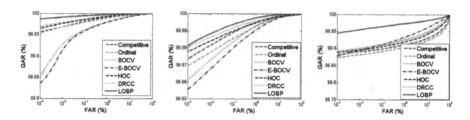

Fig. 2. ROC curves obtained based on different methods on the PolyU, M_Green, and IITD databases, respectively.

shown as in Fig. 2. It is seen from the figure that the proposed method always obtain a higher GAR than other methods on a certain FAR on three palmprint databases. Therefore, the proposed method can achieve the smallest Equal Error Rate (EER) among all methods. In addition, we also test the LBP method on palmprint recognition. However, the result is a very bad, and thus not included in this paper.

It is worth mentioning that the proposed method performs much better than other methods on the IITD database. The possible reason is that the palmprint images of IITD database present serious variances on projection, rotation and translation. The LOBP method generally based on the differences of the center points within neighbor sets, which effectively improve the robustness to the illumination changes.

3.3   Palmprint Identification

Palmprint identification [8] is the process of one-against-many palmprint comparison, which answers the question that which palm of a query palmprint image is from. In general, some palmprint images with already known labels are selected as the training samples in advance. Then, a query palmprint image is compared with all the training samples, and find out the label of the most similar training sample with the query sample. In our experiments, we randomly determine $n(n = 1, 2, 3, 4)$ palmprint images from a palm as the training samples, and correspondingly use the rest palmprint images as the query samples. In the experiment, we employ the rank-1 identification accuracy to measure the performance of palmprint identification. Also, the representative methods, including the competitive code, ordinal code, BOCV, E-BOCV, HOC and DRCC methods, are run and compared with the LOBP method. In addition, all cases are performed for 5 times, and the mean identification accuracies are reported. The comparative experimental results on different palmprint databases are summarized as Fig. 3. It is seen that, with the same situation, the proposed method can achieve the highest accurate rate among all methods.

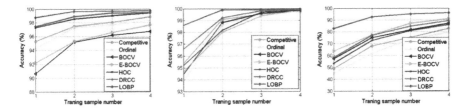

Fig. 3. Accuracy (%) of palmprint identification with using different methods on the PolyU, M_Green, and IITD databases, respectively.

3.4   Comparison of OBP and CBP

To verify the effectiveness OBP and CBP, we perform palmprint verification with using single OBP and single CBP, respectively. Specifically, we respectively use the block-wise histograms of OBP and CBP to form two kinds of palmprint descriptors, and the Chi-square distance is used in the matching stage. The ROC curves of using OBP descriptor and CBP descriptor on three palmprint databases are respectively shown in Fig. 4, in which the ROC curve of LOBP is also included. From the comparative results, we can see that the LOBP performs better than both the OBP and CBP. Therefore, combining the OBP with CBP, that is LOBP, can effectively improve the performance of palmprint recognition.

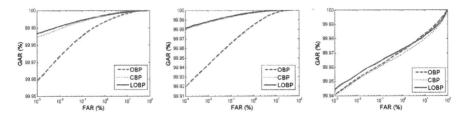

Fig. 4. The ROC curves obtained based on the OBP, CBP and LOBP on the PolyU, M_Green, and IITD databases, respectively.

4   Conclusions

In this paper, for exploiting the principal orientation features and corresponding orientation confidence, a novel local orientation binary pattern (LOBP) is proposed for palmprint recognition. Specifically, the principal orientation is compared within the neighboring sets to obtain the orientation binary pattern (OBP), and the orientation confidence is binarized by thresholding within a local patch to obtain the confidence binary pattern (CBP). The block-wise histograms of OBP and CBP are combined to form the LOBP of palmprint. Extensive experimental results on three widely used palmprint databases have demonstrated the effectiveness of the proposed method.

Acknowledgment. This paper is partially supported by Guangdong Province high-level personnel of special support program (No. 2016TX03X164), and Shenzhen Fundamental Research fund (JCYJ20160331185006518).

References

1. Jia, W., Zhang, B., Lu, J., Zhu, Y., Zhao, Y., Zuo, W., Ling, H.: Palmprint recognition based on complete direction representation. IEEE Trans. Image Process. **26**(9), 4483–4498 (2017)
2. Fei, L., Zhang, B., Xu, Y., Yan, L.: Palmprint recognition using neighboring direction indicator. IEEE Trans. Hum.-Mach. Syst. **46**(6), 787–798 (2016)
3. Jain, A.K., Feng, J.: Latent palmprint matching. IEEE Trans. Pattern Anal. Mach. Intell. **30**, 1032–1047 (2009)
4. Huang, D.S., Jia, W., Zhang, D.: Palmprint verification based on principal lines. Pattern Recogn. **41**, 1316–1328 (2008)
5. Fei, L., Xu, Y., Tang, W., Zhang, D.: Double-orientation code and nonlinear matching scheme for palmprint recognition. Pattern Recogn. **49**, 89–101 (2016)
6. Kong, A.K., Zhang, D.: Competitive coding scheme for palmprint verification. In: 17th International Conference on Pattern Recognition, pp. 520–523 (2004)
7. Sun, Z., Tan, T., Wang, Y., Li, S.: Ordinal palmprint represention for personal identification. In: IEEE Conference on Computer Vision and Pattern Recognition, pp. 279–284 (2005)
8. Fei, L., Xu, Y., Zhang, D.: Half-orientation extraction of palmprint features. Pattern Recogn. Lett. **69**, 35–41 (2016)
9. Xu, Y., Fei, L., Wen, J., Zhang, D.: Discriminative and robust competitive code for palmprint recognition. IEEE Trans. Syst. Man Cybern.: Syst. (2016). doi:10.1109/TSMC.2016.2597291.
10. Zhang, D., Zuo, W., Yue, F.: A comparative study of palmprint recognition algorithms. ACM Comput. Surv. **44**, 1–37 (2012)
11. Ojala, T., Pietikainen, M., Maenpaa, T.: Multiresolution gray-scale and rotation invariant texture classification with local binary patterns. IEEE Trans. Pattern Anal. Mach. Intell. **24**, 971–987 (2002)
12. Huang, D., Shan, C.F., Ardabilian, M., Wang, Y.H.: Local binary patterns and its application to facial image analysis: a survey. IEEE Trans. Syst. Man Cybern. Part C (Appl. Rev.) **41**, 765–781 (2011)
13. Michael, G., Connie, T., Teoh, A.: Touch-less palm print biometrics: novel design and implementation. Image Vis. Comput. **26**, 1551–1560 (2008)
14. Guo, Z., Zhang, D., Zhang, L., Zuo, W.: Palmprint verification using binary orientation co-occurrence vector. Pattern Recogn. Lett. **30**, 1219–1227 (2009)
15. Zhang, L., Li, H., Niu, J.: Fragile bits in palmprint recognition. IEEE Sig. Process. Lett. **19**, 663–666 (2012)

Multi-scaling Detection of Singular Points Based on Fully Convolutional Networks in Fingerprint Images

Jin Qin, Congying Han$^{(\boxtimes)}$, Chaochao Bai, and Tiande Guo

University of Chinese Academy of Sciences, Beijing, China
{qinjin13,baichaochao12}@mails.ucas.ac.cn, {hancy,tdguo}@ucas.ac.cn

Abstract. Most of the existing conventional methods for singular points detection of fingerprints depend on the orientation fields of fingerprints, which cannot achieve the reliable and accurate detection of poor quality fingerprints. In this paper, a novel algorithm is proposed for fingerprint singular points detection, which combines multi-scaling fully convolutional networks (FCN) and probability model. Firstly, we divide fingerprint image into overlapping blocks and pose them into a classification problem. And we propose a convolutional neural network (ConvNet) based approach for estimating whether the center of a block is one singularity point. Then, we transform the ConvNet into FCN and fine-tuned. Finally, we adopt probabilistic methods to determine the actual positions of singular points. The performance testing was conducted on NIST DB4 and FVC2002 DB1 database, which concluded that the proposed algorithm gives better results than competing approaches.

Keywords: Fully convolutional networks · Singular points

1 Introduction

Fingerprint is widely used in biometrics identification technology. It is used in authentication or recognition system to verify the identity of an individual. As a global feature of fingerprint, singular points play very important roles in fingerprint identification system. Furthermore, singular points can be used in fingerprint classification [1] to reduce search space in large database and as reference points in fingerprint minutiae matching [2]. Lots of methods have been proposed for extracting singular points. The traditional method for singular points detection is the Poincare index introduced by Kawagoe and Tojo [3]. Improved method [4] based on Poincare index, usually calculates the cumulative changes along a counter-clockwise closed contour in orientation field to judge whether there exists a singular point. Almost algorithms based on Poincare index evaluation have used local information to detect singular points and can easily be affected by noise. Further more, Poincare index is a method which is fully dependent on fingerprint orientation field. Fan et al. [5] proposed an algorithm which combined Zero-pole Model and Hough Transform to detect singular points. Orientation of

© Springer International Publishing AG 2017
J. Zhou et al. (Eds.): CCBR 2017, LNCS 10568, pp. 221–230, 2017.
https://doi.org/10.1007/978-3-319-69923-3_24

singular points is defined on the basis of the Zero-pole Model. Contrary to orientation field generation, detection of singular points is simplified to determine the parameters of the Zero-pole Model. Hough Transform uses rather global information of fingerprint images to detect singular points. Finally, Poincare index is used to refine positions of the candidate singular points. So, the results of singular points detection are limited by the accuracy of the Poincare index. By now, most methods of singular points detection need orientation field estimation, furthermore, their results overly depend on the accuracy of orientation field. In this paper, we will propose a novel method which is fully independent of orientation field.

In sections below, singular points detection algorithm will be presented in detail. Section 2 constructs the multi-scaling FCN for fingerprint images and detect the region of singular points. Section 3 describes about probabilistic algorithm for detecting singular points. Section 4 shows our experimental results tested on NIST-4 and FVC2002. Finally, Sect. 5 presents the conclusions of this paper.

2   Construct Multi-scaling FCN for Fingerprint Images and Detect the Region of Singular Points

Convolution neural networks is an effective identification method developed in recent years that caused widespread attention. In Recent years, ConvNets have demonstrated excellent performance at tasks such as hand-written digit classification and face detection [6,7]. Inspired by the superiority of ConvNets for various classification and recognition tasks, we propose a method for fingerprint singular points detection based on fully convolutional network.

2.1   ConvNet Production

The ConvNet architecture used in this paper is shown in Fig. 1. We define this ConvNet as CNN-C. A block is input to a convolutional layer (conv1) with 16 kernels of size 11×11, closely followed by the max pooling layer with a stride of 2 pixels. The second convolutional layer (conv2) takes as input the (max pooled) output of the first convolutional layer (conv1) and filters it with 32 kernels of size 5×5. Similar operations are described in Fig. 1 for conv3 and conv4. Then the outputs of conv4 are fed to a spatial pyramid pooling layer [8] which takes max pooling and outputs a 10×10 feature map. The output layer of the CNN-C will provide a fully-connected softmax to predict the probability distribution over three different classes.

To utilize the representation and classification power of ConvNet, we need a large number of fingerprints to train the ConvNet. There is a fingerprint database which contains 10 million people's fingerprints in our laboratory. These fingerprints are provided by some of the province's Public Security Bureau of China. We randomly selected 15000 fingerprints including various types and different qualities from this database. The size of these fingerprint images is all 640×640

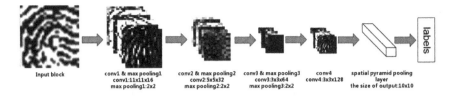

Fig. 1. Outline of the CNN-C architecture.

pixels. All fingerprint patches (80×80 pixels, 120×120 pixels, 160×160 pixels) with the center of the singular point were extracted. These patches are binarization processed, the obtained blocks are regarded as training data. Singular points position of each fingerprint image should be marked out artificially to get exact training data, which is a time-consuming and labor-intensive work. In order to generate enough training data, it is better to mark out the singular points by automatic method. In this paper, we use the singular points detection algorithm of [5] to automatically extract the singular points position of the 15000 fingerprints. The ConvNet are trained to classify a fingerprint block as one of the patterns (core pattern, delta pattern and nonsingular point pattern). A large number of fingerprint blocks for each pattern are then selected to train the ConvNet.

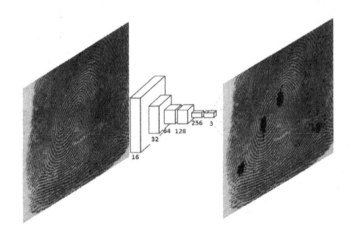

Fig. 2. Fully convolutional networks make singular points predictions.

2.2 Singular Point Region Detection

If we only use ConvNet to estimate whether a pixel point of a fingerprint image is a singular point or not, there are several drawbacks: (a) High storage overhead. We need extract the image block windows for each pixel. These windows input to ConvNet to be classified, so that the required storage space is rapidly increased with the number and size of the sliding windows; (b) Low computational efficiency. The adjacent windows are essentially repetitive, and the convolution is calculated one by one for each pixels' window. This calculation also has a large degree of repetition. (c) The size of the pixels' window limits the size of the perceptual region. Usually the size of the pixels' window is much smaller than the size of the whole image, and only some local features can be extracted, resulting in the performance of the classification being limited.

We transformed the well trained ConvNet into FCN, which is efficient and effective. Then, FCN can learn to make dense predictions, which is illustrated in Fig. 2. The transform details (convolutionalizing and upsampling) are described in [9].

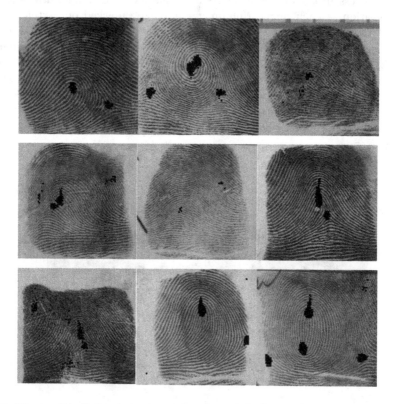

Fig. 3. The results of singular point region detection of some fingerprint images from NIST-4 by using FCN.

In order to improve the detection speed, it's not necessary to predict each pixel. The size of heatmap (i.e. output of FCN), only need be set $1/n$ of the original size. In our experiments, we find that $n = 5$ is the best choice. Figure 3 shows the results of singular point region detection. Each black spot in Fig. 3 is estimated as a singular point by FCN. For each point of FCN outputs, if its singular probability is larger than a threshold w, this point is estimated as a singular point. The value of the w is 0.95 in Fig. 3.

2.3 Multi-scaling

As shown in Fig. 4(a), the fingerprints whose ridges near the singular points are missing, we cannot detect the singular point when the training patch size is not large enough. However, the larger training patch size makes detection accuracy decline. That is similar to human's visual system. When we look for a singular point in fingerprints by our eyes, our visual range descends from wide to narrow. Finally, our sight line will focus on the singular point. Inspired by this phenomenon, we present multi-scaling detection of singular points region by using ConvNet with a spatial pyramid pooling layer [8].

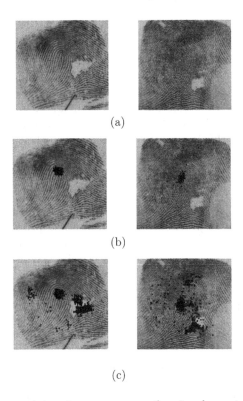

(a)

(b)

(c)

Fig. 4. (a) Two fingerprints whose area near the singular point are missing from NIST-4. (b) The results of singular point region detection for Fig. 4(a) by using FCN-SingleScale80. (c) The results of singular point region detection for Fig. 4(a) by using FCN-SingleScale160.

In CNN-C, the size of the input blocks limits the size of the receptive fields. Usually the size of the input block is much smaller than the size of the whole image, and only some local features can be extracted, resulting in the performance of the classification being limited in some situations.

In order to proof-test the effectiveness of the multi-scale, we conducted a comparative experiment. We trained another two ConvNets, CNN-CSingleScale80 and CNN-CSingleScale160. The architecture of these two ConvNets are same as CNN-C, but the training patch size is single. All training patch size used in CNN-CSingleScale80 is 80×80 pixels. All training patch size used in CNN-CSingleScale160 is 160×160 pixels. FCN-SingleScale80 and FCN-SingleScale160 are produced by CNN-CSingleScale80 and CNN-CSingleScale160 respectively.

As shown in Fig. 4, FCN-SingleScale160 can detect the singular points which are hidden in the missing areas of fingerprint. But due to the larger size of the visual block, its' estimation accuracy is lower than FCN-SingleScale80. This phenomenon is similar to our visual system, when we use wide visual range to look for an object, we cannot see clearly.

3   Singular Point Position Determination by Probability Computation

We can find that there are some black spots in nonsingular areas in Fig. 3 above. These black spots are error detection pixels. We define these black spots as noise points. There are few noise points on high quality fingerprint images by using FCN detection. With the decline of the fingerprint quality, the number of noise points increases. For example there are some noise points in the upper-left areas in the third row first column image of Fig. 3, because this area is like a core area. We determine the singular point accurate position after singular region detection, following by three steps:

3.0.1 Step 1: As far as possible to remove noise points. The threshold w (Sect. 2.2) strongly influences the precision of the singular point region detection. As the value of w increases, the precision of the singular point region would be higher and the number of noise points will be decreased, but some singular point also would be missed. We determine w adaptively in our algorithm. The value of w is defined as the max probability minus a threshold $\varepsilon = 0.01$.

$$w = max\{f(p) \mid \forall p \in SP\} - \varepsilon, \tag{1}$$

where SP is the points set that include all points which output pattern is core pattern or delta pattern. $f(p)$ is the probability output of p.

After the adaptive singular point region detection by FCN, to each black spot P_i detected, we count the number NBP_i (the number of black spots in the mask whose center is P_i, the mask size is 5×5 pixels in our algorithm). If the value of NBP_i less than a threshold NBW (NBW is 6 in our algorithm), the black spot is regarded as a noise spot and remove this black spot.

3.0.2 Step 2: Determine the deltas position. In fingerprint recognition, we must determine the exact number and position of singular point. So we need to estimate whether there is a delta, two deltas or no delta in the results of singular point region detection. The methods to determine the deltas position go as follows:

(a) If the number of black points whose output pattern is delta pattern is less than a threshold, we determine that there is no delta exist in the fingerprint image.

(b) Compute the diameter of the point set DP (all points whose output pattern is delta pattern). The diameter d of the point set DP is defined as:

$$d = max\{\|p_i - p_j\|_2 \mid \forall p_i, p_j \in DP\}, \tag{2}$$

where $\|p_i - p_j\|_2$ is the Euclidean distance between p_i and p_j.

If the diameter is less than a threshold, we determine that there is a delta in the fingerprint image. The coordinate of this delta $P_d(x, y)$ is:

$$P_d(x, y) = (\frac{\sum_{i=1}^{n} x_i * v_i}{\sum_{i=1}^{n} v_i}, \frac{\sum_{i=1}^{n} y_i * v_i}{\sum_{i=1}^{n} v_i}). \tag{3}$$

where $p_i(x, y)(i = 1 \ldots n)$ are all points coordinate of set DP, v_i is the probability output of p_i.

(c) If the diameter defined in (b) is larger than a threshold, we determine that there are two deltas in the fingerprint image. Then the set DP is divided into two parts by perpendicular bisector of the diameter in which each part belongs to only one of the deltas. According to the method described in (b), we can determine the coordinate of the two deltas.

3.0.3 Step 3: Determine the cores position. Likewise, we define the CP as the points set that consists of all points whose output pattern is core pattern. If the CP's diameter is larger than a threshold, we can determine that there exists two cores. If the diameter of CP is less than the threshold, we can't determine that there is only one core in this fingerprint image like the case of delta. It is caused by the characteristics of the fingerprint singular point distribution. It is generally true that there is a certain distance between two deltas in a fingerprint, but the distance between two cores in a fingerprint can be very small. It causes the results of core region detection are similar between a core situation and two cores situation.

In order to distinguish the number of cores, we plot the probability outputs of all pixel points which on the diameter, as illustrated in Fig. 5. All fingerprints we used satisfy the previous described situation, then the actual number of singular points in each fingerprint is known.

We find that the curves present low probability on both sides and high probability in the middle such as Fig. 5(a) below, then there are two cores. And the curve looks serrated as Fig. 5(b) below, then there is only a core.

The methods used to determine the cores position go as follows: (1) The method determine whether there is no core is the same as delta determination step (a); (2) If the CP's diameter is larger than a threshold, we can determine that there are two cores in the fingerprint image. The coordinates of cores can

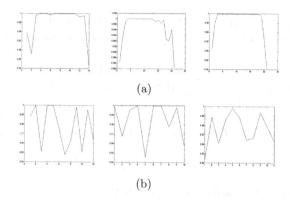

(a)

(b)

Fig. 5. The probability curve of the CP's diameter from top to bottom in fingerprint image. (a) The curve is plotted when there are two cores in the fingerprint image. (b) The curve is plotted when there is a core in the fingerprint image.

be computed as the same as delta determination step (c); (3) We calculate $\xi = \sum_{i=2}^{n} |p_i - p_{i-1}|$, where p_i is the probability of points on the CP's diameter. If ξ is larger than a threshold, there is only one core exists in the fingerprint image, otherwise there are two cores.

4   Experimental Results

We extract 480,000 patches(various sizes) from 15,000 selected fingerprints which is described in Sect. 2.1. Moreover, 400000 patches are used to train the CNN-C and 80000 patches for testing. The fingerprint patches in the training set are different from the testing set. In our experiment, we test the proposed method on NIST-4 [10] and FVC2002 DB1 [11]. Some fingerprints of these databases have a variety of noise, like creases, scars, smudges, dryness, dampness and blurs, etc. NIST-4's images are 512×512 with 8 bits per pixel. The size of each image in FVC2002 DB1 is 388×387. The singular points of all fingerprints in testing are manually labeled beforehand to obtain ground truth. For a ground truth singular point $SP'(x', y', type')$ and a detected singular point $SP(x, y, type)$, we calculate Dis which is the Euclidean distance between SP and SP': $Dis = \|SP' - SP\|_2$. If $Dis < 6$ and $type' = type$, SP is a true detection, otherwise, SP is a spurious detection.

We compare the proposed detection algorithm with the methods [4,5,12] which are dependent on Poincare index and the accuracy of orientation field. The traditional methods for computing orientation field are sensitive to noise. So the method [4,5,12] perform badly on some bad quality fingerprints. Our method performs well on these low quality situation by learning large amounts of data. Tables 1 and 2 show a comparison of our method with these methods. As clearly seen from the comparison, our method has better performance than others. From the result, we can see that the singular points can be detected more robustly by using our algorithm and the detected positions are reasonably accurate. We believe that our method would perform better if using more accuracy (artificial mark totally) and much larger data to train the ConvNet.

Table 1. The comparison results of different algorithms on NIST-4.

Method	Detection rate (%)		False alarm rate (%)	
	Cores	Deltas	Cores	Deltas
Our method	88.60	94.26	6.43	3.71
Fan's [5]	88.76	91.45	13.77	9.92
Zhou's [4]	86.13	89.51	8.47	6.15
Chikkerurs [12]	85.40	86.66	9.93	8.70

Table 2. The comparison results of different algorithms on FVC2002 DB1.

Method	Detection rate (%)		False alarm rate (%)	
	Cores	Deltas	Cores	Deltas
Our method	95.39	98.26	1.03	4.10
Fan's [5]	95.64	96.95	1.88	10.84
Zhou's [4]	95.78	96.98	2.27	9.97
Chikkerurs [12]	95.89	92.75	6.93	8.16

5   Conclusion

This paper combines FCN, probability method and multi-scaling analysis to detect singular point. We pose singular points detection to a classification problem in ConvNet. And training multi-scaling ConvNet, transforming the well trained ConvNet into FCN, and fine-tuning. Then we propose an adaptively and frequency statistics algorithm to rectify the detection result of FCN and obtain the actual positions of singular points. Experimental results on NIST-4 and FVC2002's DB1 database demonstrate the superior performance of the previous method. Compared to traditional singular point detection method, our method does not need to compute orientation field or enhancing by filter. And we can make full use of the information provided by the big database. Using big data to train the ConvNet makes our algorithm fairly robust to noise. In our future work, we will evaluate the effect of the visual block size to improve the multi-scaling analysis. And we will also rectify the method of removing noise points which is important to improve the accuracy of our method.

Acknowledgments. This work was funded by the Chinese National Natural Science Foundation (11331012, 11571014).

References

1. Jain, A.K., Prabhakar, S., Hong, L.: A multichannel approach to fingerprint classification. IEEE Trans. Pattern Anal. Mach. Intell. **21**(4), 348–359 (1999)
2. Chan, K.C., Moon, Y.S., Cheng, P.S.: Fast fingerprint verification using subregions of fingerprint images. IEEE Trans. Circuits Syst. Video Technol. **14**(1), 95–101 (2004)
3. Kawagoe, M., Tojo, A.: Fingerprint pattern classification. Pattern Recogn. **17**(3), 295–303 (1984)
4. Gu, J., Zhou, F. Chen, F.: A novel algorithm for detecting singular points from fingerprint images. IEEE Trans. Pattern Anal. Mach. Intell. **31**(7), 1239–1250 (2009)
5. Fan, L., Wang, S., Wang, H., Guo, T.: Singular points detection based on zero-pole model in fingerprint images. IEEE Trans. Pattern Anal. Mach. Intell. **30**(6), 929–940 (2008)
6. Hinton, G.E., Srivastava, N., Krizhevsky, A., Sutskever, I., Salakhutdinov, R.R.: Improving neural networks by preventing co-adaptation of feature detectors. Comput. Sci. **3**(4), 212–223 (2012)
7. Krizhevsky, A., Sutskever, I.: Hinton, G.E.: Imagenet classification with deep convolutional neural networks. Adv. Neural Inf. Process. Syst. **25**(1), 1097–1105 (2012)
8. He, K., Zhang, X., Ren, S., Sun, J.: Spatial pyramid pooling in deep convolutional networks for visual recognition. IEEE Trans. Pattern Anal. Mach. Intell. **37**(9), 1904–1916 (2015)
9. Long, J., Shelhamer, E., Darrell, T.: Fully convolutional networks for semantic segmentation. In: Proceedings of the IEEE Conference on Computer Vision and Pattern Recognition, pp. 3431–3440 (2015)
10. Watson, C.I., Wilson, C.L.: Nist special database 4 (1992)
11. Maio, D., Maltoni, D., Cappelli, R., Wayman, J.L., Jain, A.K.: FVC2002: second fingerprint verification competition. In: Proceedings of 16th International Conference on Pattern recognition, vol. 3, pp. 811–814. IEEE (2002)
12. Chikkerur, S., Ratha, N.: Impact of singular point detection on fingerprint matching performance. In: Fourth IEEE Workshop on Technologies, Automatic Identification Advanced, pp. 207–212. IEEE (2005)

An Efficient Slap Fingerprint Segmentation Algorithm Based on Convnets and Knuckle Line

Siqi Tang[1], Jin Qin[1], Yan Liu[1], Congying Han[1,2(✉)], and Tiande Guo[1,2]

[1] School of Mathematical Science, University of Chinese Academy of Sciences
(UCAS), Beijing, China
{tangsiqi14,qinjin13,liuyan515}@mails.ucas.ac.cn,
{hancy,tdguo}@ucas.ac.cn
[2] Key Laboratory of Big Data Mining and Knowledge Management,
School of Mathematical Science, UCAS, Beijing, China

Abstract. We propose a novel and efficient technique to extract individual fingerprints from a slap-image and identify them into their corresponding indices i.e. index, middle, ring or little finger of left/right hand. We pose the orientation of the hand to a classification problem, and present an approach based on Convolutional Neural Networks (ConvNets) to address the angle of the hand. Geometrical and spatial properties of hand are applied to split a single finger and detect the knuckle line. The proposed algorithm solves the challenges of segmentation like the large rotational angles of the hand and non-elliptical shape of components. Extensive experimental evaluations demonstrate the success of this approach.

Keywords: Slap fingerprint · Segmentation · Convolutional Neural Networks · Knuckle line

1 Introduction

Finger ridge configurations do not change throughout the life of an individual except due to accidents such as bruises and cuts on the fingertips. This property makes fingerprint a very attractive biometric identifier [1]. Over the past few years, the increasing security requirement has led to a large scale application and deployment of automated fingerprint identification systems (AFIS). In order to improve the performance of fingerprint recognition system, slap-fingerprint scanners capable of recording multiple fingers at the same time, are deployed. Figure 1(a) shows a typical slap fingerprint image. Multiple fingerprints can be acquired simultaneously. However, fingerprint images can not be matched against an image of a group of fingers. So the slap fingerprints are necessary to be fast and accurately segmented into individual fingerprint images. The whole process where the slap image is divided up into individual images is called slap fingerprint segmentation [2]. An example of the segmented fingerprint image is shown in Fig. 1(b).

© Springer International Publishing AG 2017
J. Zhou et al. (Eds.): CCBR 2017, LNCS 10568, pp. 231–239, 2017.
https://doi.org/10.1007/978-3-319-69923-3_25

Since 2004, the United States has held two sessions of slap fingerprint segmentation algorithm competition [2,3]. A variety of fingerprint segmentation algorithms have been summarized in [1], i.e. using a global or local thresholding technique, local histogram of ridge orientations, according to the variance of gray-levels and the average magnitude of the gradient in each image block. In [2], each slap-image is binarized and several pairs of parallel lines with equal spacing are drawn on the image at various angles. It fails when users place the hand at will. Moreover, various angles can increase the time of computation. The method in [4] is based on the mean-shift algorithm and ellipse-fitting. But the seed of the mean-shift algorithm is obtained by interval sampling, which leads to a large number of seeds. Thus it reduces the accuracy and speed of the algorithm. In the meantime, the algorithm of [4] performs poorly if non-elliptical shaped components or dull prints are presented in the slap-image. Connected-components which are labeled based on 8-neighborhood connectivity [5] can be used for component detection. Further improvement has been reported in [6] where quality of components is used to eliminate several non-fingerprint components. Force field and heuristics have been used in [7] for the components detection. The above methods which adopt the global pixel to cluster the component are highly time consuming. In order to remove the part that is not belonging to the fingertip, several algorithms like Radon transform [5] and cumulative sum analysis [8] take a variety of different ways to detect the knuckle line.

(a)   (b)

Fig. 1. (a) A typical slap fingerprint image, (b) an example of the segmented fingerprint image.

Convolutional Neural Networks (ConvNets) [9] have delivered outstanding performance on different challenging classification tasks [10]. Especially in recent year, the applications of fingerprint based on the deep learning have been obtained a higher accuracy. Inspired by the superiority of ConvNets for various classification and recognition tasks, we pose orientation estimation to a classification problem and train a ConvNet to solve it.

The rest of this paper is organized as follows. In Sect. 2, we describe the proposed segmentation technique. Experimental results have been analyzed in Sect. 3. Finally, we draw some conclusions in the last section.

2   Proposed Algorithm

The proposed segmentation technique consists of major tasks i.e. preprocessing stage, correcting orientation by using ConvNets, dividing fingers, detecting knuckle line, hand classification and labeling. First, we take the traditional method to preprocess the image. Then we correct the orientation of the slap-image by using ConvNets. Next, the finger is divided by the integral projection method. The knuckle line is detected by cumulative sum in the fourth step and components below the knuckle line are removed as well. Finally, fingerprint components are detected and labeled as index, middle, ring or little finger of left/right hand. The flow of the whole algorithm is shown in Fig. 2.

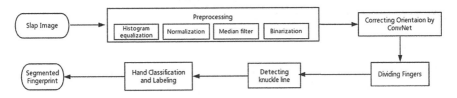

Fig. 2. The flow of the whole algorithm.

2.1   Preprocessing Stage

Preprocessing involves four steps, histogram equalization, normalization, median filter and binarization. In order to make sure not to change the structure of the ridge and the valley, we need to adjust the contrast of the different fingerprint images and the gray level to a fixed level. The original slap image is enhanced based on histogram equalization. It is observed that a histogram equalization on a dull quality image improves the segmentation accuracy. Then we use normalization so that it has the pre-specified zero mean and one variance.

$$G(i,j) = \begin{cases} M_0 + \sqrt{\frac{VAR_0((I(i,j)-M(I))^2)}{VAR}}, & I(i,j) > M(I) \\ M_0 - \sqrt{\frac{VAR_0((I(i,j)-M(I))^2)}{VAR}}, & I(i,j) \le M(I) \end{cases}, \qquad (1)$$

where $G(i,j)$ is the modified pixel value, $M(I)$ and VAR are the mean and variance of the image after histogram equalization, M_0 and VAR_0 are preset mean and variance respectively. Then the median filter is used to reduce noise. Finally the image is binarized by using an adaptive thresholding method.

2.2   Correcting Orientation by Using ConvNet

It has been observed that the orientation of the hand is not always vertical. In order to improve the segmentation accuracy, we need to correct the direction of the slap-image. The orientation of the slap-image can be easily distinguished

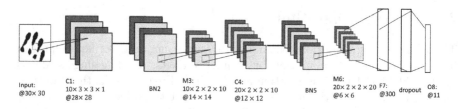

Input: C1:   M3:   C4:   M6:
@30×30   10×3×3×1   BN2   10×2×2×10   20×2×2×10   BN5   20×2×2×20 F7:   dropout   O8:
             @28×28   @14×14   @12×12   @6×6   @300   @11

Fig. 3. Convolution neural network for image processing.

by human. But when it comes to automatic rotation by computers, it is not an easy task, especially in images with low quality. Convolutional neural network, as one of the best deep neural networks, can realize a form of regularization and provide some degree of robustness automatically.

2.2.1 Training Data Preparation

Limited to the size of the slap fingerprint device, the slap-image can not rotate too large angle, so we take $-50°$ to $50°$, every ten degrees for a class of ways for training. In order to obtain a large number of samples to avoid overfitting, we rotate the samples of each class two degrees to the left and right sides. The preprocessed image is resampled to 1/50 of the original size.

2.2.2 ConvNet Architecture

Our algorithm can be viewed as a convolutional neural network with three important ingredients: convolution, batch normalization (BN) [11] and pooling. First, at a convolutional layer, the previous or the input layers feature maps are convolved with learnable kernels. Next, to accelerate convergence and achieve invariance to local deformations, we employ batch normalization and max pooling. Our convolutional neural network is constructed by replicating two times the same stage composed of the above three important ingredients. The overall model can be interpreted as a six-layered network (see Fig. 3). At last, following full-connected layer is a dropout layer [12] and softmax classifier.

$$y_i = \frac{exp(x_i)}{\sum_{j=1}^{N} exp(x_j)}, \tag{2}$$

where x_i and y_i are the input and output, respectively, of the i_{th} neuron at the output layer. We use the adaptive moment estimation (Adam) [13] to maximize the likelihood of the label.

2.3 Dividing Fingers

The images after preprocessed and downscaled are input to the trained neural network in order to get label. Then we rotate the preprocessed image according to the label. The rotated fingerprint image is segmented based on the integral projection along the horizontal axis. Then we use the cubic spline interpolation to smooth the integral projection curve. According to the center of the two maximum point, we cut the slap-image along with pairs of parallel lines into four parts.

2.4   Detecting Knuckle Line

We firstly detect the knuckle line of each finger and then remove the non-fingertip components. Obviously, the knuckle line is a kind of special line shaped pattern, so we can extract it by adopted the cumulative sum analysis. Considering creases or bad quality of fingertip components may seriously affect the location accuracy and reliability, it is necessary to enhance edge with canny edge detector [14] and smooth it with appropriate algorithm.

We adopt scanning line by line to locate the fingertip vertex and the left/right boundary of the fingertip. The ratio of fingertip vertex to knuckle line distance and the length of the fingertip semi-minor axis is always maintained in a certain range. Detecting the knuckle line in this range can not only ensure the accuracy of the results, but also accelerate the algorithm speed.

We are inspired by previous work [5] that makes use of the Radon transform to detect the knuckle lines directly. Radon transform gives the integral projection of the image intensity along a radial line oriented at a special angle. The transform,

$$Radon_l(P, \theta) = \int_{-\infty}^{+\infty} f(x, y)\delta(P - x\cos\theta - y\sin\theta)dl, \qquad (3)$$

where

$$\delta(P - x\cos\theta - y\sin\theta) = \begin{cases} 0, P - x\cos\theta - y\sin\theta \neq 0 \\ 1, P - x\cos\theta - y\sin\theta = 0 \end{cases},$$

$f(x, y)$ represents the image function, P represents the distance of l from the origin and θ is the angle the normal vector to l. Through the above step, we have corrected the orientation of the slap image. So the Radon transform degenerates to a one-dimensional problem. In fact, the mathematical essence of the degenerated Radon transform is the cumulative sum. Considering the noise of the finger edges, so we do not use the Radon transform directly. A rectangular detection frame with a length of 2/3 fingertip semi-minor axis and a width of 2 pixel is constructed. Then we align the center of the rectangle with the center of the finger which we got from the second step. Suppose that $F(\Omega)$ denotes the sum of the pixel within the search box.

$$F(\Omega) = \sum_{\Omega} I(x_i, y_j), \qquad (4)$$

where Ω represents points in the rectangle, $I(x_i, y_j)$ is the pixel value of the (x_i, y_j).Making it easier for observation and post-computer analysis, the pixel of the image has been reversed. Therefore, search box corresponding to the knuckle line should have a low peak value. Due to the presence of scars and crease, $F(\Omega)$

also has various peaks at various locations where there are no knuckle lines. It may happen that knuckle line location is not the global minimum as well.

To eliminate the influence of creases, dry or wet fingerprints, the $F(\Omega)$ is smoothen using Savitzky-Golay filter (S-G filter) [15]. Then we use the Fourier function to fit the smoothed curve. Finally, we find the minimum point on a adequate range between $2 \times r$ and $3 \times r$, where r represents the semi-minor axis of the fingertip. Value of the range is defined by experiments and statistical methods. Figure 4 shows the entire process. Area below this knuckle line is removed.

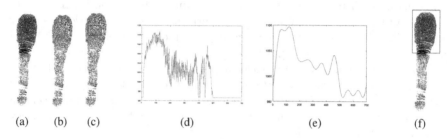

(a)   (b)   (c)   (d)   (e)   (f)

Fig. 4. The entire process of detecting the knuckle line: (a) the original finger, (b) the image processed by canny edge detector, (c) the width of the red rectangle is magnified to give details of the observation. Actually, the width of the rectangular detection frame is two pixels, (d) the cumulative sum of the finger, (e) the smooth curve of the cumulative sum, (f) the bounding box of the fingertip. (Color figure online)

2.5 Hand Classification and Labeling

The geometric property of the hand is the main basis to distinguish the left and right hand. It can be observed that the middle finger has two fingers in the left side for the left hand and has two fingers in the right side for the right hand. Therefore we first determine the middle finger according to the location of the fingertip. Then we determine the number of fingerprints on both sides of

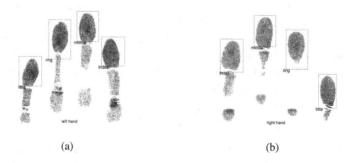

(a)   (b)

Fig. 5. Hand geometry for left hand right hand showing labeling: (a) left hand, (b) right hand.

the middle finger. And we use the geometric properties of the hand sequentially determined label of the left/right hand. The result of the label of the left/right hand is shown in Fig. 5.

3   Experimental Results

There does not exist any publicly available database, as all of the evaluation data was considered sensitive and could not be distributed to participants. We create our own database which consists of 500 slap-images acquired from 50 subjects. In order to ensure the diversity of samples, we collect the slap-image from teachers and students of different ages in different environments during three months. Each slap image is with 1500×1600 and 500 dpi as shown in Fig. 1(a). Because there is not publicly available database, criteria of the experimental results for correct segmentation is based on the NIST fingerprint segmentation algorithm (NFSEG) and humans examination.

3.1   Accuracy of Each Part of the Algorithm

The experiments about Convnet are carried out with the deep learning framework Caffe [16], which is developed by the Berkeley Vision and Learning Center (BVLC) and community contributors.

The overall architecture used in this paper is shown in Fig. 3. A fingerprint patch of size 30×30 pixels is input to a convolutional layer (C1) with 10 filters of size 3×3 and stride of 1 (denoted by $10 \times 3 \times 3 \times 1@28 \times 28$). Then we adopt the ReLU activation function to model the output of the neurons. A batch normalization layer (BN2) is applied to reduce internal covariate shift of the weights. Then the resulting 10 feature maps (of size 28×28) are then separately fed to a max-pooling layer (M3) which takes the max over 2×2 spatial neighborhoods with a stride of 2. We denote this max-pooling layer by $10 \times 2 \times 2 \times 10@14 \times 14$. Similar definitions are used for layers C4, BN5, M6 (see Fig. 3 for additional details). A fully-connected layer (F7) follows the last local response normalization layer (L6). After F7, a dropout [12] regularization method sets the output to zero with probability 0.4 to encourage sparsity of the neurons and to avoid overfitting.

The trained ConvNet can achieve a high accuracy with 98.125% on the test set. In experiments, we adopt different approaches to improve the performance of the network, such as local response normalization. Those methods have no obvious influence on the accuracy. But the batch normalization can be applied to significantly accelerate the convergence. In the application period, we calculate the rotation angle according to the label. In fact, the training error for each wrong sample is no more than $10°$. The single finger acquired from the next step is robust within ten degrees. Therefore the error of classification has no influence on the rotation of the original image.

In order to increase the diversity of samples, we take some images where the users press their fingers very tightly together. Surprisingly, it is nearly impossible to produce images without a space in-between the fingers. Using our method, the accuracy of divided finger is around 99.87%.

Total 500 such fingers are used to evaluate the knuckle line detection algorithm. The algorithm (Algorithm-1) which used the Radon transfer directly and our proposed algorithm (Algorithm-2) are compared on the database. By counting the number of the falsely segmented slaps, the successful segmentation rates are calculated simultaneously. Table 1 shows the comparison of the performance. It has shown that the performance of Algorithm-2 is much better than that of the Algorithm-1. Through the above experiment, we can find that our proposal method can get the comparatively accurate detection result on the edge blurring images.

Table 1. Performance Comparison

Algorithm	Total number	True number	Acc
Algorithm-1	500	469	93.8%
Algorithm-2	500	489	97.8%

3.2 Failure Case

Through experiments we find that the main reason for the error classification of the algorithm is the knuckle line detecting. Figure 6 shows the failure segmentation cases. It has been observed that most of the failure cases fall into category where the knuckle line is not obvious, this leads to the location of the minimum point doesn't represent the knuckle line. We hope to improve the smooth function to increase the correct rate in the future.

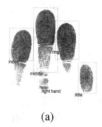
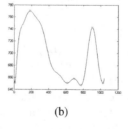

(a)   (b)   (c)

Fig. 6. The failure segmentation case. (a) The failed segmented fingerprint image, (b) the smooth function of the cumulative sum, (c) inaccuracy bounding-box.

4   Conclusion

This paper proposes an efficient and novel slap fingerprint segmentation algorithm. The whole process we used is independent of any shape constraint, and it is significant in these dull print regions. The success of the algorithm is shown clearly by the presented experimental results and error rate. Our future work includes speeding-up our algorithm and making the algorithm more reliable to segment those challenged slap images.

Acknowledgment. This work was funded by the Chinese National Natural Science Foundation (11331012, 11571014, 1731013).

References

1. Maltoni, D., Maio, D., Jain, A., Prabhakar, S.: Handbook of Fingerprint Recognition. Springer Science and Business Media, London (2009)
2. Ulery, B., Hicklin, A., Watson, C., et al.: Slap fingerprint segmentation evaluation 2004. Slapseg04 analysis report (2005)
3. Watson, C., Flanagan, P., Cochran, B.: SlapSegII: slap fingerprint segmentation evaluation II. NIST, Gaithersburg, MD, USA, Int. Rep. 7553 (2009)
4. Hödl, R., Ram, S., Bischof, H., et al.: Slap fingerprint segmentation (2009)
5. Gupta, P., Gupta, P.: An efficient slap fingerprint segmentation and hand classification algorithm. Neurocomputing **142**, 464–477 (2014)
6. Gupta, P., Gupta, P.: Slap fingerprint segmentation using symmetric filters based quality. In: International Conference on Advances in Pattern Recognition, pp. 1–6 (2015)
7. Tiwari, K., Gupta, P.: An efficient technique for automatic segmentation of fingerprint ROI from digital slap image. Neurocomputing **151**, 1163–1170 (2015)
8. Zhang, Y.L., Xiao, G., Li, Y.M., et al.: Slap fingerprint segmentation for live-scan devices and ten-print cards. In: International Conference on Pattern Recognition, pp. 1180–1183 (2000)
9. Hinton, G.E., Salakhutdinov, R.R.: Reducing the dimensionality of data with neural networks. Science **313**(5786), 504–507 (2006)
10. Krizhevsky, A., Sutskever, I., Hinton, G.E.: Imagenet classification with deep convolutional neural networks. In: Advances in Neural Information Processing Systems, pp. 1097–1105 (2012)
11. Ioffe, S., Szegedy, C.: Batch normalization: accelerating deep network training by reducing internal covariate shift. In: International Conference on Machine Learning, pp. 448–456 (2015)
12. Srivastava, N., Hinton, G.E., Krizhevsky, A., et al.: Dropout: a simple way to prevent neural networks from overfitting. J. Mach. Learn. Res. **15**(1), 1929–1958 (2014)
13. Chilimbi, T., Suzue, Y., Apacible, J., et al.: Project Adam: building an efficient and scalable deep learning training system. In: USENIX Symposium on Operating Systems Design and Implementation, OSDI 2014, pp. 571–582 (2014)
14. Jain, R., Kasturi, R., Schunck, B.G.: Machine Vision. McGraw-Hill, New York (1995)
15. Savitzky, A., Golay, M.J.E.: Smoothing and differentiation of data by simplified least squares procedures. Anal. Chem. **36**(8), 1627–1639 (1964)
16. Jia, Y., Shelhamer, E., Donahue, J., Karayev, S., Long, J., Girshick, R., Guadarrama, S., Darrell, T.: Caffe: convolutional architecture for fast feature embedding. arXiv preprint arXiv:1408.5093 (2014)

An Adaptive Contrast Enhancement Method for Palm Vein Image

Xiongwei Sun[1,3(✉)], Xiubo Ma[2], Chunyi Wang[3], Zede Zu[1],
Shouguo Zheng[1], and Xinhua Zeng[1]

[1] Institute of Technology Innovation, Hefei Institutes of Physical Science,
Chinese Academy of Sciences, Hefei 230088, Anhui, China
xiongweisun@163.com, xwsun_ustc@163.com
[2] Department of Computer Engineering, Anhui Sanlian University,
Hefei 230601, China
xiuboma@163.com
[3] Science Island Branch of Graduate School,
University of Science and Technology of China, Hefei 230031, Anhui, China

Abstract. Contrast enhancement plays an important role in palm vein image processing applications. However, the over enhancement of noise the commonly used enhancement method produces in relatively homogeneous regions is still a challenging problem. This paper proposes a low-complexity gray-level transformation method for this contrast enhancement problem. Firstly, we calculate a grid size based on the image's dimension and extract the high frequency from each patch as a weighting matrix. Then we construct a Gaussian model to express the expected contrast-stretching ratio based on the analysis of patch's high-frequency distribution. Finally, we use the intensity of each pixel as an index to find its mapping at the four closest neighboring grid points and then interpolate among these values to get the gray scale transformation. Experimental results for some of the widely accepted criterions demonstrate its superiority to the conventional contrast enhancement techniques in enhancement performance and anti-noise capability.

Keywords: Contrast enhancement · Gray-level transformation · Gaussian fitting

1 Introduction

Nowadays palm vein based technologies are becoming more and more widely used for its superiority in security and flexible interaction. The normally vein patterns are obtained by exposing the palm to infrared rays and these captured palm veins are unique to individuals. As different people have different skin absorption and scattering coefficient, the patterns in the captured images are usually nonuniform and low contrast in nature. The image enhancement's duty is to improve the quality so that the palm vein patterns become more suitable for further processing. Even though in the past few decades, a large number of contrast enhancement algorithms have been proposed, most of which are largely ad hoc or too complicated to use. Due to the lack of simple and

J. Zhou et al. (Eds.): CCBR 2017, LNCS 10568, pp. 240–249, 2017.
https://doi.org/10.1007/978-3-319-69923-3_26

reasonable approach to contrast enhancement, histogram equalization and its variations seem to be a folklore synonym for contrast enhancement in the literature and in textbooks of image processing and computer vision. Although this intuition is backed up by empirical observations in many cases, the relationship between histogram and contrast has not been precisely quantified. In fact, histogram equalization can be detrimental to biologic images (lots of homogeneous regions) interpretation if carried out mechanically without care. To alleviate these shortcomings, large numbers of techniques were proposed to modify the histogram equalization algorithm [1, 5]. One of the most influential work initiated by Pisano et al. is the contrast-limited adaptive histogram equalization (CLAHE) [5, 6]. Pursuing the contrast enhancement, these authors limit the contrast by empirical observations in many cases. Despite its lack of mathematical basis for the uniformity of the processed histogram, it is clearly superior to histogram equalization (HE) in perceptual quality, as well recognized in the existing literature and among practitioners. However, CLAHE is somewhat still week in over enhancement of noise in relatively homogeneous regions, particularly in the balance of sharp details and contrast enhancement in biologic image.

Compared with the aforementioned techniques, this paper presents a more reasonable approach by relocating the contrast gain according to the statistics of image's high frequency. The basic procedure of this method is first to calculate a grid size based on the maximum dimension of the image and extract the high frequency pixels of each patch as a weighting matrix taken by the normalized high-frequency intensity. Then a Gaussian model is calculated to express the expected contrast-stretching ratio by analyzing the intensity distribution of patch's high-frequency. Finally, we use the intensity of each pixel as an index to find its mapping at the four closest neighboring grid points based on their cumulative distribution functions, and then interpolate among these values to get the scale transformation.

The remainder of the paper is organized as follows. In the next section, we introduce some definitions related to the notions of our adaptive contrast enhancement. In Sect. 3, we discuss the progressive manners according to palm vein application requirements within the proposed framework. Experimental results and discussions are reported in Sect. 4, Finally, the conclusion is provided in Sect. 5.

2 Gaussian Fitting Based Transformation Model

Contrast enhancement is an integer-to-integer transfer processing and it is achieved by a gray levels remapping strategy for the increase of difference between two adjacent gray levels [7–9]. Such a remapping technology is actually the reasonable selection of the contrast gain distribution in limited gray levels. In this paper, we use Gaussian function to distribute the growth of gray levels from the minimum to the maximum, then the transfer function can be accumulated by contrast gain from each gray level. In essence, this transfer function is actually subject to the distribution of contrast variance as shown in Fig. 1. Therefore we can say that the process of constructing a gray scale transformation is the process of optimization to the variance distributions of different gray levels.

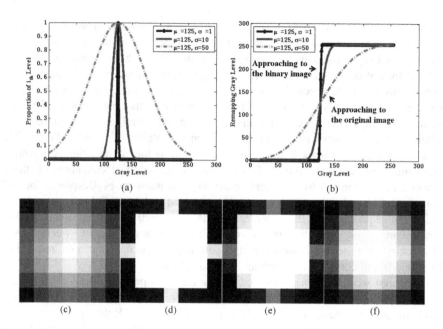

Fig. 1. Gaussian-fitting method for the gray-level transformation. (a) Gaussian function. (b) Transfer function for gray levels. (c) Original mesh image. (d) Gaussian-fitting gray levels transformation with $\mu = 125, \sigma = 1$. (e) Gaussian-fitting gray levels transformation with $\mu = 125, \sigma = 10$. (f) Gaussian-fitting gray levels transformation with $\mu = 125, \sigma = 50$.

To balance between noise immunity and contrast enhancement we introduce a Gaussian function to describe the contrast variance distribution. The Gaussian function can be expressed by the parameters of mean μ and variance σ. By the analytical expression of Gaussian function, we obtain for different values of μ and σ a family of gray-level transformations, as illustrated in Fig. 1. The case $\sigma \gg 50$ ($\forall \mu \in [1, 255]$) corresponds to the approximate linear gray-level stretching. For the very small values of σ ($\sigma \ll 1$) the transformation tend toward a threshold function with single threshold of μ. Thus, our analytic expression defines a wide class of gray-level transformations ranging from the linear stretching to the threshold transformation.

Generally speaking, the improving of contrast enhancement depends much on the high frequency of a biological image. Therefore we construct a weighting matrix which is used to emphasize the influence of the high spatial frequency information without loss of normally flat regions in the image. In order to obtain the high frequency of an image, we extract the low frequency obtained by Gaussian filtering first, then, calculate the weighting matrix by taken the subtraction of original image with blurred image and normalized this weighting matrix. The basic procedure can be illustrated in Fig. 2.

As is stated above, the normalized weighting matrix can be defined as

$$W(x,y) = \frac{|I(x,y) - G(x,y,s) \otimes I(x,y)|}{max|I(x,y) - G(x,y,\sigma) \otimes I(x,y)|}. \tag{1}$$

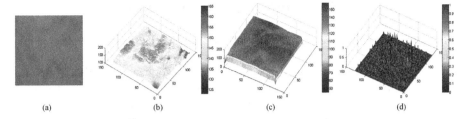

Fig. 2. Weighting matrix. (a) Original palm vein image. (b) 3D plot of the Grey-scale original image. (c) 3D plot of Gaussian filtered image. (d) 3D plot of weighting matrix.

Where, (x,y) is the coordinate of the original image I, $\otimes$ is the operator of convolution and $G(x,y,\sigma)$ can be defined as

$$G(x,y,\sigma) = \frac{1}{2\pi\sigma^2}e^{\frac{-(x^2+y^2)}{2\sigma^2}}. \tag{2}$$

Using this $W(x,y)$, we develop a Gaussian distribution to express the layout of contrast variance arrangements. Here, M and N are the rows and columns of the original image, the parameters mean μ_w and variance σ_w of the Gaussian function can be formulated as

$$\begin{cases} \mu_w = \dfrac{\sum\limits_{y=1}^{M}\sum\limits_{x-1}^{N}(1+\lambda W(x,y))I(x,y)}{\sum\limits_{y=1}^{M}\sum\limits_{x=1}^{N}(1+\lambda W(x,y))} \\ \sigma_w = (\dfrac{\sum\limits_{y=1}^{M}\sum\limits_{x=1}^{N}((1+\lambda W(x,y))I(x,y)-\mu_w)^2}{\sum\limits_{y=1}^{M}\sum\limits_{x=1}^{N}(1+\lambda W(x,y))})^{\frac{1}{2}} \end{cases}. \tag{3}$$

To adjust the influence of high frequency, λ is set as the value of $\lambda = 1.0$ by empirical analysis. Finally, the gray levels transformation can be defined as follows

$$\begin{cases} D(\mu_w,\sigma_w,l) = \dfrac{1}{\sqrt{2\pi}\sigma_w}e^{\frac{-(l-\mu_w)^2}{2\sigma^2}} \\ M(s_i) = v_{min} + \dfrac{\sum\limits_{k=v_{min}}^{s_i}D(\mu_w,\sigma_w,k)}{\sum\limits_{i=v_{min}}^{v_{max}}D(\mu_w,\sigma_w,i)}(v_{max}-v_{min}) \end{cases}. \tag{4}$$

Where contrast gain function can be set as $D(\mu_w,\sigma_w,l)$, l is a gray level $(\forall l \in [0,255])$. We define v_{min} and v_{max} as the minimum and maximum values of gray image I (If do not stretch out the range of gray values), for any original gray level s_i, the corresponding gray level can be calculated by formula $M(s_i)$.

3 Adaptive Gaussian Fitting Based Transformation

For palm vein images which contain lots of low contrast bright or dark regions, global enhancement won't work effectively. A modification of gray levels transformation method called the adaptive Gaussian fitting based transformation (AGFT) is used on such images for the better results. Adaptive Gaussian Fitting works create the local Gaussian fitting functions by considering only small piece of regions and each region performs contrast enhancement independently. In order to reunite individual sections, AGFT use the "tiled windows with interpolated mapping" strategy started by Pizer [5, 10]. The main steps performed by this method are:

$$
\begin{cases}
l^{UL} = \dfrac{d^R d^D}{(d^L + d^R)(d^U + d^D)} \\[2mm]
l^{UR} = \dfrac{d^D d^L}{(d^L + d^R)(d^U + d^D)} \\[2mm]
l^{DL} = \dfrac{d^U d^R}{(d^L + d^R)(d^U + d^D)} \\[2mm]
l^{DR} = \dfrac{d^U d^L}{(d^L + d^R)(d^U + d^D)} \\[2mm]
M^{tar}(k) = l^{UL} M^{UL}(k) + l^{UR} M^{UR}(k) + l^{DL} M^{DL}(k) + l^{DR} M^{DR}(k)
\end{cases}
\tag{5}
$$

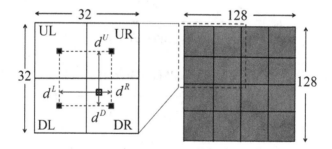

Fig. 3. Interpolate local patch transformation value.

- Calculate a grid size based on the maximum dimension of the palm vein image. As shown in Fig. 3, the grid size is set as 32 pixels square by the empirical analysis according to the bench mark ROI size 128 pixels square.
- For each grid area, calculate the Gaussian distribution function and obtain the patch image's gray levels transformation by the strategy mentioned earlier. As shown in Fig. 3, we can obtain the four gray-level transformation functions from the close-up four image patches: $M^{UL}(k)$, $M^{UR}(k)$, $M^{DL}(k)$ and $M^{DR}(k)$.
- Using the current pixel intensity value k as an index, find its mapping at the four grid points based on the gray-level distribution functions.

- Interpolate among these values to get the mapping at the current pixel location. The fused transformed gray level can be defined as the equation given in (5). Map this intensity to the range between global minimum and maximum of the original image and put it in the target image.

As is shown in Fig. 3, the AGFT method put its focus on the high-frequency details exaggeration and pays equal attention to the fusion of adjacent patches. This design brings better performance of vein texture enhancement and anti-noise capability in homogeneous regions.

4 Experimental Results

In this section, we present some sample images from PolyU palm vein database [11] that are enhanced by our technique in comparison with those produced by the conventional histogram equalization method (HE), such as the well-known adaptive histogram equalization (AHE) and contrast limited adaptive histogram equalization (CLAHE).

4.1 Comparison of Palm Vein Enhancement Methods

The histograms are plotted in accompany with the corresponding enhancement results to show different behaviors of the techniques in different images. The proposed algorithm has been successfully tested on a variety of test images and only a few of the results are shown in this paper.

HE or its variations capture excellent results in the best utilization of the pixel values dynamic range for the maximum of contrast. However, in many cases, the contrast of the image is maximized at the expense of amplified noise. As can be observed clearly in Fig. 4, the bright spikes which are caused by having high slope in the histogram mapping function will seriously affect the subsequent analysis of palm vein patterns. By comparison to the conventional techniques HE, our proposed method GFT shows richer intensity information with no additional high contrast noise. The distribution of gray levels in Fig. 4 clearly proved it.

In practice, palm vein image capturing process is often affected by the uneven illumination environment and uneven surface of palm skin. With regard to complex lighting environment during the image acquisition process, we use the Retinex theory [12] to weaken the influence of uneven infrared illumination. It is obvious that combined with the simplified SSR preprocessing, all the contrast enhancement methods mentioned above have better performances. However, the expense of the amplified noise still limited the effectiveness of HE or its variations. Even though CLAHE is clearly superior to HE and AHE in perceptual quality, it is somewhat inferior to our method in overall image quality, particularly in the balance of sharp details and anti-noise ability.

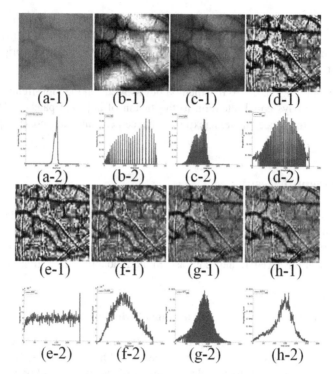

Fig. 4. Palm vein enhancement. (a-1) Original. (b-1) HE result. (c-1) GFT result. (d-1) AHE result. (a-2) histogram of Original. (b-2) histogram of HE. (c-2) histogram of GFT. (d-2) histogram of AHE. (e-1) SSR + AHE. (f-1) SSR + CLAHE. (g-1) SSR + GFT. (h-1) SSR + AGFT. (e-2) histogram of SSR + AHE. (f-2) histogram of SSR + CLAHE. (g-2) histogram of SSR + GFT. (h-2) histogram of SSR + AGFT.

4.2 Image Quality Assessment

There are some conventional quality assessment methods are proposed to evaluate the effectiveness of the proposed method, such as Entropy, Peak signal-to-noise ratio (PSNR), and Structural similarity (SSIM).

Entropy is used to measure the content of an image. Higher value of entropy indicates an image with richer detials and more information brought from the image.

As HE method is a double-edged sword (clearly shown in the Fig. 4(b-1)), it always suffer from the shortage of over enhancement of noise in homogeneous regions. Therefore, the entropy values of HE test cases are excessive high than the other methods. However, the entropy results from Fig. 5 shows that the proposed AGFT method improves the contrast of the image in a better way, which is numerically indicated by greater or approximately equal values as compared to one of the best contrast enhancement techniques CLAHE, no matter in the independent running or combination with the preprocessing SSR.

PSNR is a measure used in science and engineering that compares the level of a desired signal to the level of background noise. It is defined as the ratio of signal power

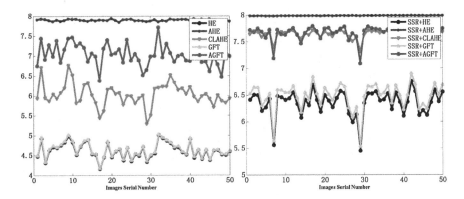

Fig. 5. Comparison of entropy results.

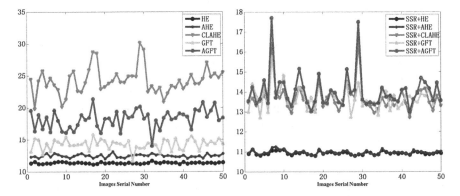

Fig. 6. Comparison of PSNR results.

to the noise power, often expressed via the mean squared error. Here, it is more reasonable to discuss the enhanced performance in the premise of illumination equalization. By analysing these SSR preprocessed values, it is found that the AGFT produces obviously greater or approximated PSNR values as compared to the conventional method CLAHE. Figure 6 shows the results of palm vein images obtained by the various existing methods and proposed method.

The SSIM index is a full reference quality metric which is designed to improve on traditional quality asscesment methods, which have been proved have a better performance in consistent with human visual perception. The SSIM index is calculated on various windows of an image. Higher SSIM indicates the better vein pattern preservation of the image.

The SSIM values are analysed using Fig. 7, from which it can be concluded that the structural similarity index is much higher when compared to other conventional methods. Thus the proposed method has been found effective in enhancing contrast of palm vein images in comparison to the conventional methods mentioned above based on qualitative and quantitative analysis.

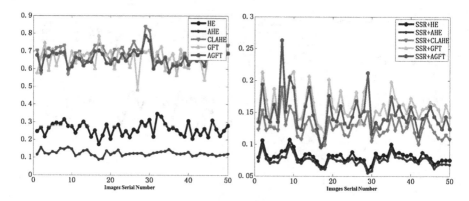

Fig. 7. Comparison of SSIM results.

5 Conclusion

In this work, an adaptive gray-level transformation method is presented for image contrast enhancement. The conventional contrast enhancement methods usually cause over enhancement of noise in the palm vein images' relatively homogeneous regions. For this issue, proposed method uses the adaptive Gaussian fittings to transform the gray levels smoothly, which can effectively preserve the patterns of palm vein images and prevent the expense of amplified noise. The experimental results showed that proposed method produces a sufficient contrast enhancement while preserving the original patterns of an image with less noise.

Acknowledgements. This work was supported by the Special Scientific Research Fund of Meteorological Public Welfare Profession of China (No. GYHY201106002-03), the Fundamental Research Funds for the Central Universities of China (No. JB140315), National Natural Science Foundation of China No. 31401285 and No. 61475163, the National Natural Science Foundation of Anhui No. 1508085QC65 and No. 1608085QF127.

References

1. Wu, X.: A linear programming approach for optimal contrast-tone mapping. IEEE Trans. Image Process. Publ. IEEE Sig. Process. Soc. **20**(5), 1262–1272 (2011)
2. Deng, G.: A generalized unsharp masking algorithm. IEEE Trans. Image Process. Publ. IEEE Sig. Process. Soc. **20**(5), 1249 (2011)
3. Stark, J.A.: Adaptive image contrast enhancement using generalizations of histogram equalization. IEEE Trans. Image Process. **9**(5), 889–896 (2000)
4. Grigoryan, A.M., Agaian, S.S.: Transform-based image enhancement algorithms with performance measure. IEEE Trans. Image Process. Publ. IEEE Sig. Process. Soc. **130**(3), 165–242 (2004)
5. Pizer, S.M., Amburn, E.P., Austin, J.D., et al.: Adaptive histogram equalization and its variations. Comput. Vis. Graph. Image Process. **39**(3), 355–368 (1987)

6. Kim, Y.T.: Contrast enhancement using brightness preserving bi-histogram equalization. IEEE Trans. Consum. Electron. **43**(1), 1–8 (1997)
7. Kim, T.K., Paik, J.K., Kang, B.S.: Contrast enhancement system using spatially adaptive histogram equalization with temporal filtering. IEEE Trans. Consum. Electron. **44**(1), 82–87 (1998)
8. Arici, T., Dikbas, S., Altunbasak, Y.: A histogram modification framework and its application for image contrast enhancement. IEEE Trans. Image Process. **18**(9), 1921–1935 (2009)
9. Wang, Y., Chen, Q., Zhang, B.: Image enhancement based on equal area dualistic sub-image histogram equalization method. IEEE Trans. Consum. Electron. **45**(1), 68–75 (2002)
10. Pisano, E.D., Zong, S., Hemminger, B.M., et al.: Contrast limited adaptive histogram equalization image processing to improve the detection of simulated spiculations in dense mammograms. J. Digit. Imaging **11**(4), 193–200 (1998)
11. http://www4.comp.polyu.edu.hk/ ~ biometrics/
12. Land, E.H.: The retinex. Am. Sci. **52**(2), 247–264 (1964)

A Scheme of Template Selection and Updating for Palmprint Authentication Systems

Xi Chen[1,2(✉)], Ming Yu[1], Feng Yue[2], and Bin Li[2]

[1] School of Electronic and Information Engineering,
Hebei University of Technology, Tianjin 300401, People's Republic of China
csxichen@outlook.com
[2] Beijing Institute of New Technology Applications,
Beijing Academy of Sciences and Technology,
Beijing 100094, People's Republic of China

Abstract. The representativeness of templates is a fundamental problem in palmprint authentication systems, where false rejection rate rises if the enrolled templates are less representative of intra-class variations such as posture changes, lighting conditions, and scars. In order to solve this problem, existing techniques typically store multiple templates for the sake of temporary variations such as posture changes, and followed by templates updating to manage the periodical and permanent variations. However, the techniques in the literature do not combine template selection and updating organically to make the system maintain or even improve the representativeness of templates. In this paper, we propose a scheme to provide effective solutions to two important issues of palmprint authentication system: how to automatically select representative templates in a number of candidate samples, and how to update the templates if they are insufficient or are no longer representative of intra-class variations. In enrollment stage, the proposed scheme performs Chameleon clustering and selects the most representative template from each cluster. During authentication stage, the proposed scheme updates the templates in online mode based on historical hit-counts and incoming samples. The experimental results on our palmprint database have demonstrated the effectiveness of our templates selection and updating scheme.

Keywords: Palmprint authentication · Representativeness of templates · Intra-class variations · Template selection · Template updating

1 Introduction

Palmprint is the surface of palm, which contains sufficient and unique texture features such as principal lines, wrinkles, ridges, etc. Even identical twins have different palmprints [1, 2]. As one of the most accurate biometrics technologies, palmprint recognition received considerable research interest in recent years [3–5]. There are two essential modules in a typical palmprint authentication system, enrollment and authentication. In enrollment module, features are extracted from palmprint images and stored as templates. In authentication module, features are extracted from incoming images and compared with stored templates to determine the user's identity.

© Springer International Publishing AG 2017
J. Zhou et al. (Eds.): CCBR 2017, LNCS 10568, pp. 250–258, 2017.
https://doi.org/10.1007/978-3-319-69923-3_27

As for practical palmprint authentication systems, the representativeness of template is susceptible to intra-class variations, which can be roughly classified as temporary variations, periodical variations and permanent variations. Temporary variations are incidental and irregular variations, such as palm posture changes (as shown in Fig. 1), hand with new scars, etc. Periodical variations are mainly caused by environmental factors (e.g., palmprints are slightly different between winter and summer) [6]. Permanent variations are referred to as irreversible and slow changes of palmprints because of skin condition, climate, habits of using hands and on-site environment [7, 8], etc. In order to improve the robustness against such variations, a typical system usually stores multiple templates for each palm [9]. The remaining problems are how to automatically select representative templates in a number of candidate samples, and how to update the templates if they are insufficient or are no longer representative of intra-class variations.

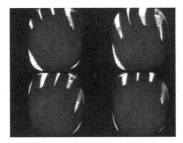

Fig. 1. Palmprint images from the same user with different postures.

For biometrics technologies, much research effort is put into the feature extraction and matching algorithms, while relatively little attention has been paid to template selection and updating. Jiang and Ser [16] proposed a recursive technique that computes average values of minutiae included in each instance to improve fingerprint templates. Other known methods are biometric trait independent. In [6], Uludag et al. proposed two algorithms to select adaptive templates in fingerprint recognition systems. The first is called DEND, which groups N fingerprint impressions into K clusters based on their similarity. The second is called MDIST, which sorts the fingerprint impressions based on their average distance to other impressions, and selects the impressions with the K smallest average distance. Then, the methods are applied periodically to update the selected templates. These two algorithms takes powerful hold of latter work of biometric templates selection. The work in [8] discusses a method of the most 'typical one' selection in every cluster and later, [12] uses a quality-based clustering, followed by a special criterion for the selection to improve DEND.

During the enrollment stage of palmprint authentication systems, experienced users may consciously change their posture, while the others are unlikely to change the posture. Therefore, it is inappropriate to use a fixed number of templates for every user. Meanwhile, for existing methods, it is difficult to deal with the 'dirty image' (e.g., an image with motion blur or incomplete palmprint as shown in Fig. 2), because they look like exactly 'typical' to be selected as templates.

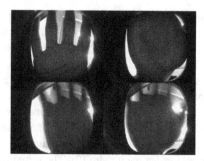

Fig. 2. Palmprint images with inappropriate posture. In the first row, images contain incomplete palm. In the second row, motion blur appears in images. These images are 'typical' in the database, but they are 'dirty images' as templates.

In this paper, we propose a scheme that combines template selection and updating organically. The scheme automatically evaluates if the images contain inappropriate posture and select templates number and representative samples based on clustering. Then the scheme adaptively updates templates in online mode based on historical hit-counts to make the system maintain or even improve the representativeness of templates. Although palmprint authentication system is our test-bed, we believe the technique presented in the paper can be applied to other biometric systems such as fingerprint and face authentication systems as well.

The paper is structured as follows: In Sect. 2 we present the Chameleon clustering based templates selection method. In Sect. 3, we detail the online updating method and the scheme of the combination of templates selection and updating. In Sect. 4, we evaluate the proposed scheme and give our experimental results. We conclude in Sect. 5 with a discussion of the results and future research directions.

2   Chameleon Clustering Based Templates Selection

The procedure of palmprint templates selection may be posed as follows: For a new user, acquire a number of palmpint images in a specific palm posture. Then change the palm posture slightly (e.g., change the angle between palm and sensor, move palm in horizon and vertical directions), and select K templates that 'best' represent the user's biometric. In order to select the 'best' templates, two important issues should be taken into account: (1) Evaluate whether an image contains inappropriate posture; (2) Choose the most representative image in every palm posture.

In a word, the principle of a good templates database includes enough similarity to meet the security requirement and enough dissimilarity to meet the robustness. The algorithm of templates selection we presented is expected to result in a better performance in 'best representative ones' selection compared to a random selection and a solution to 'bad image' elimination.

In the paper, N palmprint images corresponding enrollment are grouped into K clusters based on Chameleon [11]. Chameleon algorithm is a hierarchical clustering algorithm. To start with a graph, the nodes in graph is palmprint feature vector, from each node edges are created to its k-nearest neighbors weighted by similarity measure [12].

We take dissimilarity matrix as similarity measure [13, 14]. The algorithm process is divided into three parts: (1) Eliminate bad images from samples based on dissimilarity matrix; (2) Cluster the images corresponding to matching distance; (3) Choose the most representative image in every cluster. More specifically, for a single user, templates selection algorithm is described as follows:

> **Step 1:** Generate the $N \times N$ dissimilarity matrix M, where N represents the number of input images and $W(i,j)$ is an element of M which represents weight between image i and j, i.e., reciprocal of matching distance. It means that the more similar between the image pair the higher $W(i,j)$ is obtained.
>
> **Step 2:** For M, $SumT(i) = W(i,0) + W(i,1) + \ldots + W(i,N-1)$ is sum of weights in row i in a row-major order, i.e., and eliminate the image i from samples in condition of $SumT(i) < W_{thre}$, where W_{thre} is the weight threshold that defined as:
>
> $$W_{thre} = N \times (1/\delta_{aut}) \tag{1}$$
>
> δ_{aut} is the authentication threshold. Repeat the step until $i = N$, and get a resized $N' \times N'$ matrix M'.
>
> **Step 3:** Perform Chameleon algorithm to group these N' images based on M' and generate K clusters set S.
>
> **Step 4:** For each image in cluster $S_m, m = 1, 2, \ldots, K$, calculate sum of weights to the other images in the same cluster, choose the maximum one as the template for S_m.

It's important to note that for a typical biometric system, the number of templates $\overline{K}$ is predefined, but the initial number of clusters K is obtained by clustering algorithm automatically. In our scheme, we make $K \leq \overline{K}$ after templates selection. In the condition of $K < \overline{K}$, it means that an inexperienced users takes insufficient palm posture changes during enrollment stage, this issue will be discussed in later Sect. 3. If $K > \overline{K}$, we pick two templates with the maximum weight to each other and remove the element with a lower $SumT$, repeat this until $K = \overline{K}$.

3 Adaptive Templates Database Updating Scheme

In a biometric system, user's palmprint feature can be considered as a fresh one for every time the authentication module is invoked [12]. False rejection rate rises if templates are insufficient or are no longer representative of intra-class variations. In this section, our updating algorithm is described in detail and the combination of templates selection and updating is introduced.

For a registered user i, let $T_i, (i = 1, 2, \ldots, N)$ be the templates from a system contains N enrolled users. T_i is composed of K_i images which selected from the templates selection algorithm presented in previous section. Tc_i is candidate templates composed of Kc_i images, $Kc_i = 0$ as be initialized. Let consider $Hit_{(i,j)}$, $(j = 1, \ldots, K_i + Kc_i)$, as the historical hit-counts of jth template from user i, they are also initialized as zero. For the system, we have $KN = K_1 + K_2 + \ldots + K_N$ templates and $KcN = Kc_1 + Kc_2 + \ldots + Kc_N$ candidates.

Img_{in} is considered as an input image during authentication stage, we obtain the minimum distance $m\_dis_{(i,j)}$ from KN times matching iterations, where $i \leq N, j \leq K_i$. In the presented updating scheme, Tc_i is the candidate templates set, and in the authentication stage, it is not matched against Img_{in}.

If $m\_dis_{(i,j)} \geq \delta_{aut}$, we believe that Img_{in} is not came from a genuine user, where δ_{aut} is the authentication threshold as mentioned before. Otherwise, the updating module works. The diagram of our updating algorithm is shown in Fig. 3.

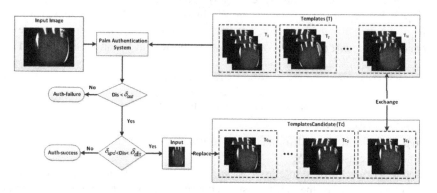

Fig. 3. Diagram of updating algorithm.

For the user i, we obtain a $(K_i + Kc_i) \times 1$ matching distance vector vc_dis_i between Img_{in} and $\{T_i, Tc_i\}$, if every element in vc_dis_i satisfies the Eq. 2, Img_{in} is considered as a new proper candidate template. In Eq. 2, δ_{upd} and δ_{dis} are the updating and dissimilarity thresholds respectively. As a rule of thumb, we set $\delta_{upd} = 0.8 \cdot \delta_{aut}$ and $\delta_{dis} = 0.8 \cdot \delta_{upd}$. δ_{upd} ensures templates will not be contaminated, and δ_{dis} ensures the dissimilarity of templates.

$$\begin{cases} vc\_dis_p \leq \delta_{dis} \\ vc\_dis_p \geq \delta_{upd} \end{cases}, p = 1, 2, \ldots, K_i + Kc_i \qquad (2)$$

Then, we have $q = \arg\min(vc\_dis)$, and make $Hit_{(i,q)} = Hit_{(i,q)} + 1$. q is the index of template in $\{T_i, Tc_i\}$.

In our algorithm, we regard Hit as the quantitative criterion of templates evaluation and we sort templates in ascending order, because every time the value grows, it means the template is the best at least in the moment. As time goes on, the intra-variations caused by templates aging make some templates can't be matched as the best one, so its Hit stop growing and the scheme will update them to better ones.

As mentioned in Sect. 2, in enrollment stage, because of the insufficient palm posture change, T_i is probably incomplete, i.e., $K_i < \overline{K}$. In this situation, the updating algorithm performs different strategies based on K_i and Kc_i.

Firstly, if $K_i < \overline{K}$, it means that T_i is incomplete and Tc_i is empty. Img_{in} is added to T_i as a new template directly and make $K_i = K_i + 1$ until $K_i = \overline{K}$.

And then, if $K_i = \overline{K}$ and $Kc_i < \overline{Kc}$, where $\overline{Kc}$ is predefined too. Img_{in} is added to candidate templates Tc_i as a candidate template and make $Kc_i = Kc_i + 1$ until $Kc_i = \overline{Kc}$.

In the end, if $K_i = \overline{K}$ and $Kc_i = \overline{Kc}$, it means that templates T_i and candidate templates Tc_i are complete databases. As mentioned before, templates and candidate templates databases are sorted by Hit_i, so $Hit_{(i,\overline{Kc})}$ is the minimum historical hit-count in Tc_i. Img_{in} replaces $Tc_{(i,\overline{Kc})}$. In next, if $Hit_{(i,\overline{K})} < Hit_{(i,\overline{K}+1)}$, it proves that the minimum hit-count in T_i is less than the maximum in Tc_i, we will replace it to a better template form Tc_i for authentication, so we exchange $T_{(i,\overline{K})}$ and $Tc_{(i,1)}$.

The presented scheme combines the templates selection and updating together, updating module improves the lack of templates after templates selection. Under our scheme, a new template replace the 'worst' one in Tc rather than in T directly, because temporary variations are incidental and irregular variations with a very short validity, it is very prone to concussion effect if replacing T many times in a short period, it also brings the risk of templates degeneration [18–20].

4   Experimental Results

The experiments have been performed on a palmprint authentication system based on the matcher called competitive-code based palmprint recognition [5]. We use two palmprint databases that collected from the same device. Database2 (DB-2) is collected in three months consecutively after Database1 (DB-1) was collected. Each of them contains more than 500 images captured from 20 different users' palm, where 20–30 images were collected for each palm. Around 10% 'dirty' images with motion blur or incomplete palmprint in DB-1, as shown in Fig. 4.

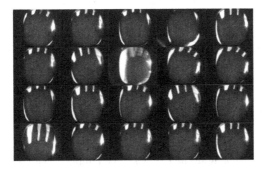

Fig. 4. Part of images in DB-1 from the same person. These samples contain 3 'dirty' images. The image with motion blur in row 2 column 3 and images with incomplete palm in row 1 column 4 and row 4 column 1.

In our experiment, the proposed scheme performs templates selection algorithm in DB-1, and then, performs updating algorithm in DB-2. After enrollment stage, dirty images will be rejected by authentication module, so there are no dirty image in DB-2.

As stated in Sect. 2, in templates selection stage, we calculate $W(i,j)$, where $i,j = 1, 2, \ldots, N$ in DB-1 and build the dissimilarity matrix M. As shown in Fig. 5, for a user contains palm images set with 29 samples in DB-1, experiment generates a 29×29 matrix M, positive diagonal matrix is null as shown in green label, means that the weight is zero between one image to itself. We set $\delta_{aut} = 0.38$ based upon empirical observation. According to Eq. 1, $W_{thre} = 76.3$.

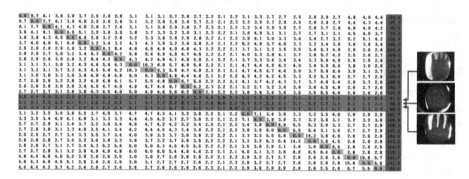

Fig. 5. Dissimilarity matrix and elimination of 'dirty' images.

In Fig. 5, we have labeled 3 rows blue which $SumT < W_{thre}$, where $SumT$ are labeled as red. Right side of the figure shows the images that corresponding to blue rows, they are 'dirty' images with motion blur, incomplete upper part of palm, incomplete lower part of palm from top to bottom.

The result indicates the presented operation with the dissimilarity matrix could find the 'dirty' images and remove them, this characteristic makes no-manual intervention during enrollment, i.e., select templates automatically.

It's difficult to evaluate an updating algorithm with quantitative measures [21, 22]. In order to test the effectiveness of algorithm under the scheme, we set a relatively small templates and candidate templates size to speed up the updating procedure.

In our experiment, we set $\overline{K} = 2$ and $\overline{Kc} = 1$. Besides, in order to verify the validity of algorithm in facing of temporary variations intervention, posture changes have been set with practical significance and operability, for this, some particular palm postures are not presented in DB-1, these postures are presented more and more frequent with the collection process of DB-2.

As shown in Fig. 6, we get 2 templates and 1 candidate template by presented template selection module. After this, two events occurred at 107th and 320th updating round.

The first event is exchanging in T and Tc, the template that ranks first in the initial state becomes candidate template after 2 times exchange.

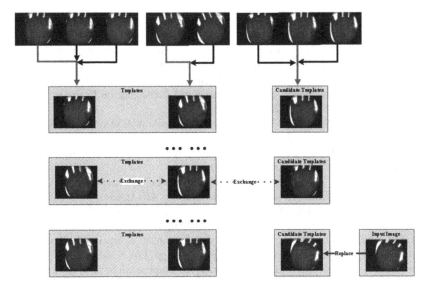

Fig. 6. The updating procedure.

The second is the candidate template stated in the first event is replaced by an input image, because the new posture obtained a higher frequency of occurrence, i.e., historical hit-count.

Although we accelerate and simplify the updating process, it seems that our verification experiment is prone to concussion effect, the complete of procedure are still ensured. Benefit from. $\delta_{aut}, \delta_{upd}$ and δ_{dif}, the updating algorithm of scheme is relatively strict and the risk of template degeneration is controlled well.

5 Conclusions

In this paper, we propose an effective scheme to select representative templates automatically and update them in online mode to prevent template aging. The scheme has been validated by a simplified simulation experiment and promising results have been obtained.

In the future, we are going to carry out a long-term experiment in real environments and study this scheme in more depth, and consider the feasibility of the scheme in other biometric fields.

Acknowledgements. This work was granted by Tianjin Sci-tech Planning Projects (Grant No. 14RCGFGX00846), the Natural Science Foundation of Hebei Province, China (Grant No. F2015202239), Tianjin Sci-tech Planning Projects (Grant No. 15ZCZDNC00130), National Natural Science Foundation of China (Grant No. 61305107) and partially supported by the Innovation Team Program of Beijing Academy of Science and Technology.

References

1. Kong, A., Zhang, D.: Competitive coding scheme for palmprint verification. In: Proceedings of IEEE International Conference on Pattern Recognition, pp. 520–523 (2004)
2. Sun, Z., Tan, T., Wang, Y., Li, S.: Ordinal palmprint representation for personal identification. In: Proceedings of IEEE International Conference on Computer Vision and Pattern Recognition, pp. 279–284 (2005)
3. Zhang, D., Kong, W.K., You, J., Wong, M.: On line palmprint identification. IEEE Trans. Pattern Anal. Mach. Intell. 25(9), 1041–1050 (2003)
4. Zhang, D., Zuo, W., Yue, F.: A comparative study of palmprint recognition algorithms. ACM Comput. Surv. 44(1), Article 2 (2012)
5. Yue, F., Zuo, W.M., Zhang, D., Wang, K.Q.: Competitive code - based palmprint recognition using FCM-based orientation selection. Pattern Recogn. 42(11), 2841–2849 (2009)
6. Uludag, U., Ross, A., Jain, A.: Biometric template selection and update: a case study in fingerprints. Pattern Recogn. 37(7), 1533–1542 (2004)
7. Trokielewicz, M.: Linear regression analysis of template aging in iris biometrics. In: International Workshop on Biometrics and Forensics, pp. 1–6. IEEE (2015)
8. De Marsico, M., et al.: GETSEL: gallery entropy for template selection on large datasets. In: IEEE International Joint Conference on Biometrics, pp. 1–8. IEEE (2014)
9. Sanchez-Reillo, R., Sanchez-Avila, C., Gonzalez-Marcos, A.: Biometric identification through hand geometry measurements. IEEE Trans. Pattern Anal. Mach. Intell. 22(10), 1168–1171 (2000)
10. Jia, W., Huang, D., Zhang, D.: Palmprint verification based on robust line orientation code. Pattern Recogn. 41(5), 1521–1530 (2008)
11. Karypis, G., Han, E.H., Kumar, V.: Chameleon a hierarchical clustering algorithm using dynamic modeling. Computer 32(8), 68–75 (2008)
12. Abboud, A.J., Jassim, S.A.: Biometric templates selection and update using quality measures. In: Proceedings of SPIE - The International Society for Optical Engineering, vol. 8406, p. 7 (2012)
13. Khan, S.H., et al.: Secure biometric template generation for multi-factor authentication. Pattern Recogn. 48(2), 458–472 (2015)
14. Moujahdi, C., et al.: Biometric template protection using spiral cube: performance and security analysis. Int. J. Artif. Intell. Tools 25(01), 150601230114001 (2016)
15. Lanitis, A.: A survey of the effects of aging on biometric identity verification. Int. J. Biom. 2(1), 34–52 (2009)
16. Jiang, X., Ser, W.: Online fingerprint template improvement. IEEE Trans. Pattern Anal. Mach. Intell. 24(8), 1121–1126 (2002). United States of America
17. Rattani, A., et al.: A dual-staged classification-selection approach for automated update of biometric templates. Inf. Fusion 25, 121–133 (2015)
18. Rattani, A., Marcialis, G.L., Granger, E., et al.: A dual-staged classification-selection approach for automated update of biometric templates. Inf. Fusion 25, 121–133 (2015)
19. Fernandez-Lozano, C., et al.: Texture classification using feature selection and kernel-based techniques. Soft Comput. 19(9), 1–12 (2015)
20. García, S., et al.: Prototype selection for nearest neighbor classification: taxonomy and empirical study. IEEE Trans. Pattern Anal. Mach. Intell. 34(3), 417–435 (2012)
21. Grosso, E., Pulina, L., Tistarelli, M.: Modeling biometric template update with ant colony optimization. In: iAPR International Conference on Biometrics, pp. 506–511. IEEE (2012)
22. Lanitis, A., Tsapatsoulis, N.: Quantitative evaluation of the effects of aging on biometric templates. IET Comput. Vis. 5(5), 338–347 (2011)

Supervised Hashing with Deep Convolutional Features for Palmprint Recognition

Jingdong Cheng, Qiule Sun, Jianxin Zhang$^{(\boxtimes)}$, and Qiang Zhang

Key Lab of Advanced Design and Intelligent Computing, Ministry of Education,
Dalian University, Dalian, People's Republic of China
zjx99326@163.com

Abstract. Palmprint representations using multiple filters followed by encoding, i.e. OrdiCode and SMCC, always achieve promising recognition performance. With the similar architecture but distinct idea, we propose a novel learnable palmprint coding representation, by integrating the two recent potentials, e.g. CNN and supervised Hashing, called as deep convolutional features based supervised hashing (DCFSH). DCFSH performs the CNN-F network to extract palmprint convolutional features, whose 13-layer features distilled by the PCA are used for the coding. To learn the compact binary code, the column sampling based discrete supervised hashing, which directly obtains the hashing code from semantic information, is employed. The proposed DCFSH is extensively evaluated by using various code bits and samplings on the PolyU palmprint database, and achieves the verification accuracy of EER = 0.0000% even with 128-bit code, illuminating the great potential of CNN and Hashing for palmprint recognition.

Keywords: Palmprint recognition · DCFSH · CNN · Hashing code

1 Introduction

Biometrics, such as face, fingerprint, palmprint, iris and vein recognition, have been widely studied. Among these biometric technologies, palmprint recognition, with the advantages of abundant discriminant features, high accuracy, well stability and low cost of acquisition, is regarded as a potential biometric technology and receives wide attentions. In recent years, a lot of palmprint recognition methods have been proposed based on various palmprint features, i.e., structure-based methods [1, 2], coding-based or texture-based methods [3, 4], subspace-based methods [5, 6] and statistics-based method [7]. Among them, coding-based methods, i.e., PalmCode [3], Competitive Code (CompCode) [8], OrdiCode [9], Sparse Multiscale Competitive Code (SMCC) [4] and Half-orientation Code [10] extracting texture information from palmprint image through a bank of filters followed by coding, have achieved the most promising performance for palmprint recognition. Especially, SMCC, which is proposed by Zuo et al., achieves the optimal verification accuracy of EER = 0.0140%. Though very high accuracy is obtained with low storage capacity, the accuracy of EER = 0.0000% is still failed to get. Meanwhile, few attentions are paid to the learning-based palmprint coding representation method which may achieve better recognition performance.

© Springer International Publishing AG 2017
J. Zhou et al. (Eds.): CCBR 2017, LNCS 10568, pp. 259–268, 2017.
https://doi.org/10.1007/978-3-319-69923-3_28

Recently, as one of the most potential technologies, convolutional neural network (CNN) is successfully applied for multimedia and vision applications, attracting more and more attentions from both academy and industry. The various CNNs, i.e., AlexNet [11], CNN-F [12], VggNet [13] and ResNet [14], designed by stacking convolutions followed by nonlinear activation functions, pooling operations and fully-connected layers, achieve excellent performance on many multimedia and vision tasks. CNNs learned from large-scale databases can extract genetic features with good generalization ability, which are conveniently transplanted onto other applications [11–16]. On the other hand, Hashing is becoming much more popular as an approximate nearest neighbor search method [17–19]. The hashing methods, i.e., the column sampling based discrete supervised hashing (COSDISH) [20] and latent factor hashing (LFH) [21], can directly learn the hashing code from samples based on optimizing algorithm. Moreover, several recent works also illuminate that hashing code produced by deep convolutional features provide remarkable performance [19, 22]. In this paper, motivated by great success of CNNs and Hashing, we propose novel deep convolutional features based supervised hashing (DCFSH) method for palmprint presentation. We employ the CNN-F architecture to extract the palmprint convolutional features, in which the 13-layer features followed by a PCA for dimensionality reduction are chosen to obtain the final binary coding representation by COSDISH. The experimental results show that the proposed DCFSH can achieve the remarkable verification accuracy of EER = 0.0000% with 128-bit code. The framework of the proposed DCFSH method is given in Fig. 1.

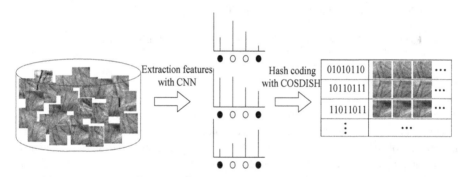

Fig. 1. The framework for supervised hashing code with deep features. Our proposed DCFSH method consists of two key components. The first component is a convolutional neural network to learn the initial palmprint convolutional features from pixels. The second component is a hashing function obtained by COSDISH method to map convolutional features to hashing code. We effectively integrate two components and obtain a novel coding method for palmprint representation.

The main contributions of this paper are listed as follows. (1) We, to our best knowledge, make the first attempt to directly obtain a coding-based palmprint representation through the learnable method. (2) To this end, we propose a novel DCFSH method for palmprint representation by assembling the CNN and Hashing, which directly learns the hashing code from the reduced palmprint convolutional features. (3) We extensively evaluate the proposed DCFSH method by using various coding bits and samplings on the PolyU palmprint database, in which it achieves the verification accuracy of EER = 0.0000% even with 128 bits code.

The rest of this paper is organized as follows: Sect. 2 describes the proposed DCFSH method, including the palmprint convolutional features extraction and COSDISH coding. Section 3 includes the evaluation results of proposed DCFSH method on the PolyU palmprint database, and the conclusions are given in Sect. 4.

2   The Proposed DCFSH Method

For the proposed DCFSH method, the CNN-F architecture is firstly adopted to extract the palmprint convolutional features, in which the 13-layer convolutional features processed by a PCA for dimensionality reduction are used for the further binary coding. Then, the recent COSDISH is performed to learn the compact binary coding representation on the reduced convolutional features.

2.1   Palmprint Convolutional Features

The proposed DCFSH method adopts the recent deep network CNN-F [12], with the similar architecture to AlexNet [11], to extract the palmprint convolutional features. The CNN-F has a total of 21 layers, including 5 convolutional layers, 3 pooling layers, 7 RELU layers, 2 normalization layers, 3 fully connected (FC) layers and softmax layer, respectively. The convolutional and FC layers are also called as learnable layers, including a number of convolutional filters learning from the input. The basic architecture of CNN-F is shown in Table 1, and the more details of CNN-F can be referred to [12].

Table 1. Configuration of the CNN-F network, where 'filter' includes the number and size information of convolutional filters, 'stride' represent the size of the convolutional kernel movement, 'pad' indicates the number of pixels added to each side of the input, and '–' stands for null value.

Layer	Filter	Stride	Pad	Layer	Filter	Stride	Pad
conv1	$64 \times 3 \times 11 \times 11$	4	0	relu4	–	–	0
relu1	–	–	0	conv5	$256 \times 256 \times 3 \times 3$	1	0
norm1	–	1	0	relu5	–	–	0
pool1	3×3	2	1	pool5	3×3	2	1
conv2	$256 \times 64 \times 5 \times 5$	1	2	fc6	$4096 \times 256 \times 6 \times 6$	1	0
relu2	–	–	0	relu6	–	–	0
norm2	–	1	0	fc7	$4096 \times 4096 \times 1 \times 1$	1	0
pool2	3×3	2	1	relu7	–	–	0
conv3	$256 \times 256 \times 3 \times 3$	1	1	fc8	$1000 \times 4096 \times 1 \times 1$	1	0
relu3	–	–	0	softmax	–	–	0
conv4	$256 \times 256 \times 3 \times 3$	1	1				

Recent works illuminate that the pre-trained CNN-F on large database provides outstanding representation ability in many multimedia and vision tasks. Moreover, the intermediate layers of CNN-F mainly mine the middle level features of the input image, and they possess better texture representation ability for palmprint image than the low and high layers. Hence, in our work, based on the pre-trained CNN-F network [12], we extract the layer-13 features, and denote its by $\mathbf{X} \in R^{h \times w \times c}$, where h, w and c represent the height, width and number of feature maps. Then, the layer-13 features are reshaped into a vector denoted as $\mathbf{x} \in R^d$, where d equals $h \times w \times c$. Finally, a PCA is performed on $\mathbf{x}$ for dimension reduction to get a lower dimensional feature vector $\mathbf{f} \in R^m$, where m equals 1024 in our evaluation.

2.2   Convolutional Features Coding with COSDISH

The recent COSDISH method [20] is employed to encode the aforementioned low dimensional convolutional features. COSDISH tries to resolve the problem of sampling and discrete optimization for the supervised hashing by minimize the following function:

$$\min_{\mathbf{B}^M, \mathbf{B}^Z} ||q\tilde{\mathbf{L}}^Z - \mathbf{B}^Z[\mathbf{B}^M]^T||_F^2 + ||q\tilde{\mathbf{L}}^M - \mathbf{B}^M[\mathbf{B}^M]^T||_F^2 \tag{1}$$

where $|| \cdot ||_F$ denotes the Frobenius norm, q represents the length of hashing code, $\tilde{\mathbf{L}}^M$ and $\tilde{\mathbf{L}}^Z$ are binary sub-matrix, $\mathbf{B}^M$ and $\mathbf{B}^Z$ are coding sub-matrix.

To resolve the Eq. (1), COSDISH adopts the strategy of alternatively optimizing matrix $\mathbf{B}^M$ and $\mathbf{B}^Z$. When $\mathbf{B}^M$ is fixed, after changing the loss from Frobenius norm into L_1 norm, the optimized function of $\mathbf{B}^Z$ can be given as:

$$F_2 = \min_{\mathbf{B}^Z} ||q\tilde{\mathbf{L}}^Z - \mathbf{B}^Z[\mathbf{B}^M]^T||_1 \tag{2}$$

Then, optimization function of $\mathbf{B}^M$ using optimal $\mathbf{B}^Z$ is rewritten as:

$$F_3 = \min_{\mathbf{B}^M} ||q\tilde{\mathbf{L}}^Z - \mathbf{B}^Z[\mathbf{B}^M]^T||_F^2 + ||q\tilde{\mathbf{L}}^M - \mathbf{B}^M[\mathbf{B}^M]^T||_F^2 \tag{3}$$

Equation (3) belongs to a general discrete optimization programming problem which can be transformed into an equivalent clustering problem to resolve. The two procedures repeat for several times to finish the optimization. Then, the final training sample hashing code $\mathbf{B} = [\mathbf{B}^M; \mathbf{B}^Z]$ is achieved.

To predict the hash coding of test set, the COSDISH learns a q bit binary classifiers, according to the training sample features matrix and hashing code matrix $\mathbf{B}$. After inputting the low dimensional convolutional features to the binary classifier, we can achieve the binary DCFSH coding for palmprint representation.

3   Experiment Results

In this section, we give a simple description of the adopted palmprint database, and extensively evaluate the proposed DCFSH method with various samplings, coding bits and training sample ratios. In coding matching step, the Hamming distance is employed to compute the similarity of two palmprint images. Moreover, the comparative result and analysis among DCFSH with state-of-the-art methods are illuminated. All the programs are developed with MatLab R2015b, and run on the PC equipped with 3.30 GHz CPU and 4 GB RAM.

3.1   Experiment Database and Setting

The PolyU palmprint database is regarded as one of the most authoritative public palmprint databases, containing 7752 grayscale images from 386 different palms. In the database, each palm has around 20 samples collected in two sessions, where about 10 samples are captured in the first session and the rest are belonged to the second session. The experiment uses the total samples of the first session. Each ROI is segmented from original image with the size of 128 × 128 pixels. Several segmented ROI images from two palms in the database are shown in Fig. 2.

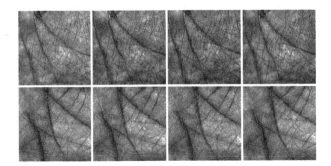

Fig. 2. Palmprint ROI images in PolyU palmprint database.

We use CNN to denote the vectorized convolutional features and CNN + PCA to represent features of PCA dimensionality reduction. The comparative performance results achieved by CNN and CNN + PCA features on the PolyU palmprint database are given in Fig. 3, in which illuminates that the two features achieve very similar performance, with corresponding EERs of 0.2623% and 0.2643%, respectively. Therefore, the CNN + PCA features are adopted in the evaluation experiments.

The following experiments mainly include three folds: (1) The proposed DCFSH method is performed with different samplings and code bits to observe their influences on palmprint recognition performance. (2) The generalization ability of the DCFSH is evaluated by using various training samples proportion, ranging from 30% to 70% with an interval of 10%. (3) Comparative experiment results and analysis among DCFSH with several state-of-the-art methods are illuminated.

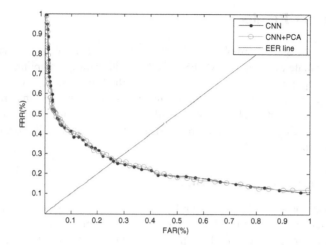

Fig. 3. The ROC curves achieved by basic convolutional features.

3.2 Experimental Results

In this experiment, the semantic information matrix is randomly column sampled from a group number of 256, 128 to 64, and the CNN + PCA features are correspondingly encoded into 256-bit, 128-bit or 64-bit hashing code, where the coding bits should not be larger than the sampling numbers, i.e., 128 columns are randomly selected from the matrix, the features can only encode 128 bits or 64 bits. The comparative experiment results based on the different sampling and coding bit are illuminated in Table 2.

Table 2. The comparative results using various samplings and coding bits

Number of sampling	Hashing code bits	EER (%)
256	256	0.0000
256	128	0.0000
128	128	0.0000
256	64	0.1231
128	64	0.2761
64	64	1.1173

It can be seen from Table 2 that the recognition accuracy of EER obtained by 64 sampling and 64-bit hashing code is 1.1173%. With the increase of coding bits and sampling, the recognition accuracy gradually improves. When using 128 sampling number and 128 coding bits, it turns to achieve the remarkable recognition accuracy of EER = 0.0000%. Generally speaking, because the given method is mainly inspired by the supervised training model, the longer hashing code will lead to the longer time consumption. Meanwhile, we also describe the matching degree distribution curve with 128 sampling and 128-bit code in Fig. 4, which the true matching denotes features matching from the same palm, and the false matching denotes feature matching from different palms. Figure 4 shows that all of the true matching scores are smaller than 13, and more than 70% of the scores are less than 3, while matching scores from different palms are larger than 40. Hence, there is a clear gap between the true matching scores and the false matching scores. In other word, this encoding method can distinguish inter-class images.

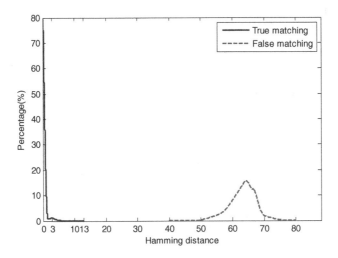

Fig. 4. Matching curves of Inter-class and Intra-class

Then, we perform the experiment to test the generalization ability of the DCFSH by using various training samples. The corresponding experiment results are given in Table 3, in which we list the EER value of the training sample and the test sample under different proportion, and the value of GAR at FAR = 0.1000%, FAR = 0.0100% respectively.

As can be seen from Table 3, the proportion of training set increases from 30% to 70%, EER decreases from 0.7097% (0.4187%) to 0.0000%, and when the training set reaches 50%, EER has become 0.0000%. We can get the good recognition accuracy

Table 3. Number of sampling and hashing code bits are 128 and 256, GAR$_{-3}$ (GAR$_{-4}$) denotes the genuine acceptance rate at FAR = 0.0010 (FAR = 0.0001).

Training sample ratio (%)	128			256		
	EER (%)	GAR$_{-3}$ (%)	GAR$_{-4}$ (%)	EER (%)	GAR$_{-3}$ (%)	GAR$_{-4}$ (%)
70	0.0000	100.00	100.00	0.0000	100.00	100.00
60	0.0000	100.00	100.00	0.0000	100.00	100.00
50	0.0000	100.00	100.00	0.0000	100.00	100.00
40	0.0801	99.95	99.79	0.0341	100.00	99.97
30	0.7097	98.67	96.89	0.4187	99.99	99.92

without too much training set. We also compute the GAR in different proportion. As the proportion of training increases, the rate of genuine acceptance has ascended significantly. The change rule of GAR is consistent with that of EER. And the result of the 256-bit encoding is significantly better than the 128-bit. Therefore, our proposed DCFSH method has a magnificent generalization capability.

Moreover, we compare our method to several state-of-the-art methods. The comparison results are listed in Table 4, where the results are reported by the SMCC [4]. Our proposed learning DCFSH method achieves the lowest EER value and uses the least coded bits. Therefore, the DCFSH is a very promising method for palmprint presentation.

Table 4. Comparison of EER of different palmprint recognition methods, the number "184320" is estimate value.

Methods	EER (%)	Template size (bytes)
OrdiCode [9]	0.1040	384
CompCode [8]	0.0380	384
MCC [23]	0.0230	480
BOCV [24]	0.0190	768
SMCC [4]	0.0140	384
RAC [25]	0.0100	184320
DCFSH (Ours)	0.0000	16

4 Conclusion

In this paper, we propose novel deep convolutional features based supervised hashing method for palmprint presentation. We employ CNN-F architecture to extract the palmprint convolutional features, followed by learning binary coding from distilled deep features. The experimental results show that the DCFSH can achieve the remarkable verification accuracy of EER = 0.0000% with the 128-bit code. In the future work, we will further research the scalability of DCFSH coding method in others palmprint database and the deep hashing method of end-to-end for palmprint recognition.

Acknowledgements. This work is supported by the National Natural Science Foundation of China (No. 61202251, 91546123), Program for Changjiang Scholars and Innovative Research Team in University (No. IRT_15R07), the Liaoning Provincial Natural Science Foundation (No. 201602035) and the High-level Talent Innovation Support Program of Dalian City (No. 2016RQ078).

References

1. Zhang, D., Shu, W.: Two novel characteristics in palmprint verification: datum point invariance and line feature matching. Pattern Recogn. **32**, 691–702 (1999)

2. Jain, A.K., Feng, J.: Latent palmprint matching. IEEE Trans. Pattern Anal. Mach. Intell. **31**, 1032–1047 (2009)

3. Zhang, D., Kong, W.-K., You, J., Wong, M.: Online palmprint identification. IEEE Trans. Pattern Anal. Mach. Intell. **25**, 1041–1050 (2003)

4. Zuo, W., Lin, Z., Guo, Z., Zhang, D.: The multiscale competitive code via sparse representation for palmprint verification. In: Computer Vision and Pattern Recognition (CVPR), pp. 2265–2272 (2010)

5. Lu, G., Zhang, D., Wang, K.: Palmprint recognition using eigenpalms features. Pattern Recogn. Lett. **24**, 1463–1467 (2003)

6. Yan, Y., Wang, H., Chen, S., Cao, X., Zhang, D.: Quadratic projection based feature extraction with its application to biometric recognition. Pattern Recogn. **56**, 40–49 (2016)

7. Krishneswari, K., Arumugam, S.: Intramodal feature fusion using wavelet for palmprint authentication. Int. J. Eng. Sci. Technol. **3**(2), 1597–1605 (2011)

8. Kong, A.-K., Zhang, D.: Competitive coding scheme for palmprint verification. In: Pattern Recognition, pp. 520–523 (2004)

9. Sun, Z., Tan, T., Wang, Y., Li, S.Z.: Ordinal palmprint representation for personal identification. In: Computer Vision and Pattern Recognition (CVPR), pp. 279–284 (2005)

10. Fei, L., Xu, Y., Zhang, D.: Half-orientation extraction of palmprint features. Pattern Recogn. Lett. **69**, 35–41 (2016)

11. Krizhevsky, A., Sutskever, I., Hinton, G.E.: Imagenet classification with deep convolutional neural networks. In: Advances in Neural Information Processing Systems, pp. 1097–1105 (2012)

12. Chatfield, K., Simonyan, K., Vedaldi, A., Zisserman, A.: Return of the devil in the details: delving deep into convolutional nets. Computer Science. arXiv:1405.3531 (2014)

13. Simonyan, K., Zisserman, A.: Very deep convolutional networks for large-scale image recognition. Computer Science. arXiv preprint arXiv:1409.1556 (2014)

14. He, K., Zhang, X., Ren, S., Sun, J.: Deep residual learning for image recognition. In: Computer Vision and Pattern Recognition (CVPR), pp. 770–778 (2016)

15. Shen, X., Tian, X., He, A., Sun, S., Tao, D.: Transform-invariant convolutional neural networks for image classification and search. In: ACM on Multimedia Conference (ACM), pp. 1345–1354 (2016)

16. Yandex, A.B., Lempitsky, V.: Aggregating local deep features for image retrieval. In: Computer Vision (ICCV), pp. 1269–1277 (2015)

17. Zhang, D., Wang, J., Cai, D., Lu, J.: Self-taught hashing for fast similarity search. In: International ACM SIGIR Conference on Research and Development in Information Retrieval, pp. 18–25 (2010)

18. Lin, G., Shen, C., Suter, D., Hengel, A.V.D.: A general two-step approach to learning-based hashing. In: Computer Vision (ICCV), pp. 2552–2559 (2013)

19. Xia, R., Pan, Y., Lai, H., Liu, C., Yan, S.: Supervised hashing for image retrieval via image representation learning. In: AAAI, pp. 2156–2162 (2014)

20. Kang, W.C., Li, W.J., Zhou, Z.H.: Column sampling based discrete supervised hashing. In: AAAI, pp. 1230–1236 (2016)

21. Zhang, P., Zhang, W., Li, W.J., Guo, M.: Supervised hashing with latent factor models. In: International ACM SIGIR Conference on Research and Development in Information Retrieval, pp. 173–182 (2014)

22. Erin Liong, V., Lu, J., Wang, G., Moulin, P., Zhou, J.: Deep hashing for compact binary codes learning. In: Computer Vision and Pattern Recognition (CVPR), pp. 2475–2483 (2015)

23. Zuo, W., Yue, F., Wang, K., Zhang, D.: Multiscale competitive code for efficient palmprint recognition. In: Pattern Recognition, pp. 1–4 (2008)

24. Guo, Z., Zhang, D., Zhang, L., Zuo, W.: Palmprint verification using binary orientation co-occurrence vector. Pattern Recogn. Lett. **30**, 1219–1227 (2009)
25. Han, Y., Sun, Z., Tan, T., Hao, Y.: Palmprint recognition based on regional rank correlation of directional features. In: Tistarelli, M., Nixon, M.S. (eds.) ICB 2009. LNCS, vol. 5558, pp. 587–596. Springer, Heidelberg (2009). doi:10.1007/978-3-642-01793-3_60

Contrast Research on Full Finger Area Extraction Method of Touchless Fingerprint Images Under Different Illuminants

Kejun Wang, Yi Cao, and Xianglei Xing[✉]

College of Automation, Harbin Engineering University, Harbin 150001, China
xingxl@hrbeu.edu.cn

Abstract. Touchless fingerprint recognition with high acceptance, high security, hygiene advantages, is currently a hot research field of biometrics. The background areas of touchless fingerprints are more complex and bigger than those of the contact. So the general methods for contact fingerprint images are difficult to achieve a good effect when extracting the full finger area. The purpose of this research is to compare the performance of finger area extraction based on different color model and illuminants, and then lays the foundation for touchless fingerprint identification. The fingerprint images are respectively collected under blue, green and red illuminants. And then, the Otsu based on YCbCr model, HSV model, and YIQ model is adopted to extract the finger area. Experimental results show that the Otsu based on the Cb component of YCbCr model and S component of HSV model can achieve excellent extraction results under blue illuminant.

Keywords: Touchless fingerprint · Full finger area extraction · Illuminant · Otsu · Color model

1 Introduction

With its high practicability and feasibility, fingerprint identification technology has become the most common and legally binding biometric technology. Even so, since the fingerprint image is collected by a touchable sensor, there are still many problems in the conventional fingerprint identification like fingerprint deformation, fingerprint residue, sensitive to skin conditions and the spread of germs at the time of collection, etc. In contrast, touchless fingerprint can not only eliminate these negative factors, but also has high recognition performance and anti-counterfeiting performance.

The background areas of touchless fingerprints are more complex and bigger than those of the contact as Fig. 1 shows. Fingerprint image will appear rotation and translation phenomenon. What's more, the contrast of the ridge and valley lines is much lower. Many scholars have studied touchless fingerprint recognition. The shape-from-silhouette method can get a three-dimensional fingerprint image with five cameras from multiple perspectives, and then expand it into an equivalent two-dimensional fingerprint image [1]. Choi et al. [2] proposed a new touchless fingerprint sensing device capturing three different views at one time and a method for

© Springer International Publishing AG 2017
J. Zhou et al. (Eds.): CCBR 2017, LNCS 10568, pp. 269–278, 2017.
https://doi.org/10.1007/978-3-319-69923-3_29

mosaicking these view-different images. They can get a high-quality fingerprint template to solve problems caused by a touch-based sensing device such as a view difference problem and a limited usable area due to perspective distortion and rotation. The device is large and expensive, so its application scope is limited.

 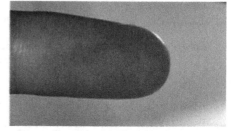

Contact fingerprint   Touchless fingerprint

Fig. 1. The contact fingerprint image and touchless fingerprint image

Scholars conducted a study of touchless fingerprint identification technology based on simple acquisition devices in order to overcome these difficulties. Literature [3] obtained the fingerprint image with mobile cameras and delved into a low contrast between ridges and valleys. Kumar and Kwong [4] developed a 3-D fingerprint identification system that employs only single camera and a new representation of 3D finger surface features using Finger Surface Codes which is very effective in matching three dimensional fingerprints. Assogba [5] presented a contactless fingerprint system based on supervised contactless image acquisition with only an ordinary camera and a ridge minutiae extraction method based on orientation computation. This kind of method, using the cheap fingerprint acquisition device and simple fingerprint acquisition method, has broad prospects. However, its fingerprint image quality is relatively poor. The recognition algorithm's effect of touchless fingerprint recognition is so poor now.

Fingerprint image preprocessing directly affects the performance of the fingerprint identification. Using the color information of fingerprint images, literature [6] proposed a fingerprint segmentation method based on skin color and the adaptive threshold point. However, the characteristics of touchless fingerprint image cannot be fully considered by these methods without targeted treatment measures. So the touchless fingerprint recognition algorithm still needs further study.

The study found that fingerprint images show more detail changes under blue light [7]. The touch-based fingerprint device, Digital Personal 4500, uses blue lights instead of red lights. This paper lays a foundation for dual-model recognition system [8] based on touchless fingerprint and finger-vein. In this paper, a fingerprint sampling device, which is made up of a common CMOS camera, is adopted under blue, green and red lights. And then, the Otsu based on different components of three color models is adopted to extract the finger area. Since there is no literature about the selection of illuminants and color models at home and abroad, this paper illustrates the best choice of the light source and color model in contactless fingerprint preprocessing which is extremely necessary.

2 Touchless Fingerprint Images Collection

The size of fingerprint image collected by the finger fingerprint acquisition system in our lab is 1280 × 720 pixels. The device is made up of a CMOS camera and a set of led. As is shown in Fig. 1, there is distortion and fracture in contact fingerprint images, and in touchless fingerprint images, background region takes so much space of the image that processing the whole image will not only increase computational cost, but also takes up more storage space. To reduce the background region interference, we need to extract the finger area.

Figure 2 shows the R/G/B components of fingerprint images collected in blue, green and red illuminants. By observing the fingerprint images in Fig. 2, we can see that fingerprint images collected in blue illuminant shows more details which are extremely important in touchless fingerprint identification than those collected in green and red illuminants.

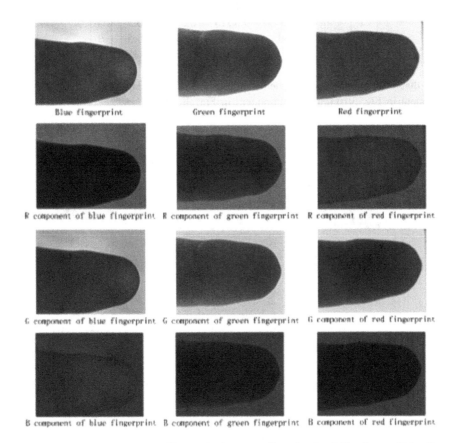

Fig. 2. The R/G/B components of fingerprint images collected under 3 illuminants (Color figure online)

3   Fingerprint Images in Different Color Models

By observing the fingerprint images in Fig. 1, we can see that finger area in touchless fingerprint images is mainly the blue part while the background is not. According to this feature, this paper converts the RGB images collected into 3 different color spaces to compare the performance of each component and then finds the best one which can perfectly separate the full finger area from the whole image.

3.1   Color Model Based on YCbCr Space

The YCbCr color model uses CaR601 as the encoding. Y/Cb/Cr refers to the luminance/blue color/red color component, YCbCr space has the characteristic to detach the color component from the luminance component. The YCbCr format can be linear changed from the RGB format as is shown in the Eq. (1):

$$\begin{bmatrix} Y \\ Cb \\ Cr \\ 1 \end{bmatrix} = \begin{bmatrix} 0.2990 & 0.5870 & 0.1140 & 0 \\ -0.1687 & -0.3313 & 0.5000 & 0.5 \\ 0.5000 & -0.4187 & -0.0813 & 0.5 \\ 0 & 0 & 0 & 1 \end{bmatrix} \begin{bmatrix} R \\ G \\ B \\ 1 \end{bmatrix} \tag{1}$$

So that we can get the component diagram of the gray-scale map in Fig. 3(a), Cb component in Fig. 3(b) and Cr component in Fig. 3(c):

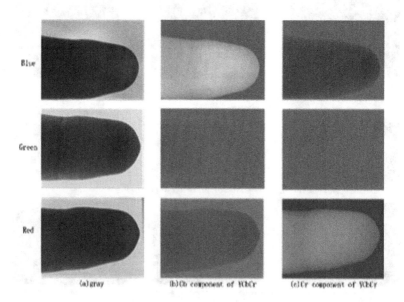

Fig. 3. The component diagrams of YcbCr

As is shown in Fig. 3, the pixel difference of the target and background in Cb component diagram under blue illuminant is more apparently than that in Cr component diagram.

3.2   Color Model Based on YIQ Space

The YIQ color model belongs to NTSC (National Television Standards Committee) system. Y refers to luminance (Brightness), which means the gray value of an image, and I and Q refer to chrominance. I component shows the change of color from orange to cyan, and Q shows the change of color from purple to yellow-green. YIQ space has the characteristic to detach the color component from the luminance component. The YIQ format can be linear changed from the RGB format as is shown in the Eq. (2):

$$\begin{bmatrix} Y \\ I \\ Q \end{bmatrix} = \begin{bmatrix} 0.299 & 0.587 & 0.114 \\ 0.596 & -0.274 & -0.322 \\ 0.211 & -0.523 & 0.312 \end{bmatrix} \begin{bmatrix} R \\ G \\ B \end{bmatrix} \tag{2}$$

So that we can get the component diagram of the Y component (Fig. 4(a)), I component (Fig. 4(b)) and Q component (Fig. 4 (c)) in Fig. 4:

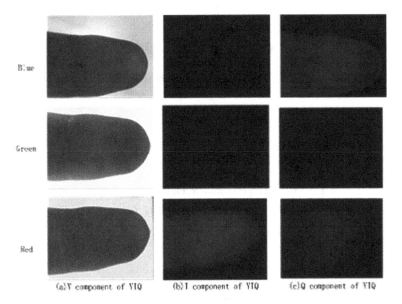

Fig. 4. The component diagrams of YIQ

As is shown in Fig. 4, the pixel difference of the target and background in three component diagrams of YIQ space is less apparently than that in Cb component diagram of YCbCr space.

3.3   Color Model Based on HSV and HSI Space

The HSV color model is defined in terms of vision based on color identification of human eyes. H/S/V refers to hue/saturation/value. Compared to RGB space, the HSV space can visually express the shades, hue and brightness of color. Figure 5 shows the space model of HSV.

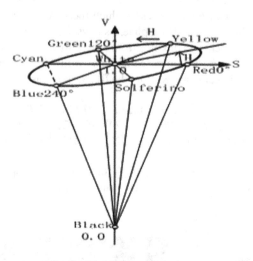

Fig. 5. The space model of HSV

The HSV format can be linear changed from the RGB format as is shown in the Eq. (3):

$$V = \max(R, G, B)$$

$$S = \begin{cases} \frac{V - \min(R,G,B)}{V} & \text{if } V \neq 0 \\ 0 & \text{otherwise} \end{cases}$$

$$H = \begin{cases} 60(G - B)/(V - \min(R, G, B)) & \text{if } V = R \\ 120 + 60(B - R)/(V - \min(R, G, B)) & \text{if } V = G \\ 240 + 60(R - G)/(V - \min(R, G, B)) & \text{if } V = B \end{cases} \tag{3}$$

$$\text{if } H < 0 \text{ then } H = H + 360$$

So that we can get the component diagram of the H component (Fig. 6(a)), S component (Fig. 6(b)) and V component (Fig. 6(c)):

As is shown in Fig. 6, the pixel difference of the target and background in S component diagram under blue illuminant is more apparently than the others.

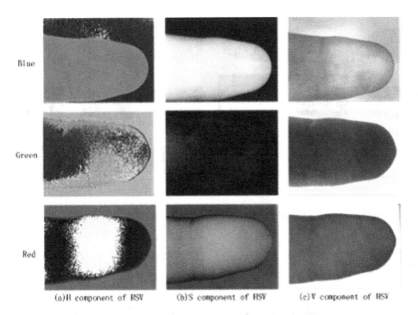

(a)H component of HSV   (b)S component of HSV   (c)V component of HSV

Fig. 6. The component diagrams of HSV

4 The Otsu Based on Different Components of Three Color Models

The Otsu based on different components of different color models is adopted to extract the finger area. Otsu [9] is a kind of adaptive threshold selection method which analyzes the class attribute. The optimum threshold is obtained, when the variance between the target one and the fingerprint image background is maximal. In Otsu, we first obtain the probability of each gray value from a m gray-level image. Secondly, we divide them into two parts with variable T and then calculate the probability of each part and the inter-class variance $\delta^2(T)$:

$$\delta^2(T) = \omega_0(\mu_0 - \mu)^2 + \omega_1(\mu_1 - \mu)^2 \tag{4}$$

where μ_0, μ_1 is the average gray-value of each part, ω_0, ω_1 are their probability, μ is the average gray-value of the whole image. The variable T, changing from 0 to m − 1, is the threshold when δ^2 is the biggest.

Otsu, utilizing the statistical property of the gray value, is strict with the size of the target picture, which means the finger area should be neither too big nor too small. The finger area extraction of components of three color models under blue illuminant is shown in Fig. 7. The finger area extraction of components of three color models under green illuminant is shown in Fig. 8. The finger area extraction of components of three color models under red illuminant is shown in Fig. 9. Figure 10 shows the extraction result of blue fingerprint with complex background.

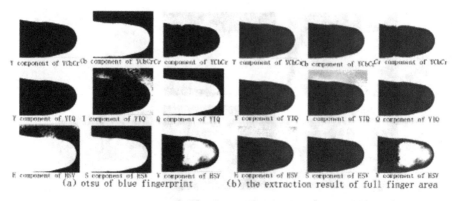

Fig. 7. Extract finger area in components of three color models under blue illuminant

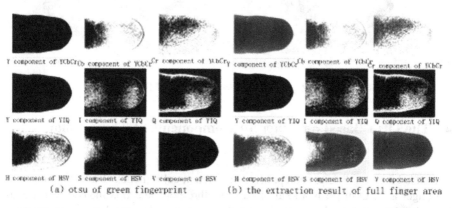

Fig. 8. Extract finger area in components of three color models under green illuminant

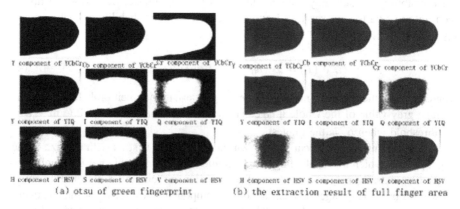

Fig. 9. Extract finger area in components of three color models under red illuminant

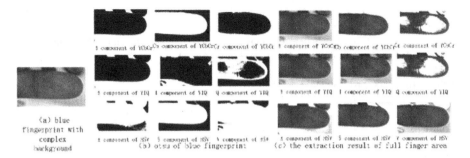

Fig. 10. Extract finger area from blue fingerprint image with complex background in components of three color models (Color figure online)

Through experimental analysis, the gray-map of fingerprint in blue illuminant shows more details and better extraction performance than that in green and red illuminant. The Otsu based on Cb component of YCbCr color model and S component of HSV color model can get better result in full finger extraction.

5   Conclusion

Taking example by the traditional touch-based fingerprint image collection and pre-processing algorithm and the existing touchless fingerprint image collection and pre-processing algorithm, the paper compares the performance of full finger area extraction of fingerprint images collected under different illuminants in different color spaces:

(1)   Fingerprint images collected under blue illuminant can achieve excellent extraction results and shows more details than those collected under green and red illuminants.

(2)   As is shown in Fig. 7, the Otsu based on the Cb component of YCbCr model and the S component of HSV model can achieve excellent extraction results under blue illuminant.

(3)   As formula (1) and (3) shows, the calculation of HSV color model is more complex than that of YCbCr color model. So the Cb component of YCbCr color model is the best choice in full finger area extraction.

Acknowledgments. This work was supported by the Fundamental Research Funds for the Central Universities of China, Natural Science Foundation of China, and Natural Science Fund of Heilongjiang Province of China under Grand No. HEUCFJ170404, 61573114, 61703119, F2015033 and QC2017070.

References

1. Parziale, G., Diaz-Santana, E., Hauke, R.: The surround Imager^{TM}: a multi-camera touchless device to acquire 3D rolled-equivalent fingerprints. In: Zhang, D., Jain, A.K. (eds.) ICB 2006. LNCS, vol. 3832, pp. 244–250. Springer, Heidelberg (2005). doi:10.1007/11608288_33

2. Choi, H., Choi, K., Kim, J.: Mosaicing touchless and mirror-reflected fingerprint images. IEEE Trans. Inf. Forensics Secur. **5**(1), 52–61 (2010)
3. Derawi, M.O., Yang, B., Busch, C.: Fingerprint recognition with embedded cameras on mobile phones. In: Prasad, R., Farkas, K., Schmidt, A.U., Lioy, A., Russello, G., Luccio, F.L. (eds.) MobiSec 2011. LNICSSITE, vol. 94, pp. 136–147. Springer, Heidelberg (2012). doi:10.1007/978-3-642-30244-2_12
4. Kumar, A., Kwong, C.: Towards contactless, low-cost and accurate 3D fingerprint identification. IEEE Trans. Pattern Anal. Mach. Intell. **37**(3), 681–696 (2015)
5. Assogba, M.K., Ali, A.N.: Fingerprint characteristic extraction by ridge orientation: an approach for a supervised contactless biometric system. Int. J. Comput. Appl. **16**(6), 14–19 (2011)
6. Kaur, P., Jain, A., Mittal, S.: Touch-less fingerprint analysis—a review and comparison. Int. J. Intell. Syst. Appl. (IJISA) **4**(6), 46 (2012)
7. Angelopoulou, E.: Understanding the color of human skin. In: Photonics West 2001-Electronic Imaging. International Society for Optics and Photonics, pp. 243–251 (2001)
8. Yang, J., Zhang, X.: Feature-level fusion of fingerprint and finger-vein for personal identification. Pattern Recogn. Lett. **33**(5), 623–628 (2012)
9. Xie, F., Zhao, D., et al.: Visual C++ Digital Image Processing, pp. 285–288. Electronic Industry Press, Beijing (2008)

Fingerprint Pore Extraction Using U-Net Based Fully Convolutional Network

Haixia Wang, Xicheng Yang, Lingtao Ma, and Ronghua Liang$^{(\boxtimes)}$

College of Information Engineering, Zhejiang University of Technology,
Hangzhou 310023, People's Republic of China
rhliang@zjut.edu.cn

Abstract. The public demand for personal safety is increasing rapidly. Fingerprint features as the most commonly used bio-signature need to improve their safety continuously. The third level features of fingerprint (especially the sweat pores) can be added to the automatic fingerprint recognition system to increase the accuracy of fingerprint identification in a variety of environments. Due to perspiration activities, the shape and size sweat of pores are varying spatially and temporally. Extraction of fingerprint pores is both critical and challenging. In this paper, we adapt a novel fully convolutional neural network called U-net for ridges and sweat pores extraction. The PolyU High-Resolution-Fingerprint (HRF) database is used for testing of the proposed method. The results show the validity of the proposed method. With the majority of the pores correctly extracted, the proposed method can serve for fingerprint recognition using Level 3 features.

Keywords: Fingerprint · Pores extraction · U-net

1 Introduction

Fingerprint is one of the most common bio-signatures in the world due to its uniqueness, permanence and convenience to use. Fast development of automatic fingerprint recognition system (AFRS) in recent years has make fingerprint identification part of our daily life. There are three levels of features in fingerprint [1]. Level 1 features refer to the general ridge flows, the positions and types of singular points, which are often used for coarse identification. Level 2 features are based on the positions and orientations of special ridge points, called minutiae points. The ridge bifurcations and endings are most frequently used minutiae points. Level 3 features are commonly recognized as the sweat pores lying in the ridges of the fingerprints, which can only be captured in fingerprint images of more than 1000 dpi. Since the standard resolution of most fingerprint recognition systems is 500 dpi, level 1 and level 2 features have been widely used in current AFRS system for personal recognition [2].

With the development of fingerprint capturing techniques, the image resolution has been much increased. Fingerprint capturing systems of more than 1000 dpi become available [3]. High image resolution makes the level 3 features part of the fingerprint recognition possible. The level 3 features have been proven to be as unique and permanent as the level 2 features. The effectiveness of sweat pores in personal

J. Zhou et al. (Eds.): CCBR 2017, LNCS 10568, pp. 279–287, 2017.
https://doi.org/10.1007/978-3-319-69923-3_30

identification has been statistically analyzed and validated [4, 5]. They are especially useful when only partial fingerprint is captured and the identified minutiae points in it are not sufficient for identification, such as in the criminal investigation. Sweat pores can be used together with the existing levels one and two features for the auxiliary judgment [6, 7]. Decided by sweating or not, the pores are categorized as open or closed pores, as shown in Fig. 1. A closed pore is entirely enclosed while an open pore intersects with the valley lying between two ridges [6]. The status of a pore is changing according to its perspiration activities. Thus, the sizes and shapes of pores are varying both spatially and temporal, which makes pore extraction challenging.

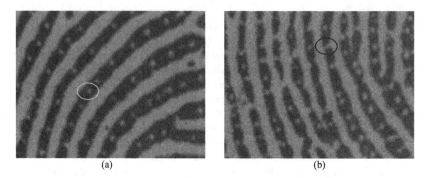

(a)   (b)

Fig. 1. Open and closed pores demonstration. (a) A fingerprint image with closed pore highlighted; (b) A fingerprint image with open pore highlighted.

Methods have been proposed to extract pores from fingerprint images. Skeleton-tracking-based methods [8] have been an early trend of pore extraction which estimate pore locations by tracking the ridges of fingerprints. This type of methods requires higher than 2000 dpi of fingerprint images and is sensitive to noise. Currently, the filtering-based methods are widely used. Ray et al. [9] proposed an isotropic pore model based on a modified 2-dimensional Gaussian function to extract pores from fingerprint images, which however does not fit with the varying pore scales and ridge/valley widths even in the same fingerprint. Jain et al. [6] proposed to use the Mexican hat wavelet transform to extract pores based on the high negative frequency response due to abrupt intensity change from bright to dark at the pores. It has difficulties in adapting to varying pore conditions. Parsons et al. [5] proposed to use DoG filter for fingerprint extraction, but circular assumption of pores does not hold well on real fingerprint images. To take different pore conditions into consideration, Zhao proposed a dynamic anisotropic pore model for pore extraction [10] by introducing the ridge orientation and frequency into consideration. Compared with designing specific models for pores, machine learning methods can well adapt to different pore conditions. Genovese et al. proposed to use neural network with pore features to identify pores [11]. Labati et al. proposed a CNN-D network to coarsely identify the pore location and a CNN-R network to refine the results [12]. It achieves good results for fingerprints on different fingerprint databases.

Convolutional neural network (CNN) seems to be a good solution for pore extraction. It has attracted wide attention in both research and engineering fields due to its excellent performances on generic visual recognition tasks. Compared with traditional methods where human interactions are often required to identify the features, CNN uses multi-layer convolutions to extract features automatically. However, conventional CNNs are not well suited for image segmentation due to the down-sampling operations, i.e. the sweat pore extraction in this paper. To solve this problem and identify each individual locations of the objects, a sliding window is often used which however results in high computational complexity.

In this paper, we propose to use a fully convolutional networks (FCN) [13] to segment pores from the fingerprint images, which overcomes the above difficulty and exhibits good results in the processing of the image semantic segmentation task. In the rest of the paper, a novel fully convolutional neural network U-net [14] is adapted to sweat pore extraction in Sect. 2. The experimental results using the U-net network in PolyU High-Resolution-Fingerprint (HRF) database [16] and discussions are given in Sect. 3. A conclusion is drawn in Sect. 4.

2   The Proposed Method

U-net is a state-of-the-art FCN for biomedical image segmentation. It can deal with possible pore variations by learning the salient features of the pores without any assumption on the image characteristics. In this section, we adapt U-net to sweat pore identification and estimate the centroid coordinates (x, y) of each pore in the fingerprint image. The overall processing flow is shown in Fig. 2, including (i) the fingerprint image preprocessing and the data augmentation, (ii) U-net network training and segmentation, (iii) post processing for spurious and false pores removal.

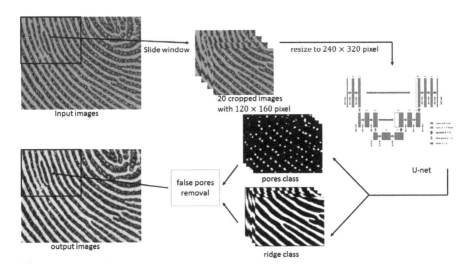

Fig. 2. U-net processing flow.

2.1 U-Net

U-net is an expansion of a convolution neural network. It is composed of one to many convolution, pooling, and up-sampling layers. The U-net network has two characteristics. First, the up-sampling outputs are combined with high resolution features before pooling. Based on the combined features, a more precise output can be assembled by a successive convolution layer. Second, a large number of feature channels are presented in the up-sampling part, which allows the network to propagate context information to higher resolution layers. Thus, instead of one single classification decision for the while image as in conventional CNN, U-net can produce a decision for each single pixel and thus better solve the image segmentation problem.

Figure 3 and Table 1 show the network structure and specific parameters of the U-net. It consists of a "contracting" and an "expanding" stage. In the contracting stage, convolution and pooling operators are used, where the size of the input is reduced while the number of feature maps is increased. In each layer, two consecutive unpadded convolutions are applied each followed by a rectifier linear unit (ReLU) activation and a 2×2 max pooling operation. As a result, at each layer, the number of extracted features is doubled. In the expanding stage, up-sampling operators are used instead of pooling operators which increases the resolution of the output and halves the number of features from the previous layer. The resultant features are also concatenated with the features from the corresponding contraction layer. Finally, a 1×1 convolution is applied to map the features from the last layer to the number of class labels. A binary decision if a pixel is contaminated or not is then made. Compared with the Skeleton-tracking-based methods [8] and filtering-based methods [5, 6, 9, 10], the U-net can adapt to pores with varying shapes and sizes. Compared with CNN, the U-net produces whole-image segmentation results directly.

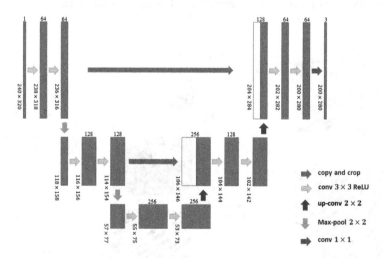

Fig. 3. U-Net architecture. A blue box represents a particular layer with number of feature maps on top of the box and map size in the left corner. White boxes represent copied feature maps. The arrows denote the different operations as indicated in the figure. (Color figure online)

Table 1. U-net parameters

Layer	Filter size	Features	Layer	Filter size	Features
conv1-1	3 × 3	64	ups-1	2 × 2	256
conv1-2	3 × 3	64	conv4-1	3 × 3	128
pool-1	2 × 2	64	conv4-2	3 × 3	128
conv2-1	3 × 3	128	ups-2	2 × 2	128
conv2-2	3 × 3	128	conv5-1	3 × 3	64
pool-2	2 × 2	128	conv5-2	3 × 3	64
conv3-1	3 × 3	256	conv6-1	1 × 1	3
conv3-2	3 × 3	256			

2.2 Data Preprocessing

The size of fingerprint images used in this paper is 240 × 320 pixels, and the size of the sweat pores is generally between three pixels to thirty pixels [6]. To better cope a pore at different scales and to increase the training data, we use resizing operation to expand the data set. For each fingerprint image, it is cut into four parts with a size of 120 × 160 pixels. Each of the image segment is then expanded to 240 × 320 pixels for training. In addition to resizing operations, 180 degree image rotation is also used for data augmentation. Meanwhile, since fingerprint images taken under different conditions have different gray value distribution. A min-max normalization is used for image normalization both for training and testing [15].

2.3 U-Net Training

We used marked fingerprint images for U-net training, with the pixels labeled into three categories: pores class, ridge class, background class. The identified ridge can be used for spurious and false pores removal as well as fingerprint recognition. Parameters are set as recommend in Ref. [14]. The initial weights from a Gaussian distribution are sets with a standard deviation of $\sqrt{2/N}$, where N denotes the number of incoming nodes of one neuron. A cross-entropy loss function is optimized to train the parameters using a momentum-based stochastic gradient decent with an exponentially decaying learning rate at an initial value of 0.2. Each network is trained for 100 epochs each with a training mini-batch size of 32 on one fingerprint image with a resolution of 240 × 320 pixels. The optimization ends when the loss function reaches a minima and remains stable. Dropout layers with a probability of 0.5 in all convolutions are used to avoid data overfitting. The network training is performed using Tensorflow on the NVIDIA Kepler K40 GPU.

2.4 Testing and Post-processing

After the network is trained, it can be used for sweat pore extraction. For better recognition of small pores, sliding window operation is used to extract multiple testing images from a fingerprint image. For an image I, a window of 120 × 160 pixels with a step of 40 pixels is used to traverse I. Thus for the fingerprint image of size 240 × 320,

20 sub-images are extracted and denoted as $I_{si}, i = 1, 2 \ldots 20$. They are resized to 240×320 again and denoted as $I_{s2i}, i = 1, 2 \ldots 20$. For each image I_{s2i}, after the testing using U-net, a three dimensional probability map of size $200 \times 280 \times 3$ is obtained and denoted as $P_i, i = 1, 2 \ldots 20$, with each dimension indicating the possibility belonging to pores, ridge, backgrounds, respectively. The total possibility of three dimensions is equal to 1. Due to the convolution operations, 40 boundary pixels are removed. A threshold is then required to establish the binary decision. In this paper, we set the threshold *thr* to 0.3 experimentally. Thus

$$\begin{cases} M_{pi}(x, y) = 1, P_i(x, y, 1) \geq thr \\ M_{pi}(x, y) = 0, P_i(x, y, 1) < thr \end{cases},\qquad(1)$$

where $M_{pi}(x, y)$ is the mask indicating the pore location. The ridge mask $M_{ri}(x, y)$ can be estimated similarly. Thus, the pores and ridges of the fingerprint image are identified. As shown in Fig. 4, where the circles highlight the pores identified by the U-net, there are spuriously or falsely identified pores which are either too small or not in the ridge as indicated by yellow and green circles. Same rules in Ref. [10] are applied to remove spurious and false pores for post-processing. I.e. the size of the identified pores is limited to 12–120 pixels after resizing, the eccentricity is above 0.9, and the pores lie in the ridge. One thing to note is that the proposed U-net estimates the fingerprint ridges along with the sweat pores. So using the ridge location to remove false pores requires no extra processing. After false pore removal, only pores highlighted by red circle are considered as true pores and saved for further usage. In the last, the pore mask M_{pi} is resize back to 100×140 pixels. The overlapped 20 boundary pixels in M_{pi} are combined by binary or operation and a $220 \times 300 \times 3$ decision map is obtained. Due to the resizing operation, only 10 pixels in each boundary side of the image are lost. The centroid coordinates are then obtained by evaluating the geometric center of each pores.

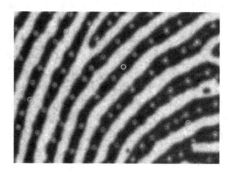

Fig. 4. True and false pores demonstration. (Color figure online)

3 Results and Discussion

3.1 Database

The PolyU High-Resolution-Fingerprint (HRF) database [16] is used for training and testing in this paper. It is built using a custom-built fingerprint scanner. The image size is 240 × 320 pixels and the resolution is 1200 dpi. Sweat pores can be observed in these images. In the database, 30 fingerprint images are marked. In our experiment, we marked the sweat pores in 70 fingerprints from the database as the training data. The 30 marked images are used for testing and evaluation.

3.2 Performance Discussion

An example of pore extraction result is shown in Fig. 5. Figure 5(a) shows the original fingerprint image. Figures 5(b) and (c) are the extracted ridges and pores from U-net. Figure 5(d) is a comparison with the labeled mask with the red points representing the correctly detected pores, the blue points representing the falsely detected pores and green points representing the missed pores. The identified result seems satisfactory. Our methods are also compared with five pore extraction methods [5, 6, 9, 10, 12] according to the correct rate and error rate, which are Ray's method [9], Jain's method [6], adaptive DoG method [5], DAPM method [10] and Ruggero's convolution neural network method [12]. We used two indicators: the true detection rate R_T and the false

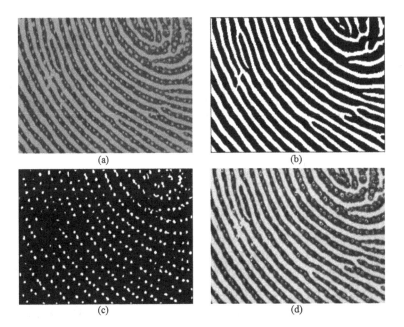

Fig. 5. Pore extraction demonstration. (a) A original fingerprint image of size 240 × 320; (b) extracted ridge map of size 220 × 300; (c) extracted pore map of size 220 × 300; (d) comparison with ground true.

detection rate R_F for comparison. R_T represents the ratio of the number of detected real pores to the number of all true pores present in the image. R_F indicates the ratio of the number of falsely detected pores to the total number of detected pores. The optimal values for R_F and R_T are zero and one, respectively. Lower error rates and higher correct rates indicate better performances of the extraction system while smaller standard deviations of correct rates and error rates indicate higher robustness of the system. We calculated the average R_F and R_T as well as their standard deviations on the 30 fingerprint images using six methods. The quantitative compassion results are shown in Table 2. Our method achieves lower error rate and standard deviation than the other methods. In terms of the correct rate, our method is better than Ray's method, Jain's method and adaptive DoG method, while similar with DAPM method and Ruggero's method. The standard deviation of correct rate in our method is lower than all methods except DAPM. Our method produces satisfactory results for sweat pore extraction.

Table 2. Average performance metrics in percentage and standard deviation for 30 test images of PolyU High-Resolution-Fingerprint (HRF) database.

	Ray et al. [9]	Jain et al. [6]	DoG [5]	DAPM [10]	CNN [12]	U-net
R_T	60.6 (11.9)	75.9 (7.5)	80.8 (6.5)	84.8 (4.5)	84.69 (7.81)	83.65 (6.41)
R_F	30.5 (10.9)	23.0 (8.2)	22.2 (9.0)	17.6 (6.3)	15.31 (6.2)	13.89 (5.4)

4 Conclusion

In this paper, we propose to use a fully convolution neural network U-net for the fingerprint pore extraction. It is compared with five existing pore extraction methods on a PolyU High-Resolution-Fingerprint (HRF) database. Our method can adapt to different pore conditions and produce both accurate and robust results.

Acknowledgments. This research is partially supported by Natural Science Foundation of China (61602414, 61402411).

References

1. Pankanti, S., Prabhakar, S., Jain, A.: On the individuality of fingerprints. IEEE Trans. Pattern Anal. Mach. Intell. **24**, 1010–1025 (2002)
2. Maltoni, D., Maio, D., Jain, A.: Handbook of Fingerprint Recognition. Springer, Dordrecht (2006)
3. Zhang, D., Liu, F., Zhao, Q., Lu, G., Luo, N.: Selecting a reference high resolution for fingerprint recognition using minutiae and pores. IEEE Trans. Instrum. Meas. **60**(3), 863–871 (2011)
4. Roddy, A., Stosz, J.: Fingerprint features-statistical analysis and system performance estimates. Proc. IEEE **85**(9), 1390–1421 (1997)

5. Parsons, N., Smith, J., Thonnes, E., Wang, L., Wilson, R.: Rotationally invariant statistics for examining the evidence from the pores in fingerprints. Law Probab. Risk **7**(1), 1–14 (2007)
6. Jain, A., Chen, Y., Demirkus, M.: Pores and ridges: high-resolution fingerprint matching using level 3 features. IEEE Trans. Pattern Anal. Mach. Intell. **29**(1), 15–27 (2007)
7. Ashbaugh, D.R.: Quantitative-Qualitative Friction Ridge Analysis: An Introduction to Basic and Advanced Ridgeology. CRC Press Inc., Boca Raton (1999)
8. Kryszczuk, K.M., Morier, P., Drygajlo, A.: Study of the distinctiveness of level 2 and level 3 features in fragmentary fingerprint comparison. In: Maltoni, D., Jain, A.K. (eds.) BioAW 2004. LNCS, vol. 3087, pp. 124–133. Springer, Heidelberg (2004). doi:10.1007/978-3-540-25976-3_12
9. Ray, M., Meenen, P., Adhami, R.: A novel approach to fingerprint pore extraction. In: Proceedings of the 37th South-Eastern Symposium on System Theory, SSST, pp. 282–286 (2005)
10. Zhao, Q., Zhang, D., Zhang, L., Luo, N.: Adaptive fingerprint pore modeling and extraction. Pattern Recogn. **43**(8), 2833–2844 (2010)
11. Genovese, A., Munoz, E., Piuri, V., Scotti, F., Sforza, G.: Towards touchless pore fingerprint biometrics: a neural approach. In: IEEE Congress on Evolutionary Computation (CEC). IEEE (2016)
12. Labati, R.D., Genovese, A., Muñoz, E., Piuri, V., Scotti, F.: A novel pore extraction method for heterogeneous fingerprint images using convolutional neural networks. Pattern Recogn. Lett. (2017)
13. Long, J., Shelhamer, E., Darrell, T.: Fully convolutional networks for semantic segmentation. In: IEEE Conference on Computer Vision and Pattern Recognition (CVPR), vol. 79, pp. 3431–3440. IEEE (2015)
14. Ronneberger, O., Fischer, P., Brox, T.: U-net: convolutional networks for biomedical image segmentation. In: Navab, N., Hornegger, J., Wells, W.M., Frangi, A.F. (eds.) MICCAI 2015. LNCS, vol. 9351, pp. 234–241. Springer, Cham (2015). doi:10.1007/978-3-319-24574-4_28
15. Snelick, R., Indovina, M., Yen, J., Mink, A.: Multimodal biometrics: issues in design and testing. In: Proceedings of the 5th International Conference on Multimodal Interfaces, ICMI, Vancouver, pp. 68–72 (2003)
16. Zhao, Q., Zhang, L., Zhang, D., Luo, N.: Direct pore matching for fingerprint recognition. In: Tistarelli, M., Nixon, M.S. (eds.) ICB 2009. LNCS, vol. 5558, pp. 597–606. Springer, Heidelberg (2009). doi:10.1007/978-3-642-01793-3_61

Fingerprint Pore Extraction Based on Multi-scale Morphology

Yuanrong Xu[1], Guangming Lu[1(✉)], Feng Liu[2], and Yanxia Li[1]

[1] Shenzhen Graduate School, Harbin Institute of Technology,
University Town of Shenzhen, Shenzhen 518055, China
luguangm@hit.edu.cn
[2] College of Computer Science and Software Engineering,
Shenzhen University, Shenzhen 518055, China

Abstract. This paper proposes a new method to extract pores on high resolution fingerprints. The basic idea of this method is to binarize the fingerprint images based on multi-scale morphological transformation, and then extract pores by different strategies. The closed pores are extracted by the size of connected regions, and the open pores are detected using the skeleton of valleys. The noise and false detected points are finally removed by using a comprehensive selection rule. Experimental results have shown that the proposed method can improve the accuracy of existing methods.

Keywords: Fingerprint identification · Pore extraction · Biometrics

1 Introduction

Sweat pores and other extended features have attracted a lot of attention in recent years because of their uniqueness and stability over time [1, 2]. Most of the existing AFRS use minutia features for recognition. The performance of these systems needs to be improved when a large population is involved or a high security level is required [3]. By this reason, pores on fingerprints have been researched by more and more researchers [4, 5]. They have been proven to be very contributing to the accuracy improvement of existing automatic fingerprint recognition systems AFRS [6, 7]. This paper focuses on the extraction of pores.

Existing pore matching method can be divided into two categories: skeleton-tracking-based [8, 9] and filtering-based methods [10–12]. Skeleton based algorithms tend to get pores using the skeleton of ridges of fingerprints. These methods are time consuming and sensitive to the noise. Filter based methods use a model to imitate the structure of pores, and then filter the fingerprint images. Earlier filter based pore detection algorithm attempt to use an isotropic pore model to filter the fingerprint images. Such as Ray's model [11], Jain's model [9, 10], and the DoG (difference of Gaussian) model [12]. However, these models are not accurate enough to imitate the various pores (close and open pores) because they are isotropic and static. In order to represent the pores more accurately, Zhao [3] proposed a new band pass filter model, named DAPM. Compare to previous pore models, this model can be more adaptive to the size and shape of pores, thus can be more efficient than previous models.

© Springer International Publishing AG 2017
J. Zhou et al. (Eds.): CCBR 2017, LNCS 10568, pp. 288–295, 2017.
https://doi.org/10.1007/978-3-319-69923-3_31

A big drawback of existing pore extraction methods is that they are trying to use a same strategy to extract closed and open pores. In fact, each kind of pores has their own characteristics, and these characteristics can be used for detection. For example, as closed pores are entirely enclosed by ridges, and not connected with valleys, they look like isolated brightened points on the image. On the contrary, open pores are connected with valleys and look like short branches of valleys. Figure 1 shows an example of closed and open pores.

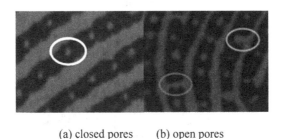

(a) closed pores   (b) open pores

Fig. 1. Two types of pores in the fingerprint image

In this paper, we propose a method to detect pores. According to this method, closed and open pores are extracted by different strategies. The fingerprint image is binarized in the first step. Then closed pores are extracted by the size of connected regions, and open pores are detected using the skeleton of valleys. The noise and false detected points are finally removed by using a comprehensive selection rule. Experimental results have shown that the proposed method can greatly improve the accuracy of existing methods.

2 The Proposed Method

2.1 Multi-scale Morphological Transformation

Let $f(x, y)$ be the input image function, $g(i, j)$ be the structuring function, where $(x, y), (i, j) \in Z^2$. The two fundamental operation which are dilation ($\oplus$) and erosion ($\ominus$) of $f(x, y)$ using $g(i, j)$ are defined as follows [13, 14]:

$$(f \ominus g)(x, y) = max_{i,j}\{f(x - i, y - j) + g(i, j)\} \tag{1}$$

$$(f \ominus g)(x, y) = min_{i,j}\{f(x + i, y + j) - g(i, j)\} \tag{2}$$

In this paper, we use the thresholding operation given by Eq. (3) to binarize the input fingerprint image [14].

$$(f \oslash g_\sigma)^k(x,y) = \begin{cases} 1, & \text{if } \Psi_1^k(x,y) - f(x,y) \le f(x,y) - \Psi_2^k(x,y) \\ 0, & \text{otherwise} \end{cases} \quad (3)$$

where $\Psi_1^k(x,y) = (f \oplus g)^k(x,y)$ is the dilation of $f(x,y)$ with the scaled structuring function $g(i,j)k$ times. Similarly, $\Psi_2^k(x,y) = (f \ominus g)^k(x,y)$. The structuring function $g(i,j)$ is defined as:

$$g_\sigma(i,j) = -|\sigma|^{-1}\max\{i^2, j^2\} \quad (4)$$

Finally, by continually practiced and compared, $\sigma^{-1} = 10$ and $k = 10$ are confirmed for all images. Figure 2 shows the result of fingerprint image binarization.

Fig. 2. An example of fingerprint image binarization

2.2 Closed Pore Extraction

The strategy we used in this paper is to extract open pores and closed pores separately. The first step is to extract closed pores: after getting the binary image, we use the area of connected regions to remove the bigger ones, and take the ones which has the similar size to the pores, so we can extract closed pores inside the ridges preliminarily. But it will also extract some pseudo pores close in distance or near the true pores as if they were true, as shown in Fig. 3. (a) (Pores in black rectangle boxes are true and in red circles are pseudo). Therefore, we use a selection rule to remove the pseudo ones based on the initial set of pores. In this paper, the reliability of a pore is decided by two features: (1) the brightness contrast between a pore and its surrounding points, and (2) the distance of a pore to the nearest one. The detailed process of deleting noise is shown as Algorithm 1.

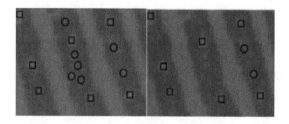

Fig. 3. Result of removing noise: initial set of pore (left one) and pores after removing noise (the right one) (Color figure online)

Algorithm 1 Process of removing pseudo pores

Input: initial set of closed pores

Output: final set of closed pores

1) Calculate the distance of the i-th pore to its nearest one, denoted as $minDis(i)$;

2) Compute the mean gray of each pore area PoreGray(i), and the mean difference of each pore and their surrounding pixels DifGray(i).

3) Compute the mean gray of each pore area PoreGray(i), and the mean difference of

---

each pore and their surrounding pixels DifGray(i).

4) Calculate average gray value of all pores areas, denoted as $meanPoreGray$;

5) Calculate the probability of each pore as true:

$$pros(i) = \frac{1}{1 + \exp(z(i))} \qquad (5)$$
$$z(i) = -(w_1 \cdot Dif\text{Gray}(i) + w_2 \cdot (\text{PoreGray}(i) - meanPoreGray))$$

6) Construct model on distance and remove the pseudo pores:

For $m = 0.1:0.1:0.5$

For $k = 1:5$

Construct distance model for each candidate pore:

$$proDis(i) = \frac{1}{1 + \exp(w_3 \cdot (minDis(i) - k))} - i \qquad (6)$$

Fusion the gray level and distance:

$$PorePro(i) = w_4 \cdot pros(i) + w_5 \cdot proDis(i) \qquad (7)$$

If $PorePro(i) < 0.5$, then delete the i-th point, and recalculate $minDis(j)$ for the j-th point if its nearest point is the i-th one.

End

End

2.3   Open Pore Extraction

As mentioned in the previous section, open pores are connected with its neighboring valleys and looks like a branch of a valley. The thinned image of the binarized contains the skeleton of valleys, and also pores. After removing the bifurcations in the skeleton image, one can separate the skeleton of open pores with the valleys. Thus the skeleton open pores can be detected. The result of this step is shown in Fig. 4.

Fig. 4. Binary image of valley with open pores (the left one), the thinned image of the binary image (the middle one), and the detected open pores (the right one).

3   Experimental Results and Performance Evaluation

3.1   Pore Detection Accuracy

In this section, we evaluate the proposed method by conducting an experiment in comparison with some state of the art methods. The database used in our experiment is as the same as the ones in paper [3]. It contains 30 high resolution fingerprint images with ground truth pores labeled manually. Figure 5 shows an example of image with true pores in this database (the left one) and the result of pore extraction using the proposed method (the right one).

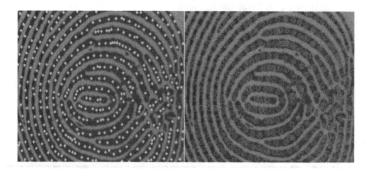

Fig. 5. Real pores and detected pores in a fingerprint image

The true detection rate (RT) and false detect rate (RF) of the proposed method are calculated and listed in Table 1. It can be seen from this table that the proposed method achieves a highest true detection rate with a lowest false detection rate over the existed methods.

Table 1. The average pore detection accuracy of the four methods

	DoG [12]	Jain's model [10]	DAPM [3]	The proposed method
RT	75.72%	75.9%	84.8%	85.7%
RF	25.55%	23.0%	17.6%	11.90%

Figures 6 and 7 show the specific difference between the proposed method and the existed methods on each of the 30 test fingerprint images. It can be seen from these images that the proposed method can get higher true detection rate and lower false detect rate than others in most conditions. Only the comparison results between the proposed method and the DAPM method are shown in these figures since the DAPM method performs best among the existing methods.

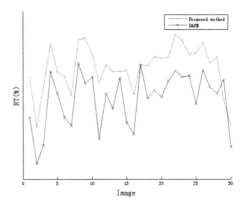

Fig. 6. True detection rate of the proposed method and DAPM method on each test image

3.2   Pore Based Fingerprint Identification

In this section, we test the contribution of the proposed pore extraction method to a fingerprint recognition system. The process of this section consists of five steps: minutiae extraction, minutiae matching, pore extraction, pore matching, and matching score fusion. The minutiae and pore matching methods used in this paper are the same with paper [3]. We also choose a partial high resolution fingerprint image database which was used in paper [3] to evaluate these methods. The database contains 1480 fingerprint images from 148 fingers, each finger have 10 samples collected in two sessions. The images in this database are 320 pixels in width and 240 pixels in height.

The following matches were carried out: Genuine matches and imposter matches. Each images in the first session was matched to all images in the second session from the same finger, thus 3700 genuine matches are generated. The first fingerprint image in

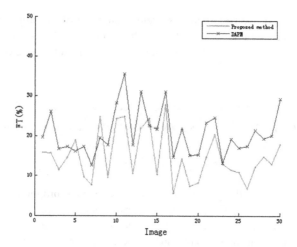

Fig. 7. False detection rate of the proposed method and DAPM method on each test image

Table 2. EERs obtained by different methods on partial fingerprint image database

	DoG	Jain's model	DAPM	The proposed method
EER	14.18%	12.4%	11.51%	10.93%

the first session of each finger was matched to the first image in the second session of all the different fingers, leading to 21756 imposter matches. The best EERs obtained by the four methods on the database are listed in Table 2. It can be seen from this table that the proposed method obtained the best fingerprint recognition accuracy among the four methods. Figure 8 shows the ROC curve obtained by different methods on the partial fingerprint image database.

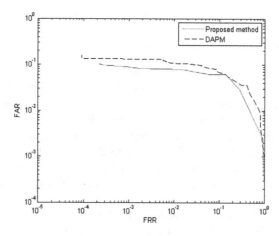

Fig. 8. ROC curve obtained by different methods on the partial fingerprint image database

4   Conclusions

In this paper, we introduced a new approach to extract pores on high resolution fingerprint image. This method detects open and closed pores based on different strategies. The fingerprint images were binarized based on multi-scale morphological transformation. Then pores were detected based on their respective characteristics. A pore selection scheme was designed to delete the wrong detected pores and noise. Experimental results show that our algorithm can detect pores more accurately than the well-known state-of-the-art methods.

Acknowledgments. The work is supported by the NSFC funds (61332011, 61271344, 61403257), Shenzhen Fundamental Research funds JCYJ20140508160910917, JCYJ20150403 161923528, JCYJ20150324140036868, Medical Biometrics Perception and Analysis Engineering Laboratory, Shenzhen, China.

References

1. Pyo, M., Lee, J., Baek, W., et al.: Sweat pore mapping using hydrophilic polymer films. J. Nanosci. Nanotechnol. **16**(12), 12263–12267 (2016)
2. Zhao, Q., Zhang, D., Zhang, L., et al.: High resolution partial fingerprint alignment using pore-valley descriptors. Pattern Recogn. **43**(3), 1050–1061 (2010)
3. Zhao, Q., Zhang, D., Zhang, L., et al.: Adaptive fingerprint pore modeling and extraction. Pattern Recogn. **43**(8), 2833–2844 (2010)
4. Malathi, S., Maheswari, S.U., Meena, C.: Fingerprint pore extraction based on marker controlled watershed segmentation. In: The 2nd International Conference on Computer and Automation Engineering, vol. 3, pp. 337–340. IEEE (2010)
5. Johnson, P., Schuckers, S.: Fingerprint pore characteristics for liveness detection. In: International Conference on Biometrics Special Interest Group, pp. 1–8. IEEE (2014)
6. Ratha, N., Bolle, R.: Automatic Fingerprint Recognition Systems. Springer, New York (2004). doi:10.1007/b97425
7. He, Y., Tian, J., Li, L., Chen, H., Yang, X.: Fingerprint matching based on global comprehensive similarity. IEEE Trans. Pattern Anal. Mach. Intell. **28**(6), 850–862 (2006)
8. Champod, C., Lennard, C.J., Margot, P., et al.: Fingerprints and Other Ridge Skin Impressions. CRC Press, Boca Raton (2016)
9. Kryszczuk, K., Drygajlo, A., Morier, P.: Extraction of level 2 and level 3 features for fragmentary fingerprints. In: Proceedings of Second COST Action, vol. 275, pp. 83–88 (2004)
10. Jain, A.K., Chen, Y., Demirkus, M.: Pores and ridges: high-resolution fingerprint matching using level 3 features. IEEE Trans. Pattern Anal. Mach. Intell. **29**(1), 15–27 (2007)
11. Ray, M., Meenen, P., Adhami, R.: A novel approach to fingerprint pore extraction. In: The 37th Southeastern Symposium on System Theory, pp. 282–286. IEEE (2005)
12. Parsons, N.R., Smith, J.Q., Thönnes, E., et al.: Rotationally invariant statistics for examining the evidence from the pores in fingerprints. Law Probab. Risk **7**(1), 1–14 (2008)
13. Leite, N.J., Dorini, L.B.: A scaled morphological toggle operator for image transformations. In: 19th Brazilian Symposium on Computer Graphics and Image Processing, pp. 323–330 (2006)
14. Dorini, L.B., Leite, N.J.: A scale-space toggle operator for morphological segmentation. In: 8th ISMM, pp. 101–112 (2007)

Finger Vein Presentation Attack Detection Using Convolutional Neural Networks

Xinwei Qiu[1], Senping Tian[1], Wenxiong Kang[1(✉)], Wei Jia[2], and Qiuxia Wu[3]

[1] School of Automation Science and Engineering,
South China University of Technology, Guangzhou, China
auwxkang@scut.edu.cn
[2] School of Computer and Information,
Hefei University of Technology, Hefei, China
[3] School of Software Engineering, South China University of Technology,
Guangzhou, China

Abstract. As an emerging biometric modality, finger vein recognition has received considerable attentions. However, recent studies have shown that finger vein biometrics is vulnerable to presentation attacks, i.e. printed versions of authorized individuals' finger veins could be used to gain access to facilities or services. In this paper, we have designed a specific shallow convolutional neural network (CNN) for finger vein presentation attack detection (PAD), which is called as FPNet for short. The proposed FPNet has been evaluated on a public-database and an intra-database. Lots of $h \times h$ patches have been extracted from vein images with a stride s for dataset augmentation and then used to train our networks without any pre-trained model. For further improving models' generalizability and robustness, training patches of two databases have been mixed together and our best model has achieved an accuracy of 100% on both test datasets, clearly outperforming state-of-the-art methods.

Keywords: Finger vein recognition · Presentation attack detection · Convolutional neural networks

1 Introduction

Biometrics techniques, especially for the face and the fingerprint, have been widely used in many fields, such as identity management, financial payment, access control systems and consumer electronics. However, these biometric traits also face potential threats involving fake data that can be used to break into systems. For example, face recognition systems are apt to be spoofed by fake face photographs, recorded videos, and three-dimensional artificial face models [1]. Similarly, fingerprint recognition systems are also vulnerable to attack by forged images made from commonly available materials, such as gelatin and latex [2]. Under these circumstances, promising vein recognition technologies represented by finger veins recognition [3] and palm veins recognition [4] are growing quickly, since vein patterns are almost invisible to the naked eye under natural lighting conditions and can be acquired in vivo only when

© Springer International Publishing AG 2017
J. Zhou et al. (Eds.): CCBR 2017, LNCS 10568, pp. 296–305, 2017.
https://doi.org/10.1007/978-3-319-69923-3_32

employing infrared illumination, which theoretically can effectively prevent attempted presentation attacks. But recent studies [5, 6] have shown that finger vein recognition systems are also vulnerable to presentation attacks from print vein images, with a spoofing false accept rate as high as 86% [6]. Hence, the studies on finger vein PAD have gradually gained attention among researchers during the past four years.

Several finger vein PAD methods [5, 7–9] have been proposed, most of which utilize hand-crafted features such as local binary pattern (LBP) [8] to capture texture differences between real and forged finger vein images. It will take much time and effort to design deliberate hand-crafted features and these features may have poor generalizability particularly when they are transferred to different databases or different application scenarios. In contrast, convolutional neural network (CNN) is able to extract and learn discriminative features automatically due to its favorable nonlinear mapping capability and self-adaptive learning capability. It shows strong generalizability and achieves great success in other biometric PAD fields [10, 11], such as face [10] and fingerprint [11]. To the best of our knowledge, PAD methods for finger vein based on CNN have not been implemented at present. One important reason is that current finger vein spoof databases are small and even much less than fingerprint and face spoof databases, which may easily lead to overfitting of CNN models. In this paper, we use CNN for finger vein PAD and extent training datasets tens or even hundreds of times by extracting all $h \times h$ patches from original images with a stride s. Additionally, all patches' scores of the same finger vein image are integrated to combine global and local information and thus to make a higher quality decision. This process has another advantage, that is, an input image with any resolution can be classified without image resizing which will lead to loss in high frequency information.

The main contributions of this work are summarized as follows: (1) a specific shallow CNN is firstly designed for finger vein PAD without any pre-trained model; (2) dataset augmentation is extended tens or even hundreds of times by directly extracting $h \times h$ patches from original images which meanwhile avoids loss in high frequency discriminative information; (3) a higher quality decision is made by integrating all patches scores of the input image by which an image with any resolution can be classified without resizing.

2 Related Work

Finger vein PAD methods can be broadly divided into two categories with respect to the cues used to detect presentation attacks. (1) Texture-based methods [5, 8, 9] explore the differences between the qualities of images of real and forged veins, which are mainly reflected in the texture resolutions and noise levels of the images. They deal with a single vein image and are rather simple and convenient. Thus, most existing methods belong to this category such as Fourier spectrum bandwidth energy (FSBE) [8], binarized statistical image feature (BSIF) [8], monogenic scale space (MSS) [8], local phase quantization–Weber local descriptor (LPQ-WLD) [8], residual local binary pattern (RLBP) [8] and W-DMD [9]. (2) Liveness-based methods [7, 12] determine whether a finger vein is real by detecting evidence of the liveness or vital signs of the finger and can be more accurate and reliable than texture-based methods. However, these methods have the disadvantage that they either need successive acquisition of image sequence, or heavily rely on additional hardware equipment, and are not applicable in some real scenarios. For example, Qin et al. [12] explored a kind of vital sign that involves the oxygen saturation of human blood and the heart rate, and Raghavendra et al. [7] measured the liveness of particular samples by magnifying the blood flow through the finger vein. Both methods of Qin and Tome require capturing, storing, and processing a sequence of infrared images, leading to the incensement of time and memory consumption.

By aid of its strong learning ability from data and high efficient feature representation ability, we use CNN to learn and represent discriminative texture features from real and forged images. The proposed method is also a kind of texture-based methods, but our experiments show that it has a higher accuracy and stronger generalizability than other existing texture-based methods.

3   Proposed Method

In this section, we will describe the methodology of our proposed method, including the specific network we have designed, the detailed implementation of dataset augmentation and the final decision making for an input finger vein image.

3.1   FPNet

Considering the success of CNNs in feature learning for image classification [13] and biometric PAD tasks [10, 11], we choose to use CNNs for finger vein PAD. An interesting fact is that new models fine-tuned on pre-trained models tend to achieve better results than those trained with randomly initialized weights, which are viewed as the success case of transfer learning for this technique. However, we didn't use any pre-trained models because our goal is to design a specific network for finger vein PAD and make it as shallow as possible to reduce time and memory consumption.

The proposed FPNet, as shown in Fig. 1, is composed of two convolutional layers and pooling layers followed by two fully-connected layers. The Conv1 layer kernel size and stride are set as 11×11 and 2, and the Conv2 layers kernel size and stride are set as 5×5 and 2. These two convolution layers output 32 and 64 feature maps, respectively, followed by Rectified Linear Units (ReLUs). We apply Batch Normalization (BN) transform to our proposed network as it helps to train networks faster and achieve higher accuracy.

3.2   Dataset Augmentation

Dataset augmentation plays an important role in reducing overfitting on image data and making classifiers more robust against small variations that may be presented in the data. It's necessary for training FPNet because the forged finger vein data is far insufficient for training a completely new network. Besides, the size of cropped images (i.e. ROIs) tends to be different for different subjects or different imaging equipment. But scale normalization is omitted for those images to avoid the loss of discriminative

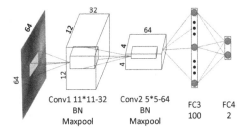

Fig. 1. The illustration of the architecture of our CNN

information in high frequency. Based on the above considerations, we extract all $h \times h$ patches with a stride s from original vein images, and then train our network on these extracted patches. The illustration of our dataset augmentation scheme is shown in Fig. 2 and the parameter settings for extracting patches in our experiments are described in Table 1. As a result, we obtain a dataset that is tens or even hundreds of times larger than the original one.

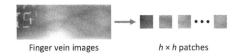

Finger vein images $h \times h$ patches

Fig. 2. Patches extracting for dataset augmentation

Table 1. Dataset augmentation for training $h \times h$ network

Dataset	Image (num)	h	s	Patch (num)
d1-train	240	64	17	43200
d2-train	1440	64	40	47232

3.3 Classification and Decision Making

Our dataset augmentation scheme extends the size of finger vein datasets tens or even hundreds of times, but a new problem on decision making arises. As shown in Fig. 2, a patch is only a small part of a finger vein image and thus its discriminative power will be reduced a lot due to loss in entropy information as well as loss in global information. Thus, we integrate all patches classification results of the same image to combine global and local information and to make a higher quality decision, which is similar to boosted learners like AdaBoost that integrates multiple weak-learners into a powerful learner. By this means, input images with any resolution don't need to be resized in training and test phases, so loss in high frequency information such as noise is avoided.

Suppose n patches are extracted from a vein image and the score of the i-th patch is s_i ($s_i = 1$ when the patch is classified as real and $s_i = 0$ otherwise). Then the detection function for a whole finger vein image can be formalized as follows:

$$y = \begin{cases} 1, & if \quad S > \tau \\ 0, & if \quad S \leq \tau \end{cases} \tag{1}$$

$$S = \frac{1}{n} \sum_{i=1}^{n} s_i \tag{2}$$

where τ is a threshold which can be determined on development set. For simplicity, we set it to 0.5 in our experiments. Through experiments we found that if n is larger, the decision accuracy is higher while the time consumption is more. To trade off between decision accuracy and time consumption in the test phase, the stride s is set to h, the height of patches.

4   Databases and Performance Metrics

To obtain an unbiased assessment, experiments are conducted on a publicly accessible database, the Idiap Research Institute (IDIAP) finger vein presentation attack database (FVD) [6], and the South China University of Technology (SCUT) FVD, the latter of which is constructed by us. In the last part of the section, we will briefly describe the metrics used to evaluate PAD performance.

4.1   IDIAP FVD

The IDIAP FVD consists of cropped and full versions of real and forged images from 110 clients. The forged images were generated from corresponding real finger vein samples from the VERA database, which were simply preprocessed and printed on paper and then recaptured with the finger vein sensor. Following the protocol in FV Competition, IDIAP FVD is divided into three sub-groups, i.e., training set with 240 (120 real + 120 forged) images, development set with 240 (120 real + 120 forged) images, and test set with 400 (200 real + 200 forged) images. The training set is used to train the classifier, whereas the development set is used to obtain the decision threshold which is determined when *APCER* (Attack Presentation Classification Error Rate) and *BPCER* (Bona Fide Presentation Classification Error Rate) are equal. The test set is used to estimate the final performance with the obtained threshold. For simplicity, we use d1-train, d1-dev and d1-test to represent the three sub-groups, respectively. Figure 3(a) shows two samples, and Table 2 describes the details of the IDIAP FVD.

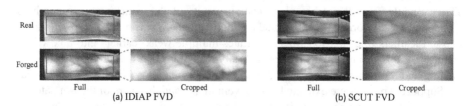

Fig. 3. Samples from IDIAP FVD and SCUT FVD

Table 2. Database descriptions of IDIAP FVD and SCUT FVD

Database	Class	Clients	Hands	Fingers	Shot number	Total
IDIAP	Real	110	2	1 (Index)	2	440
	Forged	110	2	1 (Index)	2	440
SCUT	Real	100	2	3 (Index, Middle and Ring)	6	3600
	Forged	100	2	3 (Index, Middle and Ring)	6	3600

4.2 SCUT FVD

Through close observation and analysis of the IDIAP FVD, we found that the disparity between the real and forged finger vein images was relatively large, reducing the difficulty of spoofing detection to some extent. To extend IDIAP's work and narrow the disparity between the types of images, which would be more in line with a realistically elaborate presentation attacks, we improved the forgery method to produce the new SCUT FVD, which consists of cropped and full versions of 3600 real and 3600 forged images from 600 fingers. The images are also divided into three sub-groups and the ratio of the sample size is 2:2:6. Thus, the training, development and sets each contains 1440 (720 real + 720 forged) images, and the test set contains 4320 (2160 real + 2160 forged) images. For simplicity, we use d2-train, d2-dev and d2-test to represent the three sub-groups, respectively. Figure 3(b) shows two samples from the new database, and Table 2 gives the details.

4.3 Performance Metrics

To achieve a fair and reasonable comparison between the different PAD algorithms, the classification results were evaluated by the Average-Classification-Error-Rate (*ACER*) which is the same metric as *HTER* used in FV Competition [8]. *ACER* is defined as

$$ACER = (APCER + BPCER)/2 \tag{3}$$

where *APCER* and *BPCER* is the PAD metrics in ISO/IEC 30107-3 [14]. *APCER* was once defined as the proportion of attack presentations and incorrectly classified as bona fide presentations in a specific scenario, whereas *BPCER* was defined as the proportion of bona fide presentations and incorrectly classified as attack presentations in a specific scenario. A lower value of *ACER* indicates better PAD performance.

5 Experimental Result

Both IDIAP FVD and SCUT FVD provide two versions of vein images, full original images without any processing and cropped images which contain only regions-of-interest (ROIs). Existing researches suggest that detecting presentation attacks with cropped images is more challenging and cost less time consumption than with full images. Thus, following experiments are all conducted on cropped version.

5.1 Effect of Resolution

The cropped images' resolutions of different databases are different and should be normalized when the images are trained with CNNs. But image resizing will affect the preference of PAD due to loss in high frequency discriminative information such as noise. The resolution of normalized images is lower, the loss of discriminative information is more. We choose two different resolutions, 64×128 and 128×256, as the input resolution of the proposed architecture showed in Fig. 1, respectively. Then both two networks are trained on the mixed dataset which is extended by image translations and rotations. Table 3 describes the detail about dataset augmentation for training 64×128 and 128×256 networks and experimental results are shown in Table 4.

Table 3. Dataset augmentation for training 64×128 and 128×256 networks

Dataset	Original (num)	Translation (time)	Rotation (time)	Total (num)
d1-train	240	80	20	24240
d2-train	1440	48	12	87840

Table 4. Performances of FPNet with different resolution inputs

Resolution	d1-test			d2-test		
	APCER	BPCER	ACER	APCER	BPCER	ACER
64×128	4.50	0.50	2.50	0.19	0.00	0.10
128×256	3.00	1.50	2.25	0.00	0.00	0.00
64×64	0.00	0.00	0.00	0.00	0.00	0.00

Table 4 shows that although training on the same dataset and with the same network architecture, the network "128×256" is superior to the "64×128" on both IDIAP FVD and SCUT FVD. This is consistent with the above analysis that images with larger resolution would keep more discriminative information. "64×64" doesn't mean resizing images to 64×64, but refers to extracting 64×64 patches from original images without scale normalization. Obviously, the method "64×64" achieves the best overall performance, i.e., 100% accuracy and zero $ACER$ for both test sets, and thus is selected as our proposed method in this paper.

5.2 Optimal Network Selection

As showed in Fig. 1, we design a shallow network which contains only two convolutional layers. When the depth of network is fixed, the model's performance will be affected by the width of each layer. If the width was increased, the use of computational resources would be increased too. We design 4 shames to choose the modest widths to trade off accuracy and computational resources, and results are showed in Table 5.

From Table 5 we can find that only scheme 1 and 2 achieves 100% (and zero $ACER$) PAD on both d1-test and d2-test. But the size of scheme 1 is 1.7 MB and 2.7 times larger than scheme 2 (635 KB), meaning the computational requirement of the

Table 5. Performance comparison for trading off models' size and accuracy

Width		Dataset	Size	d1-test			d2-test		
Conv1	Conv2	(train)	(network)	APCER	BPCER	ACER	APCER	BPCER	ACER
64	128	d1-train,	1.7 MB	0.00	0.00	0.00	0.00	0.00	0.00
32	64	d2-train	635 KB	0.00	0.00	0.00	0.00	0.00	0.00
16	32		268 KB	2.00	0.00	1.00	0.00	0.00	0.00
8	16		123 KB	2.00	0.00	1.00	0.00	0.00	0.00

former is larger than the latter. Thus, the widths of Conv1 and Conv2 in our proposed network are set to 32 and 64, respectively.

5.3 Performance Comparison

To compare the performance of our proposed method with of other existing methods, another 4 schemes are designed according to the combinations of IDIAP FVD and SCUT FVD. Besides, two existing methods, RLBP and FSBE, are implemented here and the results are showed in Table 6.

Table 6. ACER of different methods and performance comparison between them

Training set	Test set	FPNet	RLBP [8]	FSBE [8]	BSIF [8]	MSS [8]	W-DMD [9]
d1-train	d1-test	0.25	0.00 (0.00*)	17.75 (20.50*)	2.75*	1.25*	1.59* (EER)
d2-train	d2-test	0.00	3.31	41.62	–	–	–
d1-, d2-train	d1-test	0.00	4.50	32.25	–	–	–
d1-, d2-train	d2-test	0.00	3.45	56.06	–	–	–

"*" indicates that the data is taken directly from the original literature.

Obviously, when the training and test sets are d1-train and d1-test respectively, RLBP archives the best result and FPNet ranks second and follows close behind RLBP. However, in the other three schemes, RLBP and FSBE cannot correctly classify all of the samples while FPNet achieves 100% PAD accuracy. That means our proposed FPNet is more robust and shows the best performance. It is noted that when d2-train is added to the training set, the ACER of FPNet has dropped from 0.25% to 0 on the test set of d1. Table 1 shows 43200 training patches of d1 which is extracted from only 240 finger vein images with a small stride ($s = 17$), meaning the nearest-neighbor patches contain much more repeated information. Thus, FPNet is easy to overfits d1-train. Adding d2-train to d1-train will increase the diversity of training set and improve the model's accuracy and robustness.

6 Conclusions

In this paper, we have designed a specific network named FPNet for finger vein PAD. It is a shallow network with two convolutional layers and has been trained without any pre-train model. Existing datasets for finger vein PAD are insufficient and thus dataset augmentation plays an important role in improving models' performance. On one hand, 64×64 patches have been extracted from vein images by which datasets can be extended tens or even hundreds of times. On the other hand, different training sets, d1-train and d2-train, have been mixed together to further increase data diversity. With highly nonlinear and self-learning ability of CNNs, FPNet yields the best results and outperforms state-of-the-art methods in both intra-database and public-database testing scenarios. In our future work, we will aim to improve the presentation attack technologies and construct a more challengeable database with fewer differences between the real and forged images. Meanwhile, corresponding studies using this new database would be conducted to more comprehensively meet the requirements of real applications.

Acknowledgments. This work was supported by the National Natural Science Foundation of China (Nos. 61573151, 61673157, 61374104, 61503141), the Guangdong Natural Science Foundation (No. 2016A030313468), Science and Technology Planning Project of Guangdong Province (No. 2017A010101026), the Science and Technology Program of Guangzhou (201510010088).

References

1. Tirunagari, S., Poh, N., Windridge, D., Iorliam, A., Suki, N., Ho, A.T.: Detection of face spoofing using visual dynamics. IEEE Trans. Inf. Forensics Secur. **10**(4), 762–777 (2015)
2. Sousedik, C., Busch, C.: Presentation attack detection methods for fingerprint recognition systems: a survey. IET Biom. **3**(4), 219–233 (2014)
3. Himaga, M., Kou, K.: Finger vein authentication technology and financial applications. In: Ratha, N.K., Govindaraju, V. (eds.) Advances in Biometrics, pp. 89–105. Springer, London (2008). doi:10.1007/978-1-84628-921-7_6
4. Kang, W., Wu, Q.: Contactless palm vein recognition using a mutual foreground-based local binary pattern. IEEE Trans. Inf. Forensics Secur. **9**(11), 1974–1985 (2014)
5. Nguyen, D.T., Park, Y.H., Shin, K.Y., Kwon, S.Y., Lee, H.C., Park, K.R.: Fake finger-vein image detection based on fourier and wavelet transforms. In: IEEE Conference on Digital Signal Processing, pp. 1401–1413 (2013)
6. Tome, P., Vanoni, M., Marcel, S.: On the vulnerability of finger vein recognition to spoofing. In: Proceedings of the IEEE BIOSIG, pp. 1–10 (2014)
7. Raghavendra, R., Avinash, M., Marcel, S., Busch, C.: Finger vein liveness detection using motion magnification. In: IEEE Biometrics: Theory, Applications and Systems (BTAS), pp. 1–7 (2015)
8. Tome, P., Raghavendra, R., Busch, C., Tirunagari, S., Poh, N., Shekar, B.H., Gragnaniello, D., Sansone, C., Verdoliva, L., Marcel, S.: The 1st competition on counter measures to finger vein spoofing attacks. In: 2015 International Conference on Biometrics (ICB) (2015)

9. Tirunagari, S., Poh, N., Bober, M., Windridge, D.: Windowed DMD as a microtexture descriptor for finger vein counter-spoofing in biometrics. In: 2015 IEEE International Workshop on Information Forensics and Security (WIFS), pp. 1–6. IEEE (2015)
10. Patel, K., Han, H., Jain, A.K.: Cross-database face antispoofing with robust feature representation. In: You, Z., Zhou, J., Wang, Y., Sun, Z., Shan, S., Zheng, W., Feng, J., Zhao, Q. (eds.) CCBR 2016. LNCS, vol. 9967, pp. 611–619. Springer, Cham (2016). doi:10.1007/978-3-319-46654-5_67
11. Nogueira, R.F., de Alencar Lotufo, R., Machado, R.C.: Fingerprint liveness detection using convolutional neural networks. IEEE Trans. Inf. Forensics Secur. **11**(6), 1206–1213 (2016)
12. Qin, B., Pan, J.F., Cao, G.Z., Du, G.G.: The anti-spoofing study of vein identification system. In: 2009 International Conference on Computational Intelligence and Security (2009)
13. Krizhevsky, A., Sutskever, I., Hinton, G.E.: Imagenet classification with deep convolutional neural networks. In: Advances in Neural Information Processing Systems (2012)
14. The ISO/IEC Standards for Testing of Presentation Attack Detection. http://www.christoph-busch.de/files/Busch-PAD-standards-170329.pdf

Fingerprint Minutiae Detection Based on Multi-scale Convolution Neural Networks

Huinan Jiang and Manhua Liu[(✉)]

Department of Instrument Science and Engineering, School of EIEE,
Shanghai Jiao Tong University, Shanghai 200240, China
mhliu@sjtu.edu.cn

Abstract. Minutiae points are defined as the minute discontinuities of local ridge flows, which are widely used as the fine level features for fingerprint recognition. Accurate minutiae detection is important and traditional methods are often based on the hand-crafted processes such as image enhancement, binarization, thinning and tracing of the ridge flows etc. These methods require strong prior knowledge to define the patterns of minutiae points and are easily sensitive to noises. In this paper, we propose a machine learning based algorithm to detect the minutiae points with the gray fingerprint image based on Convolution Neural Networks (CNN). The proposed approach is divided into the training and testing stages. In the training stage, a number of local image patches are extracted and labeled and CNN models are trained to classify the image patches. The test fingerprint is scanned with the CNN model to locate the minutiae position in the testing stage. To improve the detection accuracy, two CNN models are trained to classify the local patch into minutiae v.s. non-minutiae and into ridge ending v.s. bifurcation, respectively. In addition, multi-scale CNNs are constructed with the image patches of varying sizes and are combined to achieve more accurate detection. Finally, the proposed algorithm is tested the fingerprints of FVC2002 DB1 database. Experimental results and comparisons have been presented to show the effectiveness of the proposed method.

1 Introduction

Fingerprint is a kind of ridge friction pattern on finger tips, which have been widely used for personnel recognition in the commercial and forensic areas. After over thirty years of development, there are tremendous advances made on automatic fingerprint recognition [10,13]. In general, fingerprint friction ridge details are described in a hierarchical order at three different levels: level 1, level 2 and level 3 features [13]. Level 1 features describe global structures of the ridge flow shape such as the orientation field and ridge frequency field. Level 2 features capture more minute details of the ridge flow patterns such as minutiae points, which are discriminative enough to determine the uniqueness of fingerprints for personnel recognition. Level 3 features such as pores and ridge contours capture more fine details of ridge flows, which carry significant discriminatory information. But

© Springer International Publishing AG 2017
J. Zhou et al. (Eds.): CCBR 2017, LNCS 10568, pp. 306–313, 2017.
https://doi.org/10.1007/978-3-319-69923-3_33

reliable extraction of these features requires high-resolution image. Since a vast majority of fingerprint matching algorithms rely on minutiae matching, minutiae points are regarded as highly significant features for automatic fingerprint recognition.

Minutiae points are defined as the discontinuities of local ridge flows. According to different configurations, there are about 150 different types of minutiae points categorized [4]. Among these minutia types, ridge ending and bifurcation are the most commonly used, since all the other types of minutiae points can be considered as the combinations of them. There are around 40 to 100 minutiae points in a full fingerprint image of good quality. The minutiae location and orientation are often used as its representation [13]. Most of automatic fingerprint recognition systems use minutiae as the main representation feature, which can reduce the complex image recognition problem to a point pattern matching problem.

There are a lot of minutiae detection methods proposed in the literature [1,2,6,11]. These methods can be broadly classified into two categories: binary image based methods [1,2] and direct gray-scale image based methods [6,11]. Usually, image pre-processing is required to improve the detection performance. In the binary image based methods, fingerprint is preprocessed by segmentation, enhancement of ridge details and binarization, and the minutiae points are detected by inspecting the patterns of localized pixels. The method [2] detect the minutiae points from skeletonized binary image, where the binary image is thinned and the ridge flow pattern is eight-connected. A mathematical morphology based method was proposed to detect minutiae points in [1]. In this method, the binary image was preprocessed with morphological operators to remove spurs and spurious bridges etc. and then the morphological Hit or Miss transform (HMT) was used to detect true minutiae points. In the binary image based methods, binarization and thinning may cause information lost, more computation and spurious minutiae. Direct gray-scale minutiae detection attempts to overcome these problems [6,11]. It employs ridge path following or tracing the ridge flow from an initial point to a minutiae points. However, the existing methods require strong prior knowledge to define the patterns of minutiae points and are sensitive to noises. Accurate detection of minutiae points is still a challenging task and still needs much research efforts.

Convolutional Neural Networks (CNNs) are a special kind of multi-layer neural networks, which are trained with a back-propagation method. In recent years, CNNs have been successfully applied in image recognition and computer vision tasks [3,5,8]. Deep CNN was introduced to significantly improve image classification accuracies by training with a large amount of labeled images on the ImageNet [8]. The hierarchical rich image representations were learned with convolutional deep belief networks for face verification [3]. Recently, a novel minutiae extraction approach was proposed based on 2 deep CNNs [5]. First, a JudgeNet was built to pick out the candidate patches that may contain one or more minutiae points. The candidate patches are then imported to a LocateNet to decide the minutiae location (9 locations in total) in these patches. This method can take the advantage of the strong representative capacity of deep CNNs and directly detect minutiae points from the raw fingerprint images. But it cannot discriminate the types of minutiae points. In addition, the LocateNet were trained to discriminate 9 different neighboring locations which is not an easy task.

Motivated by the success of CNNs in image representation and classification, we propose a learning based algorithm for fingerprint minutiae point detection based on Multi-scale CNNs. The problem of minutiae point detection is converted to image classification problem. The proposed algorithm is divided into the offline training and online testing stages. In the offline stage, a number of local image patches are extracted and labeled, and CNN models are trained to classify the image patches. In the online testing stage, the test fingerprint image is scanned with the CNN models to detect the minutiae position. To improve the detection accuracy, two deep CNNs are trained to classify the local patch into minutiae v.s. non-minutiae and into ridge ending v.s. bifurcation, respectively. In addition, multi-scale CNNs are constructed with the image patches of varying sizes and are combined to achieve the noise robustness and accurate detection. Finally, the proposed algorithm is tested on FVC2002 DB1 fingerprint database.

2   Proposed Minutiae Detection Algorithm

In this section, we will present the proposed algorithm based on learning multi-scale CNNs for detection of fingerprint minutiae points. Figure 1 shows an overview of our proposed minutiae detection algorithm. In general, the proposed algorithm consists of offline training and online testing stages. In the training stage, a number of multi-scale image patches are extracted and labeled, and deep CNNs are trained to classify the image patches. In the online testing stage, the whole fingerprint is scanned with the CNN models to locate the minutiae position and discriminate the type of minutiae points.

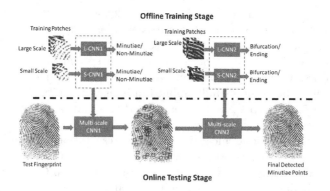

Fig. 1. Overview of the proposed minutiae detection algorithm.

There are three main advantages to apply deep CNNs for our minutiae detection task. First, the deep complex architecture can extract the low-, mid- to high-level features to capture the minutiae variations from a high volume of training patches. Second, they can make use of the spatial structure of image patch and learn the filters useful for the classification task. Finally, by stacking multiple layers, deep CNNs can extract a hierarchy of complex features representing large spatial regions, finally providing the robust minutiae detection.

2.1   Training Multi-scale CNNs

The fingerprint ridges often flow smoothly except for minutiae points, which are the special discontinuity patterns. In this work, we just consider to detect two commonly used minutiae points, i.e., ridge ending and bifurcation since the other types of minutiae can be considered as the combinations of these two points. CNNs were designed to recognize visual patterns directly from gray images with minimal preprocessing. In general, more context information is required to discriminate minutiae from non-minutiae, while local ridge details are more important to discriminate different types of minutiae, i.e., ridge ending and bifurcation. To achieve better detection accuracy, minutiae detection task is divided into two image classification tasks, i.e., classifications of minutiae v.s. non-minutiae and ridge ending v.s. bifurcation. First, we build a CNN ("CNN1") to classify the image patches into minutiae or non-minutiae, and then another CNN ("CNN2") to classify the minutiae candidates into ridge ending or bifurcation.

In addition, fingerprint images are usually corrupted by various kinds of noises. The main challenging problem is to reduce noise while achieving reliable minutiae detection. The patch size is important for minutiae detection. A large patch can suppress noise but it cannot discriminate ridge details well. A small patch can capture well the ridge details but it is sensitive to noise. To address this problem, we build the CNN models at multiple scales for two classification problems. At the same scale, CNN1 and CNN2 are built with the same architecture. To train deep CNN, the first step is to extract a number of image patches from training set. We use the marked minutiae points as ground truth which are available in [7]. The image patches centered at the manually marked minutiae points are extracted from training fingerprints as the training set labeled with minutiae type. The non-minutiae patches are randomly extracted from the non-minutiae regions. The patch size is varied to train the CNNs at multi-scales.

The second step is to build the architectures of CNN models. The multi-scale CNN models have different network architectures, which are shown in Fig. 2. Each deep CNN consists of convolutional layers followed by max pooling, full connection and softmax layers. A typical convolutional layer usually convolves the input image with a number of learned kernel filters, followed by adding a bias term and applying a non-linear activation function. It finally produces a feature map for each filter. Then, $Tanh$ is adopted as the activation function following each convolution layer. After each convolutional layer, there may be a pooling layer, which takes a small rectangular block of feature maps and produces a single output from that block. The maxpooling layer is adopted by replacing each non-overlapping block with their maximum. Through maxpooling, the features become more compact and efficient from low to higher layer, which makes them robust to some variations such as shift, scale and rotation at a certain level.

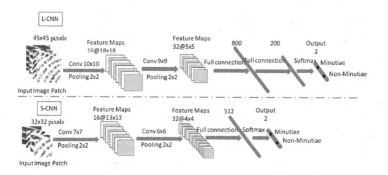

Fig. 2. The architectures of deep CNNs at two scales, denoted with the sizes of input, convolution, maxpooling and output layers, and the numbers and sizes of feature maps.

The third type of layer is the fully connected layer. After several convolutional and max pooling layers, the high-level reasoning in the neural network is done by fully connected layers. All feature maps are flattened and concatenated into a 1D feature vector as the input of fully connected layer. A fully connected layer takes all neurons in the previous layer and connects them to every output neuron. Finally, a softmax classification layer is appended to the last fully connected layer and is fine-tuned by back-propagation with negative log-likelihood to predict class probability. The outputs of softmax layer can be interpreted as prediction probabilities ranging from 0 and 1 with their sum equal to 1.

In the training stages, the convolutional kernels are randomly initialized from the Gaussian distribution. The other trainable parameters of network are tuned using the standard back-propagation with stochastic gradient descent by minimizing the cross entropy loss. In addition, the dropout strategy is employed to reduce the overfitting problem and improve generalization capability.

2.2   Online Minutiae Detection

In the online testing stage, the minutiae points are detected with the CNN1 models to scan the test fingerprint from the coarse to fine levels. At the coarse level, CNN1 is applied to detect the initial minutiae positions. Large image patches are input into the CNN1 as to make full use of more context information for robust minutiae detection. In addition, deeper network structures help to learn high-level features. At the fine level, the CNN1 at small scale, which are designed with a shallower structure, are employed to refine the initial detection for accurate detection in small regions, where the disruption from the irrelevant areas is reduced significantly. To further improve the performance of minutiae detection, we propose to combine the features learned from multi-scale CNNs to locate the positions of minutiae points. However, there might be a few groups of detected points clustered which are from the same minutiae point. These minutiae points are filtered according to the prediction score and a defined range. We choose the point with highest score within 2×2 range as the final one.

Finally, the trained CNN2 models are applied to discriminate the types of minutiae points detected by CNN1. To improve the classification accuracy, the prediction scores of CNN2 at the large and small scales are combined by weights to make the final classification decision on the types of minutiae points.

3 Experiments

In this section, we conduct the experiments to evaluate the effectiveness of the proposed algorithm. The goal of minutiae detection is to obtain the accurate minutiae points for reliable fingerprint representation and recognition. To evaluate the accuracy of minutiae detection, the proposed algorithm is tested on a well known fingerprint database, i.e., FVC2002 DB1 [12]. FVC2002 DB1 set A contains 800 fingerprints of 100 fingers with 8 images per finger. For training the deep CNN models, FVC2002 DB1 set A is partitioned into two halves used for training and testing sets and cross validation is performed to evaluate the accuracy of minutiae detection. FVC2002 DB1 set B is used as the validation set to determine the optimal parameters of CNN models. The fingerprints of training set is used to extract the image patches for training the CNNs models, while the testing set is used to detect the minutiae points for evaluation. Figure 3 shows the minutiae detection results of sample fingerprints including original fingerprints, located minutiae points and the detected minutiae type.

In our experiments, two measures are computed to evaluate the minutiae detection accuracy. The first one is True Detection Rate (TDR), which is defined as the proportion of truly detected minutiae points with respect to the total number of labeled minutiae points. The second measure is False Detection Rate (FDR), which is defined as the proportion of falsely detected minutiae points with respect to the total number of detected minutiae points. The manually marked minutiae points in [7] are downloaded and used as the ground truth for comparison. A detected minutia is considered as correct detection if there is a minutia point in the manually marked minutia set whose distance to the detected minutia point is less than a threshold (10 pixels in our experiments). As we can see, a higher TDR and a lower FDR are desired in minutia detection.

The first experiment is to test the effects of patch size on minutiae detection. The patch size is fixed to 32×32 and 45×45 in CNN1 based minutiae detection for comparison in Table 1. The proposed algorithm combines the CNN1 models at two scales, denoted as "Proposed with combined patch". The second experiment compares the proposed algorithm with other methods. The FDR and TDR of the proposed algorithm are compared with those of Liu and Cao [9] and Verifinger SDK 6.5 on FVC2002 DB1. Minutiae detection is automatically conducted using a commercial fingerprint matcher, Neurotechnology VeriFinger

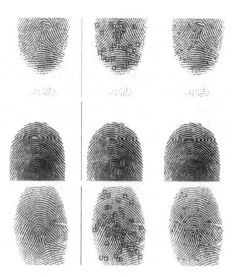

Fig. 3. The minutiae detection results of some sample fingerprint images: original fingerprint (left), located minutiae points (middle) and detected minutiae type (right).

SDK 6.5 (http://www.neurotechnology.com) and the results reported in [9] are directly used for comparison. Table 1 shows performance comparison of different patch sizes and various methods on FVC2002 DB1. From these results, we can see that the CNN1 trained with 45×45 patch can achieve higher accuracy than those with 32×32 patch. The proposed algorithm by combining multi-scale CNNs further improves the minutiae detection accuracy with higher TDR and lower FDR. Compared with other methods, our proposed algorithm achieves higher TDR. But our proposed algorithm operates on the raw fingerprint image without image preprocessing which causes higher FDR than other two methods.

Table 1. Performances comparison of minutiae detection algorithms on FVC2002 DB1.

Algorithm	TDR (%)	FDR (%)
Verifinger SDK 6.5	79.28	9.44
Liu and Cao [9]	59.79	22.73
Proposed with patch 32×32	79.28	29.26
Proposed with patch 45×45	82.11	28.07
Proposed with combined patch	84.50	23.10

The third experiment is to test classification accuracy of CNN2 on discrimination of ridge ending and bifurcation. Two measures i.e., precision and recall are computed to evaluate the minutiae classification accuracy. Precision denotes the proportion of ridge endings which are correctly classified. Recall is the proportion of ridge bifurcations correctly classified. In our experiments, precision is 71.31% while recall is 73.66 % on the FVC2002 DB1.

4   Conclusions

This paper proposes a fingerprint minutiae detection algorithm based on multi-scale deep CNNs. The minutiae detection task is converted two image classification problems i.e., classification of image patches into minutia and non-minutiae and classification of candidate minutia into ridge ending and bifurcation. We have built deep CNN models at multiple scales, which are combined to make the classification decision. The proposed algorithm can work directly on the gray level fingerprints without image preprocessing. Experimental results and comparison demonstrate the effectiveness of the proposed algorithm.

Acknowledgement. This work was supported by NSFC grants (No. 61773263, 61375112).

References

1. Bansal, R., Sehgal, P., Bedi, P.: Effective morphological extraction of true fingerprint minutiae based on the hit or miss transform. Proc. Int. J. Biom. Bioinform. (IJBB) **4**, 71–85 (2010)
2. Farina, A., Kovacs-Vajna, Z.M., Leone, A.: Fingerprint minutiae extraction from skeletonized binary images. Pattern Recogn. **32**(5), 877–889 (1999)
3. Huang, G.B., Lee, H., Learned-Miller, E.: Learning hierarchical representations for face verification with convolutional deep belief networks. In: Proceedings of IEEE Computer Society Conference on Computer Vision and Pattern Recognition (CVPR), Providence, Rhode Island, 16–21 June 2012
4. Jain, A.K., Hong, L., Bolle, R.: On-line fingerprint verification. IEEE Trans. Pattern Anal. Mach. Intell. **19**(4), 302–314 (1997)
5. Jiang, L., Zhao, T., Bai, C., Yong, A., Wu, M.: A direct fingerprint minutiae extraction approach based on convolutional neural networks. In: International Joint Conference on Neural Networks, pp. 571–578 (2016)
6. Jiang, X.D., Yau, W.-Y., Ser, W.: Detecting the fingerprint minutiae by adaptive tracing the gray-level ridge. Pattern Recogn. **34**(5), 999–1013 (2001)
7. Kayaoglu, M., Topcu, B., Uludag, U.: Standard fingerprint databases: manual minutiae labeling and matcher performance analyses. Eprint Arxiv (2013)
8. Krizhevsky, A., Sutskever, I., Hinton, G.: Imagenet classification with deep convolutional neural networks. In: The 13th Annual Conference on Neural Information Processing Systems (NIPS), Harrahs and Harveys, Lake Tahoe, 03–08 December 2012
9. Liu, E., Cao, K.: Minutiae extraction from level 1 features of fingerprint. IEEE Trans. Inf. Forensics Secur. **11**(9), 1893–1902 (2016)
10. Liu, M., Yap, P.T.: Invariant representation of orientation fields for fingerprint indexing. Pattern Recogn. **45**(7), 2532–2542 (2012)
11. Maio, D., Maltoni, D.: Direct gray-scale minutiae detection in fingerprints. IEEE Trans. Pattern Anal. Mach. Intell. **19**(1), 27–39 (1997)
12. Maio, D., Maltoni, D., Cappelli, R., Wayman, J.L., Jain, A.K.: FVC2002: 2nd fingerprint verification competition. In: Proceedings of 16th International Conference of Pattern Recognition, Quebec City, Canada, vol. 3, pp. 811–814, August 2002
13. Maltoni, D., Maio, D., Jain, A.K., Prabhakar, A.: Handbook of Fingerprint Recognition. Springer, New York (2003)

Customized Local Line Binary Pattern Method for Finger Vein Recognition

Haiying Liu[1], Lingfei Song[1], Gongping Yang[1], Lu Yang[2], and Yilong Yin[1(✉)]

[1] School of Computer Science and Technology, Shandong University,
Jinan 250101, People's Republic of China
ylyin@sdu.edu.cn
[2] School of Computer Science and Technology,
Shandong University of Finance and Economics, Jinan, People's Republic of China

Abstract. Finger vein images present plenty of oriented features. Local line binary pattern (LLBP) and its variance are very good oriented feature representation methods, but their discrimination may be limited, since they does not utilize the class labels in the process of extracting features. In this paper, a class based orientation-selectable PLLBP method, called customized local line binary pattern (CLLBP), is proposed for finger vein recognition. We first calculate the average genuine scores using components of PLLBP at different orientations for each class on the training set, respectively. Secondly, we sort these average genuine scores from the different orientations for each class to rank each component in their relative importance. Thirdly, we choose the k most important components at the top-k orientations for each class. Lastly, given a testing image and an enrolled image, we only use the components at the top-k orientations of the enrolled class to calculate the matching score. Experimental results on the PolyU database verify the better performance of the proposed method than other algorithms, such as LBP and LLBP.

Keywords: Finger vein recognition · Oriented feature · Local line binary pattern · Biometrics

1 Introduction

Finger vein recognition, which is convenient, no-invasive and high-security, has been an important topic in the field of biometric for decades [1]. Finger veins are subcutaneous structures that randomly grow into a network and distribute along a finger. The physiological characteristic of the veins makes them highly secure and easy collectability [2]. Furthermore, compared with the traditional biometrics (i.e., fingerprint, face, DAN, ear, palmprint, etc.), the system of finger vein recognition has the merit of small imaging device, low cost, liveness, universality and acceptability [3]. Therefore, finger vein recognition is a promising biometric solution for personal identification in the future.

© Springer International Publishing AG 2017
J. Zhou et al. (Eds.): CCBR 2017, LNCS 10568, pp. 314–323, 2017.
https://doi.org/10.1007/978-3-319-69923-3_34

Recent years, a large quantities of works have been proposed from different perspectives for finger vein recognition, such as region of interest (ROI) extraction [4], image restoration [5,6], image enhancement [7], image representation [8,9,18]. Among all related problems, finger vein representation plays an important role in finger vein recognition. Lots of vein-pattern-based methods, which are relied on the segmented blood vessel network and use the geometric shape or topological structure of vein patterns for matching, have developed for representation of finger vein image. For instance, Miura et al. [1] introduced an extraction method based on repeated line tracking (RLT) from various starting position and demonstrated good extraction performance with regard to image shading. In later research [10], Miura et al. discovered that the finger vein region is darker than the skin area, and the intensity of the cross-sectional profile in the finger vein is represented as a valley. Based on this discovery, they obtained the vein centerlines by calculating the local maximum curvatures in cross-sectional profiles. Song et al. [11] designed vascular features by mean curvature. Qin et al. [12] proposed a vein pattern extraction method by running a region growing operator based on different seeds. Kumar and Zhou [13] presented a finger vein extraction approach using the Gabor filters. However, if the quality of the captured images is low, the network may not be segmented properly. Consequently, the extracted features based on an improper network will make the performance of the recognition degrade dramatically.

To alleviate the difficulty of segmentation, several approaches to extracting the local features in finger vein images have been developed. For example, Lee et al. [14] proposed a feature fusion method that uses simple binarization, local binary pattern (LBP) and local derivative pattern (LDP) for finger vein recognition, which shows improved recognition accuracy and reduced process time. Rosdi et al. [15] applied the local line binary pattern (LLBP) approach on finger vein recognition. The main different between LBP and LLBP is that LLBP adopts the line-shaped neighborhood, instead of the square neighborhood in LBP. The performance using the LLBP is better than with the LBP [14] due to the veins pattern inside the finger in the piecewise-linear style. Considering the veins randomly grow inside a finger and LLBP can only extract horizontal and vertical line patterns, Yu et al. proposed two variants of LLBP for finger vein representation to furtherly improve the discriminative ability. One is polydirectional local line binary pattern (PLLBP) [16], and the other one is generalized local line binary pattern (GLLBP) [17]. PLLBP [16] extracts line pattern in arbitrary orientation and enhances the discriminative ability of local features. GLLBP [17] selects three most discriminative orientation of PLLBP to calculate the matching score.

However, LLBP and PLLBP are limited in that they have low discriminative ability and a great deal of redundant information [17]. Since the veins grow inside a finger with random orientations and different finger have roughly different growing orientations for veins pattern, we believe that the relative importance (discriminability) of the features at different orientations are different between different classes. To test this, we calculate the genuine score for each component of PLLBP at eight orientations, respectively. (For convenience, we name the orientations at which genuine scores are the most k largest as the top-k orientations for this class.) As show in Table 1, for class 1 the top-three orientations are $0°$, $45°$ and $180°$, while for class 2 they are $90°$, $225°$ and $270°$. That is to say, different class has different top-k orientations. Inspired by these phenomena, we calculate the matching scores for different enrolled class using different top-k orientations. If we use this matching strategy, three advantages will come: (1) the redundant information of the local feature will be eliminated; (2) the discriminative ability of features will be increased; (3) the matching time will be reduced.

Table 1. Comparison of average genuine score at different orientations on training set

θ	$0°$	$45°$	$90°$	$135°$	$180°$	$225°$	$270°$	$315°$
Class 1	0.80	0.77	0.69	0.71	0.81	0.72	0.68	0.75
Class 2	0.81	0.82	0.84	0.80	0.82	0.84	0.85	0.83
Class 3	0.86	0.88	0.89	0.90	0.87	0.92	0.90	0.87
Class 4	0.67	0.71	0.83	0.78	0.70	0.79	0.85	0.72

In order to fulfil this goal, this paper introduces a novel class-based orientation-selectable PLLBP method, i.e., a customized local line binary pattern (CLLBP) for finger vein recognition. Instead of using whole PLLBP to calculate the matching score, we propose a simple and effective method to evaluate the importance of PLLBP's component at each orientation and select several relative important components of PLLBP for each class. Specifically, our method includes following procedure. First, we calculate the genuine scores of components at each orientations for each class on the training set, respectively. Secondly, we sort these average component genuine scores from the different orientations for each class to rank each component in their relative importance. Then, we choose the k most important orientations as the top-k orientations for each class. In the subsequent recognition process, we only use the components at the top-k orientations of the enrolled class to calculate the matching score between a testing image and the enrolled image. Our methods have following advantage. (1) Class separability for training stage. Due to seeking the top-k orientations for a class is irrelative to other classes, these operation for each class can be parallelized. (2) Discriminability the top-k components are different from individual to individual since ranking the relative importance of components to a class and choosing the top-k components both are based on the genuine score for each class. Thus, the discriminability of recognition system will be enhanced by using different top-k orientations for different class to calculate the matching score. (3) Low matching time. PLLBP uses all components to compute the matching score, while CLLBP only chooses components at the top-k orientations. That is to say, CLLBP uses shorter code than PLLBP to calculate the matching scores. Hence, the matching time is reduced.

Experimental results on the PolyU database clearly demonstrate the effectiveness of the proposed method.

The structure of this paper is organized as follows. Section 2 presents our proposed approach. Section 3 provides experimental results. Section 4 concludes the paper.

2   Proposed Approach

In this section, we introduce our proposed method: customized local line binary pattern (CLLBP) for finger vein recognition. Our method mainly involves extracting every components of PLLBP, a training stage and a recognition stage. In the following parts, we introduce them sequentially.

2.1   Extracting Components of PLLBP

LBP have been used in finger vein recognition [14]. In term of the case that finger veins are located inside a finger in the line style, Rosdi et al. [15] applied the local line binary pattern (LLBP) for finger vein recognition. Unlike the shapes of neighborhoods are square in LBP, the shapes in the LLBP are straight lines. The limitation of LLBP is only extracting the horizontal component and vertical component, Yu et al. [16] proposed PLLBP which could extract arbitrary orientation components.

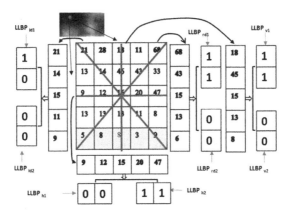

Fig. 1. Illustration of extracting of components of the PLLBP

Generally, constructing a PLLBP for a pixel can be decomposed into two steps. First, all components at all orientations are extracted. Specifically, for a certain orientation, we compute the difference vector between one pixel and its neighboring pixel in a straight line, and then encode this vector with a fixed threshold to obtain a components of PLLBP at this orientation. Same steps can be performed to get component of PLLBP at the arbitrary orientation. Second, all the components at different orientations are concatenated together as whole PLLBP.

In this paper, considering that the operation of bilinear interpolation for computing components at certain orientations is required, we only extract the components at 0°, 45°, 90°, 135°, 180°, 225°, 270° and 315°. Extracted components at these eight orientations are showed in Fig. 1.

Let N represents the number of pixels in the line, h_n, v_n, ld_n and rd_n denote the pixel value along the horizontal, vertical, diagonal and anti-diagonal lines, respectively. $c = (N+1)/2$ is the position of the center pixel. h_c, v_c, ld_c and rd_c denote the center pixels located in the corresponding horizontal, vertical, diagonal and anti-diagonal lines, respectively. $LLBP_{h1}(x,y)$, $LLBP_{h2}(x,y)$, $LLBP_{v1}(x,y)$, $LLBP_{v2}(x,y)$, $LLBP_{ld1}(x,y)$, $LLBP_{ld2}(x,y)$, $LLBP_{rd1}(x,y)$ and $LLBP_{rd2}(x,y)$ denote the PLLBP's components extracted from 180°, 0°, 90°, 270°, 135°, 315°, 45° and 225°, respectively. By employing Eq. (1), the component of PLLBP at the 180° extracts a $(N-1)/2$ number of binary vector for the center pixel. The same numbers of binary vector can be extracted for the components of PLLBP at rest orientations using Eqs. (2) to (8), respectively. We treat each extracted component as a complete feature in the following sections.

$$LLBP_{h1}(x,y) = [h_1 - h_c, \cdots, h_{c-1} - h_c] \tag{1}$$

$$LLBP_{h2}(x,y) = [h_{c+1} - h_c, \cdots, h_N - h_c] \tag{2}$$

$$LLBP_{v1}(x,y) = [v_1 - v_c, \cdots, v_{c-1} - v_c]. \tag{3}$$

$$LLBP_{v2}(x,y) = [v_{c+1} - v_c, \cdots, v_N - v_c]. \tag{4}$$

$$LLBP_{ld1}(x,y) = [ld_1 - ld_c, \cdots, ld_{c-1} - ld_c]. \tag{5}$$

$$LLBP_{ld2}(x,y) = [ld_{c+1} - ld_c, \cdots, ld_N - ld_c]. \tag{6}$$

$$LLBP_{rd1}(x,y) = [rd_1 - rd_c, \cdots, rd_{c-1} - rd_c]. \tag{7}$$

$$LLBP_{rd2}(x,y) = [rd_{c+1} - rd_c, \cdots, rd_N - rd_c]. \tag{8}$$

After obtaining all the components of PLLBP in the image, we will evaluate the relative importance of each component to each class. In the next part, we will describe the details of our algorithm.

2.2   Training Stage

The aim of training stage is to learn the top-k orientations for each class. That is to say, we will rank each component in their relative importance for each class based on the genuine scores.

Supposing that there are m training samples (i.e. $Sample_1^w$, $Sample_2^w$, $\cdots$, $Sample_m^w$) of the class w and $codeA_{il}^w$ is the component of PLLBP code of $Sample_i^w$ at lth orientation. In learning process, we will use the genuine score function to measure the similarity of two components at one direction of two genuine PLLBPs. The formula is given in Eq. (9).

$$HD_{ijl}^w = 1 - \frac{\left\| codeA_{il}^w \otimes codeA_{jl}^w \right\|}{CodeLength}. \qquad (9)$$

where $\otimes$ is a Boolean exclusive-OR operator between corresponding pair of bits. CodeLength is the total number of bits of the $codeA_{il}^w$.

The process of learning the top-k orientations is given as follows:

(1) Calculate the genuine score for every class in the training samples at each orientation, separately. The genuine score $gen\_score_{il}^w$ at lth orientation for class w is the average similarity between the current sample i and the rest samples in the same class, which can be expressed by Eq. (10):

$$gen\_score_{il}^w = mean_{j=1,\cdots,m \cap j \neq i} \left(HD_{ijl}^w \right). \qquad (10)$$

For every orientations from the training samples, the genuine scores are calculated. In our system, the total orientations is eight, so l can be $1, 2, \cdots, 8$.

(2) Obtain the top-k orientations for each class.

Firstly, sort all the genuine scores for each class in descending order, this sorted genuine scores determinate which orientations are the importance to the current class. Then we chose orientations corresponding the largest k genuine scores for each class as the top-k orientations. The number k is empirically decided.

The process of learning the top-k orientations for enrolled class is summarized in Algorithm 1.

2.3   Recognition Stage

After the top-k orientations of each enrolled class have been learned in the training stage, the final step is matching the test image and the enrolled image. Different from LLBP and PLLBP, we only use the components of PLLBP at the top-k orientations of current enrolled class to compute the final matching score. Given a test image and an enrolled image, we use Eq. (11) to calculate their matching score. The sum rule is used to fusion.

Algorithm 1. Learning the top-k orientations algorithm.

Require:
    Training samples $Sample_1^w$ to $Sample_m^w$ of an enrolled class w;
Ensure:
    The top-k orientations of LLBP for class w;
1: Initialize $gen\_score_1^w = [\ \ ]$, $l = 1, \cdots, L$;
2: While $l \leq L$ do   //L is the number orientations of LLBP
3: While $i \leq m$ do   // m is the number of training samples for class w
4: Get $gen\_score_1^w = gen\_score_1^w + gen\_score_{il}^w$
5: End While
6: Get $gen\_score_1^w = gen\_score_1^w / m$
7: End while
8: Sort $gen\_score_1^w$, $gen\_score_2^w$, $\cdots$, $gen\_score_L^w$
9: **return** the top-k orientations corresponding largest k genuine scores;

$$HD_{ij}^w = \sum_{l=1}^{k} \left(1 - \frac{\left\| codeA_{il}^w \otimes codeA_{jl}^w \right\|}{CodeLength} \right). \tag{11}$$

where HD_{ij}^w represent the matching score between the test image i and a enrolled image j from class w, and k is the number of components to be used.

3 Experiments and Results

In this section, we first introduce the experimental database and experimental settings. And then, the experiments about the parameters determination and recognition performance comparison are given.

3.1 Database

In this study, all the experiments are implemented in MATLAB R2013a and conducted on a computer with a 3.60 GHz $i7 - 4790$ CPU and a 16 GB RAM. The proposed method is evaluated on the PolyU database [13].

The PolyU database consists of 3,132 finger images collected from 156 volunteers over a period of eleven months. The finger images were acquired in two separate sessions. In each session, each of the volunteer provided six image samples from the index finger to the middle finger, respectively. As only 105 subjects turned up for the imaging during the second session, in our experiments, we use 1,872 finger vein images (156 subjects $\times$ 2 fingers $\times$ 6 images) captured in first session. That is to say, the database include of 312 classes and each class has 6 images. We use 3 images from each class for training and 3 images for testing. The original spatial resolution of the finger vein image is 513×256 pixels, and after ROI extraction, size normalization and gray normalization, the size of the region used for feature extraction is reduced to 96×64 pixels. In this paper, we evaluate the recognition performance by the equal error rate (EER), which is the value where the false accept rate (FAR) is equal to the false reject rate (FRR).

3.2   Parameter Determination

It is well known that the values of parameters will influence the performance of recognition system. So we need to perform a series of experiments to explore the proper parameters. We use PolyU database to do parameters determination experiments. As mentioned above, 3 images for training and 3 images for testing from each classes are randomly selected.

We have two parameters (k and the code length of each component of PLLBP) to determine, where k is the number of components of PLLBP using for calculating the matching score in the testing stage. To make the experiment results more clearly, we first fix the code length while vary k, then, we fix k while vary the code length. Based on the optimal value of two parameters, we apply these parameters for all the following experiments.

First, we set the length of PLLBP's component at each orientations as 10, and examined the performance of our proposed method with varied k for testing stage on PolyU database.

Figures 2 and 3 show the EER and the corresponding processing time with the varied values k. From Fig. 2, the EER is decreasing as the value of k is increasing from 1 to 3. But further increasing k from 3 to 8, the EER is tend to increase. Thus when the value of k is 3, the lowest EER can be obtained. This results can be explained from two aspects: (1) when k is smaller than 3, less information is included in features. Therefore, the performance of system is poor. (2) when the value of k is larger than 3, the shared information between class are increasing. This resulted in reducing the discriminability of feature and negative effect to system. In terms of processing time, the matching time keeps increasing with increasing k, which is shown in Fig. 3. This is attributed to increasing feature size. These results also prove that advantages to using partly components of PLLBP in recognition stage is not only reducing matching time but also enhancing the discriminability of features.

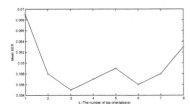   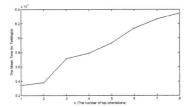

Fig. 2. Mean EER of our method versus varying the number orientations.   **Fig. 3.** Mean time of our method versus varying the number orientations.

Second, we set k (the number of directional components of PLLBP) in the recognition stage as 3, and examined the performance of our proposed method with different length of component of LLBP at each orientation on PolyU database. Figure 4 shows the mean EER of our method with different length of component at each orientation. We see that the EER is decreasing when the length

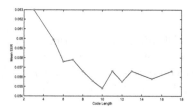
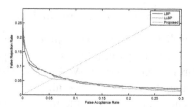

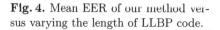

Fig. 4. Mean EER of our method ver-   **Fig. 5.** ROC curves by different meth-
sus varying the length of LLBP code.   ods.

of each component is increasing from 3 to 10, the EER is tend to increase as
further increase of the length from 10 to 17. The lowest EER can be obtained
when the length of each component of PLLBP is set as 10. Hence, in the later
experiments, the optimal length of component is 10.

Table 2. Performance of different traditional methods on PolyU database.

Methods	LBP [14]	LLBP [15]	Proposed
EER	0.65	0.062	0.055

3.3   Comparison with Other Methods

In order to show the effectiveness of the proposed method, similar methods such
as LBP and LLBP are implemented for comparison. EER is used to evaluate
the matching performance. In the experiment, the optimal parameter values
obtained in previous experiment are used. For fair comparison, all the algorithms
are performed on ROIs from PolyU database without any post-processing like
image denoising or image enhancement. Except the feature, the rest condition
are all same. The experimental results are listed in Table 2 and the corresponding
ROCs are show in Fig. 5. The experimental results from Table 2 and Fig. 5 shows
that the matching performance using the proposed method outperforms the LBP
and LLBP.

4   Conclusion

This paper presented a finger vein recognition method named customized local
line binary pattern (CLLBP). Through utilizing the different distribution of
individual finger vein pattern and poly-directions of PLLBP, CLLBP not only
enhances the discriminative ability of PLLBP, but also reduces the matching
time. Experimental results show that the recognition performance of proposed
method is better in comparison with the existing LLBP-based methods.

Acknowledgments. This work is supported by the National Science Foundation of
China under Grant Nos. 61472226, 61573219 and 61703235.

References

1. Miura, N., Nagasaka, A., Miyatake, T.: Feature extraction of finger-vein patterns based on repeated line tracking and its application to personal identification. Mach. Vis. Appl. **15**(4), 194–203 (2004)
2. Xie, S.J., Yoon, S., Yang, J., Lu, Y., Park, D.S., Zhou, B.: Feature component-based extreme learning machines for finger vein recognition. Cogn. Comput. **6**(3), 446–461 (2014)
3. Yanagawa, T., Aoki, S., Ohyama, T.: Human finger vein images are diverse and its patterns are useful for personal identification. MHF Prepr. Ser. **12**, 1–7 (2007)
4. Yang, L., Yang, G., Yin, Y., Xiao, R.: Sliding window-based region of interest extraction for finger vein images. Sensors **13**(3), 3799–3815 (2013)
5. Lee, E.C., Park, K.R.: Image restoration of skin scattering and optical blurring for finger vein recognition. Opt. Lasers Eng. **49**(7), 816–828 (2011)
6. Yang, J., Zhang, B., Shi, Y.: Scattering removal for finger-vein image restoration. Sensors **12**(3), 3627–3640 (2012)
7. Shin, K.Y., Park, Y.H., Nguyen, D.T., Park, K.R.: Finger-vein image enhancement using a fuzzy-based fusion method with gabor and retinex filtering. Sensors **14**(2), 3095–3129 (2014)
8. Dong, L., Yang, G., Yin, Y., Liu, F., Xi, X.: Finger vein verification based on a personalized best patches map. In: 2014 IEEE International Joint Conference on Biometrics (IJCB), pp. 1–8. IEEE, September 2014
9. Liu, F., Yang, G., Yin, Y., Xi, X.: Finger-vein recognition based on fusion of pixel level feature and super-pixel level feature. In: Sun, Z., Shan, S., Yang, G., Zhou, J., Wang, Y., Yin, Y.L. (eds.) CCBR 2013. LNCS, vol. 8232, pp. 274–281. Springer, Cham (2013). doi:10.1007/978-3-319-02961-0_34
10. Miura, N., Nagasaka, A., Miyatake, T.: Extraction of finger-vein patterns using maximum curvature points in image profiles. IEICE Trans. Inf. Syst. **90**(8), 1185–1194 (2007)
11. Song, W., Kim, T., Kim, H.C., Choi, J.H., Kong, H.J., Lee, S.R.: A finger-vein verification system using mean curvature. Pattern Recogn. Lett. **32**(11), 1541–1547 (2011)
12. Qin, H., Qin, L., Yu, C.: Region growth based feature extraction method for finger-vein recognition. Opt. Eng. **50**(5), 057208 (2011)
13. Kumar, A., Zhou, Y.: Human identification using finger images. IEEE Trans. Image Process. **21**(4), 2228–2244 (2012)
14. Lee, E.C., Jung, H., Kim, D.: New finger biometric method using near infrared imaging. Sensors **11**(3), 2319–2333 (2011)
15. Rosdi, B.A., Shing, C.W., Suandi, S.A.: Finger vein recognition using local line binary pattern. Sensors **11**(12), 11357–11371 (2011)
16. Lu, Y., Xie, S.J., Yoon, S., Park, D.S.: Finger vein identification using polydirectional local line binary pattern. In: 2013 International Conference on ICT Convergence (ICTC), pp. 61–65. IEEE (2013)
17. Lu, Y., Yoon, S., Xie, S.J., Yang, J., Wang, Z., Park, D.S.: Finger vein recognition using generalized local line binary pattern. KSII Trans. Internet Inf. Syst. **8**(5), 11357–11371 (2014)
18. Xi, X., Yang, L., Yin, Y.: Learning discriminative binary codes for finger vein recognition. Pattern Recogn. **66**, 26–33 (2017)

Fingerprint Segmentation via Convolutional Neural Networks

Xiaowei Dai[1], Jie Liang[1], Qijun Zhao[1(✉)], and Feng Liu[2]

[1] National Key Laboratory of Fundamental Science on Synthetic Vision, College of Computer Science, Sichuan University, Chengdu, China
qjzhao@scu.edu.cn
[2] School of Computer Science and Software Engineering, Shenzhen University, Shenzhen, Guangdong, China

Abstract. In automatic fingerprint identification systems, it is crucial to segment the fingerprint images. Inspired by the superiority of convolutional neural networks for various classification and regression tasks, we approach fingerprint segmentation as a binary classification problem and propose a convolutional neural network based method for fingerprint segmentation. Given a fingerprint image, we first apply the total variation model to decompose it into cartoon and texture components. Then, the obtained texture component image is divided into overlapping patches, which are classified by the trained convolutional neural network as either foreground or background. Based on the classification results and by applying morphology-based post-processing, we get the final segmentation result for the whole fingerprint image. In the experiments, we investigate the effect of different patch sizes on the segmentation performance, and compare the proposed method with state-of-the-art algorithms on FVC2000, FVC2002 and FVC2004. Experimental results demonstrate that the proposed method outperforms existing algorithms.

Keywords: Fingerprint segmentation · Convolutional neural network · Fingerprint recognition

1 Introduction

A fingerprint image usually consists of two components, which are called the foreground and background. The foreground (i.e., Region of Interest, ROI) originates from the effective fingerprint area. It is a typical flow-like pattern formed by ridges and valleys. The background contains noisy and irrelevant contents that should be discarded in the following processing steps. When feature extraction algorithms are applied on a fingerprint image without segmentation, lots of false features would be extracted due to the presence of noisy background, and eventually lead to matching errors in the later stage. The goal of fingerprint segmentation is thus to segment out the foreground fingerprint region from the background, and thus to reduce the number of false features and improve the fingerprint matching accuracy. As one of the typical fingerprint image processing steps, segmentation is critical to the performance of automated fingerprint identification systems.

J. Zhou et al. (Eds.): CCBR 2017, LNCS 10568, pp. 324–333, 2017.
https://doi.org/10.1007/978-3-319-69923-3_35

Many methods have been proposed for fingerprint segmentation. Bazen and Gerez [1] use grayscale features including coherence, local mean and variance of fingerprint images. The coherence gives a measure how well the gradients are pointing in the same direction. Usually the coherence will be much higher in the foreground than in the background, but it may be influenced significantly by boundary signals and line noise signals. Kang and Zhang [2] introduce the gray histogram-based weighting as feature. Then, an automatic modified FCM clustering algorithm is used for fingerprint segmentation. Marques and Thome [3] take the frequency of fingerprint as its feature and use an MLP network to discriminate the regions containing fingerprint fragments from the rest of the image.

In addition, Fourier spectrum energy [4, 5], Gabor features [6, 7], Gaussian-Hermite Moments [8], and Harris Corner Points [9] have been applied to fingerprint segmentation. Ridges and valleys in a fingerprint image are generally observed as a sinusoidal-shaped plane wave with a well-defined frequency and orientation [10], and non-ridge regions does not hold this surface wave model. Thai and Gottschlich [11] decompose a fingerprint image into cartoon, texture and noise parts. After decomposition, the foreground region is obtained from the non-zero coefficients in the texture image using morphological processing.

The performance of these conventional methods depends heavily on the classifier. However, the designs of the robust features and excellent classifiers are difficult things. In addition to these methods, there are a number of approaches [12–15] for segmentation of latent fingerprint, but they are inappropriate for rolled/slap fingerprints. Inspired by the success of convolutional neural networks in a variety of pattern recognition tasks such as image classification [16, 17], edge-aware filtering [29], and retinal blood vessel segmentation [30], we approach fingerprint segmentation as a classification problem, and learn suitable fingerprint feature representation and classifier via convolutional neural networks for segmentation.

The rest of the paper is organized as follows. In Sect. 2, we present in detail the proposed method. In Sect. 3, we report the evaluation benchmark and experimental results. Finally, we conclude the paper in Sect. 4.

2 Proposed Method

The basic idea of our proposed method is to predict the category (foreground or background) for a given fingerprint patch using a convolutional neural network. Given a fingerprint image, (i) a preprocessing step is used to remove large scale background (also called the cartoon component) and enhance the potential ridge structure; (ii) Each fingerprint patch is fed to the trained convolutional neural network to predict its category; (iii) The predicted category from each patch is quilted together to construct the whole fingerprint segmentation; (iv) Morphological operations are used to post-proceed the classification results and obtain the final foreground. Experimental results on the NIST SD4, FVC2000, FVC2002 and FVC2004 [24–27] show that the performance of the proposed algorithm outperforms state-of-the-art algorithms. A large number of fingerprint patches are used to train the convolutional neural network. Figure 1 shows the flowchart of the proposed algorithm.

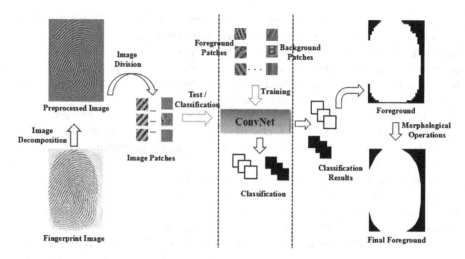

Fig. 1. Flowchart of the proposed convolutional neural network based fingerprint segmentation algorithm.

2.1 Fingerprint Image Decomposition

In the following, we assume that the fingerprint image can be represented by the function $f : (x, y) \in \Omega \to R$. Here Ω is an open subset of R^2, which is usually rectangular or square. Assuming that the image f is defined on R^2 the continuous domain, we obtain the continuous image by interpolating its corresponding digital image (which is defined on the discrete pixel set). We decompose f into two components [18, 19]:

$$f = u + v \tag{1}$$

where u represents a cartoon component of f, while v represents the oscillatory or texture component of f. The oscillatory part contains essentially the texture. Most of the structure noises in fingerprints have been successfully removed while retaining the friction ridge pattern (see Fig. 2).

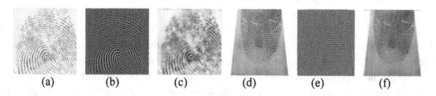

(a)   (b)   (c)   (d)   (e)   (f)

Fig. 2. Illustration of fingerprint image decomposition. (a, d) fingerprint images; (b, e) texture component images; (c, f) cartoon component images.

2.2   Training Data Preparation

In order to train a reliable network, we prepare the training data in the following ways:

(1) Fingerprint selection. NIST Fingerprint Image Quality (NFIQ) [21] is used to select 1000 fingerprints from NIST SD14 [20]. NFIQ has five-level quality, i.e., $NFIQ = 1$ is highest quality, while $NFIQ = 5$ is lowest quality. The distribution of the 1000 fingerprint images is 200 for per quality level.

(2) Manual segmentation. In order to ensure the accuracy of the training data, we obtain the ground truth foreground of the 1000 fingerprint images by manual segmentation.

(3) Fingerprint decomposition. Each of the selected fingerprint images is decomposed by using the method in Sect. 2.1. The texture component is divided into patches of $n \times n$ pixels, while the cartoon component is discarded.

(4) Fingerprint division. Each fingerprint is divided into patches by moving a rectangle window across the fingerprint with a fixed step size (8 pixels in this paper). If more than 50% of a patch is background, the patch is classified into the background category. Finally, about one million texture patches (500,000 for each of the foreground and background classes) are obtained from the 1000 NIST SD14 [20] fingerprints for training the convolutional neural network.

Figure 3 shows some examples of foreground and background patches.

Foreground: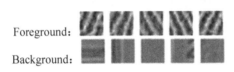
Background:

Fig. 3. Examples of background and foreground 24 × 24 training patches.

2.3   Convolutional Neural Network

The convolutional neural network (CNN) is trained to classify a fingerprint patch as one of two classes, i.e., foreground or background. The overall architecture of the CNN used in this paper is shown in Fig. 4 (taking patches of 24 × 24 pixels as an example). A fingerprint patch of size 24 × 24 pixels is input to a convolutional layer (C1) with 32 filters of size 5 × 5 and stride of 1 (denoted by 32 × 5 × 5 × 1(1) @ 20 × 20). The ReLU activation function ($f(x) = \max(0, x)$) is adopted to model the output of the neurons. The resulting 32 feature maps (of size 20 × 20) are then separately fed to a max-pooling layer (P1) which takes the max over 2 × 2 spatial neighborhoods with a stride of 2 (denoted by 32 × 2 × 2 × 32(2) @ 10 × 10). Local response normalization [17] is then applied, which aids generalization. Similar definitions are used for layers C2 and C3.

The fully-connected layer (F1) is connected to all neurons in the previous layer. It follows the last convolutional layer (C3). The output of the last fully-connected layer is fed to a 2-way Softmax which produces a distribution over the 2-class (foreground and background) label. Caffe framework [22] is used to implement the convolutional neural network architecture.

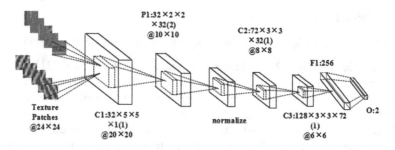

Fig. 4. Outline of the convolutional neural architecture.

2.4 Fingerprint Segmentation

After training the convolutional neural network, the segmentation process should be executed according to the following steps: (i) the image is decomposed as in Sect. 2.1 to obtain texture component of the input fingerprint image; (ii) The texture component is divided into overlapping patches (of size 24 × 24 pixels) with step size of 8 pixels; (iii) Each patch is directly fed into the trained convolutional neural network which outputs label of the patch; (iv) The results of these texture patches are quilted together to segment the whole fingerprint; (v) To obtain final segmentation results, morphological operations (dilation and opening) [23] are applied to remove small foreground blocks as well as to fill holes inside the foreground. The convex hull of the foreground blocks is computed to determine the final segmentation result. The effect of the morphological operations is shown in Fig. 5.

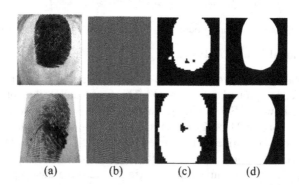

Fig. 5. Illustration of fingerprint segmentation. (a) fingerprint image; (b) texture component image; (c) mask before morphological operations; (d) mask after morphological operations.

3   Experiments

Our experiments are conducted on a PC with i7-4790 CPU @ 3.60 GHz, 32 GB memory and a NVIDIA 980 Ti GPU. We use the selected data (refer to Sect. 2.2) from NIST SD14 to train the proposed fingerprint segmentation CNN model, and then evaluate the model on four different fingerprint databases (FVC2000, FVC2002, FVC2004 and NIST SD4 [24–27]). NIST SD4 [24] contains 2000 8-bit gray rolled fingerprint image pairs. The databases of FVC2000, FVC2002 and FVC2004 [25–27] are publicly available and established for Fingerprint Verification Competition. Each competition contains four sub-databases, the first three of which are real fingerprint images acquired by different sensors and the last consists of synthetic fingerprint images.

3.1 Patch Size Assessment

The final goal of a fingerprint segmentation algorithm is to improve the fingerprint matching accuracy. Thus, we conduct experiments to evaluate the accuracy by measuring the fingerprint matching performance using a commercial off the shelf (COTS) matcher [28]. In this part, we investigate the impact of patch size on the performance of the proposed method.

The Cumulative Match Characteristic curves on the NIST SD4 [24] are shown in Fig. 6. It can be seen that the 24 × 24 pixels patch size achieves the best performance among the three set-ups. We believe that this is because a medium patch size makes a good balance between the sufficiency of true fingerprint details and the distraction of noisy information. Moreover, a larger patch size has more apparent boundary effect. Figure 7 gives the segmentation results of the proposed method with different patch sizes on some fingerprint images.

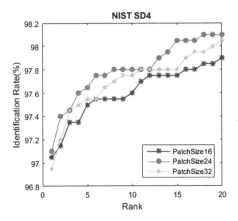

Fig. 6. CMC curves on the NIST SD4. PatchSize16: the patch size of 16 × 16 pixels; PatchSize24: the patch size of 24 × 24 pixels; PatchSize32: the patch size of 32 × 32 pixels.

3.2 Comparison with State-of-the-Art Algorithms

The aim of this evaluation is to analyze the segmentation accuracy by comparing the segmentation results to the manual markup (ground truth) that is available on the web site [5]. The segmentation accuracy is evaluated based on two error measurements: M_f

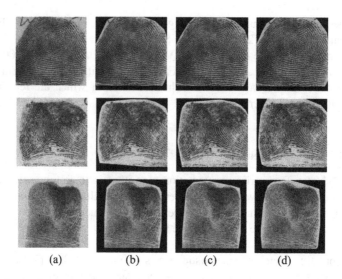

(a)   (b)   (c)   (d)

Fig. 7. (a) fingerprint image; (b) the proposed segmentation image with the path size of 16×16 pixels; (c) the proposed segmentation image with the path size of 24×24 pixels; (d) the proposed segmentation image with the path size of 32×32 pixels.

refers to the number of pixels which are marked as foreground by human experts and estimated as background by an algorithm (missed/misclassified foreground); M_b refers to the number of pixels which are marked as background by human experts and estimated as foreground by an algorithm (missed/misclassified background). Let N_1 and N_2 be the width and height of the fingerprint image in pixels. The average total error per image is defined as:

$$Err = \frac{M_f + M_b}{N_1 \times N_2} \tag{2}$$

According to the above experimental assessment results, we use the patch size of 24×24 pixels to segment fingerprint on FVC2000, FVC2002 and FVC2004 [25–27]. We use the validation sets in these databases (i.e., the '_b' sets, totally $80 \times 12 = 960$ fingerprints) to fine-tune the network that has been trained on the NIST SD14 [20] fingerprint images. As shown in Table 1, the proposed method outperforms the other methods on nine of twelve databases and yields a satisfactory performance judged by visual inspection (see Fig. 8). These demonstrate the effectiveness of the proposed method for fingerprint segmentation.

Table 1. Error rates (average percentage of misclassified pixels) computed using the manually marked ground truth segmentation.

FVC	DB	GFB [7]	HCR [9]	MVC [1]	STFT [4]	FDB [5]	G3PD [11]	The proposed
2000	1	13.26	11.15	10.01	16.70	5.51	5.69	**4.57**
	2	10.27	6.25	12.31	8.88	3.55	4.10	**3.32**
	3	10.63	7.80	7.45	6.44	2.86	2.68	**2.31**
	4	5.17	3.23	9.74	7.19	2.31	**2.06**	2.37
2002	1	5.07	3.71	4.59	5.49	2.39	**1.72**	1.92
	2	7.76	5.72	4.32	6.27	2.91	2.83	**2.28**
	3	9.60	4.71	5.29	5.13	3.35	3.27	**3.19**
	4	7.67	6.85	6.12	7.70	4.49	3.63	**2.50**
2004	1	5.00	2.26	2.22	2.65	1.40	**0.88**	1.10
	2	11.18	7.54	8.06	9.89	4.90	4.62	**2.97**
	3	8.37	4.96	3.42	9.35	3.14	2.77	**2.64**
	4	5.96	5.15	4.58	5.18	2.79	2.53	**2.26**
Avg		8.33	5.78	6.51	7.57	3.30	3.06	**2.62**

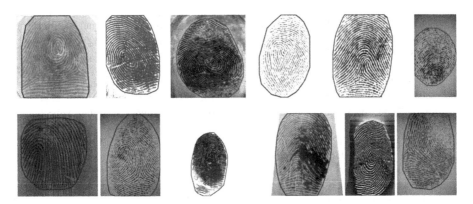

Fig. 8. Example fingerprint images from different databases. The red curves illustrate the ROI of fingerprint images obtained by the proposed method.

4   Conclusions

We have proposed a fingerprint segmentation method based on convolutional neural networks. Convolutional neural network is an excellent tool, which integrates the feature extraction and classification. Experimental results on NIST SD4 [24] have demonstrated that the proposed method can effectively improve the fingerprint matching accuracy with the patch size of 24×24 pixels. We have performed a comparison between the proposed method and some state-of-the-art fingerprint segmentation algorithms on FVC2000, FVC2002 and FVC2004 [25–27]. It has found that the proposed method outperforms the competitors in terms of fingerprint segmentation accuracy on average.

Acknowledgements. This work is supported by the National Natural Science Foundation of China (No. 61202161), and Shenzhen Fundamental Research funds JCYJ20150324140036868 (No. 61403257).

References

1. Bazen, A.M., Gerez, S.H.: Segmentation of fingerprint images. In: ProRISC 2001 Workshop on Circuits, Systems and Signal Processing, pp. 276–280 (2001)
2. Kang, J., Zhang, W.: Fingerprint image segmentation using modified fuzzy c-means algorithm. In: Bioinformatics and Biomedical Engineering, pp. 1–4 (2009)
3. Marques, A.P., Thome, A.G.: A neural network fingerprint segmentation method. In: Hybrid Intelligent Systems, pp. 6–pp (2005)
4. Chikkerur, S., Govindaraju, V., Cartwright, A.N.: Fingerprint image enhancement using STFT analysis. In: Singh, S., Singh, M., Apte, C., Perner, P. (eds.) ICAPR 2005. LNCS, vol. 3687, pp. 20–29. Springer, Heidelberg (2005). doi:10.1007/11552499_3
5. Thai, D.H., Huckemann, S., Gottschlich, C.: Filter design and performance evaluation for fingerprint image segmentation. PLoS ONE **11**(5), e0154160 (2016)
6. Alonso-Fernandez, F., Fierrez-Aguilar, J., Ortega-Garcia, J.: An enhanced gabor filter-based segmentation algorithm for fingerprint recognition systems. In: Image and Signal Processing and Analysis, pp. 239–244 (2005)
7. Shen, L., Kot, A., Koo, W.: Quality measures of fingerprint images. In: Bigun, J., Smeraldi, F. (eds.) AVBPA 2001. LNCS, vol. 2091, pp. 266–271. Springer, Heidelberg (2001). doi:10.1007/3-540-45344-X_39
8. Wang, L., Suo, H., Dai, M.: Fingerprint image segmentation based on gaussian-hermite moments. In: Li, X., Wang, S., Dong, Z.Y. (eds.) ADMA 2005. LNCS, vol. 3584, pp. 446–454. Springer, Heidelberg (2005). doi:10.1007/11527503_54
9. Wu, C., Tulyakov, S., Govindaraju, V.: Robust point-based feature fingerprint segmentation algorithm. In: Lee, S.-W., Li, Stan Z. (eds.) ICB 2007. LNCS, vol. 4642, pp. 1095–1103. Springer, Heidelberg (2007). doi:10.1007/978-3-540-74549-5_114
10. Hong, L., Wan, Y., Jain, A.: Fingerprint image enhancement: algorithm and performance evaluation. IEEE Trans. Pattern Anal. Mach. Intell. **20**(8), 777–789 (1998)
11. Thai, D.H., Gottschlich, C.: Global variational method for fingerprint segmentation by three-part decomposition. IET Biom. **5**(2), 120–130 (2016)
12. Zhang, J., Lai, R., Kuo, C.C.: Latent fingerprint segmentation with adaptive total variation model. In: 2012 5th IAPR International Conference on Biometrics (ICB), pp. 189–195 (2012)
13. Zhang, J., Lai, R., Kuo, C.C.: Latent fingerprint detection and segmentation with a directional total variation model. In: 2012 19th IEEE International Conference on Image Processing (ICIP), pp. 1145–1148 (2012)
14. Choi, H., Boaventura, M., Boaventura, I.A., Jain, A.K.: Automatic segmentation of latent fingerprints. In: 2012 IEEE Fifth International Conference on Biometrics: Theory, Applications and Systems (BTAS), pp. 303–310 (2012)
15. Cao, K., Liu, E., Jain, A.K.: Segmentation and enhancement of latent fingerprints: a coarse to fine ridge structure dictionary. IEEE Trans. Pattern Anal. Mach. Intell. **36**(9), 1847–1859 (2014)
16. LeCun, Y., Kavukcuoglu, K., Farabet, C.: Convolutional networks and applications in vision. In: Proceedings of 2010 IEEE International Symposium on Circuits and Systems (ISCAS), pp. 253–256 (2010)

17. Krizhevsky, A., Sutskever, I., Hinton, G.E.: Imagenet classification with deep convolutional neural networks. In: Advances in Neural Information Processing Systems, pp. 1097–1105 (2012)
18. Goldstein, T., Osher, S.: The split Bregman method for L1-regularized problems. SIAM J. Imaging Sci. **2**(2), 323–343 (2009)
19. Gilles, J., Osher, S.: Bregman implementation of Meyer's G-norm for cartoon + textures decomposition. UCLA Cam Report, pp. 11–73 (2011)
20. NIST special database 14. http://www.nist.gov/srd/nistsd14.cfm
21. Tabassi, E., Grother, P.: Fingerprint Image Quality. Springer, US (2015)
22. Jia, Y., Shelhamer, E., Donahue, J., Karayev, S., Long, J., Girshick, R., Guadarrama, S., Darrell, T.: Caffe: Convolutional architecture for fast feature embedding. In: Proceedings of the 22nd ACM international conference on Multimedia, pp. 675–678 (2014)
23. Sonka, M., Hlavac, V., Boyle, R.: Image Processing, Analysis, and Machine Vision. Cengage Learning, Boston (2014)
24. NIST special database 4. http://www.nist.gov/srd/nistsd4.cfm
25. FVC2000 database. http://bias.csr.unibo.it/fvc2000/
26. FVC2002 database. http://bias.csr.unibo.it/fvc2002/
27. FVC2004 database. http://bias.csr.unibo.it/fvc2004/
28. Neurotechnology Inc., VeriFinger. http://www.neurotechnology.com/
29. Xu, L., Ren, J., Yan, Q., Liao, R., Jia, J.: Deep edge-aware filters. In: Proceedings of the 32nd International Conference on Machine Learning, pp. 1669–1678 (2015)
30. Liskowski, P., Krawiec, K.: Segmenting retinal blood vessels with deep neural networks. IEEE Trans. Med. Imaging **35**(11), 2369–2380 (2016)

Feature Guided Fingerprint Pore Matching

Feng Liu[✉], Yuanhao Zhao, and Linlin Shen

College of Computer Science and Software Engineering, Shenzhen University,
Shenzhen, Guangdong, China
feng.liu@szu.edu.cn

Abstract. The huge number of sweat pores in fingerprint images results in low efficiency of direct pore (DP) matching methods. To overcome this drawback, this paper proposes a feature guided fingerprint pore matching method. It selects "distinctive" pores around the minutiae and singular points from fingerprint images which extremely reduced the number of pore features for matching. And then, the selected "distinctive" pores are matched using the-state-of-the-art DP matching methods. We also consider to take the select "distinctive" pores together with the extracted minutiae and singular points as a whole feature set for matching. The experimental results have shown that the matching time of the proposed method can be reduced to a quarter of the original time when the recognition accuracy is kept at the same level. Both of the matching time and recognition accuracy are improved when multi-features are taken as a whole set for matching.

Keywords: Fingerprint recognition · Pore matching · "Distinctive" pores

1 Introduction

Since Galton quantified the uniqueness of fingerprints in 1872, fingerprints are widely used for human identification [1–5]. Fingerprints are identified by their features. In general, fingerprint features are described in a hierarchical order of three levels. Level 1 features are the overall global ridge flow patterns, including singular points, deltas and cores. The population of Level 1 features is small (fewer than 5), and they cannot be extracted exactly. Thus, Level 1 features are usually taken as reference point for coarse alignment [6]. Level 2 features refer to ridge ending and ridge bifurcation, namely minutiae points. The previous study had confirmed that Level 2 features have sufficient discriminating power to establish the individuality of fingerprints [7–9]. They are moderate in population. Level 3 features are defined as the dimensional attributes of the ridges, such as sweat pores, ridge contour, and ridge edge features. Compared with Level 2 features, Level 3 features are also permanent, immutable and unique [10]. Researches of fingerprint identification based on Level 3 features are mainly focused on sweat pores [11–13]. Locard certified that 20 to 40 pores should be enough to establish human identity [14]. This feature is used for more accuracy fingerprint matching because of its large population (about 1500 in each 640 * 480 pixels fingerprint image) but small detection bias (about 5 pixels). We summarized some attributes and performance of fingerprint recognition methods based on different features in Tabel 1. It

© Springer International Publishing AG 2017
J. Zhou et al. (Eds.): CCBR 2017, LNCS 10568, pp. 334–343, 2017.
https://doi.org/10.1007/978-3-319-69923-3_36

can be seen from the table that each feature has its own characteristics. Methods with high recognition accuracy and low computational complexity can be achieved if those features are organized in a reasonable way.

Table 1. Comparison of attribute/performance of fingerprint recognition methods based on different features.

Attribute/performance	Singular points	Minutiae	Sweat pores
Location accuracy	Low	Moderate	High
Orientation	\	Provided	\
Population	Small	Moderate	Large
Uniqueness	Moderate	High	High
Recognition accuracy	Low	Moderate	High
Computational complexity	Low	Relative low	High

Motivated by the above discussion, we proposed a feature guided fingerprint pore matching method. This method aims to make full use of the characteristics of each feature. Due to the uniqueness of singular points and minutiae, those pores which are around singular points and minutiae are defined as "distinctive" pores. Based on the small population of singular points and minutiae in a fingerprint image, the large population of sweat pores is largely reduced to "distinctive" pores set. Consequently, the computational complexity goes down when fingerprint pore matching methods are adopted. The recognition accuracy is kept or improved when singular points, minutiae and "distinctive" pores are taken as a whole feature set for matching. The effectiveness of the proposed method was proved by our experimental results.

The rest of this paper is organized as follows. Section 2 discusses existing pore matching methods and our proposed idea about performance improving. Section 3 reports and analyzes the evaluation results. Section 4 finally concludes the paper.

2 Related Work and Proposed Methodology Description

The existing pore matching methods are generally divided into two categories. One is alignment based methods. This kind of methods align the fingerprint images using other features firstly, and then match pores included in the aligned area measured by geometric distances [12, 15, 16]. The other one is direct pore matching methods. Methods in this category directly match pores in fingerprints which is independent of other fingerprint features [13, 17, 18]. Typical methods are introduced in following subsections.

2.1 Alignment Based Method

In [12, 15], Kryszczuk *et al.* proposed to first align the query fragmentary fingerprint with the full template fingerprint using the image-correlation based method, and then matched the pores in the aligned fingerprint images based on their geometric distances.

In [16], Jain *et al.* proposed to match pores after minutiae pairs are established between query and template fingerprints (denoted by MICPP). More specifically, minutiae in fingerprints are firstly extracted and matched. Then, pores lying in a rectangular neighborhood to each aligned minutiae pair are matched using a modified iterative closest point (ICP) algorithm. The experimental results given in those papers showed that the equal error rates (EER) can reach to 3.3% in their own established database. Although the accuracy was improved significantly compared with recognition methods based on low level fingerprint features, the accuracy is far away from meeting our expectations. Thus, researchers began to investigate other effective methods.

2.2 Direct Pore Matching Method

In 2009, Zhao *et al.* for the first time proposed direct pore matching method [13] (denoted by DP). A hierarchical coarse-to-fine pore matching scheme was adopted in their paper. Figure 1 shows the flowchart of the DP method. In the coarse step, local descriptor of each pore (P) was extracted and matched by calculating the similarity between two pores P_i and P_j using Eq. (1), where P_i, $i = 1, 2, \ldots$, and P_j, $j = 1, 2, \ldots$, are the sets of descriptors of the pores on the query and template fingerprints, respectively. In the fine step, the obtained pore correspondences are refined using a global transformation model shown in Eq. (2). From the experiment results shown in their paper, we can see that the accuracy get 30% improved but the computational complexity is largely increased compared with MICPP.

$$S_{ij} = P_i P_j^T \tag{1}$$

$$\begin{pmatrix} \bar{x} \\ \bar{y} \end{pmatrix} = \begin{bmatrix} a_{11} & a_{12} \\ a_{21} & a_{22} \end{bmatrix} \begin{pmatrix} x \\ y \end{pmatrix} + \begin{bmatrix} t_x \\ t_y \end{bmatrix} \tag{2}$$

In 2010 and 2011, an improved version of this method is proposed by Liu *et al.* [17, 18]. In these methods, sparse representation-based method (denoted as TD-Sparse) is using in the coarse matching step. While a weighted RANdom Sample Consensus (WRANSAC) algorithm was adopted to refine coarse pore correspondences. The experiments showed that much higher recognition accuracy is achieved than DP method. However, the computational complexity is still very high.

2.3 Proposed Methodology Description

From the discussion in Subsects. 2.1 and 2.2, we can see that the alignment based method usually has low recognition accuracy. This is because alignment based on low level fingerprint features is firstly implemented before matching pores. The final recognition accuracy heavily relies on the matching result based on low level fingerprint features, and accuracy is not high based on low level fingerprint features, as shown in Table 1. The direct pore matching method often spend too much time. This is largely due to the huge number of sweat pores extracted from fingerprint images, and each pore is considered for matching (as shown in Fig. 1).

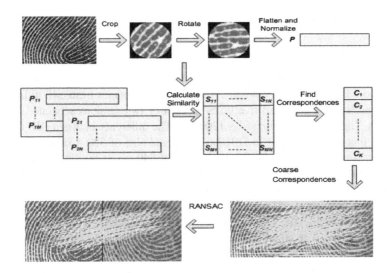

Fig. 1. The flowchart of direct pore matching method.

In order to keep relatively high recognition accuracy and reduce computational complexity, we proposed a feature guided pore matching method. Low level fingerprint features (e.g. singular points, minutiae) were firstly extracted but not used for fingerprint alignment. They were used for guiding the selection of "distinctive" pores. As shown in Fig. 2, pores near the singular points and minutiae are defined as "distinctive" pores. It is notable that the radius of the defined neighborhood is set to 15. And then, the "distinctive" pores were considered for matching using the DP method. By selecting "distinctive" pores for matching, the number of matching pores are extremely reduced so as to decrease the matching time. Via adopting the effective DP method, the recognition accuracy is guaranteed in the same level of DP matching. Since singular points and minutiae features can be treated as point features as sweat pores and the number of these features are small, we combined them with the "distinctive" pores to form a "Multi-feature" set for matching to further improve the recognition accuracy.

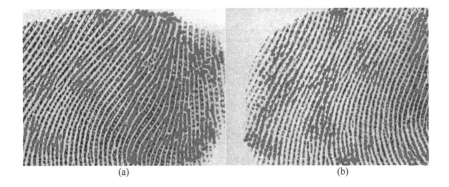

(a)   (b)

Fig. 2. Examples of "distinctive" pores selected from fingerprint image.

3 Experimental Results and Analysis

3.1 Databases and Protocols

In the experiment, two databases (denoted by DBI and DBII) were used to evaluate the performance. Both databases contain 1,480 fingerprint images from 148 different fingers, and each finger collected five times in each of two sessions separated by about two weeks. The image resolution is ~1200 dpi. The difference between DBI and DBII is just the image size. Images in DBI have a spatial size of 320 pixels by 240 pixels while images in DBII have a larger spatial size of 640 pixels by 480 pixels.

The singular points were extracted using the Poincare Index introduced in [3]. The minutiae were extracted by using the algorithm introduced in [19]. Sweat pores on the fingerprint images were extracted by using an improved version of the algorithm in [20]. DP methods in [13, 17, 18] were adopted to match "distinctive" pores and "Multi-feature" set. The equal error rates (EER) which is used to evaluate the recognition accuracy were calculated from 3,700 genuine match scores (each of the fingerprint images in the second session was matched with all the fingerprint images of the same finger in the first session) and 21,756 imposter match scores (the first fingerprint image of each finger in the second session was matched with the first fingerprint images of all the other fingers in the first session). Note that the pore match scores in our experiments were defined as the number of pairs of final matched pores in fingerprints.

3.2 Results and Analysis

At first, we compared the matching performance of proposed method (denoted by DP-MSR-select pores) with the existing DP method with modified sparse representation strategy in [17] (denoted by DP-MSR-all pores) in terms of EER and average matching time. The results evaluated in DBI were shown in Fig. 3. From the results, we can see that the matching time is reduced to be one fourth of the original time after pore selection. Meanwhile, the EER is increased but kept at the same level as the original method.

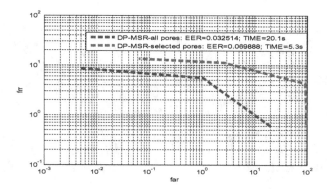

Fig. 3. The ROC curves of DP-MSR-select pores and DP-MSR-all pores.

As mentioned in Subsect. 3.1, the pore match scores were obtained by calculating the number of finally matched pores on two fingerprints. An interesting finding in the experiment is that: same match scores but obviously quite different pore correspondences are obtained when matching a pair of fingerprint images from the same finger using DP-MSR-select pores and DP-MSR-all pores. As shown in Fig. 4(a) and (b), wrong pore correspondences were obtained when all pores were used for matching, while true pore correspondences were received if "distinctive" pores were selected for matching. Thus, it can be inferred that the performance is improved using our proposed strategy and the match score defined in the paper is not reasonable.

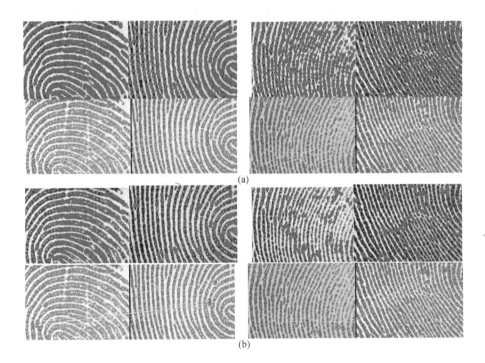

Fig. 4. Different pore correspondences with the same match score using (a) DP-MSR-all pores, and (b) DP-MSR-select pores.

To alleviate the influence of match score to recognition, we proposed a new match score which considered the number of initial matched pore correspondences. It is defined as:

$$Matchscore = \left\lceil \frac{Num_{final}}{Num_{initial}} * 10 \right\rceil \bmod 10 + Num_{initial} \tag{3}$$

where Num_{final} is the final matched pairs of the pores on fingerprint images and $Num_{initial}$ is the initial matched pairs of the pores.

We did the experiment again and drew the receiver operator characteristic (ROC) curves in Fig. 5. It can be seen that the EER is reduced to 6.1%. However, it is still higher than the method which considered all pores. We inferred that the size of initial pore set have an impact on matching results. To confirm our conjecture, we found those false rejection fingerprint pairs out from our results. As an example shown in Fig. 6, wrong pore correspondences are established by DP-MSR-select pores while right results are obtained by DP-MSR-all pores. It is because that there are small overlapping area between two fingerprint images which limited the number of matched singular points and minutiae. The defined "distinctive" pores are then easily wrong matched between two fingerprint images. Therefore, we could concluded that when matching partial fingerprints with small image size, it is better to consider all pores to guarantee the recognition accuracy. Meanwhile, since the matching results can be improved when just considering the "distinctive" pores in some situations (as the examples shown in Fig. 4), the match scores obtained by DP-MSR-select pores and DP-MSR-all pores can be fused together to further improve recognition accuracy, as the result shown in Fig. 7. The matching time is only increased a quarter of the original time.

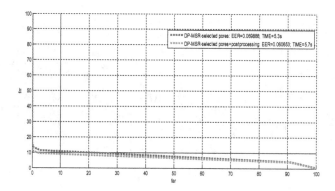

Fig. 5. The ROC curves of DP-MSR-selected pores and DP-MSR-selected pores with new match score.

Fig. 6. An example of matching results with small overlapping area between two fingerprint images. (a) Pore correspondences established by DP-MSR-all pores, (b) pore correspondences established by DP-MSR-select pores.

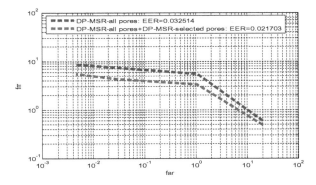

Fig. 7. The ROC curves of DP-MSR-all pores and fusion of DP-MSR-all pores and DP-MSR-selected pores

It is not obvious that large improvement can be obtained using our proposed method on DBI due to the limited number of pores (several hundreds) provided by small image size. We then evaluated our proposed method on DBII with large image size (several thousand of pores can be provided). From the results shown in Fig. 8, we can see that better results can be obtained using our proposed method. We finally compared our proposed multi-feature method with other representative pore matching methods, including MICPP, DP and TD-Sparse. The ROC curves, EERs and mean matching time were given in Fig. 9 and Table 2, respectively. It can be seen that compared with MICPP, the proposed multi-feature methods can achieve higher recognition accuracy by $\sim 37\%$ and $\sim 98\%$, respectively. By comparing with DP and TD-Sparse methods, the proposed multi-feature strategy can reduce the match time to one fifth of the original time. Moreover, the recognition accuracy are further improved (EER is decrease). The effectiveness of our proposed method is fully validated by the experiments.

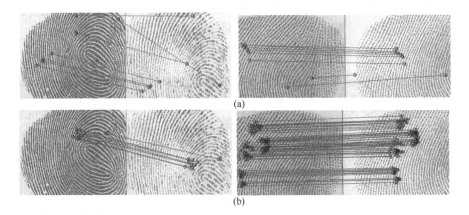

Fig. 8. Two examples of matching pore correspondences using different methods. (a) DP-MSR-all pores, and (b) DP-MSR-select pores.

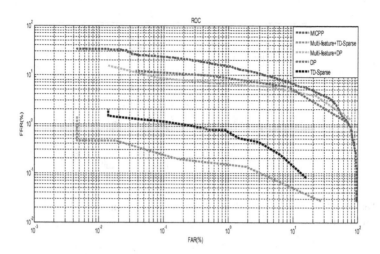

Fig. 9. The ROC curves with different methods.

Table 2. The EER and mean time of different methods.

Method	EER (%)	Mean time (s)
MICPP	7.83	~1
DP	7.05	~19.53
Multi-feature + DP	5.93	~3.01
TD-Sparse	0.53	~94.13
Multi-feature + TD-Sparse	0.17	~18.97

We believe that the improvement achieved by the proposed method owes to the following two factors. First, pores around singular points and minutiae are more "distinctive" than other pores. Second, reducing the number of pores for DP matching appropriately can decrease interference among pores.

4 Conclusion

This paper introduced an effective pore matching strategy based on pore selection. "Distinctive" pores were selected under the guidance of singular points and minutiae. The computational complexity was largely reduced with the decrease of matching pores. By taking the select "distinctive" pores together with the extracted singular points and minutiae as a whole feature set for matching, the recognition accuracy was improved. The experimental results had shown the effectiveness of the proposed method.

Acknowledgments. The work is supported by the NSFC funds 61403257 and Shenzhen Fundamental Research funds JCYJ20150324140036868.

References

1. Yoon, S., Jain, A.K.: Longitudinal study of fingerprint recognition. In: Proceedings of the National Academy of Sciences of the United States of America. vol. 112, no. 28, pp. 8555–8560 (2015)
2. Peishan, X., Yuzhen, Y.: HPTLC fingerprint identification of commercial ginseng drugs - reinvestigation of HPTLC of ginsenosides. J. High Resolut. Chromatogr. **10**(11), 607–613 (2015)
3. Maltoni, D., Maio, D., Jain, A.K., Prabhakar, S.: Handbook of Fingerprint Recognition. Springer Science and Business Media, Berlin (2009)
4. Liu, F., Zhang, D., Shen, L.: Study on novel curvature features for 3D fingerprint recognition. Neurocomputing **168**(C), 599–608 (2015)
5. Darlow, L.N., Webb, L., Botha, N.: Automated spoof-detection for fingerprints using optical coherence tomography. Appl. Opt. **55**(13), 3387 (2016)
6. Jain, A.K., Prabhakar, S., Hong, L., Pankanti, S.: FingerCode: a filterbank for fingerprint representation and matching. In: IEEE Computer Society Conference on Computer Vision and Pattern Recognition. vol. 2, no. 2, p. 193 (1999)
7. Pankanti, S., Prabhakar, S., Jain, A.K.: On the individuality of fingerprints. IEEE Trans. PAMI **24**, 1010–1025 (2002)
8. Ali, M.M.H., Mahale, V.H., Yannawar, P., Gaikwad, A.T.: Fingerprint recognition for person identification and verification based on minutiae matching. In: IEEE International Conference on Advanced Computing, pp. 332–339 (2016)
9. Jain, A.K., Hong, L., Bolle, R.: On-line fingerprint verification. IEEE Trans. PAMI **19**, 302–314 (1997)
10. Thornton, J.: Setting standards in the comparison and identification. In: 84th Annual Training Conference of the California State Division of IAI. Laughlin, Nevada (2000)
11. Kryszczuk, K., Drygajlo, A., Morier, P.: Extraction of level 2 and level 3 features for fragmentary fingerprints. In: Proceedings of the 2nd COST275 Workshop. vol. 27, no. 2, pp. 290–304 (2004)
12. Jain, A.K., Chen, Y., Demirkus, M.: Pores and ridges: fingerprint matching using level 3 features. IEEE Trans. PAMI **4**(1), 477–480 (2006)
13. Zhao, Q., Zhang, L., Zhang, D., Luo, N.: Direct pore matching for fingerprint recognition. Adv. Biom. ICB **5558**, 597–606 (2009)
14. Ashbaugh, D.R.: Quantitative-Qualitative Friction Ridge Analysis: An Introduction to Basic and Advanced Ridgeology. CRC Press, Boca Raton (1999)
15. Kryszczuk, K.M., Morier, P., Drygajlo, A.: Study of the distinctiveness of level 2 and level 3 features in fragmentary fingerprint comparison. In: Maltoni, D., Jain, A.K. (eds.) BioAW 2004. LNCS, vol. 3087, pp. 124–133. Springer, Heidelberg (2004). doi:10.1007/978-3-540-25976-3_12
16. Jain, A.K., Chen, Y., Demirkus, M.: Pores and ridges: High-resolution fingerprint matching using level 3 features. IEEE Trans. Pattern Anal. Mach. Intell. **29**(1), 15–27 (2007)
17. Liu, F., Zhao, Q., Zhang, L., Zhang, D.: Fingerprint pore matching based on sparse representation. In: Proceedings of the 20th International Conference on Pattern Recognition (2010)
18. Liu, F., Zhao, Q., Zhang, D.: A novel hierarchical fingerprint matching approach. Pattern Recogn. **44**(8), 1604–1613 (2011)
19. Feng, J.: Combining minutiae descriptors for fingerprint matching. Pattern Recogn. **41**(1), 342–352 (2008)
20. Zhao, Q., Zhang, L., Zhang, D., Luo, N.: Adaptive pore model for fingerprint pore extraction. In: International Conference on Pattern Recognition, pp. 1–4 (2008)

A CNN-Based Fingerprint Image Quality Assessment Method

Jianqi Yan[1], Xiaowei Dai[1], Qijun Zhao[1(✉)], and Feng Liu[2]

[1] National Key Laboratory of Fundamental Science on Synthetic Vision,
College of Computer Science, Sichuan University, Chengdu, China
qjzhao@scu.edu.cn
[2] School of Computer Science and Software Engineering, Shenzhen University,
Shenzhen, Guangdong, China

Abstract. Fingerprint image quality assessment is a very important task as the performance of automatic fingerprint identification systems relies heavily on the quality of fingerprint images. Existing methods have made many efforts to find out more appropriate solutions, but most of them operate either on full regions of a fingerprint image, or on local areas. Unlike previous methods, we divide fingerprint images into blocks, and define the quality levels of the blocks according to the minutiae on them and their ridge orientation certainty. With the manually prepared quality-specific fingerprint image blocks, we train a convolutional neural network (CNN) to fulfill end-to-end quality prediction for fingerprint image blocks. The global quality of a fingerprint image can be obtained by fusing the quality levels of its blocks. We evaluate the proposed method on FVC2002 DB1A and FVC2002 DB2A. Experimental results show that the proposed method can effectively distinguish good quality fingerprints from bad ones, and ensure high fingerprint recognition accuracy.

Keywords: Fingerprint image quality assessment · Minutiae · Orientation Certainty Level · CNN

1 Introduction

Fingerprint identification is one of the most popular and reliable biometric techniques and it has been wildly applied to the authentication of individuals in many scenes such as electronic personal identification card, smart phone and so on [1]. A fingerprint recognition system provides a good balance of security, privacy, convenience and accountability because of the uniqueness, invariance and accessibility of fingerprint [2]. But it is affected a lot by the quality of the input data. Poor quality fingerprint images which may be caused by scar, patchy skin, dirty sensor surface, etc. could result in many difficulties when using them for identification. Therefore, fingerprint image quality assessment is considered as an essential phase for an automatic fingerprint identification system (AFRS).

Over the last years, couples of fingerprint quality assessment algorithms have been proposed. A comparative study of them is given in [3]. It classifies the

© Springer International Publishing AG 2017
J. Zhou et al. (Eds.): CCBR 2017, LNCS 10568, pp. 344–352, 2017.
https://doi.org/10.1007/978-3-319-69923-3_37

existing methods into three categories: (1) segmentation-based methods; (2) single feature-based methods; (3) and methods based on a combination of multi-features or indexes.

Segmentation based methods divide the input fingerprint image into foreground and background components, and define the quality index based on the area ratio of qualified blocks to the whole fingerprint image. Yao *et al.* [4] proposed an approach with minutiae template which adopted the convex-hull and Delaunay triangulation to measure reasonable informative region. Usually, poor quality samples generate tiny triangles considered as unreasonable regions due to spurious minutiae points. But it depends heavily on the reliability of minutiae points and some real minutiae points may also result in tiny triangles.

Another major category pays attention to the quality metrics that rely on a single feature on fingerprint images. For example, Lee *et al.* [5] proposed a measure of the fingerprint image quality using the Fourier spectrum. The Fourier transform is very useful for distinguishing the total direction and the consistency of ridges and valleys. However, it has difficulty in evaluating local direction. Other features include local standard deviation [6], Gabor features [7] and directional contrast of local block [8], none of which, however, can gauge the total direction, persistence or consistence of fingerprint images.

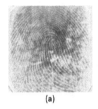 

(a)   (b)

Fig. 1. Two fingerprint images of quality (a) score $= 88$ and (b) score $= 6$ as evaluated by the Self-Organization Maps method [13].

Many existing studies qualify fingerprint images with multiple features in two aspects: linear fusion with weighted coefficients and classification. For the first aspect, Chen *et al.* [9] proposed a quality metric by linearly combining the Orientation Flow and the ridge-valley clarity features. But the weighted coefficients must be adjusted for different images. For the latter, the method, NFIQ [11, 12], employs 11-dimension feature to estimate a matching score and classifies fingerprint images to five quality levels through a trained neural network. In addition, Olsen *et al.* [13] proposed a method based on a combination of unsupervised self-organizing maps and supervised Random Forest. The Random Forest classifies fingerprints according to a prior-knowledge of matching scores. However, the matching scores between bad quality fingerprints are somehow unforeseeable. Figure 1 gives two examples whose quality are both visually bad, but obtain obviously different quality scores as evaluated by the Self Organization Maps (SOM) method in [13].

In this paper, we propose a fingerprint image quality assessment method based on CNN. Generally, the minutiae extracted from a fingerprint image of good quality are credible. In the meantime, the Orientation Certainty Level (OCL) [10] is frequently used to determine the reliability of the ridge orientation in fingerprint images. Therefore, we define the quality levels of fingerprint image blocks according to these two features, and manually prepare a set of quality-specific fingerprint image blocks to train a convolutional neural network (CNN), which can fulfill end-to-end quality prediction of fingerprint image blocks. The global quality of a fingerprint image can be obtained by fusing the predicted quality levels of its blocks. This paper is organized as follows: Sect. 2 details the proposed method. Section 3 then reports the experimental results. Finally, Sect. 4 concludes the paper.

2   Proposed Method

In this section, we first describe how we prepare the training data in detail. Then we introduce the training process of our method. Figure 2 shows the flowchart of our proposed method.

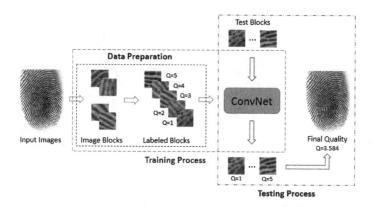

Fig. 2. The flowchart of our method.

2.1   Data Preparation

Fingerprint minutiae [14] are widely used in defining crucial quality indices of fingerprint images. Here, we employ a commercial software called VeriFinger [17] to detect the location and reliability of minutiae. VeriFinger associates a reliability score with each minutia. A higher score means a more reliable minutia. Another feature of fingerprint images worthy of attention is the orientation [9, 15,16]. A fingerprint image of good quality usually has better persistence and consistency of the ridges and valleys. OCL is considered as an important analysis method to indicate the energy concentration along the direction of ridges. It can be computed using the following equations.

$$C = \frac{1}{N} \sum_N \left\{ \begin{bmatrix} G_x \\ G_y \end{bmatrix} [G_x \ G_y] \right\} = \begin{bmatrix} G_x^2 & G_x G_y \\ G_y G_x & G_y^2 \end{bmatrix} = \begin{bmatrix} c_1 & c_3 \\ c_3 & c_2 \end{bmatrix} \quad (1)$$

$$OCL = \frac{(c_1 - c_2)^2 + 4c_3^2}{(c_1 + c_2)^2} \quad (2)$$

In Eq. 1, C is the covariance matrix of gradient vector for an image block of N pixels. G_x and G_y exhibit the intensity gradient at each pixel, which can be calculated using Prewitt, Sobel or Robert operators. Here, Sobel operator of 3 by 3 windows is used. From Eq. 2, OCL values of the image block can be computed which lies in the range of $[0, 1]$. $OCL = 1$ means that ridges and valleys in a block change consistently in the same direction, while $OCL = 0$ means that they are not consistent and may belong to the background.

Table 1. Five quality levels of fingerprint images blocks.

Quality level	Contain minutiae or not	Score of minutiae	OCL value
Q = 1	No	-	[0, 0.4)
Q = 2	No	-	[0.4, 0.6)
Q = 3	No	-	[0.6, 1]
Q = 4	Yes	[65, 85)	[0.4, 1]
Q = 5	Yes	[85, 100]	[0.4, 1]

Based on the above two features, we propose the following definition of the quality levels of fingerprint image blocks. (1) Dividing fingerprint images into blocks (block size is 24×24 or 32×32). (2) Detecting the minutiae to obtain the location and reliability scores of each block using the VeriFinger. (3) Computing the OCL value of each block. (4) Classifying each block into one of the five quality levels that are defined in Table 1 (Quality level 5 corresponds to the best quality). Figure 3 shows some example fingerprint image blocks for each quality levels.

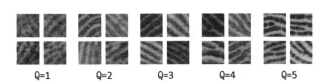

Q=1   Q=2   Q=3   Q=4   Q=5

Fig. 3. Example fingerprint image blocks of the five different quality levels.

2.2   Training CNN for Quality Prediction

The training data we use are from the 800 fingerprint images in the FVC2004 DB1A [19]. We crop from these images 801,182 patches of 24 × 24 pixels and 649,908 patches of 32×32 pixels. We adopt different network structures for different block size, and the network for size 32 × 32 has one more convolutional layer than that for size 24 × 24. Figure 4 depicts the network structure for fingerprint image blocks of 24 × 24 pixels.

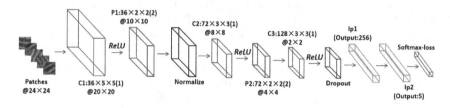

Fig. 4. Network structure of size 24 × 24.

After training, the trained model can be used for fingerprint image quality assessment. Firstly, we divide fingerprint images into blocks and use the trained model to process the image blocks. Then, the quality level of each block is obtained and used as the quality score of the block. Ultimately, we can get the global quality of the whole image from Eq. 3, in which, M is the number of the blocks and Q_i means the quality of the ith block.

$$Global_{quality} = \frac{1}{M} \sum_{i=1}^{M} Q_i \qquad (3)$$

Figure 5 gives the quality scores obtained by our proposed method for the two example fingerprint images shown in Fig. 1. We can see that the results obtained with our method are reasonable compared with the results obtained by the existing SOM method.

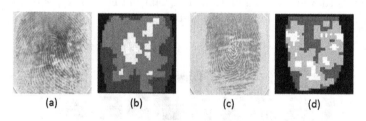

(a)   (b)   (c)   (d)

Fig. 5. The quality maps obtained by our proposed method for the two fingerprint images (a) and (c) that are shown in Fig. 1. The corresponding global quality scores for them are, respectively, $Global_{quality} = 1.818$ and $Global_{quality} = 1.814$.

3 Experiments and Results

3.1 Experimental Design

The purpose of assessing the quality of fingerprint images is to distinguish between fingerprint images of good and poor quality, so as to improve the accuracy of fingerprint matching process. In order to verify the effectiveness of the method proposed in this paper, we design the following experiment protocol.

(1) The databases we use are FVC2002 DB1A and FVC2002 DB2A [18]. Each one contains 800 fingerprint images of 100 fingers with eight images per finger. (2) The comparative method we use is NFIQ. (3) The strategy of the experiment: (a) Dividing fingerprint images into blocks, including size 24×24 and 32×32. And processing the image blocks with trained model to obtain the score of each block. Further, using Eq. 3 to get the global quality score of the whole image and sorting it from high to low on each database respectively. (b) Employing the NFIQ to classify the fingerprint images on each database individually and pairing the image under every category, including genuine match and imposter match. Then, using VeriFinger for identification experiment and calculating False Rejection Rate (FRR) and False Acceptance Rate (FAR) to analyze the relationship between FRR and FAR. (c) The same with the NFIQ, classifying the fingerprint images processed with our method into several categories, in which the category with high scores correspond to the category of good quality in NFIQ. Similarly, computing FRR and FAR, and analyzing their relationship.

3.2 Experimental Results

According to the above experimental protocol, we obtain the following results. Table 2 summarizes the number of genuine match and imposter match of each quality level on FVC2002 DB1A and FVC2002 DB2A. Usually, NFIQ classifies fingerprint images into five quality levels, but both of these two databases lack of fingerprint images from one or two quality levels. Besides, the quality level of the fingerprint image with lower quality are used as the quality level of each match. And global quality level 4 corresponds to the best quality.

Table 2. Numbers of genuine and imposter match on two databases.

Global quality level	FVC2002 DB1A		FVC2002 DB2A	
	Genuine	Imposter	Genuine	Imposter
G1	276	33,178	28	3,162
G2	1,441	180,965	391	48,473
G3	1,083	102,657	1569	200,636
G4	-	-	812	64,529

In Table 2, there are several quality levels containing few genuine matches. Thus, we incorporate the quality levels with few genuine matches into neighbor quality level. Here, we incorporate G1 into G2 on FVC2002 DB2A. Furthermore, we calculate the value of FRR when FAR is equal to 0.1%, and smaller value means better performance. Table 3 shows the results on these two databases.

Table 3. FRR(%)@FAR = 0.1% on FVC2002 DB1A and FVC2002 DB2A.

Global quality level	FVC2002 DB1A			Global Quality Level	FVC2002 DB2A		
	Blocksize		NFIQ		Blocksize		NFIQ
	24 × 24	32 × 32			24 × 24	32 × 32	
L1(G1–G3)	0.536	0.536	0.536	L1(G2–G4)	0.321	0.321	0.321
L2(G2–G3)	0.317	0.277	0.436	L2(G3–G4)	0.210	0.210	0.252
L3(G3)	0.093	0.093	0.092	L3(G4)	0.123	0.124	0.123

In Table 3, L1(G1–G3) contains fingerprint images from global quality level G1, G2 and G3. Moreover, the value of FRR is decreasing when the low quality image is removed. In order to depict the descend range of FRR intuitively, we employ the following equation to compute the value of cumulative decline, denoted as S. The larger the value of S means the larger descend range.

$$S = \sum_{i=1}^{N} \frac{L_i - L_{i+1}}{L_i} \tag{4}$$

In Eq. 4, L_i denotes the value of FRR when FAR is equal to 0.1% on the level i. Table 4 shows the value of S on FVC2002 DB1A and FVC2002 DB2A. The results show that our method has better performance.

Table 4. The value of S on FVC2002 DB1A and FVC2002 DB2A.

Database	Blocksize		NFIQ
	24 × 24	32 × 32	
FVC2002 DB1A	1.115	1.147	0.976
FVC2002 DB2A	0.760	0.755	0.727

4   Conclusions

In this paper, we propose a fingerprint image quality assessment method based on CNN. Unlike previous methods, it defines block-wise quality levels based on the minutiae and orientation features in fingerprint images, and constructs a CNN for end-to-end quality prediction of fingerprint image blocks. Experimental results prove the effectiveness of our proposed method. However, our method is relatively time-consuming, and computes global quality by simply averaging the block-wise quality levels. Therefore, our future work is to improve the efficiency of our method and try some other method to get the global quality.

Acknowledgments. This work is supported by the National Natural Science Foundation of China (Nos. 61202161, 61403257) and Shenzhen Fundamental Research Funds (No. JCYJ20150324140036868).

References

1. Ratha, N.K., Bolle, R.: Automatic Fingerprint Recognition Systems. Springer, New York (2004)
2. Maltoni, D., Maio, D., Jain, A.K., Prabhakar, S.: Handbook of Fingerprint Recognition. Springer, London (2009)
3. Yao, Z.G., Bars, J.M.L., Charrier, C., Rosenberger, C.: A literature review of fingerprint quality assessment and its evaluation. IET Biometrics 5(3), 243–251 (2016)
4. Yao, Z., Bars, J.L., Charrier, C., Rosenberger, C.: Quality assessment of fingerprints with minutiae delaunay triangulation. In: 2015 International Conference on Information Systems Security and Privacy, pp. 315–321 (2015)
5. Lee, B., Moon, J.: A novel measure of fingerprint image quality using the Fourier spectrum. In: Proceedings of SPIE - The International Society for Optical Engineering, pp. 105–112 (2005)
6. Bazen, A.M., Gerez, S.H.: Segmentation of fingerprint images. In: ProRISC 2001 Workshop on Circuits, Systems and Signal Processing, pp. 276–280 (2001)
7. Shen, L.L., Kot, A., Koo, W.M.: Quality measures of fingerprint images. In: Bigun, J., Smeraldi, F. (eds.) AVBPA 2001. LNCS, vol. 2091, pp. 266–271. Springer, Heidelberg (2001). doi:10.1007/3-540-45344-X_39
8. Ballan, M., Sakarya, F.A., Evans, B.L.: A fingerprint classification technique using directional images. In: Thirty-First Asilomar Conference on Signals, Systems and Computers, pp. 101–104 (1997)
9. Chen, T.P., Jiang, X., Yau, W.Y.: Fingerprint image quality analysis. In: International Conference on Image Processing, pp. 1253–1256 (2004)
10. Xie, S.J., Yang, J.C., Yoon, S., Dong, S.P.: An optimal orientation certainty level approach for fingerprint quality estimation. In: Second International Symposium on Intelligent Information Technology Application, pp. 722–726 (2008)
11. Tabassi, E., Wilson, C., Watson, C.: NIST fingerprint image quality. NIST Res. Rep. NIST7151 (2004)
12. Tabassi, E., Wilson, C.L.: A novel approach to fingerprint image quality. In: IEEE International Conference on Image Processing, pp. 37–40 (2005)
13. Olsen, M.A., Tabassi, E., Makarov, A., Busch, C.: Self-organizing maps for fingerprint image quality assessment. In: Computer Vision and Pattern Recognition Workshops, pp. 138–145 (2013)
14. Yao, Z., Bars, J.M.L., Charrier, C., Rosenberger, C.: Fingerprint quality assessment combining blind image quality, texture and minutiae features. In: International Conference on Information Systems Security and Privacy (2015)
15. Hong, L., Wan, Y., Jain, A.K.: Fingerprint image enhancement: algorithm and performance evaluation. IEEE Trans. Pattern Anal. Mach. Intell. 20(8), 777–789 (1998)

16. Ratha, N.K., Chen, S., Jain, A.K.: Adaptive flow orientation-based feature extraction in fingerprint images. Pattern Recogn. **28**(11), 1657–1672 (1995)
17. Neurotechnology Inc.: VeriFinger. http://www.neurotechnology.com/
18. FVC2002 database. http://bias.csr.unibo.it/fvc2002/
19. FVC2004 database. http://bias.csr.unibo.it/fvc2004/

2D Fake Fingerprint Detection for Portable Devices Using Improved Light Convolutional Neural Networks

Yongliang Zhang[1(✉)], Bing Zhou[1], Xiaoguang Qiu[2], Hongtao Wu[3],
and Xiaosi Zhan[4]

[1] College of Computer Science and Technology,
Zhejiang University of Technology, Hangzhou 310023, China
titanzhang@zjut.edu.cn
[2] Hangzhou Commnet Company Limited, Hangzhou 310012, China
[3] College of Computer Science and Engineering,
Hebei University of Technology, Tianjin 300130, China
[4] College of Computer Science and Technology,
Zhejiang International Studies University, Hangzhou 310023, China

Abstract. With the increasing use of fingerprint authentication systems on portable devices, fake fingerprint detection has become growing important because fingerprints can be easily spoofed from a variety of available fabrication materials. Recently, many smartphones are hacked successfully by 2D fake fingerprint, which is a serious threat to authentication security. In order to enhance the robustness against fake fingerprint type, this paper proposes a novel 2D fake fingerprint detection method for portable devices based on improved light Convolutional Neural Networks (CNN). To evaluate the performance of the proposed method, a new 2D fake fingerprint dataset including three fabrication materials is created from capacitive fingerprint scanner. In addition, batch normalization and global average pooling are integrated to optimize the network. Experimental results show that the proposed method has high accuracy, strong robustness and good real-time performance, and can meet the requirements on portable devices.

Keywords: Fingerprint liveness detection · 2D fake fingerprint · Convolutional Neural Networks · Batch normalization · Global average pooling

1 Introduction

With the advancement of biometric technology, Automatic Fingerprint Identification System (AFIS) for portable devices is very popular. However, fingerprints can be easily spoofed from a variety of readily available materials such as wood glue, electrosol or printed fingerprint [1, 2]. Therefore, Fake Fingerprint Detection (FFD) for portable devices has become increasingly important in the field of personal information security. Although many traditional FFD methods [3–9] have achieved good real-time performance already, their accuracy usually is not high enough to meet practical application or they need additional hardware devices.

© Springer International Publishing AG 2017
J. Zhou et al. (Eds.): CCBR 2017, LNCS 10568, pp. 353–360, 2017.
https://doi.org/10.1007/978-3-319-69923-3_38

Recently, Convolutional Neural Networks (CNN) has been applied to build image-based anti-spoofing systems [10–13] and achieved state-of-the-art performance because of its strong learning ability from data and high efficient feature representation ability. The experimental results in [10] strongly indicated that CNN-based FFD was robust to attacks already known. Experiments presented in [14] revealed good robustness with regards to unseen fabrication materials on LivDet 2011 and 2013 databases. However, compared with traditional methods [3–8], although many CNN methods reach higher accuracy, they need more computational resources which are hard implemented on portable devices.

In addition, the duplication of a fingerprint can be a cooperative process or a non-cooperative process [1, 2], and the former is named 3D fake fingerprint and the latter is named 2D fake fingerprint. In contrast, 2D fake fingerprints are easier to be obtained from many occasions and it has been confirmed that some 2D fake fingerprints made of wood glue and electrosol from photolithographic Printed Circuit Board (PCB) mold, or printed by special conductive ink can cheat many current fingerprint verification systems on smartphone, lockfast or fingerprint lock [1, 2, 15]. However, these above methods including traditional and deep learning methods mainly research on 3D FFD, but very little research on 2D FFD is reported in the field of fingerprint liveness detection.

Therefore, in order to further enhance the robustness against the attack from 2D fake fingerprint, a novel 2D FFD method for portable devices based on improved light CNN is proposed in this paper. To evaluate the performance of the proposed method, a new 2D fake fingerprint dataset including three fabrication materials is created from capacitive fingerprint scanner. In addition, Batch Normalization (BN) [16] and Global Average Pooling (GAP) [17] are integrated into CNN to further improve its efficiency and accuracy.

The rest of the paper is organized as follows. In Sect. 2, the proposed method is described in detail. Experimental results are presented completely in Sect. 3. Finally, Sect. 4 concludes the paper.

2   Proposed Method

Firstly, we improve partial architecture of original Inception module to reduce dimension and computation cost. Secondly, the light CNN is constructed based on three improved Inception module and GAP. Finally, the evaluation strategy of classification is proposed.

2.1   Improving Inception Module

Compared with local descriptor based methods [3–8], current many deep learning based methods reach higher accuracy. However, they need high-performance hardware modules so that they are difficultly implemented on portable devices [18]. Therefore, we improve the original Inception module [19] and construct a light CNN. Inception can not only increase the depth and width of CNN at a certain computation cost, but also can extract multi-scale features for FFD. In order to enhance the expression ability of Inception, the 5×5 convolution is replaced with two 3×3 convolution by increasing the depth of module. Meanwhile, 1×1 convolution is used before 3×3 convolution layers to reduce dimension and computation cost. Smaller size convolution layer focus more on local information, and the lager one focus more on global information. In addition, BN [16] is added after each convolution to solve the problem of overfitting and accelerate deep network training by reducing internal covariate shift [16]. For the activation function, Rectified Linear Units (ReLU) [20] is used after BN for each convolution. The overall framework of improved Inception module is shown in Fig. 1.

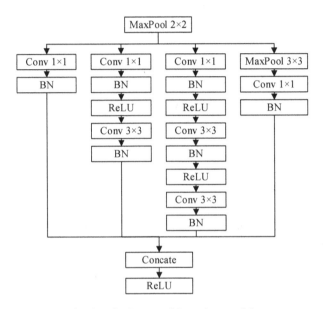

Fig. 1. The improved Inception module

2.2 Constructing Light Convolutional Neural Networks

To adopt the limited computational resources on portable devices, the proposed light network is constructed to contain only three improved Inception modules and is designed with 12 layers when counting only layers with parameters. The compete framework of the improved light CNN is depicted in Fig. 2, which includes the following auxiliary classifiers:

(1) Two 3×3 convolution for dimension reduction and rectified linear activation.
(2) One average pooling layer with 10×10 filter size and stride 1, resulting in an $1 \times 1 \times 256$ feature for the next full connected layer.
(3) One fully connected layer with 256 units and rectified linear activation.
(4) One dropout layer with 50% ratio of dropped outputs.
(5) One linear layer with softmax loss as the classifier.

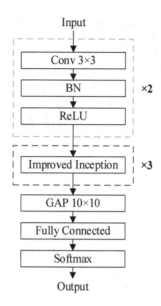

Fig. 2. The overall framework of the improved light CNN

To optimize the proposed light CNN, the traditional fully connected layer is replaced by GAP [17] to reduce overfitting and enhance the robustness of spatial translations. As shown in Fig. 3, the main idea is to generate one feature map for each corresponding category of the classification task in the last convolutional layer. The average of each feature map is calculated and the resulting feature vector is transmitted into the softmax layer directly instead of connecting fully connected layers on top of the feature maps. Compared with the fully connected layer, the advantages of GAP contain these aspects:

(1) Overfitting can be addressed effectively in this layer since it is no need to optimize any parameter in the GAP.
(2) It is more robust to spatial translations of the input because GAP evaluates the spatial information of the whole feature map.
(3) The feature maps can be easily interpreted as categories confidence maps because enforcing correspondences between feature maps and categories are more native to the convolution.

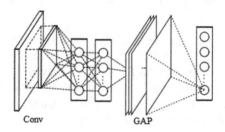

Fig. 3. Structure of global average pooling layer (GAP)

2.3   Classifier Evaluation

The improved light CNN can train a spoof detector P_{CNN} and the detection result R can be calculated as follows:

$$R = \begin{cases} 1, & P_{CNN} > T_P \\ 0, & P_{CNN} \leq T_P \end{cases} \tag{1}$$

where T_P denotes a threshold calculated from the 7-fold cross validation strategy. If $R = 1$, the input image is judged from a fake fingerprint; otherwise it is considered from a live fingerprint.

3   Experimental Results

3.1   Datasets

The published LivDet2009, LivDet2011, LivDet2013 and LivDet2015 are generally created from traditional optical fingerprint scanners. Most of them only contain 3D fake fingerprints and are with enough ideal area. To the best of our knowledge, there is no published dataset which contains 2D fake fingerprints or is created from capacitive fingerprint scanner of portable devices. The main differences between our in-house 2D fake fingerprint dataset and four published datasets of LivDet2015 is shown in Table 1.

Table 1. The differences between in-house dataset and published LivDet2015

Scanner	FPC1021	Crossmatch	Digital persona	Green Bit	Biometrika
Fingerprint type	**2D**	3D	3D	3D	3D
Image size	**160 × 160**	800 × 750	252 × 324	500 × 500	1000 × 1000
Scanner type	**Capacitive**	Optical	Optical	Optical	Optical

However, it has been confirmed that some 2D fake fingerprints made of wood glue and electrosol from photolithographic PCB mold, or printed by special conductive ink can cheat many current fingerprint verification systems on portable devices, lockfast or fingerprint lock [1, 2, 15]. Therefore, we create 2D fake fingerprints with these materials and create a new 2D fake fingerprint dataset with FPC1021 capacitive fingerprint scanner. This dataset is divided into training dataset, validation dataset and testing dataset randomly. Some examples are shown in Fig. 4, and the detail distribution of in-house dataset is listed in Table 2.

3.2   Results

To evaluate the performance of our proposed method, the performance evaluation of Fingerprint Liveness Detection Competition (LivDet) is used as follows:

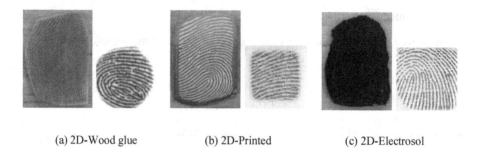

(a) 2D-Wood glue   (b) 2D-Printed   (c) 2D-Electrosol

Fig. 4. Three materials of 2D fake fingerprints and corresponding fingerprint images

Table 2. The detailed distribution of in-house 2D fake fingerprint dataset

Dataset	Training dataset	Validation dataset	Testing dataset
2D-wood glue	46276	551	11200
2D-printed	109476	2799	29354
2D-electrosol	86096	3161	13798
Live	152044	4314	25092
Total	393892	10825	79444

(1) F_corrlive: rate of correctly classified live fingerprints.
(2) F_corrfake: rate of correctly classified fake fingerprints.
(3) F_corrweight: weight average rate of correctly classified live fingerprints and fake fingerprints.

We experiment two main aspects on the in-house 2D fake fingerprint dataset. Firstly, in order to prove the effectiveness of BN and GAP, the proposed method is compared with unimproved CNN, CNN with BN, CNN with GAP respectively. Secondly, the performance of the proposed method is comprehensively compared with classical LBP [7], CLTP [8], Inception [19] and our previous AlexNet-based method [21] respectively.

The experimental platform is Inter®CPU i5-3450 and 4G Memory. As shown in Table 3, compared with unimproved CNN, CNN with BN, CNN with GAP respectively, the proposed method is confirmed to have better F_corrfake, F_corrlive and F_corrweight overall. As shown in Table 4, traditional LBP and CLTP cost less time and memory, but their accuracy is lower which can not meet the practical application. The accuracy of original Inception [19] method can reach 97.30%, but it costs so much time and memory that it is difficulty embed into the portable devices. However, the accuracy of the proposed method can reach 99.13%, and its average time and average memory only cost 69.43 MS and 43.27 MB respectively, which are also better than our previous AlexNet-based method [21].

Table 3. The accuracy of the proposed method on in-house dataset

Method	F_corrlive (%)	F_corrfake (%)	F_corrweight (%)
CNN	97.81	98.12	98.02
CNN + BN	98.43	98.72	98.62
CNN + GAP	98.16	98.50	98.39
Proposed method	**99.03**	**99.18**	**99.13**

Table 4. The performance and cost of the proposed method on in-house dataset

Method	F_corrweight (%)	Average time (MS)	Average memory (MB)
LBP [7]	91.45	5.74	5.03
CLTP [8]	96.57	10.73	5.12
Inception [19]	97.30	153.51	176.39
Previous method [21]	98.58	84.26	62.98
Proposed method	**99.13**	69.43	43.27

4 Conclusion

A novel 2D fake fingerprint detection method for portable devices is proposed, which is based on improved Inception module and light CNN. In addition, a new in-house 2D fake fingerprint dataset is created from capacitive fingerprint scanner, which includes three fabrication materials. Compared with several state-of-the-art methods, Experimental results confirm that the proposed method has higher accuracy and good real-time performance, and can be applied on portable devices.

As well as traditional fingerprint liveness detection, 2D fake fingerprint detection also faces the challenges of scanner interoperability. In the future, we will research on how to enhance the robustness of cross-device detection.

Acknowledgement. This work is supported by the Natural Science Foundation of Zhejiang Province, China (No. Y1101304), and the Science and Technology Planning Project of Hebei Province, China (No. 15210124), and the Science and Technology Research Project of Higher School in Hebei Province, China (No. Z2015105), and Hangzhou Commnet Company Limited.

References

1. Marasco, E., Ross, A.: A survey on antispoofing schemes for fingerprint recognition systems. ACM Comput. Surv. **47**(2), 1–36 (2014)
2. Sousedik, C., Busch, C.: Presentation attack detection methods for fingerprint recognition systems: a survey. IET Biom. **3**(4), 219–233 (2014)
3. Dubey, R., Goh, J., Thing, V.L.L.: Fingerprint liveness detection from single image using low-level features and shape analysis. IEEE Trans. Inf. Forensics Secur. **11**(7), 1461–1475 (2016)

4. Rattani, A., Scheirer, W.J., Ross, A.: Open set fingerprint spoof detection across novel fabrication materials. IEEE Trans. Inf. Forensics Secur. **10**(11), 2447–2460 (2015)
5. Kim, W.: Fingerprint liveness detection using local coherence patterns. IEEE Sig. Process. Lett. **24**(1), 51–55 (2017)
6. Rassem, T.H., Khoo, B.E.: Completed local ternary pattern for rotation invariant texture classification. Sci. World J. **2014**(1), 174–175 (2014)
7. Ojala, T., Pietikinen, M., Menp, T.: Multiresolution gray-scale and rotation invariant texture classification with local binary patterns. IEEE Trans. Pattern Anal. Mach. Intell. **24**(7), 971–987 (2002)
8. Gragnaniello, D., Poggi, G., Sansone, C., et al.: Local contrast phase descriptor for fingerprint liveness detection. Pattern Recogn. **48**(4), 1050–1058 (2015)
9. Jin, C., Kim, H., Elliott, S.: Liveness detection of fingerprint based on band-selective fourier spectrum. In: Nam, K.-H., Rhee, G. (eds.) ICISC 2007. LNCS, vol. 4817, pp. 168–179. Springer, Heidelberg (2007). doi:10.1007/978-3-540-76788-6_14
10. Menotti, D., Chiachia, G., Pinto, A.A., et al.: Deep representations for iris, face, and fingerprint spoofing detection. IEEE Trans. Inf. Forensics Secur. **10**(4), 864–879 (2015)
11. Wang, C., Li, K., Wu, Z., Zhao, Q.: A DCNN based fingerprint liveness detection algorithm with voting strategy. In: Yang, J., Yang, J., Sun, Z. (eds.) Biometric Recognition. LNCS, vol. 9428, pp. 241–249. Springer, Cham (2015). doi:10.1007/978-3-319-25417-3_29
12. Nogueira, R., Lotufo, R., Machado, R.: Fingerprint liveness detection using convolutional neural networks. IEEE Trans. Inf. Forensics Secur. **11**(6), 1206–1213 (2016)
13. Park, E., Kim, W., Li, Q., et al.: Fingerprint liveness detection using CNN features of random sample patches. In: IEEE the 15th International Conference of the Biometrics Special Interest Group, pp. 1–6 (2016)
14. Marasco, E., Wild, P., Cukic, B.: Robust and interoperable fingerprint spoof detection via convolutional neural networks. In: IEEE International Conference on Technologies for Homeland Security, pp. 1–6 (2016)
15. Cao, K., Jain, A.K.: Hacking portable phones using 2D printed fingerprints. MSU Technical report, MSU-CSE-16-2 (2016)
16. Ioffe, S., Szegedy, C.: Batch normalization: accelerating deep network training by reducing internal covariate shift. In: Proceedings of the 32nd International Conference on Machine Learning, pp. 448–456 (2015)
17. Lin, M., Chen, Q., Yan, S.: Network in network. In: International Conference on Learning Representations. http://arxiv.org/abs/1312.4400 (2014)
18. Kim, Y.D., Park, E., Yoo, S., et al.: Compression of deep convolutional neural networks for fast and low power portable applications. Comput. Sci. **71**(2), 576–584 (2015)
19. Szegedy, C., Liu, W., Jia, Y., et al.: Going deeper with convolutions. In: The IEEE Conference on Computer Vision and Pattern Recognition, pp. 1–9 (2015)
20. Nair, V., Hinton, E.: Rectified linear units improve restricted Boltzmann machines In: Proceedings of the 27th International Conference on Machine Learning, pp. 807–814 (2010)
21. Zhang, Y., Zhou, B., Wu, H., Wen, C.: 2D fake fingerprint detection based on improved CNN and local descriptors for smart phone. In: You, Z., Zhou, J., Wang, Y., Sun, Z., Shan, S., Zheng, W., Feng, J., Zhao, Q. (eds.) CCBR 2016. LNCS, vol. 9967, pp. 655–662. Springer, Cham (2016). doi:10.1007/978-3-319-46654-5_72

Fusing 3D Gabor and Block-Wise Spatial Features for Hyperspectral Palmprint Recognition

Mian Li, Weicheng Xie, and Linlin Shen$^{(\boxtimes)}$

School of Computer Science and Software Engineering,
Shenzhen University, Shenzhen, China
llshen@szu.edu.cn

Abstract. Hyperspectral palmprint contains various information in the joint spatial-spectral domain. One crucial task in hyperspectral palmprint recognition is how to extract spatial-spectral features. Since hyperspectral palmprint is three dimensional, most of the existing 2D based algorithms, such as collaborative representation (CR) based framework [15], may not fully explore the information on the spectral domain. Although 3D Gabor filter [18] can be utilized to encode the information on the joint spatial-spectral domain, the texture direction information such as the surface map may not be explored sufficiently. In this work, a novel response-competition (ResCom) feature is proposed to present the spectral information of hyperspectral palmprint based on 3D Gabor filters. Incorporated with the 2D surface map, the ResCom feature can encode not only the 2D texture but also the 3D response variation. Therefore, features of hyperspectral palmprint will be extracted efficiently on the joint spatial-spectral domain. By fusing Block-wise and ResCom features, the proposed approach achieves so far the highest recognition rate of 99.43% on the public hyperspectral palmprint database.

Keywords: 3D Gabor · Hyperspectral palmprint · Fusion feature

1 Introduction

Due to its similarity with the stimulation function of visual cortex cells, Gabor wavelets have been widely used in extracting features for biometrics like face and palmprint [1]. Coding-based approaches firstly apply a set of Gabor wavelets to extract local features, and then encode the responses of wavelets to a binary code for fast matching. PalmCode [2], CompCode (Competitive Code) [3] and FusionCode [4] are three examples of them. Palmcode used a finely tuned Gabor wavelet to extract the orientation and width information of the lines in the palmprint. CompCode encodes the winning wavelet's index, and FusionCode encodes the resulting wavelet's response. The experimental results of the two methods are superior to the PalmCode. The direction filters are typically used by line-based systems to represent the orientation information of principal lines and wrinkles.

© Springer International Publishing AG 2017
J. Zhou et al. (Eds.): CCBR 2017, LNCS 10568, pp. 361–369, 2017.
https://doi.org/10.1007/978-3-319-69923-3_39

Recently, multispectral imaging with different illumination sources has attracted lots of research attention due to its advantages in accuracy and anti-spoofing for biometrics applications. An empirical study by Guo et al. [5] made a conclusion that different illumination sources include yellow or magenta are the best spectral bands for palmprint recognition. Since then, Multispectral Palmprint recognition systems using the images captured by red, blue, green and Near Infrared light sources [7–9] have been developed. In [6], a hyperspectral imaging device was developed to capture the palmprint images at 69 spectral bands over spectrum 420–110 nm with a step of 10 nm. Hyperspectral palmprint contains various information on the joint spatial-spectral domain. It is an important and challenging topic to encode the features of these palmprints effectively.

A common practice is to process and identify the 2D images on each band, and then combine the results for the final decision [10]. However, a better strategy is to extract feature on the joint spatial and spectral domain using three-dimensional filters directly, such as 3D Gabor wavelets. The filters have been successfully applied on both hyperspectral palmprint recognition [11] and hyperspectral face recognition [12]. Shen et al. [11] exploited the information that contained in the hypercube data. A set of 3D Gabor wavelets were convolved with the cube data to jointly extract signal variances on spatial and spectral domains. But the dimension of the feature is very high [13], which could cause curse of dimensionality. To avoid this situation, they proposed an Affinity Propagation (AP) based method [14] to cluster the 2D bands of hyperspectral palmprint data. Then the redundant bands could be removed and 3D Gabor wavelets were convolved with the remaining bands only. Therefore, the feature size can be significantly reduced, and the efficiency can be greatly improved. Collaborative representation (CR) based framework with $l_2 - norm$ has been used on depth maps of palmprint due to its ability to robustly classify pixels by curvature and Gaussian curvature [17]. However, CR based framework has not been explored for the hyperspectral palmprint recognition.

In this paper, we propose a novel local feature named response-competition (ResCom) feature, to utilize the magnitude and phase of the maximum 3D Gabor response sufficiently. The feature vectors encoded by the look-up table imply the surface geometry characteristics. In addition to the proposed local features, this paper also combines ResCom feature with the information of the 2D images on each band. Moreover, the ResCom feature and CR Based framework with $l_2 - norm$ regularization [15] are combined to improve the recognition accuracy.

This paper is structured into the following sections. The proposed framework of palmprint recognition is presented in Sect. 2. Then the experimental results and the corresponding illustrations are demonstrated in Sect. 3. Finally, the conclusion and some discussions are presented in Sect. 4.

2   Framework of the Algorithm

2.1   3D Gabor Wavelets

The Gabor function [12] is proposed to maximize the resolution of the joint time and frequency of the signal, which is modulated by the sine function of Gaussian. Granlund first introduced the Gabor elementary functions to the 2D counterpart. Since then, 2D Gabor wavelet [13] is widely used to solve various visual problems, including feature extraction, texture classification [16,17], palmprint recognition [2] and face recognition [12]. With the extensive applications of 2D Gabor wavelets, 3D Gabor wavelets have also been utilized on 3D brain image registration, hyperspectral image classification and face recognition.

In the 3D frequency domain (u, v, w), if we represent the angle between the frequency vector f and the w axis as φ, the angle between f and uv plane as θ, 3D Gabor wavelet (x, y, b) can be defined as follows [1]:

$$
\begin{cases}
\Psi_{f,\varphi,\theta}(x,y,b) = S \times exp(-((\frac{x'}{\sigma_x})^2 + (\frac{y'}{\sigma_y})^2 + (\frac{b'}{\sigma_b})^2)) \\
\qquad\qquad \times exp(2\pi j(xu + yv + bw)) \\
u = f\sin\varphi\cos\theta, v = f\sin\varphi\sin\theta, w = f\cos\varphi \\
[x', y', b'] = R \times [x - x_c, y - y_c, b - b_c]^T
\end{cases}
\tag{1}
$$

where S is scale, (x_c, y_c, b_c) denote volume element coordinate, f is the central frequency of the sinusoidal plane wave, φ and θ are the angles of the wave vector with w axis and $u - v$ plane in frequency domain (u, v, w), R is the rotation matrix, and $\sigma_x, \sigma_y, \sigma_b$ are the widths of Gaussian envelops in different axis. For representing the local information about various frequencies and orientations, a set of $I \times J \times K$ Gabor wavelets with different frequencies are introduced to extract features from volume data:

$$
\{\Psi_{i,j,k} \triangleq \Psi_{f_i,\varphi_j,\theta_k}(x,y,b), f_i = f_{max}/2^i, \varphi_j = j\pi/J, \theta_k = k\pi/K\}
\tag{2}
$$

where f_i, (φ_j, θ_k) define the amplitude and orientations of central frequency, f_{max} is the highest possible amplitude of frequency.

Given a set of 3D Gabor wavelets $\{\Psi_l, l = 1, \cdots, L\}$ and a hyperspectral palmprint image $V(x, y, b)$, the convolution coefficient $V \otimes \Psi_l(x, y, b)$, response to the phase $P_l(x, y, b)$, the wavelet index m and the magnitude $M_l(x, y, b)$ of the position (x, y, b) are defined as follows:

$$
\begin{cases}
P_l(x,y,b) = arg\tan(\frac{Im(V \otimes \Psi_l(x,y,b))}{Re(V \otimes \Psi_l(x,y,b))}) \\
m = arg\max_l M_l(x,y,b) \\
M_l(x,y,b) = |V \otimes \Psi_l(x,y,b)|
\end{cases}
\tag{3}
$$

where the $|\otimes|$ operation extracts the size of the convolution coefficient, and the Im and Re operations are the imaginary and real parts of the complex coefficients, respectively.

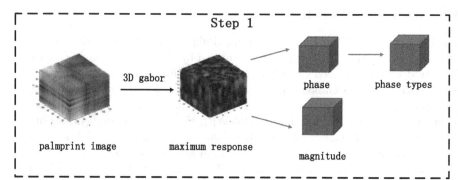

(a) Magnitude and phase types.

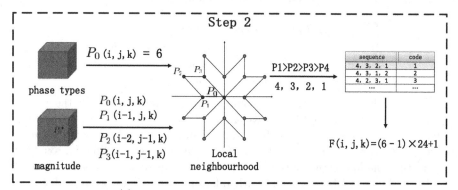

(b) Encode the pixels according to the
corresponding phase types.

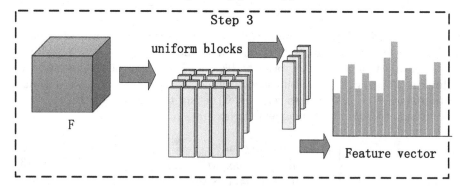

(c) Local histograms.

Fig. 1. The process of feature extraction.

2.2   The Proposed Feature

ResCom feature is the local feature extracted by the maximum response of Gabor wavelet. We produce a new cube from phase and magnitude of the response, that has the same size as the sample data. The cube is then divided into uniform blocks. And the histogram of each block is extracted to form the feature vector. As shown in Fig. 1, the feature extraction is conducted by the following steps:

- Calculate the magnitude and phase. The magnitude and phase as described in Eq. (3) can be generate from the real and imaginary parts of the maximum response produced by the 3D Gabor wavelet. As shown in Fig. 1(a), the magnitude cube and phase types cube are both with size $M \times N \times B$, where $M = 64$, $N = 64$, $B = 54$. As defined in (4), the phase values are classified into nine types.
- Encode the pixels according to the phase types. The local neighborhoods of each point in magnitude cube are divided into eight sectors as shown in Fig. 2. In other words, the sector which we choose to encode is decided by corresponding phase types. Then the sector is chosen and find the four points P_0, P_1, P_2, P_3 are found. The value at P_0, P_1, P_2 and P_3 are ranked to produce the sequence of 1–4. For example, as shown in Fig. 1(b), P_0 in phase types cube is 6 and then the sixth sector is chosen. A sequence of "4, 3, 2, 1" is used to represent the relationship of P_3, P_2, P_1, P_0. The full permutation of 1–4 by a lookup table is stored as shown in Fig. 1(b) and the sequence is mapped to the code according to the table. At last we can get code $= 1$ in this example. Then the initial feature information F is obtained by size $M \times N \times B$, according to Eq. (4).
- Compute local histograms of F. We divide F into $P \times P$ blocks and use local histograms as features, P $= 16$ in this paper. The size of each feature vector is $P \times P \times K$, where K $= 193$.

$$\text{PhaseTypes(i, j, k)} = \begin{cases} 9 & \text{if } Mag \leq 1e-6 \\ \lfloor \frac{\theta}{Span Ang} \rfloor + 1 & otherwise \end{cases} \tag{4}$$

where θ is angle value, SpanAng denotes the step size (45° in this paper, see Fig. 2 for details) and $\lfloor \cdot \rfloor$ denotes the floor operation.

$$\text{F(i, j, k)} = \begin{cases} (\text{PhaseTypes-1}) \times 24 + code & \text{if } 1 \leq K \leq 8 \\ 193 & \text{if } K = 9 \end{cases} \tag{5}$$

where code is value listed in the look-up table based on the sequence.

2.3   L2-Norm Recognition Framework

After the feature extraction, we combine ResCom and Block-wise feature in the $L2 - norm$ recognition framework. In [15], Block-Wise features performed

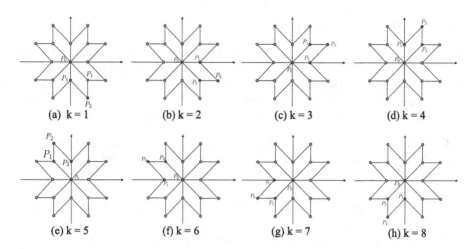

(a) k = 1　　　　(b) k = 2　　　　(c) k = 3　　　　(d) k = 4

(e) k = 5　　　　(f) k = 6　　　　(g) k = 7　　　　(h) k = 8

Fig. 2. Eight sectors of neighbourhood.

palmprint recognition based on the signs of the mean curvature H and Gaussian curvature K in Eq. (6).

$$
\begin{cases}
H = \frac{(1+f_x^2)f_{yy}+(1+f_y^2)f_{xx}-2f_xf_yf_{xy}}{2(1+f_x^2+f_y^2)^{3/2}} \\
K = \frac{f_{xx}f_{yy}-f_{xy}^2}{(1+f_x^2+f_y^2)^2}
\end{cases}
\tag{6}
$$

where f_x, f_{xx} are the first and second order partial derivatives in the x-direction. f_y, f_y are the first and second order partial derivatives in the y-direction. See Table 1 for detailed information of our algorithm.

3　Experimental Results

3.1　Database

The proposed method is tested using the HK-PolyU hyperspectral palmprint Database [9]. As shown in Fig. 3, the hyperspectral palmprint images were captured under wavelengths from 420 to 1100 nm. The samples were collected from 190 volunteers whose ages are from 20 to 60 years old. Each palm was captured at 69 spectral bands with a step-length of 10 nm over spectrum 420–1100 nm. In total, the database contains 5,240 images from 380 different palms. After preprocessing, each image is cropped into an ROI of size $M \times N$ pixels. Figure 3 shows six bands of an example palm, and the third dimension (z-axis) is the magnitude of wavelengths. The 1st and 2nd sessions of palmprint database are used as the gallery and probe sets, respectively.

Table 1. L2-norm recognition framework

Training phase:

Input: A gallery set containing hyperspectral palmprint.

Output: The dictionary matrix M.

    1. For each sample in the gallery set

       Extract the ResCom vector g;

       Divide the sample into $P \times P$ patches on each band, where each block contains

       $Q \times Q = P$ pixels, where Q=4, P=16, then B blocks are obtained for B spectral

       bands. Extract from these blocks a Block-Wise feature vector h;

       Combine g and h to form feature vector b and Normalize b to have unit $l_2 - norm$

    2. Concatenate all bs as M.

Testing phase:

Input: A query hyperspectral palmprint samples and M.

Output: Identity of the query sample.

    1. For each sample in the query set

       Extract the ResCom feature vector l;

       Extract the Block-Wise feature vector r;

       Combine l and r to form feature vector y and Normalize y to have unit $l_2 - norm$

    2. Code y over A as:

    $w_0 = argmin_w \{||y - Dw||_2^2 + \lambda_1 ||w||_2^2\}$.

    3. Compute the residuals $r_i(y) = ||y - A\delta_i(w_0)||_2$ where $\delta_i(w_0)$ is a new vector

       whose only nonzero entries are the entries in w_0 that are associated with class i.

    4. Find the label according to $id(y) = argmin_i r_i(y)$.

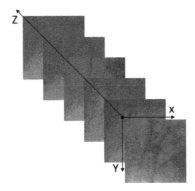

Fig. 3. A hyperspectral palmprint sample.

3.2 Results

The recognition rates of different features are summarized in Table 2. In Gabor
ResCom feature, each quadrant in Eq. (5) is divided into two sectors according
to the phase. From the above, this proposed feature can combine the phase and

Table 2. Experimental results

Employed feature	Recognition rate
Gabor maximum response	0.9719
Block-wise	0.9928
Gabor ResCom	0.9863
Block-wise + Gabor maximum response	0.9932
Block-wise + Gabor ResCom	**0.9943**

magnitude information and make feature vectors more discriminative. Using the Gabor ResCom feature, the recognition rate can reach 98.63%.

In addition to the Gabor ResCom feature, we combine ResCom feature with block-wise extracted on each band. Consider CR Based Framework with $l_2 - norm$ Regularization (Block-wise) [15], the recognition rate on hyperspectral palmprint database is 99.32%, where the curvature features on the faces $x - y$, $x - z$ and $y - z$ are extracted. In our work, The fusion of block-wise feature and ResCom achieved the accuracy of 99.43%.

4 Discussion and Conclusion

In this paper, a novel feature encoding method based on 3D Gabor wavelets is proposed for the hyperspectral palmprint recognition. The fused feature based on 3d Gabor wavelets is extracted to improve the accuracy of CR framework for hyperspectral palmprint recognition. The experimental result indicates that the CR framework can exhibit good performance for hyperspectral palmprint after combining the local information from maximum response produced by 3d Gabor filtering. Although competitive results are obtained with the proposed feature, there is still room for further improvement. More efficient features representing the 3D geometry characteristics should be devised and integrated. Finally, feature selection will be explored in our future work.

Acknowledgments. The work was supported by Natural Science Foundation of China under grands nos. 61672357 and 61602315, the Science Foundation of ShenZhen under grant no. JCY20160422144110140 and China Postdoctoral Science Foundation under grant no. 2015M572363.

References

1. Shen, L., Bai, L.: A review on Gabor wavelets for face recognition. Pattern Anal. Appl. **9**, 273–292 (2006)
2. Zhang, D., Kong, A., You, J., Wong, M.: Online palmprint identification. IEEE Trans. Pattern Anal. Mach. Intell. **25**, 1041–1050 (2003)
3. Kong, A., Zhang, D.: Competitive coding scheme for palmprint verification. In: Proceedings of the 17th International Conference on Pattern Recognition, vol. 1, pp. 520–523. Cambridge (2004)

4. Kong, A., Zhang, D.: Palmprint identification using feature-level fusion. Pattern Recogn. **39**, 478–487 (2006)
5. Guo, Z., Zhang, D., Zhang, L., Zuo, W., Lu, G.: Empirical study of light source selection for palmprint recognition. Pattern Recogn. Lett. **32**, 120–126 (2011)
6. Shen, L., Wu, S., Zheng, S., Ji, Z.: Embedded palmprint recognition system using OMAP 3530. Sensors **12**, 1482–1493 (2012)
7. Xu, X., Guo, Z., Song, C., Li, Y.: Multispectral palmprint recognition using a quaternion matrix. Sensors **12**, 4633–4647 (2012)
8. Zhang, D., Guo, Z., Lu, G., Zhang, L., Zuo, W.: An online system of multispectral palmprint verification. IEEE Trans. Instrum. Measur. **59**, 480–490 (2010)
9. Guo, Z., Zhang, D., Zhang, L., Liu, W.: Feature band selection for online multispectral palmprint recognition. IEEE Trans. Inf. Forensics Secur. **7**, 1094–1099 (2012)
10. Chang, H., Koschan, A., Abidi, B.: Fusing continuous spectral images for face recognition under indoor and outdoor illuminants. Mach. Vis. Appl. **21**, 201–215 (2010)
11. Shen, L., Wu, W., Jia, S., Guo, Z.: Coding 3D Gabor features for hyperspectral palmprint recognition. In: 2014 International Conference on Proceedings of Medical Biometrics, pp. 169–173 (2014)
12. Shen, L., Zheng, S.: Hyperspectral face recognition using 3D Gabor wavelets. In: Proceedings of International Conference on Pattern Recognition, pp. 1574–1577 (2012)
13. Shen, L., Jia, S.: Three-dimensional Gabor wavelets for pixel-based hyperspectral imagery classification. IEEE Trans. Geosci. Remote Sensing **49**, 5039–5046 (2011)
14. Shen, L., Dai, Z., Jia, S.: Band selection for Gabor feature based hyperspectral palmprint recognition. In: International Conference on Biometrics, pp. 416–421 (2015)
15. Zhang, L., Shen, Y., Li, H., Lu, J.: 3D palmprint identification using block-wise features and collaborative representation. IEEE Trans. Pattern Anal. Mach. Intell. **37**, 1730–1736 (2015)
16. Bianconi, F., Fernandez, A.: Evaluation of the effects of Gabor filter parameters on texture classification. Pattern Recogn. **40**, 3325–3335 (2007)
17. Li, M., Staunton, R.C.: Optimum Gabor filter design and local binary patterns for texture segmentation. Pattern Recogn. Lett. **29**, 664–672 (2008)
18. Shen, L., Bai, L.: 3D Gabor wavelets for evaluating SPM normalization algorithm. Med. Image Anal. **12**, 375–383 (2008)

Weighted Graph Based Description for Finger-Vein Recognition

Ziyun Ye[1], Jinfeng Yang[1(✉)], and Jose Hernandez Palancar[2]

[1] Tianjin Key Lab for Advanced Signal Processing,
Civil Aviation University of China, Tianjin, China
jfyang@cauc.edu.cn
[2] Advanced Technologies Applications Center, Havana, Cuba

Abstract. The randomness of vein networks determines the discrimination of finger veins patterns in recognition. Effectively describing the random patterns is therefore very important for finger-vein based biometrics. In this paper, a new graph-based method is proposed for finger-vein network feature representation. A block-wise action is first done for graph node generation from a finger-vein image. By applying Delaunay triangulation to these obtained nodes, the graph edges are then built for featuring the spatial relations between images blocks. For a given feature space, each of these edges can locally represent a relationship between two adjacent nodes. Considering local variations in image contents, the graph edges are further weighted node-wisely using the statistics of image blocks. Thus, a graph can globally represent a finger-vein network, and its weighted edges can locally describe the relations of image blocks. Experimental results on two image databases totally 1,200 image samples show that the proposed method performs well in finger-vein recognition.

Keywords: Finger-vein recognition · Weighted graph · Vein network

1 Introduction

Finger-vein recognition is a newly emergent biometrics based on human finger-vein patterns. Compared with some traditional biometric patterns, e.g., fingerprint, face, palmprint and iris, the finger-vein pattern itself behave outstandingly in forgery-proofness, biological liveness and user friendliness and so on [1]. These merits make finger-vein patterns very suitable for many critical security applications, such as ATM, access control, border crossing, etc. Hence, finger-vein recognition technology has progressed greatly over the past decade.

The random variation of different vein networks is the origin of the uniqueness of different finger-vein individuals. Exploring network-related feature representation methods is therefore very beneficial for improving the discrimination of finger-vein images. However, it is not a trivial thing to effectively make reliable representations of finger-vein networks. In [2–6], some methods related to orientation field [6], vector field [2, 5], included angle chain [4] and network enhancement [3] had been respectively proposed for handling the network feature description problems. For the above methods, the chain-based methods are sensitive to minutiae point extraction, while

© Springer International Publishing AG 2017
J. Zhou et al. (Eds.): CCBR 2017, LNCS 10568, pp. 370–379, 2017.
https://doi.org/10.1007/978-3-319-69923-3_40

others are usually time-consuming in practice. Hence, exploring effective methods suitable for vein network feature representation is still necessary for finger-vein recognition.

The development of graph-based methods in image content analysis motivates us using graph models for vein networks representation. In the past decades, many graph-based methods have been proposed for dealing with pattern recognition problems [7]. Luo et al. used a graph embedding method for 3D image clustering [8]. Abusham et al. proposed a local graph structure algorithm (LGS) for face recognition [9]. Based on the LGS, Song et al. proposed a multi-orientation weighted symmetric local graph structure for finger-vein feature extraction [10]. In this paper, a new weighted graph construction method is proposed for effectively representing vein networks considering local variations and global structures.

The proposed graph is asymmetric in structure. Its nodes generated by image division, its edges are formed using a triangulation algorithm, and the weights of edges are valued considering both the content variations of blocks and the similarities of two adjacent blocks. Since local image contents vary with blocks, these weighting values of edges are node-wisely readjusted by the local statistics of image blocks. This makes a graph asymmetric. Thus, compared with traditional weighted graphs, the proposed asymmetric graph is more helpful to describe the properties of finger-vein networks. In this way, a finger-vein image can be represented by a weighted graph, and the adjacency matrix of the weighted graph can be used for finger-vein recognition.

2 Weighted Graph Construction

A weighted graph can be represented by a data group $G(V, E, w)$, where V and E respectively denotes a node-set and an edge-set, w is a weighting function giving a real nonnegative value $w(v_i, v_j | v_i, v_j \in V)$ for a pair of nodes of an edge $e_{ij}(\in E)$. If $w(v_i, v_j) = w(v_j, v_i)$ is satisfying, $G(V, E, w)$ is symmetric, otherwise it is asymmetric.

The node-set V is generated by image division, $V = \{v_1, v_2, \cdots, v_i, \cdots, v_n\}$, where n is the number of image blocks, and v_i represents a node corresponds to the ith block of image. Assume that the size of a finger-vein image is $M \times N$, the size of a block is $h \times h$, and k denotes the overlap step between two adjacent blocks, we can obtain

$$n = \frac{M - k}{h - k} \cdot \frac{N - k}{h - k}. \tag{1}$$

By changing the values of h and k, as shown in Fig. 1, different block sets (corresponding to node sets), can be generated readily.

The edge-set E is generated by connecting nodes according to Delaunay triangulation, $E = \{e_{12}, e_{23}, \cdots, e_{ij}, \cdots\}$, where e_{ij} is the edge between two adjacent nodes v_i and v_j. The edge e_{ij}, if undirected, follows $j \in \{i - 1, i - r - 1, i - r, i + 1, i + r + 1, i + r | v_j \in V\}$, as shown in the left of Fig. 2, while the e_{ij}, if directed, follows $j \in \{i + 1, i + r + 1, i + r | v_j \in V\}$, where $r = M - k/h - k$, as shown in the right of Fig. 2. Compared with the undirected graph, directed graph is better in describing the local relations of an image.

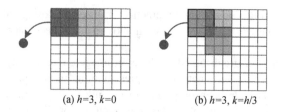

(a) $h=3, k=0$ (b) $h=3, k=h/3$

Fig. 1. Generation of node-set V.

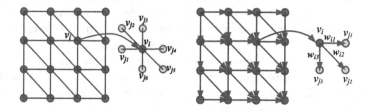

Fig. 2. Generation of edge-set E.

After generating the node-set V and the edge-set E, we need to further assign proper weights to the edges. Here, we define

$$w(v_i, v_j \mid e_{ij} \in E) = W(v_i) \times S(v_i, v_j),\qquad(2)$$

where $W(v_i)$ represents the content variations of block v_i, and $S(v_i, v_j)$ denotes a relationship between two adjacent blocks. We first give a method of computing $S(v_i, v_j)$ in Sect. 3, and then detail the expression of $W(v_i)$ in Sect. 5.1.

3 Edge Weight Assignment

To reliably represent the vein network, the weights of graph edges should be valued considering the properties of vein network. Here, the skeletons of finger-vein networks are used as finger-vein pattern supporters since they are the essential carriers indicating the randomness of finger-vein patterns. The features related to the skeletons are extracted accordingly for edge weight computation. We first obtain the finger-vein skeletons, and then the steerable filters with arbitrary orientations are used for describing the randomness energy consisting in the local blocks of skeleton image [11]. Based on the obtained local energy features, the weight $S(v_i, v_j)$ corresponding to an edge e_{ij} can be computed by using measuring the similarity between v_i and v_j.

3.1 Network Skeleton Extraction

As finger-vein images are often degraded seriously during NIR imaging, the separability is poor between the venous regions and non-venous regions. In order to reliably strength the finger-vein networks, finger-vein images need to be enhanced effectively. Here, a bank of Gabor filters with 8 orientations [1] and Weber's Law Descriptor

(WLD) [12] are combined for venous region enhancement and light attenuation elimination. In order to extract reliable finger-vein skeletons, a multi-threshold method [13] is used to obtain the binary results of the enhanced finger-vein image. A thinning algorithm proposed in [14] is used to extract the finger-vein skeletons of the binary images, some results are shown in Fig. 3.

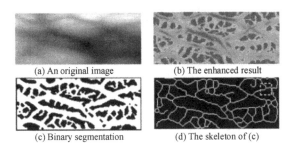

(a) An original image   (b) The enhanced result

(c) Binary segmentation   (d) The skeleton of (c)

Fig. 3. The results during skeleton extraction

3.2 Edge Weight Calculation

The steerable filter has shown good performance in primitive feature analysis, which is defined as [15]

$$h^\theta(x,y) = \sum_{j=1}^{N} k_j(\theta) f^{\phi_j}(x,y),$$ (3)

where $f(x, y)$ is a set of basic function, N is the number of $f(x, y)$, $k(\theta)$ is interpolation function, θ is the orientation of Steerable filter, ϕ_j is the orientation of $f^{\phi_j}(x,y)$.

The oriented energy $E(\theta)$ is defined as the squared convolution between a steerable filter and a block I_i at angle θ, where the I_i is the ith block of a skeleton image

$$E(\theta) = \left(\sum_{j=1}^{N} \sum_{x=1}^{X} \sum_{y=1}^{Y} \left(k_j(\theta) f^{\phi_j}(x,y) I_i(x,y) \right) \right)^2,$$ (4)

where X, Y are the size of h^θ and I_i. From Eq. (4), we can find that the oriented energy E is a function of angle θ.

In order to describe the local vein skeletons of I_i, we need to compute the $E(\theta)$ at different θ. Figure 4 illustrates an obtained energy map corresponding to block I_i located at a dot-square region in Fig. 3(d). Thus, the energy map of a block, which is used for edge weight computation, can be expressed as

$$\chi_i = \{ E(1), E(2), \cdots, E(\theta), \cdots, E(360) \mid I_i \}.$$ (5)

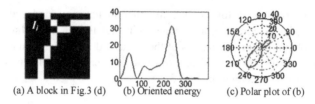

(a) A block in Fig.3 (d)   (b) Oriented energy   (c) Polar plot of (b)

Fig. 4. Oriented energy

And, the weighting function assigning values to graph edges is defined as

$$S(v_i, v_j) = \exp\left(\left(-\sum_{l=1}^{m} (\chi_i(l) - \chi_j(l))^2\right)\bigg/ 2\sigma^2\right),$$ (6)

where σ is a constant. (Here, σ is 17)

4   Weighted Graph Matching

Assume that $\mathbf{A}_G$ denotes the adjacency matrix of the weighted graph $G(V, E, w)$, $\mathbf{A}_G$ is a $n \times n$ matrix, n is the number of nodes. $\mathbf{A}_G$ can be expressed by

$$\mathbf{A}_G(i,j) = \begin{cases} w(v_i, v_j) & e_{ij} \in E \\ 0 & \text{otherwise} \end{cases}.$$ (7)

Large-scale graph-matching based on $G(V, E, w)$ is time-consuming so that it is not applicable in practice. Thus we use adjacency matrix $\mathbf{A}_G$ for matching simplification. The similarity of two adjacency matrix is measured by

$$M_s = \frac{\sum_{p=1}^{n}\sum_{q=1}^{n} (A(p,q) - \overline{A})(B(p,q) - \overline{B})}{\sqrt{\left(\sum_{p=1}^{n}\sum_{q=1}^{n} (A(p,q) - \overline{A})^2\right)\left(\sum_{p=1}^{n}\sum_{q=1}^{n} (B(p,q) - \overline{B})^2\right)}},$$ (8)

where $\overline{A}$ and $\overline{B}$ respectively denote the averages of the matrix $\mathbf{A}$ and $\mathbf{B}$.

To further improve matching efficiency, we propose a matrix reorganization method (MRM). From Fig. 2, we can see that each node of the obtained graph has 3 non-repeating weights. So $\mathbf{A}_G$ is a sparse matrix with real values only at certain positions. By reorganizing $\mathbf{A}_G$, we can generate a new low-dimension matrix with 3 rows and n columns, as shown in Table 1. In MRM, every column lists the weights of edges corresponding to a node in the directed graph $G(V, E, w)$, as shown in the right of Fig. 2.

Table 1. Adjacency matrix reorganization

Weight	Node						
	v_1	v_2	v_3	...	v_i	...	v_n
w_1	w_{11}	w_{21}	w_{31}	...	w_{i1}	...	w_{n1}
w_2	w_{12}	w_{22}	w_{32}	...	w_{i2}	...	w_{n2}
w_3	w_{13}	w_{23}	w_{33}	...	w_{i3}	...	w_{n3}

5 Experiments and Analysis

To evaluate the proposed graph-based finger-vein network feature representation method, two databases are used in our experiments. The database 1 is a homemade image set which totally contains 5000 finger-vein images from 500 individual fingers, and the database 2 is an open Homologous Multi-modal Traits Database [16] developed by Shangdong University. From these two databases, two sub-sets are respectively extracted. Each sub-set contains 600 image samples from 100 different fingers (6 images per finger).

5.1 Performance Comparisons of Different Weighting Functions

From Eq. (2), we can see that the weight of an edge e_{ij} is determined by $W(v_i)$. So different $W(v_i)$ should have different effects on recognition performance. Here we define $W(v_i)$ respectively as

$$W(v_i) = 1, \tag{9}$$

$$W(v_i) = AAD(\chi_i), \tag{10}$$

$$W(v_i) = AAD(B_i), \tag{11}$$

where AAD is an average absolute deviation operator, B_i is the *ith* block of a enhanced image. Here, for a block B_i, its size is 9×9 with 3 pixels overlap, as show in Fig. 1(b).

Some ROC curves are plotted in Fig. 6. We can see from Fig. 6 that $W(v_i)$ defined by Eq. (11) performs best in image recognition, and weighting the graph G using Eq. (9) has the lowest recognition rate. for $W(v_i) = 1$, e_{ij} only represents the similarity of two nodes v_i and v_j, so taking some statistics of image blocks into account for weighting graph is beneficial for reducing EER rates (Fig. 5).

5.2 Performance Evaluation of Matrix Reorganization Method

In order to test the performance of MRM, we evaluate it using two recognition indicators, accuracy and efficiency. Here, the block size is 9×9 with 3 pixels overlap.

From Fig. 7, we can see that MRM-based graph matching performs better than adjacency-matrix-based graph matching in graph recognition. The reorganized matrix is capable of preserving the structure information of the obtained node set, and it can

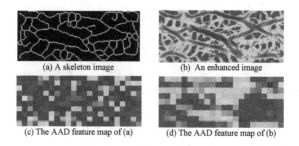

(a) A skeleton image   (b) An enhanced image

(c) The AAD feature map of (a)   (d) The AAD feature map of (b)

Fig. 5. AAD feature maps of different processed images

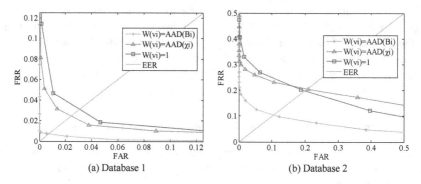

(a) Database 1   (b) Database 2

Fig. 6. ROC curves of different weighting functions

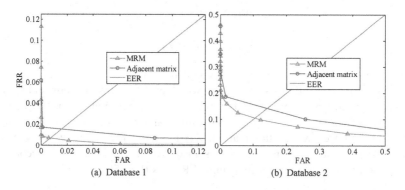

(a) Database 1   (b) Database 2

Fig. 7. Performance comparisons by using adjacent matrix and MRM

greatly reduce the redundant information of the adjacency matrix. From Table 2, we can see that MRM-based graph matching is also superior to adjacency-matrix-based graph matching in computation cost.

Table 2. The time cost of single image

Matrix	Efficiency	Database 1	Database 2
Adjacency matrix	Time cost(s)	1.0284	0.9566
Reorganized matrix	Time cost(s)	0.0354	0.0367

5.3 Image Divisions for Node-Set Generation

Different node sets may have different recognition performances in graph matching. So selecting proper image division method is helpful for recognition performance improvement. In order to find the appropriate image division method, we selecte different block sizes h and overlap step k ($k = 0$, $k = h/3$) for testing.

From Figs. 8 and 9, we can see that block divisions with overlap perform better than these without overlap in recognition, and different block sizes generate different ROC curves. By observing these ROC curves, we find that the block size with 9×9 performs best in recognition rate, and both 5×5 and 15×15 blocks make lower recognition rate. This shows that the statistics in small blocks or bigger blocks have lower discrimination for weighting the graphs.

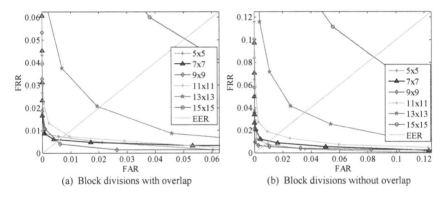

(a) Block divisions with overlap   (b) Block divisions without overlap

Fig. 8. Comparisons of different block divisions in database 1

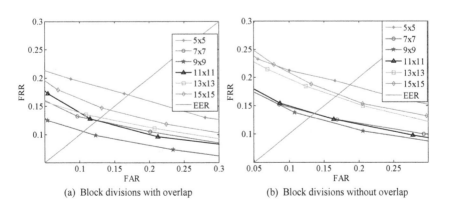

(a) Block divisions with overlap   (b) Block divisions without overlap

Fig. 9. Comparisons of different block divisions in database 2

5.4   Comparison

In order to further evaluate the performance of the proposed method, we compare the proposed method with the state-of-the-art method proposed in [17]. This paper is one of the latest results of deep learning on finger-vein recognition. Here, we compare these two methods in terms of the recognition accuracy and efficiency.

From Fig. 10, we can see that the deep representation method is slightly better than the proposed method in term of recognition performance. From Table 3, we find that the time cost of the proposed method is much less than the deep representation method. Based on these results, we will be committed to further improve the accuracy of the proposed method in future.

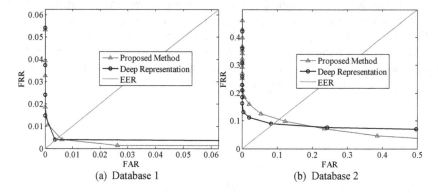

Fig. 10. Recognition performance comparisons

Table 3. The time cost of single image

Method	Efficiency	Database 1	Database 2
Proposed method	Time cost(s)	0.0354	0.0367
Deep representation	Time cost(s)	3.9603	3.6376

6   Conclusions

In this paper, a new weighted graph construction method has been proposed for finger-vein network representation. Based on two databases we have conducted a series of experiments to evaluate different weighting functions, matrix reorganization method and image division method on the recognition rates. The experimental results have shown that the proposed method could obtain a good identification performance on finger-vein recognition. However, the proposed method still has much room for improvement in further improving the robustness of the graph.

Acknowledgements. This work is jointly supported by National Natural Science Foundation of China (Nos. 61379102, U1433120, 61502498) and the Fundamental Research Funds for the Central Universities (No. 3122014C003).

References

1. Yang, J.F., Shi, Y.H.: Finger-vein ROI localization and vein ridge enhancement. PRL **33** (12), 1569–1579 (2012)
2. Yang, J.F., Shi, Y.H., Jia, G.M.: Finger-vein image matching based on adaptive curve transformation. PR **66**, 34–43 (2017)
3. Yang, J.F., Shi, Y.H.: Finger-vein network enhancement and segmentation. Pattern Anal. Appl. **17**(4), 783–797 (2014)
4. Cao, D., Yang, J.F., Shi, Y.H., Xu, C.H.: Structure feature extraction for finger-vein recognition. In: ACPR, vol. 135, pp. 567–571 (2013)
5. Yang, J.F., Wu, M.J., Wang, W.Y., Shi, Y.H.: Finger-vein matching based on adaptive vector field estimation. In: ICIP, pp. 145–148 (2012)
6. Yang, J.F., Wang, W.Y.: Finger-vein image enhancement based on orientation field. In: International Conference on Hand-Based Biometrics, pp. 198–203 (2011)
7. Pasquale, F., Gennaro, P., Mario, V.: Graph matching and learning in pattern recognition in the last 10 years. J. Pattern Recogn. Artif. Intell. **28**(01), 1428–1481 (2014)
8. Luo, B., Wilson, R.C., Hancock, E.R.: Spectral embedding of graphs. PR **36**(10), 2213–2230 (2003)
9. Abusham, E.E.A., Bashir, H.K.: Face recognition using local graph structure (LGS). In: Jacko, J.A. (ed.) HCI 2011. LNCS, vol. 6762, pp. 169–175. Springer, Heidelberg (2011). doi:10.1007/978-3-642-21605-3_19
10. Dong, S., Yang, J.C., Chen, Y.R., et al.: Finger vein recognition based on multi-orientation weighted symmetric local graph structure. KSII Trans. Internet Inf. Syst. **9**(10), 4126–4142 (2015)
11. Simoncelli, E.P., Farid, H.: Steerable wedge filters for local orientation analysis. TIP **5**(9), 1377–1382 (1996)
12. Chen, J., Shan, S.G., He, C., et al.: WLD: a robust local image descriptor. TPAMI **32**(9), 1705–1720 (2010)
13. Vlachos, M., Dermatas, E.: Vein segmentation in infrared images using compound enhancing and crisp clustering. In: Gasteratos, A., Vincze, M., Tsotsos, John K. (eds.) ICVS 2008. LNCS, vol. 5008, pp. 393–402. Springer, Heidelberg (2008). doi:10.1007/978-3-540-79547-6_38
14. Yu, C.B., Qin, H.F., Cui, Y.Z., et al.: Finger-vein image recognition combining modified Hausdorff distance with minutiae feature matching. Interdisc. Sci. Comput. Life Sci. **1**(4), 280–289 (2009)
15. Freeman, W.T., Adelson, E.H.: The design and use of steerable filters. TPAMI **13**(9), 891–906 (1991)
16. Yin, Y., Liu, L., Sun, X.: SDUMLA-HMT: a multimodal biometric database. In: Sun, Z., Lai, J., Chen, X., Tan, T. (eds.) CCBR 2011. LNCS, vol. 7098, pp. 260–268. Springer, Heidelberg (2011). doi:10.1007/978-3-642-25449-9_33
17. Qin, H., EI-Yacoubi, M.A.: Deep representation-based feature extraction and recovering for finger-vein verification. IEEE Trans. Inf. Forensics Secur. **12**(8), 1816–1829 (2017)

Iris

Iris Recognition Based on Adaptive Gabor Filter

Shuai Liu[1,2], Yuanning Liu[1,3], Xiaodong Zhu[1,3(✉)], Guang Huo[4],
Jingwei Cui[1,2], and Yihao Chen[1,3]

[1] Key Laboratory of Symbolic Computation and Knowledge Engineering of
Ministry of Education, Jilin University, Changchun 130012, Jilin, China
zhuxd@jlu.edu.cn
[2] School of Software, Jilin University, Changchun 130012, Jilin, China
[3] School of Computer Science and Technology,
Jilin University, Changchun 130012, Jilin, China
[4] Informatization Office, Northeast Electric Power University,
Jilin 132012, China

Abstract. Aiming at the problem of multi-category iris recognition, there proposes a method of iris recognition algorithm based on adaptive Gabor filter. Use DE-PSO to adaptive optimize the Gabor filter parameters. DE-PSO is composed of particle swarm optimization and differential evolution algorithm. Use 16 groups of 2D-Gabor filters with different frequencies and directions to process iris images. According to the direction and frequency of maximum response amplitude, transform iris features into 512-bit binary feature encoding. Calculate the Hamming distance of feature code and compare with the classification threshold, determine iris the type of iris. Experiment on a variety of iris databases with multiple Gabor filter algorithms, the results showed that this algorithm has higher recognition rate, the ROC curve is closer to the coordinate axis and the robustness is better, compare with other Gabor filter algorithm.

Keywords: Iris recognition · Gabor filter · Particle swarm optimization · Differential evolution · Feature encoding · Hamming distance

1 Introduction

Iris recognition has stable features, uniqueness and non – invasiveness [1], so become a popular direction for biometrics research. The iris recognition process is divided into iris image acquisition, iris localization, iris feature expression and recognition [2].

On the iris feature extraction and recognition, Daugman [3] proposed a method of extracting iris features by Gabor filter and using Hamming distance to identify. However, the specific application of the filter needs to involve multiple parameters of the adjustment, so it's necessary to optimize parameters. Zhou proposed to optimize parameters by using Particle Swarm Optimization (PSO) algorithm [4]. But PSO was likely to cause local minimum and the result may not ideal [5]. This paper use particle swarm optimization algorithm which incorporated differential evolution algorithm [6] (DE-PSO) to optimize parameters.

© Springer International Publishing AG 2017
J. Zhou et al. (Eds.): CCBR 2017, LNCS 10568, pp. 383–390, 2017.
https://doi.org/10.1007/978-3-319-69923-3_41

For iris recognition, this paper uses 16 groups of 2D-Gabor filters with different frequencies and directions to process iris image. According to the direction and frequency of maximum response amplitude, transform the iris features into binary feature encoding. Calculate the Hamming distance of feature code and compare with the classification threshold, and then determine the type of iris.

2   Iris Image Processing

The iris image processing includes iris quality evaluation, iris localization, iris image normalization and enhancement [7]. This paper through clarity, centrifugal and other indicators to assess iris quality, and then determine whether the iris can be used for iris recognition [8]. This paper used the Hough transform proposed by Dr. Wilde to achieve iris localization [9], find the location of the iris. Then use the rubber band model method [10] to develop the iris into a 512 × 64 rectangle. Enhance [11] image texture. The iris localization image is shown in Fig. 1(a). The iris normalized enhancement image is shown in Fig. 1(b).

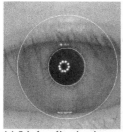 

(a) Iris localization image   (b) Iris normalized enhancement image

Fig. 1. Iris positioning and normalized image

The strongest portion of the texture in the enhanced image is cut into a 256 × 32 rectangle (This paper starts from the upper left corner of Fig. 1(b)). The cut image is shown as Fig. 2.

Fig. 2. The cut iris image

3   Iris Image Recognition

Before extract iris features, all normalized iris images need to be horizontally shifted to eliminate iris rotation [9].

3.1 Gabor Filter

The expression of the 2D-Gabor filter is defined as Eq. 1 [3].

$$G(x,y) = \exp(-\pi[(x-x_0)/\alpha^2 + (y-y_0)^2/\beta]) \times \exp(-2\pi i[u_0(x-x_0) + v_0(y-y_0)]) \quad (1)$$

(x_0, y_0) represents the texture of image. α and β represent the width and the length of Gaussian window. (u_0, v_0) defines the spatial frequency w_0, $w_0 = \sqrt{u_0^2 + v_0^2}$. Direction angle $\theta_0 = \arctan(v_0/u_0)$.

The Gabor filter kernel function expression used in this experiment are shown in Eqs. 2, 3, 4 and 5.

$$x' = x\cos\theta + y\sin\theta \quad (2)$$

$$y' = -x\sin\theta + y\cos\theta \quad (3)$$

Real expression:

$$g(x,y,\lambda,\theta,\psi,\delta,\gamma) = \exp(-(x'^2 + \gamma^2 y'^2)/2\delta^2) \times \cos(2\pi x'/\lambda + \psi) \quad (4)$$

Imaginary expression:

$$g(x,y,\lambda,\theta,\psi,\delta,\gamma) = \exp(-(x'^2 + \gamma^2 y'^2)/2\delta^2) \times \sin(2\pi x'/\lambda + \psi) \quad (5)$$

Wavelength (λ): greater than or equal to 2, less than 1/5 of the input image size. Direction (θ): direction of the Gabor function parallel stripes, range from 0° to 360°. Phase shift (ψ): value range from −180° to 180°. Aspect ratio (γ): space aspect ratio; Bandwidth (b): b is related to the δ/λ ratio. δ represented standard deviation of gauss factor of Gabor function. The relationship between δ/λ and b is shown in Eqs. 6, 7 and 8.

$$b = \log_2^S \quad (6)$$

$$S = \frac{\frac{\delta}{\lambda}\pi + \sqrt{\frac{\ln 2}{2}}}{\frac{\delta}{\lambda}\pi - \sqrt{\frac{\ln 2}{2}}} \quad (7)$$

$$\delta = 0.56\lambda \quad (8)$$

So, Gabor filter in this paper is decided by 5 parameters: (λ, θ, ψ, b, γ).

3.2 Iris Feature Extraction and Recognition

When extract iris features, change the direction and the phase shift of Gabor filter, forming 16 Gabor filters. The template image and the test image are divided into 128 sub-blocks, each with a size of 16 × 4 pixels. Every sub-block is processed by Gabor filter. The phase shift is represented by 00, 01, 10, 11 and the direction are also represented by 00, 01, 10, 11. Calculate the amplitude of all filtered results for each sub-block. Find the maximum phase shift and direction of each sub-block amplitude value. The binary code is spliced together with the direction is in the front, phase shift is in the back, each sub-block feature is represented by a 4-bit feature code, write as $F_{index-i}$. The 128 sub-block feature codes are arranged in the order from top to bottom, from left to right, express as a 512-bit feature code, record as F_{index}.

Calculate the Hamming distance (HD) [12] of F_{index} and compare with classification threshold. If less than classification threshold, the test iris and the template iris belong to the same type.

$F_{index-i}$ is shown in Eq. 9. The Hamming distance formula as shown in Eq. 10.

$$F_{index-i} = \max(\phi_{m,n}(\vec{y})) \tag{9}$$

$$HD = \frac{1}{N} \sum_{i=1}^{N} A_i \oplus B_i \tag{10}$$

$F_{index-i}$ denotes the feature code of the i-th sub-block. $\varphi_{m,n}(\vec{y})$ represents the in direction n and phase shift m, sub-block response amplitude. n take four values, respectively $0°, 45°, 90°, 135°$. m also take four values, respectively $-45°, 0°, 45°, 90°$.

A_i and B_i represent the feature code of the test iris and the template iris, N indicates the number of signature bits, in this paper, N = 512.

3.3   DE-PSO and Parameter Optimization

This paper uses DE-PSO to optimize wavelength (λ), aspect ratio (γ) and bandwidth (b) in Gabor filter. The PSO in this paper uses 30 particles, each with an initial velocity range of [− 50, 50]. Each particle contains a set of Gabor filter parameters that need to be optimized, which is equivalent to 30 sets of initial Gabor filters. The initial value of λ ranges from 20 to 40, γ ranges from 0.1 to 1, b ranges from 1 to 10. The initial *pBest* and *gBest* of the particles are set to the initial values.

When performing parameter optimization, for a specific iris library, take 5 test iris images, 5 same types of iris images, 5 different types of iris images. Using the iris feature extraction algorithm mentioned above, obtain the Hamming distance. Calculate the fitness G. The fitness function is shown in Eq. 11.

$$G = \frac{\sum\limits_{a=1}^{5} HD_a^2}{5 \times \sum\limits_{b=1}^{5} HD_b^2} \tag{11}$$

HD_a indicates Hamming distance from the iris of different type, HD_b indicates the Hamming distance from the iris of the same type. G represents the average of the HD ratio for different type and the same type. The higher value of G, the higher fitness. By 300 iterations, each calculate new fitness G, if the new G is less than the original

G. Then the new *pBest* is set to the corresponding filter parameters for the new *G*, and the filter parameters corresponding to the maximum value of *G* in the 30 group filters is set to the new *gBest*. After the new *pBest* and *gBest* are determined, the evolution of the particles are carried out according to Eqs. 12 and 13.

$$v_i^d = \omega \times v_i^d + c_1 \times rand_1^d \times (pBest_i^d - x_i^d) + c_2 \times rand_2^d \times (gBest_i^d - x_i^d) \tag{12}$$

$$x_i^d = x_i^d + v_i^d \tag{13}$$

ω represents inertia weight. c_1 and c_2 represent acceleration coefficients. ω is set to 0.729, c_1 and c_2 are set to 1.49445, which are beneficial to the convergence of the algorithm [13]. $rand_1^d$ and $rand_2^d$ are random number on the interval [0,1]. After each particle evolution, insert differential evolution algorithm, similar to mutation. Operation is completed to get new parameters, but only when the new fitness is greater than the original fitness, the filter parameters will be replaced, otherwise keep the original parameters constant.

4   Results and Discussion

In this experiment, JLU iris database [14], CASIA-V1, CASIA-V2 and CASIA-Iris-Twin iris databases [15] were selected as template iris databases. The Gabor filter [1] with no parameter optimization and the Gabor filter [4] which only uses the PSO to optimize the parameters were compared with the algorithm in this paper.

The experimental environment were Windows xp sp3, 32 bit system, 2.5 GHz Core 3 generation CPU, 8 G memory.

The ROC curve [16] is a curve representing the relationship between false reject rate (FRR) and false accept rate (FAR), which is used to reflect the matching performance of the iris recognition system. The value that FRR equal FAR is called equal error rate (EER). The smaller of EER, the better performance of the iris recognition system. In addition, correct recognition rate (CRR) is also commonly used to evaluate the performance of iris recognition system. This paper uses the highest CRR, the minimum EER, the ROC curve to evaluate the performance of the algorithm.

The number of matches within each iris database is shown in Table 1. Table 2 shows the comparison of parameters before and after optimization. The highest recognition rate is shown in Table 3. The ROC curves are shown in Fig. 3.

Not only that, this paper also carried out the experiment of running time. The algorithm is compared with the Gabor + SVM algorithm, the algorithm proposed in

Table 1. The number of matches within each iris database

Iris	Category	Sample	Total	Class match	Out-of-match	Total match
JLU	56	5	280	7840	68320	76160
CASIA-1.0	108	5	540	29160	82080	111240
CASIA-2.0	60	20	1200	144000	182400	326400
Twin	100	7	700	49000	141400	190400

Table 2. Parameters before and after optimization

	Before optimization					After optimization				
	λ	θ	ψ	b	γ	λ	θ	ψ	b	γ
non	10	45	−135	1	0.50	–	–	–	–	–
PSO	15	258	109	6	0.14	5	264	28	3	0.11
DE-PSO	30	178	54	7	0.02	28	69	23	2	0.09

Table 3. The highest recognition rate in class comparison

Iris	Gabor [1]		PSO-Gabor [4]		DE-PSO-Gabor	
	CRR	EER	CRR	EER	CRR	EER
JLU	95.12%	2.78%	96.21%	2.28%	98.35%	1.38%
CASIA-1.0	94.23%	3.21%	96.01%	2.68%	99.03%	1.64%
CASIA-2.0	96.13%	2.94%	97.56%	1.94%	98.94%	1.28%
Twin	95.09%	3.05%	97.36%	2.13%	99.05%	1.41%

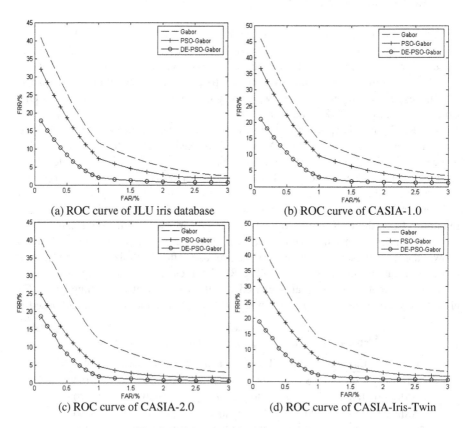

(a) ROC curve of JLU iris database

(b) ROC curve of CASIA-1.0

(c) ROC curve of CASIA-2.0

(d) ROC curve of CASIA-Iris-Twin

Fig. 3. ROC curve of each iris databases

literature [17] and the artificial neural network algorithm. Template iris database select JLU iris database. Compared the same test iris with the same 1200 iris images in the iris database by using four algorithms. The run time (T,unit:ms) and CRR of the four algorithms are shown in Table 4.

Table 4. The run time (T) and CRR of four algorithms

Algorithm	T (ms)	Number of correctly identify	CRR
DE-PSO-Gabor	1234	1198	99.83%
Gabor + SVM	2063	1176	98%
Neural network	2453	1197	99.75%
Literature [17]	1901	1143	95.25%

It can be seen from Fig. 3 and Table 3 that CRR of the algorithm is higher and EER is smaller and the ROC curve is closer to the transverse axis than the different Gabor filter algorithms in different iris databases. CRR basic can reach more than 98%. This result can be maintained in a variety of iris databases, indicating that the algorithm has good stability and robustness. As can be seen from Table 4, compare with the traditional machine learning algorithm, with the same number of iris images to identify, this algorithm runs less time.

In addition, because there is currently no suitable algorithm to determine the structure of traditional artificial neural network [18] and connection weight [19] down, it is usually artificially trained according to experience, which is cumbersome and difficult to guarantee that it is the best structure for iris recognition. The algorithm in this paper can be based on different iris databases adaptive training parameters, and then achieve a better state for iris recognition.

Therefore, it is concluded that in the multi-category iris recognition (no more than 20 images per category, within 110 categories), the algorithm in this paper can adaptively train the appropriate parameters, according to different iris databases, and then achieve a good recognition effect.

5 Conclusions

This paper proposes a method that use DE-PSO to adaptively train the Gabor filter parameters, and then to carry out iris recognition. DE-PSO is composed of particle swarm optimization and differential evolution algorithm. Use JLU iris database, CASIA-1.0, CASIA-2.0 and CASIA-Iris-Twin as template iris databases. Compare with other Gabor filter algorithm, this algorithm has higher recognition rate, the ROC curve is closer to the coordinate axis and the robustness is better. Compare with the traditional machine learning algorithm, with the same number of iris images to identify, this algorithm runs less time. And compare with the traditional artificial neural network, this algorithm is simpler and has high adaptability for different iris databases.

This paper focuses on the multi-category iris recognition, which is not considered for the problem of image noise, which will be the focus of future work.

Acknowledgments. The authors would like to thank the referee's advice and acknowledge the support of the National Natural Science Foundation of China (NSFC) under Grant No. 61471181, Natural Science Foundation of Jilin Province under Grant Nos. 20140101194JC, 20150101056JC.

References

1. Huo, G., et al.: An iris recognition method based on annule-energy feature. In: Yang, J., Yang, J., Sun, Z., Shan, S., Zheng, W., Feng, J. (eds.) Biometric Recognition. LNCS, vol. 9428, pp. 341–348. Springer, Cham (2015). doi:10.1007/978-3-319-25417-3_40
2. Zhu, L., Yuan, W.: An eyelash extraction method based on improved ant colony algorithm. J. Opto-Electron. Eng. **43**(6), 44–50 (2016)
3. Fei, H., Ye, H., Han, W., et al.: Deep learning architecture for iris recognition based on optimal Gabor filters and deep belief network. J. Electron. Imaging **26**(2), 023005 (2017)
4. Zhou, J., Ji, Z., Shen, L., et al.: PSO based memetic algorithm for face recognition Gabor filters selection. In: IEEE Workshop on Memetic Computing, Paris, France. IEEE Computer Society (2011)
5. Song, L., Li-jun, L., Man, Z.: Prediction for short-term traffic flow based on modified PSO optimized BP neural network. Syst. Eng.-Theory Pract. **32**(9), 2045–2049 (2012)
6. Wang, D.-F., Meng, L., Zhao, W.-J.: Improved bare bones particle swarm optimization with adaptive search center. Chin. J. Comput. **39**(12), 2652–2666 (2016)
7. Lu, C.: An iris recognition system based on feature fusion and optimized extreme learning machine algorithm. Comput. Appl. Softw. **33**(7), 326–333 (2016)
8. Gao, S., Zhu, X., Liu, Y., et al.: A quality assessment method of iris image based on support vector machine. J. Fiber Bioeng. Inform. **8**(2), 293–300 (2015)
9. Huan-li, L., Li-hong, G., Xiao-ming, L., et al.: Iris recognition based on SCCS-LBP. Opt. Precis. Eng. **21**(8), 2129–2136 (2013)
10. Daugman, J.G.: How iris recognition works. IEEE Trans. Circuits Syst. Video Technol. **14**(1), 21–30 (2004)
11. Bi, X., Pan, T.: An image enhancement method based on improved teaching-learning-based optimization algorithm. J. Harbin Eng. Univ. **37**(12), 1716–1721 (2016)
12. Li, H., Guo, L., Wang, X., et al.: Iris recognition based on weighted Gabor filter. J. Jilin Univ. (Eng. Technol. Edn.) **44**(1), 196–202 (2014)
13. Carlisle, A., Dozier, G.: An off-the-shelf PSO. In: Proceedings of Workshop on Particle Swarm Optimization, pp. 1–6 (2001)
14. JLU Iris Image Database. http://biis.jlu.edu.cn
15. CASIA Iris Image Database. http://www.cbsr.ia.ac.cn/IrisDatabase.htm
16. Zhao, T.: Research on iris feature extraction. School of Computer Science and Technology, Jilin University, Changchun, China (2016)
17. Yu, Z., Lu, Y., Zhang, J., et al.: Progressive semisupervised learning of multiple classifiers. IEEE Trans. Cybern. **99**, 1–14 (2017)
18. Shaikh, N.F., Doye, D.D.: An adaptive central force optimization (ACFO) and feed forward back propagation neural network (FFBNN) based iris recognition system. J. Intell. Fuzzy Syst. **30**(4), 2083–2094 (2016)
19. Olanrewaju, O.A., Mbohwa, C.: Evaluating factors responsible for energy consumption: connection weight approach. In: IEEE Electrical Power and Energy Conference, Canada (2016)

Deep Convolutional Features for Iris Recognition

Xingqiang Tang, Jiangtao Xie, and Peihua Li[✉]

School of Information and Communication Engineering,
Dalian University of Technology (DUT), Dalian 116024, China
peihuali@dlut.edu.cn

Abstract. Traditional iris recognition methods are mostly based on hand-crafted features, having limited success in less constrained scenarios due to non-ideal images caused by less cooperation of subjects. Though learned features via deep convolutional neural network (CNN) has shown remarkable success in computer vision field, it has been rarely used in the area of iris recognition. To tackle this issue, this paper proposes a novel method for robust iris recognition based on CNN models. As large-scale labeled iris images are not available, we design a lightweight CNN architecture suitable for iris datasets with small-scale labeled images. Different from existing works which use fully-connected features to capture the global texture, we propose to use the convolutional features for modeling local property and deformation of iris texture. We also develop a mechanism which can effectively combine the mask image for excluding the corrupted regions in the CNN model. The proposed method achieves much better performance than the compared methods on challenging ND-IRIS-0405 benchmark.

Keywords: Iris recognition · Convolutional neural network · Mask image

1 Introduction

Iris recognition has been studied for over twenty decades [4] and great advance has been made in different aspects, including preprocessing, feature extraction and matching. The irises of human beings have abundant, stable texture patterns uniquely distinguishing one from the others. Hence, one of the critical issues in iris recognition is to design effective filters for extracting the texture patterns.

In highly constrained scenarios where the subjects are motionless and cooperative, the captured iris images are often of good quality. Hand-crafted filters, e.g., the Gabor filters [4], Laplacian of Gaussians [18] and ordinal measure of Gaussian filters [15], have proven successful for charactering iris textures. However, in less constrained scenarios, the quality of iris images degrade greatly due to large geometric transformation, severe occlusion from eyelids or hair

---

The work was supported by the National Natural Science Foundation of China (Grant No. 61471082).

J. Zhou et al. (Eds.): CCBR 2017, LNCS 10568, pp. 391–400, 2017.
https://doi.org/10.1007/978-3-319-69923-3_42

and motion blur. Besides development of elaborate preprocessing techniques, researchers made great efforts to represent iris textures by designing a variety of hand-crafted filters to extract consistent features. Tan et al. [17] integrated ordinal measure, color histogram and semantic information for feature representation and matching. In [16], the Zernike moment-based phase encoding is proposed, which is further combined with Gabor filter-based iris coding. Yang et al. [19] proposed a method called ordinal measure of outer product tensor of SIFT features. Despite such progresses, iris recognition in less constrained or unconstrained scenarios is far from solved.

In computer vision community, deep Convolutional Neural Network (CNN) [10] has been very successful in large-scale image classification. Extremely deep CNN models (e.g. ResNet [7]) with hundreds of layers achieved accuracy surpassing human beings on ImageNet Large-Scale Visual Recognition Challenge (ILSVRC) [5]. However, few works have investigated applications of CNN models in iris recognition. Liu et al. [12] proposed deep CNN method called DeepIris, where they take a pair of images from different sensors as input, and learn the pairwise filter bank to model the relationship between the pair of images. Gangwar and Joshi [6] trained deep networks on normalized iris images, adopting the outputs of the second fully-connected layer for representing iris images.

Several difficulties exist for application of CNN in iris recognition. First, there is currently no large-scale labeled iris datasets matching the scale of ImageNet. As deep CNN often involves large number of parameters, it is important to avoid overfitting for successful training on small-scale iris datasets. Secondly, for a given input iris image, though a mask image can be obtained to exclude the corrupted regions by preprocessing, there lacks an effective mechanism to combine it in CNN architectures. Last but not least, the local geometrical deformations cannot be easily handled in existing CNN architecture. Though the two aforementioned achieved encouraging results, they failed to explicitly consider and address such challenges.

We present a novel method attempting to tackle these difficulties. We propose a lightweight deep CNN model suitable for iris recognition problems, which we call Lw-IrisNet. Notably, our design philosophy is that the network has a much smaller number of parameters and, above all, has features maps of much larger spatial size for convolutional layers. We propose to use the outputs of the last convolutional layers as features for characterizing iris textures, rather than those of the FC layers. In this way, we can model fine iris texture properties and their local deformation, as the convolutional features capture local information while FC features can only capture global one [3]. Furthermore, we extract ordinal measures on the feature maps for robustness and for compacting the iris code [19]. During matching process, we combine the masks of two iris images for excluding the occlusions.

2   Proposed Method

In this section, we first give an overview of the proposed iris method, and then describe our Lw-IrisNet architecture. Modeling of convolutional features and matching are given at last.

2.1   Method Overview

We present an overview of the proposed method in Fig. 1. Given an input iris image, we perform iris segmentation and normalization using the method introduced in [11]. We obtain a fixed size (256×256) normalized image containing only the iris region and a binary mask image where zero indicates occlusion and one otherwise. The normalized image is then inputted to the network for training. During verification process, the outputs of the last convolutional layer (conv5) are used for representing iris textures. On the feature map of conv5, we compute the ordinal measures to model the order relationship of pairs of features. For iris matching, we compute the Hamming distance while considering the masks of the iris image pair.

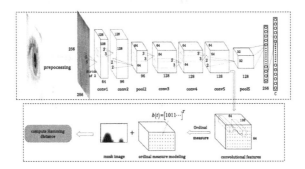

Fig. 1. Pipeline of the proposed method. Top: architecture of the proposed light-weight CNN (Lw-IrisNet), which notably has small number of parameters while with large spatial size of feature maps; Bottom: convolutional feature modeling and matching with mask image considered.

2.2   Network Architecture

Since the success of AlexNet [10] on ILSVRC, the CNN architecture becomes significantly deeper [7]. Accordingly, the number of parameters to be learned inclines to get larger. Unfortunately, the existing labeled iris datasets are much smaller than ImageNet which contains millions of training examples. To adapt to small-scale iris dtasets, we design a convolutional network, Lw-IrisNet, with 34M parameters, about half of those of AlextNet (60M) [10] and also much smaller than DeepIrisNet (55M) [6].

The architecture of Lw-IrisNet, as shown in Fig. 1 (top), is based on AlextNet [10] and shares similar structure with vgg-f network [2], but is much more narrower and, notably, has much larger spatial size per layer. It comprises seven learnable layers, including five convolutional (conv.) layers and two fully-connected layers. Each conv. layer or FC layer is sequentially followed by a Batch Normalization (BN) layer and a Rectified Linear Unit (ReLU). As suggested in [8], the BN layers can make the network converge faster and dropout not necessary. The output of the last FC layer is connected to the C-way softmax classifier, producing a vector of class probability measure. According to [14], we adopt small size filters (size: 3 × 3, stride: 1, and pad: 1) for all conv. filters except the first one where 5 × 5 filter is used.

A notable difference from previous CNN architectures is that Lw-IrisNet has much larger spatial size of feature maps. To this end, we design such that conv1 layer has a stride of 2 while all other conv. layers are of stride 1. The second and last conv. layer are respectively followed by a pooling layer (size: 2 × 2, stride: 2). Hence, the spatial size of feature map of conv5 is one fourth of the input image size (for a normalized iris image of 256 × 256, the spatial size of conv5 is 64 × 64). Such a network architecture renders the extracted features more local, and so we can model iris textures at finer spatial resolution.

2.3   Modeling and Matching of Convolutional Features

Once we have trained one Lw-IrisNet, we cut off its layers after conv5 and use it as a general feature extractor. For a normalized iris image with height h width w, we obtain $d-$dimensional features of spatial size $\frac{h}{4} \times \frac{w}{4}$. We use ordinal measure to encode the qualitative spatial relationship among features, which is more robust to noise and feature variation [15,19]. Let $\mathbf{f}(\mathbf{t}) = [f_i(\mathbf{t}), \ldots, f_d(\mathbf{t})]$ be a convolutional feature at spatial point $\mathbf{z}$ on the feature map, and $\Omega(\mathbf{z})$ be a small patch with $\mathbf{z}$ as its top-left corner. We compute the binary vector at $\mathbf{b}(\mathbf{z})$ modeling the convolutional features via ordinal measure as

$$b_i(\mathbf{z}) = H\left(\sum_{\mathbf{t} \in \Omega(\mathbf{z})} f_i(\mathbf{t}) \quad - \sum_{\mathbf{t}' \in \Omega(\mathbf{z}+\Delta\mathbf{z})} f_i(\mathbf{t}') \right), \quad i = 1, \ldots, d, \qquad (1)$$

where $b_i(\mathbf{z})$ denotes the $i^{\text{th}}-$component of $\mathbf{z}$, $H(\cdot)$ is Heaviside step function whose value is one for positive arguments and zero otherwise, and $\Delta\mathbf{z}$ denotes a displacement vector from $\mathbf{z}$. We thus obtain the final Ordinal Measure feature image.

After preprocessing stage, we can obtain an initial binary mask image of the same size with the normalized iris image, where zero indicates that the corresponding pixel on the normalized image is of non-iris, which is occluded by eyelids or polluted by highlights or noise, while one indicates a clean pixel. From the initial mask image, we compute the ratio r between the area of effective iris region and that of the whole image, which is called *effective iris region ratio* hereafter. Like the normalized image, we subject the mask image to the convolutions and pooling in sequential as defined in the Lw-IrisNet, except that every convolutional kernel is of uniform weights. Corresponding to encoding process of ordinal measure, we further compute the mask image as $w_i(\mathbf{z}) =$

$\frac{1}{|\Omega(\mathbf{z})|}$ min $\left(\sum_{\mathbf{t}\in\Omega(\mathbf{z})} r_i(\mathbf{t}), \sum_{\mathbf{t}'\in\Omega(\mathbf{z}+\Delta\mathbf{z})} r_i(\mathbf{t}')\right)$ where $|\Omega(\mathbf{z})|$ denotes the area of patch $\Omega(\mathbf{z})$. The final mask image is of the same size with the OM feature image.

If two iris images are perfectly aligned, then the Hamming distance between the corresponding feature points of the two images can be used for matching. In practice, however, two iris images to be compared are generally misaligned due to motions of the subject as well as that of the subject's eye and head. For robustness it is necessary to compensate for this misalignment [19]. Let I_1 and I_2 be a pair of images to be matched, and $\mathbf{b}^{I_1}$ and $\mathbf{b}^{I_2}$ be their OM feature images, respectively. For a OM feature $\mathbf{b}^{I_1}(\mathbf{z})$, we compare with the OM features in the neighboring region of $\mathbf{b}^{I_2}(\mathbf{z})$, not solely $\mathbf{b}^{I_2}(\mathbf{z})$, seeking the feature point $\mathbf{b}^{I_2}(\mathbf{z}^*)$ which matches $\mathbf{b}^{I_1}(\mathbf{z})$, i.e., $\mathbf{z}^* = \arg\min_{\mathbf{z}'\in\Omega(\mathbf{z})} \left(\frac{1}{d}\sum_{i=1}^d b_i^{I_1}(\mathbf{z})\oplus b_i^{I_2}(\mathbf{z}')\right)$, where $\oplus$ denotes bit-wise exclusive. By considering the mask image, we define the dissimilarity between the image pair as

$$\rho(I_1, I_2) = \frac{\sum_{\mathbf{z}} \min(w^{I_1}(\mathbf{z}), w^{I_2}(\mathbf{z}^*)) \sum_{i=1} b_i^{I_1}(\mathbf{z}) \oplus b_i^{I_2}(\mathbf{z}^*)}{d \sum_{\mathbf{z}} \min(w^{I_1}(\mathbf{z}), w^{I_2}(\mathbf{z}^*))} \tag{2}$$

3 Experiments

We mainly make experiments on ND-IRIS-0405 [9] benchmark. We first introduce this dataset and experimental settings. Then we describe implementation of our Lw-IrisNet. We evaluate thoroughly the proposed iris recognition method using convolutional features. Finally, we compare our method (called ConvOM for simplicity) with previous ones, including Gabor filter [4], dilobe ordinal filter of Sun and Tan [15], ordinal measure of outer product tensor (O^2PT) [19] and Deep Learning based method DeepIrisNet-A [6].

3.1 Dataset and Experimental Setting

The ND-IRIS-0405 benchmark consists of 64,980 grayscale iris images from 356 subjects, and 712 unique irises, captured with LG2200 iris image camera. The collection of the images contains many complex situations that the real world may encounter, such as blurring, occlusion and off-axis viewing, wearing contact lenses.

We adopt the preprocessing method introduced in [11], where the circular iris region of an input image is segmented out from the input image, then transformed to a fixed size, rectangular iris image. A companying mask image is also produced indicating whether one pixel is occluded or polluted. We discard the images in which irises can be well segmented, i.e., effective iris region ratio $r > \epsilon$, where ϵ is a threshold set to 0.5 unless specified otherwise. The remaining 62,911 images for ND-IRIS-0405 are used in experiments. By regarding the left and right eye of the same person as different iris classes, we divide the ND-IRIS-0405 into Part1 and Part2 with disjoint class labels in terms of the number of samples in each class, i.e., the identities with larger number of images are allocated to Part1 and those with fewer images are allocated to Part2. The Part1, containing

399 unique irises class, is further divided into training and validation set by a ratio of 7:1, and consequently, we obtain a training set with 47,456 images and a validation set with 6,474 images. Part2 containing 313 unique irises and 8,981 images is used for testing. Note that the *iris classes in the Part2 dataset do not appear* in network training.

We run the program on a PC with Intel i7-4790K CPU at 4.0 Ghz and NIDIA GTX 1080 8 GB GPU, under MatConvNet software package and Matlab 2015b. We adopt the mini-batch (batch size: 64) stochastic gradient descent with momentum for network training. The momentum and weight decay are set to 0.9 and 5×10^{-5}, respectively. The learning rate is initialized to 0.01, divided by 10 when the validation error stops decreasing in at most 30 epoches. the weights of conv. layers and FC layers are initialized with a Gaussian distribution with zero mean and standard deviation 0.01; all biases are initialized to zero. The data augmentation techniques include altering the pixel intensities and horizontal flip as done in [10], and horizontal translation in circular manner of the pixel over the interval $[-7, 7]$, which simulates the rotation of circular iris regions.

3.2   Evaluation of Proposed Method

Convolutional Features Against FC Features. The proposed method uses convolutional features for iris texture modeling, different from the straightforward method which adopts the outputs of the penultimate FC layer as features for representing iris image and Euclidean distance for matching [6]. Figure 2 presents comparison results between these two methods. We first observe that ConvOM has clear advantage over FCEucl on both the validation set and test set. The performance of both methods decrease on the test set, while the decline of FCEucl is much more significant while we only observe mild decrease of ConvOM. We mention that the class, not merely the images, in the test set is invisible in the training phase. The above results show that (1) the convolutional features have better capability for iris texture modeling than the FC features, and, and (2) they generalizes better than the latter for unseen classes.

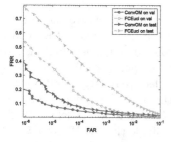

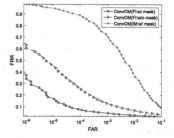

Fig. 2. ROC plot comparing ConvOM and FCEucl which respectively uses convoltuional features and FC features.

Fig. 3. ROC plot comparing ConvOM with different usages of mask.

Importance of Mask Image. Appropriate consideration of mask image can effectively excludes the effect of occlusion or pollution. In the proposed ConvOM we combine the mask in convolutional feature modeling, which is rephrased here as ConvOM(FI:w/ mask) to avoid ambiguity. We compare it with ConvOM (FI:w/o mask) which denotes the proposed method without using mask. We also compare with a straightforward scheme called ConvOM(IM:w/ mask), indicating that the mask image is considered for the input images. Specifically, for an input image, we set the intensity of one pixel to zero if it is occluded or polluted in terms of the initial mask image. Figure 3 presents comparison results on test set between these schemes. The ROC plots between ConvOM(FI:w/ mask) and ConvOM(FI:w/o mask) indicate that mask images is indispensable during matching. We also observe that ConvOM(IM:w/ mask) lead to serious performance degradation, we attribute this to setting the non-iris region of normalized iris images to zero potentially increase the similarity of the different categories of images, while the mask image is no longer used to exclude information of non-iris region during matching.

Proposed Lw-IrisNet Against Existing Network. We compare the convolutional feature modeling method (ConvOM) under two archtectures, i.e., Lw-IrisNet and the most commonly used AlexNet [10]. To avoid overfitting for AlextNet, we reduce the neuron number of each of two FC layer from 4096 to 2048. We train AlexNet from scratch with single channel, grayscale image as input, and the last convolutional layer of the trained AlextNet is used as feature extractor. For AlexNet, we resize the input image at four scales, i.e., 224, 512, 768 and 1024, and so the feature map sizes are 13, 26, 48, 52, respectively. Note that enlarging input image is equivalent to shrinking the filter size, and consequently the features at finer spatial scale can be extracted. Figure 4 and Table 1 presents comparison results.

For AlexNet, we observe that the performance overall continuously improves when the input images grows larger from 224 to 768. This shows that more local features are suitable iris texture modeling, as larger input images give arise to features at finer spatial resolution. However, enlarging input image to 1024 is

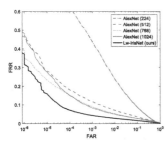

Fig. 4. ROC plot comparing ConvOM under Lw-IrisNet architecture and AlexNet architecture on test set

Table 1. Comparison of ConvOM under Lw-IrisNet architecture and AlexNet architecture on test set

Net	input size	EER	FRR (FAR@10^{-5})
AlexNet	224	0.0921	0.7815
	512	0.0471	0.2805
	768	0.0377	0.2293
	1024	0.0362	0.2715
Lw-IrisNet	256	0.0239	0.1599

inappropriate, significantly hurting the performance. In any case, the proposed Lw-IrisNet with input images of 256 × 256 consistently outperforms AlexNet by a large margin. We also note that changing input image size for Lw-IrisNet trivially affects the performance of Lw-IrisNet. This suggests that, compared to AlexNet, our designed architecture has better capability to capturing the local iris texture property.

3.3   Comparison with Existing Methods

Finally, we compare our method with Gabor filter [4], Sun and Tan [15], O^2PT [19] and DeepIrisNet-A [6]. The iris image preprocess of all methods is based on the scheme of [11]. The normalized image for these baseline methods have a image size of 64 × 256. For implementation of [4], we adopt freely available code, Osiris v4.1 [13], and we implement ourselves all the remaining methods. Figure 5(a) shows the comparison results where the effective iris region ratio threshold $\epsilon = 0.5$, i.e., the occluded or polluted area of iris images is less than 0.5. We can see that the proposed method has obvious advantage, outperforming the compared methods.

In real-world scenarios, the captured iris images may contain much smaller effective region due to severe occlusion or pollution. To test the performance of various methods in this scenario, in preprocessing stage we set the effective iris region ratio threshold $\epsilon = 0$, indicating that all test images are used for evaluation, even some of them may be severely occluded or polluted. Figure 5(b) shows the comparision results. It can be seen that compared to $\epsilon = 0.5$, the performance of all methods declines. However, it is clear that our ConvOM are less affected, demonstrating much better performance than the other methods. We attribute this superiority to better representational capability of convolutional features and robustness to interference or occlusion.

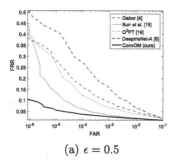
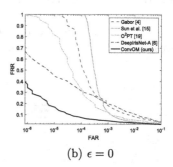

(a) $\epsilon = 0.5$ (b) $\epsilon = 0$

Fig. 5. Comparison with existing methods on test set. Figure (a) and (b) shows the effective iris region ratio threshold $\epsilon = 0.5$ and $\epsilon = 0$, respectively. Note that $\epsilon = 0$ indicates that all test images are used for evaluation, even some of them may be severely occluded ot polluted.

4   Conclusion

In this paper we designed a novel lightweight CNN architecture suitable for small-scale iris datasets. By using outputs of the last convolutional layer, we can capture local texture property and local iris deformation. We also develop an effective method which has capability to combine the mask image in the CNN model. We made experiments on ND-IRIS-0405, a realistic benchmark fit for CNN training, as it contains more images per class and more images in total than the other iris benchmarks. On this dataset, the proposed method achieved performance superior to the competing methods. In the future, we will study transferability of our method to other iris datasets (e.g., [1]), in which training CNNs from scratch is impractical as few images per class are provided.

References

1. CASIA: Casia Iris Image Database. http://biometrics.idealtest.org/
2. Chatfield, K., Simonyan, K., Vedaldi, A., Zisserman, A.: Return of the devil in the details: delving deep into convolutional nets. In: BMVC. British Machine Vision Association (2014)
3. Cimpoi, M., Maji, S., Vedaldi, A.: Deep filter banks for texture recognition and segmentation. In: CVPR, pp. 3828–3836. IEEE (2015)
4. Daugman, J.G.: High confidence visual recognition of persons by a test of statistical independence. IEEE TPAMI 15(11), 1148–1161 (1993)
5. Deng, J., Dong, W., Socher, R., Li, L.J., Li, K., Fei-Fei, L.: ImageNet: a large-scale hierarchical image database. In: CVPR. IEEE (2009)
6. Gangwar, A., Joshi, A.: Deepirisnet: deep Iris representation with applications in iris recognition and cross-sensor iris recognition. In: ICIP, pp. 2301–2305. IEEE (2016)
7. He, K., Zhang, X., Ren, S., Sun, J.: Deep residual learning for image recognition. In: CVPR, pp. 770–778. IEEE (2016)
8. Ioffe, S., Szegedy, C.: Batch normalization: accelerating deep network training by reducing internal covariate shift. In: ICML, pp. 448–456. ACM (2015)
9. Bowyer, K.W., Flynn, P.J.: Computer vision research laboratory. https://sites.google.com/a/nd.edu/public-cvrl/data-sets
10. Krizhevsky, A., Sutskever, I., Hinton, G.E.: Imagenet classification with deep convolutional neural networks. In: NIPS, pp. 1097–1105. MIT Press (2012)
11. Li, P., Liu, X., Xiao, L., Song, Q.: Robust and accurate iris segmentation in very noisy iris images. IVC 28(2), 246–253 (2010)
12. Liu, N., Zhang, M., Li, H., Sun, Z., Tan, T.: Deepiris: learning pairwise filter bank for heterogeneous iris verification. PRL 82, 154–161 (2016)
13. Petrovska, D., Mayoue, A.: Description and documentation of the biosecure software library. Project No. IST-2002-507634-BioSecure, Deliverable (2007)
14. Simonyan, K., Zisserman, A.: Very deep convolutional networks for large-scale image recognition. arXiv (2014)
15. Sun, Z., Tan, T.: Ordinal measures for iris recognition. IEEE TPAMI 31(12), 2211–2226 (2009)
16. Tan, C.W., Kumar, A.: Accurate iris recognition at a distance using stabilized iris encoding and zernike moments phase features. IEEE TIP 23(9), 3962–3974 (2014)

17. Tan, T., Zhang, X., Sun, Z., Zhang, H.: Noisy iris image matching by using multiple cues. PRL **33**(8), 970–977 (2012)
18. Wildes, R.P., Asmuth, J.C., Green, G.L., Hsu, S.C., Kolczynski, R.J., Matey, J.R., McBride, S.E.: A machine-vision system for iris recognition. Mach. Vis. Appl. **9**(1), 1–8 (1996)
19. Yang, G., Zeng, H., Li, P., Zhang, L.: High-order information for robust iris recognition under less controlled conditions. In: ICIP, pp. 4535–4539. IEEE (2015)

Mobile Iris Recognition via Fusing Different Kinds of Features

Qi Wang[1(✉)], Xia Su[1], Zhenlin Cai[1], and Xiangde Zhang[1,2]

[1] College of Sciences, Northeastern University, NO. 3-11 Wenhua Road,
Heping District, Shenyang 110819, Liaoning Province, China
wangqimath@126.com, 1849862792@qq.com, tsaizhenlin@163.com
[2] Department of Mathematics, College of Sciences, Northeastern University,
Heping District, Shenyang City, Liaoning Province, People's Republic of China
zhangxiangde@mail.neu.edu.cn

Abstract. Iris recognition is widely accepted in different kinds of applications. When it comes to mobile iris recognition, the task is quite challenging because of the low quality of iris images. To solve this problem, we propose a mobile iris recognition algorithm based on fusing features and Joint Bayesian. The iris feature representations are extracted by 2D Gabor and Ordinal Measures. Then these feature representations are fused by Joint Bayesian and the similarity of two iris images is measured by log-likelihood ratio. The experiments are conducted on MIR-Train database and a self-established low-quality iris image database (LQIID). The proposed method achieves EER at 1.2% on MIR-Train database and 0.8% on LQIID. These experiments support the effectiveness of the proposed method.

Keywords: Mobile iris recognition · Feature fusion · 2D Gabor · Ordinal measures · Joint Bayesian

1 Introduction

Iris recognition [1] is regarded as one of the most reliable and accurate biometric techniques. It is widely used in many important cases such as border controls, airport security check, bank employee or customer verification and so on. Currently, iris recognition is regarded as the most effective biometric technique for mobile devices. Since mobile iris recognition is used under different kinds of situations, the captured iris images may be influenced by ambient light intensity, different kinds of noises, movements, uncertain complex background and so on. All these cases increase the difficulty of mobile iris recognition. Thus mobile iris recognition is still a quite challenging task when it is used without enough constraints.

Most of current commercial iris recognition systems are developed based on near infrared light (NIR). These systems highly relies on users' cooperation.

© Springer International Publishing AG 2017
J. Zhou et al. (Eds.): CCBR 2017, LNCS 10568, pp. 401–410, 2017.
https://doi.org/10.1007/978-3-319-69923-3_43

And the quality of captured iris images is relative good. Daugman [1,2] proposed the first iris recognition algorithm. He extracted phase information as features by Gabor wavelet. Then the extracted features were encoded to binary codes. Finally, Hamming distance was used to measure the similarity of irises. Since then, researchers have developed different kinds of iris recognition algorithms. Wildes et al. [3] proposed the iris recognition method based on the four level Laplacian pyramid. Boles and Boashash [4] extracted zero-crossings of one-dimensional wavelet transform over concentric circles. In the matching step, the information of position and magnitude of zero-crossing representations were used. Ma et al. [5] processed the iris image by wavelet filtering, and then the position sequences of local sharp variation points were extracted as features. Sun et al. [6] extracted direction of gradient vector field as iris feature. Sun and Tan [7] developed multilobe differential filters (MLDF) for iris feature representation. They extracted ordinal features for iris recognition. Desoky et al. [8] adopted template fusion to generate one representative template for every class. Li et al. [9] proposed average local binary pattern(ALBP) achieving 99.61% on CASIA iris database.

Scholars also made great efforts in visible iris recognition. When iris images are captured in visible light, the quality of captured images is relative poor. They may be out of focus, motion-blurred and off-angle. These make iris recognition more difficult. In order to achieve better iris recognition performance, Tan et al. [10] put forward an iris matching method using multiple cues. Wang et al. [11] proposed a noisy iris verification method based on 2D Gabor and Adaboost. Besides these, some researchers also developed some competitive recognition methods [12–17].

Recently, NIR mobile iris recognition becomes a hot research topic since it is highly required by mobile market. But as we have mentioned before, mobile iris recognition is still a challenging task because the quality of iris images captured by mobile devices may be relative poor. Figure 1 shows some samples of high-quality and low-quality iris images. The high-quality samples are selected from CASIA-Iris-Lamp and CASIA-Iris-Thousand database [18]. The low-quality iris images are from Mobile Iris Recognition Train (MIR-Train) database [19] and self-established low quality iris image database (LQIID). So far, the performance of mobile iris recognition is not ideal, Zhang et al. [20] fused the Ordinal Measure (OM) features and iris representation learned by CNN for mobile iris recognitions, and they have achieved a satisfactory result, but on the whole NIR mobile iris recognition is still an open problem.

Based on fusing features and Joint Bayesian, we propose a NIR mobile iris recognition method. Section 2 introduces the procedure of iris image preprocessing. Section 3 demonstrates the proposed mobile iris recognition method. The experiments of proposed method are presented in Sect. 4. The last section illustrates conclusions of this paper.

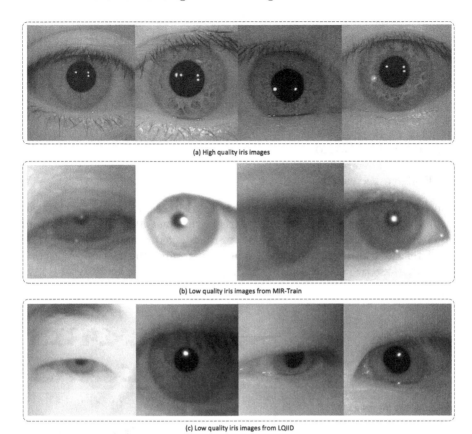

(a) High quality iris images

(b) Low quality iris images from MIR-Train

(c) Low quality iris images from LQIID

Fig. 1. Samples of high-quality and low-quality iris images

2   Image Preprocessing

It is a challenging problem to detect eye in complex scenes, especially when there are objects similar to eye. In this paper, we employ AdaBoost eye detector [11] to detect the coarse position of eyes. Then the improved Radial Symmetry Transform [21] is adopted to estimate the parameter of pupil. The boundaries of upper and lower eyelids are located by Random Sample Consensus (RANSAC). The accurate boundaries of pupil and iris are determined by integral differential algorithm [1,2]. The segmented annular iris region and corresponding noise template are normalized by Rubber Sheet Model [1,2]. Figure 2 shows the whole process of iris image preprocessing. More details could be found in [11].

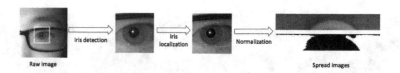

Fig. 2. Diagram of iris image preprocessing

3   Proposed Method

3.1   Feature Extraction

Texture is the most distinguishable features for iris recognition. To get excellent texture features, Daugman [1] extracted iris feature by Gabor wavelet. Sun and Tan [7] developed ordinal measure (OM) to represent iris texture by comparing ordinal relation among iris blocks. Figure 3 illustrates the feature extraction process for these two classical algorithms.

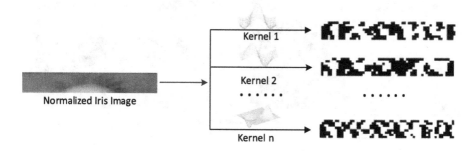

Fig. 3. Diagram of iris coding

Gabor Feature. Gabor wavelet is viewed to be similar as human visual system [22]. The Gabor function used in iris recognition [1] is

$$G(\theta, r) = e^{-iw(\theta - \theta_0)} e^{-\frac{(r - r_0)^2}{\alpha^2}} e^{-\frac{(\theta - \theta_0)^2}{\beta^2}} \tag{1}$$

Given a pixel $I(\theta, r)$ of a normalized iris sample I, its iris codes h_{Re} and h_{Im} for pixels are generated by the following formulas.

$$h_{Re} = \begin{cases} 1 & Re \int_\rho \int_\phi G(\theta_0, r_0) I(\rho, \phi) \rho \, d\rho \, d\phi \geq 0 \\ 0 & Re \int_\rho \int_\phi G(\theta_0, r_0) I(\rho, \phi) \rho \, d\rho \, d\phi < 0 \end{cases} \tag{2}$$

$$h_{Im} = \begin{cases} 1 & Im \int_\rho \int_\phi G(\theta_0, r_0) I(\rho, \phi) \rho \, d\rho \, d\phi \geq 0 \\ 0 & Im \int_\rho \int_\phi G(\theta_0, r_0) I(\rho, \phi) \rho \, d\rho \, d\phi < 0 \end{cases} \tag{3}$$

where, Re and Im represent real and imaginary parts separately.

Ordinal Measures. Sun and Tan [7] propose OM for iris recognition. They extract invariant that is the relation among adjacent pixel blocks. MLDF varies with parameter of distance, scale, position, orientation and the number of Gaussian functions. MLDF can be expressed as sum of Gaussian functions.

$$MLDF = C_p \sum_{i=1}^{N_p} \frac{1}{\sqrt{2\pi}\sigma_{pi}} e^{\frac{-(x-\mu_{pi})^2}{2\sigma_{pi}^2}} - C_n \sum_{i=1}^{N_n} \frac{1}{\sqrt{2\pi}\sigma_{ni}} e^{\frac{-(x-\mu_{ni})^2}{2\sigma_{ni}^2}} \qquad (4)$$

where μ and σ represent position and scale of 2D gaussian filter, C_p is the number of positive peaks, C_n is the number of negative peaks. The two constant coefficients N_p and N_n ensure the summation of MLDF is zero.

3.2 Feature Fusion

Feature fusion is an effective method to improve the recognition performance. The feature extracted by 2D Gabor contains rich detailed texture information [1]. Ordinal feature [7] represents the qualitative relationships among iris adjacent regions, and this may, in part, lose some detail information. We transform 2D Gabor and OM features to 1D vectors, which is regarded as the final feature.

3.3 Joint Bayesian

Generally, the similarity of a pair of features can be measured by Euclidean distance and Hamming distance etc. Then a threshold selected by ROC curves is used to classify the intra-class and inter-class samples. It makes sense when they are linearly separable. However the feature vector is linearly inseparable in most instances.

We construct joint probability distribution [23] of iris fusion features. It is assumed that the distribution of (x_1, x_2) obeys 2D Gaussian distribution, and each iris feature is constitute of two latent variables μ and ε. μ represents average feature of one class, ε is the difference between μ and the object. That is

$$x = \mu + \varepsilon \qquad (5)$$

Suppose that μ and ε obey Gaussian distribution. Note H_I as hypothesis that iris features x_1 and x_2 are from same class, H_E represents that they are from different classes. The similarity of x_1 and x_2 is measured by log-likelihood function.

$$r(x_1, x_2) = log\frac{P(x_1, x_2|H_I)}{P(x_1, x_2|H_E)} \qquad (6)$$

On hypothesis of H_I, u_1 and u_2 are same vectors, ε_1 and ε_2 are independent, then covariance of $P(x_1, x_2|H_I)$ is

$$\Sigma_I = \begin{bmatrix} S_\mu + S_\varepsilon & S_\mu \\ S_\mu & S_\mu + S_\varepsilon \end{bmatrix} \qquad (7)$$

Correspondingly, on hypothesis of H_E, both μ_1, μ_2 and ε_1, ε_2 are independent. The covariance of $P(x_1, x_2|H_E)$ is

$$\Sigma_E = \begin{bmatrix} S_\mu + S_\varepsilon & 0 \\ 0 & S_\mu + S_\varepsilon \end{bmatrix} \tag{8}$$

With the above assumption and notations, the joint distribution function of $f(x_1, x_2)$ could be deduced as the following equation. More details of this algorithm could be found in [23],

$$f(x_1, x_2; \mu, \Sigma) = \frac{1}{\sqrt{2\pi}|\Sigma|^{-2}} exp(-\frac{(x - \mu)^T \Sigma^{-1}(x - \mu)}{2}) \tag{9}$$

where Σ is the covariance of distribution. The mean value of all features must be normalized to be zero in preprocessing part. The final formula of log-likelihood is

$$r(x_1, x_2) = x_1^T A x_1 + x_2^T A x_2 - x_1^T G x_2 \tag{10}$$

where,

$$A = (S_\mu + S_\varepsilon)^{-1} - (F + G)$$

$$\begin{bmatrix} F + G & G \\ G & F + G \end{bmatrix} = \begin{bmatrix} S_\mu + S_\varepsilon & S_\mu \\ S_\mu & S_\mu + S_\varepsilon \end{bmatrix}^{-1}$$

The relationship of two irises x_1, x_2 are measured by log-likelihood $r(x_1, x_2)$. For a selected threshold θ, if $r(x_1, x_2) > \theta$, x_1 and x_2 are from the same class, otherwise not.

3.4 Learning Process

In order to learn the related parameters of two latent variables, the EM-like algorithm is adopted [23]. S_μ and S_ε are the covariance matrix of latent variable μ and ε. m is the dimension of iris feature. The learning procedure is shown in Algorithm 1.

4 Experimental Result and Discussion

4.1 Experimental Databases

In this section, the proposed method is experimented on a public iris database MIR-Train [19] and a self-established low quality iris image database (LQIID).

The distribution of iris radius in low-quality databases MIR-Train, LQIID are different from that of high-quality databases CASIA-Iris-Interval, CASIA-Iris-Lamp [18]. The radius of these two high-quality iris databases varies from 80 to 120 pixels approximately. In contrast, iris radius of MIR-Train and LQIID varies from 50 to 160 pixels, which is a larger range. This increases the difficulty of recognizing low quality mobile iris images.

Algorithm 1. EM-like algorithm

Initialize: S_μ,S_ε according to train-set,convergence condition $\sigma = 10^{-11}$

    while $(||S_\mu^{update} - S_\mu||/||S_\mu|| \geq \sigma)$ **do**

        E step:calculate F and G

$$F = S_\varepsilon^{-1}$$
$$G = -(mS_\mu + S_\varepsilon)^{-1}S_\mu S_\varepsilon^{-1}$$

        with obtained F and G, calculate

$$\mu = \sum_{i=1}^m S_\mu(F + mG)x_i$$
$$\varepsilon_j = x_j + \sum_{j=1}^m S_\varepsilon G x_j$$

        turn to M step

        M step: update S_μ and S_ε by

$$S_\mu = \frac{\sum_i \mu_i \mu_i^T}{n}$$
$$S_\varepsilon = \frac{\sum_i \sum_j \varepsilon_{ij} \varepsilon_{ij}^T}{n}$$

        continue E step

    end while

Output: F, G, S_ε, S_μ.

4.2 Evaluation Criteria

The commonly used evaluation indexes of iris recognition performance are False Accept Rate (FAR), False Reject Rate (FRR), Equal Error Rate (EER) and decidability. Decidability is used to measure the distinguishable ability of iris verification. It is defined as following

$$decidability = \frac{|\mu_1 - \mu_2|}{\sqrt{(\sigma_1^2 + \sigma_2^2)/2}} \tag{11}$$

where μ_1 and σ_1 are the mean and standard deviation of the intra-class matching while μ_2 and σ_2 are those of inter-class.

4.3 Experiment on MIR-Train

MIR-Train [19] is the training set of mobile iris recognition competition BTAS [24], which is held by the Institute of Automation, Chinese Academy of Sciences (CASIA). The database contains 4500 face images, which are captured by NIR camera of cell phone. Some of iris samples are noisy or occluded heavily. In the end, 8548 iris samples are selected from 600 classes for experiment.

Experimental results on MIR-Train database are shown in Fig. 4 and Table 1. Figure 4 shows the ROC curves of several methods. This figure indicates that the proposed method performs better than state-of-the-art methods. Table 1 demonstrates the EER and decidability of different methods. According to this table, the EERs of 2D Gabor, OM, Template Fusion and ALBP method are 4.0%, 5.3%, 4.2% and 8.0% respectively. And the proposed methods is 1.2%. The decidability of proposed methods achieves 4.2732.

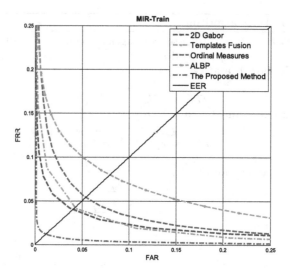

Fig. 4. The ROC curve on MIR-Train

Table 1. The performance of different algorithms on MIR-Train

Algorithm	EER	Decidability
2D Gabor [1]	0.040	2.9551
OM [7]	0.053	3.0909
Templates fusion [8]	0.042	3.3161
ALBP [9]	0.080	2.8811
Proposed method	**0.012**	**4.2732**

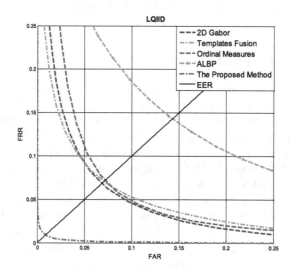

Fig. 5. The ROC curve on LQIID

4.4 Experiment on LQIID

Figure 1(a) has shown some typical iris samples from LQIID. Figure 5 and Table 2 show some experimental results on LQIID. Figure 5 shows that the proposed method achieves better performance than state-of-the-art methods. Table 2 illustrates the EER and Decidability of different methods. The EER of proposed method is 0.8%. And the EERs of 2D Gabor, OM, Template Fusion and ALBP method are 6.8%, 7.1%, 6.9% and 13.1% separately. And the decidability of proposed method is also better than those of evaluated state-of-the-art methods.

Table 2. The performance of algorithms on LQIID

Algorithm	EER	Decidability
2D Gabor [1]	0.068	2.9252
OM [7]	0.071	2.7904
Templates fusion [8]	0.069	2.7374
ALBP [9]	0.131	2.1265
Proposed method	**0.008**	**4.1674**

5 Conclusion

In this paper, we propose a NIR mobile iris recognition method based on Joint Bayesian. Firstly, the features are extracted by 2D Gabor and Ordinal Measures, then these extracted features are combined to one vector. After that, Joint Bayesian is adopted for measuring the similarity of fusion features. The experiments are conducted on a public mobile iris database (MIR-Train) and a self-established mobile database (LQIID). The experimental result demonstrates that the proposed method achieves encouraging performance for mobile iris recognition.

Acknowledgement. This research is partly supported by "the Fundamental Research Funds for the Central Universities", N160503003 and "National Natural Science Foundation of China", 61703088. The authors would like to thank "National Laboratory of Pattern Recognition, Institute of Automation, Chinese Academy of Sciences (CASIA)" for their great contributions in sharing iris image databases.

References

1. Daugman, J.G.: High confidence visual recognition of persons by a test of statistical independence. IEEE Trans. Pattern Anal. Mach. Intell. **15**(11), 1148–1161 (1993)
2. Daugman, J.: How iris recognition works. IEEE Trans. Circ. Syst. Video Technol. **14**(1), 21–30 (2004)
3. Wildes, R.P., Asmuth, J.C., Green, G.L., Hsu, S.C., Kolczynski, R.J., Matey, J.R., McBride, S.E.: A machine-vision system for iris recognition. Mach. Vis. Appl. **9**(1), 1–8 (1996)

4. Boles, W.W., Boashash, B.: A human identification technique using images of the iris and wavelet transform. IEEE Trans. Signal Process. **46**(4), 1185–1188 (1998)
5. Ma, L., Tan, T., Wang, Y., Zhang, D.: Personal identification based on iris texture analysis. IEEE Trans. Pattern Anal. Mach. Intell. **25**(12), 1519–1533 (2003)
6. Sun, Z., Wang, Y., Tan, T., Cu, J.: Robust direction estimation of gradient vector field for iris recognition. In: International Conference on Pattern Recognition, pp. 783–786 (2004)
7. Sun, Z., Tan, T.: Ordinal measures for iris recognition. IEEE Trans. Pattern Anal. Mach. Intell. **31**(12), 2211–2226 (2009)
8. Desoky, A.I., Ali, H.A., Abdel-Hamid, N.B.: Enhancing iris recognition system performance using templates fusion. Ain Shams Eng. J. **3**(2), 133–140 (2012)
9. Li, C., Zhou, W., Yuan, S.: Iris recognition based on a novel variation of local binary pattern. Vis. Comput. **31**(10), 1–11 (2014)
10. Tan, T., Zhang, X., Sun, Z., Zhang, H.: Noisy iris image matching by using multiple cues. Pattern Recognit. Lett. **33**(8), 970–977 (2012)
11. Wang, Q., Zhang, X., Li, M., Dong, X., Zhou, Q., Yin, Y.: Adaboost and multi-orientation 2D gabor-based noisy iris recognition. Pattern Recognit. Lett. **33**(8), 978–983 (2012)
12. Santos, G., Hoyle, E.: A fusion approach to unconstrained iris recognition. Pattern Recognit. Lett. **33**(8), 984–990 (2012)
13. Shin, K.Y., Nam, G.P., Jeong, D.S., Cho, D.H., Kang, B.J., Park, K.R., Kim, J.: New iris recognition method for noisy iris images. Pattern Recognit. Lett. **33**(8), 991–999 (2012)
14. Li, P., Liu, X., Zhao, N.: Weighted co-occurrence phase histogram for iris recognition. Pattern Recognit. Lett. **33**(8), 1000–1005 (2012)
15. Marsico, M.D., Nappi, M., Riccio, D.: Noisy iris recognition integrated scheme. Pattern Recognit. Lett. **33**(8), 1006–1011 (2012)
16. Li, P., Ma, H.: Iris recognition in non-ideal imaging conditions. Pattern Recognit. Lett. **33**(8), 1012–1018 (2012)
17. Szewczyk, R., Grabowski, K., Napieralska, M., Sankowski, W., Zubert, M., Napieralski, A.: A reliable iris recognition algorithm based on reverse biorthogonal wavelet transform. Pattern Recognit. Lett. **33**(8), 1019–1026 (2012)
18. Institute of Automation, Chinese Academy of Sciences: CASIA iris database. http://www.cbsr.ia.ac.cn/english/IrisDatabase.asp
19. Institute of Automation, Chinese Academy of Sciences: CASIA iris database. http://biometrics.idealtest.org/2016/MIR2016.jsp
20. Zhang, Q., Li, H., Sun, Z., He, Z., Tan, T.: Exploring complementary features for iris recognition on mobile devices. In: International Conference on Biometrics, pp. 1–8 (2016)
21. Loy, G., Zelinsky, A.: Fast radial symmetry for detecting points of interest. IEEE Trans. Pattern Anal. Mach. Intell. **25**(8), 959–973 (2003)
22. Daugman, J.G.: Complete discrete 2-D gabor transforms by neural networks for image analysis and compression. IEEE Trans. Acoust. Speech Signal Process. **36**(7), 1169–1179 (1988)
23. Chen, D., Cao, X., Wang, L., Wen, F., Sun, J.: Bayesian face revisited: a joint formulation. In: Fitzgibbon, A., Lazebnik, S., Perona, P., Sato, Y., Schmid, C. (eds.) ECCV 2012 Part III. LNCS, vol. 7574, pp. 566–579. Springer, Heidelberg (2012). doi:10.1007/978-3-642-33712-3_41
24. Zhang, M., Zhang, Q., Sun, Z., Zhou, S., Ahmed, N.U.: The BTAS* competition on mobile iris recognition. In: IEEE International Conference on Biometrics Theory, Applications and Systems, pp. 1–7 (2016)

Coarse-to-Fine Iris Recognition Based on Multi-variant Ordinal Measures Feature Complementarity

Hui Zhang[1](✉), Man Zhang[2], Zhaofeng He[3], Hang Zou[4], and Rui Wang[1]

[1] Institute of Software, CAS, Beijing, China
zhzaozao@126.com
[2] Institute of Automation, CAS, Beijing, China
[3] Beijing IrisKing Co., Ltd., Beijing, China
[4] Minzu University of China, Beijing, China

Abstract. Iris recognition inevitably need to tackle extremely large scale database matching issue which challenges the iris recognition in both computing efficiency and accuracy. As a feasible solution, the iris image classification has great potential and needs further studies. We propose a multi-variant Ordinal Measures feature complementarity based coarse-to-fine iris recognition strategy. Two OM variant feature are proposed for iris classification. One is very large scale OM feature (VLSOM), and the other is histogram statistics of OM Run-Length Coding (HOM-RLC). VLSOM, HOMRLC and OM describes overall appearance, global statistic and local characteristics of iris respectively. Extensive experiments show advantages of the proposed complementarity feature.

Keywords: Iris classification · Coarse-to-fine iris recognition · Multi-variant Ordinal Measures feature complementarity · VLSOM · HOMRLC

1 Introduction

Nowadays, iris recognition draws more attentions driven by its wide applications in web personal identity, national ID card, border control, banking, etc. Iris is the ring shaped region of human eye which includes rich texture information. Iris recognition aims to assign a unique identity label to each iris image automatically. State-of-the-art iris recognition methods include Gabor phase demodulation [1], Ordinal Measures(OM) [2], etc.

With the iris recognition application boost, the iris image database scales become larger and larger. It is time consuming to compare an query iris image with all the iris templates in a very large gallery database. Classification of all iris images in the central gallery database into multiple categories may help speed up

---

H. Zhang—This work is supported by the Natural Science Foundation of China (61503365) (61603385).

J. Zhou et al. (Eds.): CCBR 2017, LNCS 10568, pp. 411–419, 2017.
https://doi.org/10.1007/978-3-319-69923-3_44

large-scale iris identification, since one query iris image only compare to part of images. We name the first-classification and then-recognition strategy as coarse-to-fine iris recognition. The coarse-to-fine iris recognition can save computing time without accuracy reducing under several conditions: (1) The extra calculating time caused by classification is less than calculating time of comparing iris image to iris images in other categories; (2) The hit rate is high, where the correct hit means classifying the query iris image into a category including the same iris. High hit rate insure little whole database comparing; (3) Last but the most basic requirement, it does not cause error identification.

The difference of iris classification and recognition is the definition of class labels at macro or micro scale. Therefore, to some extent, iris image classification can share similar solution of iris recognition. Moreover, using similar feature for classification and recognition can save feature extraction time. We adopt the OM [2] feature as iris recognition solution. Novelly, we propose two OM based feature extraction algorithms for iris classification. One is very large scale OM feature (VLSOM) which describes overall appearance characteristics of iris image. One is histogram statistics of OM Run-Length Coding (HOMRLC) which describes statistics characteristics of iris image and OM feature. Compared to previous iris classification methods, the proposed multi-variant OM feature strategy considers the classification and recognition in the overall context.

Research about iris classification is still very limited, but it is actually a more challenging problem: (1) iris image classification needs to find the stable relationship of similar iris texture features between different subjects; (2) clustered categories have no inevitable connection to recognition, so improving the robustness of iris image classification is one of the most important factors for coarse-to-fine iris recognition efficiency. Therefore, we propose using different iris image classification methods to cooperate with each other, which aims to improve the hit rate of iris classification stage. High hit rate is conducive to reduce the whole gallery database matching rate, since the whole gallery database matching rate is mainly determined by classification ability of classifying images from an iris into a same category. We use VLSOM and HSRLC as two different iris image classification methods to conduct a robust coarse-to-fine iris recognition framework, which shows the complementarity advantages. See Fig. 1.

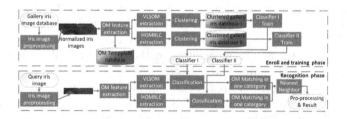

Fig. 1. Framework of multi-variant Ordinal Measures feature complementarity

2   Related Work

At the beginning, work on iris classification is mainly about iris liveness detection which protects an iris recognition system from fake iris attacks. Daugman [3], Ma et al. [4] and He et al. [5] proposed to detect printed iris images via frequency analysis. Quality based image measures were used [6]. Texture features useful for iris liveness detection include gray level co-occurrence matrix [7], statistical distribution of iris texture primitives [8], LBP [9] and HVC [10]. Besides the fake iris detection, some of these texture analysis methods were used for iris based ethnic classification [11–14]. There are a few iris image classification methods proposed for coarse iris image classification. Yu et al. [15] described iris surface using fractal dimensions features and classified iris images into four classes based on manually set thresholds. Fu et al. [16] used artificial color filter and margin setting classifier for coarse iris image classification. Qiu et al. [17] grouped iris images into five categories based on statistical description of learned Iris-Textons. Mehrotra et al. [18] used energy based histogram of multi-resolution DCT transformation to group iris images. Sunder and Ross [19] investigated iris macro-features (structures such as moles, freckles, nevi, and melanoma) for iris retrieval and matching. Our previews work [10] proposed Hierarchical Visual Codebook for several iris classification tasks. Most of these methods focus on iris classification itself, considering little about the overall efficiency of coarse-to-fine iris recognition.

3   Our Method

To tackle challenging issues of large scale iris recognition, iris image classification needs further research to match advance developed iris recognition technique. We propose an novelty coarse-to-fine iris recognition strategy including coarse classification stage and fine matching recognition stage. The classification stage and the recognition stage share basic OM feature [2], but focus on different scales. The classification stage needs to focus on large scale characteristics or global characteristics. The recognition stage needs to focus on detailed small scale matching. Sharing same basic feature has two-folds advantages: it does not introduce much feature extraction calculation; iris categories clustered based on variant OM feature is potentially related to recognition based on OM feature. For robustness of the strategy, we adopt two different feature for classification respectively, the very large scale OM feature (VLSOM) and the Histogram statistics of OM Run-Length Coding (HOMRLC). These two methods are both variant feature based on OM, but represent different aspect characteristics of iris images. These algorithms will be introduced in the next two subsections. Figure 1 shows the framework of multi-variant OM feature complementarity.

3.1   Very Large Scale OM Feature

Unlike the iris recognition with individual ground truth, the coarse iris classification has no ground truth. We try to classify iris based on appearance by large scale feature. The OM feature show advantages in iris recognition [2] due to the robustness of contrast feature. So we use OM feature at the image size scale for iris classifications. If large scale OM features of two iris images are same, then the likelihood of these two images belonging to a same category are greater. For example, see Fig. 2, the large scale OM feature of I1 and I2 are same, but different to I3, which means that I1 and I2 are more similar than I1 and I3 (I2 and I3). The conception of large scale OM is similar with people's visual processing.

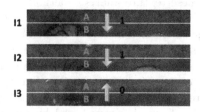

Fig. 2. Large scale OM for iris image classification

We introduce the very large scale OM feature (VLSOM) for iris classification. Three types of large scale OM are designed to classify all iris images into 4 categories. First, dividing an iris image into left half part and right half part, V_1 compares the average gray level of two parts AG_L and AG_R:

$$V_1 = \begin{cases} 1, & if \frac{|AG_L - AG_R|}{(AG_L + AG_R)/2} \geq th_1 \\ 0, & otherwise \end{cases} \tag{1}$$

th_1 is a threshold determined experimentally. Second, dividing an iris image into upper half part and bottom half part, V_2 compares the average gray level of two parts AG_U and AG_B:

$$V_2 = \begin{cases} 1, & if \frac{|AG_U - AG_B|}{(AG_U + AG_B)/2} \geq th_2 \\ 0, & otherwise \end{cases} \tag{2}$$

th_2 is a threshold determined experimentally. Third, dividing an iris image into upper half part and bottom half part, V_3 compares the average gray level of two parts AG_U and AG_B:

$$V_3 = \begin{cases} 1, & if AG_U \leq AG_B \\ 0, & otherwise \end{cases} \tag{3}$$

During classification, V_1 V_2 and V_3 are calculated in order. Iris images are classified into 4 categories by following rules. *Label* is the category label.

$$\begin{aligned} & if \ V_1 = 1, \ then \ Label = 4; \\ & if \ V_1 = 0 \cap V_2 = 1, \ then \ Label = 3; \\ & if \ V_1 = 0 \cap V_2 = 0 \cap V_3 = 1, \ then \ Label = 2; \\ & if \ V_1 = 0 \cap V_2 = 0 \cap V_3 = 0, \ then \ Label = 1; \end{aligned} \tag{4}$$

The VLSOM is designed based on observation and experiments. The VLSOM extraction and classification is very fast, which increases a little calculation while decreasing the times of matching and comparing largely.

3.2 Histogram Statistics of OM Run-Length Coding

Figure 3(a) shows some example OM feature matrixes. By observing a large number of iris OM feature matrixes, we believe that the value changing frequency in each row is relevant to iris image appearance. The statistics of the 0 and 1 change frequency is good feature for iris image classification. We propose to the novel feature called Histogram statistics of OM Run-Length Coding (HOMRLC), which borrows the idea of Run-Length Coding (RLC) [20] and is statistics of run lengths. Figure 3(b) illustrates the RLC calculation.

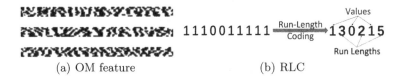

(a) OM feature   (b) RLC

Fig. 3. OM feature of iris images and Run-Length Coding

The OM feature of each iris image is an 8×128 binary matrix. Extraction of HOMRLC includes 3 steps, as shown in Fig. 4. (1) RLC feature of each line of the OM matrix is calculated; (2) A histogram of run length is calculated for each row, which includes 6 bars standing for 1–6 run length; (3) All 8 histograms are connected in series giving a 48-D vector. After feature extraction, gallery images are clustered into 4 categories by K-means. SVM is used as classifier. HOMRLC feature is a 48-D vector, so the clustering and the classifier training speed is much faster than using high dimension feature.

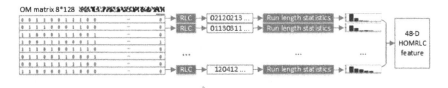

Fig. 4. Illustration of histogram statistics of OM Run-Length Coding calculation

4 Experiments

The CASIA-Iris-Thousand [21], one of the largest iris image databases in the public domain, is used as the testing database. It contains 20,000 iris images of

1,000 subjects (2,000 irises). The first five images of each iris conduct the gallery database, while the later five are query images. The baseline iris recognition method in the experiments uses a tri-lobe OM filter (5*5 Gaussian kernel as the basic lobe, horizontal orientation and inter-lobe distance is 10 pixels) to extract OM feature. The nearest neighbor (NN) method is adopted for OM feature matching. The LLC is used as baseline feature, which has been used for iris classification successfully [10,13], and SPM is adopted [1,2,4]. The linear SVM [22] is used as classifier for LLC and HOMRLC.

4.1   Classification and Clustering Results

Table 1 lists the results of iris image clustering and classification. For LLC and HOMRLC, we use K-means to cluster 10000 gallery iris images into 4 categories. For VLSOM, based on a set of pre defined threshold, we get 4 categories. Image numbers of each category spread even. HOMRLC gets better CCR than LLC.

Table 1. Clustering results and correct classification rate

Methods	No. of each categories	CCR
LLC	2620, 2925, 2470, 1985	0.844061
VLSOM	1892, 3372, 2410, 2326	-
HOMRLC	2427, 2360, 2705, 2508	0.927106

4.2   Coarse-to-Fine Iris Recognition Results

We introduce Classification Hit Rate (CHR) and final Recognition Hit Rate (RHR) index for comparison. If a query iris image is classified into a category including image of same iris, it is regarded as successful classified. N_{SC} is number of query images which are successful classified. If a query iris image matched to same iris correctly in the pre-classified category, it is regarded as successful identified. N_{SR} is number of query images which are successful identified. Then, $CHR = N_{SC}/N$ and $RHR = N_{SR}/N$, where N is total number of query images.

Table 2 lists the CHR and RHR of different methods. "Rec" stands for iris recognition without coarse classification. "Multi" stands for multi-variant OM feature complementarity method, we adopt VLSOM and HOMPLC for cooperation. The proposed VLSOM and HOMPLC outperform LLC method. It

Table 2. Classification hit rate and recognition hit rate

	Rec	LLC	VLSOM	HOMPLC	Multi
CHR	100	73.90	82.02	80.20	94.57
RHR	95.65	71.47	76.52	73.92	90.18

demonstrates that variant OM feature is suitable for iris classification tasks. The multi-variant OM feature complementarity strategy can largely improve the CHR and the RHR. It can reduce the probability of whole gallery matching caused by unsuccessful classification. The complementarity strategy guarantees the speed-up goal of coarse-to-fine iris recognition. Figure 5 shows ROCs without considering whole database matching while classification failed. The proposed multi-variant OM feature complementarity algorithm achieves the best result.

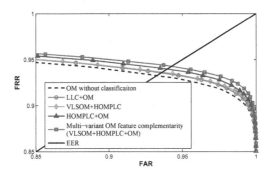

Fig. 5. ROCs of coarse-to-fine iris recognition

We conduct experiments under same operating environment on a laptop, using the Matlab2014a. Average time for VLSOM and HOMRLC extraction and classification is listed in Table 3. Average time for OM matching of two images is $2e{-}04$ s. The speed-up effect of coarse-to-fine iris recognition, for one query image, is estimated as Table 3.

Table 3. Speed-up effect of coarse-to-fine iris recognition

	Cls time	Saved matching times	Total save
VLSOM	$7.0e{-}04$ s	6150 ($10000 \times 0.75 \times 0.82$)	1.2293 s
HOMRLC	$2.0e{-}03$ s	6000 ($10000 \times 0.75 \times 0.8$)	1.1980 s
Multi	$2.7e{-}03$ s	4700 ($10000 \times 0.5 \times 0.94$)	0.9373 s

5   Conclusion

In this paper, we propose VLSOM and HOMRLC feature for iris classification, which cooperates with OM based recognition to form less time consuming coarse-to-fine iris recognition. Features for classification and recognition reflect different scales or aspects of iris images. We furthermore propose to use multi classification methods cooperation to improve the hit rate of classification. Experimental results show advantages of the proposed coarse-to-fine iris recognition strategy.

H. Zhang et al.

References

1. Daugman, J.: High confidence visual recognition of persons by a test of statistical independence. IEEE TPAMI **15**(11), 1148–1160 (1993)
2. Sun, Z., Tan, T.: Ordinal measures for iris recognition. IEEE TPAMI **31**(12), 2211–2226 (2009)
3. Daugman, J.: How iris recognition works. IEEE Trans. Circuits Syst. Video Technol. **14**(1), 21–30 (2004)
4. Ma, L., Tan, T., Wang, Y., Zhang, D.: Personal identification based on iris texture analysis. IEEE TPAMI **25**(12), 1519–1533 (2003)
5. He, X., Lu, Y., Shi, P.: A fake iris detection method based on FFT and quality assessment. In: Proceedings of CCPR, pp. 316–319 (2008)
6. Galbally, J., Ortiz-Lopez, J., Fierrez, J, Ortega-Garcia, J.: Iris liveness detection based on quality related features. In: Proceedings of ICB, pp. 271–276 (2012)
7. He, X., An, S., Shi, P.: Statistical texture analysis-based approach for fake iris detection using support vector machines. In: Lee, S.-W., Li, S.Z. (eds.) ICB 2007. LNCS, vol. 4642, pp. 540–546. Springer, Heidelberg (2007). doi:10.1007/978-3-540-74549-5_57
8. Wei, Z., Qiu, X., Sun, Z., Tan, T.: Counterfeit iris detection based on texture analysis. In: Proceedings of ICPR (2008)
9. He, Z., Sun, Z., Tan, T., Wei, Z.: Efficient iris spoof detection via boosted local binary patterns. In: Tistarelli, M., Nixon, M.S. (eds.) ICB 2009. LNCS, vol. 5558, pp. 1080–1090. Springer, Heidelberg (2009). doi:10.1007/978-3-642-01793-3_109
10. Sun, Z., Zhang, H., Tan, T., Wang, J.: Iris image classification based on hierarchical visual codebook. IEEE TPAMI **36**(6), 1120–1133 (2014)
11. Qiu, X., Sun, Z., Tan, T.: Global texture analysis of iris images for ethnic classification. In: Zhang, D., Jain, A.K. (eds.) ICB 2006. LNCS, vol. 3832, pp. 411–418. Springer, Heidelberg (2005). doi:10.1007/11608288_55
12. Qiu, X., Sun, Z., Tan, T.: Learning appearance primitives of iris images for ethnic classification. In: Proceedings of ICIP, vol. 2, pp. 405–408 (2007)
13. Zhang, H., Sun, Z., Tan, T., Wang, J.: Ethnic classification based on iris images. In: Sun, Z., Lai, J., Chen, X., Tan, T. (eds.) CCBR 2011. LNCS, vol. 7098, pp. 82–90. Springer, Heidelberg (2011). doi:10.1007/978-3-642-25449-9_11
14. Lyle, J., Miller, P., Pundlik, S., Woodard, D.: Soft biometric classification using periocular region features. In: Proceedings of BTAS (2010)
15. Yu, L., Zhang, D., Wang, K., Yang, W.: Coarse iris classification using box-counting to estimate fractal dimensions. Pattern Recogn. **38**(11), 1791–1798 (2005)
16. Fu, J., Caulfield, J., Yoo, S., Atluri, V.: Use of artificial color filtering to improve iris recognition and searching. Pattern Recogn. Lett. **26**(14), 2244–2251 (2005)
17. Qiu, X., Sun, Z., Tan, T.: Coarse iris classification by learned visual dictionary. In: Lee, S.-W., Li, S.Z. (eds.) ICB 2007. LNCS, vol. 4642, pp. 770–779. Springer, Heidelberg (2007). doi:10.1007/978-3-540-74549-5_81
18. Mehrotra, H., Srinivas, B.G., Majhi, B., Gupta, P.: Indexing iris biometric database using energy histogram of DCT subbands. In: Ranka, S., et al. (eds.) IC3 2009. CCIS, vol. 40, pp. 194–204. Springer, Heidelberg (2009). doi:10.1007/978-3-642-03547-0_19
19. Sunder, M., Ross, A.: Iris image retrieval based on macro-features. In: Proceedings of ICPR, pp. 1318–1321 (2010)
20. Christopher, D.: Smile! you're on RLE!. Transactor **7**(6), 16–18 (1987)

21. Institute of Automation, Chinese Academy of Sciences: CASIA Iris Image Database v4.0. http://biometrics.idealtest.org/
22. Fan, R., Chang, K., Hsieh, C., Wang, X., Lin, C.: LIBLINEAR: a library for large linear classification. J. Mach. Learn. Res. **9**, 1871–1874 (2008)

An Eye Localization Method for Iris Recognition

Yongliang Zhang$^{(\boxtimes)}$, Xiaozhu Chen, Xiao Chen, Dixin Zhou,
and Erzhe Cao

College of Computer Science and Technology,
Zhejiang University of Technology, Hangzhou 310023, China
titanzhang@zjut.edu.cn

Abstract. Eye localization plays a fundamental role in iris recognition, for it can define the effective regions used for iris recognition. This paper presents a new eye localization method based on light spots detection. First, images are preprocessed by Gaussian Smoothing Filter and dilation. Then, FAST feature detection algorithm is used to select candidate regions by detecting the light spots. Furthermore, we calculate the HOG features of these candidates and use the SVM classifier to obtain eye regions. If only one eye is localized, block matching algorithm is applied to fix the missed detection. The localization accuracy on two public dual-eye iris image databases, CASIA-IrisV4-Distance and MIR, keeps above 99.75%, and it shows that 98% of the samples have a normalized error value below 0.1, which demonstrates the success of the proposed method.

Keywords: Eye localization · FAST algorithm · HOG features · SVM classifier · Block matching

1 Introduction

Iris recognition has become a hot research topic in the field of computer vision in recent years. Compared with fingerprint and face, iris is considered as the most reliable modality because of its uniqueness, stability, and difficulty to be replicated. Eye localization plays a fundamental role because it is the first step in iris recognition.

1.1 Related Works

One of the most traditional algorithms is Gray projection [1]. It roughly frames out the approximate eye areas using the information of the distribution of peaks and valleys constructed by projection. Gray projection and its improved algorithms [2] perform fast, but they are not robust because of their high susceptibility to noise, illumination and posture. Template matching [3] needs eye templates based on prior knowledge of eye parameters and finds the region with the largest similarity to the template. Although being easy to implement, this method is time-consuming and not suitable for all detectors due to the differences of the human eyes. Edge extraction uses Hough transform to detect the possibly eyeball edges. The candidate circle is determined as an

© Springer International Publishing AG 2017
J. Zhou et al. (Eds.): CCBR 2017, LNCS 10568, pp. 420–427, 2017.
https://doi.org/10.1007/978-3-319-69923-3_45

eye only if its gray level contrasts to neighbors. Edge extraction needs massive pre-processing, and it is difficult to set proper parameters for Hough transform. Statistical learning-based method constructs a classifier by analyzing substantial target and non-target samples to find eyes. This method is widely used in pattern recognition for its accuracy. The mainstream algorithms include Boosting [4], Support Vector Machine (SVM) [5], neural network [6], etc. However, besides of concerning about the speed, it needs a great quantity of training samples, and is prone to over-learning.

1.2   Presence of Light Spots

An important point we noticed is that there are light spots presented around the pupils in the overwhelming majority of dual-eyes iris images. It is inevitable because of the particularity of iris cameras which use infrared light. Taking the advantage of this characteristic, we propose a novel algorithm based on light spot detection. This algorithm consists of four modules, including image preprocessing, candidate detection, eye selection and fixing detection, as illustrated in Fig. 1.

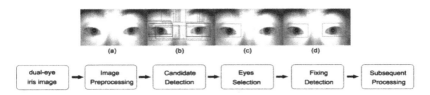

Fig. 1. The flowchart of the proposed algorithm

2   Method Description

2.1   Image Preprocessing Based on Gaussian Blur and Dilating

Preprocessing module aims to create an ideal image for the following processing, mainly in noise elimination and light spot dilation. In this paper, gaussian blur is used to reduce noise. Dilating expands the highlighted area in images, so that candidates can be detected more effectively.

2.2   Candidate Detection Based on FAST Feature Detection

An eligible candidate detection module must meet three rules: (1) Covering the whole eye regions; (2) The number of candidates is less enough; (3) Performing fast. In this paper, FAST algorithm [7] is introduced to detect light spots, which is a feature detection algorithm based on gray-scale comparison. It determines feature point by comparing the gray level of the candidate feature point with the pixels around it.

As illustrated in Fig. 2, C_p is a circle centered on p and its radius is 3. There are sixteen points on $C_p's$ circumference, named as $p[1], p[2], \ldots, p[16]$. where p is a feature point determined by the follow formula:

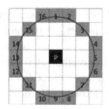

Fig. 2. Pixels around point P

$$V_{C_p} = \sum_{p' \in C_p} |I(p') - I(p)| > \varepsilon_d \qquad (1)$$

Here $I(p)$ is the gray level of point p, ε_d is a threshold of gray level difference. Only if V_{C_p} is greater than a given threshold, p is considered as a feature point. To avoid feature points of crowding together, in this paper, only one feature point is chosen in the region of 20 * 20 pixels. We calculate the value S as follow:

$$S = \sum_{i=1}^{16} |I(p'') - I(p''[i])| \qquad (2)$$

Here $p''[i](i = 1, 2, \ldots, 16)$ are points on the circumference $C_{p''}$. Remain the feature point which has the most great value S.

2.3   Eyes Selection Based on HOG Feature and SVM Classifier

Eye selection module is designed to select true eye regions from the numerous candidates detected from the previous step. We obtain the HOG features of candidates and then filter out the non-eye regions by using SVM classifier [8]. The HOG features calculate as follows:

(1) Standardize Gamma space and color space

Gamma correction is introduced to minimize the influence of light. It standardizes the color space of input images by adjusting the contrast, reducing the impact of local shadows and effectively suppressing the interference of noise.

(2) Construct the gradient direction histogram of cell

The purpose of this step is to code a local image and maintain a weak sensitivity to the posture and appearance of the target object in the image at the same time. The image is divided into several connected areas called cells. Each cell contains n * n pixels. K histograms are used to describe the gradient information of pixels. Namely, the gradient of cell is divided into K blocks (denoted by Ψ). Each pixel has different weight in gradient directions $V_k(x, y)$:

$$V_k(x,y) = \begin{cases} \theta \cdot G(x,y) & \alpha(x,y) \in \Psi_k \\ 0 & \alpha(x,y) \notin \Psi_k \end{cases} \quad 1 \leq k \leq K \tag{3}$$

Here θ is an arbitray constant, Ψ_k is the kth gradient direction, $G(x,y)$ is the gradient magnitude at (x,y), $\alpha(x,y)$ is the gradient direction at (x,y). The histogram equals the K-dimension feature vector of the cell. Each feature vector in the $Cell_i$ is expressed as $v^i = [H_1^i, H_2^i, \cdots, H_K^i]$. H_k^i is calculated as follows:

$$H_k^i = \sum_{(x,y) \in Cell} V_k(x,y) \quad 1 \leq k \leq K \tag{4}$$

(3) Combine cells and normalize the gradient histogram of block

In this step we combine the cells into a large spatially connected section called block. If there are n cells in a block, then gradient direction histogram vector of this block can be express as:

$$v_B = [v_c^1, v_c^2, \cdots v_c^n] = [H_1^1, H_2^1, \ldots, H_k^1, \ldots H_1^n, H_2^n, \ldots, H_k^n]$$
$$H_k^i = \sum_{(x,y) \in Cell} V_k(x,y) \quad 1 \leq k \leq K \tag{5}$$

Dividing the image into N blocks, for each block we calculate the gradient direction histogram vector as follow:

$$v_B^i \leftarrow v_B^i \Big/ \sqrt{\|v_B^i\|_2^2 + \varepsilon^2} \quad (i = 1, 2, \ldots, N) \tag{6}$$

Here ε is a minimal constant to avoid the case whose denominator is zero. Then HOG feature of the block is calculated by concatenating and normalizing the feature vectors of all cells in the block.

2.4   Fixing Detection Based on Image Block Matching

In rare instances, it only localizes one eye in a dual-eye iris image, so we use the fixing module based on image block matching to detect the other eye.

(1) Judge the benchmark eye

According to the prior knowledge of facial features and the coordinates of the detected eye, we can easily judge it as the left or right one. It is called benchmark eye and defined as E_b. We make $E_b = E_b^R$ if the benchmark eye is on the right while make $E_b = E_b^L$ when it on the left.

(2) Define the sliding window size

According to the coordinates of benchmark eye center, we delimit a rectangle R in the symmetrical area (For example, the symmetrical area is on the right side of the image when the benchmark eye is the left one, and vice versa). The length of R is L, and the height is H. The ordinate of the rectangle's center should be same as what the benchmark eye has. The values of L and H are calculated as follows:

$$L = \begin{cases} W_I - x - 2 * a, & if \quad E_b = E_b^L \\ x - 2 * a, & else \end{cases}$$ (7)

$$H = 8a \tan 10$$

Here W_I is the length of the image, x is the abscissa of benchmark eye's center, and a is half value of the width of benchmark eye. We define a sliding window SW which has the same size as benchmark eye. The region cut by the SW in the R is defined as a matching region and added to the set T. After several experiments we set the step length of SW to 1/10 of a.

(3) Calculate the similarity of matching regions and benchmark eye

Cutting a small block A_c with $P * Q$ pixels size in the center of the benchmark eye, and then flip A_c horizontally to get block B_c. For each matching region $T_i(i = 0, 1, ..., k)$ in the set T, similarly, cutting small blocks $T_{ic}(c = 0, 1, ..., k)$ with the same size. Then we calculate the similarity value l_i of T_{ic} and B_c:

$$l_i = \frac{\sum_{p=0}^{P-1} \sum_{q=0}^{Q-1} [T_{ic}(p,q) - \overline{T_{ic}}][B_c(p,q) - \overline{B_c}]}{\sqrt{\sum_{p=0}^{P-1} \sum_{q=0}^{Q-1} [T_{ic}(p,q) - \overline{T_{ic}}]^2 \sum_{p=0}^{P-1} \sum_{q=0}^{Q-1} [B_c(p,q) - \overline{B_c}]^2}} \quad (i = 0, 1, ..., k)$$ (8)

The higher l_i is, the more similar matching regions are to the benchmark eye.

We select the matching region T whose similarity value l is the highest of all l_i. If l is greater than the threshold τ, we believe that the matching region T is what we find. Otherwise, the matching region is abandoned, which means the fixing module do not find the other eye in the image. In this paper, the threshold value τ is set to 0.7.

3 Experimental Results

Experiments are carried out on two public dual-eye iris image database, CASIA-IrisV4-Distance (short for Distance) and MIR-Train (short for MIR). The following experiments were performed using VS2013 on an Intel Core i7-6700HQ 2.60 GHz processor with 8 Gbyte RAM.

3.1 Evaluation Protocol

In the experiments, we demonstrate the efficiency and usefulness of the proposed methods via eyes localization accuracy and the execution speed. Here, several indicators are used to measure the performance.

There are four kinds of results in an eye localization problem. The regions that the method localized are exactly human eye regions, which is called true positive (TP). In this paper, the true positive is defined only when the region localized by the method covers 100% of the iris region given by the standard answer. Oppositely, the regions that the method localized are unfortunately not human eye regions, which is defined as false positive (FP). Similarly, false negative (FN) means the human eye regions which the method fails to localize. And true negative (TN) is the non-eye regions that the method do not localized.

Two indicators are set to measure the accuracy of the proposed method. True positives rate (TPR) is defined as formula 9, the larger it is, the better. And false positive rate (FPR) is defined as formula 10, the smaller it is, the better.

$$
\begin{aligned}
\text{TPR} &= \text{TP}/(\text{TP}+\text{FN}) \\
\text{FPR} &= \text{FP}/(\text{TP}+\text{FP})
\end{aligned}
\tag{9}
$$

3.2   Results on Distance and MIR Iris Image Databases

There are 2567 images in Distance, and the first 1067th images are chosen as the train set, while the rest 1500 images are left as the test set. Table 1 shows the experimental result in Distance. From Table 1, we can see that the result is really ideal, which relates a lot with the high quality of the iris images. The distance with the volunteers and the sensor is constant, which is a great convenience for our localization.

Table 1. Performance Comparison

Iris image database	Train set no.	Test set no.	Method	Accuracy		Execution speed (ms)
				TPR	FPR	
Distance	1067	1500	our method	100.0%	0.00%	104
MIR	2500	2000	our method	99.75%	0.05%	60
Distance	1067	1500	gabor + svm	93.90%	4.50%	1800
MIR	2500	2000	gabor + svm	83.04%	5.60%	1100
Distance	1067	1500	haar + adaboost	94.10%	5.90%	650
MIR	2500	2000	haar + adaboost	90.72%	3.20%	400

And for MIR, we select the first 2500th images of all 4500 images as the training database, at the same time, leave the rest 2000 images as the testing database. Table 1 shows how our method and another two mainstream methods perform on these two image sets, and we can see that our method performs better.

3.3   Comparison Results with Mainstream Methods

Here, we introduce normalized error to measure the precision of the mainstream methods and our method. In the experiment, we use small rectangles to label the detected eyes, and naturally regard the center of the rectangle as the detected-eye center. Therefore, in order to measure the localization error, we can use the distance between the ground truth and the detected-eye center. For comparison between different methods, we employ a normalized error in our experiment. The normalized error can be measured by the quotient between the localization error and the ground-truth intraocular distance [9]. The normalized error is defined as follows:

$$err = \max(d_l, d_r)/d_{lr} \tag{10}$$

Here (d_l, d_r) is the Euclidean distance between the detected-eye's position and the actual eye's position, and d_{ij} is the Euclidean distance between actual left eye and the right eye.

First, the minimum enclosing rectangles of the pupils in Distance was marked manually. The center of rectangle is considered as the center of eyes as before. Then, the proposed method was compared with Haar + Adaboost algorithm and Gabor + SVM algorithm, which are mainstream feature learning methods. Figure 3 shows the variation of accumulative accuracy with different admissible errors.

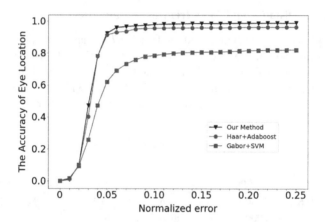

Fig. 3. Eye location accuracy of each method

92% outputs of the normalized error are below 0.05 and 98% percent outputs of the normalized error are below 0.1, which is very competitive compared with that wherein Haar + Adaboost algorithm and Gabor + SVM algorithm. But we also find the question that all the algorithms perform not well if we ask for the outputs whose normalized error less than or equal to 0.04. Two reasons may cause this result: (1) our eye localization method based on light spots detection, so it is unavoidable to bring error into the result of experiment; (2) Subjective error of manual calibration.

4 Conclusions

In this paper, we have presented an accurate and fast eye localization algorithm for dual-eye iris images. There are three major contributions.

First, a fast and accurate eye localization algorithm is proposed. It employs FAST algorithm to detect the light spot areas, and mark them as candidates. Because eyes are well-structured, HOG features are tend to be an eligible feature to represent eyes. Therefore, we train SVM classifier with HOG features to select true eye areas from the candidates.

Second, as there are cases that the algorithm can only localize one eye, we design the fixing module. Information of the detected eye is used to draw a possible area of the other eye. And comparing the similarity of the selected area and the detected eye region, we search the other eye in the possible area.

Third, because most iris cameras are designed with infrared light, and that, in most cases, there are light spots presented around pupils, our method is universal.

Extensive experimental results on two challenging public iris image databases show that the proposed method achieves state-of-the-art eye localization accuracy, while being computationally efficient. We also compare our method with other mainstream methods by the normalized error,and it shows that the result is very competitive.

Acknowledgement. This work is supported by research grants from Hangzhou Daishi Technology Co. Ltd, China.

References

1. Jianqiang, F., Wenbo, L., Shenglin, Y.: Eyes location based on gray-level integration projection. J. Computer Simulation. **22**(4), 75–76, 104 (2005)
2. Wencheng, W., Faliang, C.: A precise eye localization method based on region projection. J. Optoelectron. Laser **22**(4), 618–622 (2011)
3. Heisele, B., Serre, T., Pontil, M., Vetter, T., Poggio, T.: Categorization by learning and combining object parts. J. Adv. Neural Inf. Process. Syst. **2**, 1239–1245 (2002)
4. Xusheng, T.: Fast locating human eyes in complex background. J. Comput.-Aided Des. Comput. Graph. **18**(10), 1535–1540 (2006). in Chinese
5. Kim, H., Kim, W.: Eye detection in facial images using zernike moments with SVM. J. ETRI J. **30**(2), 335–337 (2008)
6. Fok, H.C.T., Abdesselam, B.: A hierarchical learning network for face detection with inplane rotation. J. Neurocomput. **71**(16), 3253–3263 (2008)
7. Rosten, E., Drummond, T.: Machine learning for high-speed corner detection. In: Leonardis, A., Bischof, H., Pinz, A. (eds.) ECCV 2006. LNCS, vol. 3951, pp. 430–443. Springer, Heidelberg (2006). doi:10.1007/11744023_34
8. David Sánchez A, V.: Advanced support vector machines and kernel methods. J. Neurocomput. **55**, 5–20 (2003)
9. Song, M., Tao, D., Sun, Z., Li, X.: Visual-context boosting for eye detection. J. IEEE Trans. Syst. Man Cybern. **40**(6), 1460–1467 (2010)

Visible Spectral Iris Segmentation via Deep Convolutional Network

Yuqing He[✉], Saijie Wang, Kuo Pei, Mingqi Liu, and Jiawei Lai

Key Laboratory of Photoelectronic Imaging Technology and System,
Ministry of Education of China, School of Optoelectronics,
Beijing Institute of Technology, Beijing 100081, China
yuqinghe@bit.edu.cn

Abstract. Iris segmentation is the prerequisite for the precise iris recognition. Visible spectral iris images may result in lower segmentation accuracy due to noise interference. We use deep learning method to segment the iris region in visible spectral iris images. A deep convolution neural network is designed to extract the eye features and segment the iris, pupil, sclera and background. It's an end-to-end model which requires no further processing. We collect the eye images and manually mask different part of the eye to establish the visible spectral iris dataset for training and testing. The proposed method was trained based on DeepLab framework. Experimental results show that the proposed method has efficiency on iris segmentation.

Keywords: Iris segmentation · Convolution neural network · Deep learning

1 Introduction

Iris recognition is a highly reliable and widely accepted biometrics recognition method because of its stability and uniqueness. Iris segmentation is a key technique in iris recognition, since the segmentation precision may affect the effective iris texture area and incorrect area may cause the error iris code. Near infrared images are widely used in iris recognition. Visible iris images are easier to obtain in normal conditions. But iris localization and segmentation is more difficult in visible spectrum because of its fuzzy boundary and image noise.

Many methods have been proposed for unconstrained visible spectral iris segmentation. Tan [1] used clustering for iris localization followed with prediction and curvature models for eyelid and eyelash detection. Li [2] and Sahmoud [3] localized the iris region by K-means clustering and applied Hough transform to localize the limbic boundary. Sankowski [4] and Chen [5] determined the threshold in YIQ and HIS color space respectively, and localized iris boundaries through Daugman's integro-differential operator. Wang et al. [6] localized the iris region by Circular Hough Transform in different color space of RGB and $l\alpha\beta$. Hu [7] located the iris region by a coarse iris map based on the correlation histogram of super-pixels and combined three individual models with Daugman's integro-differential operator. Soliman [8] proposed a coarse-to-fine algorithm to achieve an acceptable accuracy, during which binary transformation and morphological processing are all included. Simultaneously, Annapoorani [9] also

© Springer International Publishing AG 2017
J. Zhou et al. (Eds.): CCBR 2017, LNCS 10568, pp. 428–435, 2017.
https://doi.org/10.1007/978-3-319-69923-3_46

developed the iris segmentation method comprising reflection map computation, bilinear interpolation and edge-based segmentation technique. Ouabida [10] put forward iris segmentation algorithm through a self-ruling active contour approach based on optical correlation algorithm and featured at its less computational time and better accuracy. However, the problem of incorrect iris segmentation still exist. And these algorithms are more complex compared with the end-to-end model.

In recently years, deep learning is an efficient method because of its powerful feature extraction ability and end-to-end process. There are many researches of image segmentation using deep learning. Long et al. [11] proposed the fully convolutional network for semantic segmentation. Noh et al. [12] proposed a novel semantic segmentation algorithm by learning a deconvolution network. Chen et al. [13] proposed a "DeepLab" system that improved the pixel-level segmentation by atrous convolution and conditional random fields. Liu el at. [14] addressed semantic image segmentation by incorporating rich information into Markov Random Field and proposed a Convolutional Neural Network (CNN, or ConvNet), namely Deep Parsing Network. Chandra and Kokkinos [15] proposed a combination of the Gaussian Conditional Random Field with Deep Learning for the task of structured prediction. Badrinarayanan el at. [16] proposed a deep fully CNN architecture named SegNet for semantic pixel-wise segmentation. Most of the segmentation methods are tested on ordinary objects such as cars, people, animals. Few research is about iris segmentation. Liu et al. [17] proposed hierarchical convolutional neural network and multi-scale fully convolutional network model for iris segmentation The method only segment the iris part. It is a novel approach to use deep learning for segmenting different part of the visible spectral eye.

Here, we proposed an iris segmentation algorithm (also including pupil and sclera segmentation) based on deep convolutional network. We established a convolutional neural network for the eye segmentation. And we trained and tested the network in a dataset which built by ourselves. The CNN learned the features of iris, pupil and sclera automatically and achieved a pixel-level segmentation of the iris region.

The rest of paper is organized as follows. In Sect. 2, the algorithm framework and the deep CNN model is introduced. In Sect. 3, our experimental results are shown and compared with traditional method. Section 4 gives the conclusions.

2 Deep CNN Based Iris Segmentation Algorithm

2.1 Algorithm Framework

Traditional iris segmentation methods include some steps of the pupil edge detection, sclera edge detection and eyelids detection, separately. Each step uses different algorithm or parameters, which results in lower efficiency of the segmentation. The deep CNN based iris segmentation algorithm is an end-to-end model. In the model, the original eye images is the input, after the whole image calculation and analyzing, the segmentation results of different part of the eyes can be got. Here we divided the eye image into 4 parts, the pupil, iris, sclera and the background. The iris recognition algorithm mainly focuses on the iris part, but the other parts may also provide supplementary information for the personal recognition.

We divide the algorithm into two steps which is shown in Fig. 1. First, we build a deep convolutional neural network and train the network on the dataset. The network learns the feature of different part of the eye image automatically without manual intervention. The weight model can be got in this step. Next, we load the weight model of the network and achieve pixel-level eye segmentation.

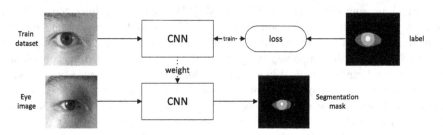

Fig. 1. The framework of the algorithm

2.2 Deep CNN Structure

In machine learning, CNN is a class of deep, feed-forward artificial neural network that have successfully been applied to analyzing visual imagery. A CNN consists of an input and an output layer, as well as multiple hidden layers. The hidden layers are either convolutional (Conv), pooling (subsampling) or fully connected (FC). The typical CNN architecture is shown in Fig. 2 [18].

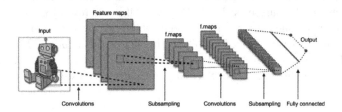

Fig. 2. Typical CNN architecture

Our deep CNN structure is modified from the DeepLab model [12]. The DeepLab model for semantic segmentation need more texture details in image. But the texture of human eye is simple so we simplify the DeepLab structure for our iris segmentation task. The proposed deep CNN structure is shown in Fig. 3. It has 5 groups including 5 Conv/Pooling layers and 3 FC layers. The ReLU activation function is used by neurons. The dropout is also be used to allow the network to learn a more robust relationship. In order to generate an equal-size mask, an interpolation layer is added before softmax layer.

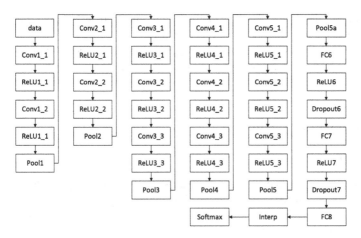

Fig. 3. Proposed CNN structure

2.3 Parameters of the Structure

The parameters of every layer are shown in Table 1. The CNN structure is similar to VGG-16 net but there are some changes such as the kernel size of pooling layers and the dilated convolution layers. Different group of the Conv/Pooling layer can reveal different features of the eye. Most of the convolutional layers' parameters are set conventionally with the kernel size is 3 and pad is 1. The dilated convolution layers lead to a larger receptive field. The stride of the forth and fifth pooling layers is changed to 1 so that the feature map of the network is denser than original VGG-16 net. Similarly to FCN [11], the fully connected layers are replaced by the convolution layers with the kernel size of 1. The dropout ratio of the dropout layers is set to 0.5. The interpolation layer magnifies the feature maps by 8 times.

During training, the stochastic gradient descent method is applied for optimization. The base learning rate is set to 0.001. The momentum and weight_decay are 0.9 and

Table 1. The parameters of proposed CNN structure

Layer name	Type	Output number	Parameters
Conv1_x	Convolution	64	kernel size = 3, pad = 1
Conv2_x	Convolution	128	kernel size = 3, pad = 1
Conv3_x	Convolution	256	kernel size = 3, pad = 1
Conv4_x	Convolution	512	kernel size = 3, pad = 1
Conv5_x	Convolution	512	kernel size = 3, pad = 2, dilation = 2
Pool1,2,3	MAX pooling	/	kernel size = 3, pad = 1, stride = 2
Pool4,5	MAX pooling	/	kernel size = 3, pad = 1, stride = 1
Pool5a	AVE pooling	/	kernel size = 3, pad = 1, stride = 1
FC6	Convolution	1024	kernel size = 3, pad = 12, dilation = 12
FC7	Convolution	1024	kernel size = 1
FC8	Convolution	4	kernel size = 1

0.0005. We use the "step" learning rate policy to automatically decrease the learning rate. The total iteration number is set to 100000.

After training, the weights in the network can be got and saved as a model file. When we use the network to segment the eye images, the weights are load in the same network and do forward propagation. We can get the eye segmentation results in the final layer.

3 Experimental Results

3.1 Dataset

We tested our proposed algorithm on a visible spectral iris dataset [6] which is captured by ourselves through MEIZU4 pro mobile phone and Sony nex5c camera. The dataset contains 350 eye images. We randomly select 270 images as training set and 80 images as test set. All images are adjusted to 321×321 pixels after preprocessing and some of the images are rotated $0 \sim \pm 45°$ to simulate the possible unconstrained conditions. We manually mark the correct label of each pixel for different part of the eye images including background, sclera, iris and pupil. Hence we produce an equal-sized mask for each image. Every image corresponds a grayscale image as label image (or the groundtruth image). In the label image, the different grayscale value represent the background, sclera, iris and pupil. The eye images and the label images are shown in Fig. 4.

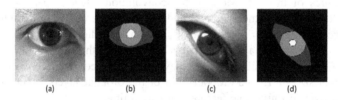

Fig. 4. The eye images and label images. (a)(c) eye images in dataset; (b)(d) the corresponding label images after image enhance.

The NIR iris image's quality is higher than the visible spectral iris images, hence the proposed method is applicable for NIR iris images theoretically. We didn't test our method in NIR iris images because the parameters we got in the visible spectral iris dataset can't be used in NIR images directly.

3.2 Results and Comparison

We use DeepLab as the development framework to train and test our iris segmentation model and analyze the algorithm. It is a state-of-art deep learning system for semantic image segmentation built on top of Caffe. The hardware of experimental platform is configured with 2.6 GHz CPU frequency, 8 GB DDR3 memory and GTX970M GPU on PC.

After training and test, we can get the segmentation results in the final layer of the deep CNN. The deep CNN model segment different regions into different grayscale values. Some segmentation results are shown in Fig. 5.

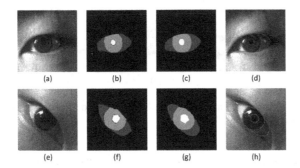

(a)　　　　(b)　　　　(c)　　　　(d)

(e)　　　　(f)　　　　(g)　　　　(h)

Fig. 5. Segmentation results of proposed method. (a)(e) eye images; (b)(f) the label images; (c) (g) the segmentation results; (d)(h) the edge of the segmentation images in the eye images.

We analyze the pixel-level error of the experimental results. The error ratio of one image is denoted as follows

$$error = \frac{segment\_pixels \oplus groundtruth\_pixels}{m \times n} \tag{1}$$

where m, n are the length and width of test image, respectively. The *segment_pixels* and *groundtruth_pixels* are respectively the generated mask and the ground truth. The $\oplus$ in the equation represents the XOR operation to evaluate the disagreeing pixels between groundtruth and segmentation result.

The proposed eye segmentation method achieves the error between 0.4%–1.5% for one image. The average error in test dataset is about 0.7%.

We also calculate the IoU (Intersection-over-Union) accuracy which is defined as follow:

$$IoU = \frac{segment\_pixels \cap groundtruth\_pixels}{segment\_pixels \cup groundtruth\_pixels} \tag{2}$$

The IoU measure gives the similarity between the predicted region and the groundtruth region for an object presented in the image, and is defined as the size of the intersection divided by the union of the two regions. The IoU accuracy of the test dataset is about 92%.

From the generated mask, we can see the error pixels only distribute on the edge of the different regions and there is no significant segmentation error in large area.

To compare the deep learning based method with the traditional segmentation method, we achieved the Xue Wang's method [6] on the same dataset. It using Circular Hough Transform on different color components to get the edge of the eye's different part. Figure 6 shows an example of the comparison. From the result, we can see the proposed method can be more accurate for the edge segmentation.

And we also test the accuracy and the execution time of the Xue Wang's method and the proposed method. We achieved the semantic segmentation network [11] for our eye image segmentation as the comparison with deep learning method. The accuracy is

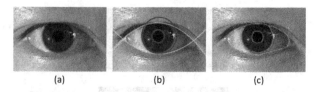

(a)   (b)   (c)

Fig. 6. Comparison of proposed method and traditional method. (a) original eye image; (b) Xue Wang's method; (c) proposed method.

evaluated by the visual inspection of each image and its segmentation result is classified as either correct or incorrect. We didn't evaluate the method by pixel-level error because we are more concerned about the overall segmentation results of the general area. The execution time is defined as every image's forward propagation time in CNN. It can also be considered as the testing time. We didn't consider the training time because we just use the parameters of the training result. The training procedure can be done before the actual use and won't affect the efficiency of the segmentation. Table 2 shows the comparison results. The semantic segmentation network can't segment the pupil well, so we didn't list the low accuracy. From the results, we can see the proposed method has higher accuracy and shorter testing time.

Table 2. Comparison between the proposed method and other methods

Method	Accuracy (%)	Execution time (s)
Wang's [6]	91.3	3.276
Semantic segmentation network [11]	/	0.416
Proposed method	97.5	0.112

Since the image label work needs a lot of efforts, we didn't process plenty samples for our experiment. And there doesn't have such kind of open dataset. Here we just use a certain number of samples to try and test the feasibility of deep learning method in visible spectral iris segmentation. Experimental results indicate that the proposed method has efficiency on iris segmentation.

4   Conclusion

In this paper, we propose a visible spectral iris segmentation algorithm based on deep learning. The method achieves the eye segmentation by building and training a deep CNN. It is verified on the dataset that is build by ourselves. Experimental results show that the proposed method can achieve good performance on visible spectral iris segmentation. It is more accurate and more efficient than traditional iris localization method. In the future, more samples should be used to verify the proposed algorithm.

Acknowledgments. This work is supported by National Science Foundation of China (No. 60905012) and International Fund of Beijing Institute of Technology.

References

1. Tan, T., He, Z., Sun, Z.: Efficient and robust segmentation of noisy iris images for non-cooperative iris recognition. J. Image Vis. Comput. **28**(2), 223–230 (2010)
2. Li, P., Liu, X., Xiao, L., Song, Q.: Robust and accurate iris segmentation in very noisy Iris images. J. Image Vis. Comput. **28**(2), 246–253 (2010)
3. Sahmoud, S.A., Abuhaiba, I.S.: Efficient iris segmentation method in unconstrained environments. J. Pattern Recogn. **46**(46), 3174–3185 (2013)
4. Sankowski, W., Grabowski, K., Napieralska, M., et al.: Reliable algorithm for iris segmentation in eye image. J. Image Vis. Comput. **28**(28), 231–237 (2010)
5. Chen, Y., Adjouadi, M., Han, C., et al.: A highly accurate and computationally efficient approach for unconstrained iris segmentation. J. Image Vis. Comput. **28**(2), 261–269 (2010)
6. Wang, X., He, Y., Pei, K., Liang, M., He, J.: Combining multiple color components for efficient visible spectral iris localization. In: You, Z., Zhou, J., Wang, Y., Sun, Z., Shan, S., Zheng, W., Feng, J., Zhao, Q. (eds.) CCBR 2016. LNCS, vol. 9967, pp. 366–373. Springer, Cham (2016). doi:10.1007/978-3-319-46654-5_40
7. Hu, Y., Sirlantzis, K., Howells, G.: Improving colour iris segmentation using a model selection technique. J. Pattern Recogn. Lett. **57**(1), 24–32 (2015)
8. Soliman, N.F., Mohamed, E., Magdi, F., et al.: Efficient iris localization and recognition. J Optik – Int. J. Light Electron Opt. **140**, 469–475 (2017)
9. Annapoorani, G., Krishnamoorthi, R., Jeya, P.G., et al.: Accurate and fast iris segmentation. Int. J. Eng. Sci. Technol. **2**(6), 1492–1499 (2010)
10. Ouabida, E., Essadique, A., Bouzid, A.: Vander Lugt Correlator based active contours for iris segmentation and tracking. Expert Syst. Appl. **71**, 383–395 (2016)
11. Long, J., Shelhamer, F., Darrell, T.: Fully convolutional networks for semantic segmentation. In: Proceedings of the IEEE Conference on Computer Vision and Pattern Recognition, pp. 3431–3440 (2015)
12. Noh, H., Hong, S., Han, B.: Learning deconvolution network for semantic segmentation. In: Proceedings of the IEEE International Conference on Computer Vision, 1520–1528 (2015)
13. Chen, L.C., Papandreou, G., Kokkinos, I., et al.: Deeplab: semantic image segmentation with deep convolutional nets, atrous convolution, and fully connected CRFs. IEEE Trans. Pattern Anal. Mach. Intell. **PP**(99), 1 (2016)
14. Liu, Z., Li, X., Luo, P., et al.: Semantic image segmentation via deep parsing network. In: Proceedings of the IEEE International Conference on Computer Vision, pp. 1377–1385 (2015)
15. Chandra, S., Kokkinos, I.: Fast, exact and multi-scale inference for semantic image segmentation with deep Gaussian CRFs. In: Leibe, B., Matas, J., Sebe, N., Welling, M. (eds.) ECCV 2016. LNCS, vol. 9911, pp. 402–418. Springer, Cham (2016). doi:10.1007/978-3-319-46478-7_25
16. Badrinarayanan, V., Kendall, A., Cipolla, R.: Segnet: a deep convolutional encoder-decoder architecture for image segmentation. IEEE Trans. Pattern Anal. Mach. Intell. **3**(99), 1 (2015)
17. Liu, N., Li, H., Zhang, M., et al.: Accurate iris segmentation in non-cooperative environments using fully convolutional networks. In: 2016 International Conference on Biometrics (ICB), pp. 1–8. IEEE (2016)
18. Wikipedia. https://en.wikipedia.org/wiki/Convolutional_neural_network

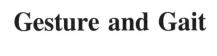

Gesture and Gait

Gesture Recognition Based on Deep Belief Networks

Yunqi Miao[1], Linna Wang[2], Chunyu Xie[1], and Baochang Zhang[1(✉)]

[1] School of Automation Science and Electrical Engineering,
Beihang University, Beijing, China
bczhang@buaa.edu.cn
[2] R&D Center, China Academy of Launch Vehicle Technology, Beijing, China

Abstract. Analyzing the data acquired from the inertial sensor in mobile phones has been proved to be an effective way in gesture recognition. This research introduces deep belief networks (DBN) to solve the inertial sensor-based gesture recognition problem and obtains a satisfactory result on the BUAA Mobile Gesture Database. The optimal architecture and the hyper parameters of DBN were tuned according to the performance of experiments in order to get a high recognition accuracy within short time. Besides, three state-of-the-art methods were tested on the same database and the comparison of results indicates that the proposed method achieved a much better recognition accuracy, which considerably improves the recognition performance.

Keywords: Deep learning · Deep belief networks · Gesture recognition

1 Introduction

As an effective way in human-computer interaction (HCI), gesture recognition [1] is widely applied in the daily life. So far, various statistical and machine learning methods have been utilized in visual recognition [2–4, 20, 21]. Traditionally, after manually extracting the features (e.g. HOG feature) of input images captured by cameras, classifiers (e.g. SVM) are used to recognize the gestures [5]. Recently, some deep learning algorithms, such as Convolutional Neural Networks (CNN) [7, 8, 10, 17], which perform better on the image classification, have been introduced to improve the performance of recognition tasks.

However, researches pay relatively less attention on gesture recognition based on data acquired from devices (e.g. inertial sensor). So far, Kratz [6] conducted Hidden Markov Model (HMM) to recognize the gestures collected by 3D accelerometer, which proved that the recognition accuracy increased with the number of HMM states, which peaked at 93%.

Inspired by the hidden layers theory in the HMM, our research introduced Deep Belief Networks (DBN) into the sensor-based gesture recognition which is capable of improving the recognition accuracy as well as speed. To our knowledge, it is the first time that DBN is introduced to sensor-driven gesture recognition. To achieve a better performance, the raw data was pre-processed as [13]. In the proposed recognition

© Springer International Publishing AG 2017
J. Zhou et al. (Eds.): CCBR 2017, LNCS 10568, pp. 439–446, 2017.
https://doi.org/10.1007/978-3-319-69923-3_47

system, the DBN is served as the feature extractor as well as the classifier to recognize different gestures with both unsupervised and supervised training stages.

2 Deep Belief Network for Gesture Recognition

2.1 Overview of DBN Framework

The architecture of the DBN is shown in Fig. 1, which is a composition of several Restricted Boltzmann machines (RBM) [12] and a Multilayer Perceptron (MLP) connecting to the stacked RBMs can be used to fine-tune the network and for classification.

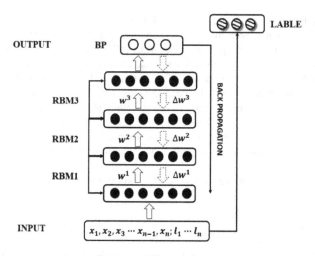

Fig. 1. DBN architecture

2.2 Training Process of DBN

The training algorithm of DBN can be described as an unsupervised pre-training of stacked RBMs followed by a supervised fine-tuning [12].

A graphical depiction of a RBM is shown in Fig. 2. $V = (v_1, v_2, \ldots, v_m)$ stands for the value of m units in the visible layer, and $H = (h_1, h_2, \ldots, h_n)$ stands for the value of n units in the hidden layer. The units are independent to each other in the same layer but fully connected with those in the separate layer with a weight matrix $W_{n \times m}$. $b = (b_1, b_2, \ldots, b_m)$ and $c = (c_1, c_2, \ldots, c_n)$ are the biases of visible and hidden units separately.

Trained in an unsupervised way, the purpose of the RBM is to probabilistically reconstruct the probability distribution of the visible units $P(v)$ [12]. The likelihood function $\mathcal{L}_\theta$ which is needed to be maximized is given by

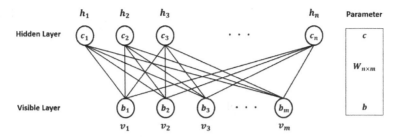

Fig. 2. RBM architecture

$$\mathcal{L}_\theta = \prod_i^m P(v_i). \tag{1}$$

To optimize the parameters, gradient ascent and a fast algorithm called Contrastive Divergence (CD) [11] are used to update the weight. Firstly, $v^{(0)}$ is initialized with the training samples and yield $v^{(k)}$ after k steps of Gibbs sampling (usually k = 1). Then, the change of weights can be approximated by

$$\Delta w_{i,j} = P\left(H_i = 1|v^{(0)}\right) \cdot v_j^{(0)} - P\left(H_i = 1|v^{(k)}\right) \cdot v_j^{(k)}. \tag{2}$$

The performance of the RBM can be estimated by the reconstruction error.

$$err = \left\|v_j^{(0)} - v_j^{(k)}\right\|. \tag{3}$$

In the fine-tuning stage, the weights of the hidden layers of a MLP are initialized with the weights that well-trained by the unsupervised stage and then the back propagation algorithm is used to minimize the training error.

3 Experiment on BUAA Mobile Gesture Database

3.1 Database and Data Pre-processing

The experiment was conducted on the BUAA Mobile Gesture Database [13]. A total of 1120 samples are collected from 8 kinds of gesture (A, B, C, D, 1, 2, 3, 4 respectively) and each sample includes three-dimensional acceleration and angular velocity of mobile phone.

To eliminate the discrimination, energy model of raw data was computed and the mean feature of each sample was extracted as the paper [13] which was a 34×2 vector and then was flatten into a 1×68 vector as the input data vector of the DBN. Also, a 14-fold cross validation was used to increase the generalization ability of the model, where each category training set had 130 samples and the test set had 10 samples.

Moreover, samples were divided into several mini-batches (size = 5) in both pre-training and fine-tuning, and weights were updated after each mini-batch, which accelerated the training process [18].

3.2 Parameters Tuning

The proposed DBN algorithm was implemented using MATLAB (R2014a). The system has i5 processor of 2.3 GHz CPU clock speed with 8 GB RAM and 64 bit operating system running with Windows 10. Initially, the optimal parameters of pre-training, including the number of the hidden layers as well as the hidden units, were initialized according to [14, 15, 18] and empirical values based on the size of training set.

Firstly, the performance of the RBMs with different number of hidden layers ($L = \{1, 2, 3, 4, 6, 8, 10\}$) was studied and the top layer's reconstruction error of each structure was analyzed. We found that one-layer RBM had the severest reconstruction error which ranged from 18 to 14 while the top layer's error of other structures can be seen in Fig. 3. Generally, the reconstruction error decreased as the layers added due to the fact that more complex features were learnt [9], except that an increase can be found when the hidden layers changed from 2 to 3.

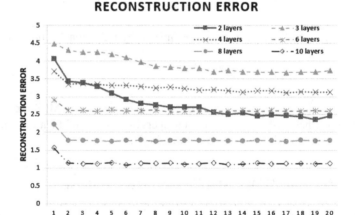

Fig. 3. The top layer's reconstruction error of RBMs with different structures

Moreover, according to paper [14, 18], besides reconstruction error, monitoring the performance on the training data in the supervised stage is also required when choosing the structure. Hence, their corresponding error on the training set was shown in Fig. 4, which showed an opposite trend with the reconstruction error in Fig. 3. Although the error in the unsupervised stage was reducing with the increase of hidden layers in the RBMs, the training error was rising at the same time, which was undesirable. Therefore, 2-layer RBMs which had the minimum training error as well as an acceptable reconstruction error was chosen.

TRAINING ERROR

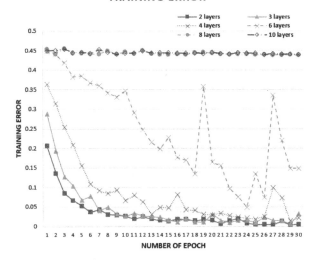

Fig. 4. Training error of RBMs with different structures

Then, according to recipe given by the guide [14, 15], the same number of hidden units on both layers ranging from 7 to 100 were tested with the step of 5 and the 18 units showed the best performance in terms of computing time as well as the correct classification rate on the test set.

After the RBMs were pre-trained, the DBN was fine-tuned in a supervised way where back-propagation (BP) algorithm was used to update the weights. The initial number of epoch was set to 200 and the curve of the first 100 epochs' training error can be seen in Fig. 5. After 60 epochs, the error became stable below 1%. Meanwhile, the corresponding recognition accuracy of the network on the test set are shown in Fig. 6. It can be found that the recognition accuracy increased as the number of fine-tuning

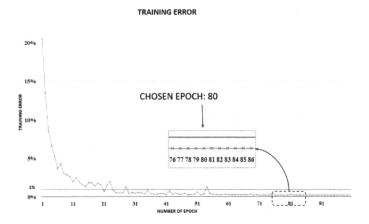

Fig. 5. Training error with the first 100 epochs

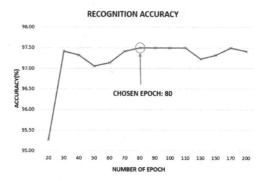

Fig. 6. Recognition accuracy of 200 epochs

epochs rising until 80, with a relatively high and stable accuracy at 97.5%. To avoid the overfitting, early stopping was introduced. Therefore, the number of epoch was fixed to 80 in the fine-tuning, before the recognition accuracy on the test set decreased [18]. In addition, the learning rate of the pre-training and fine-tuning were 0.04 and 1 respectively based on the size of mini-batch and the training set [14, 15].

Hence, the architecture considered for the DBN combined two stacked RBMs and a MLP. For the RBMs, the number of the visible units was 68, corresponding to the dimension of the input data vector and the two hidden layers both had 18 units. The output layer of MLP had 8 units, representing the 8 categories of gesture.

4   Experiment Results and Discussion

4.1   Performance of DBN

The recognition rate of each category based on DBN are shown in the Table 1. The average accuracy reaches 97.4%, proving that the proposed method is an effective way in the gesture recognition on the BUAA mobile gesture database.

Besides, Multi-layer Perceptron (MLP) without pre-training was also experimented for the recognition on the same database. The structure of the MLP was chosen

Table 1. Accuracy by category based on DBN and MLP

ALG[1] ACC[2] CATG*	DBN	MLP	ALG ACC CATG*	DBN	MLP
A	96.40%	96.43%	1	98.57%	96.43%
B	95.70%	95.00%	2	96.40%	97.86%
C	97.14%	95.00%	3	98.57%	99.28%
D	97.85%	98.57%	4	98.57%	99.28%
[1]ALG:Algorithm, [2]ACC: Accuracy, CATG*: Category					

according to the proposed DBN with 68-18-18-8 units in input layer, hidden layer and the output layer respectively. Similarly, the number of epoch was set to 80 and the batch size was set to 5. The results in terms of category can also be seen in the Table 1 and the average accuracy achieves 97.23%.

The similar accuracy can be explained by [16] that pre-training may only help when the structure is deep, so it would be interesting to see how the MLP compares to the DBN when there exists a large amount of training data. The results also give a suggestion that if the training set is relatively small, MLP without pre-training is a wise option.

4.2   Comparison with State-of-the-Art Methods

Other than DBN, three state-of-the-art statistical classification methods, specifically, SVM, KNN and HMM, were also tested on the database in order to compare the recognition performance. The SVM algorithm was conducted with LIBSVM [19] and the KNN selected the nearest Euclidean distance while the HMM used the maximum of likelihood as a decision rule. Table 2 shows the comparison of DBN, KNN and HMM in terms of recognition accuracy. It is obvious that DBN and MLP outperform the other three methods on the BUAA dataset.

Table 2. Recognition results comparison with state-of-the-art methods

Algorithm	DBN	MLP	SVM	KNN	HMM
Accuracy	**97.4%**	97.23%	93.84%	90.54%	91.79%

5   Conclusion

The paper presented a method in the inertial sensor-based gesture recognition using Deep Belief Networks (DBN). The structure and the parameters of the DBN were chosen and fixed theoretically and empirically. The effectiveness of the proposed network is verified by 14-fold cross validation on the BUAA Mobile Gesture Database with the recognition accuracy reaching more than 99% on the training set and 97% on the test set. The results indicate that the proposed method can recognize the gesture effectively and efficiently. Meanwhile, a comparative study is performed among three state-of-the-art statistical classification methods which shows that the proposed method has a much better performance.

References

1. Bansal, B.: Gesture recognition: a survey. Int. J. Comput. Appl. **139**(2), 8–10 (2016)
2. Hasan, H.S., Kareem, S.A.: Human computer interaction for vision based hand gesture recognition: a survey. Artif. Intell. Rev. **43**(1), 1–54 (2015)
3. Rautaray, S.S., Agrawal, A.: Vision based hand gesture recognition for human computer interaction a survey. Artif. Intell. Rev. **43**, 1–54 (2015)

4. Zhang, B., Li, Z., Perina, A., Del Bue, A., Murino, V., Liu, J.: Adaptive local movement modeling for robust object tracking. IEEE Trans. Circ. Syst. Video Technol. **27**(7), 1515–1526 (2017)

5. Song, Y., Davis, R.: Continuous body and hand gesture recognition for natural human-computer interaction. In: International Conference on Artificial Intelligence, pp. 4212–4216. AAAI Press (2015)

6. Kratz, L., Smith, M., Leem F.J.: Wiizards: 3D gesture recognition for game play input. In: Conference on Future Play, pp. 209–212. ACM (2007)

7. Molchanov, P., Gupta, S., Kim, K., et al.: Hand gesture recognition with 3D convolutional neural networks. In: IEEE Conference on Computer Vision and Pattern Recognition Workshops, pp. 1–7. IEEE (2015)

8. Molchanov, P., Yang, X., Gupta, S., et al.: Online detection and classification of dynamic hand gestures with recurrent 3D convolutional neural networks. In: Computer Vision and Pattern Recognition. IEEE (2016)

9. Hinton, G.E., Osindero, S., Teh, Y., et al.: A fast learning algorithm for deep belief nets. Neural Comput. **18**(7), 1527–1554 (2006)

10. Hinton, G.E., Salakhutdinov, R.R.: Reducing the dimensionality of data with neural networks. Science **313**(5786), 504 (2006)

11. Hinton, G.E.: Training products of experts by minimizing contrastive divergence. Neural Comput. **14**(8), 1771 (2002)

12. Fischer, A., Igel, C.: An introduction to restricted Boltzmann machines. In: Alvarez, L., Mejail, M., Gomez, L., Jacobo, J. (eds.) CIARP 2012. LNCS, vol. 7441, pp. 14–36. Springer, Heidelberg (2012). doi:10.1007/978-3-642-33275-3_2

13. Xie, C., Luan, S., Wang, H., Zhang, B.: Gesture recognition benchmark based on mobile phone. In: You, Z., Zhou, J., Wang, Y., Sun, Z., Shan, S., Zheng, W., Feng, J., Zhao, Q. (eds.) CCBR 2016. LNCS, vol. 9967, pp. 432–440. Springer, Cham (2016). doi:10.1007/978-3-319-46654-5_48

14. Hinton, G.E.: A practical guide to training restricted Boltzmann machines. Momentum **9**(1), 599–619 (2012)

15. Bengio, Y.: Practical recommendations for gradient-based training of deep architectures. In: Montavon, G., Orr, G.B., Müller, K.-R. (eds.) Neural Networks: Tricks of the Trade. LNCS, vol. 7700, pp. 437–478. Springer, Heidelberg (2012). doi:10.1007/978-3-642-35289-8_26

16. Vinyals, O., Ravuri, S.V.: Comparing multilayer perceptron to deep belief network tandem features for robust ASR. In: IEEE International Conference on Acoustics, Speech and Signal Processing, pp. 4596–4599. IEEE (2011)

17. Bengio, Y.: Learning Deep Architectures for AI. Now Publishers, Breda (2009)

18. Montavon, G., Orr, G., Mller, K.R.: Neural Networks: Tricks of the Trade. Springer, Heidelberg (2012)

19. Chang, C.-C., Lin, C.-J.: LIBSVM: a library for support vector machines. ACM Trans. Intell. Syst. Technol. **2**, 27:1–27:27 (2011)

20. Zhang, B., Li, Z., Cao, X., et al.: Output constraint transfer for kernelized correlation filter in tracking. IEEE Trans. Syst. Man Cybern. Syst. **PP**(99), 1–11 (2016)

21. Zhang, B., Yang, Y., Chen, C., Han, J., Shao, L.: Action recognition using 3D histograms of texture and a multi-class boosting classifier. IEEE Trans. Image Process. **26**(10), 4648–4660 (2017)

Deepgait: A Learning Deep Convolutional Representation for Gait Recognition

Xianfu Zhang[1,2], Shouqian Sun[1], Chao Li[1(✉)], Xiangyu Zhao[1], and Yuping Hu[3]

[1] College of Computer Science and Technology,
Zhejiang University, Hangzhou 310027, China
{zhangxianfu,ssq,superli,ssagittis}@zju.edu.cn
[2] Wuzhou University, Wuzhou 543002, China
[3] Shaoyang University, Shaoyang 422000, China
huyuping@163.com

Abstract. Human gait, as a soft biometric, helps to recognize people by walking. To further improve the recognition performances, we propose a novel video sensor-based gait representation, DeepGait, using deep convolutional features. DeepGait is generated by using an pre-trained VGG-D net without any fine-tuning. When compared with other traditional hand-crafted gait representations (eg. GEI, FDF and GFI etc.) experimentally on OU-ISR large population (OULP) dataset and CASIA-B dataset, DeepGait has been shown that the performances of the proposed method is outstanding under different walking variations (view, clothing, carrying bags). The OULP dataset, which includes 4007 subjects, makes our result reliable in a statically way. Even in a very low dimension, our proposed gait representation still outperforms the commonly used 11264-dimensional GEI. For further comparison, all the gait representation vectors are available.

Keywords: Gait recognition · Gait representation · Deep convolutional features large population

1 Introduction

Biometrics refers to the use of intrinsic physical or behavioral traits in order to identify humans. Besides regular features (face, fingerprint, iris, DNA and retina), human gait, which can be obtained from people at larger distances and at low resolution without subjects' cooperation has recently attracted much attention. It also has a vast application prospect in crime investigation and wide-area surveillance. For example, criminals usually wear gloves, dark sun-glasses, and face masks to invalidate finger print, eyes, and face recognition. In such scenarios, gait recognition is the only useful and effective identification method. Previous research [1,2] has shown that human gait, specifically the walking pattern, is difficult to disguise and unique to each people.

To the best of our knowledge, [3–6] also make use of deep learning for gait recognition. Recently, in [5], more complex 3D convolutional neural networks

© Springer International Publishing AG 2017
J. Zhou et al. (Eds.): CCBR 2017, LNCS 10568, pp. 447–456, 2017.
https://doi.org/10.1007/978-3-319-69923-3_48

are used while our proposed gait presentation just adopts the simple 2D convolutional neural networks; In [6], they first calculate GEI as the input of 2D convolutional neural networks, and then the deep learning features are generated. Additionally, all these deep learning based methods [3–6] need to be trained from the subsets of gait sequences while our proposed methods don't need any further training.

In this paper, a novel gait representation based on deep convolutional features in each gait cycle, DeepGait, is proposed to further improve the recognition rate. The primary aim of this paper is to propose a new gait representation and evaluate it's effectiveness so that we just consider the simple cooperative conditions. Additionally, euclidean distance based nearest neighbor (NN) method is adopted and the more powerful generative approaches [7–9] discriminative approaches [10,11] and metric learning approaches [12] will not be discussed in this paper.

1.1   Overview

The main contributions of this work are three-fold: (1) introduce the deep learning for gait recognition and propose a new gait representation, (2) improve the recognition performances on the OULP dataset and CASIA-B dataset under cooperative conditions, (3) public all the gait representations and experimental results for further comparison (https://pan.baidu.com/s/1nvv1ci1)

An earlier and preliminary version of our work was published in [13]. However [13] just focused on cross-view evaluations. Compared with [13], this paper provides a more systematic comparison with other appearance-based gait representations. Much more additional works are included: (1) Additional experiments are conducted on a new dataset and more walking variances (clothing, carrying bags) are considered; (2) This paper describes the process of DeepGait in detail, such as the preprocessing steps; (3) Detailed explanations of the mostly used hand-crafted representations are provided; (4) We public all the gait representations for further comparison.

Figure 1 shows the overview of our proposed gait representation. The outline of the paper is organized as follows. Section 2 introduces DeepGait and some famous traditional representations in detail. Section 3 describes details of gait recognition approach and performances evaluation metrics. Section 4 presents the experimental results on two public gait dataset. Section 5 offers our conclusion.

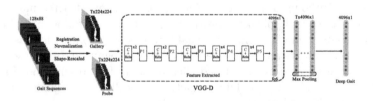

Fig. 1. An illustration of the proposed gait representation. (C: convolution, P: max-pooling, T: gait period).

2 Deep Convolutional Gait Representation

2.1 Registration and Size Normalization of Silhouette Images

CASIA-B just directly provides original gait silhouette images without any pre-processing. To eliminate the scaling effect, we perform registration and size normalization on the original silhouette images. Firstly, to obtain silhouette images' region of interest (ROI), we extracted each image's horizontal center, top and bottom regions [14,15]. Secondly, we cropped each frame according to the first step's regions to perform centralization. Finally, we scaled the ROI image with size of 128×88 and centralization were performed on ROI to make testing easier for all subjects. Figure 2 shows the original silhouette image (a) and the registration and normalization silhouette image (b). However, the OULP dataset provides high-quality silhouette image after registration and normalization with the fixed size (128×88). Thus, it is not necessary to perform preprocessing. The preprocessing makes experimental results comparable and reliable between the two dataset.

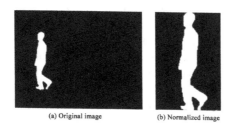

(a) Original image   (b) Normalized image

Fig. 2. Original silhouette image and normalized silhouette image.

2.2 Gait Period Estimation

Similar with the other appearance-based gait recognition method, the first step for DeepGait generation is gait period detection. As in [14,15], we calculated the Normalized Auto Correlation (NAC) of each normalized gait sequence along the temporal axis:

$$NAC(N) = \frac{\sum_{x,y} \sum_{n=0}^{N_{total}-N-1} S(x,y,n)S(x,y,n+N)}{\sqrt{\sum_{x,y} \sum_{n=0}^{N_{total}-N-1} S(x,y,n)^2} \sqrt{\sum_{x,y} \sum_{n=0}^{N_{total}-N-1} S(x,y,n+N)^2}} \tag{1}$$

where $NAC(N)$ stands for the autocorrelation for the N frame shift which can quantify periodic gait motion. N_{total} is the number of frames in each gait sequence. $S(x,y,n)$ is the silhouette gray value at position of (x,y) on the n-th frame. Empirically for the natural gait period, the domain of N is set to be $[20, 40]$ and the gait period is estimated as:

$$T_{gait} = arg \max_{N \in [20,40]} NAC(N) \qquad (2)$$

where T_{gait} is the gait period. We have made public the code and result (large deviations was manually modified) in https://pan.baidu.com/s/1eSNvMmu.

2.3 Deep Convolution Activation Features

In this paper, a state-of-the-art deep convolutional model (VGG-D) [16] which is consisting of 16 convolutional and pooling layers was first trained in a fully supervised setting. The convolutional model just uses very small convolution filters (3×3) and was the winner of ILSVRC-2014. We then used the responses from the pre-trained CNN model using ImageNet dataset [17] (classification annotations only) as generic features for gait representation generation.

Feature Extraction. In order to extract deep learned features for gait representation generalization, the size of input gait silhouette images must be compatible with VGG-D's input size which is known as 224×224 pixel size. We first rescaled each image to fixed size. Features were then computed by forward propagating a mean-subtracted and size-fixed (224×224) gait image through 17 convolutional/pooling layers and 2 fully connected layers using Caffe, a open source CNN library [18]. According to the other vision tasks [19–22], the first fully connected layer's $(fc6)$ features outcome the other layers' features. Unless otherwise specified, we extracted the 4096-dimensional $fc6$ features as deep convolutional features for gait representation generalization.

Representation Generalization. In one gait period, if there are T silhouette images, we can generate T $fc6$ features. Each element (i) of 4096-dimensional gait representation (DeepGait) can then be generated from maxing the $fc6$ features by using Eq. 3.

$$DeepGait_i = \max_{k=0}^{T-1} fc6_{i,k}, 0 \le i \le 4095 \qquad (3)$$

2.4 Gait Representations for Performance Comparison

We compared the performances of DeepGait with such state-of-the-art gait representations: Gait Flow Image (GFI) [23], Gait Energy Image (GEI) [24], Masked GEI based on GEnI (MGEI) [25], Frequency-Domain Feature (FDF) [15], and Gait Entropy Image (GEnI) [26]. Similar with the procedure of most appearance-based method, we first finished the pre-processing steps and estimated the gait sequences' period. Some examples of each feature is shown in Fig. 3. In the following sub-sections, we explain the details of such traditional hand-crafted representations.

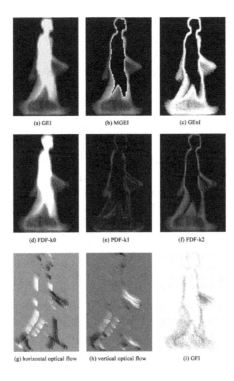

(a) GEI   (b) MGEI   (c) GEnI

(d) FDF-k0   (e) PDF-k1   (f) FDF-k2

(g) horizontal optical flow   (h) vertical optical flow   (i) GFI

Fig. 3. Examples of hand-crafted gait representations.

3   Gait Recognition

Usually, a more discriminative gait representation and a more powerful classify method can both improve the recognition performances. If the representation is discriminative enough, a simple classify method can even achieve a better result. In this paper, we just used the euclidean distance to evaluate the efficacy of DeepGait.

3.1   Euclidean Distance for Direct Matching

For gait verification, two gait sequences P_i and G_j were given, and we calculated the similar score ($SimScore$) simply using the Euclidean distance. For a better performance, L_2 normalization was applied for the gait representations. Equation 4 shows the detail.

$$SimScore_{i,j} = -||\frac{P_i}{||P_i||} - \frac{G_j}{||G_j||}||$$ (4)

For gait identification, nearest neighbor (NN), an unsupervised classification method was used. The probe sample P is classified as class i, if the final $SimScore$ with all the gallery (G_i) is the maximum as shown in Eq. 5.

$$i = arg \max_{i \in [0, N_{gallery-1}]} SimScore(P, G_i) \tag{5}$$

where $N_{gallery}$ is the number of training subjects. In the experiments, we just used the first period of the gait sequence.

4 Experiments

The first experiment was performed on the OULP dataset [14]. Because of the large population(nearly 4000 subjects), we can evaluate the performances of DeepGait in a statistically reliable manner. The second experiment was performed on the CASIA-B dataset [27] that is composed of gait sequences from a wide variety of views and has lower quality silhouette images. The recognition performances were evaluated using rank-1 and rank-5 identification rates.

4.1 OULP Dataset

The OULP dataset has nearly 4000 subjects, and each subject has two video sequences (Gallery, Probe). Because of the largest population, this experimental results can be calculated in a statistically reliable way. Based on the video sensor's recorded angle (55°, 65°, 75°, 85°), they divided each gait sequence into four subsets (**View-55, View-65, View-75** and **View-85**) respectively.

We first evaluated the performances of DeepGait under different observation angles (**View-55, View-65, View-75, View-85**) to find the views' effect on our proposed representation. Then, we compared the recognition result with traditional methods. Table 1 shows the rank-1 and rank-5 identification rates using the simple NN classifier. Compared with the others, DeepGait achieves much better performances with the largest population dataset as to rank-1 and rank-5

Table 1. Comparison of rank-1/rank-5 identification rates on the OULP dataset. (Direct Matching) (%)

Rank-1/Rank-5	Dataset	#Subjects	DeepGait	GEI	MGEI	GEnI	FDF	GFI
rank-1	**View-55**	3,706	**90.6**	85.3	79.3	75.1	83.1	61.9
	View-65	3,770	**91.2**	85.6	83.2	77.3	84.7	66.6
	View-75	3,751	**91.2**	86.1	84.6	79.1	86.0	69.3
	View-85	3,249	**92.0**	85.3	83.9	80.7	85.6	69.8
	Mean		**91.3**	85.6	82.8	78.1	84.9	66.9
rank-5	**View-55**	3,706	**96.0**	91.8	89.3	85.5	91.0	75.5
	View-65	3,770	**96.0**	92.3	91.5	87.7	92.3	79.5
	View-75	3,751	**96.1**	92.2	92.0	88.8	92.5	81.3
	View-85	3,249	**96.5**	92.6	91.9	89.3	92.3	81.9
	Mean		**96.2**	92.2	91.2	87.8	92.0	79.6

metrics. The result shows that DeepGait, using the simple classify method (NN), retains powerful discrimination even over large population condition. From the four different views' results, we can see that the performances of Deep Gait, GEI and FDF are nearly the same under different observation views. Our proposed DeepGait is independent of view change.

Table 2. The rank-1 identification rates and it's Standard Deviation (Std) using DeepGait with different number of principle components k in PCA on the OULP dataset (%).

Dataset	Number of principle components k						Std
	4096	2048	1024	512	256	128	
View-55	**90.6**	90.5	89.9	89.7	89.0	86.9	1.25
View-65	**91.2**	91.1	90.6	89.8	88.9	87.3	1.37
View-75	**91.2**	91.0	90.5	90.0	89.3	87.4	1.28
View-85	**92.0**	91.9	91.2	92.2	90.5	89.7	0.90
Mean	**91.3**	91.1	90.1	90.4	89.4	87.8	1.2

In order to evaluate the compactness of DeepGait, PCA was used to reduce the dimension of DeepGait before recognition, and only the rank-1 metric was adapted. Table 2 shows the dimension reduction results of DeepGait. More specifically, the rank-1 identification rates fluctuate very little and the mean Strand Deviation is just 1.2% among different number of principle components. Even in a very low dimension (128-D), our proposed gait representation still retains the discriminative power.

4.2 CASIA Dataset

DeepGait was further tested on the CASIA-B dataset. As in [27], we just used rank-1 identification rates to measure different methods' performances. In CASIA-B, totally 124 subjects gait data are captured from 11 views ($0°$-$180°$). Between two nearest view directions, the interval angle is $18°$. Three covariate condition changes, i.e., clothing, carrying, and view changes are considered. In this dataset, each subject has 10 gait sequences: 6 normal walking sequences (nm), 2 carrying-bag sequences (bg), and 2 wearing-coat sequences (cl).

In this section, the experiments were divided into two main parts. In the first part, we compared DeepGait with other representation under different view condition. For 6 normal sequences, the first 4 of them were taken as the gallery, and the last 2 of them were used as the probe. Table 3 shows the comparison results. In the second part, the proposed method was compared with other existing representations for three cases of different gallery and probe combinations: the gallery and probe were both chosen from normal walking sequences (nm, nm); the gallery and probe were both chosen from carrying-bag sequences (bg, bg), and the gallery and probe were both chosen from wearing-coat sequences (cl, cl) under side view ($90°$). In (nm, nm), we just chose the fifth of normal

Table 3. Rank-1 identification rates under different views on CASIA dataset (Direct Matching) (%).

Representations	0°	18°	36°	54°	72°	90°	108°	126°	144°	162°	180°	Mean
GEI	92.0	86.5	82.0	89.5	92.5	93.5	92.0	93.5	94.5	94.5	96.0	91.5
MGEI	85.5	74.5	76.0	85.5	89.5	91.0	89.0	89.5	87.5	92.0	95.0	86.8
GEnI	92.5	90.5	85.5	87.5	91.5	92.0	94.0	92.0	92.5	95.0	94.3	91.6
FDF	93.0	87.5	82.0	88.5	91.5	93.0	91.5	92.5	94.5	94.0	95.5	91.2
GFI	86.0	79.0	76.5	85.0	90.5	91.5	88.5	90.5	94.5	95.5	96.5	88.5
DeepGait	**95.4**	**91.3**	**92.1**	**94.2**	**97.1**	**97.7**	**97.7**	**96.7**	**95.8**	**97.5**	**97.1**	**95.7**

walking sequences as gallery set, and the sixth as probe set. As to (cl-cl) and (bg-bg) combinations, we chose the first sequence as gallery set and the second sequence as probe set separately. Table 4 shows the comparison results. Under a similar setting, a rank-1 identification rate of 92.5% is reported by [5] although their their experimental setting is still slightly different from ours (their model needs to be trained with a subset of dataset).

Table 4. Rank-1 identification rates under changes of clothing and carrying conditions on CASIA dataset (Direct Matching) (%).

Representations	nm-nm	bg-bg	cl-cl	Mean
GEI	85.0	75.0	91.0	83.7
MGEI	86.0	71.0	91.0	82.7
GEnI	83.0	75.0	90.0	82.7
FDF	85.0	73.0	91.0	83.0
GFI	88.0	76.0	91.0	85.0
deepCNN [4]	95.6	88.3	76.2	86.7
DeepGait	**96.0**	**90.0**	**97.0**	**94.3**

We find that DeepGait significantly outperforms the traditional hand-crafted gait representations under view, carrying bag and clothing conditions. Considering the different performances between two gait datasets, the final results also depend on the silhouette images' quality. On the other way, DeepGait also achieves a competitive with lower silhouette images' quality.

5 Conclusion

In this paper, we have proposed a new video sensor-based gait representation, DeepGait, for gait recognition. On CASIA-B and OULP dataset, DeepGait has been reported to achieve significantly better performances than previous hand-crafted gait representations. On the OULP dataset, the performances of

DeepGait is better than GEI, MGEI, GEnI, FDF, GFI in a statistically reliable manner using the direct matching. The best rank-1 average identification rate of DeepGait is 92.5%, while the most used method GEI is 87.1%, and FDF is 86.7%. Even in a very low dimension (128), our proposed gait representation still retains the discriminative power. On the CASIA-B dataset, state-of-the-art results of DeepGait indicate that the new gait representation can deal with different variation (eg. clothing, carrying bag and view) under the cooperative conditions. However, the performances decreases on the CASIA-B dataset than on the OULP dataset due to different silhouette images' quality. In the future, we will further do experiments under cross variation conditions (eg. cross view, nm-bg and nm-cl) and collect a larger gait dataset which covers the most variations and has more sequences per subject, so that we can train the deep convolutional model to achieve a better performances.

Acknowledgments. The authors would like to thank OU-ISIR and CBSR for providing access to the OU-ISIR Large Population Gait Database and CASIA-B Gait Database. This study is partly supported by the National Natural Science Foundation of China (No. 61562072).

References

1. Murray, M.P., Drought, A.B., Kory, R.C.: Walking patterns of normal men. J. Bone Joint Surg. Am. **46**(2), 335–360 (1964)
2. Cutting, J.E., Kozlowski, L.T.: Recognizing friends by their walk: gait perception without familiarity cues. Bull. Psychon. Soc. **9**(5), 353–356 (1977)
3. Hossain, E., Chetty, G.: Multimodal feature learning for gait biometric based human identity recognition. In: Lee, M., Hirose, A., Hou, Z.G., Kil, R.M. (eds.) ICONIP 2013. LNCS, vol. 8227, pp. 721–728. Springer, Berlin, Heidelberg (2013)
4. Alotaibi, M., Mahmood, A.: Improved gait recognition based on specialized deep convolutional neural networks. In: 2015 IEEE Applied Imagery Pattern Recognition Workshop, pp. 1–7. IEEE Press, New York (2015)
5. Wolf, T., Babaee, M., Rigoll, G.: Multi-view gait recognition using 3D convolutional neural networks. In: IEEE International Conference on Image Processing, pp. 4165–4169. IEEE Press, New York (2016)
6. Shiraga, K., Makihara, Y., Muramatsu, D., Echigo, T., Yagi, Y.: Geinet: view-invariant gait recognition using a convolutional neural network. In: 2016 International Conference on Biometrics (ICB), pp. 1–8. IEEE Press, New York (2016)
7. Belhumeur, P.N., Hespanha, J.P., Kriegman, D.J.: Eigenfaces vs. fisherfaces: recognition using class specific linear projection. IEEE Trans. Pattern Anal. Mach. Intell. **19**(7), 711–720 (1997)
8. Mansur, A., Makihara, Y., Muramatsu, D., Yagi, Y.: Cross-view gait recognition using view-dependent discriminative analysis. In: 2014 IEEE International Joint Conference on Biometrics (IJCB), pp. 1–8. IEEE Press, New York (2014)
9. Sharma, A., Kumar, A., Daume, H., Jacobs, D.W.: Generalized multiview analysis: a discriminative latent space. In: 2012 IEEE Conference on Computer Vision and Pattern Recognition (CVPR), pp. 2160–2167. IEEE Press, New York (2012)
10. Muramatsu, D., Makihara, Y., Yagi, Y.: View transformation model incorporating quality measures for cross-view gait recognition. IEEE Trans. Cybern. **46**(7), 1602–1615 (2016)

11. Muramatsu, D., Makihara, Y., Yagi, Y.: Cross-view gait recognition by fusion of multiple transformation consistency measures. IET Biom. **4**(2), 62–73 (2015)
12. Ben, X., Zhang, P., Meng, W., Yan, R., Yang, M., Liu, W., Zhang, H.: On the distance metric learning between cross-domain gaits. Neurocomputing **208**, 153–164 (2016)
13. Li, C., Min, X., Sun, S., Lin, W., Tang, Z.: Deepgait: a learning deep convolutional representation for view-invariant gait recognition using joint Bayesian. Appl. Sci. **7**(3), 210 (2017)
14. Iwama, H., Okumura, M., Makihara, Y., Yagi, Y.: The OU-ISIR Gait database comprising the large population dataset and performance evaluation of gait recognition. IEEE Trans. Inf. Forensics Secur. **7**(5), 1511–1521 (2012)
15. Makihara, Y., Sagawa, R., Mukaigawa, Y., Echigo, T., Yagi, Y.: Gait recognition using a view transformation model in the frequency domain. In: Leonardis, A., Bischof, H., Pinz, A. (eds.) Computer Vision - ECCV 2006. LNCS, vol. 3953, pp. 151–163. Springer, Berlin, Heidelberg (2006)
16. Simonyan, K., Zisserman, A.: Very deep convolutional networks for large-scale image recognition. arXiv preprint (2014). arXiv:1409.1556
17. Krizhevsky, A., Sutskever, I., Hinton, G.E.: Imagenet classification with deep convolutional neural networks. In: Proceedings of the 25th International Conference on Neural Information Processing Systems, New York (2012)
18. Jia, Y., Shelhamer, E., Donahue, J., Karayev, S., Long, J., Girshick, R., Guadarrama, S., Darrell, T.: Caffe: convolutional architecture for fast feature embedding. In: Proceedings of the 22nd ACM International Conference on Multimedia, pp. 675–678. ACM, New York (2014)
19. Girshick, R., Donahue, J., Darrell, T., Malik, J.: Rich feature hierarchies for accurate object detection and semantic segmentation. In: Proceedings of the IEEE Conference on Computer Vision and Pattern Recognition, pp. 580–587. IEEE Press, New York (2014)
20. Donahue, J., Jia, Y., Vinyals, O., Hoffman, J., Zhang, N., Tzeng, E., Darrell, T.: Decaf: a deep convolutional activation feature for generic visual recognition. In: Proceedings of the 31st International Conference on Machine Learning, pp. 647–655. ACM, New York (2014)
21. Tran, D., Bourdev, L., Fergus, R., Torresani, L., Paluri, M.: Learning spatiotemporal features with 3D convolutional networks. In: 2015 IEEE International Conference on Computer Vision (ICCV), pp. 4489–4497. IEEE Press, New York (2015)
22. Zhou, B., Lapedriza, A., Xiao, J., Torralba, A., Oliva, A.: Learning deep features for scene recognition using places database. In: Advances in Neural Information Processing Systems, pp. 487–495 (2014)
23. Lam, T.H., Cheung, K.H., Liu, J.N.: Gait flow image: a silhouette-based gait representation for human identification. Pattern Recogn. **44**(4), 973–987 (2011)
24. Man, J., Bhanu, B.: Individual recognition using gait energy image. IEEE Trans. Pattern Anal. Mach. Intell. **28**(2), 316–322 (2006)
25. Bashir, K., Xiang, T., Gong, S.: Gait recognition without subject cooperation. Pattern Recogn. Lett. **31**(13), 2052–2060 (2010)
26. Bashir, K., Xiang, T., Gong, S.: Gait recognition using gait entropy image. In: 3rd International Conference on Crime Detection and Prevention (ICDP 2009), pp. 1–6. IET, Stevenage Herts (2009)
27. Yu, S., Tan, D., Tan, T.: A framework for evaluating the effect of view angle, clothing and carrying condition on gait recognition. In: 18th International Conference on Pattern Recognition (ICPR 2006), vol. 4, pp. 441–444. IEEE Press, New York (2006)

Gait Identification by Joint Spatial-Temporal Feature

Suibing Tong[1], Yuzhuo Fu[1(✉)], Heifei Ling[2], and Enbang Zhang[2]

[1] Department of Computer Science and Engineering, Shanghai Jiao Tong University,
No. 800 Dong Chuan Rd, Minhang District, Shanghai 200240, China
{sjtutsb,yzfu}@sjtu.edu.cn
[2] School of Computer Science and Technology, Huazhong University of Science and
Technology, No. 1037 Luoyu Rd, Hongshan District, Wuhan 430074, China
{lheifei,u201413783}@hust.edu.cn

Abstract. In order to extract the gait spatial-temporal feature, we propose a novel Long-Short Term Memory (LSTM) network for gait recognition in this paper. Given a gait sequence, a CNNs unit with three layers convolution neural networks is used to extract the spatial feature. Then the spatial feature vector is sent to the LSTM unit, which is used to extract the temporal feature. Based on the spatial-temporal feature vector, the triplet loss function is adopted to optimize the network parameters. The CNNs and LSTM unit are jointly trained to act as a gait spatial-temporal feature extractor for the gait recognition system. Finally extensive evaluations are carried out on the CASIA-B dataset. The results turn out that our network performs better than previous state-of-the art method. It shows great potential for the practical application.

Keywords: Spatial-temporal feature · CNNs · LSTM · Triplet loss

1 Introduction

Gait refers to the style of walking of an individual. It contains the unique behavioral biometric feature. Gait recognition plays an important role in security surveillance. Compared with many other biometric traits such as fingerprints, face, and irises, gait traits have more attractive advantages. First, gait can be collected in a noncontact, noninvasive, and hidden manner. Second, gait is the only perceptible biometric at a long distance, gait recognition system still work well even though the image resolution of gait sequences is very low. Third, it is difficult to imitate or camouflage. Based on the advantages mentioned above, gait recognition technology attracts the attention from many researchers more and more.

Although gait feature has so many advantages, many factors affect the accuracy of gait recognition. Subject-related ones, the gait individual dress different coats, carry different bags or walk at different speeds. Device-related ones, such as different frame rates and sensor resolutions. Environment-related ones, such

© Springer International Publishing AG 2017
J. Zhou et al. (Eds.): CCBR 2017, LNCS 10568, pp. 457–465, 2017.
https://doi.org/10.1007/978-3-319-69923-3_49

as different light conditions and capture view angles. To construct an accurate gait recognition system, the spatial-temporal feature extraction plays a key role. The current methods consist of two categories: model-based approaches and appearance-based approaches. The former design a certain model that presents the structure and motion feature of the gait sequence. The latter extracts the gait feature in the form of Gait Energy Image (GEI) [3]. These methods all loss the temporal order feature. In order to increase the accuracy of gait recognition further, a CNNs with Long-Short Term Memory (LSTM) unit is proposed. Meanwhile, the triplet loss is adopted as the objective function to optimize the network model, which make the inter-class variations larger than intra-class variations. Compared to previous methods, our major contributions are listed as follows.

- We first propose to apply LSTM to extract the spatial-temporal gait feature;
- We design a novel network joint CNNs and LSTM to extract gait feature;
- We adopt triplet loss as the objective function to optimize our network;

The content of this paper is organized as follows. First, we give a brief survey on the gait recognition methods in Sect. 2. We introduce LSTM and give a detailed description about it in Sect. 3. We present our solution to extract the spatial-temporal feature for gait recognition in Sect. 4. Extensive evaluations are performed and analyzed in Sect. 5. We conclude the paper in Sect. 6.

2   Related Work

As we know, the feature extraction plays an important role in gait recognition, based on which the methods of gait recognition are roughly divided into two categories. Model-based approaches and appearance-based approaches. Model-based methods try to build the human body structure model and extract the feature parameters from the gait sequence. Chai et al. [4] divided human body into three parts. The combination of part variances becomes the crucial feature. These models can solve the problem of occlusion and self-occlusion as well as rotation. However, it fails to extract the temporal feature effectively. Appearance-based methods extract gait feature from video sequence directly. Liu and Sarkar apply hidden Markov models (HMM) to model human walking and generated the dynamics-normalized sequence frames to recognize the different individuals [5]. However, this method need a large number of training samples to obtain a good performance. Meanwhile, it needs the high computational cost and storage capacity for sequence matching directly. Han and Bhanu [6] extract the gait energy image (GEI) from gait sequence. But this method throws out the temporal order feature. To extract the temporal feature effectively, many methods have been proposed. Lam et al. [7] proposed gait flow image (GFI) as a novel gait feature representation. However, it fails to extract the temporal feature of the whole gait sequence. C. Wang et al. [8] carefully designed the CGI to carry temporal information by color mapping. But it still fails to represent the temporal feature of gait sequence accurately.

3 Background: LSTM

So as to extract the temporal feature effectively, we adopt a Long Short-Term Memory Units, termed as LSTM, as the base network unit to train samples. The structure of the LSTM units is described as follows.

3.1 Recurrent Neural Network (RNN)

RNN is usually used to address the sequence data. It processes an arbitrarily long time-series by mapping the input sequence to the hidden state, and the hidden state to the output via the recurrence equations (shown as Fig. 1, left):

$$h_t = g(W_{xh}x_t + W_{hh}h_{t-1} + b_h), z_t = g(W_{hz}h_t + b_z). \tag{1}$$

here x_t is the input, h_t is the hidden state with N hidden units, g is a non-linearity function, such as a sigmoid or hyperbolic tangent. z_t is the output of the recurrent unit at time t. RNN has performed well on speech recognition and text generation, but it is difficult to adopt RNN to train samples with long-term dynamics dependencies. It may result in gradient disappearance or explosion.

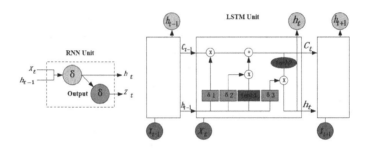

Fig. 1. Recurrent neural network architecture.

3.2 Long Short-Term Memory Units (LSTM)

The Long Short-Term Memory Unit is introduced as a special recurrent neural network in this section. Illustrated as Fig. 1, right, it consists of three gates and one cell. The three gates are used to protect and control the state of the cell.$x(t)$ is the raw input frames sequence, $h(t)$ is the hidden layer, $y(t)$ is the output layer. The principle of the LSTM is described as follows.

$$f(t) = sigmod(wf[h(t-1), x(t)] + bf) \tag{2}$$

$$I(t) = sigmod(wi[h(t-1), x(t)] + bi) \tag{3}$$

$$Ct = Ct - 1 \times ft + It \times gt \tag{4}$$

$$N(t) = sigmod(wo[h(t-1), x(t)] + bo) \tag{5}$$

$$h_t = N(t) \times tanh(Ct) \tag{6}$$

Shown as the equations above. When the input feature vector enter the LSTM unit from the former cell C_{t-1}, the forget gate δ_1 decides which part of the input data is thrown out from the former cell. The output of this layer is δ_1 . Its value ranges from 0 and 1, which means whether throw out all the information from the former cell C_{t-1} or not. The output of this layer is $f(t)$. Then δ_2 and tanh1 decides which part of information is stored in the cell C_t. The δ_2 is denoted as the input gate, its result is $I(t)$. The output of tanh1 is $g(t)$. The input gate δ_2 and forget gate δ_2 make a joint decision about which part of information is preserved in C_t. The output gate is δ_3, its value decides which part of information preserved in C_t is sent to the next LSTM unit. Which is represented as $N(t)$. The h_t is the input of next hidden layer.

4   Method

In this section, we propose a novel network model by joint CNNs and LSTM, termed as CNNs-LSTM, to extract the gait spatial-temporal feature and adopt the triplet loss function to optimize the network parameters.

4.1   Data Preprocessing

Since the gait contour can get rid of various kinds of interference due to the background noise effectively, we adopt it as input to the network. Based on the fact that the height of gait silhouettes in a gait sequence usually varies stably, and that the gravity center of silhouettes moves stably. We obtain gait contour by a heuristic approach [3], illustrated as Fig. 2. After the gait cycle estimation [6], we obtain a gait sequence. We first generate the raw silhouette by off-the-shelf background subtraction approach. Then we locate the top and bottom pixels point and record the distance between them along the vertical dimension as height in the raw silhouette, and the gravity center of gait silhouette is calculated, based on which a series of aligned gait contours are obtained by drawing a rectangle box circling the raw silhouette with a given aspect ratio, i.e., 11/16 and cropping off the region within the rectangle. Finally, we resize the gait contours into a given size (88×128) and get the standardized gait silhouettes.

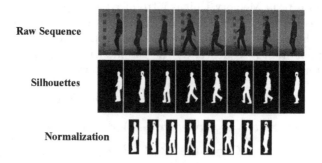

Fig. 2. Gait sequence generation.

4.2 Network Architecture

The gait recognition system consists of three parts: input layer, feature extraction layer and loss layer. Illustrated as Fig. 3, the gait contour sequences are processed by a CNNs, which consists of three layers convolution networks, includes convolution, pooling, non-linear activation operation and so on. As gait contour contains very little information, so we adopt a shallow CNNs to prevent the overfitting [9]. After that, the spatial feature maps in every cycle are sent into a single LSTM layer in turn which is adopted to extract the temporal dependency feature based on the working mechanism described in Sect. 3.2. Finally, the feature vectors from LSTM layer are sent into the loss layer, based on which the triplet loss is adopted to train the weights of our network.

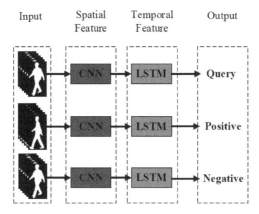

Fig. 3. Gait recognition network architecture.

4.3 Train Strategy

In our network model, the triplet loss is taken to optimize the weights of the network. The training strategy is introduced in this section.

The Triplet Loss. The feature embedding is represented by $f(x) \in R^n$. The gait sequence similarity model is learned by CNNs-LSTM. Given a gait contour sequence x as input, we can obtain its spatial-temporal feature in the last layer $f(x)$. Then, we denote the distance of two gait sequence x_1, x_2 based on the squared Euclidean distance in the feature space as Eq. 7,

$$S(X_1, X_2) = \|f(x_1) - f(x_2)\|_2^2 \tag{7}$$

The triplet loss is adopt to optimize our network. Given R present the space of input gait contour sequence x, where X_i denote the query sample, X_i^+ denote the positive sample, X_i^- denote the negative sample, $x_i, x_i^+, x_i^- \in R$, we want to make $S(X_i, X_i^-) > S(X_i, X_i^+)$. The loss is presented as follow,

$$min\frac{\lambda}{2}\|w\|_2^2 + \sum_{i=1}^{N} max\left\{0, D(X_i, X_i^+) - D(X_i, X_i^-) + M\right\} \tag{8}$$

M denotes the gap parameter between two distance which is set as 0.5, w denotes the weights of the network, N denotes the number of samples, λ denotes weight decay that is set as 0.0005.

Negative Samples Selection. In order to ensure the network fast convergence, it is important to select the negative samples conform to the triplet constraint. There are usually two methods to select the negative sample: the offline method and the online one. The former select negative sample every n steps, adopt the latest network check-point and compute the loss value on a subset of gait data. The latter select negative samples randomly, and then the hard negative samples are adopted from these selected samples by a certain algorithm. In this paper, we adopt the latter method. In the training phase, we randomly select the top hardest negative samples to construct the triplet samples. Then we apply the sum of the loss value on the matched negative samples as the total loss and back-propagate it to update the network weights. After every training cycle, the negative samples are shuffled randomly, so that the query-positive sample pairs can match with each different negative sample. Optimized by this method, our network can extract the spatial-temporal feature of gait sequence effectively.

5 Experiments

5.1 Datasets

To evaluate the performance of our network model, we select the CASIA-B dataset. It contains 124 persons, and 110 gait sequences every person. Namely, there are eleven view angles and ten gait sequences per individual at each view angle. Among the ten gait sequences, six of them are taken under the normal walking condition (nm). Another two are taken with bags (bg). The rest two are taken with coats (cl). The gait sequences are collected at the rate of 25 frames every second, and the image resolution of each frame is 320 × 240.

5.2 Implementation Details

In this paper, we design a CNNs-LSTM network, which consists of three layers convolution networks and one LSTM layer. The LSTM layer and the loss layer are connected by two additional full-connect layers. The triplet samples are constructed so as to apply the triplet loss function effectively. We optimize our network model by the triplet loss on a GTX TITAN X GPU with 12 G memory. We set the learning rate as le-3. The batch size is set as 100, the top hardest negative sample number is set as 30.

5.3   Evaluation on CASIA-B Dataset

Compared with Different Methods. In this section, the CASIA-B dataset is selected as the gait dataset and two other methods NN [8] CNN [3] are adopted to compare. The result of NN is adopted as the baseline, and the method of CNN designs a two-stream network to extract the spatial feature and temporal feature. To evaluate the performance of the three kinds of methods, we select 100 individuals as gallery and the rest 24 individuals as probe. All the triplet samples are captured under the normal walking condition. During the training phase, we select two kinds of angles difference $18°$ and $36°$. For the former, the view angles of the query samples range from $54°$ to $126°$, such as $54°$, $90°$, $126°$. While the positive view range from $36°$ to $144°$, such as $36°$, $72°$, $108°$, $144°$. For the latter, the query view angles range from $36°$ to $144°$, such as $36°$, $90°$, $144°$, and the positive view angles range from $0°$ to $180°$, such as $0°$, $54°$, $72°$, $108°$, $126°$, $180°$. The experiment results are listed as Table 1, it is not difficult to find that our network performs best, especially as the query view angle is taken under $90°$ its recognition scores reach 94.2% and 84.7% corresponding to the two kinds of angle difference respectively.

Table 1. The results of samples (nm) with the angle difference under $18°$ and $36°$.

Query view	Positive view	Ours	NN	CNN	Query view	Positive view	Ours	NN	CNN
54°	36°	91.8	73.8	79.8	36°	0°	77.8	69.8	78.1
54°	72°	92.3	81.5	87.1	36°	72°	82.7	65.1	71.8
90°	72°	87.2	86.7	91.3	90°	54°	**84.7**	71.5	76.3
90°	108°	**94.2**	80.9	88.7	90°	126°	79.2	67.9	75.2
126°	108°	90.1	84.6	83.1	144°	108°	78.3	65.1	77.3
126°	144°	85.7	76.3	81.9	144°	180°	69.1	73.1	74.5

Compared with Different Walking Conditions. To evaluate the robustness of our model, other two groups of experiments are carried out based on the gait sequences with bags and coats. We adopt NN [8] and CNN [3] to compare as before. In this section, we only take $18°$ as the angle difference to consider. The sample individuals are selected as before and the view angles of the query samples range from $54°$ to $126°$, such as $54°$, $90°$, $126°$. While the positive view range from $36°$ to $144°$, such as $36°$, $72°$, $108°$, $144°$. The experiment results are listed as Table 2. It is not difficult to find that our network performs best for the two kinds of gait sequences. Its identification scores reach 85.7% and 87.6% corresponding to the two kinds of different gait sequences respectively.

Based on the experiment results above, we find our network performs better than the traditional ones due to the LSTM unit which can extract the temporal gait feature effectively. Meanwhile, all three networks get better identification scores when the query view angles are taken around $90°$, that's because the gait sequences around this view angle contain more discriminating gait feature.

Table 2. The results of samples (bg/cl) with the angle difference under $18°$.

Query view	Positive view	Ours(cl)	NN(cl)	CNN(cl)	Ours(bg)	NN(bg)	CNN(bg)
$54°$	$36°$	81.8	62.8	71.4	80.2	67.8	77.1
$54°$	$72°$	83.2	76.4	82.5	76.7	71.4	75.3
$90°$	$72°$	82.1	78.3	81.7	**87.6**	69.4	76.4
$90°$	$108°$	**85.7**	65.1	77.2	79.2	67.9	71.7
$126°$	$108°$	77.5	62.7	74.8	78.3	67.1	78.3
$126°$	$144°$	81.7	68.3	80.1	79.1	73.1	77.4

5.4 Evaluation on Different Network Depths

In this section, we adopt a three layers convolution network as the base CNNs unit. Besides, we select two other network units, such as AlexNet, VGG16 [10], to extract the spatial feature instead of our CNNs unit, and then we evaluate the performance of these networks based on the gait sequences with normal walking condition. The triplet samples are selected by the method described in Sect. 5.3. The results are listed in Table 3. We find our network gets the best performance. So it is important to design a proper network to extract the spatial feature of gait sequence, which should be neither too deep nor too shallow.

Table 3. The results of the samples (nm) with the angle difference under $18°$.

Query view	Positive view	Ours	AlexNet	VGG16
$54°$	$36°$	90.4	86.2	79.8
$54°$	$72°$	91.8	89.2	77.2
$90°$	$72°$	**94.2**	87.4	80.5
$90°$	$108°$	92.3	86.7	84.1
$126°$	$108°$	88.7	82.1	78.4
$126°$	$144°$	89.2	80.4	77.6

6 Conclusion

In this paper, we propose a novel network model, termed as triplet-based CNNs-LSTM network, to extract the spatial-temporal feature of the gait sequence. This network takes the gait contour sequences as input, and extracts the spatial-temporal feature by the CNNs and LSTM unit respectively. Finally, the triplet loss function is adopted to optimize the network parameters based on the spatial-temporal vectors feature. Masses of evaluations are carried out to evaluate the performance of our network. The results show that our network can extract the spatial-temporal gait feature more effectively than the previous state-of-the art ones even if the gait sequence is taken under abnormal walking conditions. We refresh the gait recognition scores once again, which means that the technology of gait recognition strides a step closer to the practical applications.

Acknowledgements. This work was supported by the National Science Fund of China under Grants (No. 61472244, No. U1536203, No. 61272409), in part by the Major Scientific and Technological Innovation Project of Hubei Province under Grant No. 2015AAA013.

References

1. Murray, M.P., Drought, A.B., Kory, R.C.: Walking patterns of normal men. J. Bone and Jt. Surg. **46–A**(2), 335–360 (1964)
2. Murray, M.P.: Gait as a total pattern of movement. Am. J. Phys. Med. **46**, 290–332 (1967)
3. Wu, Z., Huang, Y., Wang, L., Wang, X., Tan, T.: A comprehensive study on cross-view gait based human identification with deep CNNs. IEEE Trans. Pattern Anal. Mach. Intell. **39**, 209–226 (2016)
4. Chai, Y., Wang, Q., Jia, J.P., Zhao, R.: A novel human gait recognition method by segmenting and extracting the region variance feature. In: Proceedings of International Conference on Pattern Recognition, vol. 4, pp. 425–428 (2006)
5. Liu, Z., Sarkar, S.: Improved gait recognition by gait dynamics normalization. IEEE Trans. Pattern Anal. Mach. Intell. **28**(6), 863–876 (2006)
6. Han, J., Bhanu, B.: Individual recognition using gait energy image. IEEE Trans. Pattern Anal. Mach. Intell. **28**(2), 316–322 (2006)
7. Lam, T.H.W., Cheung, K.H., Liu, J.N.K.: Gait flow image: a silhouette-based gait representation for human identification. Pattern Recogn. **44**(4), 973–987 (2011)
8. Yu, S., Tan, D., Tan, T.: A framework for evaluating the effect of view angle, clothing and carrying condition on gait recognition. In: ICPR (2006)
9. Sundaresan, A., Roy-Chowdhury, A., Chellappa, R.: A hidden Markov model based framework for recognition of humans from gait sequences. In: Proceedings of International Conference on Image Processing, vol. 2, pp. 93–96 (2003)
10. Krizhevsky, A., Sutskever, I., Hinton, G.: ImageNet classification with deep convolutional neural networks. In: NIPS (2012)

A Convolutional Neural Network for Gait Recognition Based on Plantar Pressure Images

Yanlin Li, Dexiang Zhang, Jun Zhang, Lina Xun, Qing Yan,
Jingjing Zhang, Qingwei Gao, and Yi Xia$^{(\boxtimes)}$

School of Electrical Engineering and Automation,
Anhui University, Hefei 230601, China
xiayi@ahu.edu.cn

Abstract. This paper proposed a novel gait recognition method that is based on plantar pressure images. Different from many conventional methods where hand-crafted features are extracted explicitly. We utilized Convolution Neural Network (CNN) for automatic feature extraction as well as classification. The peak pressure image (PPI) generated from the time series of plantar pressure images is used as the characteristic image for gait recognition in this study. Our gait samples are collected from 109 subjects under three kinds of walking speeds, and for each subject total 18 samples are gathered. Experimental results demonstrate that the designed CNN model can obtain very high classification accuracy as compared to many traditional methods.

Keywords: Gait recognition · Convolutional Neural Network · Plantar pressure images · Peak pressure image

1 Introduction

Until now, there has been rapid growth in the field of person identification techniques for the intent of security and personalized services. Among a great many person identification means, gait identification as a behavioral biometric has attracted remarkable attention in recent years. Basically, gait recognition technologies developed so far can be divided into two categories: (1) that based on the video system by extracting gait pose kinematics; and (2) that based on force or pressure sensing system by extracting gait kinetic information. Gait recognition based on the video system, due to its easy installation and cheap acquisition, has been studied extensively and yielded fruitful gait analysis methods [1] including the key frame, time normalization, projection, class energy map [2, 3] and so on. However, typical obstacles in the computer vision area such as perspective, climate interference and other clothing shelter problems also posed great challenges to be tackled. Comparatively speaking, gait recognition based on plantar kinetic information has various advantages such as long-effecting distance, not easy to be mimicked and no privacy-intrusion problem. Correspondingly, there are a plenty of research activities both in the health and security industries. For instance, Moustakidis et al. [4] proposed a valid subject recognition approach by measuring human gait with ground reaction force (GRF). The original GRF data is transformed into time–frequency domain through wavelet packet (WP) transform and

© Springer International Publishing AG 2017
J. Zhou et al. (Eds.): CCBR 2017, LNCS 10568, pp. 466–473, 2017.
https://doi.org/10.1007/978-3-319-69923-3_50

then they realized optimal WP decomposition for wavelet feature ranking using a fuzzy-set-based criterion. Vera-Rodriguez et al. [5] also utilized GRF for footstep identification, and they proposed two new features that are upper and lower contour coming from the maxima and minima of the sensors for each time sample independently of the spatial distribution of the sensors.

In addition to the above GRF-based methods for gait analysis, with the continuous improvement of force sensitive sensors, there is also a research activity by analyzing plantar pressure image to achieve subject identification. For example, in an early work, Jung et al. [6] realized gait recognition based on a hidden Markov model and a Levenberg-Marquart learning method, and they found that dynamic-footprint could be used to identify 8 men with an average of 64% recognition rate. More recently, Pataky et al. [7] demonstrated that by using relatively simple image processing and feature extraction, dynamic foot pressures can be utilized to identify 104 subjects with an overall accuracy of 99.6%.

The gait recognition technique based on plantar dynamics information doesn't need active cooperation of the subjects when they are collecting data. In addition, for gait plantar imaging, there is no complex background interference, occlusion, camera angle, illumination, and so on. Thus, it has great development potential as compared to other identification technologies. However, the current gait database for plantar dynamics is small either at the number of subjects or the number of the images for each subject. Considering such a situation and also being encouraged by the fruitful results reported in previous studies, this study first establishes a gait database with plantar pressure images collected from 109 young students with different walking speeds, and then a gait recognition method based on CNN is proposed. The input to the CNN is the so-called Peak Pressure Image (PPI) that is defined as the maximum pressure experienced by each part of the foot over the course of stance-phase during the walking process. An image registration among different intra-subject PPI images is first applied for the enhancement of the classification performance. After that, a CNN with four convolutional layers is realized for an end-to-end gait recognition. As a comparison, some traditional feature-extraction-based methods are equally implemented. The excellent classification performance obtained using the proposed method indicates that CNN can extract stable and high unique characteristics directly from the input peak pressure image, which solves the feature-extraction difficulties encountered by the traditional methods.

2 Methods

2.1 Preparation of the Feature Images

As we know, the plantar image collected during the walking process is a time series, that is, it takes the form of 3D data. Though CNN can accept 3D data as its input, for simplicity, this study adopts the 2D peak pressure image (PPI) as the feature image that is fed into the CNN. The PPI is defined as the maximum pressure experienced by each sensor under the foot during walking, and it can well represent the kinetic characteristics of gait. It is often used to check for plantar tissue overloading and also for gait recognition [7]. The PPI can be denoted as follows:

$$\text{PPI}(x, y) = \max I(x, y, t), t \in [0, T] \tag{1}$$

where $I(x, y, t)$ represent a plantar image, x, y is the position coordinate and t is the time, T is the maximum time that has pressures on the sensors. Figure 1 displays an example of how PPI is generated from a plantar pressure series.

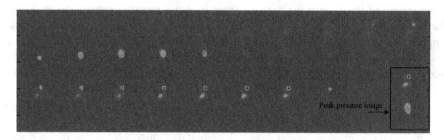

Fig. 1. A plantar pressure time series (only some typical frames are shown) and the final peak pressure image.

As the position and the angle for the plantar pressure images collected during each experiment are often different, some alignment among intra-subject PPI images are necessary to ensure that: (1) the size of the image fed into the CNN is same; (2) the postures of all PPI footprints is similar. For such purpose, this study performs a preprocessing step mentioned in [8] due to its efficiency and effectiveness. The algorithm includes three basic steps:

- Calculate the principal axis (PA) direction and the center point of the PPI using a method based on image moments [9]. Adjust the original coordinate system to a transformed one where the PA of PPI image coincides with the Y axis of the new coordinate system, and the center point is positioned at the origin.
- The alignment of intra-subject PPIs is realized by selecting one image as a template and the other images are aligned to this template by an optimization algorithm [8] to minimize the following objective function

$$f_{XOR} = \frac{|I_0 \oplus I_1|}{|I_0| + |I_1|} \times 100\% \tag{2}$$

where $|I_0|$ and $|I_1|$ are binary template as well as source images, respectively, the symbol $\oplus$ is an exclusive OR operation.
- All the PPIs used in this study are cropped and centered to be with a size of 59×59. Figure 2 displays a series of PPIs for one subject and their aligned versions.

2.2 The Proposed CNN for Gait Recognition

Since a breakthrough work of [10], CNNs have had a major impact on computer vision, and image understanding in particular, essentially replacing traditional image

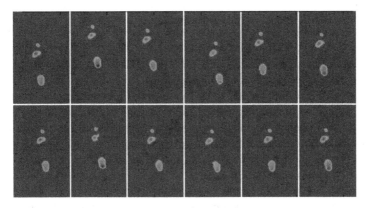

Fig. 2. A plantar pressure time series (upper row) and their corresponding aligned versions (down row).

representations such as all kinds of manually-designed features. In general, the basic structure of the CNN includes two kinds of layers: (1) the first is the feature extraction layer, where the input of each neuron is connected to the local acceptance domain of the previous layer for the purpose of extracting local features [11]; and (2) the second is the feature mapping layer, which constitutes the computational layer of the network [12]. Besides these two layers, CNN can also include other layers such as batch normalization, drop-out for better representation or fully connection, softmax for classification or regression. The proposed CNN for gait recognition is illustrated in Fig. 3. It mainly consists of two parts.

The first part is the so-called feature extraction pipeline, where four convolutional layers take different kernel size to produce different pieces of feature maps. The convolution kernel is slid in the effective area of the input pressure image with a stride of 1 in all convolutional operations. After convolutional layers, as indicated in Fig. 3, other layers such as Rectified Linear Units (ReLU), Max-Pooling (MP) or Batch normalization (BN) is immediately followed. The ReLU layer, which takes the form of

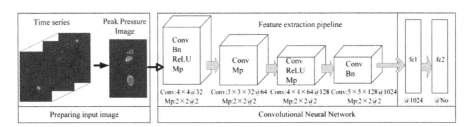

Fig. 3. The proposed gait recognition framework based on CNN. Note that "conv", "Bn", "ReLU", "fc", and "MP" are the abbreviations of "convolutional layer", "Batch normalization", "Rectified Linear Unit", "fully connected layer" and "Max pooling layer" respectively. The numbers before "@" refer to the kernel parameters of the corresponding operation and the number after "@" refers to the number of feature maps in convolutional layers or the output dimension of the fully connected layers.

$y = \max(0, x)$, can enhance the nonlinear properties of the decision function and of the overall network without affecting the receptive fields of the convolution layer. In comparison to the other non-linear functions used in CNNs, the advantage of a ReLU is that the network trains many times faster. MP layer reduces the resolution of the output features and makes the features robust against noise and distortion. The proposed CNN is done on the MAX operation due to its significant virtues such as faster integration, controlling overfitting, improving generalization as well as selecting superior invariant features. The max pooling operation takes a big step by using a filter with a size of 2×2 that can make every input feature image subsampling by 2 along both height and width. By normalizing the data in each mini-batch not only once at the beginning but also all over other places in the CNN, BN can reduce internal covariate shift in neural networks, and thus lead to faster learning and higher overall accuracy [13].

The second part of the proposed CNN realizes the classification of the target samples. It mainly includes two fully connected layers prior to a top-level softmax layer. These layers mathematically sum a weighting of the previous layer of features, indicating the precise mix of "ingredients" to determine a specific target output result. The proposed CNN is implemented by using MatConvNet [14], which is a widely used MATLAB toolbox for building and training deep learning networks. For efficiency, the input data is segmented into mini-batches with the size of 128 during training and testing. The training and testing have been performed on a computer equipped with a NVIDIA GTX 1060 GPU card with a Pascal architecture, CUDA Cores 1280 and 6 GB memory.

3   Experiments

3.1   Data Set

The plantar pressure images used in this study are collected at a sampling rate of 100 Hz by using a pressure-sensing-mat system (Zebris FDM-S system, Germany). The sensing area is 54.2×33.9 cm with a physical resolution of 1.4 sensors/cm^2. A total of 109 young students were recruited for this study. Their characteristic details are listed in Table 1.

Each subject was asked to perform a total of six trials of self-pacing with a speed that can be normal, fast and slow. By using such a protocol, for each subject at each speed, there are six volumetric samples while each one consists of a sequence of

Table 1. Subject characteristics. Average, with s.d. in parentheses. Note that BMI is the abbreviation of body mass index

	Female	Male
n	12	97
Age (years)	25.6 (2.3)	20.8 (4.3)
Mass (kg)	47.7 (2.3)	66.5 (8.7)
Height (cm)	160 (4.4)	173.7 (5.2)
BMI (kg cm^{-2})	18.6 (0.9)	22 (2.5)

images from the beginning frame when the subject's foot touches on the mat to the end frame when the foot departs the mat.

3.2 Optimal Parameters are Based on CNN

In this experiment, the meaning of two important parameters is discussed, which are used to select network architectures. The testing error with training epoch for different pooling method and activation function is plotted in Fig. 4. It can be found that the convergence is faster and better performance can be obtained by using ReLU function than sigmoid function. By using ReLU as activation function, the mean pooling and max pooling perform equally well with regards to the classification accuracy, but the convergence curve is smoother for the latter method.

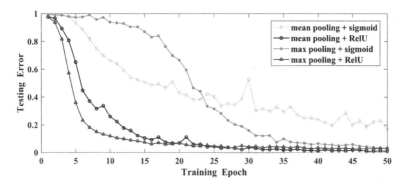

Fig. 4. The effect of different pooling methods and activation functions on model performance

3.3 Performance Evaluation

To compare the proposed approach with traditional gait recognition methods that depend on hand-crafted features, we also implemented several algorithms [7, 15], proposed in other studies that also use plantar pressure images as the sole information source for recognition. The features include PPI itself [7], Spatio-Temporal Histogram of Oriented Gradients (STHOG) [15], and the HOG of the PPI (PPIHOG) that is a new feature designed in this study. For these traditional features, the classification was performed by the famous LIBSVM package which implemented the support vector machine (SVM) classifier [16]. The parameters of SVM are manually tuned with a trial-and-error process to achieve the best performance. The comparative results evaluated by a 10-fold cross-validation process are shown in Table 2.

The results in Table 2 demonstrate that the proposed CNN-based approach can obtain significantly higher classification accuracy than other traditional methods. One important advantage for CNN is its capability of learning discriminative features automatically by exploring deep architecture at multiple levels of abstracts from raw data without any domain knowledge. As for other traditional features, though the difference is not obvious, the PPI feature performs worst as compared to other two

Table 2. Performance comparison of different methods.

Method	Model	Accuracy(%)
STHOG	SVM	85.25
PPI	SVM	83.64
PPIHOG	SVM	84.31
Ours	CNN	98.47

features. This result is not strange since the PPI has no additional feature extraction process. However, we notice that one previous study [7] reported that PPI can obtain excellent classification accuracy (99.6%) on a dataset of 104 subjects. The significant difference of PPI's classification performance between these two studies can be attributed to the following two factors: first the sensor resolution (8 mm between two sensing units) in this study is lower than their case (5 mm between two sensing units), thus leading to a less sensitive plantar pressure distribution; second, the subjects in this study are mainly students from university, thus they have similar ages and BMIs, while ages (female: 30 ± 10.8, male: 34.4 ± 8.6) and BMI ranges (female: 22 ± 2.4, male: 24.1 ± 2.2) of the subjects in the Ref. [7] are much broader than the case in our studies.

4 Conclusion

This paper proposed a novel CNN-based approach for gait recognition that used plantar pressure images as the sole evidence. The CNN can realize automatic feature extraction and a subsequent built-in classification, thus leading to an end-to-end gait recognition except a simple image alignment preprocessing. We validate our method via several contrast experiments, and the high recognition accuracy (98.47%) on a dataset of 109 subjects demonstrates the feasibility and utility of a trained CNN for the single modal gait recognition investigated in this study.

Acknowledgments. This work is supported by Anhui Provincial Natural Science Foundation (grant number 1608085MF136); China Postdoctoral Science Foundation (2015M582826); Major University Science Research Project of Anhui Province (grant number KJ2016SD33); Anhui Province Science and Technology Major Project (grant number 1603081122); National Natural Science Foundation of China (NSFC) for Youth (grant numbers 61402004, 61602002).

References

1. Ben, X., Xu, S., Wang, K.: Review on pedestrian gait feature expression and recognition. Pattern Recognit. Artif. Intell. **25**, 71–81 (2012)
2. Liu, J., Zheng, N.: Gait history image: a novel temporal template for gait recognition. In: 2007 IEEE International Conference on Multimedia and Expo, pp. 663–666. IEEE (2007)
3. Yang, J., Wu, X., Peng, Z.: Gait recognition based on difference motion slice. In: 2006 8th International Conference on Signal Processing. IEEE (2006)

4. Moustakidis, S.P., Theocharis, J.B., Giakas, G.: Subject recognition based on ground reaction force measurements of gait signals. IEEE Trans. Syst. Man Cybern. Part B: Cybern. **38**, 1476–1485 (2008)
5. Vera-Rodriguez, R., Mason, J.S., Fierrez, J., Ortega-Garcia, J.: Comparative analysis and fusion of spatiotemporal information for footstep recognition. IEEE Trans. Pattern Anal. Mach. Intell. **35**, 823–834 (2013)
6. Jung, J.-W., Bien, Z., Lee, S.-W., Sato, T.: Dynamic-footprint based person identification using mat-type pressure sensor. In: Proceedings of the 25th Annual International Conference of the IEEE Engineering in Medicine and Biology Society, pp. 2937–2940. IEEE (2003)
7. Pataky, T.C., Mu, T., Bosch, K., Rosenbaum, D., Goulermas, J.Y.: Gait recognition: highly unique dynamic plantar pressure patterns among 104 individuals. J. R. Soc. Interface **9**, 790–800 (2012)
8. Pataky, T.C., Goulermas, J.Y., Crompton, R.H.: A comparison of seven methods of within-subjects rigid-body pedobarographic image registration. J. Biomech. **41**, 3085–3089 (2008)
9. Jia, W., Hu, R.-X., Gui, J., Lei, Y.-K.: Newborn footprint recognition using band-limited phase-only correlation. In: Zhang, D., Sonka, M. (eds.) ICMB 2010. LNCS, vol. 6165, pp. 83–93. Springer, Heidelberg (2010). doi:10.1007/978-3-642-13923-9_9
10. Krizhevsky, A., Sutskever, I., Hinton, G.E.: Imagenet classification with deep convolutional neural networks. In: Advances in Neural Information Processing Systems, pp. 1097–1105 (2012)
11. Bazzani, L., Cristani, M., Murino, V.: Symmetry-driven accumulation of local features for human characterization and re-identification. Comput. Vis. Image Underst. **117**, 130–144 (2013)
12. Acharya, Y.R.: Mapping layer 2 LAN priorities to a virtual lane in an Infiniband™ network. Google Patents (2006)
13. Ioffe, S., Szegedy, C.: Batch normalization: accelerating deep network training by reducing internal covariate shift. arXiv preprint arXiv:1502.03167 (2015)
14. Vedaldi, A., Lenc, K.: MatConvNet: convolutional neural networks for MATLAB. In: Proceedings of the 23rd ACM International Conference on Multimedia, pp. 689–692. ACM (2015)
15. Xia, Y., Ma, Z., Yao, Z., Sun, Y.: Gait recognition based on spatio-temporal HOG of plantar pressure distribution. Pattern Recognit. Artif. Intell. **26**, 529–536 (2013)
16. Chang, C.-C., Lin, C.-J.: LIBSVM: a library for support vector machines. ACM Trans. Intell. Syst. Technol. (TIST) **2**, 27 (2011)

Pose-Based Temporal-Spatial Network (PTSN) for Gait Recognition with Carrying and Clothing Variations

Rijun Liao[1], Chunshui Cao[2], Edel B. Garcia[3],
Shiqi Yu[1]($^{(\boxtimes)}$), and Yongzhen Huang[2]

[1] College of Computer Science and Software Engineering, Shenzhen University,
Shenzhen 518060, China
2150230306@email.szu.edu.cn, shiqi.yu@szu.edu.cn
[2] National Laboratory of Pattern Recognition, Institute of Automation,
Chinese Academy of Sciences, Beijing 100190, China
ccs@mail.ustc.edu.cn, yongzhen.huang@nlpr.ia.ac.cn
[3] Advanced Technologies Application Center (CENATAV), 7ma A 21406, Playa,
Havana, Cuba
egarcia@cenatav.co.cu

Abstract. One of the most attractive biometric techniques is gait recognition, since its potential for human identification at a distance. But gait recognition is still challenging in real applications due to the effect of many variations on the appearance and shape. Usually, appearance-based methods need to compute gait energy image (GEI) which is extracted from the human silhouettes. GEI is an image that is obtained by averaging the silhouettes and as result the temporal information is removed. The body joints are invariant to changing clothing and carrying conditions. We propose a novel pose-based gait recognition approach that is more robust to the clothing and carrying variations. At the same time, a pose-based temporal-spatial network (PTSN) is proposed to extract the temporal-spatial features, which effectively improve the performance of gait recognition. Experiments evaluated on the challenging CASIA B dataset, show that our method achieves state-of-the-art performance in both carrying and clothing conditions.

Keywords: Gait recognition · Pose-based · PTSN network

1 Introduction

Gait is a kind of behavioral biometric feature, that is suitable for human identification at a distance. In consequence, gait recognition technology has attracted increasing attention in video surveillance.

There have been mainly two categories of gait approaches with different highlights. The first one is model-based methods [3] which employ modelling of human body structure and local movement patterns of different body parts.

© Springer International Publishing AG 2017
J. Zhou et al. (Eds.): CCBR 2017, LNCS 10568, pp. 474–483, 2017.
https://doi.org/10.1007/978-3-319-69923-3_51

The second category of gait approach is appearance-based methods [4,5] which directly extract gait representations from videos. Gait energy image (GEI) is the feature most applied, because of its good compromise between recognition rate and simplicity of computation. However, there are different cons concerning the use of human silhouettes, first, in wild conditions the extraction is affected by illumination changes and many silhouettes appear incomplete. Second, even when the extraction step is performed correctly, the shape depends on the view angles, clothes variations and the carring conditions.

Some authors faced this problem removing the parts of silhuoettes affected by variations and retain only those uninfluenced parts to eliminate the effects of clothing and carried objects. But, recognition rates are not good enough. In order to handle with the clothing and carrying variations, Huang and Boulgouris [13] increase robustness to some classes of structural variations by fusing Shifted Energy Image and the Gait Structural Profile. In [12], Hossain et al. analyze the discrimination capability of different parts through dividing the human body into eights parts. Yu et al. [21] employ the Stacked Progressive Auto-Encoders (SPAE) trying to transform the clothing and carrying conditions into normal walking. In [1] the authors propose a novel covariate cognizant framework to deal with the presence of such clothes and carring covariates. They describe gait motion by forming a single 2D spatio-temporal template from video sequence. Guan et al. [10] proposed a random subspace method (RSM) framework for clothing-invariant gait recognition by combining multiple inductive biases for classification. In Liang et al. [16] the golden ratio takes the characteristics of clothing into consideration, enabling all the clothing parts to be discarded and the unaffected parts of the gait to be retained. Choudhury and Tjahjadi [7] introduced the use of rotation forest ensemble classifier in gait recognition, and experimentally demonstrates its superiority to random subspace method in this field.

Some researchers have studied the problem as a pose-based gait recognition, for example [15] uses skeleton data provided by the low-cost Kinect sensors. In [9] instead of using binary silhouette to describe each frame, they use the human body joint heatmap. They feed the joint heatmap of consecutive frames to Long Short Term Memory (LSTM). The hidden activation values at the last timestep is used as their gait feature.

Our approach is based on early studies on gait perception that showed that joints' motion over time is sufficient for humans to identify familiar persons. Until now, only structural feature was not enough to human identification problem in gait analysis, since pose estimation requires accurate tracking of body parts, which is known to be a very challenging problem considering the nonrigidness and self-occlusion of the human body. However, a recently bottom-up method [6] for pose estimation using deep learning opens the door to retake approaches based on dynamic parameters. We believe the body joint is invariant to changing clothing and changing carrying conditions. Our contribution in this paper is a pose based temporal-spatial network that combines a LSTM and Convolutional Neural Network (CNN) to capture the dynamic and static information of a gait sequence. Our method is robust to the clothing variations and carring conditions.

2   Our Method

In this paper, a novel pose-based gait recognition approach is proposed to deal with clothing and carrying condition variations. The work-flow of proposed method is illustrated in Fig. 1. The first step is to estimate the pose information from the given consecutive frames. Then, the pose coordinate sequences is extracted and preprocessed. Finally, a pose-based temporal-spatial network (PTSN) is proposed to extract the temporal features and spatial features from gait pose rather than image, which effectively improve the performance. In this section, we will illustrate our method in detail.

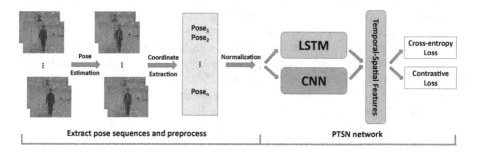

Fig. 1. Work-flow of our pose-based gait recognition approach.

2.1   Pose Information

The proposed method employs the pose information to extract the invariant feature for clothing and carrying conditions. For the appearance-based methods, one common pipeline is to evaluate the similarities between pairs of gait energy image (GEI). However, the GEI would be greatly changed by the clothing and carrying condition variations which directly lead to decrease the recognition rate. Besides, the GEI is computed by averaging the silhouettes, which will eliminate the temporal information in the process of walking. In contrast, the human pose is less affected by these variations due to it does not depend on human body appearance and shape. In addition, gait is a process of movements, the pose sequences has powerful representation capacity to capture the invariant features from consecutive frames. Consequently, the invariant features that are robust to clothing and carrying conditions, are extracted from the pose sequences rather than human shape.

We use a pre-trained model of multi-person 2D pose estimation [6] to acquire the human pose. Cao et at. propose the Part Affinity Fields which directly estimate the association between anatomical parts. The pre-trained model can estimate 18 joints, namely Nose, Neck, RShoulder, RElbow, RWrist, LShoulder, LElbow, LWrist, RHip, RKnee, Rankle, LHip, LKnee, LAnkle, Reye, LEye, Rear and Lear, as shown in Fig. 2. Before we use the pose information, we should normalize and select the effective joints in order to extract more robust feature.

Fig. 2. Normal walking, walking with a bag, and walking with a coat sequences from CASIA B dataset: 18 human joints are shown.

Normalization: The distance between people and camera will change at all the time when people walk through the fixed camera. In order to avoid the influence of this distance change, each joint needs to be normalized. In the process of people walking, the Neck and the center of Hip are two relatively more stable joints than others. As a result, the normalization should be based on that two joints. The equation of normalization is defined as follows:

$$P'_i = \frac{P_i - P_{neck}}{H_{nh}} \tag{1}$$

where $P_i \in \mathbb{R}^2$ be the coordinate of body joint i, P'_i be the normalized coordinate of P_i, P_{neck} is the Neck coordinate, the H_{nh} is the height between the Neck position and the center of Hip position.

Selection of Effective Joints: One of the most important features is the change of human leg movement. Cunado et al. [8] used the legs as a model, as they found harmonics from the motion of legs. In addition, from the Fig. 2, we can find the width of shoulder in the walking with a coat is little bigger than the normal walking and the walking with a bag. Therefore, not all of the joints can effectively boost the performance of gait recognition, and even some joints will perform worse. As the Neck already was used as a base point for normalization, we do not have to choose Neck as an effective joint. Consequently, we choose the RHip, RKnee, Rankle, LHip, LKnee, LAnkle as the effective joints of gait feature. These six effective joints not only have rich representation capacity for gait recognition, but also more robust to the clothing and carrying condition variations than other joints.

2.2 PTSN for Gait Temporal-Spatial Features

We borrow the idea of Deep Evolutional Spatial-Temporal Networks [23], and propose a pose-based temporal-spatial network (PTSN) to capture the dynamic and static information of gait pose. The proposed PSTN mainly consists of two kinds of networks, as shown in Fig. 1. Firstly, we use the Long Short-Term Memory (LSTM) [11] to extract the temporal features from gait pose sequences. Secondly, the Convolutional Neural Network (CNN) is used to extract the spatial features from static gait pose frames. Finally, the two types of features are combined to capture the dynamic-static information of gait pose, which has powerful representation capacity to extract invariant features from different gaits.

LSTM for Temporal Features: As gait is a process with a series of movements, it is natural to consider to extract the dynamic information from the walking sequence. Simonyan and Zisserman [19] trained an additional network on top of optical flow in order to capture temporal information under the framework of CNN. Although CNN can achieve state-of-the-art performance on image classification tasks, it has not yet been shown to be effective in capturing dynamic information. In contrast, the Long Short-Term Memory is supposed to better handle with temporal sequences. Therefore, we employ the LSTM to extract the temporal features from consecutive pose frames.

CNN for Spatial Features: The LSTM can effectively extract the dynamic information, but it has not enough capacity to extract the static information of gait, such as the length between Ankle and Knee. In order to complement the information of static appearance, Zhang et al. [23] proposed a multi-signal convolutional neural network (MSCNN) to extract spatial features from static frames. Unlike the MSCNN, we fuse CNN with LSTM in the top fully convolutional layer, which effectively boost the performance of gait recognition.

2.3   Definition of Loss Function

In order to extract the temporal-spatial features with large between-gait variations and reduce the within-gait variations, we adopt a multi-loss strategy to optimize the PTSN network. The Cross-entropy Loss classifies each gait sequence into different gaits, and the Contrastive Loss constrains the relationship between the temporal-spatial features.

Cross-Entropy Loss: In the task of recognition, many researchers [23] use the recognition signal as supervision. Because of features have to be classified into different classes, so the Cross-entropy Loss is useful to pull apart the temporal-spatial features of different gaits. The Cross-entropy Loss can promote the temporal-spatial features with large between-gait variations, it is defined as:

$$CELoss = -\sum_i y_i \log(p_i) \tag{2}$$

where y_i is the true distribution of sample i, and p_i is the predicted probability of gaits.

Contrastive Loss: The Cross-entropy Loss can push temporal-spatial features apart, but it has not a strong capacity to reduce the variations of identical human gaits. Many researchers employ another loss function to constrain the feature, such as Zhang et al. [23] use the VeLoss and Wen et al. [20] adopt the center loss. In order to extract powerful features, we adopt an additional Contrastive Loss, which is not only helpful to enlarge the between-gait variations, but also can reduce the within-gait variations. The Contrastive Loss is defined as:

$$CTLoss = \frac{1}{2}y\|f_i - f_j\|_2^2 + \frac{1}{2}(1 - y)max(\lambda - \|f_i - f_j\|_2^2, 0) \qquad (3)$$

where f_i and f_j are features of two input sequences. $y = 1$ when the two input sequences are from the same human gait, then the f_i and f_j will to be close. $y = 0$ means that the two input sequences are from different human gaits. In this case, the distance of f_i and f_j is limited to be larger than margin λ.

3 Experiments and Analysis

3.1 Experimental Setting

To evaluate the performance of the proposed pose-based gait recognition approach, several experiments are performed on the challenging CASIA B gait dataset [22]. CASIA B dataset is one of the largest public gait databases. It has 124 subjects in total (31 females and 93 males). There are 10 sequences for each subject, 6 sequences of normal walking (NM), 2 sequences of walking with bag (BG) and 2 sequences of walking with coat (CL). The three kinds of sequences as shown in Fig. 2. In these 10 sequences, each sequence has 11 views which were captured from 11 cameras, the view angle set of camera is $\{0°, 18°, \cdots, 180°\}$. Like the experimental setting of SPAE [21] and GaitGAN [18], we also set the first 62 subjects as the training set and the rest of subjects as the test set. In the test set, the gallery set consists of the first 4 normal walking sequences of each subjects and the probe set consists of the rest of sequences, as be shown in Table 1.

Table 1. Experimental setting on CASIA B dataset.

Training	Test	
	Gallery set	Probe set
ID: 001-062	ID: 063-124	ID: 063-124
Seqs: NM01-NM06	Seqs: NM01-NM04	Seqs: NM05-NM06
BG01-BG02, CL01-CL02		BG01-BG02, CL01-CL02

3.2 Experimental Results on CASIA B Dataset

Our experimental results on test set of CASIA B dataset are shown in Table 2. The gallery set of Table 2 is the first 4 normal walking sequences at a specific view, the probe sets has three types which are the last 2 normal sequences, 2 carrying bags sequences and 2 with coats sequences, respectively. In the tables, each column represents a view of gallery set and probe set.

Table 2. The recognition rate for 11 single views on CASIA B dataset.

View	0°	18°	36°	54°	72°	90°	108°	126°	144°	162°	180°	Mean
Probe NM 5-6	96.77	99.19	98.39	98.39	94.35	96.77	95.97	95.97	96.77	98.39	95.16	96.92
Probe BG 1-2	89.52	95.16	92.74	87.90	83.87	79.03	84.68	83.06	83.06	90.32	74.19	85.78
Probe CL 1-2	53.23	83.87	87.90	72.58	61.29	61.29	75.00	66.94	70.97	70.16	45.97	68.11

3.3   Comparisons with GEI + PCA, SPAE and GaitGAN

We compare the average recognition rates without view variation with GEI+PCA [17], SPAE [21] and GaitGAN [18], as is shown in Fig. 3. The average recognition rates without view variation are computed by averaging the recognition rates on the 11 single views. The corresponding values for GEI + PCA, SPAE and GaitGAN are obtained in the same way. In normal walking condition, our method achieves comparable performance with GEI + PCA, SPAE and GaitGAN. In walking with carrying condition, the proposed method outperforms these three methods greatly, its recognition rate is higher than the best result by 13%. For walking with clothing condition, our method achieves a high average recognition rate of 68.11%, which exceeds the best result by more than 22%. The comparison shows that our method can effectively handle with carrying and clothing condition variations.

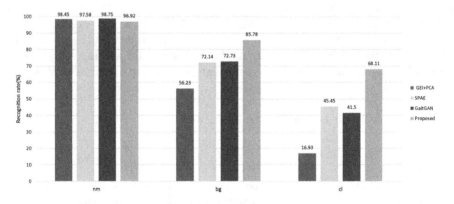

Fig. 3. The average recognition rates compared with GEI + PCA, SPAE and GaitGAN.

3.4   Comparisons with State-of-the-art

For further illustrate the performance of our method, we also compare the proposed method with state-of-art methods. Including Shanableh et al. [2], Huang and Boulgouris [13] and Jeevan et al. [14] which are all appearance-based methods for the 90° view. Since our method does not adopt the fusion scheme, we only compare the nine single-level methods (R1-R9) of Shanableh et al. In addition, we want to emphasize that our method contains only one model to handle with any single view. The 90° view is the best angle for appearance-based methods because of captures more dynamic information, but not for our pose-based method due to many joints are invisible in 90° view. So we use both 90° and 36° views to compare with these methods, the result is listed in Fig. 4. The comparison shows that proposed method achieves comparable performance with state-of-the-art in normal walking, better than many methods in carrying and clothing conditions. Besides, the comparison of average recognition rate of NM, BG and CL shows that our method achieves good performance, especially for the 36° view.

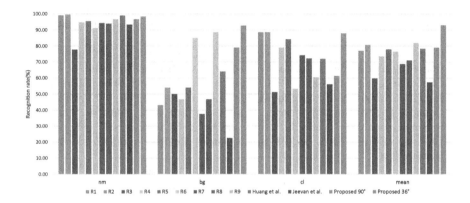

Fig. 4. Comparing with state-of-the-art methods.

4 Conclusions and Future Work

In this paper, we proposed a novel pose-based gait recognition approach to handle with clothing and carrying condition variations. In order to extract the dynamic and static information for gait poses from a sequence of frames, a pose-based temporal-spatial network (PTSN) is proposed which can greatly boost the performance. Experimental results show that our method can improve recognition rate greatly especially for the clothing condition, and achieve state-of-the-art performance.

In the future, we will extend this method to handle with other challenging variations, such as view condition. The view variation is an important challenging in gait recognition. The pose-based gait recognition approach has greatly potential to deal with all variations in gait recognition.

Acknowledgments. The work is supported by the Science Foundation of Shenzhen (Grant No. JCYJ20150324141711699).

References

1. Aggarwal, H., Vishwakarma, D.K.: Covariate conscious approach for gait recognition based upon Zernike moment invariants. CoRR, abs/1611.06683 (2016)
2. Al-Tayyan, A., Assaleh, K., Shanableh, T.: Decision-level fusion for single-view gait recognition with various carrying and clothing conditions. Image Vis. Comput. **61**, 54–69 (2017)
3. Ariyanto, G., Nixon, M.S.: Model-based 3D gait biometrics. In: 2011 International Joint Conference on Biometrics (IJCB), pp. 1–7. IEEE (2011)
4. Ben, X., Meng, W., Yan, R., Wang, K.: An improved biometrics technique based on metric learning approach. Neurocomputing **97**, 44–51 (2012)
5. Ben, X., Zhang, P., Meng, W., Yan, R., Yang, M., Liu, W., Zhang, H.: On the distance metric learning between cross-domain gaits. Neurocomputing **208**, 153–164 (2016)
6. Cao, Z., Simon, T., Wei, S.-E., Sheikh, Y.: Realtime multi-person 2D pose estimation using part affinity fields. arXiv preprint arXiv:1611.08050 (2016)
7. Choudhury, S.D., Tjahjadi, T.: Clothing and carrying condition invariant gait recognition based on rotation forest. Pattern Recogn. Lett. **80**, 1–7 (2016)
8. Cunado, D., Nixon, M.S., Carter, J.N.: Using gait as a biometric, via phase-weighted magnitude spectra. In: Bigün, J., Chollet, G., Borgefors, G. (eds.) AVBPA 1997. LNCS, vol. 1206, pp. 93–102. Springer, Heidelberg (1997). doi:10.1007/BFb0015984
9. Feng, Y., Li, Y., Luo, J.: Learning effective gait features using LSTM. In: 23rd International Conference on Pattern Recognition, ICPR 2016, Cancún, Mexico, 4–8 December 2016, pp. 325–330 (2016)
10. Guan, Y., Li, C., Hu, Y.: Robust clothing-invariant gait recognition. In: Eighth International Conference on Intelligent Information Hiding and Multimedia Signal Processing, IIH-MSP 2012, Piraeus-Athens, Greece, 18–20 July 2012, pp. 321–324 (2012)
11. Hochreiter, S., Schmidhuber, J.: Long short-term memory. Neural Comput. **9**(8), 1735–1780 (1997)
12. Hossain, M.A., Makihara, Y., Wang, J., Yagi, Y.: Clothing-invariant gait identification using part-based clothing categorization and adaptive weight control. Pattern Recogn. **43**(6), 2281–2291 (2010)
13. Huang, X., Boulgouris, N.V.: Gait recognition with shifted energy image and structural feature extraction. IEEE Trans. Image Process. **21**(4), 2256–2268 (2012)
14. Jeevan, M., Jain, N., Hanmandlu, M., Chetty, G.: Gait recognition based on gait pal and pal entropy image. In: 2013 20th IEEE International Conference on Image Processing (ICIP), pp. 4195–4199. IEEE (2013)
15. Kastaniotis, D., Theodorakopoulos, I., Fotopoulos, S.: Pose-based gait recognition with local gradient descriptors and hierarchically aggregated residuals. J. Electron. Imaging **25**(6), 063019 (2016)
16. Liang, Y., Li, C., Guan, Y., Hu, Y.: Gait recognition based on the golden ratio. EURASIP J. Image Video Process. **2016**, 22 (2016)
17. Man, J., Bhanu, B.: Individual recognition using gait energy image. IEEE Trans. Pattern Anal. Mach. Intell. **28**(2), 316–322 (2006)
18. Yu, S., Chen, H., Reyes, E.B.G., Norman, P.: Gaitgan: invariant gait feature extraction using generative adversarial networks. In: Proceedings of the IEEE Conference on Computer Vision and Pattern Recognition Workshops (2017)

19. Simonyan, K., Zisserman, A.: Two-stream convolutional networks for action recognition in videos. In: Advances in neural information processing systems, pp. 568–576 (2014)

20. Wen, Y., Zhang, K., Li, Z., Qiao, Y.: A discriminative feature learning approach for deep face recognition. In: Leibe, B., Matas, J., Sebe, N., Welling, M. (eds.) ECCV 2016. LNCS, vol. 9911, pp. 499–515. Springer, Cham (2016). doi:10.1007/978-3-319-46478-7_31

21. Yu, S., Chen, H., Wang, Q., Shen, L., Huang, Y.: Invariant feature extraction for gait recognition using only one uniform model. Neurocomputing **239**, 81–93 (2017)

22. Yu, S., Tan, D., Tan, T.: A framework for evaluating the effect of view angle, clothing and carrying condition on gait recognition. In: 18th International Conference on Pattern Recognition, ICPR 2006, vol. 4, pp. 441–444. IEEE (2006)

23. Zhang, K., Huang, Y., Du, Y., et al.: Facial expression recognition based on deep evolutional spatial-temporal networks. IEEE Trans. Image Process. **26**, 4193–4203 (2017)

Windowed DMD for Gait Recognition Under Clothing and Carrying Condition Variations

Jiawei Wang[1]([✉]), Edel B. Garcia[2], Shiqi Yu[3], and Dexin Zhang[4]

[1] College of Physics and Energy, Shenzhen University, Shenzhen, China
2014180065@email.szu.edu.cn
[2] Advanced Technologies Applications Center, Havana, Cuba
egarcia@cenatav.co.cu
[3] College of Computer Science, Shenzhen University, Shenzhen, China
shiqi.yu@szu.edu.cn
[4] Tianjin iSecure Technology Co. Ltd., Tianjin, China
zhangdexin@isecure-technology.com

Abstract. In this paper, we introduce a method based on Windowed Dynamic Mode Decomposition to enhance the texture of body parts on the *Gait Energy Image* that are not affected by the clothing and carrying condition variations, in order to improve the gait recognition accuracy under these kinds of variations. We obtain the best accurracy (71.37%) for *large carrying condition variations* reported in the literature for CASIA-B dataset. Unlike the deep learning based approaches the proposal method is simple and does not need training.

Keywords: Gait recognition · Windowed-DMD · Gait energy image · Textural extraction

1 Introduction

Gait is a biometric trait based on the pattern of human's movement of limb and body while they are walking. Normally, each person has his own identical pattern to walk, which make gait recognition possible for identity authentication. In recent years, gait recognition methods and their relevant algorithms have gained more and more interest from security service providers and computer vision researchers.

There are two main categories of gait recognition approaches. The first one is model-based approach, which employs modelling of human body structure and local movement patterns of different body parts [9,11]. The second one is appearance-based approach, which extracts the gait pattern directly from the video frame [13].

The most prevalent gait feature is gait energy image (GEI) [14], which is obtained by simply aggregating the silhouette sequence over one gait period. Extracting a gait pattern from a sequence of video frames is considered a challenge because when capturing a subject's walking pattern using cameras, so

© Springer International Publishing AG 2017
J. Zhou et al. (Eds.): CCBR 2017, LNCS 10568, pp. 484–492, 2017.
https://doi.org/10.1007/978-3-319-69923-3_52

many other variations are also captured in the video, including different view angles, body shape variation due to the clothing, accessories bringing with the subject like bags. Even when the subject is wearing the exact same clothes and accessories, the movement of limbs and body might still be slightly different from the gallery set captured previously.

In order to handle with the clothing and carrying variations many methods have been proposed. As a GEI represents a mixture of static and dynamic parts, some approaches focus more on dynamic parts to mitigate clothing and carrying status variation because such variations mainly affect the static parts. Many authors process the GEI to increase the robustness. For example, the GEI can be divided into parts and the relevant silhouette parts are selected to be used in the classification process. Also, it is possible to compute the Histogram of Oriented Gradients (HOG) of the GEI. Then, the HOG templates can be used for classification.

In this paper, we introduce a method based on Windowed Dynamic Mode Decomposition to enhance the texture of body parts on the GEI that are not affected by the clothing and carrying condition variations, in order to improve the gait recognition accuracy under these kind of variations.

2 Proposed Method

2.1 Dynamic Mode Decomposition

Dynamic Mode Decomposition (DMD) method separates an image into several maps, called dynamic modes, which are associated with Fourier frequencies and can be used to highlighting the image texture when is locally applied. For examples, on GEI image, the area associated to the superpositions of legs movements shows more high frequencies than other body parts. Our motivation is to use DMD to enhance the texture for body parts unaffected by the clothing and carrying condition variations. Our methodological framework is show in Fig. 1 and consists of the following: (i) Computing the GEI from the gait sequences. (ii) Applying the W-DMD method. (iii) Selection of the DMD mode that highlights the GEI texture of legs movement part.

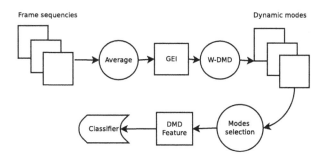

Fig. 1. Flow chart showing the steps involved in the methodological framework.

Windowed-DMD is a variant of original DMD method mainly to capture the textural information by analysing an image by row (or by column) instead of analysing a video sequence by frames. DMD algorithm for textural information is defined as followed:

Let P be an image whose column are given by $\{p_1, p_2, \cdots, p_n\}$. We can assume that there exists a linear mapping A for one column to the consecutive ones, due to the consecutive columns or rows are linearly correlated, resulting P can be represented as the span of Krylov subspace.

$$P = [p_1, Ap_1, A^2 p_1, A^3 p_1, \cdots, A^{N-1} p_1] \tag{1}$$

In Windowed-DMD, we employ DMD algorithm limited to w column sliding window. To simply the notation here we will use $w = 3$

In this case the Krylov subspace is reduced to:

$$P_w = [p1, Ap_1, A^2 p_1] \tag{2}$$

then

$$[p_2, p_3] = A[p_1, p_2] \tag{3}$$

and can be represented using two matrices

$$V_2^3 = [p_2, p_3] \tag{4}$$

and

$$V_1^2 = [p_1, p_2] \tag{5}$$

hence

$$V_2^3 = AV_1^2 + re_2^T \tag{6}$$

The system A captures the textural information within the window, with an vector r representing the residuals that cannot be completely described by A.

If the GEI has a height of m pixels and width of n pixels, applying W-DMD by column, the size of unknown matrix A would be $m \times m$. Unfortunately, solving A is computationally expensive for large image dimensions. In this paper we use a method called the SVD-Based Approach:

We first perform an SVD of V_1^2:

$$V_1^2 = U\Sigma W^T \tag{7}$$

where the matrices U, Σ and V are left singular vectors, singular values and right singular vectors respectively. The inversions of these matrices are then multiplied with V_2^3 subspace to obtain the full-rank matrix $\widetilde{S}$

$$V_2^3 = AU\Sigma W^T + re_2^T \tag{8}$$

Next we leave out the residual re_2^T and multiply U^T on both sides of the Eq. (8) to obtain:

$$U^T V_2^3 = U^T AU\Sigma W^T$$
$$U^T AU = U^T V_2^3 W\Sigma^{-1} \equiv \widetilde{S} \tag{9}$$

Since A and $\widetilde{S}$ are related via similarity transform, the eigenvalues of $\widetilde{S}$ are the eigenvalues of A. If y is the eigenvector of $\widetilde{S}$, then Uy is the eigenvector of A, which is the DMD mode for the window P_w.

Because we only perform DMD on the first three columns $\{p_1, p_2, p_3\}$, we can obtain two DMD modes from the algorithm. For N columns, DMD algorithm can obtain $N-1$ DMD modes [15]. Next step is to slide the window, by excluding the first column and apply procedure to $\{p_2, p_3, p_4\}$, followed by $\{p_3, p_4, p_5\}$, $\{p_4, p_5, p_6\}$ and so on until to $\{p_{n-2}, p_{n-1}, p_n\}$. Finally, we concatenate all DM modes by window to obtain W-DMD modes for the input GEI.

2.2 Gait Energy Image

To apply the Windowed-DMD algorithm in gait recognition we need to obtain an image representing its gait sequence.

Gait Energy Image is defined as

$$G(x, y) = \frac{1}{N} \sum_{t=1}^{N} I(x, y, t) \tag{10}$$

where N determines how many frames are captured during the sequence, I represents a calibrated frame which the test subject is fixed in the center of the canvas. t indicates the tth frame of the sequence and x and y defines the coordinates of the image.

3 Experiments and Analysis

3.1 Dataset

In this section, we test the proposed method on 11 directions of view of the CASIA-B database, which contains 124 subjects. For each person, there are 6 normal walking sequences, 2 sequences walking with a coat and 2 sequences walking carring a bag. Some GEIs from the database are shown in Fig. 2. CASIA-B database provides image sequences with background subtraction for each person. We obtain the GEI feature of each sequences and after the W-DMD is applied to better describe the gait on clothing and carrying condition variations.

(a) Walking normally   (b) Walking with a coat   (c) Walking with a bag

Fig. 2. Walking under different conditions

3.2 Experiments Design and Results

The framework [14] is used to evaluate the performance of our recognition algorithm. For all the experiments there are not variations on the view angle. We are interested in to evaluate the method robustness the clothes and carrying condition variations. We put in the gallery the first four sequences of normal walking (nm) of each person. We image that person is enrolled with normal walking. Then, we use as probe different walking sequences of a person, trying to identify that person from 2 sequences of normal walking (nm), 2 sequences of walking with a coat (cl) and 2 sequences of walking with a carried object (bg). We use the *Correct Classification Rates (CCRs)* as measure of classification performance. This experimental setup is used to study the case of large variations (nm-bg, nm-cl) between the gallery and the probe. The combination (bl-cl) is not taken into account because the number of this kind of sequences is small in the CASIA-B dataset.

We apply the W-DMD using a windows size of 4 rows. In Fig. 3 the three modes are shown. We can see in Fig. 3(c) that the microtexture corresponding to the legs movement is highlighting and these body parts are less affected by the carrying conditions variations.

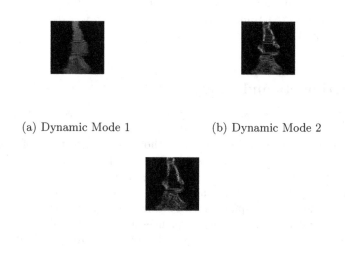

(a) Dynamic Mode 1   (b) Dynamic Mode 2

(c) Dynamic Mode 3

Fig. 3. Dynamic modes. Windows size = 4

Experiment A uses *Sequence Normal #5–#6* as probe set to evaluate the *Correct Classification Rates* on normal walking condition. Person in the gallery and probe are walking under the same view angle. In the gallery and probe the person is walking in normal (nm) conditions. First, the *Correct Classification Rates* are computed for Basic GEI feature. Second, the W-DMD is computed on the Basic GEI. We want to study if the W-DMD feature improves the results reported for the baseline [14] or not. The results are shown in the first rows (Exp. A nm-nm) of Tables 1 and 3.

Table 1. Correct classification rates for large variations for basic GEI.

	0°	18°	36°	54°	72°	90°	108°	126°	144°	162°	180°
Exp. A nm-nm	99.60%	99.60%	97.98%	96.77%	97.18%	97.58%	95.16%	96.77%	96.77%	96.77%	99.60%
Exp. B nm-cl	16.13%	16.53%	20.16%	16.94%	14.92%	14.52%	15.32%	15.32%	20.56%	16.13%	16.94%
Exp. C nm-bg	73.39%	64.11%	56.85%	51.21%	39.11%	31.45%	38.71%	47.58%	45.56%	57.26%	72.98%

Table 2. Evaluation metrics for basic GEI

Metrics	Exp. A nm-nm	Exp. B nm-cl	Exp. C nm-bg
C_Δ	97.62%	16.68%	52.56%
σ	1.45%	1.98%	13.85%

Table 3. Correct classification rates for large variations for GEI+W-DMD.

	0°	18°	36°	54°	72°	90°	108°	126°	144°	162°	180°
Exp. A nm-nm	100%	98.79%	97.98%	96.77%	**97.58%**	**96.77%**	**97.58%**	98.39%	96.77%	97.58%	99.19%
Exp. B nm-cl	29.84%	36.69%	42.74%	47.98%	**55.24%**	50.40%	**50.40%**	46.77%	43.15%	34.27%	35.08%
Exp. C nm-bg	83.47%	75.81%	72.58%	74.60%	**77.82%**	**71.37%**	70.97%	72.18%	73.39%	74.19%	80.65%

Experiment B uses *Sequence Coat #1–#2* as probe set to evaluate how clothing affect the performance in gait recognition and the robustness of the algorithm to body shape variation(e.g. subject wearing a coat). Person in the gallery and probe are walking under the same view angle. In the gallery the person is walking in normal (nm) conditions and in the probe person is walking with a coat (cl). First, the *Correct Classification Rates* are computed for Basic GEI feature. Second, the W-DMD is computed on the Basic GEI. The results are shown in the second rows (Exp. B nm-cl) of Tables 1 and 3.

Experiment C uses *Sequence Bag #1–#2* as probe set to evaluate how accessories affect the performance in gait recognition and the robustness of the algorithm to carrying condition variations (e.g. subject carrying a bag). Person in the gallery and probe are walking under the same view angle. In the gallery the person is walking in normal (nm) conditions and in the probe person is walking with a carried object (bg). First, the *Correct Classification Rates* are computed for Basic GEI feature. Second, the W-DMD is computed on the Basic GEI. The results are shown in the threeth rows (Exp. C nm-bg) of Tables 1 and 3.

From Tables 2 and 4 we can see that W-DWD feature improves the accuracy for all the view angles and experiments. Especially, for carrying condition variations the performance is increased from 52.56% to 75.18%. Even more, the Correct Classification Rate for normal walking conditions is increased from 97.62% to 97.95%.

Table 4. Evaluation metrics for GEI with W-DMD enhancement

Metrics	Exp. A nm-nm	Exp. B nm-cl	Exp. C nm-bg
C_Δ	97.95%	42.96%	75.18%
σ	1.06%	8.06%	3.98%

3.3   Comparisons with Other Existing Methods Under Large Variation of Clothing and Carrying Condition

The proposed method is further compared with other existing methods in the literature, under changes of clothing and carrying condition. Table 5 shows the comparison results. These cases are under one viewing angle which is 90°.

The proposed method has reported for 90° of viewing angle, almost the same performance that the Basic GEI (96.77% vs 97.6%), for the case of no variation (nm-nm) and achieved significantly better performance for the case of large variations caused by clothing (nm-cl) and carrying condition (nm-bg) changes. We can see at the Table 5 that it obtains the best accuracy (71.37%) for *large carrying condition variations* (nm-bg) reported in the literature for CASIA-B dataset.

Table 5. Comparisons with other existing methods under large variation of clothing and carrying condition. The viewing angle is 90°.

Gallery-probe	Exp. A nm-nm	Exp. B nm-cl	Exp. C nm-bg
GEI-framewok [14]	97.6	32.7	52.0
GEI-2DLPP [10]	95.2	44.4	55.7
EGEI-2DLPP [10]	95.7	48.4	48.8
GEI+CDA [7]	99.4	22.0	60.2
RF+FSS [3]	99.4	22.0	60.2
RF+FSS+CDA [3]	100.0	33.1	50.0
RF+FSS+MDA [3]	99.6	33.9	46.0
Mj+ACDA [2]	99.6	33.0	54.9
LF+AVG [12]	71.4	20.2	43.1
LF+DTW [12]	61.9	25.0	21.4
LF+oHMM [12]	63.8	22.6	19.7
LF+iHMM [12]	94.0	42.9	45.2
GEI+PCA+LDA [4]	90.5	22.6	44.1
GPPE [5]	93.4	22.4	56.1
GEnI [6]	92.3	26.5	56.1
STIPs [8]	95.4	52.0	60.9
Proposal	96.77	50.40	71.37

4   Conclusions

The proposed method is effective for person identification under carrying conditions variations. The Correct Classification Rate is increased from 52.56% to 75.18% averaging for all the viewing angles. In particular for 90° of viewing angle the performance was increased from 31.45% to 71.37%. In this case, the W-DMD feature increased the performance for clothing condition variations from 14.52% to 50.40%. It shows again, that clothing changes are difficult to solve. The method can be used in scenery where there is not change on the viewing angle. A variation between 72° and 108° of view angle can be a good compromise because for normal walking conditions the performance is almost the same that for Basic GEI. Unlike the deep learning based approaches the proposal method is simple and does not need training.

References

1. Tirunagari, S., Poh, N., Bober, M., Windridge, D.: Windowed DMD as a microtexture descriptor for finger vein counter-spoofing in biometrics. In: 2015 IEEE International Workshop on Information Forensics and Security (WIFS), pp. 1–6, November 2015
2. Bashir, K., Xiang, T., Gong, S.: Gait recognition without subject cooperation. Pattern Recognit. Lett. **31**(13), 2052–2060 (2010)
3. Dupuis, Y., Savatier, X., Vasseur, P.: Feature subset selection applied to model-free gait recognition. J. Image Vis. Comput. **31**(8), 580–591 (2013)
4. Sarkar, S., Phillips, P.J., Liu, Z., Vega, I.R., Grother, P., Bowyer, K.W.: The human ID gait challenge problem: data sets, performance, and analysis. IEEE Trans. Pattern Anal. Mach. Intell. **27**(2), 162–177 (2005)
5. Jeevan, M., Jain, N., Madasu, H., Chetty, G.: Gait recognition based on gait pal and pal entropy image. In: Proceedings IEEE International Conference on Image Process, pp. 4195–4199, September 2013
6. Bashir, K., Xiang, T., Gong, S.: Gait recognition using gait entropy image. In: Proceedings of International Conference on Crime Detection and Prevention, pp. 1–6, December 2009
7. Bashir, K., Xiang, T., Gong, S.: Feature selection for gait recognition without subject cooperation. In: Proceedings of British Machine Vision Conference, pp. 1–10, September 2008
8. Kusakunniran, W.: Recognizing gaits on spatio-temporal feature domain. IEEE Trans. Inf. Forensics Secur. **9**(9), 1416–1423 (2014)
9. Kovac, J., Peer, P.: Human skeleton model based dynamic features for walking speed invariant gait recognition. Math. Probl. Eng. **2014**(6), 15 (2014)
10. Zhang, E., Zhao, Y., Xiong, W.: Active energy image plus 2DLPP for gait recognition. Sig. Process. **90**(7), 2295–2302 (2010)
11. Haiping, L.: A Full-Body Layered Deformable Model for Automatic Model-Based Gait Recognition. Hindawi Publishing Corporation, Cairo (2008)
12. Hu, M., Wang, Y., Zhang, Z., Zhang, D., Little, J.J.: Incremental learning for video-based gait recognition with lbp flow. IEEE Trans. Syst. Man Cybern. B Cybern. **43**(1), 77–89 (2013)

13. Wang, L., Tan, T., Ning, H., et al.: Silhouette analysis-based Gait recognition for human identification. IEEE Trans. Pattern Anal. Mach. Intell. **25**(12), 1505–1518 (2003)
14. Yu, S., Tan, D., Tan, T.: A framework for evaluating the effect of view angle, clothing and carrying condition on Gait recognition. In: International Conference on Pattern Recognition, pp. 441–444. IEEE Computer Society (2006)
15. Tirunagari, S., Poh, N., Windridge, D., et al.: Detection of face spoofing using visual dynamics. IEEE Trans. Inf. Forensics Secur. **10**(4), 762–777 (2015)

Emerging Biometrics

Research on Dig-Imprint Detection
of Three-Dimensional Footprints

Han Sun$^{(\boxtimes)}$, Yunqi Tang, and Wei Guo

School of Forensic Science, People's Public Security University of China,
Beijing 10038, China
sunhan_930708@outlook.com, 64136997@qq.com,
gd928@sina.com

Abstract. In Chinese forensic science, a three-dimensional footprint can provide us lots of information, such as sex, age and gait. Dig-imprint is one of the impressions in three-dimensional footprints that can show the biometric. However, the three-dimensional footprints are still analyzed artificially by forensic investigators, which is inefficient and subjective. In this research an algorithm for the automatic detection of dig-imprints of three-dimensional footprints was developed. Haar-like and LBP features were extracted from the dataset. Next, two classifiers were constructed with Adaboost algorithm using these two features. A dig-imprint database is constructed for evaluating the performance of the proposed method. Pictures of three-dimensional footprints were taken by the way of criminal scene photography. Then the dig-imprints were cut out as positive samples. The negative samples were also cut out from three-dimensional footprints. Experimental results shows that the proposed method achieves good detection accuracy.

Keywords: Footprints · Haar feature · Local binary pattern · Adaboost

1 Introduction

In Chinese forensic science, three-dimensional footprints can indicate a lot of information of human. Experts can get to know the sex, age and even gait from three-dimensional footprints [1]. As a biological pattern, three-dimensional footprints contain so much information because of different kinds of impressions in them. Dig-impression is one of the impressions in three-dimensional footprints, which appears just behind the front edge of three-dimensional footprints. It is a major impression created in the process of lifting a foot because toes are pushing the ground to make one's body move forward. Dig-impression is a depressed hole shaped like an arc (Fig. 1). This impression shows the speed, strength and angle when someone walks by. Generally, young people have a higher possibility to leave this impression than middle-aged people and the position of this impression is relatively stable. Chinese public security experts can estimate the pedestrian's age with this impression. However, the analysis of three-dimensional footprints is still conducted artificially only by technicians with rich experience, and this is inefficient and subjective.

Researches on automatic way to analyze footprints are still at the initial stage. However, great contributions have been made by lots of researchers. Wu et al.

© Springer International Publishing AG 2017
J. Zhou et al. (Eds.): CCBR 2017, LNCS 10568, pp. 495–502, 2017.
https://doi.org/10.1007/978-3-319-69923-3_53

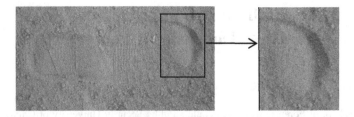

Fig. 1. The dig-imprint

(2010) use 3D scanner to create a 3-dimensional model of a footprint for comparing. Liu et al. (2017) developed a system combined of laser-ranging sensor, computer controlling and image processing for analyzing three-dimensional footprints. This system measure some depth, length and angle for comparing. Some researchers focus on the plantar pressure. Queen et al. [2], analyzed the plantar pressure characteristics of 50 healthy testers with standard and flat feet to study the influence caused by different foot characteristics. Researchers in Chinese Academy of Sciences Institute of Automation implemented personal recognition using wavelet packet coefficients of plantar pressure as the gait feature [3]. Principal component analysis method was adopted in plantar pressure analysis by Muniz, and it shows a good result in identify normal and abnormal gait [4]. Han et al. studied the stability of plantar pressure under normal walking condition [5]. Beside face recognition [6], the technique of object detection is widely used in many areas. Zhao et al., developed an algorithm to detect ripe tomatoes based on Haar-like algorithm [7]. Tambasco Bruno et al. presented a method to describe texture in breast cancer tissues based on LBP [8]. García-Olalla et al. used LBP combined with LOSIB to develop an automatic process to determine tool wear in machining procedures [9]. Li et al. presented a new way to recognize hand-dorsa vein for personal identification based on improved PLBP [10].

However, these researches ignored the shape of three-dimensional footprints. Inspired by objection detection technology, in this paper we used Adaboost algorithm to develop a computer vision approach to detect dig-imprints in three-dimensional footprints, in order to make a first step in automatically analyzing three-dimensional footprints in Chinese traditional forensic science way.

2   Technical Details

Figure 2 shows the developing and usage process of this algorithm. We established a dataset and tried two feature extraction method. Then, Adaboost algorithm was adopted to train classifiers. Finally, we chose a better classifier for detection according to the test result.

2.1   Haar-like Feature

Haar-like features have been popularly employed in face detection for its efficiency. Papageorgiou et al. (1998) firstly proposed to represent objects in terms of a subset of

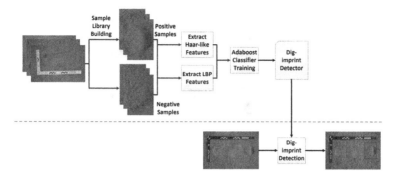

Fig. 2. Flow diagram of the proposed method

over-complete dictionary of Haar wavelet basis functions [11]. Haar-like features reflect the gray scale of the pixels in the region. A Haar-like filter consists of two different square regions, the white squares and the black squares. In a Haar-like filter, the feature value is equal to the sum of white region pixels minuses black region pixels.

To calculate Haar-like features rapidly, an integral image method could be very useful [12]. With this method, the sum of grey scale pixel values within any rectangular region could be computed by referencing only four points of rectangular from the integral image. As shown in Fig. 3(a), in an integral image the value of P is equal to the sum of pixels of the gray part. So, in integral image the sum of the pixels in rectangle in Fig. 3(b) is equal to $d + a - b - c$.

(a)Value of a point in an integral image   (b)Calculate the sum of pixels in a rectangle

Fig. 3. Principle of integral image

There are many types of Haar-like features. In this research, 10 kinds of Haar-like features are chosen (Fig. 4). In this research, we set the step of Haar-like features is 2 pixels and the length of the square has 1, 2 and 5 pixels three types.

2.2 Local Binary Pattern (LBP)

The technique of local binary patterns (LBP) [13] was first introduced by Ojala in 1994 to describe the texture of grayscale images. Now it is widely used in face detection. When given a central pixel, the value of LBP is computed by comparing its value with the pixels around it according to the following equation:

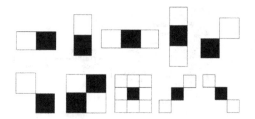

Fig. 4. 10 Haar-like features used in this research

$$LBP_{P,R} = \sum_{p=0}^{p-1} s(g_p - g_c)2^p \quad s(x) = \begin{cases} 1 \ if \ x \geq 0 \\ 0 \ if \ x \prec 0 \end{cases} \quad (1)$$

where g_c is the value of central pixel, g_p is the value of one of the neighboring pixel, P is the number of neighbors and R is the radius of neighborhood. However, original LBP may produce 2^P patterns, which is too many. Ojala et al. created uniform LBP to solve this problem [14]. It can be defined as:

$$U(LBP_{P,R}) = \left| s(g_{p-1} - g_c) - s(g_0 - g_c) \right| + \sum_{p=1}^{p-1} \left| s(g_p - g_c) - s(g_{p-1} - g_c) \right| \leq 2 \quad (2)$$

In this research, we used uniform LBP, the radius was 1 and the number of sampling points was 8. So there were 59 patterns in all. To compute LBP feature, a sample photos should be divided into small blocks of small size. Then, calculated the histogram of uniform LBP of each blocks. At last, histograms are concatenated into a global histogram as a feature vector. In this work, we divided samples into blocks of 10 × 10 pixels.

2.3   Adaboost

Adaboost is an adaptive boosting iterative method [15]. The input of this algorithm is an S of N dataset. $S = (x_i, y_i)$, $i = 1, ..., N$ $x_i \in X$ is the feature vector and $y_i \in Y = \{0, 1\}$ is the class label. 1 represents positive samples and 0 represents negative samples. A weak learning algorithm will be conducted repeatedly for several rounds. At the beginning, all the samples will be assigned the same weight. After each round of training, the weight of incorrectly classified examples is increased in order to focus on them in the next round. In each round of training, Adaboost will generate an optimal classifiers called weaker classifiers. Finally, it linearly combines these weaker classifiers with their weights together to form a strong classifier.

3   Experiments and Analysis

In this research, all algorithm development steps and experiments were performed on MATLAB (R2013a) with 64-bit Intel®Core i7® 2.5 GHz CPU.

3.1   Dataset Construction

For developing proposed algorithm, 300 university students were invited to walk on the bunker. Before a student started walking, the bunker had been swept to make sure it was flat. After a student had walked by, we took a photo of each footprints. The proposed algorithm is developed mainly for public security, so the footprints were shot in the way of criminal scene photography, which requires camera is perpendicular to footprint and the footprints must be distinguishable (Fig. 5). The camera in this research is Nikon D7000. The condition is natural daylight.

Fig. 5. A three-dimensional footprint image

After shooting the footprints, each photo was checked. If there is a dig-imprint in the footprints, we cut out the dig-imprint as a positive sample. The length-width ratio maintained 3:2. Then the positive samples were resized to 300 × 200 pixels using the nearest neighbor interpolation algorithm. In this research, 1100 positive samples were collected (Fig. 6). 1000 positive samples were taken as training set, 100 were taken as test set.

Fig. 6. Some positive samples

Because the proposed algorithm is used in forensic science, the negative samples were also cut out from the footprint photos. Dig-imprints only appear behind the front edge of footprints, so the front part of footprints without dig-imprint has great importance in negative examples. If there is not a dig-imprint in the footprint photo, the front part of this footprint was also cut out as a negative sample. 1132 negative samples were cut out from the front part of footprints and 2201 negative samples were cut out from other parts of the photos (Fig. 7). In training set, there are 1000 negative samples from the front part of footprints, 2000 negative samples from other parts of the photos. The rest 333 negative samples were taken as test set.

Fig. 7. Some negative samples

3.2   Features Extraction and Training

Samples of 300 × 200 pixels are too big. Too many useless features will be calculated and the computation will be large. So, every sample had been resized to 30 × 20 pixels and converted into gray images before extracting features.

First, extract features with Haar-like algorithm. In this way, 3157 Haar-like features were extracted in a sample. Secondly, extract features with LBP algorithm. There are 354 LBP features in a sample. At last, these two kinds of features were individually trained with Adaboost algorithm. In this paper, the highest number of iteration was 3000 with Haar-like features and 340 of LBP features. When the times of iteration reaches the highest, the algorithm would stop. Finally, two strong classifiers were developed.

3.3   Results and Analysis

After 3000 times of iteration, the test results of algorithm developed with Haar-like were as shown in Table 1. It shows that after 1174 times of iteration, the TPR (True Positive Rate) reaches the highest of 95.00% and the FPR (False Positive Rate) reaches 10.81%.

After 340 times of iteration, the test results of algorithm developed with LBP were as shown in Table 1. We can see that after 311 times of iteration, the TPR reaches 98.00% and the FPR reaches the lowest of 12.01%.

Table 1. Part of test results

Using Haar-like features	Iteration	467	711	1174	1384	2000	3000
	TPR	0.9500	0.9400	0.9500	0.9400	0.8900	0.8700
	FPR	0.1231	0.1021	0.1081	0.1081	0.1141	0.1081
Using LBP features	Iteration	24	101	168	208	311	313
	TPR	0.9800	0.9900	0.9900	0.9900	0.9800	0.9800
	FPR	0.1832	0.1622	0.1351	0.1351	0.1201	0.1201

To analyze the performance of this two algorithm, Receiver Operating Characteristic (ROC) curves were drawn and the area under the ROC curve (AUC) was calculated. The closer the ROC curve is to the point (0,1), the more the AUC is approaching 1 and the better this algorithm performs. As shown in Fig. 8, the algorithm developed with LBP features got an AUC of 0.9672, which is bigger than 0.9492 of LBP. So the algorithm developed with LBP and Adaboost was chosen as the dig-imprint detector.

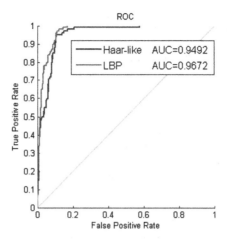

Fig. 8. ROC curve of the two algorithm

4   Conclusion and Future Work

In this research, two methods of feature extraction were conducted and they all showed a good result in test. However, LBP algorithm showed a better result in ROC curve analysis. So we choose the algorithm developed with LBP and Adaboost as the detection algorithm. This research was conducted in order to analyze three-dimensional footprints efficiently. The developed algorithm is accurate enough to help technicians detect dig-imprints.

In the future, the amount of samples could be larger and the algorithm would be more reliable. Dig-imprint is only one of the impressions in three-dimensional foot-prints. Feature work is to detect more impressions with high accuracy. In Chinese traditional forensic science, these impressions can be used to calculate for identifica-tion. So the calculation process could be added into the algorithm in the future to achieve the ultimate goal of personal identification.

Acknowledgments. This work is supported by the National Natural Science Foundation of China (Grant No. 61503387).

References

1. Shi, L., et al.: Footprint足迹学. People's Public Security University of China, Beijing (2007)
2. Queen, R.M., Abbey, A.N., Wiegerinck, J.I., et al.: Effect of shoe type on plantar pressure: a gender comparison. J. Gait Posture **31**, 18–22 (2013)
3. Xu, S., Zhou, X., Sun, Y.: A novel platform system for gait analysis. In: Proceedings of the 2008 International Conference on Human System Interactions, pp. 1045–1049 (2008)
4. Manfio, E.F., Nadal, J., Muniz, A.M.S., et al.: Principal component analysis of vertical ground reaction force: a powerful method to discriminate normal and abnormal gait and

assess treatment. In: International Conference of the IEEE Engineering in Medicine & Biology Society, pp. 2294–2297. IEEE, New York (2006)

5. Han, D., Yunqi, T., Wei, G.: Research on the stability of plantar pressure under normal walking condition. In: Tan, T., Li, X., Chen, X., Zhou, J., Yang, J., Cheng, H. (eds.) CCPR 2016. CCIS, vol. 662, pp. 234–242. Springer, Singapore (2016). doi:10.1007/978-981-10-3002-4_20

6. Viola, P., Jones, M.J.: Robust Real-Time Face Detection. Kluwer Academic Publishers, Netherlands (2004)

7. Zhao, Y., Gong, L., Zhou, B., Huang, Y., Liu, C.: Detecting tomatoes in greenhouse scenes by combining AdaBoost classifier and colour analysis. J. Biosyst. Eng. **148**, 127–137 (2016)

8. Tambasco Bruno, D.O., do Nascimento, M.Z., Ramos, R.P., Batista, V.R., Neves, L.A., Martins, A.S.: LBP operators on curvelet coefficients as an algorithm to describe texture in breast cancer tissues. J. Expert Syst. Appl. **55**, 329–340 (2016)

9. García-Olalla, O., Alegre, E., Barreiro, J., et al.: Tool wear classification using LBP-based descriptors combined with LOSIB-based enhancers. J. Procedia Eng. **132**, 950–957 (2015)

10. Li, K., Zhang, G., Wang, Y., Wang, P., Ni, C.: Hand-dorsa vein recognition based on improved partition local binary patterns. Biometric Recognition. LNCS, vol. 9428, pp. 312–320. Springer, Cham (2015). doi:10.1007/978-3-319-25417-3_37

11. Papageorgiou, C., Oren, M., Poggio, T.: A general framework for object detection. In: Proceedings of International Conference on Computer Vision, pp. 555–562. IEEE Press, New York (1998)

12. Viola, P., Jones, M.: Rapid object detection using a boost cascade of simple features. In: Proceedings of Conference on Computer Vision and Pattern Recognition, pp. 511–518. IEEE Press, New York (2001)

13. Ojala, T., Pietikainen, M., Harwood, D.: A comparative study of texture measures with classification based on feature distributions. J. Pattern Recognit. **29**, 51–59 (1996)

14. Ojala, T., Pietikainen, M., Maenpaa, T.: Multiresolution gray-scale and rotation invariant texture classification with Local Binary Patterns. J. IEEE Trans. Pattern Anal. Mach. Intell. **24**, 971–987 (2002)

15. Goldberg, D.E.: Genetic algorithm in search. J. Optim. Mach. Learn. **1**(7), 2104–2116 (1989)

ECG Based Identification by Deep Learning

Gang Zheng, Shengzhen Ji$^{(\boxtimes)}$, Min Dai, and Ying Sun

Tianjin Key Laboratory of Intelligent Computing and Novel Software
Technology, Tianjin University of Technology, Tianjin 300384, China
kenneth_zheng@vip.163.com, shulinji@163.com,
{daimin, sunying}@tjut.edu.cn

Abstract. Strategies were proposed for Electrocardiogram (ECG) based identification. Firstly, a selecting mechanism based on information entropy was used
to obtain whole heart beat signal; Secondly, a Depth Neural Network (DNN)
based on Denoising AutoEncoder (DAE) was adopted in feature selection
unsupervised, by which, the robustness of the recognition system could be
improved in recognizing. Finally, 98.10% and 95.67% recognition rate were
obtained on self-collected calm and high pressure data sets respectively, and
94.39% rate on combined data sets of MIT arrhythmia database (mitdb) and
self-collected data averagely.

Keywords: Deep learning · Waveform selecting · Emotion status · ECG based
identification

1 Introduction

Nowadays, identity technologies are becoming part of our social life, identification
security and its convenience usage have been drawn more attention, therefore, biometric techniques based identification have becoming hot research spot gradually. The
biometric contains face [1], fingerprint [2], iris [3] and so on. ECG waveform reflects
heart electric activity by voltage changing [4]. Since ECG waveform can only exist on
living creature, it can hardly be forged, and this character makes it unique to other
biometric. The studies of it on identification have lasting two more decades.

Studies on ECG based identification were in two ways, one is on ECG fiducial
features, the other is non-fiducial features [5]. In fiducial features studies, combination
of temporal, amplitude, angle between or among peak or valley points of ECG
waveform and time length of heart beat (R-R interval, changeable) were used [6–10],
see Fig. 1(a). The accuracy rate of identity is tightly related to the recognition degree of
peak and valley point of ECG waveform.

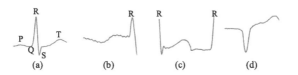

Fig. 1. Examples of complete (a), and incomplete (b), (c), (d) single periodic ECG signal

© Springer International Publishing AG 2017
J. Zhou et al. (Eds.): CCBR 2017, LNCS 10568, pp. 503–510, 2017.
https://doi.org/10.1007/978-3-319-69923-3_54

In nonfiducial features studies, single or more periods ECG waveform (each amplitude value of ECG) were used for identification. One difficulty in studies was to orientate R point firstly, and ECG waveform as input data [11–14]. Misrecognition of R point may resulted in incomplete periodic ECG extraction, shown as Fig. 1(b)(c)(d).

Data used in ECG based identification studies were mostly collected in calm status. To solve the problem, firstly, the paper proposed a screening mechanism for ECG data integrity by the help of information entropy. The method can make ECG waveform segmentation and data selection work beyond man's participating, and improve accuracy rate of ECG based identification. Secondly, deep learning was used in feature extracting and human identifying. Different from artificial feature extraction in traditional methods, it can search ECG features automatically and effectively, and it can also achieve good classification results. Finally, in order to verify the robustness of the proposed method, the paper ran test on self collected ECG signals in calm and pressure status, and promising results were gotten. The whole procedure was shown in Fig. 2.

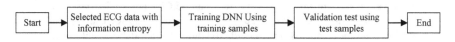

Fig. 2. Flowchart of the proposed method

2 Information Entropy Based ECG Signal Selecting Mechanism

In the paper, $T = \{(X_i, Y_i)\}_{i=1}^{n}$ was assumed as training set, it was composed of n single periodic ECG signals as input data. X_i stands for i^{th} ECG signal, it was composed of m amplitude value, $X_i = \{x_1^i, x_2^i, x_3^i, \ldots x_m^i\}$, and Y_i was test data tag.

Information entropy is a measurement of confusion and dispersion degree of data set. The information entropy of X_i was shown in formula (1), b is the class number of X_i, p_a is the appearing probability of the ath class of amplitude in the X_i.

$$E(X_i) = \sum_{a=1}^{b} -p_a \log_2 p_a \tag{1}$$

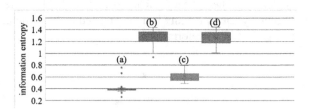

Fig. 3. Information entropy of ECG data on different ECG data set self-collected data set: (a) completed ECG data, (b) incompleted ECG data; mitdb data set: (c) completed ECG data (d) incompleted ECG data

Randomly selected 100 complete and 100 incomplete single beat ECG signals from mitdb and self-collected data set respectively. From computing result, when p_a was 100%, $E(X_{\text{complete}})$ was less than 1, $E(X_{\text{incomplete}})$ was greater than 1, and 1 was the separating value of the two kinds of ECG data, shown in Fig. 3.

3   ECG Signal Based Identification by Deep Learning

3.1   Pre-training: Unsupervised Feature Learning by DAE

Pre-training was to restrain all weight matrices and bias vectors in a certain parameter space, and optimizing system parameter of neural network smoothly. DAE relies unsupervised training and layer by layer greedy algorithm to learn features from sample data set. Noise was added to input data for improving the robustness of feature representation, shown in Fig. 4(a).

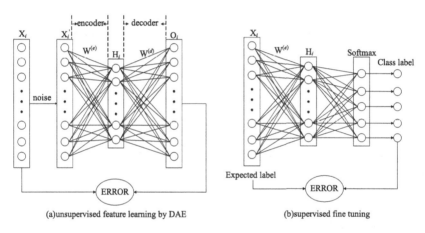

(a)unsupervised feature learning by DAE   (b)supervised fine tuning

Fig. 4. DNN architecture

DAE consists of two parts: encoding and decoding. In the encoding process, the noisy input X'_i was mapped to the hidden layer H_i, shown as formula (2).

$$H_i = f(W^{(e)}X'_i + b^{(e)}) \tag{2}$$

The $W^{(e)}$ represented as weight matrix and $b^{(e)}$ as bias vector in encoding process, f is activation function, the sigmoid function was usually chosen, shown in formula (3).

$$f(v) = 1/(1 + e^{-v}) \tag{3}$$

The decoding process was actually using hidden layer features of H_i to reconstruct the input layer data X_i, it was the procedure that the hidden layer H_i was mapped to output layer O_i, shown in formula (4).

$$O_i = f(W^{(d)}H_i + b^{(d)}) \tag{4}$$

$W^{(d)}$ represented as weight matrix and $b^{(d)}$ as bias vector in the decoding process, f was same to formula (3). The process of training DAE was to find the minimum reconstruction error of the parameter $\theta = \{W^{(e)}, b^{(e)}, b^{(d)}\}$ on the training sample set X. Expression of reconstruction error was shown in formula (5).

$$J = \sum_{X_i \in X} L(X_i, O_i) \tag{5}$$

L is the reconstruction error function, it adopted the cross entropy loss function shown in formula (6), the greater the error, the faster the weight updated.

$$L(X_i, O_i) = -\sum_{i=1}^{d_x} X_i \log O_i + (1 - X_i) \log(1 - O_i) \tag{6}$$

The basic steps of the whole pre-training stage can be summarized as follows:

(1) The weight matrix $W^{(e)}$ and $W^{(d)}$ are randomly initialized, the first layer of the neural network was trained in an unsupervised manner, and the output was used as the original input to minimize the reconstruction error, and the error was controlled within a certain range;

(2) The output of each hidden layer element serves as input to the next layer of neural networks, and step (1) was repeated. The weight matrix $W^{(e)}$ and $W^{(d)}$ were adjusted until a specified number of hidden layer training was performed;

(3) The parameters such as node settings and weights of unsupervised networks were preserved to initialize a supervised neural network.

3.2 Fine Tuning Stage

The supervised neural network was initialized and the network parameters were tuned by training the sample set repeatedly. After pre-training, a supervised neural network with the same structure as the pre -training was constructed. In this paper, BP neural network was selected, and the soft-max function was added in the network output layer to construct multiple classifiers. The core idea of fine tuning was to use a supervised training data set to further adjust neural network obtained from pre-training stage meticulously in many iterations, as shown in Fig. 4(b).

The basic steps can be summarized as follows:

(1) The network was initialized by network parameters such as the weight matrix W (e) and the bias vectors b (e) obtained from the pre-training phase;

(2) Supervised neural networks were trained by a tagged sample set;

(3) Calculated the error between the layers of the network and adjusts the weights and bias vectors based on the error;

(4) Repeat training until the entire network output had met the desired requirements.

In order to reduce the network cost function, the weight attenuation strategy was applied to the BP neural network, and the error function formula (7) is shown below:

$$E = 0.5 \sum_i (X_i - O_i)^2 + 0.5\,\mu \sum_{ij} [W_{ij}/(1 + W_{ij}^2)] \tag{7}$$

μ is weight attenuation activation factor, when $\mu = 0$, weight attenuation function is activated, the weight updating formula (8) is shown below.

$$\Delta W_{ij} = -\frac{\alpha E}{W_{ij}} = \alpha\,H_i(X_i - O_i)O_i(1 - O_i) - \alpha\mu \frac{W_{ij}}{1 + W_{ij}^2} \tag{8}$$

α is the learning rate, when learning rate was greater, the weight change was faster, and the convergence rate was faster. But if the value was too large, it was easy to cause system oscillation. The weight attenuation strategy [16] strengthens the higher weights, but weakens the smaller weights, and applies different degrees of punishment to the different weights, this accelerates the convergence speed, reduces the error, and enhances the robustness of the neural network.

4 Experimental Results and Analysis

4.1 Data Description

The experimental data were in three groups; one was from mitdb, sampling rate 360 Hz; self-collected ECG data in the real environment, sampling rate 250 Hz, ECG device was produced by us; and different emotion status data (pressure and calm) that derived from Zheng team [17], sampling rate 250 Hz.

4.2 Experimental Scheme

Three data sources were use in the paper, first one, 13 individuals from the mitdb, aged 32–84 years old, including 8 male and 5 female; second one, 28 individuals from self-collected ECG database, aged 23–26 years old, including 14 male and 14 female, and third one, 19 individuals with different emotion status, aged 20–22 years, 10 male and 9 female. In the experiment, we randomly selected 400 ECG data from each individual in two groups: one was filtered by selecting mechanism, the other was not. Traditional BP neural network and the DNN were use for classifying in three experiment scenarios.

Experiment 1: In mitdb and self-collected database, from each individual, we randomly select 120 data as training set, and 280 data to construct test set.

Experiment 2: In Zheng's [17] data set, 200 data in pressure and calm status of each individual were randomly selected, 60 for training, 140 data were to build test set.

Experiment 3: After normalizing the sample rate of above three data sources, 60 individuals were involved, 400 data from each person were randomly select, 120 for training, and 280 for test.

4.3   Experiment Result Analysis

Results of above experiment were shown in Tables 1, 2, 3 and 4.

Table 1. Correct recognition rates of BP and DNN on the mitdb and self-collected database

Data source	Amount of sample	The correct recognition rates			
		BP		DNN	
		Raw data	Filtered data	Raw data	Filtered data
mitdb	13	90.33%	92.39%	94.24%	96.63%
Self-collected database	28	90.63%	91.57%	97.16%	98.10%

Table 2. The correct recognition rates of BP and the DNN on different emotion status data

Emotion status	Amount of sample	The correct recognition rates			
		BP		DNN	
		Raw data	Filtered data	Raw data	Filtered data
Calm and high pressure	19	84.13%	85.26%	94.54%	95.67%
Calm	19	91.24%	91.24%	96.02%	96.02%
High pressure	19	77.81%	78.31%	94.35%	94.85%

Table 3. The correct recognition rates of BP and the DNN on 60 normalized data

Data source	Amount of sample	The correct recognition rates			
		BP		DNN	
		Raw data	Filtered data	Raw data	Filtered data
Normalized data	60	–	–	92.54%	94.39%

Table 4. Comparison of convergence rate on different data sets

Data source	Amount of sample	Convergence rate (second)	
		BP	DNN
		Filtered data	Filtered data
mitdb	13	30 s	8 s
Self-collected database	28	60 s	12 s
ECG database of calm and high pressure	19	70 s	16 s
Normalized data	60	–	40 s

Symbol '–' meant that no result was gotten dues to non-converge in training process of traditional BP. In contrast to experimental results of raw data and filtered data expressed in Tables 1, 2, 3, screening mechanism proposed in this paper can effectively filter out the incomplete single periodic ECG signals.

Tables 1 and 2 showed that the proposed identification method can be applied to different data sources, and achieve good recognition effects on mitdb and data under different emotion status. The results shown in Table 2 imply that the correct recognition rate of ECG data collected in the calm emotion was higher 2% than the data collected in the high pressure emotion. It means that the accuracy of using one's different status of ECG data for identification was slightly different. In the third experiment, during training, the traditional BP neural network could not converge, resulting in no final prediction results. However, the depth learning method used in this paper can get a high accuracy of recognition. In the Table 4, the convergence rate of the DNN in each data set was much higher than that of the traditional BP neural network, which means that the DNN has strong feature learning ability.

By comparing the results and analysis of the three groups of experiments, the following conclusions were given in this paper.

(1) In this paper, a method of screening incomplete single periodic ECG signals was proposed, and has been validated in self-collected database and mitdb, which effectively reduced the effect of ECG waveform segmentation errors on ECG identification results;

(2) A new identification method based on ECG signal was used in this paper, which could automatically learn ECG signal features, reduced the human intervention. This method was suitable for self-collected database, mitdb and self-collected ECG signal database under different emotion status, which achieved a good classification effect and had high robustness;

(3) The deep learning method used in this paper realizes the identification of ECG signals in the scale of 60 samples whose ECG data were collected in different status, and achieved the correct recognition rate of 94.39%. This method had a strong learning ability and classification function compared with the traditional BP neural network;

(4) The ECG signals of different emotion status were used in this paper for identification experiments, although the ECG signal identification results were affected by the emotion changes, the ECG signal identification results under different emotion status still reached 95.67%, which showed the ECG signals under different emotion status as the basis for identification with high reliability.

5   Summary and Further Work

In this paper, a selecting strategy based on information entropy was proposed, which can successfully filter incomplete single periodic ECG signals out, reduce its effect of identification accuracy. DAE was used in this paper can automatically learn the features of ECG signals, and ECG identification was done by the DNN. In the future work, we will expand the scale of the identification sample, and use the ECG signals of more status for identification.

Acknowledgments. The paper was supported by Tianjin Natural Science Foundation 16JCYBJC15300 (2016.04–2019.03) and Tianjin Natural Science Foundation 15JCYBJC15800 (2015.04–2018.03).

References

1. Ghazi, M.M., Ekenel, H.K.: A comprehensive analysis of deep learning based representation for face recognition. In: Computer Vision & Pattern Recognition Workshops, pp. 102–109 (2016)
2. Ali, M.M.H., Mahale, V.H., Yannawar, P., Gaikwad, A.T.: Fingerprint recognition for person identification and verification based on minutiae matching. In: IEEE International Conference on Advanced Computing, pp. 332–339 (2016)
3. Garagad, V.G., Iyer, N.C.: A novel technique of iris identification for biometric systems. In: International Conference on Advances in Computing, pp. 973–978 (2014)
4. Ramos, J., Ausín, J.L., Lorido, A.M., Redondo, F., Duque-Carrillo, J.F.: A wireless multi-channel bioimpedance measurement system for personalized healthcare and lifestyle. Stud. Health Technol. Inform. **189**, 59–67 (2013)
5. Odinaka, I., Lai, P.H., Kaplan, A.D., O'Sullivan, J.A., Sirevaag, E.J.: ECG biometric recognition: a comparative analysis. IEEE Trans. Inf. Forensics Secur. **7**, 1812–1814 (2012)
6. Singh, Y.N.: Human recognition using Fisher's discriminant analysis of heartbeat interval features and ECG morphology. Neurocomputing **167**, 322–335 (2015)
7. Hamdi, T., Ben Slimane, A., Ben Khalifa, A.: A novel feature extraction method in ECG biometrics. In: Image Processing, Applications & Systems Conference, pp. 1–5 (2014)
8. Paulet, M.V., Salceanu, A., Salceanu, A.: Automatic recognition of the person by ECG signals characteristics. In: International Symposium on Advanced Topics in Electrical Engineering (ATEE), pp. 281–284 (2015)
9. Choi, H.S., Lee, B., Yoon, S.: Biometric authentication using noisy electrocardiograms acquired by mobile sensors. IEEE Access **4**, 1266–1273 (2016)
10. Porée, F., Kervio, G., Carrault, G.: ECG biometric analysis in different physiological recording conditions. Signal Image Video Process. **10**, 267–276 (2016)
11. Zhang, Y., Shi, Y.: A new method for ECG biometric recognition using a hierarchical scheme classifier. In: IEEE International Conference on Software Engineering and Service Science, pp. 457–460 (2015)
12. Tantawi, M.M., Revett, K., Salem, A.B., Tolba, M.F.: A wavelet feature extraction method for electrocardiogram (ECG)-based biometric recognition. Signal Image Video Process. **9**, 1271–1280 (2015)
13. Page, A., Kulkarni, A., Mohsenin, T.: Utilizing deep neural nets for an embedded ECG-based biometric authentication system. In: Biomedical Circuits & Systems Conference, pp. 1–4 (2015)
14. Jahiruzzaman, M., Hossain, A.B.M.A.: ECG based biometric human identification using chaotic encryption. In: International Conference on Electrical Engineering and Information Communication Technology (2015)
15. Deng, J., Zhang, Z., Eyben, F., Schuller, B.: Autoencoder-based unsupervised domain adaptation for speech emotion recognition. IEEE Signal Process. Lett. **21**, 1068–1072 (2014)
16. Lecun, Y., Bengio, Y., Hinton, G.: Deep learning. Nature **521**, 436–444 (2015)
17. Zheng, G., Chen, Y., Dai, M.: HRV based stress recognizing by random forest. In: Fuzzy Systems and Data Mining II, pp. 444–458 (2016)

Realtime Human-UAV Interaction Using Deep Learning

Ali Maher[1], Ce Li[2], Hanwen Hu[1], and Baochang Zhang[1(✉)]

[1] School of Automation Science and Electrical Engineering,
Beihang University, Beijing, China
ali_mtc@hotmail.com, huhanwenxxx@163.com, bczhang@buaa.edu.cn
[2] China University of Mining and Technology, Beijing, China
celi@cumtb.edu.cn

Abstract. In this paper, we propose a realtime human gesture identification for controlling a micro UAV in a GPS denied environment.
Exploiting the breakthrough of deep convolution network in computer
vision, we develop a robust Human-UAV Interaction (HUI) system that
can detect and identify a person gesture to control a micro UAV in real
time. We also build a new dataset with 23 participants to train or fine-
tune the deep neural networks for human gesture detection. Based on the
collected dataset, the state-of-art YOLOv2 detection network is tailored
to detect the face and two hands locations of a human. Then, an interpreter approach is proposed to infer the gesture from detection results, in
which each interpreted gesture is equivalent to a UAV flying command.
Real flight experiments performed by non-expert users with the Bebop 2
micro UAV have approved our proposal for HUI. The gesture detection
deep model with a demo will be publicly available to aid the research
work.

Keywords: Human gesture · Micro UAV · YOLO · Deep learning

1 Introduction

The Unmanned Air Vehicle (UAV), also knows as a drone have mainly two types
of control; Remotely piloted and autonomous flight by means of On Board Computer (OBC). Most remotely piloted Uavs are driven by means of a physical
remote controller. However, the Natural User Interface (NUI) has been proposed
recently instead of the physical remote to drive the UAV. Visual human gesture
is one of the most appealing method to build a HUI system. It is a computer
vision with body language challenges based mainly on how accurately detect
and interpret visual human gestures. In this work, we propose a Human-UAV
Interaction based on deep detection framework running on a local machine's
GPUs. The proposed interpreter developed in the system maps the detected
human gesture to a certain UAV flying command. Our contribution mainly are
three folds: (1) We introduce an intuitive realtime system for controlling a low
cost UAV using our pre-designed set of human gestures. (2) We optimize and

© Springer International Publishing AG 2017
J. Zhou et al. (Eds.): CCBR 2017, LNCS 10568, pp. 511–519, 2017.
https://doi.org/10.1007/978-3-319-69923-3_55

deploy a state-of-the-art object detection architecture, YOLOv2 [1], in the context of Human-UAV interaction. (3) We build a large dataset for human gesture experiments that is efficient and adequate for deep detection framework training. Figure 1(a) shows our proposal being tested indoor with two different UAVs.

Fig. 1. (a) Our HUI proposal being tested with Parrot AR. drone 2.0 *(up)* and Bebop 2 *(down)*. (b) Samples from our dataset were taken in different environments.

The rest of the paper is structured as follows. Section 2 reviews and compares other similar works. Section 3 introduces our human gesture dataset. Section 4 presents the overall system architecture and explains the gesture's interpreter in detail. Section 5 describes the implementation of the proposed deep detection network. Sections 6 and 7 are experimental results and conclusions, respectively.

2   Related Work

Plentiful amounts of research projects proposed a UAV navigation using human gestures based interface. Most of them [2–4] have used the Microsoft Kinect sensor device at the ground station. They exploited its depth and RGB images to deduce the human skeleton model. Although, many gestures can be built from the skeleton model. But, involving the Kinect with its driver and API library made the system costlier and has a noticeable latency. The author of [5] introduced a HUI proposal based on leap motion sensor which has two monochromatic IR to track hand and fingers. Then, leap motion controller software will analyze tracked gestures on the ground station. Our HUI proposal differs from those; we have used a conventional USB digital camera to acquire human gestures at the ground station. Moreover, we can use the UAV's onboard camera directly instead of the USB one with our proposal, which cannot be applied for Kinect or leap motion based systems. In [6], the author used the UAV's onboard camera to detect and track the operator's face using a Harr cascade classifier with a Kalman filter. Then, applying color-based segmentation to detect colored (by means of gloves) right and left hands. Our proposal also differs from that proposal. Where, we detected the operator's hands and face by means of high level features which have more discriminating power than the hand crafted one. Also, we applied a simple trick in our interpreter to discriminate between left and right hand not by wearing a colored glove which eased hand-tracking by color matching. So far as we know, HUI with hand gestures based on deep detection network has not been proposed yet. In this paper, we focus on involving YOLOv2 framework in controlling a micro UAV with simple and intuitive human gesture.

3 Human Gesture Dataset

Our dataset includes 6223 images focusing on human's hands and faces. There are 23 volunteers involved in the collection of this dataset. The camera resolution is of 1920 × 1080, 30 frames per second, and the duration of each video is about 30 s. There are 48 videos were taken into two backgrounds - indoor (18) and outdoor (38). We obtain one frame from videos every 5 frames, then all the images are filtered in order to discard redundant data. Aiming to get the key information about human's hands and faces, we crop images to remove the extra background. Ultimately, each image's resolution is 1200×1000 or less. Figure 1(b) presents some random samples from our dataset.

4 System Architecture Overview

Our HUI proposal tele-navigate the UAV in a denied GPS environment with the hand postures. Figure 2 shows a high level description of our proposed system and its fundamental components. All of them were implemented in the

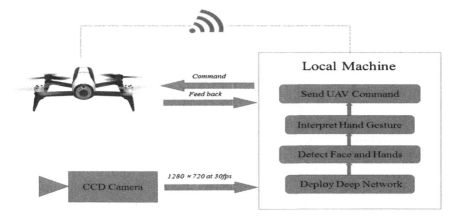

Fig. 2. High level architecture of our proposed HUI with Bebop 2 drone.

Robot Operating System (ROS) framework as nodes. Where, each node can (publish/subscribe) communicate with the other nodes via ROS transport protocol [7]. The ground station is a laptop (with an Intel core i7-5500 @ 2.4 GHz and equipped with NVIDIA GPU GeForce GTX 840M). The proposal being tested with two Parrot's UAVs; AR. drone 2 and Bebop 2.

4.1   Gesture Interpreter

The deep detection network will detect the operator gesture in each frame, therefore it will work as an observation model [8,9] but in the absence of the motion model. So, the detected gesture in the current frame and the previous one does not relate to each other. This led us to use static (posture) not dynamic (sequence of postures) gesture recognition in our proposal. Where, the control command depends on detected gesture in the current frame and will not change until the threshold is breached again by a new gesture [10].

4.2   Gesture Design

The operator's face, right and left hands were used as gesture source. The deep detection node will publish three bounding boxes annotated with hand, face and hand. The interpreter will take the hand which has lower horizontal location (x-value) as a *right* hand and the other one as a *left* hand. We use the ratios between vertical centers (y-values) of the three bounding boxes to build the gestures.

$$R_1 = \frac{Y_{cf}}{Y_{rh}}, R_2 = \frac{Y_{cf}}{Y_{lh}} \tag{1}$$

Figure 3(a) demonstrates how the R_1 and R_2 (yellow lines margins) are determined from the bounding boxes of the detected gesture. Thus, these ratios provide the scale invariance, so, it does not matter where the operator will stand in front of the ground station camera. A total of nine natural static hands postures are designed for the UAV controlling. Table 1 summarizes the correspondence between hand postures and UAV controlling commands. Figure 3(b) shows different gesture postures designed using human's hands and face. We state three important rules in designing the gesture interpreter as follows: (1) To avoid the effect of the false positive gesture, the interpreter will be invoked if and only if (two hands and one face) are detected and with high confidence scores. (2) We use the UAV current state flags (Taking off, Landed, Hovering, Flying) to avoid the conflict which may come from disordered commands (taking off should be after landing or controlling command should be after hovering, etc.). (3) Hovering is a default command when the operator gesture does not satisfy any threshold mentioned in Table 1. The UAV states are acquired within UAV navigation data which measured by its on board sensors. Finally, the interpreter maps the detected human gesture to a controlling command as mentioned previously.

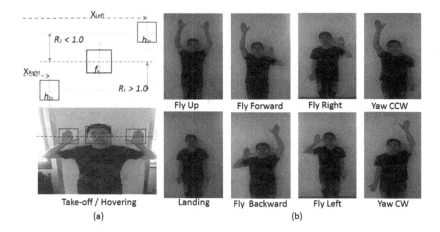

Fig. 3. (a) Demonstrates of how the ratios R_1 and R_2 are determined from the bounding boxes. (b) Different gestures are designed to control the UAV. (Color figure online)

Table 1. The correspondence between postures and the UAV controlling commands.

Hand's postures w.r.t face	R_1	R_2	Corresponding command
All Aligned vertically	0.9 : 1.1	0.9 : 1.1	Take-Off/ Hovering
Two hands aligned vertically and beneath the face	0.4 : 0.6	0.4 : 0.6	Landing
Two hands aligned vertically and above the face	2.0 : 2.2	2.0 : 2.2	Fly up
Right hand aligned with the face and left hand above	0.9 : 1.1	> 2.4	Fly backward
Left hand aligned with the face and right hand above	> 2.4	0.9 : 1.1	Fly forward
Right hand aligned with the face and left hand beneath	0.9 : 1.1	< 0.5	Fly left
Left hand aligned with the face and right hand beneath	< 0.5	0.9 : 1.1	Fly right
Right hand above the face and left hand beneath	> 2.4	< 0.5	Yaw CCW
Left hand above the face and right hand beneath	< 0.5	> 2.4	Yaw CW

5 Deep Detection Network

We trained Faster RCNN [11] and Tiny-Yolo [1] by 3733 images from our dataset. The remaining unseen frames (2490) were used in testing to get an indication for the network accuracy. Although, Tiny-YOLO is fast, but it achieved gesture detection with a speed of *15* FPS when running on our ground station laptop. Tiny-YOLO comprises 9 convolutional layers, only 6 of them followed by pooling layers for down sampling. We modified Tiny-Yolo architecture to be 6 convolutional layers, only 4 of them followed by pooling layers. This will aid our detection system in two aspects: (1) 6-layers Tiny-YOLO achieved gesture detection with speed more than *21* FPS when running on our ground station laptop. (2) Reducing number of the pooling layers will preserve more spatial information (such as face and hand postures) which is crucial for our application. The running time was measured in terms of the ROS topic publishing rate of the deep detection node. Thus, the pre-processing for image conversion, image loading and parsing of the detection results are included.

The architecture of the proposed 6-layers is set in the Yolo configuration file as follows: *C1,P1,C2,P2,C3,P3,C4,P4,C5,C6*. Where, *C* is for convolutional layer and *P* for pooling. Leaky ReLU activation was used with all convolutional layers, except last one (*C6*) was activated by a linear function. All kernels sizes are 3×3 with stride 1 and padding 1 except for last layer the kernel size is 1×1. The number of filters (feature maps) for C1,C2,C3,C4,C5,C6 are 16,32,64,128,1024,14 respectively. We tailored the anchors (reference boxes) to fit the detected gestures aspects ratios and scales. Where, k-mean clustering algorithm was applied to get the centroids (reference boxes) of our training dataset. We used the silhouette [12] average score to determine the best number of centroids (k). We got two anchors *(k = 2)* for each network (Tiny-YOLO and 6 layers Tiny-YOLO).

6   Experiments

6.1   Experiments on Face and Hands Detection

Tailoring the bounding box is very important in our application, where the success of the interpreter relies on how accurately the detection network localizes the gesture with a tight bounding box. Figure 4 shows how the anchors adaptation affects the detection results. Multi-scale training is activated (resize the network input image) from 320×320 up to 608×608 with a step of 32. This will aid the deep network to detect properly the operator gesture with many resolutions (gives some flexibility to use different digital cameras) at the ground station.

Faster RCNN is trained and tested to have a baseline for a comparison with the trained Tiny-YOLO and 6-layers Tiny-YOLO. Table 2 presents the mean Average Precession mAP for Faster RCNN, Tiny-YOLO and proposed 6-layers Tiny-YOLO on our data testing set. From Table 2 obviously, we can achieve the required real time for gesture detection beside preserving the same detection accuracy in terms of mAP. It is noticed that the detection results are almost high and equal. Where, the detection (not recognition) of human physical characteristic (such as the face) with a massive training set is not a complex task.

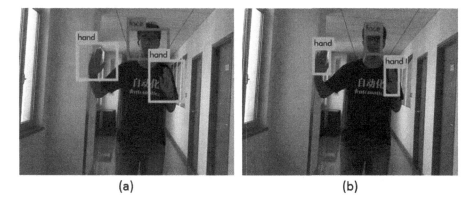

(a)   (b)

Fig. 4. Shows detection results using (a) (VOC) anchors, (b) our determined anchors.

Table 2. Detection accuracy results, the speed was measured on our local machine.

Method	Hand	Face	mAP	Speed (FPS)
Faster R-CNN	0.9034	0.9088	0.9061	1
Tiny-YOLO	**0.909**	**0.909**	**0.909**	15
6-layers Tiny-YOLO	0.9085	0.9088	0.9087	**21**

Inferring that, our proposed dataset for human gesture is large enough and sufficient. Finally, in our system, we used the proposed 6-layers Tiny-YOlO with 21 FPS, which achieves real time interaction in controlling the micro UAV.

6.2   Experiments on Human-UAV Interaction

We use the same evaluation done by [2,4] to judge the performance of our HUI proposal. Where, real indoor flight test with gesture control was conducted inside a room of 6.5 m × 15 m × 3.5 m Dimensions. So, the UAV position was not tracked by the GPS. We collected all navigation data measured by Bebop's onboard sensors which mentioned before. To test all proposed gesture, a non-expert user performed gestures to fly the Bebop 2 UAV in this sequence; take-off, flying up, flying forward, flying left, flying backward, flying right, yawing 180° CCW, yawing 180° CW then landing. Figure 5(a) shows the 3D plot of the acquired (x, y, z) position data. The total flight time for the mentioned flying sequence was around 85 s. Figure 5(b) illustrates the UAV's attitude *(yaw, pitch, roll)* during the flight test. Where, the UAV made pitch and roll angles to fly forward/backward and right/left, respectively. Before the end of the flight (from the second 67 to 77), the UAV made yawing 180° CW then CCW.

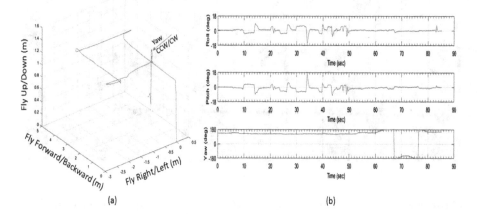

(a)   (b)

Fig. 5. (a) 3D plot of the acquired position data for the UAV during real flight test, (b) Illustrates the UAV attitude during the real flight test *roll, pitch* and *yaw.*

7   Conclusion

In this paper, we introduce an intuitive realtime system for controlling a low cost UAV using human gestures. With our new collected dataset built for human gesture, we design an interpreter mapping each gesture to a controlling command. We investigate how to deploy the state-of-the-art object detection framework YOLOv2 in the context of HUI. Our proposal with that investigation achieved real time and preserved high gesture detection accuracy.

Acknowledgments. The work was supported in part by the Natural Science Foundation of China under Contract 61672079, 61473086 and 61601466. The work of B. Zhang was supported in part by the Program for New Century Excellent Talents University within the Ministry of Education, China, and in part by the Beijing Municipal Science and Technology Commission under Grant Z161100001616005. Baochang Zhang is the correspondence.

References

1. Redmon, J., Farhadi, A.: Yolo9000: better, faster, stronger. arXiv preprint arXiv:1612.08242 (2016)
2. Mashood, A., Noura, H., Jawhar, I., Mohamed, N.: A gesture based kinect for quadrotor control. In: 2015 International Conference on Information and Communication Technology Research (ICTRC), pp. 298–301. IEEE (2015)
3. Boudjit, K., Larbes, C., Alouache, M.: Control of flight operation of a quad rotor AR. drone using depth map from microsoft kinect sensor. Int. J. Eng. Innov. Technol. (IJEIT) **3**, 15–19 (2008)
4. Sanna, A., Lamberti, F., Paravati, G., Manuri, F.: A kinect-based natural interface for quadrotor control. Entertain. Comput. **4**(3), 179–186 (2013)

5. Suarez Fernandez, R., Sanchez Lopez, J.L., Sampedro, C., Bavle, H., Molina, M., Campoy Cervera, P.: Natural user interfaces for human-drone multi-modal interaction. In: Proceedings of 2016 International Conference on Unmanned Aircraft Systems (ICUAS), ETSI_Informatica (2016)
6. Nagi, J., Giusti, A., Di Caro, G.A., Gambardella, L.M.: Human control of UAVs using face pose estimates and hand gestures. In: Proceedings of the 2014 ACM/IEEE International Conference on Human-robot Interaction, pp. 252–253. ACM (2014)
7. Quigley, M., Conley, K., Gerkey, B., Faust, J., Foote, T., Leibs, J., Wheeler, R., Ng, A.Y.: ROS: an open-source robot operating system. In: ICRA Workshop on Open Source Software, vol. 3, p. 5, Kobe (2009)
8. Zhang, B., Perina, A., Li, Z., Murino, V., Liu, J., Ji, R.: Bounding multiple gaussians uncertainty with application to object tracking. Int. J. Comput. Vision 118(3), 364–379 (2016)
9. Zhang, B., Li, Z., Perina, A., Del Bue, A., Murino, V., Liu, J.: Adaptive local movement modeling for robust object tracking. IEEE Trans. Circuits Syst. Video Technol. 27(7), 1515–1526 (2017)
10. Zhang, B., Yang, Y., Chen, C., Yang, L., Han, J., Shao, L.: Action recognition using 3D histograms of texture and a multi-class boosting classifier. IEEE Trans. Image Process. 26(10), 4648–4660 (2017)
11. Ren, S., He, K., Girshick, R., Sun, J.: Faster R-CNN: towards real-time object detection with region proposal networks. In: Advances in Neural Information Processing Systems. pp. 91–99 (2015)
12. Zhou, H.B., Gao, J.T.: Automatic method for determining cluster number based on silhouette coefficient. In: Advanced Materials Research, vol. 951, pp. 227–230. Trans Tech Publ (2014)

Adapting Convolutional Neural Networks on the Shoeprint Retrieval for Forensic Use

Yang Zhang[1,2], Huanzhang Fu[3(✉)], Emmanuel Dellandréa[2], and Liming Chen[2]

[1] Beihang University, 100191 Beijing, China
[2] Ecole Centrale de Lyon, 36 Avenue Guy de Collongue, Ecully 69130, France
yang.zhang@auditeur.ec-lyon.fr, {emmanuel.dellandrea,lchen}@ec-lyon.fr
[3] Institute of Forensic Science, No. 17 Muxidinanli, Beijing 100038, China
fuhuanzhang@gmail.com

Abstract. Shoeprint is an important evidence for crime investigation. Many automatic shoeprint retrieval methods have been proposed in order to efficiently provide useful information for the identification of the criminals. In the mean time, the convolutional neural network shows great capacity in image classification problem but its application in shoeprint retrieval is not yet investigated. This paper presents an application of VGG16 network as feature extractor in shoeprint retrieval and a data augmentation method to fine-tune the neural network with a very small database. Our method shows a much better performance compared with state-of-the-art methods on a same database with crime-scene-like shoeprints.

Keywords: Shoeprint retrieval · Feature extraction · Deep learning · Convolutional neural network · Fine-tuning

1 Introduction

Shoeprint is one of the most abundant forms of evidence left at crime scenes, and a study shows that it can be found in more than 30% of the burglary scenes [1]. Although it can't be used in most cases as a reliable proof on the court to testify the crime under the current scientific level, it is still considered as an importance soft biometric evidence in forensic science that can provide useful information about the height, age and gait for the primary identification of the suspect and the linking of several criminal cases in the investigation stage. The common practice of using the shoeprint collected from a crime scene is to match it with the police database for similar shoeprints. The database may contain reference images from the manufactories or shoeprints from other crime scenes. This work is still challenging because of the high increasing number of outsole patterns, the low image quality, the incompleteness, the noise etc.

In recent years, deep learning methods based on the Convolutional Neural Networks (CNN) have achieved great progress and they have been successfully applied in many fields including image classification, object detection, facial

© Springer International Publishing AG 2017
J. Zhou et al. (Eds.): CCBR 2017, LNCS 10568, pp. 520–527, 2017.
https://doi.org/10.1007/978-3-319-69923-3_56

recognition, video analysis etc. The strength of CNN is its ability of learning meaningful features by itself for the specific task during its training, which are proved to be better than the human designed features [2]. The algorithms based on CNN even performed better than human beings on the object localization task of ImageNet Large Scale Visual Recognition Challenge [3]. However, the performance of CNN on the shoeprint retrieval problem is rarely studied. In [4], the neural network has been used but only to classify features extracted by traditional methods. To this end, we propose in this paper a novel technique to the problem of automatic shoeprint image retrieval by adapting the CNN.

In Sect. 2 we give a review on the researches of automatic shoeprint retrieval algorithms; in Sect. 3 we present briefly our proposed method and in Sect. 4 we show the detail of the experiment and the discussion of the results.

2   Related Works

Many research works have been reported in the domain of automatic shoeprint retrieval and a variety of feature extraction and matching algorithms have been published. One part of these works consists in computing the features from the entire image, for example, the fractal decomposition theory [5], Hu's moment [6] and Zernike moment [7] etc. Moreover, in terms of the frequency space feature, algorithms using the power spectrum density (PSD) [8], phase only correlation (POC) [9], cross power spectrum [10] and Fourier-Mellin transformation (FMT) [11] have been proposed. In addition to the Fourier transformation, the Gabor wavelet has also been used [12]. Methods of this category are usually based on the global information of the images and have good invariance against transformations and rotations. However, some of them are not suitable for partial images where the local information plays a more important role.

The other part interests rather in the local features. The local interest point based methods are implemented with the SIFT descriptor [13]. A graph-based shoeprint descriptor [14] had good performance too, by construction an Attributed Relational Graph (ARG) using the detection of geometric shapes and their relative position information. This kind of methods is especially robust against to rotation and missing parts but requires a rather high image quality to ensure the correct detection of local descriptors or shapes.

Some efforts have been made to compare different methods on same data-bases under same experimental configurations [15,16]. In [15], the author has tested PSD, POC and a new Mahalanobis distance based method on synthetic shoeprint images as well as real crime scene images. The result shows that POC outperforms the other two methods on both databases while all of them suffer from significant performance loss on the real scene images. More recent com-parison work [16] using crime scene simulated images also shows that the POC method has better resistance towards dust and blood trace distortion than the Fourier-Mellin transformation and the SIFT method. Despite of these compari-son works, the domain of shoeprint retrieval still suffers from the lack of data, especially the well-recognized, large and common database.

We should note that although most of the methods have achieved good results on the images of laboratory condition, the real crime scene shoeprint retrieval remains a major challenge, since there are always potential unpredictable factors that might cause the degradation of the shoeprint. Generally, the handcrafted features can relatively easily be designed to overcome one or a series of known degradations, however it will be more difficult for them to deal with the unpredictable ones. While the CNN features are proved to be capable to learn powerful features with enough training data for a specific task. This is also our motivation to adapt CNN to our research topic.

3   CNN Feature Based Image Retrieval

A typical image retrieval process aims at finding similar images to the query image in a database according to the similarity between their features extracted by a feature extractor.

Our method consists of using the CNN as feature extractor in the process to compute image features for the retrieval. Studies have proved that the output of the CNN before the classification layer have also great representative capacity that can be served as a feature vector [17]. Consequently, it should also have good performance when used in retrieval problems instead of classification. However, this method faces a huge difficulty when applied to the shoeprint retrieval problem since there doesn't exist a common database with large quantity of labeled shoeprint images as we mentioned before, while CNN needs enough data for training to guarantee a satisfying performance.

Thus we novelly proposed two techniques in order to make the training of a CNN possible for shoeprints:

Use a Pre-trained CNN Model with Fine-Tuning. As studied in [18], the low level convolutional layers often learns general representations of image characteristics. It makes them also useful when the network is used on a new database. As a result, it makes sense to use a pre-trained network model rather than a completely new model as the network won't need to relearn the general low-level features and we only need to fine-tune the network's parameters for our specific task. This fine-tuning requires much less data than training a network from scratch.

Use Data Augmentation to Generate More Data. Data augmentation is a popular method to enlarge a database when facing the lack of data. Nevertheless, the detailed technique should still be well designed so as to prevent the over-fitting of the network. As we mentioned previously, the major degradations of shoeprints in the real crime scene are the incompleteness and noise. We wish the network could be resisting these distortions by simulating these two phenomena in the training. Hence, we tried two methods for data augmentation: (a) Regular shape based random pixel removal to simulate the incompleteness and

(b) Adding Gaussian noise with different variance to simulate the natural noise. Detailed presentation about data augmentation is described in the Sect. 4.1.

Once the features are extracted from the images, they need to be matched using a similarity metric. What we used in our study is the correlation coefficient. Given two feature vectors $X = (x_1, x_2, ..., x_n)$ and $Y = (y_1, y_2, ..., y_n)$, their correlation is defined as:

$$r = \frac{\sum_{i=1}^{n}(x_i - \overline{x})(y_i - \overline{y})}{\sqrt{\sum_{i=1}^{n}(x_i - \overline{x})^2(y_i - \overline{y})^2}} \tag{1}$$

With this definition of similarity, we compare each feature vector of the query image with all features of the reference images and it creates one ranking list for each query image with the most similar reference images on the top.

4   Experiments

4.1   Database and Data Preparation

In order to test the efficiency of our proposed method, the database published in [16] has been chosen for our experiments. This choice presents us the following advantages: firstly, it is one of the few shoeprint databases opened for public access; secondly, it offers both high quality reference images and crime scene simulation images so that we may evaluate the performance on real-case-like test images; thirdly, the author also presented in [16] the performances of some popular image retrieval algorithms on this database, so we are able to compare our method with them using the same experimental configuration.

The database consists of 4 parts of images whose resolution is $869 * 869$ for use: (1) A reference set of 100 distinct shoeprint high quality images; (2) A simulated set of 66 dust shoeprint images; (3) A simulated set of 53 blood shoeprint images; (4) The same 53 blood simulated samples enhanced by LCV. Figure 1 shows some of the shoeprint images in this database. Please refer to [16] for the detailed creation process.

(a)   (b)   (c)   (d)   (e)

Fig. 1. Shoeprint image examples from database. (a)(b) Reference images, (c) dust simulated image, (d) blood simulated image, (e) blood simulated image enhanced by LCV

For our experiments, we use the high-quality reference images to generate training and validation dataset for the fine-tuning, while the degraded simulation images are used in retrieval test to evaluate the performance. Moreover, we found 12 pairs of extremely similar images in the reference set and only one image of each pair is kept for future use since we are only interested in recognizing the types of the shoeprint patterns not the individual shoe itself for the current study. Therefore, the class numbers are reduced from 100 to 88.

Concerning the generation of training images, we first add random Gaussian noise to the shoeprint pixels. The Gaussian distribution we used is always of 0 means and the variance is chosen from 5 levels $\{0, 0.03, 0.06, 0.09, 0.12\}$. A higher variance value will cause greater degradation to the image. Then on each noised image, we perform the regular shape based random pixel removal by a loop until the ratio of the removed pixel reaches a certain threshold interval. This term is defined as $threshold = P_{removed}/P_{initial}$, where $P_{removed}$ is the total number of removed pixels and $P_{initial}$ is the initial number of non-background pixels. For our experiments, we used 5 threshold levels: $\{0.2-0.3, 0.3-0.4, 0.4-0.5, 0.5-0.6, 0.6-0.7\}$. The form, position and size of shape are determined randomly. Both the variance and threshold levels are selected based on a simple human analysis according to the quality of the generated data (Fig. 2).

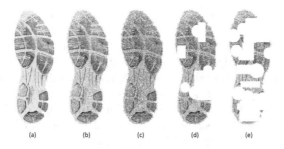

(a)   (b)   (c)   (d)   (e)

Fig. 2. Generated shoeprint examples. (a) Original HQ shoeprint, (b)(c) noisy shoeprint of variance 0.03 and 0.09, (d)(e) noisy shoeprint with 25% and 65% pixel removed.

Finally, we have respectively generated 3 datasets for fine-tuning to test our method: **Dataset D1**: only random pixel removal. For each class, 10 images are generated per removal ratio, which makes 50 images per class and in total 4400 images. **Dataset D2**: Gaussian noise + random pixel removal. For each class, 1 image is generated per noise level and based on it 2 images are generated per removal ratio, which makes 50 images per class and in total 4400 images. **Dataset D3**: more Gaussian noise + random pixel removal. For each class, 5 images are generated per noise level and based on it 2 images are generated per removal ratio, which makes 250 images per class and in total 22000 images. In each database, 10% of the images are kept as validation set. D1 and D2 are prepared respectively to make the CNN features robust to incompleteness and noise; D3 aims for a better robustness by trying to have more data.

4.2   Network Structure and Fine-Tuning

The network we used is the VGG16 network [19] pre-trained on the ImageNet database and implemented using Keras [20]. In order to adapt VGG16 to our specific problem, we brought several modification to it. That is to say, we replaced all the fully connected layers at the end by one layer of batch normalization and one classifier with softmax. No hidden layer is added between them for preventing over-fitting due to model complexity. Only the convolution part of the network is used for feature extraction. Our modified network is presented in Fig. 3.

Feature vector during retrieval

Fig. 3. The modified VGG16 network used in our study.

At the beginning of the fine-tuning, the convolutional layers are initialized with the pre-trained ImageNet weights. The fine-tuning is performed separately on all three datasets with the same parameters and progressive steps: we first freeze all convolutional layers to train only the new added ones; then we open progressively the last 3, 6, 9 and all convolutional layers for training.

After some random searches for hyperparameters, we added a L2 regularization with strength of 0.001 to the last fully connected layer. The learning process used stochastic gradient descent method with decay $= 1e-6$ and nesterov momentum $= 0.9$. The learning rate for the first step is at 0.004 and is reduced to 0.00004 for the rest.

4.3   Evaluation Method and Experimental Results

The measurement of performance is the cumulative match characteristic (CMC) score as it is the same method used in [16]. It is defined as $Q_{success}/Q_{total} * 100\%$, where Q_{total} is the total number of test queries (here $66 + 53 + 53 = 172$) and $Q_{success}$ is the number of the queries that we find the correct reference image by looking at the top n results of the retrieval output.

Table 1 shows the results of 3 fine-tuned networks as well as those of the methods in [16]. As we can see, the network trained with only pixel removal method (D1) outperform already the best result in [16] (POC) on the blood and blood+LCV sets but not on the dust set. With the Gaussian noise added (D2), we note a huge improvement on the dust set from 15.1% to 45.5% of the top 1 accuracy. Finally, the network trained with a bigger database (D3) shows a further improvement on the dust set from 45.5% to 56.1% of the top 1 accuracy. Despite the slight decreasing on blood and blood+LCV set, this result

Table 1. Cumulative scores on 3 different test set of the methods in [16], and fine-tuned network by three different training set

Test set	Rank position	SIFT+RANSAC	FMT	POC	D1	D2	D3
Dust	1	6.10%	7.58%	47.0%	15.1%	45.5%	**56.1%**
	2	10.6%	12.1%	47.0%	25.8%	59.1%	**62.1%**
	3	15.2%	16.7%	51.5%	43.9%	66.7%	**68.2%**
	4	21.2%	19.7%	51.5%	45.5%	**74.2%**	**74.2%**
	5	22.7%	22.7%	54.5%	53.0%	**80.3%**	75.6%
Blood	1	1.90%	18.9%	45.3%	66.0%	67.9%	**71.7%**
	2	3.80%	18.9%	50.9%	79.2%	79.2%	**84.9%**
	3	13.2%	18.9%	54.7%	86.8%	86.8%	**88.7%**
	4	17.0%	20.8%	64.2%	**92.4%**	88.7%	90.6%
	5	18.9%	20.8%	66.0%	92.4%	**94.3%**	**94.3%**
Blood+LCV	1	17.0%	13.2%	58.5%	79.2%	**84.9%**	79.2%
	2	24.5%	18.9%	66.0%	90.1%	**92.5%**	90.6%
	3	28.3%	26.4%	71.7%	92.5%	**94.3%**	**94.3%**
	4	32.1%	34.0%	81.1%	**96.2%**	94.3%	94.3%
	5	34.0%	34.0%	83.0%	**96.2%**	**96.2%**	94.3%

still outperforms the best result in [16] by at least 9%, 26% and 20% separately on the dust, blood and blood+LCV sets. The improvement on dust set is possibly because the data augmentation methods we used happens to simulate the dust effect on shoeprints, which helped increase the resistance of the network towards this kind of distortion but not those of the blood images.

5 Conclusion

In this paper, we studied the possibility of using features extracted by convolutional neural network for shoeprint retrieval. The data augmentation method we applied proves that we can fine-tune a neural network for better performance even with an extremely small database at hand. The result shows that CNN can outperform existing methods with satisfying performance on crime-scene-images, which shows the great potential of CNN in the shoeprint retrieval problem. Several directions can be envisaged for future works, including the use of blood shoeprint simulated data for training, the systematic optimization of data generation parameters and the design of task-adapted neural network structure etc. We might expect more progress in the application of deep learning methods in the shoeprint retrieval if a large labeled database can be created.

References

1. Alexandre, G.: Computerized classification of the shoeprints of burglars' soles. Forensic Sci. Int. **82**(1), 59–65 (1996)

2. Zeiler, M.D., Fergus, R.: Visualizing and understanding convolutional networks. In: Fleet, D., Pajdla, T., Schiele, B., Tuytelaars, T. (eds.) ECCV 2014. LNCS, vol. 8689, pp. 818–833. Springer, Cham (2014). doi:10.1007/978-3-319-10590-1_53
3. He, K., Zhang, X., Ren, S., Sun, J.: Deep residual learning for image recognition. In: Proceedings of the IEEE Conference on Computer Vision and Pattern Recognition, pp. 770–778 (2016)
4. Geradts, Z., Keijzer, J.: The image-database REBEZO for shoeprints with developments on automatic classification of shoe outsole designs. Forensic Sci. Int. **82**(1), 21–31 (1996)
5. Alexander, A., Bouridane, A., Crookes, D.: Automatic classification and recognition of shoeprints (1999)
6. AlGarni, G., Hamiane, M.: A novel technique for automatic shoeprint image retrieval. Forensic Sci. Int. **181**(1), 10–14 (2008)
7. Xiao, R., Shi, P.: Computerized matching of shoeprints based on sole pattern. Comput. Forensics **5158**, 96–104 (2008)
8. De Chazal, P., Flynn, J., Reilly, R.B.: Automated processing of shoeprint images based on the fourier transform for use in forensic science. IEEE Trans. Pattern Anal. Mach. Intell. **27**(3), 341–350 (2005)
9. Gueham, M., Bouridane, A., Crookes, D.: Automatic recognition of partial shoeprints based on phase-only correlation. In: IEEE International Conference on Image Processing. vol. 4, pp. IV–441. IEEE (2007)
10. Cervelli, F., Dardi, F., Carrato, S.: A translational and rotational invariant descriptor for automatic footwear retrieval of real cases shoe marks. In: 2010 18th European Signal Processing Conference, pp. 1665–1669. IEEE (2010)
11. Gueham, M., Bouridane, A., Crookes, D., Nibouche, O.: Automatic recognition of shoeprints using Fourier-Mellin transform. In: NASA/ESA Conference on Adaptive Hardware and Systems, pp. 487–491. IEEE (2008)
12. Patil, P.M., Kulkarni, J.V.: Rotation and intensity invariant shoeprint matching using Gabor transform with application to forensic science. Pattern Recogn. **42**(7), 1308–1317 (2009)
13. Li, Z., Wei, C., Li, Y., Sun, T.: Research of shoeprint image stream retrival algorithm with scale-invariance feature transform. In: International Conference on Multimedia Technology (ICMT), pp. 5488–5491. IEEE (2011)
14. Srihari, S.N.: Analysis of Footwear Impression Evidence. BiblioGov, Columbus (2012)
15. Cervelli, F., Dardi, F., Carrato, S.: Comparison of footwear retrieval systems for synthetic and real shoe marks. In: Image and Signal Processing and Analysis, pp. 684–689. IEEE (2009)
16. Richetelli, N., Lee, M.C., Lasky, C.A., Gump, M.E., Speir, J.A.: Classification of footwear outsole patterns using fourier transform and local interest points. Forensic Sci. Int. **275**, 102–109 (2017)
17. Athiwaratkun, B., Kang, K.: Feature representation in convolutional neural networks. arXiv preprint arXiv:1507.02313 (2015)
18. Yosinski, J., Clune, J., Bengio, Y., Lipson, H.: How transferable are features in deep neural networks? In: Advances in Neural Information Processing Systems, pp. 3320–3328 (2014)
19. Simonyan, K., Zisserman, A.: Very deep convolutional networks for large-scale image recognition. In: arXiv preprint arXiv:1409.1556 (2014)
20. Chollet, F., et al.: Keras. https://github.com/fchollet/keras (2015)

Motion Analysis Based Cross-Database Voting for Face Spoofing Detection

Lifang Wu, Yaowen Xu, Meng Jian$^{(\boxtimes)}$, Wei Cai, Chuncan Yan, and Yukun Ma

Faculty of Information Technology, Beijing University of Technology,
Beijing 100124, China
lfwu@bjut.edu.cn, xuyao_wen@126.com, jianmeng648@163.com, cwlcfj@126.com,
chuncanyan@emails.bjut.edu.cn, yukuner@126.com

Abstract. With the rapid development of face recognition systems in various practical applications, numerous face spoofing attacks under different environment and devices have emerged. The countermeasure of face spoofing attacks in cross-database have caused increasing attention. This paper proposes a face spoofing detection method with motion analysis based cross-database voting. We employ the consistency motion information of different databases like eye-blink, mouth movements and facial expression etc. Then the motion information maps of a video is classified to real or fake by CNN model. Furthermore, cross-database voting strategy is constructed to transfer motion characteristics from a database to another for face spoofing inference. Experimental results demonstrate that the proposed method outperforms its comparisons taking benefits of motion analysis based CNN classification and cross-database voting.

Keywords: Face spoofing · Cross-database · Motion analysis · Voting strategy

1 Introduction

In recent years, face recognition has been widely applied in various identity authentication system [1], e.g., face recognition system embedded in smart phones used to unlock, and self-service identity authentication system in train station. Face spoofing occurs as someone attack the face recognition system by photos or videos recorded from legal users [2,3]. It takes a great risk for security of personal information and possessions. Face spoofing detection, which is intended to distinguish between real faces and fake faces is particularly necessary. Face spoofing includes print, photo, and video attacks, where the difference of print and photo attacks lays in the display of paper and device respectively.

Real faces and fake faces generally share considerable features, which leads to great challenges in spoofing detection. In addition, the variation of environment and devices for face acquisition, e.g., light intensity, background, proportion of face to image, resolution, and image size, also leads to great challenges for face spoofing detection. Considering the requirements of spoofing detection

© Springer International Publishing AG 2017
J. Zhou et al. (Eds.): CCBR 2017, LNCS 10568, pp. 528–536, 2017.
https://doi.org/10.1007/978-3-319-69923-3_57

in complex environments of practical applications, in this work, we investigate cross-database spoofing inference.

A number of face spoofing detection methods have been proposed [4]. In [5], CNN was adopted to extract features from original frames in videos and classify real and fake faces for spoofing detection. Alotaibi and Mahmood [6] proposed a method to extract facial shape edges as the input of CNN. They indicated that preprocessing of images by hand-drafted features is necessary which is able to avoid the influence of background and noise for spoofing detection. Boulkenafet et al. [7] proposed a face spoofing detection approach using colour texture analysis, that extracted different local descriptors in the different colour spaces. [8] performed spoofing detection by using Local Binary Pattern (LBP), an effective texture operator, to extract local texture information. These works were designed for spoofing detection on a single database which consisted of videos from the same environment and device rather than those from various environments and devices across databases. Therefore, we consider the robust motion information to prevent influence of illumination, background, resolution etc. There exist many motion analysis based spoofing detection methods [9,10]. [9] analyzed local motion by detecting eye-blink for spoofing inference. [10] extracted global motion for spoofing detection, which learnt head movements together with motion style. In this work, we employ both local and global motion analysis to extract cross-database consistent features for CNN based spoofing inference.

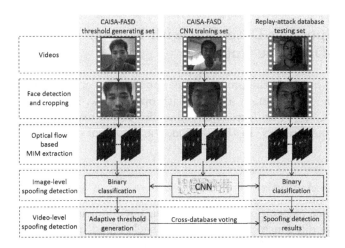

Fig. 1. The framework of the proposed face spoofing detection method with motion analysis and CNN based cross-database voting. (MIM: motion information map).

In this paper, we propose a face spoofing detection method based on motion analysis and cross-database voting strategy. Firstly, the proposed method preforms motion analysis with optical flow [11] and extracts motion information map(MIM) from neighboring frames. Then CNN is contacted to extract features and classify each MIM of a video as real or fake face. Finally, we formulate a cross-database voting strategy to adaptively generate a cross-database voting threshold and provide the corresponding video a category of real or fake for face spoofing detection. Figure 1 illustrates the framework of the proposed face spoofing detection method. The main contributions of this work are summarized as follows:

The proposed method investigates face spoofing detection in case of cross-database with different environment and imaging devices, which is promising to meet the requirements in reality.

- We employ motion analysis by optical flow and leverage effectively its robustness to illumination, background, resolution, etc. for spoofing detection.
- We construct a cross-database voting strategy by adaptively generating cross-database threshold, which effectively transfers motion characteristics of one database to another in spoofing detection.

The experimental results demonstrate that the proposed method is capable of detecting face spoofing with the help of both motion analysis and cross-database voting.

The remainder of the paper is organized as follows. Section 2 provides the details of the proposed face spoofing detection method. The experimental results and its corresponding analysis are given in Sect. 3. Finally, Sect. 4 draws the conclusions.

2 Face Spoofing Detection with Motion Analysis Based Cross-Database Voting

As illustrated in Fig. 1, the proposed face spoofing detection method consists of three main modules: motion analysis with optical flow, image-level MIM classification by CNN, video-level binary classification of real and fake with cross-database voting strategy. In this section, the details of each module would be described.

2.1 Motion Analysis

In practical face recognition systems, various environment and imaging devices would lead to differences in illumination, background, resolution, etc., which become great obstacles for spoofing detection. However these differences have no effects on motion information of faces which means motion information are relatively consistent to different video sources. Therefore, in this work, motion analysis is implemented firstly on the frames to alleviate the variations of faces.

In order to extract a consistent feature across databases, we adopt optical flow method to trace blinking, face micro motion and head movement, which take significant differences between real and fake faces. Till now, lots of outstanding optical flow methods have been proposed. One of the most popular sparse optical flow methods is LK Pyramid optical flow [12] and one of the most popular dense optical flow methods is Gunnar Farneback optical flow [13]. For face spoofing detection problem, it is required to implement dense optical flow to express the dense movement of the entire face. Actually, LK Pyramid optical flow is also able to form dense optical flow field by taking the complete key points [14], but it's very inefficient. Consequently, we employ Gunnar Farneback optical flow to extract motion information of faces.

In addition, both the non-unified image size and proportion of face to image from different databases interfere face spoofing detection. Therefore we pre-process the entire videos before motion analysis. We perform viola Jones face detector [15] to crop face region of videos per frame, but the size and location of face regions between different frames have a small shift. It would significantly distort the motion information which is not desirable in this work. For this reason, we crop all the frames in an video with the same size and location of the face region detected in the first frame, which effectively preserve the original motion information with the cropped videos. Then the face regions extracted from different videos are resized to the same scale for convenience in the following motion extraction and CNN based spoofing detection.

We leverage optical flow to track the motion of corresponding pixels of two adjacent frames in a video sequence. First we obtain displacement vectors for all the pixels in every frame from dense optical flow field, and then calculate all the displacement amplitudes which represent the movement details of the face in the corresponding video. In order to make the extracted motion information in MIMs fit for the following CNN processing, we visualize the displacement amplitudes of MIMs. The principle of visualization is that the pixel value corresponding to no displacement amplitude is set as zero and the pixel value corresponding to max displacement amplitude is embedded to 255, while other amplitudes follow uniform quantification in $[0, 255]$. The visualization function could be represented as follows:

$$P = 255 \times \frac{D}{\max_{i \in A}\{D_i\}} \qquad (1)$$

where P is a pixel value in the extracted MIM, D is the displacement amplitude of the corresponding pixel, and A represents all the pixels in the map. Figure 2 provides MIMs of real and fake faces from Replay-Attack and CASIA-FASD databases. The first column is the MIMs of real face, the second column is from fake face of photo attack and the third column is from video attack. It can be observed that photo attack has almost no motion information while video attack has a wide range of motion information which is considerably hazy. Different from these attacks, the real faces have a specific and clear motion. The maps of the first row and second row are from Replay-Attack and CASIA-FASD databases, respectively, but the MIMs of faces are distributed similarly between the two databases which is conducive to face spoofing detection with cross-database.

2.2 Image-Level Spoofing Detection on CNN

As illustrated in Fig. 2, the MIMs of real and fake faces are very different visually and the same category (real, photo attack, or video attack) between different

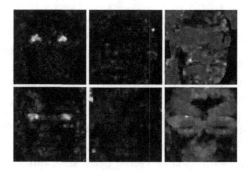

Fig. 2. Motion information maps of real faces (the first column) and fake faces (photo attack in the second and video attack in the third column) from Replay-Attack database (the first row) and CASIA-FASD (the last row).

databases has a high similarity in motion distribution. Therefore, we conduct face spoofing binary classification of real and fake faces with MIMs of video frames. We train AlexNet [16], a classic CNN, and classify MIMs of video frames to real or fake faces. Specifically, The last fully-connected layer has 2 neurons and is connected with a 2-way softmax classifier. The CNN model is employed to perform image-level classification of MIMs extracted from videos. As shown in Fig. 1, CNN model is trained on CASIA-FASD CNN training set, and preformed on CASIA-FASD threshold generating set to create fake score limitation which is combined with image-level spoofing detection on Replay-Attack database for video-level spoofing detection inference.

2.3   Video-Level Spoofing Detection by Cross-Database Voting

In practice, each video corresponds to a consistent category of real, photo attack, or video attack. However the image-level spoofing detection by CNN mentioned above may produce different classification results for different MIMs in the same video. Therefore, it is required intuitively to make a unified decision from all the MIMs for the video by voting.

We can not simply assign a video as real face, even if the number of MIMs in the video classified to real is more than that to fake. We take the ratio of the MIMs classified as fake to all MIMs from a video as a video-level spoofing inference measurement. The ratio is regarded as a fake score of the video. When the fake score does not exceed a threshold, the video is classified as real, vise versa. However by observation of the image-level spoofing detection results, we figure out a phenomenon that the limitation ratio of image-level real and fake inference in a video can not be set with exhaustive experiments for video-level inference. It is hard to select an appropriate threshold for video-level spoofing inference. Thanks to the similar motion distribution property across databases, in this work we propose a cross-database voting strategy to transfer the adaptive generated threshold from a database to another.

The CASIA-FASD threshold generating set involves videos with labels of real or fake faces. Besides, each video is given a fake score from image-level spoofing detection by CNN as Fig. 1. Then we could generate a threshold to separate the real and fake faces by their fake scores. In fact this is a one-dimensional classification problem. The maximum and minimum fake scores of each category are removed to prevent bias caused by the extreme situations. The mean of the lowest fake scores of fake videos and the highest fake scores of real videos is regarded approximately as the voting threshold which takes minimum sum of distance to all the fake scores of videos. Finally, the generated voting threshold from CASIA-FASD is transferred to Replay-Attack database and combined with the image-level spoofing detection results to voting a video-level spoofing inference for the videos in Replay-Attack database.

3 Experiments

To verify the effectiveness of the proposed method in face spoofing detection, we perform experiments on publicly available databases including Replay-Attack database and CASIA-FASD [17]. The extraction of MIM is implemented by Microsoft Visual Studio 10 with OpenCV, and the CNN framework is conducted on Caffe whose operating environment is ubuntu with TITAN X.

3.1 Database

CASIA Face Anti-Spoofing Database has 600 videos, including 3 different video sequences in quality from 3 different cameras. The resolution of 3 quality video is 640×480, 480×640 and 1280×720, respectively. Real face videos are acquired from 50 people. And the database covers 3 kinds of fake faces: warped photo attack, cut photo attack and video attack.

Replay-Attack database consists of 1200 videos which include 200 valid access videos and 1000 attack videos. The resolution of all videos is 320×240. The attack videos were generated with 3 techniques (print attack, mobile attack, and high-definition attack) and designed to 2 kinds of attacks (photo attack and video attack).

3.2 Experimental Setup

All frames in the video are cropped by the face area of the first frame and resized to 256×256 resolution, which guarantees the following optical flow to extract the motion information effectively. The parameters of the Gunnar Farneback optical flow method used to extract the motion-information are set as: 0.5 for the pyramid interlayer relationship, 3 for the number of pyramid layers, and 10 for the mean window.

CASIA-FASD is divided into three data sets including 70% as training set, 20% as validation set and 10% as testing set. The first two data sets are used as CNN training sets, and the last one is voting threshold generating set. We test all videos in Replay-Attack database to verify the effectiveness of the proposed cross-database spoofing detection method.

3.3   Experimental Comparison

We compare the proposed spoofing detection method with several state-of-the-art approaches, LBP [18], LBP-TOP [18], CNN [5], Correlation [18], Spectral cubes [19], Colour Texture [7]. The experimental results are evaluated by Half-Total Error Rate (HTER). HTER is defined as the mean of the False Rejection Rate and the False Acceptance Rate. We calculate the HTER on image-level spoofing detection results and video-level spoofing detection results by the proposed method, respectively. Table 1 provides the spoofing detection results of the proposed method compared with LBP [18], LBP-TOP [18], CNN [5], Correlation [18], Spectral cubes [19], Colour Texture [7]. It shows that the HTER of image-level spoofing detection without voting reaches 32.9% which is better than that of CNN. This indicates that MIMs extracted by optical flow work more effective compared to the original frames in videos. The proposed voting strategy reduces HTER from 32.9% to 25.3% by comparing video-level spoofing detection with image-level spoofing detection in the proposed method. It implies that cross-database voting strategy captures the consistency effectively across databases for face spoofing detection. It can be observed that the proposed method outperforms the other comparisons with a HTER 25.3%. It can be concluded that the proposed method is capable of leveraging cross-database consistency in motion information for spoofing detection.

Table 1. The results of cross-database (train on CASIA-FASD, test on Replay-Attack database) experiment compared with related studies

Method	HTER (%)	Method	HTER (%)
Correlation [18]	50.2	LBP-TOP [18]	49.7
CNN [5]	48.5	LBP [18]	45.9
Spectral cubes [19]	34.4	Colour texture [7]	30.3
image-level	32.9	Proposed	25.3

4   Conclusion

In this paper, we have proposed a face spoofing detection method with motion analysis based cross-database voting. Motion analysis extracts consistent motion information effectively across databases which is robust to illumination, background, resolution, etc. from environment and imaging devices. Cross-database voting employs the motion consistency across databases to perform video-level face spoofing inference with CNN based MIM binary classification. The experimental results and its corresponding analysis demonstrate that the proposed method outperforms its comparisons on face spoofing detection. Consequently, the proposed method enhances the face spoofing detection taking benefits from the cross-database consistency of motion information.

Acknowledgment. This work was supported in part by the Beijing Municipal Education Commission Science and Technology Innovation Project under Grant KZ201610005012.

References

1. Chihaoui, M., Elkefi, A., Bellil, W., Amar, C.B.: A survey of 2D face recognition techniques (2016)
2. Li, Y., Xu, K., Yan, Q., Li, Y., Deng, R.H.: Understanding OSN-based facial disclosure against face authentication systems. In: ACM Symposium on Information, Computer and Communications Security, pp. 413–424. ACM (2014)
3. Omar, L., Ivrissimtzis, I.: Evaluating the resilience of face recognition systems against malicious attacks. In: Uk British Machine Vision Workshop, pp. 5.1–5.9 (2015)
4. Chakraborty, S., Das, D.: An overview of face liveness detection. Comput. Sci. (2014)
5. Yang, J., Lei, Z., Li, S.Z.: Learn convolutional neural network for face anti-spoofing. Comput. Sci. **9218**, 373–384 (2014)
6. Alotaibi, A., Mahmood, A.: Enhancing computer vision to detect face spoofing attack utilizing a single frame from a replay video attack using deep learning. In: International Conference on Optoelectronics and Image Processing, pp. 1–5. IEEE (2016)
7. Boulkenafet, Z., Komulainen, J., Hadid, A.: Face spoofing detection using colour texture analysis. IEEE Trans. Inf. Forensics Secur. **11**(8), 1818–1830 (2016)
8. Chingovska, I., Anjos, A., Marcel, S.: On the effectiveness of local binary patterns in face anti-spoofing. In: Biometrics Special Interest Group, pp. 1–7. IEEE (2012)
9. Bharadwaj, S., Dhamecha, T.I., Vatsa, M., Singh, R.: Computationally efficient face spoofing detection with motion magnification. In: Computer Vision and Pattern Recognition Workshops, vol. 13, pp. 105–110. IEEE (2013)
10. Tirunagari, S., Poh, N., Windridge, D., Iorliam, A., Suki, N., Ho, A.T.S.: Detection of face spoofing using visual dynamics. IEEE Trans. Inf. Forensics Secur. **10**(4), 762–777 (2015)
11. Bao, W., Li, H., Li, N., Jiang, W.: A liveness detection method for face recognition based on optical flow field. In: International Conference on Image Analysis and Signal Processing, pp. 233–236. IEEE (2009)
12. Bouguet, J.Y.: Pyramidal implementation of the lucas kanade feature tracker description of the algorithm. Opencv Doc. **22**(2), 363–381 (1999)
13. Farnebäck, G.: Two-frame motion estimation based on polynomial expansion. In: Bigun, J., Gustavsson, T. (eds.) SCIA 2003. LNCS, vol. 2749, pp. 363–370. Springer, Heidelberg (2003). doi:10.1007/3-540-45103-X_50
14. Wu, L., Xu, Y., Xu, X., Qi, W., Jian, M.: A face liveness detection scheme to combining static and dynamic features. In: You, Z., Zhou, J., Wang, Y., Sun, Z., Shan, S., Zheng, W., Feng, J., Zhao, Q. (eds.) CCBR 2016. LNCS, vol. 9967, pp. 628–636. Springer, Cham (2016). doi:10.1007/978-3-319-46654-5_69
15. Viola, P., Jones, M.J.: Robust Real-Time Face Detection. Kluwer Academic Publishers, Dordrecht (2004)
16. Krizhevsky, A., Sutskever, I., Hinton, G.E.: ImageNet classification with deep convolutional neural networks. In: International Conference on Neural Information Processing Systems, vol. 25, pp. 1097–1105. Curran Associates Inc (2012)

17. Zhang, Z., Yan, J., Liu, S., Lei, Z.: A face antispoofing database with diverse attacks. In: IAPR International Conference on Biometrics, pp. 26–31. IEEE (2012)
18. Pereira, T.D.F., Anjos, A., Martino, J.M.D., Marcel, S.: Can face anti-spoofing countermeasures work in a real world scenario? In: International Conference on Biometrics, pp. 1–8. IEEE (2013)
19. Pinto, A., Pedrini, H., Schwartz, W.R., Rocha, A.: Face spoofing detection through visual codebooks of spectral temporal cubes. IEEE Trans. Image Process. 24(12), 4726 (2015). A Publication of the IEEE Signal Processing Society

Personal Identification Based on Content-Independent EEG Signal Analysis

Yifan Li, Yinghui Zhao, Taifeng Tan, Ningjie Liu,
and Yuchun Fang[✉]

School of Computer Engineering and Science,
Shanghai University, Shanghai, China
ycfang@shu.edu.cn

Abstract. Interests in the use of biological signals have been rapidly growing in the past decades. Biometrics recognition based on electroencephalogram (EEG) has become a hotspot. In this paper, we propose a novel EEG biometrics system. The system contains automatic channel selection, wavelet feature extraction and Deep Neural Network (DNN) classifier. The channel selection can not only reduce the computational redundancy, but also improve the accuracy. A strategy of fusing EEG and physiological signal is adopted in the system. As a very useful supplement to other previous work, we specially endeavor to handle content-independent EEG biometrics. The proposed system is validated on a multimodal dataset, i.e. DEAP [1] for the authentication of the identity. We perform data augmentation through splitting the EEG signal by down sampling with different shift. An accuracy of 94% ± 3% is obtained in 10-fold validations. The results demonstrate the possibility of EEG biometrics under content-independent scenario.

Keywords: EEG · Discrete wavelet analysis · Deep Neural Network · Data fusion

1 Introduction

Interests in the use of biological signals have been rapidly growing in the past decades. Biometrics-based recognition has become a hotspot. Fingerprints [2], irises, retinas, faces [3] and even odors [4] are used to identify individual traits, which are known as "biological features". Personal safety and public safety has become a hot issue, and many researchers are working on the use of various biometric authentication to achieve individual identification.

There are many literatures on the analysis of the causes of EEG variations [5–7]. Besides, EEG signals, as an emerging biometric, have unique recognition advantages [8]. The unique fluctuations of EEG signals show how the subjects react to stimuli. As for identification theft, each individual who can maintain the state of physiological activity can produce brainwave signals, and these signals are unique. The EEG signal is difficult to thieve and copy for it is not available over a certain distance. Näpflin et al. used EEG signals to validate the individual signature [9]. Brigham and Kumar used EEG signals for subject identification during imagined speech [10]. There are

© Springer International Publishing AG 2017
J. Zhou et al. (Eds.): CCBR 2017, LNCS 10568, pp. 537–544, 2017.
https://doi.org/10.1007/978-3-319-69923-3_58

individual recognition studies based on EEG neural networks [11], as well as research on biometrics based on EEG [12].

EEG is more widely used in emotional recognition, which provides reference for designing better personal identification models. Naser and Saha [13] used a double tree complex wavelet packet transform (DT-CWPT) on the basis of the DEAP dataset. In [14], facial expressions and heart rates were recorded while a total of 24 female undergraduates watching 48 pictures. Torres et al. used the recursive feature elimination (RFE) to study the DEAP database [15].

The previous researches on EEG personal identification show the feasibility of EEG biometrics in several aspects. Poulos et al. used the LVQ neural network for classification of unclassified EEG signals, and the correct recognition rate was 80% [11]. Su et al. proposed the importance of Covert Warning as a feature in individual recognition, and used KNN to classify self-collected EEG samples with an accuracy of 95% [16]. Campisi and Rocca conducted an in-depth study of the closed resting state acquisition protocol (Closed Eyes), which performed EEG acquisition of 45 healthy subjects, using Monte Carlo and other methods [8]. However, there are few researches on content independent EEG personal identification.

In this paper, we present a new approach on a complex emotional dataset for content-independent personal identification. Content-related EEG personal identification fixes the same specified content for the stimulus. While in this paper, we explore the possibility of content-independent personal identification in EEG biometrics, and the data used is the EEG signal is generated by each subject receiving the stimulus of different content. Content-independent recognition has a higher degree of freedom than content-related recognition, which is less affected by the content, so it is more practical in real applications.

2   Method

The flowchart of the proposed algorithm is shown in Fig. 1. It contains three major parts, i.e. selection of the appropriate channel, feature extraction with wavelet analysis and DNN based classifier.

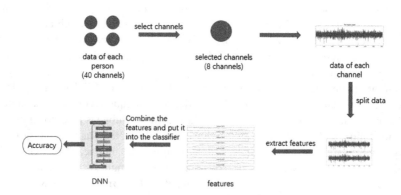

Fig. 1. The flow chart

2.1 Channel Selection

It is important to select the channel, which is better support of the identification from the complex emotional signals. By selecting the channel, some redundant information is removed, and the data is down-sampled, which reduces the computational complexity and improves the computational efficiency.

The Euclidean distances of two channels are calculated to measure the variance between arbitrary channels intra- or inter-subjects. The two sets of distances for each channel are merged into two one-dimensional vectors, which are used to describe the support of each channel for distinguishing the subjects as shown in Eq. (1),

$$J = \frac{|\overline{d_{intra}} - \overline{d_{inter}}|}{\sigma_{intra}\sigma_{inter}} \tag{1}$$

where d_{intra} means the Euclidean distance of the data of each channel of the same subject, and d_{inter} means the Euclidean distance of the data of each channel between the subjects. The higher the value of J, the higher the degree of distinction with the others. We select the EEG channels with the largest J value. Through channel selection, we can reduce the dimension of the data and keep the most distinguishing information in personal identification meanwhile.

2.2 Feature Extraction with Discrete Wavelet Transform

The data for each channel is large and an appropriate feature extraction scheme is required. Discrete wavelet transform can obtain the approximation of the original signal in the time domain. We perform the fifth-order discrete wavelet transform on the data of each channel, and get the approximate signal as the feature of this channel by Eq. (2). The features of the eight channels of the same video are merged together as a feature of the subject. Db4 waveform and EEG waveform are similar, we can extract the effect of a good approximation signal.

$$WT(a, \tau) = \frac{1}{\sqrt{a}} \int_{-\infty}^{\infty} f(t) \times \psi\left(\frac{t - \tau}{a}\right) dt \tag{2}$$

2.3 Classifier

In this paper, we classify the extracted features by DNN classifier and compare the classification effect of the DNN classifier and traditional classifiers.

There is no better network construction method yet. Determining the structure and weight coefficients of the neural network can describe a given mapping or approximate an unknown mapping, and only through the learning method to meet the requirements of the network model. When designing a network, the main method is to experiment with a variety of model schemes, which are improved in the experiment until a satisfactory solution is selected.

There are the following steps: first only using a hidden layer; using very few hidden layer nodes, increasing the number of hidden layer nodes until the satisfaction of the performance so far, otherwise using two hidden layers repeat the above process. When having determined the network layer, the number of nodes per layer, transfer function, the initial weight coefficient and learning algorithm, etc., it is identified the network. There are certain rules to determine these options, but most of them are according to experience and trial. The DNN adopted consists of four dense layers, two dropout layers and a loss layer. The activation function used in the network is Sigmoid, ReLu and Softmax. The architecture of the adopted DNN is shown in Fig. 2.

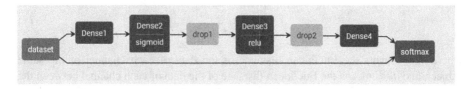

Fig. 2. DNN architecture diagram

3   Experiments

We perform content-independent personal identification experiments on the DEAP dataset after augmenting the number of samples.

3.1   Data Augmentation

We use the emotional dataset named DEAP [1]. The dataset was collected from 32 volunteers. 40 pieces of music video, each contains 40 channels of data, and the data for each channel is 8064-length vector. 32 channels are EEG signals and 8 channels are physiological signal. After down-sampling to 128 Hz, each channel is divided into two parts for down sampling. And the segmentation method is the array subscript parity division, in order to preserve the overall characteristics, as shown in Fig. 3.

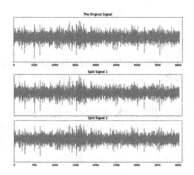

Fig. 3. Split data

3.2 Channel Selection

We select the *J* value of the highest 8 channels, normalized by Min-Max Normalization to extract features. The number and the channel content of the 8 channels are displayed in Table 1, and the distribution is shown in Fig. 4.

Table 1. The selected EEG signal channels.

Channel no.	Channel content
10	CP1
11	P3
13	PO3
16	Pz
25	C4
28	CP2
30	P8
32	O2

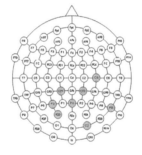

Fig. 4. Selected EEG signal channel's distribution

3.3 Feature

The data in the channel is processed after discrete wavelet transform, normalized by Min-Max Normalization. 8-channel 4032 dimensions data is handled with fifth-order discrete wavelet transform and merged into obtain 1056 dimensions features (as shown in Fig. 5). Eventually we get 40 video features for 32 subjects (32 * 40 * 1056 dimensions).

3.4 Classifier Comparison

For the EEG signal data, we select five kinds of classifiers for training and classification. By comparing the prediction accuracy in Table 2, we get the DNN, SVM and the Logical Regression to get the better classification result.

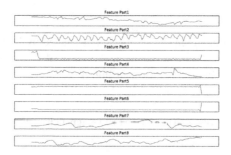

Fig. 5. The eight parts of each feature correspond to a selected channel

Table 2. Single EEG signal classification results.

Classifier	Average accuracy
Decision Tree	40% ± 4%
Random Forest	60% ± 7%
Logical Regression	85% ± 5%
SVM	85% ± 4%
DNN	88% ± 4%

3.5   Fusion of Features

In the experiment, we find that physiological signals have an important role in the identification, such as the 38th channel breathing zone, whose breathing for himself is unique. We select eight higher J-value channels for classification, which contain EEG channels and physiological signal channels (as shown in Table 3).

Table 3. The Selected EEG channels and physiological signal channels

Channel no.	Channel content
10	CP1
11	P3
16	Pz
30	P8
33	hEOG (horizontal EOG, hEOG1 - hEOG2)
34	vEOG (vertical EOG, vEOG1 - vEOG2)
37	GSR (values from Twente converted to Geneva format (Ohm))
38	Respiration belt

When the physiological signal is added to the feature, the five classifiers have achieved better results (as shown in Table 4). The predictive accuracy of the Decision Tree is improved from 40% to 80%, and the predictive accuracy of the Random Forest is improved from 60% to 89%. The predictive accuracy of the Logistic Regression is improved from 85% to 87%, DNN's prediction accuracy is improved from 88% to

Table 4. Comparison of single feature and mixed feature classification.

Classifier	Single EEG features	Single physiological features	Mixed features
Decision Tree	40% ± 4%	73% ± 4%	80% ± 2%
Random Forest	60% ± 7%	85% ± 2%	89% ± 2%
Logical Regression	85% ± 5%	83% ± 3%	87% ± 3%
SVM	85% ± 4%	78% ± 2%	88% ± 2%
DNN	88% ± 4%	70% ± 3%	94% ± 3%

94%. Thus, we can see the mixed features of EEG and physiological signals outperforms the simple EEG feature or simple physiological features. The mixed feature improves the recognition accuracy.

4 Conclusion

In this paper, we present automatic channel selection, wavelet feature extraction and Deep Neural Network (DNN) classifier for content-independent identification. In the single EEG signal data, we compared five classifiers. DNN get the best results, the accuracy of 88% ± 4%. In the fusion of signal, the highest accuracy is 94% ± 3% of DNN in 10-fold validations. We use the discrete wavelet transform to extract the rough feature of the data, which effectively reduces the training time of DNN. In DNN, its training process integration feature extraction, so the classification effect is better than traditional classifier.

The results demonstrate the possibility of EEG biometrics under content-independent scenario. And the channel selection method not only effectively reduces computational redundancy, but also improves the accuracy. The fusion of EEG and physiological signals have better support for identity than a single EEG signal feature or a single physiological signal feature.

94% of the predictive accuracy in the practical application is far from enough. In the future work, we will optimize the neural network architecture and adjust the network parameters to improve the recognition rate.

Acknowledgements. The work is funded by the National Natural Science Foundation of China (No. 61170155), Shanghai Innovation Action Plan Project (No. 16511101200) and the Open Project Program of the National Laboratory of Pattern Recognition (No. 201600017).

References

1. Koelstra, S., Soleymani, M., Lee, J.-S., Yazdani, A., Ebrahimi, T., Pun, T., Nijholt, A., Patras, I.: DEAP: a database for emotion analysis using physiological signals. IEEE Trans. Affect. Comput. **3**, 18–31 (2012). New York
2. Cao, K., Yang, X., Chen, X., Zang, Y., Liang, J., Tian, J.: A novel ant colony optimization algorithm for large-distorted fingerprint matching. Pattern Recogn. **45**, 151–161 (2012)

3. Shin, A.-Y., Wallraven, C., Bülthoff, H., Lee, S.-W.: Building a 3D morphable face model based on implicit surfaces. In: Proceedings of the Korea Computer Congress, vol. 37, pp. 339–342 (2010)
4. O'Dwyer, T., Nevitt, G.: Individual odor recognition in procellariiform chicks: potential role for the major histocompatibility complex. Ann. N. Y. Acad. Sci. **1170**, 442–446 (2009)
5. Peterson, C.K., Harmon-Jones, E.: Circadian and seasonal variability of resting frontal EEG asymmetry. Biol. Psychol. **80**, 315–320 (2009)
6. Vogel, F., Schalt, E.: The electroencephalogram (EEG) as a research tool in human behavior genetics: psychological examinations in healthy males with various inherited EEG variants. Hum. Genet. **47**, 81–111 (1979)
7. van Beijsterveldt, C.E., Molenaar, P.C., de Geus, E.J., Boomsma, D.I.: Heritability of human brain functioning as assessed by electroencephalography (EEG). Am. J. Hum. Genet. **58**, 562–573 (1996)
8. Campisi, P., La Rocca, D.: Brain waves for automatic biometric-based user recognition. IEEE TIFS **9**(5), 782–800 (2014). New York
9. Näpflin, M., Wildi, M., Sarnthein, J.: Test–retest reliability of resting EEG spectra validates a statistical signature of persons. Clin. Neurophysiol. **118**, 2519–2524 (2007)
10. Brigham, K., Kumar, B.V.: Subject identification from electroencephalogram (EEG) signals during imagined speech. In: Proceedings of the IEEE 4th International Conference on BTAS, New York, pp. 1–8 (2010)
11. Poulos, M., Rangoussi, M., Alexandris, N.: Neural network based person identification using EEG features. In: Proceedings of the IEEE International Conference on Acoustics, Speech, Signal Processing, New York, vol. 2, pp. 1117–1120 (1999)
12. Riera, A., Soria-Frisch, A., Caparrini, M., Grau, C., Ruffini, G.: Unobtrusive biometric system based on electroencephalogram analysis. EURASIP J. Adv. Sig. Process. **2008**, 1–8 (2008)
13. Naser, D.S., Saha, G.: Recognition of emotions induced by music videos using DT-CWPT. In: 2013 Indian Conference on Medical Informatics and Telemedicine (ICMIT), pp. 53–57 (2013)
14. Kortelainen, J., Tiinanen, S., Huang, X., Li, X., Laukka, S., Pietikäinen, M., Seppänen, T.: Multimodal emotion recognition by combining physiological signals and facial expressions: a preliminary study. In: The 34th Annual International Conference of the IEEE Engineering in Medicine and Biology Society, EMBC 2012, New York, pp. 5238–5241. IEEE Press (2012)
15. Torres, C.A., Orozco, Á.A., Álvarez, M.A.: Feature selection for multimodal emotion recognition in the arousal-valence space. In: 35th Annual International Conference of the IEEE EMBS Osaka, New York, pp. 3–7. IEEE Press (2013)
16. Su, F., Zhou, H., Feng, Z., Ma, J.: A biometric-based covert warning system using EEG. In: 5th IAPR International Conference on Biometrics ICB, pp. 342–347 (2012)

Handwaving Authentication: Unlocking Your Smartwatch Through Handwaving Biometrics

Zhao Wang, Chao Shen$^{(\boxtimes)}$, and Yufei Chen

Xi'an Jiaotong University, No. 28 Xianning West Road, Xi'an 710049, China
{zhaowang,cshen,yfchen}@sei.xjtu.edu.cn

Abstract. The increasing usage of smartwatches to access sensitive and personal data while being applied in health monitoring and quick payment, has given rise to the need of convenient and secure authentication technique. However, traditional memory-based authentication methods like PIN are proved to be easily cracked or user-unfriendly. This paper presents a novel approach to unlock smartwatches or authenticate users' identities on smartwatches by analyzing a users' handwaving patterns. A filed study was conducted to design typical smartwatch unlocking scenarios and gather users' handwaving data. Behavioral features were extracted to accurately characterize users' handwaving patterns. Then a one-class classification algorithm based on scaled Manhattan distance was developed to perform the task of user authentication. Extensive experiments based on a newly established 150-person-time handwaving dataset with a smartwatch, are included to demonstrate the effectiveness of the proposed approach, which achieves an equal-error rate of 4.27% in free-shaking scenario and 14.46% in imitation-attack scenario. This level of accuracy shows that these is indeed identity information in handwaving behavior that can be used as a wearable authentication mechanism.

Keywords: Wearable devices · Smartwatch unlocking · User authentication · Motion sensor

1 Introduction

Recently, smart wearable devices gradually come into people's vision. They bring new means to human-computer interaction, and are also applied to instant messaging, quick payment and other fields, which usually store contact information, bank account password and other privacy information. Unfortunately, these devices are easy to be stolen for their portable and small size, even be attacked by malware [1]. Under such circumstances, it's emergency to solve the security problems of smart wearable devices.

The unlocking and identity authentication method is an indispensable part of smart wearable devices. Classical identity authentication methods are usually memory-based. The most widely used one is PIN unlock method. However, it's inconvenient to set a long password due to the small screen and frequent unlocking request especially in smart wearable devices, but short passwords are

© Springer International Publishing AG 2017
J. Zhou et al. (Eds.): CCBR 2017, LNCS 10568, pp. 545–553, 2017.
https://doi.org/10.1007/978-3-319-69923-3_59

vulnerable to be cracked by guessing, peeping or brute-force attack. So, the traditional unlocking approaches seem to be not feasible for smart wearable devices.

Biometric methods are explored to meet the urgent demand for security and usability of the wearables, which can be divided into two main categories [2]: physiological characteristics and behavioral characteristics. The former contain voice, fingerprints, face, iris, etc., which are sensitive to external environment or personal status. While the latter, including gesture, typing habit, gait, mouse using habit, etc., which are not easy to be affected by external circumstance and performs well in most situations especially in terms of stability and reliability.

Compared with other behavioral characteristics, handwaving has its own advantages in biometric authentication for wearable devices. which is more unique, reliable and unduplicable, as it corresponds with physiological structure and behavioral habits. It has already been applied and proved feasible in some areas (e.g. smartphone unlock and authentication) preliminarily [3]. Meanwhile, handwaving based authentication is labour-saving, especially for smartwatch users.

However, how to extract a unique and stable pattern from handwaving gestures is still a challenging task. In this paper, we propose a handwaving based unlocking system, Alertor, for wearable devices, which is lightweight and user-friendly. The system first reads accelerometer data when user waves hand, and then preprocesses the raw data via shaking functions. And then it adopts Manhattan scaled one-class classifier to discriminate the true user and imposters. We recruited 10 volunteers and established a 150-person-time handwaving dataset with a Samsung Gear 2 smartwatch in multiple scenarios. Alertor achieves an EER of 4.27% in the free-shaking scenario and 14.46% in the imitation-attack scenario, demonstrating that our system is feasible and applicable.

2   Background and Related Work

In this section, we briefly review multiple applications of biometric methods.

2.1   Gait Authentication

Previous studies composed several different identity authentication methods based on user's gait habit [4–6]. But most results are claimed under an experimental environment. Actually, authentication accuracy may show an unstable behavior when facing various ground environments. For example, when people stand above the grass or snowfield or wet road, the precision rate may fluctuate observably. Besides, it can't be used while the user remains stationary. That is to say, this method's application is a bit limited.

2.2   Touch Authentication

The authentication based on touch gesture in literature started in 2013. Frank et al. published a paper about utilizing touchscreen swipe behavior to conduct continuous authentication [7]. After that, researchers concentrate on touchscreen click, swipe, drag and drop and other behavior features [8–10]. These previous studies proved the feasibility of identity authentication based on touch gesture: under the circumstance of a single environment and neglecting the observation time, the accuracy can reach more than 90% across current small data set. However, the stability of this method is not ideal since the numerical value of extracted feature vector is small. Feature will be indistinctive especially when the user has other drastic actions.

2.3   Accelerator Authentication

In biometrics areas, accelerator is an important data source for actions or behaviors sensing. There are several researches parallel to this study, utilizing accelerator to collect raw data of user's behavior pattern and extract features from these data to identify the user [11,12]. Just like what mentioned in [11], the user is asked to conduct a specific secret gesture in air to execute the authentication. Likewise, in [12], the user needs to hold a detection device and shake it up and down for 5 times. Both of the two means are similar to traditional PIN authentication method as they request for a specific behavior (or we can call it *gesture password*). So they have security vulnerabilities: once the gesture password has been recorded or glimpsed by someone else, the device may be hacked in without a hitch by action imitation.

3   Data Collection and Feature Extraction

In this section, we give a detailed introduction to data collection, establishment of dataset, and feature extraction.

3.1   Shaking Data Collection

We recruited 10 subjects into our experiment, including 7 males and 3 females, who are all students of campus. There are 9 right-handed and 1 left-handed. We developed a third-party application running in the background on a Samsung Gear S2 smartwatch to collect accelerometer data. All the data are recorded as a sequence of tuples in the form of (x_t, y_t, z_t), where x, y, z donate the acceleration in x-axis, y-axis and z-axis respectively, and t represents the timestamp.

In our experiment, we considered different attacker scenarios. In each session we select a user as the genius user and others as imposters, and all the subjects form a group. Then we divide the whole group into four classes (one genius-user type and three attacker types) with different tasks: firstly, the genius user shakes the smartwatch for three times and we record a video of him, where every single shaking procedure consists of one second waiting and nine seconds shaking. And then, we choose three imposters to watch the shaking video and shake the smartwatch for three times with recalling the gesture. Meanwhile, we select other three imposters to watch the video and imitate with the video while shaking the smartwatch for three times. At last, we choose all the remaining three imposters to shake the smartwatch for three times as they want. In this way, we collect 30 times shaking data for every single group, then we choose another genius user for data acquisition, we call it Group 2.

We can get data of Group 3 to Group 5 by repeating the steps. After 5 times collection, we have a total of 150 sets of shaking data (10 subjects × 3 times shaking × 5 different genius users). Finally, we has obtained approximately 150,000 raw tuples in total.

3.2 Data Preprocessing

Although in the data collection stage we set a built-in method to filter the outliers beyond the preset range, there are still some data not satisfied with our experiment. Therefore, we have to design a filter to remove these improper data, such as the data of the initial and end stage, whose value is too low to be recognized. The filter must have the properties of efficiency and robustness. We design a filter presented as follows:

$$\sum_{i=1}^{r}(A_i - m) \times \frac{(2b+1)}{(r-l+1)} < \alpha \tag{1}$$

where A_i is the acceleration of time i, m is the mean value of raw data, r is the right boundary and l is the left boundary. b is the longest length of low-value data you can accept, a is the threshold which represents the lowest value you put into your experiment. The effect of this filtering algorithm is depicted in Fig. 1. It's obvious that the initial stage with low-value data have been removed.

3.3 Feature Extraction

The raw shaking data can't be used directly to anomaly detectors. So, we need to design a feature extraction procedure before system implementation. To investigate the raw data characteristics, we present several subjects' raw shaking data in Fig. 2, where the user 1 test1 and test2 represent two operations of same user, and the user 2 and 3 represent another two users' single operation respectively.

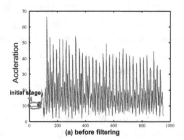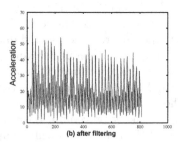

Fig. 1. Filter effect picture

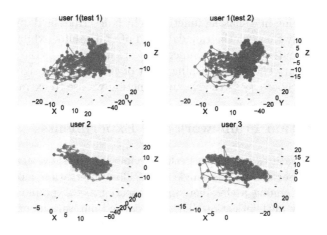

Fig. 2. User wave data contrast

Apparently, the raw data resemble across one test to another of the same subject, but differ from each other through different subjects. In order to depict the data characteristics, we define a shaking function, which is given by:

$$f = S(A) \tag{2}$$

where $A = \{(x_0, y_0, z_0), (x_1, y_1, z_1), \ldots, (x_n, y_n, z_n)\}$. A is the acceleration data sequence of subjects. We select A as the input and compute feature vector f as

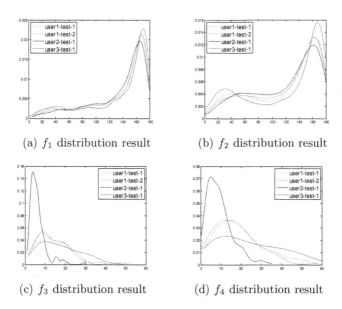

(a) f_1 distribution result   (b) f_2 distribution result

(c) f_3 distribution result   (d) f_4 distribution result

Fig. 3. Shaking function distribution result

the output. We bring in 4 shaking functions which describe the data in angle and distance and apply them to the raw data and obtain results exhibited in Fig. 3. Obviously, the results of these four functions are satisfactory as the distinction of the features is clear. The distinguishing effect of f_4 is the most significant above all, so we finally choose f_4 as the shaking function we use to extract features.

4   Classification Framework and Experiments

Empirically, the features we extract in the previous section show a larger variance across different user than for a single user. This observation motivates us to classify the users among a classifier. In this section, we expound the classifier we use to identity authentication. Then we carried out various experiments to investigate the feasibility of the system we designed.

4.1   Choice of Classifiers

A classifier is designed to utilize the feature vector to distinguish the genius user and imposters. In the process of our experiment, we use Manhattan (scaled) classifier to classification. This classic detector was described by Araújo et al. [13]. In the training stage, the mean of feature vector matrix is computed, and the mean average deviation is also calculated. In the test stage, we calculate the Manhattan distance and make it to the similarity of two feature vectors, and choose it as the user score, the anomaly score is calculated by $\sum_{i=1}^{p} |x_i - y_i|/a_i$, where x_i and y_i are the value of i-th dimension of test and mean vector respectively, and a_i is the mean average deviation.

4.2   Influence of Application Scenarios

Safety guarantee varies with the application context and environment. If we set a high security level, the true user may be locked out of our system, while if it is too low, the imposters may easily hack in the system and theft of user's secret. Therefore, there must be a trade-off between usability and security. To measure the performance of our system, we use the FAR and FRR to generate a ROC curve, where FAR is *false acceptance rate*, representing the rate of imposters who has been accepted by our system; and FRR is the *false rejection rate*, representing the rate of genius user who has been rejected by our system. A ROC curve example of Manhattan (scaled) detector and SVM detector is shown in Fig. 4. We choose the point where the FAR equals to the FRR, and call it as EER (equal-error rate).

As described in Sect. 3, we consider three types of application scenarios, which are: imitating, imitating with video and the shake as what you like. Instinctively the first two scenarios may have a high ability to break into the system, but the last is weaker. For this reason, we experimentally analyze three different authentication scenarios.

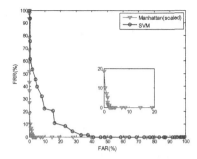

Fig. 4. ROC curve example

We train our system and test it as follows:

1. In every single test, we choose one genius user, and let the rest of the group subjects as imposters.
2. Then, we train our system with the first set of shaking data of the true user.
3. Finally, we test the system with the remaining data of the true user and all the three sets of data of imposters.

This progress is repeated among 5 groups, designating single person in every group as the genius user in turn, and train the system the corresponding three-time shaking data. After training 150 times (10 subjects × 5 groups × 3 times) and testing for all datasets we collected for 4350 times(29 Non-training data × 30 individual data in every group × 5group), we have got 150 sets EERs (10 subjects × 5 groups × 3 times) in total. Then we calculate the mean value of them, and present the experiment result in Table 1 and Fig. 4. In general, the performance of our system works well in the case of uninformed imposters, and the video imitators can enter the system more easily than the imitators of memory.

Table 1. Different scenarios authentication accuracy

User type	Video imitation	Recall imitation	Free shaking
Mean EERs	0.2314	0.0578	0.0427

5 Conclusion

The trend to access and store privacy information using wearable devices has stressed an urgent demand of applicable and handy authentication mechanism for wearable devices. To the best of our knowledge, our work is the first to systematically design and evaluate the biometric authentication scheme on smart wearable devices. From data acquisition and preprocessing, feature extraction to classification, we provide a detailed implementation of handwaving-gesture authentication system on wearable devices. Furthermore, we collected handwaving data from 10 subjects and have established a 150-person-time dataset to evaluate authentication performance and facilitate future research. Our experimental results indicate that our system is capable of discriminating genuine user and resisting imitation attacks.

Aknowledgement. This work was supported in part by the National Natural Science Foundation of China under Grant 61403301 and Grant 61773310, in part by the China Postdoctoral Science Foundation under Grant 2014M560783 and Grant 2015T81032, in part by the Natural Science Foundation of Shaanxi Province under Grant 2015JQ6216, and in part by the Fundamental Research Funds for the Central Universities under Grant xjj2015115.

References

1. Shrestha, B., Saxena, N., Harrison, J.: Wave-to-access: protecting sensitive mobile device services via a hand waving gesture. In: Abdalla, M., Nita-Rotaru, C., Dahab, R. (eds.) CANS 2013. LNCS, vol. 8257, pp. 199–217. Springer, Cham (2013). doi:10.1007/978-3-319-02937-5_11
2. Alzubaidi, A., Kalita, J.: Authentication of smartphone users using behavioral biometrics. IEEE Commun. Surv. Tutor. **18**(3), 1998–2026 (2016)
3. Blasco, J., Chen, T.M., Tapiador, J., Peris-Lopez, P.: A survey of wearable biometric recognition systems. ACM Comput. Surv. (CSUR) **49**(3), 43 (2016)
4. Gafurov, D., Helkala, K., Søndrol, T.: Biometric gait authentication using accelerometer sensor. JCP **1**(7), 51–59 (2006)
5. Kwapisz, J.R., Weiss, G.M., Moore, S.A.: Cell phone-based biometric identification. In: 2010 Fourth IEEE International Conference on Biometrics: Theory Applications and Systems (BTAS), pp. 1–7. IEEE (2010)
6. Mantyjarvi, J., Lindholm, M., Vildjiounaite, E., Makela, S.M., Ailisto, H.A.: Identifying users of portable devices from gait pattern with accelerometers. In: IEEE International Conference on Acoustics, Speech, and Signal Processing, 2005. Proceedings. (ICASSP 2005), Vol. 2, pp. ii-973. IEEE (2005)
7. Frank, M., Biedert, R., Ma, E., Martinovic, I., Song, D.: Touchalytics: on the applicability of touchscreen input as a behavioral biometric for continuous authentication. IEEE Trans. Inf. Forensics Secur. **8**(1), 136–148 (2013)
8. Saravanan, P., Clarke, S., Chau, D.H.P., Zha, H.: Latentgesture: active user authentication through background touch analysis. In: Proceedings of the Second International Symposium of Chinese CHI, pp. 110–113. ACM (2014)
9. Zhang, H., Patel, V.M., Fathy, M., Chellappa, R.: Touch gesture-based active user authentication using dictionaries. In: 2015 IEEE Winter Conference on Applications of Computer Vision (WACV), pp. 207–214. IEEE (2015)
10. El Masri, A., Wechsler, H., Likarish, P., Grayson, C., Pu, C., Al-Arayed, D., Kang, B.B.: Active authentication using scrolling behaviors. In: 2015 6th International Conference on Information and Communication Systems (ICICS), pp. 257–262. IEEE (2015)
11. Liu, J., Zhong, L., Wickramasuriya, J., Vasudevan, V.: User evaluation of lightweight user authentication with a single tri-axis accelerometer. In: Proceedings of the 11th International Conference on Human-Computer Interaction with Mobile Devices and Services, p. 15. ACM (2009)

12. Okumura, F., Kubota, A., Hatori, Y., Matsuo, K., Hashimoto, M., Koike, A.: A study on biometric authentication based on arm sweep action with acceleration sensor. In: 2006 International Symposium on Intelligent Signal Processing and Communications, ISPACS 2006, pp. 219–222. IEEE (2006)
13. Araújo, L.C., Sucupira, L.H., Lizarraga, M.G., Ling, L.L., Yabu-Uti, J.B.T.: User authentication through typing biometrics features. IEEE Trans. Signal Process. **53**(2), 851–855 (2005)

Identification of the Normal and Abnormal Heart Sounds Based on Energy Features and Neural Network

Ting Li[1(✉)], Hong Tang[2], and Xiao-ke Xu[1]

[1] School of Information and Communication Engineering,
Dalian Minzu University, Dalian, China
liting@dlnu.edu.cn
[2] School of Electronic Information and Electrical Engineering,
Dalian University of Technology, Dalian, China

Abstract. A normal and abnormal heart sound identification method was put forward in the paper. The wavelet packet energy features of the heart sounds were extracted and LM-BP neural network was used as the classifier. Experimental results showed that the proposed algorithm converged much faster than traditional BP neural network, and achieved better results compared with two traditional heart sound processing methods based on STFT and Spectrogram analysis.

Keywords: Heart sounds · Identification · Wavelet packet energy · LM-BP neural network

1 Introduction

Heart disease is the most common overall cause of death for people worldwide. The heart sound reflects the mechanical action of the heart and the cardiovascular system, including the physiology and pathology information of various parts of the heart. Therefore, in all the heart disease detecting methods, heart sound analysis is a non-invasive, economical, easy and efficient method which is widely used to diagnose heart disease and evaluate heart functions during medical check-ups for adults and children.

However, the traditional heart auscultation is over-dependent on the ear sensitivity and the subjective experience of physicians, which can not meet the high accuracy requirement under clinical conditions [1]. In recent years, many features of heart sounds are extracted to describe the heart sound, such as wavelet envelope [2], wavelet-time entropy [3, 7], frequency feature matrix [4] and linear band frequency cepstra [5]. And various classification algorithms have been employed to identify the normal and abnormal heart sounds, such as SVM [2–4], dynamic time warping algorithm [5], adaptive neuro-fuzzy inference system [6, 9], and neural network [8].

However, identification of the normal and abnormal heart sound is still not a straightforward task, with a number of challenges to overcome. The first challenge is the feature extraction and selection to represent the heart sound properties. The features

© Springer International Publishing AG 2017
J. Zhou et al. (Eds.): CCBR 2017, LNCS 10568, pp. 554–561, 2017.
https://doi.org/10.1007/978-3-319-69923-3_60

should provide distinguishing quantitative measures to classify the normal and abnormal heart sounds. The second challenge is the construction of the classifiers. Due to the limited amount of available data, there might be considerable amount of bias if the classifier was not conducted properly.

The aim of this paper is to establish an efficient method to extract the features from pre-processed heart sound signals and identify the normal and abnormal heart sounds. The energy features of the heart sounds using wavelet technology are extracted and LM-BP neural network is used as the classifier. The paper is organized as follows. In Sect. 2, the structure diagram of heart sound identification system is designed, and the basic theories and realization process of the technologies used in this paper are introduced briefly. In Sect. 3, the actual heart sounds (including normal and abnormal heart sounds) are processed according to the proposed feature extraction method and identification method. Finally, discussion and conclusion are presented in Sect. 4.

2   Methodology

The normal and abnormal heart sounds identification process we design is shown in Fig. 1, which consists of three parts: preprocessing, feature extraction and identification. In the next sections, the basic theories will be introduced respectively.

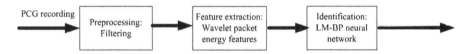

Fig. 1. Structure diagram of heart sound identification process

2.1   Wavelet Packet Decomposition

Wavelet transform (WT) can be used to decompose a signal into sub-bands with low frequency (approximate components) and sub-bands with high frequency (detail components) [11]. Although wavelet analysis has the characteristics of multi-resolution, it only breaks up as an approximation version, that is to say, in the WT, each level is calculated by passing only the previous wavelet approximation coefficients through the discrete-time low and high pass quadrature mirror filters. Wavelet packet decomposition (WPD) proposed by M. V. Wicker et al. has solved this problem. In the WPD, it has the same frequency bandwidth in each resolution.

Define sub-space U_j^n as the close packet space of function $u_n(t)$, then the orthogonal wavelet packet is defined as [3]

$$u_{2n}(t) = \sqrt{2} \sum_{k \in Z} h_k u_n(2t - k) \tag{1}$$

$$u_{2n+1}(t) = \sqrt{2} \sum_{k \in Z} g_k u_n(2t - k) \tag{2}$$

where h_k and g_k are the quadrature mirror filters associated with the predefined scaling function and mother wavelet function, respectively. The wavelet packet coefficients are given by:

$$d_{j,n}(k)= \int_{-\infty}^{+\infty} x(t)2^{\frac{j}{2}}u_n(2^jt - k)dt \qquad (3)$$

where $x(t)$, j, k and n are the signal, scale, band and surge parameter, respectively.

Wavelet packet decomposition is to divide the band into several layers, and to select corresponding sub-band adaptively according to the characteristics of the signal analyzed, which will promote the time-frequency resolution. The structure of the 4-layer wavelet packet decomposition tree is shown in Fig. 2. Moving from top to bottom of Fig. 2, frequencies are divided into small segments. Each layer which emanates down and to the left of a node represents a low-pass filtering operation (h), and to the right a high-pass filtering operation (g). The nodes which have no further nodes emanating down are referred to as terminal nodes, leaves or sub-bands. The other nodes are referred to as non-terminal, or internal nodes. The first layer represents the original signal bandwidth. The other nodes are computed from their father by one application of either the low-pass or high-pass quadrature mirror filters. The bandwidth is 50% decreased with each filtering operation. In the bottom layer, each sub-band is a sixteenth of the original signal bandwidth. Thus, multi-resolution is achieved.

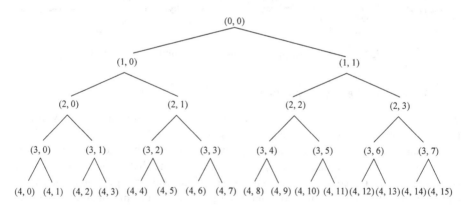

Fig. 2. Tree diagram of wavelet packet decomposition - depth 4

2.2 LM-BP Neural Network

BP neural network, known as a "feed-forward back-propagation network", is widely used in pattern recognition, machine learning, prediction and classification, because it is easy to understand and to be implemented. A multi-layer BP neural network typically has an input layer, an output layer, and one or more hidden layers, in which neurons are arranged in layers and there is a connection among the neurons of other layers. The inputs are applied to the input layer the output layer contributes to the output directly. Other layers between input and output layers are called hidden layers. Inputs are propagated in gradually modified form in the forward direction, finally reaching the output layer. The back-propagation learning algorithm has been used in the feed-forward, single hidden layer neural network. A tangent sigmoid transfer function has been used for both the hidden layer and the output layer [8]. On account of the limitations of the BP algorithm, such as local minimum and slow convergence, Levenberg-Marquardt algorithm, based on optimizing theory, is used to improve BP algorithm. The LM-BP neural network has faster convergence speed and higher accuracy.

Suppose the tth layer has n_L nodes, the error function can be expressed as [12]

$$E(W) = \frac{1}{2}\sum_{i=1}^{n_L} e_i^2(W) = \frac{1}{2}\mathbf{e}^T(W)\mathbf{e}(W) \tag{4}$$

where $\mathbf{e}^T(W) = [e_1, e_2, \ldots, e_{n_L}]$, and $\mathbf{W}^T = \left[W_{11}^1, W_{21}^1, \ldots \theta_1^1, \ldots, \theta_{n_1}^1, W_{11}^1, \ldots, \theta_{n_L}^2\right]$.

According to LM algorithm, we have

$$\mathbf{W}(k+1) = \mathbf{W}(k) - [\mathbf{J}^T(W_k)\mathbf{J}(W_k) + \mu_k I]^{-1}\mathbf{J}^T(W_k)\mathbf{e}(W_k) \tag{5}$$

$$\mathbf{G} = \mathbf{J}^T(W_k)\mathbf{J}(W_k) + \mu_k I = \mathbf{H} + \mu_k I \tag{6}$$

The gradient of $E(W)$ is

$$E(W) = \sum_{i=1}^{n_L} e_i(W)\frac{\partial e_i(W)}{\partial W} = \mathbf{J}^T(W)\mathbf{e}(W) \tag{7}$$

where $\mathbf{J}^T(W) = \begin{bmatrix} \frac{\partial e_1(W)}{\partial W_{11}^1} & \frac{\partial e_1(W)}{\partial W_{21}^1} & \cdots & \frac{\partial e_1(W)}{\partial W_{n_1 n_L}^2} & \frac{\partial e_1(W)}{\partial \theta_1^1} & \cdots & \frac{\partial e_1(W)}{\partial \theta_{n_L}^2} \\ \frac{\partial e_2(W)}{\partial W_{11}^1} & \frac{\partial e_2(W)}{\partial W_{21}^1} & \cdots & \frac{\partial e_2(W)}{\partial W_{n_1 n_L}^2} & \frac{\partial e_2(W)}{\partial \theta_1^1} & \cdots & \frac{\partial e_2(W)}{\partial \theta_{n_L}^2} \\ \vdots & \vdots & & \vdots & \vdots & & \vdots \\ \frac{\partial e_{n_L}(W)}{\partial W_{11}^1} & \frac{\partial e_{n_L}(W)}{\partial W_{21}^1} & \cdots & \frac{\partial e_{n_L}(W)}{\partial W_{n_1 n_L}^2} & \frac{\partial e_{n_L}(W)}{\partial \theta_1^1} & \cdots & \frac{\partial e_{n_L}(W)}{\partial \theta_{n_L}^2} \end{bmatrix}$ is called Jacobi matrix.

So,

$$E^2(W)_{kj} = \mathbf{J}^T(W)\mathbf{J}(W) + \mathbf{S}(W) \tag{8}$$

where $\mathbf{S}(W)$ can be neglected.

The steps of LM-BP neural network is shown in Fig. 3.

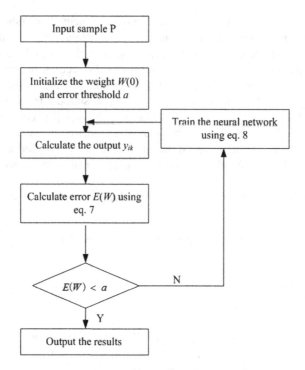

Fig. 3. The steps of LM-BP neural network

3   Experimental Results

3.1   Data Acquisition

The heart sound data are downloaded from Internet or collected in the authors' lab. The subject laid on his back on an examination bed and was kept under stable conditions. A sensor was placed on mitral site. ECG and heart sounds were recorded synchronously. The bandwidth of heart sounds is about 500 Hz. The aural environment in the lab was controlled to allow recording to be low-noise heart sounds. All heart sound data are preprocessed as follows. First, heart sound signals are filtered by linear low-pass filters whose stop frequency is 2 kHz. Second, heart sound signals are down sampled to 4 kHz. Third, heart sound signals are normalized. There is a total of 100 heart sound recordings, given as.wav format, from 100 subjects/patients, lasting from 5 s to 120 s. The recordings were divided into two types: normal and abnormal recordings with a confirmed cardiac diagnosis. The number "1" was used to present abnormal (50 recordings) and "−1" to present normal (50 recordings).

3.2   Feature Extraction Using Wavelet Packet Energy

In this paper, wavelet packet energy features are extracted from a heart sound recording. According to the characteristics of the heart sounds, they are divided into 4 layers, i.e. 16 frequency bands. They are 0–125 Hz, 126–250 Hz, 251–375 Hz, 376 –500 Hz, 501–625 Hz, 626–750 Hz, 751–875 Hz, 876–1000 Hz, 1001–1125 Hz, 1126–1250 Hz, 1251–1375 Hz, 1376–1500 Hz, 1501–1625 Hz, 1626–1750 Hz, 1751–1875 Hz, 1876–2000 Hz. According to the general properties of representative normal wavelet family functions (including Daubechis, Coiflets, Symlets and so on) and former work of others [3, 13], Db6 is chosen as the wavelet type. The normal heart sound is shown in Fig. 4 and its wavelet packet energy features are shown in Fig. 5. We can see that after 4-layer decomposition, the energy of normal heart sound is mainly concentrated on the first four frequency bands. The first heart sound mainly exists in the first and second bands, i.e. 0–250 Hz. The second heart sound mainly exists in the first, second and third bands, i.e. 0–375 Hz. The abnormal heart sound is shown in Fig. 6 and its wavelet packet energy features are shown in Fig. 7. We can see that after 4-layer decomposition, the energy of abnormal heart sound is covered almost all the frequency bands.

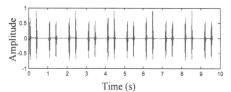

Fig. 4. A normal heart sound

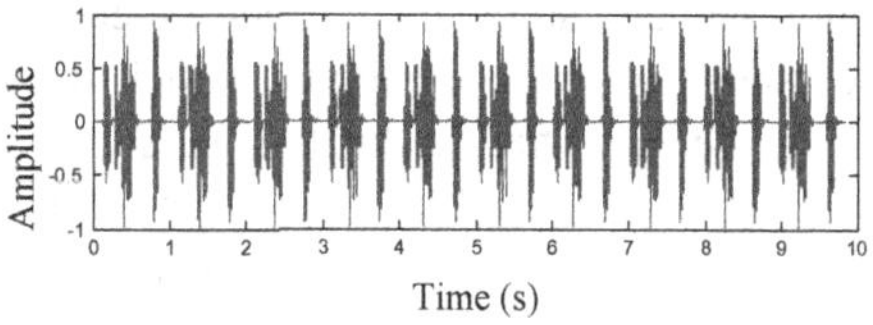

Fig. 6. An abnormal heart sound

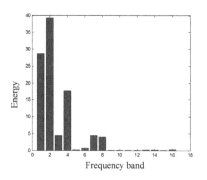

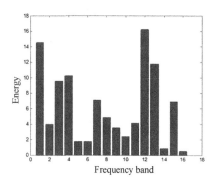

Fig. 5. Energy features of a normal heart sound

Fig. 7. Energy features of an abnormal heart sound

3.3 Identification Results

After extracting the wavelet packet energy features of the heart sounds, a classifier using 3-layer LM-BP neural network is implemented. In order to test the performance of the proposed method, identification accuracy, sensitivity and specificity are defined below [3]:

$$Accuracy = \frac{TP+TN}{TP+FP+FN+TN} \times 100\% \tag{9}$$

$$Sensitivity = \frac{TP}{TP+FN} \times 100\% \tag{10}$$

$$Specificity = \frac{TN}{FP+TN} \times 100\% \tag{11}$$

where TP is the number of true positives, which means that some subjects with abnormal heart sound are correctly identified as ones with abnormal heart sound; FN is the number of false negatives, which means that some subjects with abnormal heart sound are identified as healthy persons; TN is the number of true negatives, which means that some healthy persons are correctly identified as healthy persons; and FP is the number of false positives, which means that some healthy are identified as patients with abnormal heart sound.

Thirty samples (15 normal heart sounds and 15 abnormal heart sounds) are chosen to train the neural network and seventy to test. To study the validity of the features in this paper, we take two other popular heart sound processing methods for comparison: Short Time Fourier Transform (STFT) and Spectrogram analysis. Table 1 shows the comparison results of three methods mentioned above. As we can see, the proposed method obtained the best results, with the accuracy of 83.15%, the sensitivity of 81.96% and the specificity of 87%.

Table 1. Comparisons of three methods

Feature extraction methods	Accuracy	Sensitivity	Specificity
STFT	76.04%	71.32%	84%
Spectrogram analysis	78.65%	80.19%	81%
The proposed method	83.15%	81.96%	87%

4 Conclusion

In this paper, a normal and abnormal heart sounds identification method is proposed, which is based on wavelet packet energy and LM-BP neural network. This algorithm converged much faster than traditional BP neural network, and achieved better results compared with two traditional heart sound processing methods based on STFT and Spectrogram analysis. Moreover, the identification results of heart sounds also depend on the heart sound data, the selected training samples, the type of wavelet, and the kind of neural network. In future studies, we will focus on extracting more features and choosing more efficient classification methods to acquire better performance.

Acknowledgements. This work was supported in part by the National Natural Science Foundation of China under Grant Nos. 61601081, 61471081; Fundamental Research Funds for the Central Universities under Grant Nos. DC201501056, DCPY2016008, DUT15QY60, DUT1 6QY13; Dalian Youth Technology Star Project Supporting Plan under Grant No. 2015R091.

References

1. Plett, M.I.: Ultrasonic arterial vibrometry with wavelet based detection and estimation. Ph.D. thesis, University of Washington (2000)
2. Hanbay, D.: An expert system based on least square support vector machines for diagnosis of the valvular heart disease. Expert Syst. Appl. **36**, 4232–4238 (2009)
3. Wang, Y., Li, W., et al.: Identification of the normal and abnormal heart sounds using wavelet-time entropy features based on OMS-WPD. Future Gener. Comput. Syst. **37**, 488–495 (2014)
4. Sun, S.: An innovative intelligent system based on automatic diagnostic feature extraction for diagnosing heart diseases. Knowl.-Based Syst. **75**, 224–238 (2015)
5. Chen, X., Ma, Y., et al.: Research on heart sound identification technology. Sci. Chin. Inf. Sci. **55**(2), 281–292 (2012)
6. Sengur, A.: An expert system based on linear discriminant analysis and adaptive neuro-fuzzy inference system to diagnosis heart valve diseases. Expert Syst. Appl. **35**, 214–222 (2008)
7. Avci, E., Turkoglu, I.: An intelligent diagnosis system based on principle component analysis and ANFIS for the heart valve diseases. Expert Syst. Appl. **36**, 2873–2878 (2009)
8. Das, R., Turkoglu, I., et al.: Diagnosis of valvular heart disease through neural networks ensembles. Comput. Methods Progr. Biomed. **93**, 185–191 (2009)
9. Harun, U.: Adaptive neuro-fuzzy inference system for diagnosis of the heart valve diseases using wavelet transform with entropy. Neural Comput. Appl. **21**(7), 1617–1628 (2012)
10. Chen, T.H., Han, L.Q., et al.: Research of denoising method of heart sound signals based on wavelet transform. Comput. Simul. **12**(27), 401–405 (2010)
11. Bhatnagar, G., Wu, J., et al.: Fractional dual tree complex wavelet transform and its application to biometric security during communication and transmission. Future Gener. Comput. Syst. **28**(1), 254–267 (2012)
12. Hou, Y., Li, T.: Improvement of BP neural network by LM optimizing algorithm in target identification. J. Detect. Control **30**(1), 53–58 (2008). (in Chinese)
13. Cheng, X., Yang, H.: Analysis and comparison of five kinds of wavelet in processing heart sound signal. J. Nanjing Univ. Posts Telecommun. (Nat. Sci. Ed.) **35**(1), 38–46 (2015). (in Chinese)

The Android-Based Acquisition and CNN-Based Analysis for Gaze Estimation in Eye Tracking

Wei Wen[1], Tong Chen[1], and Meng Yang[1,2($\boxtimes$)]

[1] College of Computer Science and Software Engineering, Shenzhen University,
Shenzhen 518000, China
wenwei2016@email.szu.edu.cn, chentongsnow@gmail.com,
yang.meng@szu.edu.cn
[2] School of Data and Computer Science,
Sun Yat-Sen University, Guangzhou 510000, China

Abstract. Over the past several years, the demand for eye tracking is increasing across fields of computer vision and pattern recognition, especially in commercial applications. However, the low prediction accuracy and the restriction of datasets and methods for special eye tracking equipment have been obstacles of the wide application of gaze estimation. In this paper, we develop an Android-based acquisition software named EyeTracker, to collect the first Chinese gaze dataset. And then we proposed a convolutional neural network framework for gaze estimation in eye tracking based on a single image. We evaluate our proposed analysis model on our dataset-EyeTrackD (tablet) and Gazecapture (part of phone data). Our model achieves a prediction error of 4.33 cm and 2.25 cm on these two datasets respectively, which are better than the previous method using the same data. Extensive experiments under different network settings show the effectiveness of our convolutional neural network framework.

Keywords: Eye tracking · Gaze estimation · Convolutional neural network (CNN)

1 Introduction

Eye tracking is the process of measuring either the point of gaze (where one is looking) or the motion of an eye relative to the head. It has shown great potential in human-computer interaction, as a new form of this area, it can play a great role on many modern devices. One of key issues of eye tracking is the estimation of gaze, which is the externally-observable indicator of human visual attention. Gaze estimation is a hot topic in computer vision and pattern recognition, and many researchers have attempted to study it, dating back to the late eighteenth century [1].

Gaze estimation methods can be divided into model-based and appearance-based [2]. Model-based methods use a geometric eye model and can be further divided into corneal-reflection and shape-based methods, which depend on whether requiring external light sources to detect eye features. Early works on corneal reflection-based

© Springer International Publishing AG 2017
J. Zhou et al. (Eds.): CCBR 2017, LNCS 10568, pp. 562–571, 2017.
https://doi.org/10.1007/978-3-319-69923-3_61

methods focused on stationary settings [3, 4] and were extended to handle arbitrary head poses using multiple light sources or cameras [5, 6]. On the other hand, shape-based methods [7–9] directly estimation gaze directions from eye shapes, such as pupil center and iris edges. These approaches are usually ineffective for low quality image and variable lighting conditions.

Appearance-based gaze estimation methods directly use eye images and other related images as input. Appearance-based methods treat the pixels or features extracted from the eye region image as a high dimensional vector, and learn a regression mapping model from such vector to the point of gaze (or gaze direction) through labeled training data. Such methods have the potential to be non-intrusive, free of calibration and can operate free of external hardware [11], and it is believed [10] able to generalize well to novel faces without needing user-specific data. Thus, this kind of model does not have to rely on visual saliency maps [12, 13] or key presses [14] to achieve accurate calibration-free gaze estimation.

Today, there are many solutions in eye tracking, but most of them have a variety of problems as follow: high cost (e.g., Tobii X2-60) or inaccuracy under real-world conditions (e.g. [15–17]). Even in recent work [10], the accuracy is still unsatisfactory. Above factors prevent eye tracking becoming a popular technology, even in the era of advanced technology.

Despite the obstacles existing in gaze estimation, we believe the following reasons will make estimating gaze in eye tracking more accurate in future. First, with the development of deep learning, many computer vision tasks are nearly to be solved. It is a reasonable way to address image-based gaze estimation based on deep learning. Moreover, many new milestones of network and constraint methods emerged in recent year, such as GooLeNet, ResNet, Batch normalization [18–20]. Second, the increasing computing power of computer allows us to experiment using more complex algorithms. Last but not the least, the daily use of mobile devices allows us to gather data more easy and reliable.

In this paper, we develop an Android-based acquisition software to collect data for gaze estimation, and propose a convolutional neural network framework to solve the problem of image-based gaze estimation. There are few databases for gaze estimation, preventing the development of eye tracking. In order to solve this issue, we utilize our acquisition system to build the first Chinese gaze dataset, including face images, eye images and the gaze ground truth of multiple subjects. Then we propose an end-to-end CNN framework to more accurately estimate the location of gaze, where head position estimation or any pre-training features for estimation are not necessary. Two datasets are used to evaluate our proposed method, which clearly show the advantages of our proposed method.

Our main contributions are summarized as follows.

1. We explore how to collect data effectively by modern mobile devices, and create the first Chinese gaze dataset, EyeTrackD, for eye tracking.
2. We propose a convolutional network framework named EyeTrackNet to reduce error in eye tracking. Under the same experimental setup, our network can achieve better effect and show the advantages of our framework.

3. We observe the influence on the final accuracy by changing the processing of the input data, including image super-resolution [21], number and size of input data. We believe that this work will serve as a new direction for the next generation of eye tracking solution.

The rest of this paper is organized as follows. Section 2 introduces the acquisition software and our built gaze dataset. Section 3 describes the proposed gaze estimation model based on the convolutional neural network. Section 4 conducts the experiments and Sect. 5 concludes the paper.

2   Acquisition Software and Dataset Collection

In this section, we develop an Android-based acquisition software named EyeTracker, to collect unconstrained face and eye image data, then we create an unconstrained mobile gaze dataset, EyeTracker Dataset named EyeTrackD, which should be the first Chinese gaze dataset.

2.1   Acquisition Software

EyeTracker is mainly divided into four modules, point module, storage module, camera module and coordinate module, and the four modules contain most of functions of EyeTracker.

Point Module: The point module is primarily responsible for the point. As shown in Fig. 1, the control point, which attracts the attention of people, appears on the screen. The point module also handles the user's click event.

Each point will be displayed on the screen for approximately 3 s so as to be well observed. For Reliability, each point has location information (L or R of the screen)

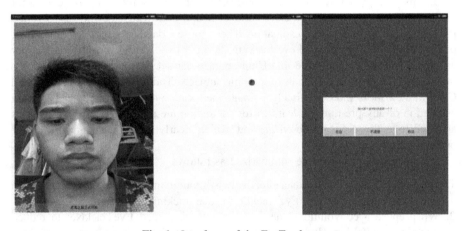

Fig. 1. Interfaces of the EyeTracker.

that needs confirmation by the participant. If participants tap the wrong side (as shown in Fig. 1), the data collected just now will be asked to re-acquire.

Storage Module: The storage module is mainly responsible for data storage, data processing and data deletion.

The storage module creates a folder for each participant, and this folder stores all of this participant's data which include 40 pictures collected by camera module and coordinate information passed from coordinate module. Storage module will delete some pictures which taping wrong side by participant.

Coordinate Module: The coordinate module is responsible for the generation of coordinate points and the transformation of pixel coordinates into physical coordinate points.

The coordinate module generates two random numbers within a certain range which represent the pixel coordinate of the point, then after some coordinate module parameter adjustment, the pixel coordinate is converted to physical coordinate, in which the camera is the coordinate origin. Then the physical coordinate will be sent to storage module to name the corresponding picture.

Camera Module: The camera module involves many functions, such as preview, face detection, camera function and timing function.

Preview function (as shown in Fig. 1) allows the participant to put the head in the right position, and participants will be warned when no face be detected by face detection function. For camera function, front camera will take pictures when the point appearance on screen, all picture will be sent to storage module. It is worth mentioning that participants are asked to collect data based on four directions of the camera in order to best leverage the power of datasets. The point shown on screen will change position randomly every 3 s because of timing function, the timing information will be transferred to the point module by timing function.

Above four modules we described complement each other, together constitute the EyeTracker.

2.2 Dataset Collection

In this section, our goal is to build the Chinese gaze dataset using EyeTracker (as described in Sect. 2.1). Our software has the following advantages.

Scalability: We develop EyeTracker based on android system, which is the most popular mobile system today.

Reliability: We take measures to ensure that participants completed the entire process of data collection intently. Except for some of measures we introduced in 2.1, participants can not begin collecting until they turn on flight mode, which ensures that the collection process will not be affected by other notifications.

Variability: In order to learn a robust eye tracking model, data diversity is important. We expect to gain a lot of data various in pose, appearance and illumination, we encourage participants to move their head in collection process.

Overall, EyeTrackD has collected data from over 90 people consisting of 4322 images. EyeTracker will collect more and more high quality data by taking the above measures, and the amount of data will continue to increase. Some sample images of our built Chinese gaze dataset, EyeTrackD, are shown in Fig. 2.

Fig. 2. Sample images from our EyeTrackD dataset.

3   CNN-Based Analysis Approach

In this section, we introduce our framework, EyeTrackNet, for gaze estimation in eye tracking. With the development of neural network, convolutional neural network has achieved a series of successes in computer vision, such as face detection and recognition [22, 23], image classification [24, 25], semantic segmentation [26, 27] and landmark detection [28, 29]. Meanwhile the computational speed of deep learning was mainly boosted by the efficient use of GPUs. We believe that convolutional neural network can handle eye tracking using enough and accurate data, we can learn end-to-end model to tackle eye tracking without the need of manually hand-craft features and additional information such as head angle and eye angle.

3.1   Network Structure Selection

In view of the specificity of eye tracking, we used multi-input and single-output neural network (as shown in Fig. 3) to forecast the true location of gaze. Our input include left eye, right eye, face images detected and cropped from the original frame (all of size 224 × 224), and face grid used to indicate the location and size of the head in the original frame (of size 25 × 25). The output is the distance from the camera location (in centimeters).

We analyze some import factors on the choice of network structure. First, gaze estimation is a high-level task which needs a holistic face feature, so we use the face as an import input. Second, in order to produce a more accurate output, we give some fine inputs such as left eye and right eye which can eliminate the effects of other positions on the face, while facial position alleviates the error caused by the distance from camera. Moreover, by combining spatially nearby features extracted at lower layers (left eye and right eye), neurons at higher layers can extract features from the whole, and high-level features are highly non-linear, making eye tracking possible.

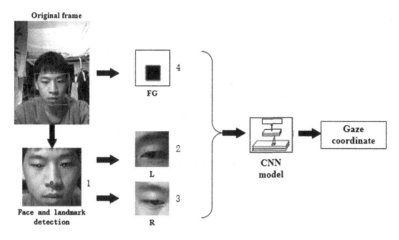

Fig. 3. Overview of our method for eye tracking.

3.2 Batch Normalization for CNNs

EyeTrackNet is a modified version based on AlexNet [25], we modify the convolutional kernel size of 3×3 which can obtain better feature maps. Moreover, Batch normalization [20] is crucial for successful training and convergence. Architectures with batch normalization allow for using much higher learning rates and hence yield in models with better generalization ability. So, we further modified EyeTrackNet by adding a batch normalization layer between each convolutional and activation unit layer as well as between each inner product and activation unit layer. And we removed the local response normalization and dropout layer. The overall structure of Eye-TrackNet is shown in Table 1.

Overall, the model trained by EyeTrackNet is a data-driven appearance-based model learned end-to-end.

Table 1. Overall structure of EyeTrackNet.

Layer name	Type	Kernel size	Output size
Conv1_x/BN	Convolutional	3×3/96	111*111
Conv2_x/BN	Convolutional	3×3/256	54*54
Conv3_x/BN	Convolutional	3×3/384	25*25
Conv4_x/BN	Convolutional	3×3/64	5*5
FC1_x/BN	Fully Connected	128	128
FC2_x/BN	Fully Connected	64	64
FC1/BN	Fully Connected	128	128
FC2	Fully Connected	2	2

4   Experiments

We conduct the experiments and corresponding analysis to verify the performance of our framework for eye tracking. We evaluate our approach on Gazecapture [10] and EyeTrackD which we created. Overall, under the same data scale and experimental settings, we outperform latest approaches achieving an average error of 4.33 cm on EyeTracker dataset (test data collected based on tablet, as shown in Fig. 2), and 2.25 cm on Gazecapture dataset (test data collected based on phone, as shown in Fig. 4). Further, we demonstrate the influence of different data processing, and verify the importance of having a large-scale dataset as well as having variety in the data.

Fig. 4. Sample images from Gazecapture dataset.

Data Preparation: Here we introduce the data preparation of the two datasets. For Gazecapture (sample images as shown in Fig. 4), we select 103,146 frames of 116 people that have both face and eye detections, serving as the inputs to the EyeTrackNet (as shown in Fig. 3). Then, we divide frames into train, validation, and test splits consisting of 71, 19, 26 people and 78,000, 12,000, 13,146 frames respectively. In contrast, for EyeTrackD (sample images as shown in Fig. 2), we select 4322 frames and divided into train, validation, and test splits consisting of 56, 16, 18 people and 2981, 718, 823 frames respectively. For the validation and test dataset, we select subjects which contain all directions (data collected in four directions based on camera), which ensures credibility of prediction result. In order to adapt to the Eye-TrackNet, we crop eye and face from original image using face and landmark detection [30], and obtain corresponding face grid which represent location information about face. Further, we evaluate the performance of our approach by changing data processing, more details will be described in Results and Analysis.

Implementation Details: our model was implemented using caffe [31]. It was trained from scratch on two dataset (Gazecapture, EyeTrackD) for 80000 iterations with batch size of 96. We used an initial learning rate of 0.001, used a momentum of 0.9 and weight decay of 0.0005 throughout the training procedure, the optimization method we used is Adam [32], and the momentum2 is 0.999.

Evaluation Metric: Similar to [10], we report the error in terms of average Euclidean distance (in centimeters) from the location of true coordinate based on camera position. Although the test set for the two dataset are based on tablet (EyeTrackD) and iphone

Table 2. Results of the latest network iTracker [10] and our network EyeTrackNet.

Network	EyeTrackD (tablet) error (cm)	Gazecapture (phone) error (cm)
iTracker	5.10	2.93
EyeTrackNet	**4.58**	**2.46**

(Gazecapture) respectively, they all apply to this evaluation metric due to device independence of EyeTracker. The result of error in our experiment is the average error of the test set.

Results and Analysis: As described above, we train and test iTracker and Eye-TrackNet on the corresponding data respectively. And the results are shown in Table 2, it is clear that our proposed network gain better effect both on EyeTrackD and Gazecapture.

We observe the influence on the final accuracy by changing the processing of the input data, these processing include image super-resolution (SR) [20] and data centralization. The results are summarized in Table 3, and we can conclude that data centralization tend to generate a more robust model, and convolutional neural network is not sensitive to the quality of the input image. Adding more information (L,R eye in one image) to the network will get better effect.

Table 3. Performance of EyeTrackNet using different data processing on input data

Network	Data processing	EyeTrackD (tablet) error (cm)	Gazecapture (phone) error (cm)
EyeTrackNet	None	4.58	2.46
EyeTrackNet	Centralization	**4.39**	**2.27**
EyeTrackNet	Centralization, SR	4.43	2.32
EyeTrackNet	Centralization, Double-eye	**4.33**	**2.25**

Further, we analysis some typical cases. Some samples with accurate prediction (error less than 0.5 cm) are shown in the left of Fig. 5, and some samples with wrong prediction (error more than 4 cm) are shown in the right of Fig. 5. We can conclude that some major factors affect the prediction accuracy such as lower lighting, smaller pupil and the reflex of glasses.

Fig. 5. Sample images of accurate prediction (at left) and wrong prediction (at right).

5 Conclusion

Here we developed an acquisition software, built the first Chinese gaze dataset, and presented an effective convolutional neural network to estimate gaze in eye tracking. We demonstrated gaze data can be captured in the Android system, which has great potential to collect a large scale gaze data. The proposed CNN-based analysis model for gaze estimation has achieved a lower average error on two datasets under the same setting. And we believe that the EyeTrackNet deserve idealized results with the amount of data increases, and we can get a more robust model for gaze estimation. In the future, we will explore more effective network and collect more data with high quantity and variety using our software.

Acknowledgements. This work is partially supported by the National Natural Science Foundation for Young Scientists of China (no. 61402289), and National Science Foundation of Guangdong Province (no. 2014A030313558).

References

1. Huey, E.B.: The psychology and pedagogy of reading. J. Philos. **18**(5), 500–502 (1908)
2. Hansen, D.W., Ji, Q.: In the eye of the beholder: a survey of models for eyes and gaze. IEEE Trans. Pattern Anal. Mach. Intell. **32**(3), 478–500 (2010)
3. Hennessey, C., Noureddin, B., Lawrence, P.: A single camera eye-gaze tracking system with free head motion. In: Proceedings of ETRA, pp. 87–94 (2006)
4. Yoo, D.H., Chung, M.J.: A novel non-intrusive eye gaze estimation using cross-ratio under large head motion. Comput. Vis. Image Underst. **98**(1), 25–51 (2005)
5. Zhu, Z., Ji, Q.: Eye gaze tracking under natural head movements. In: Proceedings of CVPR, pp. 918–923 (2005)
6. Zhu, Z., Ji, Q., Bennett, K.P.: Nonlinear eye gaze mapping function estimation via support vector regression. In: Proceedings of ICPR, pp. 1132–1135 (2006)
7. Chen, J., Ji, Q.: 3D gaze estimation with a single camera without IR illumination. In: Proceedings of ICPR, pp. 1–4 (2008)
8. Yamazoe, H., Utsumi, A., Yonezawa, T., Abe, S.: Remote gaze estimation with a single camera based on facial-feature tracking without special calibration actions. In: Proceedings of ETRA, pp. 245–250 (2008)
9. Valenti, R., Sebe, N., Gevers, T.: Combining head pose and eye location information for gaze estimation. IEEE Trans. Image Process. **21**(2), 802–815 (2012)
10. Krafka, K., Khosla, A., Kellnhofer, P., Kannan, H., Bhandarkar, S., Matusik, W.: Eye tracking for everyone. In: Proceedings of CVPR, pp. 2176–2184 (2016)
11. Huang, Q., Veeraraghavan, A., Sabharwal, A.: TabletGaze: unconstrained appearance-based gaze estimation in mobile tablets. Comput. Sci. (2015)
12. Chen, J., Ji, Q.: Probabilistic gaze estimation without active personal calibration. In: CVPR 2011, pp. 609–616 (2011)
13. Sugano, Y., Matsushita, Y., Sato, Y.: Appearance-based gaze estimation using visual saliency. PAMI **35**(2), 329–341 (2013)
14. Sugano, Y., Matsushita, Y., Sato, Y., Koike, H.: An incremental learning method for unconstrained gaze estimation. Comput. Sci. **5304**(3), 656–667 (2008)

15. Mora, K.A.F., Monay, F., Odobez, J.M.: EYEDIAP: a database for the development and evaluation of gaze estimation algorithms from rgb and rgb-d cameras. In: ACM Symposium on Eye Tracking Research and Applications, pp. 255–258 (2014)

16. Sugano, Y., Matsushita, Y., Sato, Y.: Learning-by-synthesis for appearance-based 3D gaze estimation. In: CVPR 2014, pp. 1821–1828 (2014)

17. Zhang, X., Sugano, Y., Fritz, M., Bulling, A.: Appearance-based gaze estimation in the wild. In: CVPR 2015, pp. 4511–4520 (2015)

18. Szegedy, C., Ioffe, S., et al.: Inception-v4, Inception-ResNet and the impact of residual connections on learning. In: AAAI 2016, pp. 4278–4284 (2016)

19. He, K., Zhang, X., Ren, S., Sun, J.: Identity Mappings in Deep Residual Networks. In: Leibe, B., Matas, J., Sebe, N., Welling, M. (eds.) ECCV 2016. LNCS, vol. 9908, pp. 630–645. Springer, Cham (2016). doi:10.1007/978-3-319-46493-0_38

20. Ioffe, S., Sergey C.: Batch normalization: accelerating deep network training by reducing internal covariate shift. Comput. Sci. (2015)

21. Jiwon, K., Jung, K.L., Kyoung, M.L.: Accurate image super-resolution using very deep convolutional networks. In: Proceedings of CVPR 2016, pp. 1646–1654 (2016)

22. Sun, Y., Wang, X., Tang, X.: Deep learning face representation from predicting 10,000 classes. In: IEEE Conference on CVPR, pp. 1891–1898 (2014)

23. Zhu, X., Ramanan, D.: Face detection, pose estimation,and landmark localization in the wild. In: CVPR 2012, pp. 2879–2886 (2012)

24. Russakovsky, O., Deng, J., Su, J.: ImageNet Large Scale Visual Recognition Challenge. Int. J. Comput. Vis. 115(3), 211–252 (2015)

25. Krizhevsky, A., Sutskever, I., Hinton, G.E.: ImageNet classification with deep convolutional neural networks. In: International Conference on Neural Information Processing Systems Curran Associates Inc., pp. 1097–1105 (2012)

26. Long, J., Shelhamer, E., Darrell, T.: Fully convolutional networks for semantic segmentation. IEEE Trans. Pattern Anal. Mach. Intell. 39(4), 640–651 (2017)

27. Simonyan, K., Zisserman, A.: Very deep convolutional networks for large-scale image recognition. In: ICRL 2015, pp. 1–14 (2015)

28. Sun, Y., Wang, X., Tang, X.: Deep convolutional network cascade for facial point detection. In: IEEE Conference on Computer Vision and Pattern Recognition, pp. 3476–3483. IEEE Computer Society (2013)

29. Zhou, E., Fan, H., Cao, Z.: Extensive facial landmark localization with coarse-to-fine convolutional network cascade. In: IEEE International Conference on Computer Vision Workshops, pp. 386–391. IEEE (2013)

30. Zhang, K., Zhang, Z., Li, Z.: Joint face detection and alignment using multitask cascaded convolutional networks. IEEE Sig. Process. Lett. 23(10), 1499–1503 (2016)

31. Jia, Y., Shelhamer, E., Donahue, J., Karayev, S., Long, J., Girshick, R., Guadarrama, S., Darrell, T.: Caffe: convolutional architecture for fast feature embedding. arXiv:1408.5093 (2014)

32. Kingma, D., Diederik, P., Ba, J.: Adam: a method for stochastic optimization. Comput. Sci. (2014)

Voice and Speech

Efficient Audio-Visual Speaker Recognition via Deep Heterogeneous Feature Fusion

Yu-Hang Liu[1,2], Xin Liu[1,2(✉)], Wentao Fan[1,2],
Bineng Zhong[1,2], and Ji-Xiang Du[1,2]

[1] Department of Computer Science, Huaqiao University, Xiamen 361021, China
xliu@hqu.edu.cn
[2] Xiamen Key Laboratory of Computer Vision and Pattern Recognition,
Huaqiao University, Xiamen 361021, China

Abstract. Audio-visual speaker recognition (AVSR) has long been an active research area primarily due to its complementary information for reliable access control in biometric system, and it is a challenging problem mainly attributes to its multimodal nature. In this paper, we present an efficient audio-visual speaker recognition approach via deep heterogeneous feature fusion. First, we exploit a dual-branch deep convolutional neural networks (CNN) learning framework to extract and fuse the high-level semantic features of face and audio data. Further, by considering the temporal dependency of audio-visual data, we embed the fused features into a bidirectional Long Short-Term Memory (LSTM) networks to produce the recognition result, though which the speakers acquired under different challenging conditions can be well identified. The experimental results have demonstrated the efficiency of our proposed approach in both audio-visual feature fusion and speaker recognition.

Keywords: Audio-visual speaker recognition · Deep heterogeneous feature fusion · Dual-branch deep CNN · Bidirectional LSTM

1 Introduction

Multi-modal biometric person recognition has received a lot of attention in recent years due to the growing security demands in commercial and law enforcement applications. In particular, speaker recognition is one of the active research problems in biometric community, and audio-visual (AV) biometrics generally offer complementary information sources for speaker identity characterization. Among them, face and voice features, incorporating the advantages of non-intrusiveness and easy acquisitions, have become economically feasible, but the appropriate fusion between these two heterogeneous modalities is still a non-trivial task.

In the past, different kinds of approaches have been exploited to fuse the face and voice data. In general, the audio-visual integration can be divided into four categories: sensor-level, feature-level, matching-level and decision-level. Since the sensor-level based fusion approaches require that the input data types must be

© Springer International Publishing AG 2017
J. Zhou et al. (Eds.): CCBR 2017, LNCS 10568, pp. 575–583, 2017.
https://doi.org/10.1007/978-3-319-69923-3_62

the same, such that there are more matching-level and decision-level fusions. For instance, Cheng et al. [2] utilized the proposed IKFD method to obtain the face recognition scores and employed GMMs to produce the voice recognition scores then fused the scores. Similarly, Feng et al. [3] utilized the GMM to fuse face scores and audio scores. Later, Soltane et al. [12] addressed an adaptive Bayesian method to fuse the scores of face and speech modalities. These matching-level or decision-level fusion functions could not take full advantage of the information.

To utilize more information, some researchers attempted to fuse the face and voice in feature level module. In the early years, researchers mainly used common feature transformation functions. For instance, Bredin et al. [1] utilized the canonical correlation analysis (CCA) to fuse the audio-visual features for speaker recognition, while Haghighat et al. [6] proposed discriminant correlation analysis (DCA) to fuse the audio-visual features for identification. These methods would cause information loss when transform features.

Recently, deep networks have been successfully applied to unsupervised feature learning for multimodal deep learning [10]. Benefit from this finding, Hu et al. [7] and Geng et al. [4] used CNN to fuse face features and audio features and achieved good results. However, they did not find the position in CNN that is most suitable for feature fusion. Ren et al. presented a multimodal LSTM networks for speaker identification, but the features are not fused actually.

In this paper, as shown in Fig. 1, we present an efficient audio-visual speaker recognition approach via deep heterogeneous feature fusion. The proposed approach first exploits a dual-branch deep CNN learning framework to extract the high-level semantic features of face and audio data, whereby the learned heterogeneous features between these two modalities can be well fused. Further, by considering the temporal dependency of audio-visual data, we embed the fused features into a bidirectional Long Short-Term Memory (LSTM) network to produce the speaker recognition result, featuring more discriminative power. The experimental results have its outstanding performance.

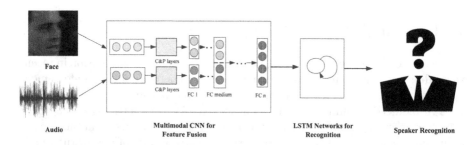

Fig. 1. The pipline of our proposed speaker recognition framework, in which the face features and audio features are fused by our proposed dual-branch deep CNN model.

2   Feature Fusion and Recognition Architecture

In this part, we explore how to use CNN to extract and fuse the features of face and audio, and further propose a dual-branch CNN model for feature extraction and fusion. In addition, we utilize the bidirectional LSTM networks associated with the fused information to get a reliable recognition result.

2.1   Dual-Branch CNN Model for Feature Fusion

In our deep feature fusion learning architecture, face features and audio features are extracted via the CNN model, which consists of convolutional and pooling layers and fully connected layers:

$$h_i = \begin{cases} P(\sigma(conv(W_i, h_{i-1}) + b_i)), \ i = 1, \ldots, m, \\ \sigma(W_i \cdot h_{i-1} + b_i), \ i = m+1, \ldots, n, \end{cases} \tag{1}$$

where h_i is the output of the i-th layer and h_0 is the raw input of the networks, W_i is the weight matrix and b_i is the bias term for the i-th layer, σ stands for the nonlinear activation function, e.g., tanh, sigmoid, or ReLU [9], P represents the pooling function. To explore the best position for fusion in CNN, four kinds of dual-branch CNN models are illustrated as shown in Fig. 2.

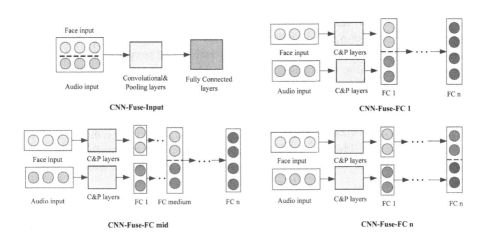

Fig. 2. Four kinds of dual-branch CNN Models for feature fusion.

CNN-Fuse-Input: In this case, the raw face input and audio input are concatenated as the input of CNN:

$$h_0 = concatenate(h_0^{face}, h_0^{audio}) \tag{2}$$

CNN-Fuse-FC 1: Convolved face features and audio features are concatenated as the input of fully connected layers:

$$h_i^j = P(\sigma(conv(W_i^j, h_{i-1}^j) + b_i^j)), \ i = 1, \ldots, m, \tag{3}$$

$$h_m = concatenate(h_m^{face}, h_m^{audio}), \tag{4}$$

where j represents the modality, i.e. face or audio.

CNN-Fuse-FC mid: Face and audio features extracted by different C&P layers and FC layers are concatenated as the input of the remaining FC layers:

$$h_i^j = \begin{cases} P(\sigma(conv(W_i^j, h_{i-1}^j) + b_i^j)), \ i = 1, \ldots, m, \\ \sigma(W_i^j \cdot h_{i-1}^j + b_i^j), \ i = m + 1, \ldots, m + mid, \end{cases} \tag{5}$$

$$h_{m+mid} = concatenate(h_{m+mid}^{face}, h_{m+mid}^{audio}), \tag{6}$$

CNN-Fuse-FC n: We first use two CNN models to extract deep face features and audio features separately, and then concatenate them:

$$h_n = concatenate(h_n^{face}, h_n^{audio}), \tag{7}$$

After training, the deep fused features could be extracted from h_n directly.

2.2 Bidirectional LSTM Networks for Recognition

In general, the face images are always influenced by the bad image quality, exaggerated expression, or illumination, which would degrade the recognition accuracy. To solve this problem, the bidirectional LSTM networks incorporating the temporal modeling ability is employed. In LSTM networks the hidden units are LSTM cells. The spirit of the LSTM cell is that for every step the cell would choose some information to "remember" and some to "forget", so that LSTM networks could learn longer information dependencies than simple RNN. In particular, bidirectional LSTM networks has been proved to be more effective for recognition [5]. Therefore, BILSTM is employed for recognition purpose. Specifically, three different methods are employed to get the recognition result:

$$y'_{last} = softmax(h_n) \tag{8}$$

$$y'_{vote} = \max_i(\sum_{t=1}^{n} I(y'_t = i)), i = 1, \ldots, c \tag{9}$$

$$y'_{mean} = softmax(W \cdot (\frac{1}{n}\sum_{t=1}^{n} h_t)) \tag{10}$$

In Eq. (8), we select the last output as the final result. In Eq. (9), the final result is generated by voting of the outputs of every results. In Eq. (10), we average the outputs of every step and utilize the softmax to classify the average value. Our whole feature fusion and recognition framework can be expressed in Fig. 3.

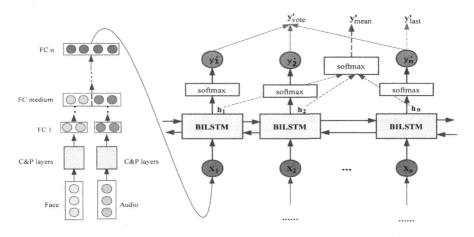

Fig. 3. Our proposed feature fusion and recognition framework.

3   Experiments and Results

The public available audio-visual dataset collected by Hu et al. [7] are selected for the evaluation. The face images and audio clips are extracted from nine episodes of two TV series, i.e. "Friends" and "The Big Bang Theory"("BBT"), in which the leading roles are selected for testing, including six actors in "Friends", i.e., Rachel, Monica, Phoebe, Joey, Chandler and Ross, and five actors in "BBT", i.e., Sheldon, Leonard, Howard, Raj and Penny. For "Friends", the faces and audio are collected from five episodes of different seasons, and we use the data of S01E03 (Season 01, Episode 03), S04E04, S07E07 and S10E15 for training and the data of S05E05 for testing. In total, there are 87273 face images involved for training and 29539 face images for testing. For "BBT", we choose S01E04, S01E05, S01E06 for training and S01E03 for testing, and total numbers of faces for training and testing are 90034 and 28554, respectively.

3.1   Multimodal CNN Model for Feature Fusion

For feature fusion, we first resize all the face images to 50×50 and convert them to gray-level images, and dimension of each face vector is 2500. Similar to the work [7], we utilize the mel frequency cepstral coefficients (MFCCs) [11] to preliminarily extract audio feature, and we acquire a 375D feature vector for every audio sample.

After extracting the primary features, we carried experiments on the four different feature fusion models, all the configurations in CNN are the same in different models. In addition, we add dropout [13] and batch normalization [8] to optimize our networks. Table 1 shows the recognition accuracies on "Friends" dataset and "BBT" dataset of different feature fusion models.

It can be found that the model "CNN-Fuse-Input" performed even worse than face modality only, which indicates that the raw features of different modalities

Table 1. Recognition accuracy of different feature fusion models

Model	Accuracy(%) on "Friends"	Accuracy(%) on "BBT"
Only face	94.0	93.6
CNN-Fuse Input	92.3	92.1
CNN-Fuse-FC 1	94.6	95.0
CNN-Fuse-FC mid	**95.6**	**95.4**
CNN-Fuse-FC n	95.0	94.9

are not suitable for fusion directly. Meanwhile, the "CNN-Fuse-FC mid" model has produced a better result than that of "CNN-Fuse-FC 1" model. That is, the high-level features extracted by CNN model are suitable for fusion. Note that, the "CNN-Fuse-FC mid" model also performs better than model "CNN-Fuse-FC n", that is because in the last two fully connected layers the concatenated features are fused better by nonlinear feature transformation. We can conclude that the middle layer of fully connected layers is the best place for feature fusion.

Table 2. Recognition accuracy of different feature fusion methods.

Method	Accuracy(%) on "Friends"	Accuracy(%) on "BBT"
PCA+LDA+SVM	84.0	85.4
PCA+MDA+SVM	83.0	83.9
CCA+SVM	82.9	83.4
DCA+SVM	84.5	85.6
Hu et al.	88.5	-
CNN-Fuse-FC mid	**95.6**	**95.4**

In order to prove the effectiveness of our model for feature fusion, we also conducted experiments of some common feature fusion methods mentioned above and contrasted the experimental results, in which the typical SVM [14] was chosen to classify the fused features. The recognition results obtained by different approaches were listed in Table 2. It can be found that our feature fusion model is more effective than the common feature fusion methods. The main reason lies that the deep learning networks has an advantage in automatic feature transformation and extraction.

3.2   Bidirectional LSTM Networks for Recognition

For speaker recognition, we select to extract the fused features from the last fully connected layer as the input of bidirectional LSTM networks, in which the dimension of fused face and its corresponding audio vector is 1000. There are 24 frames per second in the video, and we choose 0.5 s for temporal characterization. In the experiments, the fused features extract from the aforementioned four models are embedded into the bidirectional LSTM networks for recognition. Meanwhile, we compare the proposed approach with the basic voting scheme, and the recognition results are shown in Table 3.

Table 3. Recognition accuracy obtained by different fusions and classifiers.

Method	Accuracy(%) on "Friends"	Accuracy(%) on "BBT"
Only face+BILSTM	96.4	96.1
CNN-Fuse-Input+BILSTM	94.5	94.0
CNN-Fuse-FC 1+BILSTM	97.4	97.4
CNN-Fuse-FC n+BILSTM	97.6	97.2
CNN-Fuse-FC mid+vote	97.3	97.2
CNN-Fuse-FC mid+LSTM	97.8	97.5
CNN-Fuse-FC mid + BILSTM	**98.2**	**97.8**

It can be clearly observed that the "CNN-Fuse-FC mid" model associated with the bidirectional LSTM networks has achieved the best results. That is, "CNN-Fuse-FC mid" is more discriminative for audio-visual heterogeneous feature fusion. Under the same fused features, the bidirectional LSTM networks have produced the better result than ordinary LSTM networks and voting scheme. As shown in Fig. 4, we also implemented three methods mentioned above to get the recognition result of bidirectional LSTM networks. From the experimental results, it can be found that the voting scheme and the utilization of mean value perform nearly and better than selection of last step.

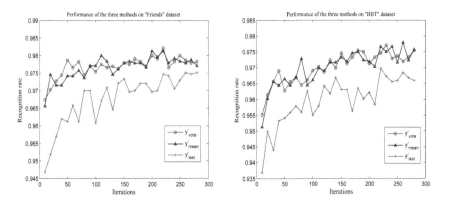

Fig. 4. Performance of the three operations in bidirectional LSTM networks.

4 Conclusion

In this paper, we have presented an efficient audio-visual speaker recognition approach via deep heterogeneous feature fusion. The proposed approach exploits a dual-branch deep CNN learning framework to extract and fuse the face and voice features in high-level semantic space. Meanwhile, by considering the temporal dependency of audio-visual fused features, a bidirectional Long Short-Term Memory networks is utilized to produce the recognition result. Accordingly, the speakers acquired under different challenging conditions can be well identified. The experimental results have shown that our proposed audio-visual speaker recognition approach performs well in both feature fusion and speaker recognition. It is expected that our proposed learning framework would be well extensible for other types of feature fusion, e.g., iris, ear or gait.

Acknowledgment. The work described in this paper was supported by the National Science Foundation of China (No. 61673185, 61502183, 61572205, 61673186), National Science Foundation of Fujian Province (2017J01112), Promotion Program for Young and Middle-aged Teacher in Science and Technology Research (No. ZQN-PY309), the Promotion Program for graduate student in Scientific research and innovation ability of Huaqiao University (No. 1611314014).

References

1. Bredin, H., Chollet, G.: Audio-visual speech synchrony measure for talking-face identity verification. In: Processing of IEEE International Conference on Acoustics, Speech and Signal Processing, pp. 233–236 (2007)
2. Cheng, H.T., Chao, Y.H., Yeh, S.L., Chen, C.S.: An efficient approach to multi-modal person identity verification by fusing face and voice information. In: Processing of IEEE International Conference on Multimedia and Expo, pp. 542–545, 2005
3. Feng, W., Xie, L., Zeng, J., Liu, Z.Q.: Audio-visual human recognition using semi-supervised spectral learning and hidden markov models. J. Vis. Lang. Comput. **20**(3), 188–195 (2009)
4. Geng, J., Liu, X., Cheung, Y.: Audio-visual speaker recognition via multi-modal correlated neural networks. In: IEEE/wic/acm International Conference on Web Intelligence Workshops, pp. 123–128 (2016)
5. Graves, A., Fernández, S., Schmidhuber, J.: Bidirectional LSTM networks for improved phoneme classification and recognition. In: Duch, W., Kacprzyk, J., Oja, E., Zadrożny, S. (eds.) ICANN 2005. LNCS, vol. 3697, pp. 799–804. Springer, Heidelberg (2005). doi:10.1007/11550907_126
6. Haghighat, M., Abdel-Mottaleb, M., Alhalabi, W.: Discriminant correlation analysis: real-time feature level fusion for multimodal biometric recognition. IEEE Trans. Inf. Forensics Secur. **11**(9), 1984–1996 (2016)
7. Hu, Y., Ren, J.S.J., Dai, J., Yuan, C., Xu, L., Wang, W.: Deep multimodal speaker naming. In: Proceedings of Annual ACM International Conference on Multimedia, pp. 1107–1110 (2015)
8. Ioffe, S., Szegedy, C.: Batch normalization: accelerating deep network training by reducing internal covariate shift. In: Proceeding of IEEE International Conference on Machine Learning, pp. 448–456 (2015)

9. Maas, A.L., Hannun, A.Y., Ng, A.Y.: Rectifier nonlinearities improve neural network acoustic models. In: Processing of IEEE International Conference on Machine Learning Workshop, pp. 1–6 (2013)
10. Ngiam, J., Khosla, A., Kim, M., Nam, J., Lee, H., Ng, A.Y.: Multimodal deep learning. In: Proceedings of IEEE International Conference on Machine Learning, pp. 689–696 (2011)
11. Sahidullah, M., Saha, G.: Design, analysis and experimental evaluation of block based transformation in MFCC computation for speaker recognition. Speech Commun. 54(4), 543–565 (2012)
12. Soltane, M., Doghmane, N., Guersi, N.: Face and speech based multi-modal biometric authentication. Process. IEEE Int. J. Adv. Sci. Technol. 21(6), 41–56 (2010)
13. Srivastava, N., Hinton, G., Krizhevsky, A., Sutskever, I., Salakhutdinov, R.: Dropout: a simple way to prevent neural networks from overfitting. J. Mach. Learn. Res. 15(1), 1929–1958 (2014)
14. David Sánchez, A.V.: Advanced support vector machines and kernel methods. Neurocomputing 55(1C2), 5–20 (2003)

Prioritized Grid Highway Long Short-Term Memory-Based Universal Background Model for Speaker Verification

Jianzong Wang$^{(\boxtimes)}$, Hui Guo, and Jing Xiao

Ping An Technology (Shenzhen) Co., Ltd., Shenzhen, China
{wangjianzong347,guohui783,xiaojing661}@pingan.com.cn

Abstract. Prioritized grid long short-term memory (pGLSTM) has been shown to improve automatic speech recognition efficiently. In this paper, we implement this state-of-the-art model of ASR tasks for text-independent Chinese language speaker verification tasks in which DNN/i-Vector (DNN-based i-Vector) framework is adopted along with PLDA backend. To fully explore the performance, we compared the presented pGLSTM based UBM to GMM-UBM and HLSTM-UBM. Due to constraint of the amount of Chinese transcribed corpus for ASR training, we also explore an adaptation method by firstly training the pGLSTM-UBM on English language with large amount of corpus and use a PLDA adaptation backend to fit into Chinese language before the final speaker verification scoring. Experiments show that both pGLSTM-UBM model with corresponding PLDA backend and pGLSTM-UBM with adapted PLDA backend achieve better performance than the traditional GMM-UBM model. Additionally the pGLSTM-UBM with PLDA backend achieves performance of 4.94% EER in 5 s short utterance and 1.97% EER in 10 s short utterance, achieving 47% and 51% drop comparing to that of GMM. Experiment results imply that DNN from ASR tasks can expand the advantage of UBM model especially in short utterance and that better DNN model for ASR tasks could achieve extra gain in speaker verification tasks.

Keywords: DNN · RNN · i-Vector · UBM · Speaker verification · pGLSTM · VAD · Long short-term memory

1 Introduction

A popular framework for speaker verification (SV) is Gaussian Mixture Model (GMM) based Universal Background Model (UBM) where the speaker feature i-Vector is extracted from sufficient statistics of GMM with Probabilistic Linear Discriminant Analysis (PLDA) backend for decision making [1,2]. However, GMM-based framework is conceptually an unsupervised way to discriminate speakers from given speech utterances. Specifically, the UBM is trained to cluster MFCCs into unsupervised clusters [3]. This fact decreases the performance

© Springer International Publishing AG 2017
J. Zhou et al. (Eds.): CCBR 2017, LNCS 10568, pp. 584–592, 2017.
https://doi.org/10.1007/978-3-319-69923-3_63

when two speakers pronounce the same phone from the same relative point (a supervised tied tri-phone state). What's more, GMM-based framework could lose robustness when background contains much noise, especially when it comes to voices overlapping situation.

To better address the challenges mentioned above, the Deep Neural Network-based (DNN) framework has been introduced into speaker recognition tasks [4–6]. One of the great improvements is implementing DNN into the UBM framework by substituting the GMM posterior with phonetic posterior [5]. We call this DNN based-UBM model, or DNN-UBM for short in this paper. [4] presents a context-aware system that efficiently leverages information of input data and separate context difference from total difference for speaker feature extraction. In DNN based UBM model, phonetic posteriors from DNN are used in place of GMM component and the name DNN/i-Vector (DNN-based i-Vector) is used instead of i-Vector. Studies have shown that DNN outperforms the traditional GMM by 30% on large scale speech recognition tasks [7]. Recently, acoustic models in DNN structure for ASR gained great improvement with different network architectures, especially highway Long Short-Term Memory (hLSTM) recurrent neural networks (RNNs). HLSTM is capable of using dynamically changing contextual windows over the sequence history [8]. Later prioritized grid LSTM improves hLSTM by introducing temporal-LSTM and depth-prioritized-LSTM within grids. PGLSTM achieves the state-of-the-art performance [9] with 2% extra gain to HLSTM in Word Error Rate (WER). While allowing more different level of information in phonetic sequence, pGLSTM has a better modeling performance in phonetic recognition with less parameter.

In DNN/i-Vector framework, the DNN is trained with transcribed corpus which cannot be always obtained in the desired amount. One simple idea is to train the model in another language with large amount of training corpus, and then adapt this model to the target language. Studies have introduced adaptation method between models, such as domain adaptation and duration mismatch adaptation [10,14]. In the lacking of transcribed corpus case, it is possible that the target model can be attained by adapting another model from another language.

In this paper, we implement this pGLSTM model in the DNN/i-Vector framework, named pgLSTM-UBM to improve the speaker verification performance. We also explore a PLDA adaptation strategy to solve the problem of lacking of transcribed corpus. To test the presented model, GMM based and highway LSTM based UBM models are used as baseline models. we build up our pGLSTM models both on 150-h Chinese transcribed corpus with PLDA scoring and on 1000 h English corpus with gaussian PLDA adaptation to Chinese. Comparisons of these models to the baseline model are reported. As a result, the presented pGLSTM-UBM model outperforms the baseline models and achieves state-of-the-art performance. Experiments also show that by PLDA adaption from the DNN/i-Vector model of another language outperforms the original DNN/i-Vector with cosine similarity.

The rest of the paper is organized as follows. In Sect. 2, we describe the LSTM and pGLSTM models that we used for our speaker verification system. We summarize the experimental setup and report experimental results in Sect. 3, and the related works are presented in Sect. 4. Finally, we concluded in Sect. 5.

2   Model Description

2.1   pGLSTM

The grid LSTM RNN was first introduced in [11]. Unlike traditional LSTM RNN models organizes LSTM blocks as a temporal chain, grid LSTM RNN models arrange LSTM blocks into multidimensional grids such that each grid contains one set of LSTM blocks for each dimension, including the depth dimensions. This architecture introduces per-dimension gated linear dependencies between adjacent cell states, which mitigates the vanishing gradient problem along all dimensions. Here we consider a two-dimensional grid LSTM model for acoustic modeling, which are time and depth dimensions. The computations in each grid are defined as follow equations. The input to depth-LSTM is updated after time-LSTM of the same grid that is firstly processed. That's why it's called time-prioritized grid LSTM model, that's pGLSTM for short. Data flows can be found in Fig. 1.

$$x_{t,l}^{T} = [h_{t,l-1}^{D}; h_{t-1,l}^{D}] \tag{1}$$

$$(h_{t,l}^{T}, c_{t,l}^{T}) = TIME - LSTM(x_{t,l}^{T}, c_{t-1,l}^{T}, \Theta^{T}) \tag{2}$$

$$x_{t,l}^{D} = [h_{t,l-1}^{D}; h_{t,l}^{D}] \tag{3}$$

$$(h_{t,l}^{D}, c_{t,l}^{D}) = DEPTH - LSTM(x_{t,l}^{D}, c_{t-1,l}^{D}, \Theta^{D}) \tag{4}$$

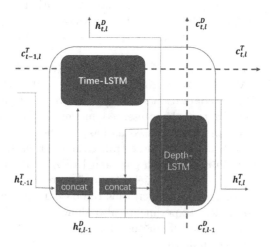

Fig. 1. Block of pGLSTM

3   Experiments

3.1   Dataset

Our experiments to implement pGLSTM in SV were based on the HKUST Mandarin Conversational Telephone Speech (LDC2005S15) dataset, which is a medium-sized corpus containing 150 h of conversational telephone speech from Mandarin speakers, recorded at an 8k sampling rate. The dataset is split into training and development sets with 873 and 24 calls respectively, of which we use the development set for evaluation.

3.2   Model Setup

Beside the traditional GMM-UBM model, we consider these two DNN-UBM structures: (1) HLSTM-UBM, (2) pGLSTM-UBM. For the GMM-UBM model, we use the configuration of [5] with 2048 GMM and 600 dimensional i-Vector. For HLSTM model, we carefully follow the configurations reported in [8]. Each layer contains 1024 memory cells, and a 512-node linear projection layer is added on top of each layer's output. For our pGLSTM models, we chose the same configuration for both time-LSTM and depth-LSTM as for the HLSTM baseline models [9].

3.3   Training

The whole DNN-UBM system with PLDA backend is trained in four stages including HMM-GMM training stage, DNN training, UBM model and i-Vector extractor training stage and PLDA training. Except for the DNN training, all the other training stages are performed on Kaldi.

Firstly, MFCC feature extraction by training of initial HMM-GMM models and context-dependent speaker adapted acoustic models with decoding are performed within standard Kaldi recipes of HKUST dataset [12]. In this stage, forced alignment is performed to generate labels for neural network acoustic model training. For later DNN training, a feed-forward neural network model is trained and used to re-generate forced alignment.

Secondly, 80 dimensional log Mel filterbank features with 3 dimensional pitch features are computed every 10 ms. For each frame, features of 11 consecutive frames including 5 frames in front and 5 frames on behind make up the input feature to DNN model. CNTK [13] is used for DNN training because it allows different connection in nodes of different layers which helps a lot to expand the LSTM structure. All weights are randomly initialized from the uniform distribution with range $[-0.05, 0.05]$, and all biases are initialized to 0. The neural network models are trained with cross-entropy (CE) criterion with truncated back-propagation-through-time (BPTT) for optimization. No momentum is used for the first epoch, and a momentum of 0.9 is used for all the other epochs. L2 regularization with weight 10^5 is applied. The output targets are context-dependent tri-phone states, of which the numbers are determined by the last HMM-GMM training stage. A softmax layer is added on top of the DNN model to achieve the probabilities of all the tri-phone states [9].

Thirdly, i-Vector extractor is computed. First, voiced activity detection (VAD) of each training utterance is computed on MFCC features. Subsequently, the DNN output probabilities of tri-phone states are filtered by VAD. Then the tri-phone probabilities are used to substitute the posteriors in the traditional UBM framework to compute per-utterance GMM representation. Finally, GMM information is collected for i-Vector extractor. In this point, we have a DNN model to generate posteriors and an i-Vector extractor. When a test audio comes in, we could extract the i-Vector by probabilities of tri-phone states computation and then i-Vector extraction.

Fourthly, a speaker verification corpus with multi-utterances per speaker is used to compute PLDA model as described in Related Work. i-Vectors are firstly extracted with the model in the third step. Then the inter-speaker and intra-speaker information is extracted. In i-Vector scoring stage, this information is used to transform i-Vector before two i-Vectors' similarity is computed.

3.4   Performance

The performances of speaker verification systems are evaluated with detection error tradeoff (DET) graph. Figures 2 and 3 show the DET curves of GMM-UBM, hLSTM-UBM, pGLSTM-UBM models. All models are tested in 5 s, 8 s,10 s durations in both cosine similarity and PLDA similarity. From DET curves, we could found EER of each model as Table 1. We refer the pGLSTM and LSTM as DNN models in following discussion to differentiate from the GMM model. Notice that DET curves of all the models have fatter tails in coordinate axis of false accept rate than of false reject rate. This is mainly because of the unbalance target and non target trials in one-to-all style, one utterance versus all enrolled speakers, in verification stage.

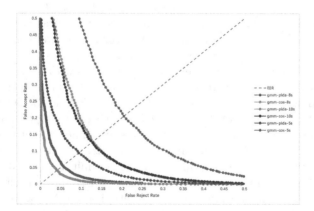

Fig. 2. The traditional GMM-UBM model with cosine or PLDA similarity, testing in 5 s, 8 s, 10 s duration

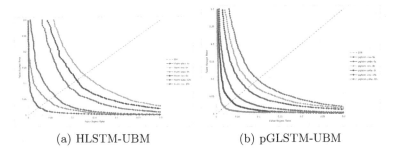

(a) HLSTM-UBM   (b) pGLSTM-UBM

Fig. 3. The HLSTM-UBM & pGLSTM-UBM model with cosine or PLDA similarity, testing in 5 s, 8 s, 10 s duration

Table 1. EER performance

Model	5 s	8 s	10 s
GMM-cosine	20.49%	12.93%	12.52%
GMM-plda	9.39%	5.43%	4.05%
HLSTM-cosine	12.69%	10.94%	9.05%
HLSTM-plda	6.02%	4.52%	2.35%
pGLSTM-cosine	9.81%	8.53%	7.09%
pGLSTM-plda	4.94%	3.65%	1.97%

In GMM performance as shown in Fig. 2, PLDA similarity achieves about 50% improvement than cosine similarity, comparing 9.39% to 20.49%, 5.43% to 12.93%, 4.05% to 12.52%. This also happens in DNN based UBM models which indicates that PLDA is a sophisticated backend to i-Vector system. Considering PLDA's well performance, the remaining of this paper mainly discuss models with PLDA backend. We can also find that in each line of the EER Table 1, data with 10 s achieves better performance than that with 8 s and 5 s. That's to say all models perform better in longer duration given other condition unchanged. Longer speech is proved to contain more speaker information for the UBM model.

When focusing on short utterance SV, the first column in Table 1, we could see out that GMM model doesn't work well in 5 s short utterance while pGLSTM is much better. With the problems of not enough speaker information in one speech and overwhelming channel and spoken noise, traditional text independent speaker verification systems require input utterance of more than 10 s in duration. However, experiments show that this situation has been improved by 47% drop in EER, comparing GMM and pGLSTM based SV model in 5 s utterance, 9.39% to 4.94% in Table 1.

Comparing different durations in pGLSM-UBM-PLDA pipeline, the last row in Table 1, 8 s utterance sees a relative 26% drop in performance to that of 5 s, and 10 s utterance has a relative drop of 60% to 5 s utterance. While comparing hLSTM-UBM and GMM-UBM models, we get 25% and 61% in HLSTM, and

42% and 57% in GMM. DNN-UBM is more stable in 5 s to 8 s transition with 26% and 25%. And GMM has less drop than the DNN-UBMs in 10 s to 5 s transition with 57%. We attribute this to the insufficient of modeling capability in GMM in various durations. As to DNN-UBM, durations has less effect on ASR tri-phone probability, and only the i-Vector extractor stage is affected. This proves the robustness of DNN-UBM in 5 s utterance SV.

Considering two DNN based models, row 3 and 5 in Table 1, better performance could be found in pGLSTM based SV system with an additional 20% drop in EER compared with that of HLSTM, in 5 s utterance. In our model, both DNN models have 2798 states in DNN output. It's reported that the pGLSTM ASR model has 32.06% Word Error Rate (WER) [9], achieving 2% relative gain compared to HLSTM model in HKUST dataset. This 2% WER improvement help specify the DNN output states, which boosts the subsequent speaker information collection. Within better ASR model, we could expect better performance in DNN-UBM text independent SV tasks.

3.5 PLDA Adaptation

Considering more ASR training material could achieve better performance in speech recognition, this part discuss about our idea of adapting SV models from a language with a great amount of training material to the Chinese language SV task. PLDA from the pGLSTM-UBM model in English corpus with LDC SRE10 evaluation project training dataset is adapted to Chinese Language as the gaussian PLDA adaptation mentioned in [10]. We compare this adaptation with Chinese language DNN/i-Vector model in cosine and PLDA scoring. Experiments result is shown in Table 2. The original PLDA method achieves 50% drop in EER to the cosine similarity, while only 18% drop to PLDA language adaptation. This adaptation gives better discriminative performance of the PGLSTM model with not enough material to train the DNN model. Even though the adaptation method is inferior to the original PLDA method, it's better than the cosine similarity in the case of lacking enough DNN training material. This experiment shows that when there's not enough transcribed corpus to train a good enough DNN model in the target language, PLDA adaptation between different language could achieve some improvement. However, the improvement is limited for that there're phonetic difference between different languages, which leads to the situation that some phonetic feature in one language may not be fully represented in another language.

Table 2. EER by different scoring methods in 5 s duration

Model	Cosine	PLDA	PLDA adapt
pGLSTM	9.81%	4.94%	8.02%

4   Related Works

The DNN/i-Vector framework is first introduced by [4] and developed by [5]. Since pGLSTM considers distance of both time and depth scales in speech information and achieves better performance in ASR [8], we adopted it as the posterior probability generation step in the framework of [5]. This should improve the tie-state recognition in ASR and result in more accurate representation of speaker feature. However, when facing very short utterance, say shorter than 5 s, which contains little content, posterior distribution of input utterance may only cover a few phones leaving duration mismatch problem in enrollment and test utterances. This also happens in GMM-UBM model.

In DNN speaker verification, end-to-end model is receiving many researching interest. [15] introduces an end-to-end system trained by discriminating between same-speaker and different-speaker utterance pairs. It works for text-dependent very short utterance by implementing cosine scoring after the DNN speaker representation network. [16] even improves the scoring method by with PLDA [2] like similarity and NIN layer for the task of 10 s duration text-independent speaker recognition. One of the trend is to combine end-to-end DNN speaker features with DNN/i-Vector which will be our next move.

5   Conclusion

In this paper, we present a novel pGLSTM-UBM framework based on state-of-the-art ASR model for text-independent speaker verification tasks achieving 4.94% and 1.97% in 5 and 10 s utterance. Experiment shows that this pGLSTM-UBM model outperforms the GMM-based i-Vector SRE schema by about 47% in EER and about 18% improvement in HLSTM for 5 s utterance. Compared to HLSTM, this pGLSTM model has better interpretation in ASR phonetic recognition and also have better discriminative performance in SV. Though experiments of adaptations could not outperform the PLDA in-domain trained and in-domain verification methods, adaptations of PLDA have better discriminative performance than the basic cosine similarity. Experiments also show that better DNN model for ASR tasks can achieve better performance while implementing in SV task, and that DNN models tend to work better in short utterance speaker verification.

References

1. Dehak, N., Kenny, P., Dehak, R., Dumouchel, P., Ouellet, P.: Front-end factor analysis for speaker verification. IEEE Trans. ASLP **19**, 788–798 (2010)
2. Burget, L., Plchot, O., Cumani, S.: Discriminatively trained probabilistic linear discriminant analysis for speaker verification. In: IEEE International Conference on Acoustics, Speech, and Signal Processing (ICASSP), pp. 4832–4835 (2011)
3. McLaren, M., Castan, D., Ferrer, L., Lawson, A.: On the issue of calibration in DNN-based speaker recognition systems. In: INTERSPEECH, pp. 1825–1829 (2016)

4. Lei, Y., Scheffer, N., Ferrer, L.: A novel scheme for speaker recognition using a phonetically-aware deep neural network. In: IEEE International Conference on Acoustics, Speech and Signal Processing (ICASSP), pp. 1695–1699 (2014)
5. Snyder, D., Garcia-Romero, D., Povey, D.: Time delay deep neural network-based universal background models for speaker recognition. In: 2015 IEEE Workshop on Automatic Speech Recognition and Understanding (ASRU), pp. 92–97 (2016)
6. Richardson, F., Reynolds, D., Dehak, N.: Deep neural network approaches to speaker and language recognition. IEEE Sig. Process. Lett. 22(10), 1671–1675 (2015)
7. Pan, J., Liu, C., Wang, Z., Hu, Y., Jiang, H.: Investigation of deep neural networks (DNN) for large vocabulary continuous speech recognition: why DNN surpasses GMMs in acoustic modeling. In: 8th International Symposium on Chinese Spoken Language Processing (ISCSLP), pp. 301–305 (2012)
8. Zhang, Y., Chen, G., Yu, D., Yaco, K., Khudanpur, S., Glass, J.: Highway long short-term memory RNNS for distant speech recognition. In: IEEE International Conference on Acoustics, Speech and Signal Processing (ICASSP), pp. 5755–5759 (2016)
9. Hsu, W., Zhang, Y., Jim, G.: A prioritized grid long short-term memory RNN for speech recognition. In: Spoken Language Technologies Workshop (SLT), San Diego, California, USA, December 2016
10. Garcia-Romero D., Zhang X., Mccree A.: Improving speaker recognition performance in the domain adaptation challenge using deep neural networks. In: Spoken Language Technology Workshop. IEEE (2015)
11. Nal, K., Ivo, D., Alex, G.: Grid long short-term memory. arXiv preprint arXiv:1507.01526 (2015)
12. Povey, D., Ghoshal, A., Boulianne, G., Burget, L., Glembek, O., Goel, N., Silovsky, J.: The Kaldi speech recognition toolkit. In: IEEE 2011 Workshop on Automatic Speech Recognition and Understanding (No. EPFL-CONF-192584). IEEE Signal Processing Society (2011)
13. Dong, Y., Adam, E., Mike, S., Kaisheng, Y., Zhiheng, H., Brian, G., Oleksii, K., Yu, Z., Frank, S., Huaming, W.: An introduction to computational networks and the computational network toolkit. Technical report, MSR, Microsoft Research (2014)
14. Taufiq, H., Rahim, S., John, H.L.H., David, V.L.: Duration mismatch compensation for i-vector based speaker recognition systems. In: IEEE International Conference on Acoustics, Speech and Signal Processing (ICASSP), pp. 4516–4519 (2013)
15. Heigold, G., Moreno, I., Bengio, S., Shazeer, N.: End-to-end text-dependent speaker verification. In: IEEE International Conference on Acoustics, Speech and Signal Processing (ICASSP), pp. 5115–5119 (2016)
16. David, S., Pegah, G., Daniel, P., Daniel, G., Yishay, C., Sanjeev, K.: Deep neural network-based speaker embedding for end-to-end speaker verification. In: IEEE Spoken Language Technology Workshop (SLT), San Diego, CA, pp. 165–170 (2016)

Assistance of Speech Recognition in Noisy Environment with Sentence Level Lip-Reading

Jianzong Wang, Yiwen Wang, Aozhi Liu, and Jing Xiao[✉]

Ping An Technology (Shenzhen) Co., Ltd., Shenzhen, China
jing.xiaoj@gmail.com,
{wangjianzong347,wangyiwen849,liuaozhi092,xiaojing661}@pingan.com.cn

Abstract. Acoustic speech recognition, as a technique to decode text from a speech, receives a great success in recent years. The trained model of Ping An Technology (ShenZhen) Co., Ltd results in a word error rate (WER) of 8.4%, which shows competitive performance among popular business products. However, an assumption of the achievement is the quiet environment of the speech. In a noisy environment, the accuracy will decrease 10%–20%. For the improvement in such environment, a multi-modal biometric system integrating acoustic speech-recognition with sentence level lip-reading is designed. In several noisy situations, the 5.7% averaged word error rate (WER) of the results of our integrated system indicates a significant improvement to the pure acoustic speech-recognition system.

Keywords: Biometric · Mutil-modal · Speech recognition · Lip-reading

1 Introduction

State-of-art machine learning algorithms have great contribution to acoustic speech recognition. The design of Expectation-Maximization (EM) algorithm makes it easy to implement Gaussian Markov Model (GMM) to build connection between Hidden Markov Model (HMM) and the acoustic input. As a result, work on the combination of GMM and HMM lasts for a few decades. With the advance of hardware development and the progress of deep learning, acoustic speech recognition is being developed from a stage of basic research to an era of business implementation. The long-term researched method of GMM-HMM is considered limited in the performance of acoustic recognition. Rather than using the traditional approach, a deep neural network (DNN) with many hidden layers is applied in the system of Ping An acoustic speech recognition. The low word error rate of the system indicates the high accuracy and reliability of the Ping An acoustic speech recognition.

However, an advanced acoustic recognition system has to be robust in even noisy situations. Unfortunately, most of the announced perfect system have good performance only in basically quiet environment. In noisy place such as a skittle-alley, a carsino or a running train, the recognition accuracy decrease dramatically. While the single-modal biometric recognition system fails to show decent

J. Zhou et al. (Eds.): CCBR 2017, LNCS 10568, pp. 593–601, 2017.
https://doi.org/10.1007/978-3-319-69923-3_64

performance, a multi-modal biometric integration has advantages on the complement of the single system. Therefore, a visual speech recognition approach is applied as an assistance. Lip-reading is a technique to obtain text by learning the visual movement of a speaker's mouth. It has great potential to be integrated with the acoustic speech recognition in noisy environment.

Over a few decades, great changes of lip-read learning from video stream has taken place due to the advance of deep learning. LipNet, as an end to end sentence-level lip-reading technology, outperform the traditional lip-reading approach that treats lip-read in word level. In this paper, we present a method of the integration of acoustic speech recognition and lip reading. If a segment of a voice is noisy, its signal-noise ratios will be low. The text decode from acoustic speech recognition technique is subsequently not reliable. We replace the text of these segments with the decoded results from LipNet and compute the word error rate (WER) on the test data. The WER decreases from 8.4% to 5.7%. This research ensures that, the lip-reading technology is a sounded supplement for acoustic speech recognition in noisy environment.

2   Approach

In the paper, we offer an integrated approach with DNN-based acoustic modeling for Chinese-speakers' speech recognition. Our test has two part: DNN-HMM model prediction using the pre-trained model in Ping An technology and Lip-reading derivation with pre-trained model of the open source LipNet network.

2.1   DNN-HMM Model Prediction

Unlike the classic neural network, deep neural network has more than one hidden layers. In acoustic speech recognition, it has 6 to 7 or even more layers. The initialization of the network is realized by the weights of a DBN (Deep Belief Network) network that has the same structure of it.

Generally, an unsupervised learning pretraining method is applied to initialize the connected weights and construct Softmax activation between the hidden layer and the output layer. Finally, the supervised learning approach will be used to adjust the network parameters. While building GRBM (Gaussian-Bernouli RBM) as the figure shown, the input layer is the voice data of Gaussian while the output is hidden units activation probability obtained by the RBM (Restricted Boltzmann Machine) network. While the GRBM is trained, the ouput of GRBM is treated as the input data of the next RBM to be trained. Through this iteration, DBN is derived to initialize a DNN network. The loss function to be minimized is the cross entroy. In our train, the output of the DNN is then applied as an estimation of the HMM's state (Fig. 1).

2.2   LipNet Network

LipNet [8] is a neural network designed specifically for lip-reading. There're three main components of the network. One is the Spatiotemporal Convolutional Neural Networks (STCNNs) while another one is the Gated Recurrent

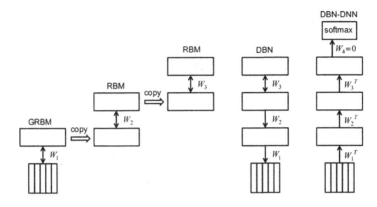

Fig. 1. DNN network build and train

Units (GRU). The final one is a Linear layer. The loss function selected is the Connectionist Temporal Classification (CTC) for the purpose of easy labeling. The LipNet Archetecture is shown with Fig. 2. Sequantially, the Bi-GRU is executed with the results of STCNNs as an input, and followed by a linear layer with a Softmax activation.

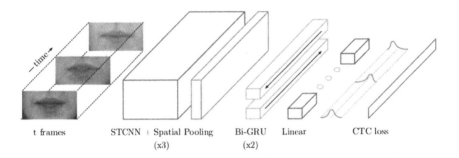

Fig. 2. LipNet architecture [8]

The convolution of STCNNs regards not only the 2D plane dimensions but also a time-sequence dimension (Karpathy et al. [1]).

$$[stconv(\boldsymbol{x}, \boldsymbol{w})]_{c'tij} = \sum_{c=1}^{C} \sum_{t'=1}^{k_t} \sum_{i'=1}^{k_w} \sum_{j'=1}^{k_h} w_{c'ct'i'j'} x_{c,t+t',i+i',j+j'} \quad (1)$$

This formula shows the principle of STCNNs where x is the image input and w indicates the weights.

Another component of the LipNet is the so-called Gated Recurrenct Unit (GRU). This is actually a type of Recurrent Neural Networks (RNNs). The optimization of GRU upon RNNs is the well-designed "gate" to filter out or to enhance the flowing information in the networks. The standard formulation is:

$$[\boldsymbol{u}_t, \boldsymbol{r}_t]^T = sigm(\boldsymbol{W}_z\boldsymbol{z}_t + \boldsymbol{W}_h\boldsymbol{h}_{t-1} + b_g)$$
$$\hat{\boldsymbol{h}}_t = \tanh[\boldsymbol{U}_z\boldsymbol{z}_t + \boldsymbol{U}_h(\boldsymbol{r}_t \odot \boldsymbol{h}_{t-1}) + b_h]$$
$$\boldsymbol{h}_t = (1 - \boldsymbol{ut}) \odot \boldsymbol{h}_{t-1} + \boldsymbol{u}_t \odot \hat{\boldsymbol{h}}_t$$

The sequence $\{z_1, ..., z_T\}$ is the input of GRU while the symbol $\odot$ indicates an element-wise multiplication. The *sigm* denotes the standard sigmoid function.

Specifically, the GRU applied in LipNet is the so called Bi-GRU. The key of "Bi" is in the prediction process. Suppose there's a sequence of strings with indices of 1, 2, 3, 4, 5. U-GRU (with only one GRU) predicts the third strings with strings of index 1 and index 2. Bi-GRU, on the other hand, predicts the third strings of with strings of index 1, index 2, index 4 and index 5. Bi-GRU predicts result in both order of a sequence.

There's a lot of loss function for selection in terms of training. LipNet choose the connectionist temporal classification (CTC) loss because it is unnecessary of the alignment between input data and output data (Amodei et al. [6]; Graves and Jaitly [4]; Maas et al. [3]).

In another word, CTC is specifically designed for the cases that the alignment of the input data and the output data is unknown, which makes the labeling procedure convenient. Define a function f that map the original sequence $\tilde{S}^*$ to the sequence $\tilde{S}$ that deletes the blank (with notaion -) tokens and the duplicate characters. The equation $f(a - ab-) = f(-aa - abb) = aab$ gives an example to the function of f, which maps "a-ab-" or "-aa-abb" into "aab". For a labeled sequence $y \in S^*$ and T as the time step, the probability $p(y|\mathbf{x}) = \sum_{u \in f^{-1}s.t.|u|=T} p(u_1, ..., u_T|\mathbf{x})$ is computed to define the CTC. If $T = 3$ and the input string is "cd", then the probability of $p(ccd) + p(cdd) + p(c - d) + p(cd-)$ is computed for the further maximum likelihood.

2.3   Visual-Acoustic Combination

The key idea of the combination of visual-acoustic recognition is to replace the texts from recognition in noisy part. The texts will first decoded from the

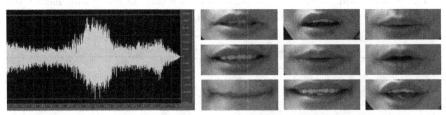

Living's know ways the best.   Life is not always that bad.

Fig. 3. Replacement by the lip-read results

DNN-HMM trained model. A simulated noise is added to the audio followed by this procedure. Then the texts are decoded again. The first comparison is made between the texts from the original audio and the texts from the noisier audio. Subsequently, a threshold of signal-noise ratio is applied to select the noisy part of audio. The full sentences of the selected noisy part will be replaced by the results from the texts obtained from LipNet prediction (Fig. 3).

3 Experiment

As a test data, we have 1000 sections of video with speech in average-time of 10.2 min. First of all, the word error rate (WER) of each video clip will be evaluated to describe the accuracy of the speech without noise. Later on, 8 kinds of noise will be added to the video clips. Every 125 video clips will be distributed in a test group. In this case, A WER of each video as well as the average WER of each group will be demonstrated the decreased accuracy. Finally, the full sentences of the part with signal-noise ratio lower than 5 dB will be replaced with the results from lip-reading.

3.1 Acoustic Speech Prediction

The acoustic-only result is evaluated on each video clips. The WER changes differently in terms of each clip. The average WER is 8.4% (Fig. 4).

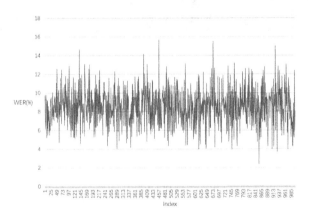

Fig. 4. Word error rate of each video clip

3.2 Noise Addition

Another test is necessary to check how does the WER change with respect to the noise addition. The waveform of the original hunman voice is shown in Fig. 5. The 8 kind of additional noises are generated with various noise models shown

Fig. 5. Human voice signal

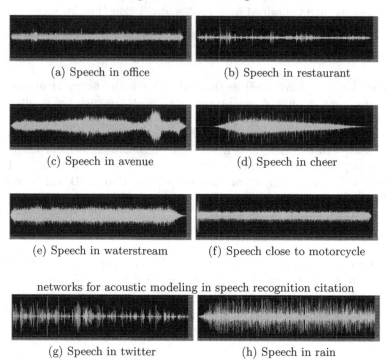

(a) Speech in office (b) Speech in restaurant

(c) Speech in avenue (d) Speech in cheer

(e) Speech in waterstream (f) Speech close to motorcycle

networks for acoustic modeling in speech recognition citation

(g) Speech in twitter (h) Speech in rain

Fig. 6. Noises addition to the human voice

in Fig. 6. They include noise in office, noise in restaurant, noise in avenue, noise in cheer, noise in water-stream, noise close to motorcycle, noise in twitter and noise in rain.

In terms of new video clips, the WER goes up in an overall level. The average WER is 17.7% in this case. On the other hand, the 1000 videos are grouped into 8 sets. WER of Every 125 videos are computed to figure out the accuracy of the text from noisy case. Although different noises addition have various effects on the recognition, they generally increase the WER in a similar level (Fig. 7).

3.3 Prediction with LipNet Replacement

For a full paragraph decoded from acoustic speech recognition, if a sentence is derived from a segment of speech with low signal-noise ratio, it will be replaced with the text obtained from lip-reading. The averaged number of replaced sentences of these 1000 videos is 7. For all videos, the increased WER is declined back to 9.2%, which is much smaller than the WER without lip-reading integration (Fig. 8).

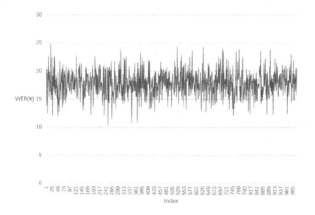

Fig. 7. Word error rate of each video clip with noises addition

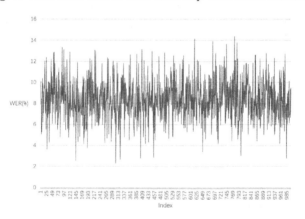

Fig. 8. WER with lip-read sentences replacement in terms of video clips

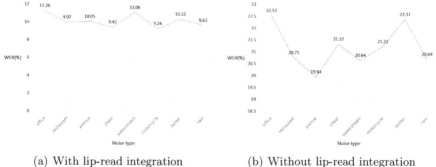

(a) With lip-read integration   (b) Without lip-read integration

Fig. 9. WER with lip-read sentences replacement in terms of groups

For the experiments of each group, the noise of twitter has significant effect on the accuracy of the speech recognition. In contrary, noise of the avenue has relatively smaller effect on the word error rate. On average, the WER of all of the groups decrease from a the high average value 18.42% back to 8.98% (Fig. 9).

4 Related Work

Contributions on visual-only text decoding or acoustic-only decoding are notable. Recently, deep learning algorithms are applied as popular approaches in both fields. Goldschen et al. [2] tried on sentence-level lip-reading. But his trained model is based on a small data set, which is not reliable enough on the result. Neti et al. [5] made effort to fuse the hand wirting visual effect into acoustic recogniton, but the research has no good practical value. On the aspect of acoustic speech recognition, Song and Cai [7] proposed an end-to-end speech recognition with deep neural networks, which is a good work but ignored the case of relatively noisy environment. There're a lot of work on only acoustic text decoding or lip-reading. In this paper, an innovative idea of combining acoustic speech recognition as well as lip-reading will be provided to improve the text-reading accuracy. LipNet, as an outstanding lip-reading deep network will be applied to improve the accuracy of acoustic-only speech recognition in noise case. The part of the speech that are added with noise will be replaced with the result from lip-reading.

5 Conclusion

The replacement approach of this examination ensures the value of fusing the visual lip-reading results with the acoustic recognition result. The remaining problem is how to automatically extract the full texts from noisy part rather than to pick them out manually. As this problem is solved, this multi-modal biometric combination will be a robust system of text decoding from speech recognition.

Acknowledgments. This work was primarily supported by PingAn Deep Learning Group.

References

1. Karpathy, A., Toderici, G., Shetty, S., Leung, T., Sukthankar, R., Fei-Fei, L.: Large-scale video classification with convolutional neural networks. In: Proceedings of the IEEE Conference on Computer Vision and Pattern Recognition, pp. 1725–1732 (2014)
2. Goldschen, A.J., Garcia, O.N., Petajan, E.D.: Continuous automatic speech recognition by lipreading. In: Shah, M., Jain, R. (eds.) Motion-Based Recognition, pp. 321–343. Springer, Dordrecht (1997). doi:10.1007/978-94-015-8935-2_14

3. Maas, A.L., Xie, Z., Jurafsky, D., Ng, A.Y.: Lexicon-free conversational speech recognition with neural networks. In: NAACL (2015)
4. Graves, A., Jaitly, N.: Towards end-to-end speech recognition with recurrent neural networks. In: International Conference on Machine Learning, pp. 1764–1772 (2014)
5. Neti, C., Potamianos, G., Luettin, J., Matthews, I., Glotin, H., Vergyri, D., Sison, J., Mashari, A.: Audio visual speech recognition. Technical report, IDIAP (2000)
6. Amodei, D., Anubhai, R., Battenberg, E., Case, C., Casper, J., Catanzaro, B., Chen, J., Chrzanowski, M., Coates, A., Diamos, G., et al.: Deep speech 2: end-to-end speech recognition in English and Mandarin. arXiv preprint arXiv:1512.02595 (2015)
7. Song, W., Cai, J.: End-to-End Deep Neural Network for Automatic Speech Recognition, Stanford CS224D reports (2015)
8. Assael, Y.M.: LipNet: end-to-end sentence-level lipreading. In: ICLR (2017)

Video Surveillance

Rich Features and Precise Localization with Region Proposal Network for Object Detection

Mengdie Chu$^{(\boxtimes)}$, Shuai Wu, Yifan Gu, and Yong Xu

Computer Science and Technology,
Harbin Institute of Technology, Harbin, China
chumengdd@126.com

Abstract. Deep Network greatly accelerates the development of object detection. Recent advances in object detection are mainly attributed to the combination of deep network and region proposal methods [1–3]. However, the accuracy of object detection on the complicated datasets is still not satisfied, especially on small object detection. This is mainly because of the coarseness of the convolution feature maps. In this paper, we design a new strategy for generating region proposals and propose a new localization method for object detection. Compared with previous baseline detectors such as Fast R-CNN [4] and Faster R-CNN [5], Our method makes use of the adjacent-level feature maps at all scales to generate region proposals and also adopts the cascaded region proposal network (RPN) to fine-tune the location of the bounding box. Compared with other state-of-the-art methods, our method achieves the best recall and object detection accuracy.

Keywords: Object detection · Proposal · Features · Localization · Cascaded

1 Introduction

Object detection is one of the most fundamental researches in computer vision [6, 7]. The purpose of object detection is to detect and localize all instances of pre-defined classes in one image [8, 9]. Basically, most object detection methods localize the instances via bounding boxes. Object detection problem can also be treat as the classification problems with the sliding window strategy [10, 11]. However, sliding window is very time-consuming because the windows are generated from all possible locations with different scales and aspect ratios. Recently, a two-stage approach has been proposed to integrate recognition and localization stages [12] into a region-based convolution neural network. It firstly generates a series of object proposals by using a proposal generator, and then determines whether an instance with exact class label exists in the ROI. Both stages are on basis of a deep neural network.

Recently, Faster R-CNN [5] is proposed to integrate proposal generation stage, classification stage and bounding boxes regression stage into a unified process through a deep convolutional network. It applies the RPN substructure to generate proposals and uses fast-RCNN to perform classification and bounding boxes regression. Faster R-CNN [5] achieve impressive performance on public benchmarks and has become the

© Springer International Publishing AG 2017
J. Zhou et al. (Eds.): CCBR 2017, LNCS 10568, pp. 605–614, 2017.
https://doi.org/10.1007/978-3-319-69923-3_65

baseline framework. However, Faster R-CNN [5] suffers from small object detection, this is mainly because it applies the deep convolution feature map which contains more semantic information while has limited effect on localization to perform the final classification and bounding boxes regression. The target region of small object after mapping on the feature map is too coarse to get expectable performance [13]. A satisfactory object detection system needs a proposal generator that can obtain a small number of region boxes with high recall [14–16]. Deeper convolutional layers usually contain powerful semantic information and are benefit for finding the region of interests with high recall. However, deeper layers are not appropriate for localization because of the limited feature map size [17]. In comparison, the lower layers could effectively localize the region of interests [18].

Considering the two situations above, we apply a multi-scale feature extraction strategy which combines the advantage of both deeper layers and lower layers. In this paper, we apply the strategy proposed in [19], which designs a top-down pathway that increasingly expand the top feature map and merge them with the corresponding layers in the backbone Network. Then all the merged feature map with multi-scale sizes will be used to generate proposals. The advantage of the top-down pathway is that it can make full use of the low-resolution feature map with powerful semantic information and high resolution feature map with efficient localization capability [20]. According to the empirical experience in classification problem, multiple representations of objects are very beneficial for recognition. Our method predicts the specific-scale proposals independently on every new feature map with multi-scale sizes.

In addition, the object detection task needs precise localization which is free effect from translation variant. For example, translation of an object inside a candidate box should produce meaningful responses for describing how well the candidate box overlaps the object [21, 22]. In order to obtain high-quality proposals, we apply a more precise localization strategy [23]. After firstly generating proposals by region proposal network(RPN), we treat these proposals as new anchors to be sent to the RPN again, which can finely tune the location of these proposals. We called this operation cascaded RPN. We evaluate our method based on the VOC detection benchmark [24] with three different baseline models. More convincingly, we verify the effect of these two improvements respectively. First, we use the top-down pathway to generate proposals without fine-tuning the location, our model significantly increases the accuracy by 0.8 points on the ResNet101 baseline network. And then, we add the cascaded region proposal network without using new features, the final result also improves 0.9 points. So, we can find that our improvements are both effective. For the final object detect, we add these two improvements together into the original Faster R-CNN, and improves the mAP by 2.0 point on ResNet101 baseline network. These results suggest that our method is an effective way for improving object detection accuracy.

2   Our Approach

In this paper, we apply the strategy in [19] that merges the adjacent-level semantic feature maps to generate proposals. However, our model is different with [19] in terms of region proposals network (RPN). We apply the cascade-RPN which could be considered as two-stage RPN after each merged feature map in [19]. The cascade-RPN treats the proposals in first stage as new anchors and sends them into the second-stage RPN. Finally, these new proposals are classified and adjusted based on the detection module. We explain our two improvements in detail respectively.

2.1 Feature Production

In order to exploit the advantage of different layers and generate richer features, we apply the strategy in [19] which is illustrated in Fig. 1. Because feature maps of different-levels have different implications, it designs a top-down pathway to generate powerful semantic feature maps of multi-scales and merge them with the corresponding layers in the backbone network. In real application, we take a single-scale image of arbitrary size as input, and regard the corresponding at multiple level feature map as outputs. The top-down pathway is independent of backbone convolutional architectures which in this paper we apply ResNet model. In ResNet, there are many output layers with the same size and we say these layers are in the same network stage, ResNet has five stages in all. As for the strategy in [19], we use the output of the last layer of each stage as our reference set of feature maps and this strategy enriches feature representation. Because every layer of the same stage has the same feature map size and the deepest layer of each stage should represent the strongest features. For conv2_x, conv3_x, conv4_x, conv5_x, we remark the output of these last residual blocks as {F2, F3, F4, F5} and each of them has strides of {4, 8, 16, 32} respectively. In our paper, we do not include the output of conv1 into the reference set, owing to its large memory footprint.

Higher-level feature maps contain powerful semantic information while coarse boundary information. Lower-level feature maps have weak semantic information but

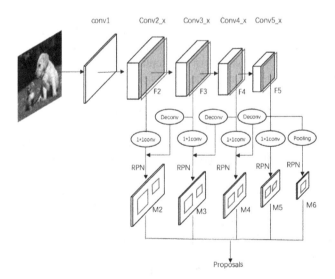

Fig. 1. Feature production architecture

are more beneficial in localization because of the limited subsampling times. The top-down pathway deconvolutes the spatial resolution of F5 by a factor 2 to powerful semantic feature maps with multi-scales. As shown in Fig. 1. the deconvoluted [25] feature maps are merged with the corresponding feature map in the backbone network (In this paper, ResNet). Before merging, the lower-level feature map undergoes a 1 * 1 convolutional layer to reduce channel dimensions. This process is iterated until the finest resolution map is generated. Because F5 is the highest-level feature map, there is no higher-level feature map to merge with it. To start the iteration, we simply attach a 1 * 1 convolutional layer after F5 to produce the coarsest resolution map. Expect for those operations, in order to reduce the aliasing effect of up-sampling, we also connect a 3 * 3 convolution on each merged map to generate the final feature map. So, we regard these final merged feature maps as {M2, M3, M4, M5}, corresponding to {F2, F3, F4, F5} and they all have the same spatial sizes.

Region Proposal Network is a huge improvement for generating proposals in Faster R-CNN [5]. It is a sliding-window class-agnostic object detector. We adapt RPN to multi-scale feature maps {M2, M3, M4, M5} instead of the single-scale feature map. Like Faster R-CNN [3], we also attach a 3 * 3 convolutional layer and two siblings 1 * 1 convolution to every new feature map. For our new generated feature maps, every new merged feature represents special scales respectively. It is not necessary to have multi-scale anchors on these merged feature maps. So [19] chooses a single scale for each new feature map. Formally, they set the anchors to have scales of {32, 64, 128, 256, 512} pixels on {M2, M3, M4, M5, M6} respectively. M6 is simply a stride of two subsampling of M5. It is used only for covering a larger anchor scale of 512, and still different aspect ratios {1:2, 1:1, 2:1} are used at each level. So, there are 15 anchors over these features in total.

2.2   Fine-Tuning of Proposals

An ideal proposals generator should generate as few proposals as possible while covering almost all object instances. With the help of strong abstraction ability of CNN, RPN could generate limited number of proposals with high recall. However, the output of general object proposal algorithms still contains a large proportion of background regions [26]. The existence of many negative samples makes the representation feature less sensitive to identify between the object category and background, causing many false positives on ambiguous object categories. In addition, due to the resolution loss caused by CNN pooling operation and the fixed aspect ratio of sliding windows, RPN is weak at covering objects with extreme scales and shapes. In this paper, we finely tune the location of proposals using cascade-RPN, which makes the localization more precise and is illustrated in Fig. 2.

In our paper, after each new merged feature maps, we apply a two-stage cascade RPN, we treat the proposals generated in first stage as new anchors, and then input these new anchors into the second stage RPN to generate the final proposals. This work makes the object proposals more compact and better localized.

As illustrated in Fig. 2, the first stage RPN is trained regularly in a sliding window manner to generate a series of anchors at special scales and various aspect ratios in an image, with the same parameters as in [5]. For every generated anchor, it is followed by

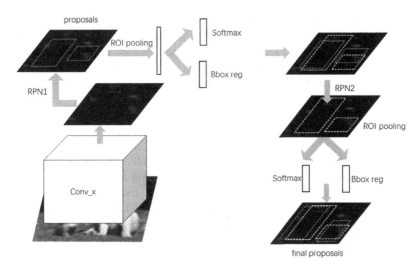

Fig. 2. Cascade RPN architecture

a region of interest (ROI) pooling layer to extract a fixed-length feature vector from the feature map, which the ROI pooling layer is simply the special-case of the spatial pyramid pooling layer used in SPPnets [27] in which there is only one pyramid level. And each feature map is fed into two sibling fully-connected layers, one for estimating whether this anchor enwrap an object or not, and another one for estimating four real-valued numbers for localization of the object. In details applications, we use three different aspect ratios for a special scale on each new merged feature, so the Bbox regression outputs has 4 * 3 channels encodes the 4 coordinates of 3 anchors, and the Softmax-layer outputs has 2 * 3 channels that estimate probability of object or non-object for each proposal. When we get the proposals from the first-stage RPN, we feed these proposals into the second stage RPN again without any operation, treat these proposals as new anchor location for fine-tuning the location of these anchors and generated final proposals.

For each image, there are about 30 K candidate boxes with different sizes and aspect ratios. After each candidate box is scored and adjusted, some region proposals extremely overlap with each other. To reduce redundancy, we adopt greedy non-maximum suppression(NMS) [28] on the regions in terms of their scores. Formally, an anchor is assigned a positive label if it has the highest IoU for a given ground-truth box or an IoU over 0.7 with any ground-truth box, and a negative label if it has IoU lower than 0.3 for all ground-truth boxes. We select the top-k ranked region proposals for detection after NMS. We train the detection network using top-300 region proposals.

2.3   Implementation

We train the RPN net and detection network with shared convolution network. We use the NMS method to restrict the number of positive and negative samples for the generated proposals. And then input these proposals into the detection network.

When we train the detection network, we use the same convolutional network as in RPN, so it can achieve shareable parameter, which have 13 shareable convolutional layers in VGG16 [29], 49 and 100 convolutional layers in ResNet50 [30] and ResNet101 [30] respectively, all of three basic models drop the full connected network. For fair comparisons with original RPN [5], we set the same parameter with it.

3   Experimental Evaluation

We evaluate our approach on PASCAL VOC 2007 and 2012 challenges [24] detection benchmarks. These datasets consist of about 20 k trainval images and 5 k test image over 20 categories. We train our models bases on VGG16 [29], ResNet-50 [30] and ResNet-101 [30] which is pre-trained on the ILSVRC CLS-LOC dataset [31], and compare results with other state-of-the-art methods [18, 20, 21, 32]. Object detection accuracy is measured by mean Average Precision (mAP). We also provide deep analysis of our approach affection to object proposal and detection performances.

We resize the shortest side to 600 pix, and the longest side to 1000 pix, which are same with Faster R-CNN [5]. We fine-tune the resulting model using SGD with a weight decay of 0.0005 and a momentum of 0.9. We train the model with 1 GPUs. We fine-tune our model using a learning rate of 0.001 for 20 k mini-batches and 0.0001 for 10 k mini-batches on VOC.

3.1   On the Impact of Feature Representation

In order to verify our merged feature strategy is effective, we compute the recall of proposals at different IoU ratios with ground-truth boxes. The results are shown in Fig. 3.

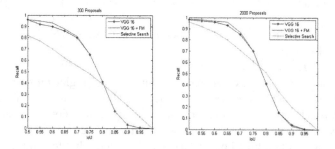

Fig. 3. Recall vs IoU overlap ratio on the PACAL VOC 2007 test set

We set the IoU ratio is 0.5 as baseline. The plots show that our merged feature method behaves gracefully when the number of proposals drops from 2000 to 300. This explains why our method has a good ultimate detection Map when using as few as 300 proposals. As we can see, this property is mainly attributed to the classify of the RPN. The recall of selective search drops quickly than our new method when the proposals are fewer. So, our new feature represent is feasible.

We compare our first improvement based on the new feature generation with basic Faster R-CNN on PACAL VOC 2007 and 2012. We test this method on three different models (VGG-16, ResNet-50, ResNet-101). The comparative results are shown in Table 1.

Table 1. Results on PASCAL VOC 2007 test set. Baseline denote the original Faster R-CNN method, FM denotes our new feature merged method. We set IoU = 0.5

Approach	mAP	Aero	Bike	Bird	Boat	Bottle	Bus	Car	Cat	Chair	Cow	Table	Dog	...
Baseline + VGG16	73.8	78.2	79.2	73.3	62.5	57.7	84.0	84.1	86.9	56.0	81.4	64.9	83.7	...
Baseline + Res50	76.4	79.1	79.9	76.5	69.2	63.1	85.1	85.4	89.2	58.4	83.5	67.5	87.1	...
Baseline + Res101	76.7	78.7	79.6	78.8	66.4	64.4	86.0	86.4	87.4	62.2	83.8	68.4	88.0	...
FM + VGG16	74.8	86.5	83.1	77.4	59.1	57.3	79.1	78.7	91.2	54.7	79.6	58.8	89.7	...
FM + Res-50	77.3	86.8	83.8	76.6	65.8	59.6	81.8	82.7	90.8	60.0	81.1	64.2	88.1	...
FM + Res-101	77.5	88.7	85.2	76.7	64.9	61.3	85.1	84.0	90.1	59.8	82.7	61.8	88.6	...

Faster R-CNN based in VGG-16 achieves a mAP of 73.8%, and 76.4% on ResNet-50 and 76.7% on ResNet-101. And our improvement method achieves a mAP of 74.8% on VGG-16, 1 points higher than Faster R-CNN, for the Res50 and Res101, are 0.9 points higher and 0.8 points higher respectively than original feature. As we shown in Table 3, this is because proposals generated by our new feature are more accurate than traditional single-scale feature map. Reasonable resolution of our new feature makes for better object localization, especially for small' object. These results demonstrate that our feature merge strategy can give excellent performance for high-quality proposals and can get better accuracy.

3.2   On the Impact of Region Proposals

We take the same train strategy as above to verity that whether cascade RPN is efficient or not. We add the cascade strategy on original Faster R-CNN without using our feature improvement. we also test this method on three different models (VGG-16, ResNet-50, ResNet-101). The comparative results are shown in Table 2.

Table 2. Results on PASCAL VOC 2007 test set. Baseline denote the original Faster R-CNN method, C-RPN denote our cascade RPN method. We set IoU = 0.5.

Approach	mAP	Aero	Bike	Bird	Boat	Bottle	Bus	Car	Cat	Chair	Cow	Table	Dog	...
Baseline + VGG16	73.8	78.2	79.2	73.3	62.5	57.7	84.0	84.1	86.9	56.0	81.4	64.9	83.7	...
Baseline + Res50	76.4	79.1	79.9	76.5	69.2	63.1	85.1	85.4	89.2	58.4	83.5	67.5	87.1	...
Baseline + Res101	76.7	78.7	79.6	78.8	66.4	64.4	86.0	86.4	87.4	62.2	83.8	68.4	88.0	...
C-RPN + VGG16	75.0	86.8	83.2	77.7	59.2	57.4	79.4	79.0	91.3	54.8	79.9	59.1	89.8	...
C-RPN +Res50	77.2	86.8	83.6	76.7	65.8	59.4	81.8	82.5	90.8	60.0	81.1	64.0	88.1	...
C-RPN + Res101	77.4	88.9	85.2	76.9	64.9	61.5	85.1	84.2	90.1	60.0	82.7	62.0	88.6	...

As we shown in Table 2, three different basic models are all obtain improvement compare with original Faster R-CNN. Our cascade RPN method gets 1.2 points, 0.8

points and 0.7 point higher respectively on basic method than original Faster R-CNN. In the fact, in the matching step, most of the default boxes are negatives, especially when the number possible and negative training is large. This introduces a significant imbalance between the positive and negative training examples. Instead of using all the negative examples, we sort them using the highest confidence loss for each default box and pick the top ones so that the ratio between the negative and positives is at most 1.5:1. We found that this leads to faster optimization and a more stable training. We show the results in Table 3. We can observe that when we restrict the ratio between positive and negative examples, the results have improvements more or less.

Table 3. Results on PASCAL VOC 2007 test set. Baseline denote the original Faster R-CNN method, CRPN denote our cascade RPN method. CRPN-ex denote the method add neg-pos example restrict. We set IoU = 0.5

Approach	mAP	Aero	Bike	Bird	Boat	Bottle	Bus	Car	Cat	Chair	Cow	Table	...
Baseline + VGG16	73.8	78.2	79.2	73.3	62.5	57.7	84.0	84.1	86.9	56.0	81.4	64.9	...
Baseline + Res50	76.4	79.1	79.1	79.9	76.5	69.2	63.1	85.1	89.2	58.4	83.5	67.5	...
Baseline + Res101	76.7	78.7	79.6	78.8	66.4	64.4	86.0	86.4	87.4	62.2	83.8	68.4	...
CRPN + VGG16	75.0	86.8	83.2	77.7	59.2	57.4	79.4	79.0	91.3	54.8	79.9	59.1	...
CRPN +Res50	77.2	86.8	83.6	76.7	65.8	59.4	81.8	82.5	90.8	60.0	81.1	64.0	...
CRPN + Res101	77.4	88.9	85.2	76.9	64.9	61.5	85.1	84.2	90.1	60.0	82.7	62.0	...
CRPN-ex + VGG16	75.2	87.0	83.4	77.9	59.4	57.6	79.6	79.2	91.5	55.0	80.1	59.3	...
CRPN-ex + Res50	77.5	88.8	85.1	76.8	64.8	61.4	85.0	84.1	90.0	59.9	82.6	61.9	...
CRPN-ex + Res101	77.6	79.7	78.6	80.8	67.4	65.4	87.0	87.4	86.4	64.2	84.8	69.4	...

3.3   Final Result

We merged all elevated methods and the results are shown in Table 4, we compare our method with other object detection method.

Table 4. Results on PASCAL VOC 2007 test set. C-FM denotes our final method

Approach	mAP	Aero	Bike	Bird	Boat	Bottle	Bus	Car	Cat	Chair	Cow	Table	...
Faster + VGG16 [5]	73.2	76.5	79.0	70.9	65.5	52.1	83.1	84.7	86.4	52.0	81.9	65.7	...
Faster + Res101	76.4	76.4	79.1	76.5	69.2	63.1	85.1	85.4	89.2	58.4	83.5	67.5	...
ION + VGG16 [19]	74.6	78.2	79.1	76.8	61.5	54.7	81.9	84.3	88.3	53.1	78.3	71.6	...
ION + R+VGG16 [19]	75.6	79.2	83.1	77.6	65.6	54.9	85.4	85.1	87.0	54.4	80.6	73.8	...
Hyper + VGG16 [35]	76.3	77.4	83.3	75.0	69.1	62.4	83.1	87.4	87.4	57.1	79.8	71.4	...
SDD512 + VGG [20]	76.8	82.4	84.7	78.4	73.8	53.2	86.2	87.5	86.0	57.8	83.1	70.2	...
R-FCN + Res101 [25]	79.5	82.5	83.7	80.3	69.0	69.2	87.5	88.4	88.4	65.4	87.3	72.1	...
C-FM + VGG16	**75.9**	87.4	83.6	76.8	62.9	59.6	81.9	82.0	91.3	54.9	82.6	59.0	...
C-FM + Res101	**78.4**	79.1	80.3	79.7	69.8	68.2	86.9	87.4	88.4	65.5	84.7	67.7	...

Some detection results are shown in Fig. 4.

Fig. 4. Some detection results

4 Conclusion

We presented two improvements for feature representation and location of object proposals. We use the new feature representation to generate high-quality proposal, which we can get better classification and proposals. For the location task, we apply the cascade RPN strategy which is a simple but accurate and efficient way to fine-tuning of the location of proposals. Our method achieves consistent and considerable improvements over state-of-the-art methods on PASCAL VOC benchmark, while being complementary to many other advanced in object detection.

References

1. Uijlings, J.R., van de Sande, K.E., Gevers, T., Smeulders, A.W.: Selective search for object recognition. Int. J. Comput. Vis. **104**, 154–171 (2013)
2. He, K., Zhang, X., Ren, S., Sun, J.: Spatial pyramid pooling in deep convolutional networks for visual recognition. In: Fleet, D., Pajdla, T., Schiele, B., Tuytelaars, T. (eds.) ECCV 2014. LNCS, vol. 8691, pp. 346–361. Springer, Cham (2014). doi:10.1007/978-3-319-10578-9_23
3. Redmon, J., Divvala, S., Girshick, R., Farhadi, A.: You only look once: unified, real-time object detection. arXiv preprint arXiv:1506.02640 (2015)
4. Girshick, R.: Fast R-CNN. In: ICCV (2015)
5. Ren, S., He, K., Girshick, R., Sun, J.: Faster R-CNN: towards real-time object detection with region proposal networks. In: NIPS (2015)
6. Hosang, J., Benenson, R., Doll'ar, P., Schiele, B.: What makes for effective detection proposals? IEEE Trans. Pattern Anal. Mach. Intell. **38**, 814–830 (2015)
7. Szegedy, C., Reed, S., Erhan, D., Anguelov, D.: Scalable, high-quality object detection. arXiv:1412.1441 (v1) (2015)
8. Gidaris, S., Komodakis, N.: Object detection via a multi-region and semantic segmentation-aware CNN model. In: ICCV (2015)
9. Hariharan, B., Arbel'aez, P., Girshick, R., Malik, J.: Hyper columns for object segmentation and fine-grained localization. In: CVPR (2015)
10. Viola, P., Jones, M.J.: Robust real-time face detection. IJCV **57**, 137–154 (2004)

11. Liu, M.-Y., Mallya, A., Tuzel, O., Chen, X.: Unsupervised network pretraining via encoding human design. In: 2016 IEEE Winter Conference on Applications of Computer Vision. pp. 1–9. IEEE (2016)

12. Sermanet, P., Eigen, D., Zhang, X., Mathieu, M., Fergus, R., LeCun, Y.: Overfeat: integrated recognition, localization and detection using convolutional networks. In: ICLR (2014)

13. Ghodrati, A., Pedersoli, M., Tuytelaars, T., Diba, A., Gool, L.V.: Deep proposal: hunting objects by cascading deep convolutional layers. In: ICCV (2015)

14. Hua, Y., Alahari, K., Schmid, C.: Online object tracking with proposal selection. In: ICCV (2015)

15. Jia, Y., Han, M.: Category-independent object-level saliency detection. In: ICCV (2013)

16. Guo, K., Wu, S., Xu, Y.: Face recognition using both visible light image and near-infrared image and a deep network. Caai Trans. Intell. Technol. 2(1), 39–47 (2017)

17. Cai, Z., Fan, Q., Feris, R.S., Vasconcelos, N.: A unified multi-scale deep convolutional neural network for fast object detection. In: Leibe, B., Matas, J., Sebe, N., Welling, M. (eds.) ECCV 2016. LNCS, vol. 9908, pp. 354–370. Springer, Cham (2016). doi:10.1007/978-3-319-46493-0_22

18. Bell, S., Zitnick, C.L, Bala, K, et al.: Inside-outside net: detecting objects in context with skip pooling and recurrent neural networks. pp. 2874–2883 (2016)

19. Lin, T.Y, et al.: Feature pyramid networks for object detection (2016)

20. Xu, Y., Zhang, B., Zhong, Z.: Multiple representations and sparse representation for image classification. Pattern Recogn. Lett. 68, 9–14 (2015)

21. Dai, J., Li, Y., He, K., et al.: R-FCN: object detection via region-based fully convolutional networks (2016)

22. Dollár, P., Appel, R., Belongie, S., Perona, P.: Fast feature pyramids for object detection. PAMI 36(8), 1532–1545 (2014)

23. Yang, B., Yan, J., Lei, Z., et al.: Craft objects from images. pp. 6043–6051 (2016)

24. Everingham, M., Eslami, S.M.A., Van Gool, L., Williams, C.K.I., Winn, J., Zisserman, A.: The pascal visual object classes challenge: a retrospective. IJCV 111, 98–136 (2015)

25. Lin, G., Milan, A., Shen, C., et al.: Refine net: multi-path refinement networks for high-resolution semantic segmentation (2016)

26. Ghodrati, A., Pedersoli, M., Tuytelaars, T., Diba, A., Van Gool, L.: Deep boxes: hunting objects by cascading deep convolutional layers. In: Proceedings ICCV (2015)

27. He, K., Zhang, X., Ren, S., Sun, J.: Spatial pyramid pooling in deep convolutional networks for visual recognition. In: Fleet, D., Pajdla, T., Schiele, B., Tuytelaars, T. (eds.) ECCV 2014. LNCS, vol. 8691, pp. 346–361. Springer, Cham (2014). doi:10.1007/978-3-319-10578-9_23

28. Shrivastava, A., Gupta, A., Girshick, R.: Training region based object detectors with online hard example mining. In: CVPR (2016)

29. Simonyan, K., Zisserman, A.: Very deep convolutional networks for large-scale image recognition. Comput. Sci. (2015)

30. He, K., Zhang, X., Ren, S., Sun, J.: Deep residual learning for image recognition. In: CVPR (2016)

31. Russakovsky, O., Deng, J., Su, H., Krause, J., Satheesh, S., Ma, S., Huang, Z., Karpathy, A., Khosla, A., Bernstein, M., Berg, A.C., Fei-Fei, L.: Imagenet large scale visual recognition challenge. IJCV 115, 211–252 (2015)

32. Kong, T., Yao, A., Chen, Y., et al.: HyperNet: towards accurate region proposal generation and joint object detection. pp. 845–853 (2016)

Sparse Similarity Learning with a Local Appearance Model for Person Tracking

Xiang Li, Min Xu$^{(\boxtimes)}$, Zeqiang Wei, and Liming Shao

College of Information Engineering, Capital Normal University,
Beijing 100048, China
xumin@cnu.edu.cn

Abstract. In this paper, we propose a novel approach to robust person tracking that combines an online bilinear similarity metric learning with a local appearance model in particle filter framework. Due to various appearance and motion changes of the target person in challenging scenarios, conventional pre-defined similarity metrics are prone to drifting in dealing with challenging sequences. To this end, we propose to learn a discriminative metric to distinguish the target object from the background by using a sparse online bilinear similarity function parameterized by a diagonal matrix. In addition, most metric learning based appearance models only consider the holistic representation and hence are sensitive to partial occlusion and cluttered background. To address this issue, we employ a local appearance model and a simple template update strategy to build a robust person tracker. Experimental results on several challenging person videos show that our tracker achieves superior performance to several state-of-the-art trackers.

Keywords: Visual tracking · Person tracking · Similarity learning · Local appearance model

1 Introduction

Visual tracking is one of the most active research topics in computer vision due to its wide range of applications, such as motion analysis, traffic control, human-computer interaction, intelligent video surveillance, video games and activity recognition. Over the past two decades, substantial visual tracking methods have been proposed in the literature. However, person tracking is still a challenging problem due to the drastic appearance variations of the target person between successive frames including fast motion, occlusion, background clutter, illumination variation, pose and scale changes, shape deformation, and so on.

Conventional similarity metrics for visual analysis proposed in the literature are often pre-defined, for example, Euclidean distance [1], Kullback-Leibler divergence [4], Matusita metric [2], and Bhattacharyya coefficient [3]. The abovementioned pre-specified similarity metrics are generally incapable to capture semantic information of the targets due to large appearance variations of the target person in two consecutive frames, and therefore, these methods have only very limited discriminative power and cannot accurately measure the target template distribution in the feature space. To

© Springer International Publishing AG 2017
J. Zhou et al. (Eds.): CCBR 2017, LNCS 10568, pp. 615–624, 2017.
https://doi.org/10.1007/978-3-319-69923-3_66

address this, some representative works which employ similarity learning have been recently introduced to learn a discriminative similarity metric for visual tracking task [5–7]. However, most previous distance metric learning methods only consider the holistic object representation to learn a Mahalanobis distance metric. Although the discriminative information can be learned, these methods have more possibility to fail in handling the partial occlusion, or to track non-target by mistake when there are similar objects around the target. To address these problems, Wang et al. [8] proposed a weighted local cosine similarity (WLCS) to measure the visual similarity between the target and candidates. WLCS is robust to partial occlusion and background clutter problem by using local features; however, it does not likely to guarantee the closest match to be the true target because the cosine similarity has similar limitation as the pre-specified distance metrics in practice.

In this paper, we propose a visual tracking method that is featured with two components: (1) an online sparse bilinear similarity learning method, and (2) a patch-based local appearance model. In addition, we design a robust and efficient tracker under the particle filter framework by integrating the two components in a unified form. The computation complexity is a key issue since real-time tracking capability is a very common requirement for visual tracking application. In the context of the computational efficiency, the proposed method shows the superiority to most existing metric learning based tracking methods, as we use a sparse diagonal matrix rather than a full matrix with $d * d$ dimensionality in our similarity metric model, where d is the dimensionality of the template feature. Consequently, computational complexity of our proposed similarity distance metric is drastically reduced from $O(d^3)$ to $O(d^2)$.

The reminder of this paper is organized as follows: Sect. 2 briefly discusses related works. Section 3 details our proposed method. Section 4 presents the experimental results, and the conclusion is made in the last section.

2   Related Work

Existing visual tracking models can be generally divided into two categories: generative and discriminative trackers. The objective of generative trackers is to learn a visual model to represent the appearance of the target object, and then search for the candidate which is most similar to the tracked object. The most representative work of generative trackers is the incremental visual tracker (IVT) [9]. IVT proposes a low-dimensional subspace appearance-based model using incremental principle component analysis. Besides IVT, Mei and Ling [1] introduce a sparse linear representation via solving an L1-regularized optimization problem (LlT), in which the tracked object is represented as a series of objects and trivial templates with the sparsity constraint. The sparse representation-based trackers show encouraging performance, however, their tracking speed is very inefficient due to complicated L1-norm convex optimization problem. In summary, the generative tracking methods are typically based on the template, subspace or sparsity representation.

Instead of focusing on learning an appearance model, discriminative trackers focus on finding the tracked object from the background, which treat visual tracking as a binary classification task. Babenko et al. [12] propose an online multiple instance learning (MIL) classifier to separate the target from the background with the real-time performance. Zhang et al. [13] present a compressive tracking algorithm (CT) and online discriminative feature selection (ODFS) [14]. Henriques et al. [15] derive a new Kernelized Correlation Filter (KCF), and propose a fast multi-channel extension of linear correlation filters. Hare et al. [16] design a framework (Struck) which uses a kernelized structured output support vector machine for adaptive visual tracking. Henriques et al. [17] exploits the circulant structure with non-linear Kernels (CSK) in fast tracking-by-detection framework. In this paper, we propose a robust tracking algorithm using online similarity metric learning approach, which exploits a diagonal matrix to instead of the square matrix to model the distance metric. Furthermore, our proposed method integrates the merits of both generative and discriminative tracking models.

3   Proposed Approach

3.1   Observation Model

Designing an effective and efficient observation likelihood model is a crucial issue in the particle filter framework. In this paper, we develop a new observation model by learning a discriminative similarity metric and utilizing a local model to obtain the effective weights. First, we divide the candidate image into M local blocks, and the candidate feature vector x is represented as the concatenation of M local feature vector $x = \left[x_1^T, x_2^T, \ldots, x_M^T\right]^T$. Meanwhile, the template is reorganized by its M blocks in the same way. Then, the aim of local model is to learn a discriminative vector $w = [w^1, w^2, \ldots, w^M]$ by exploiting some positive samples and negative samples, where w_i denotes the weight of i block and $\sum_{i=1}^{M} w_i = 1$. Finally, we propose an online similarity metric approach, which focuses on learning a similarity metric function S parameterized by matrix A as follows:

$$S_A(x, t) = x^T diag(A)t \tag{1}$$

where $x, t \in R^d$, and $A \in R^{d*d}$.

Based on the local model and the proposed similarity learning approach, we build our likelihood function as:

$$p\left(o^j \mid s^j\right) = \sum_{i=1}^{M} w_{t-1}^i S_A\left(t_i, o_i^j\right) \tag{2}$$

for $j = 1, 2, \ldots, N$, where $w_{t-1} = \left[w_{t-1}^1, w_{t-1}^2, \ldots, w_{t-1}^M\right]$ is the weight vector learned in the prior frame, and $t = [t_1, t_2, \ldots, t_M]$ denotes the template including M local feature vector.

3.2   Similarity Learning

To design a more robust visual tracker, we present a novel online similarity metric learning approach to learn a distance metric matrix, which is diagonal and sparse.

Data Preparation. Formally, let D be the training set, which contains N_p positive samples $D^+ = \{x_i \mid i = 1, 2, \ldots, N_p\}$ and N_n negative samples $D^- = \{y_i \mid j = 1, 2, \ldots, N_n\}$. First, N_p positive samples are sampled near from the target object in the target-centered region of radius d_α. We collect N_n negative samples from the larger target-center region with radius from d_β to d_γ After obtaining the positive and negative samples, we construct K positive-negative sample triplets to learn our similarity metric matrix. Each sample triplet consists of two randomly selected samples from N_p positive samples, and one randomly chosen sample in N_n negative samples.

Formulation. In order to achieve a discriminative metric A, we model the bilinear similarity function in (3) and ensure that the distance between positive samples is as small as possible; in the meanwhile, the distance between negative pairs is as large as possible. We restrict each positive pair has higher similarity score than negative pair in all sample triplets (x_i, x_j, y_k) as follow:

$$S_A(x_i, x_j) > S_A(x_i, y_k) + 1 \tag{3}$$

where $i, j \in [1, N_p], i \neq j$, and $k \in [1, N_n]$.

To learn a similarity measurement that follows the constraints in (3), a loss function for a single triplet is defined as:

$$\ell_A(x_i, x_j, y_k) = max(0, 1 - S_A(x_i, x_j) + S_A(x_i, y_k)) \tag{4}$$

To minimize the loss ℓ_A, our similarity learning is based on the online passive-aggressive algorithm [18]. It is formulated as the following convex optimization problem with a certain margin:

$$\begin{aligned} A^i = \arg \min_A \tfrac{1}{2} \|A - A^{i-1}\|_F^2 + C\xi \\ Subject\ to\ \ell_A(x_i, x_j, y_k) \leq \xi\ and\ \xi \geq 0 \end{aligned} \tag{5}$$

To deal with the problem in Eq. (5), we define the Lagrangian as:

$$L(A, \tau, \xi, \lambda) = \frac{1}{2}\|A - A^{i-1}\|_T^2 + C\xi + \tau(1 - \xi - x_i^T A(x_j - y_k)) - \lambda\xi \tag{6}$$

Where $\tau, \lambda \geq 0$. The optimal solution can be obtained when the gradient vanishes.

$$\partial L(A, \tau, \xi, \lambda)/\partial A = A - A^{i-1} - \tau V^i = 0 \tag{7}$$

Where V^i is the gradient matrix:

$$V^i = \partial \ell_A / \partial A = x_i (x_j - y_k))^T \tag{8}$$

Finally, we can solve the optimization problem according to Eqs. (6)–(8) and the solution to A can be achieved by:

$$A^i = A^{i-1} + \tau V^i \tag{9}$$

$$\tau = min\left\{ C, \frac{\ell_{A^{i-1}}(x_i, x_j, y_k)}{\|V_i\|^2} \right\} \tag{10}$$

3.3   Weight Learning and Update

To address the partial occlusion and background clutter problem, we utilize the local model for visual tracking, in which we design an optimization method to learn the discriminative weights. For the samples, we make use of the same sample set as similarity metric learning in the weight learning process. To learn the effective feature weights, we define the objective function as follows:

$$G(W) = \frac{1}{|D^+|} \sum_{i \in D^+} S_A(t, o^i) - \frac{1}{|D^-|} \sum_{i \in D^-} S_A(t, o^i) + \frac{\mu}{2} \sum_{j=1}^{M} \left(w_j - w_j' \right)^2 \tag{11}$$

where the first two terms denote the average local-weighted similarity of positive samples and negative samples, respectively. We add a regularization term as the last term to avoid model degradation, in which $w' = \left[w_1', w_2', \ldots, w_M' \right]^T$ serves as a reference weight vector and it is set as the discriminative weight from the previous frame. Note that in the first frame, the discriminative weight of each component is initialized as equal value. The aim of the first two terms is to assure that the average local-weighted similarity of positive samples is as large as possible; simultaneously, the average local-weighted similarity of negative samples is as small as possible. Hence, the discriminative weights can be achieved by solving the optimization problem, that is, $max\, G(w)$, subject to $\sum_{i=1}^{M} w_i = 1, w_i \geq 0, For\, i = 1, 2, \ldots, M$. Then, the maximization problem is equivalent to the minimization problem $min\, J(w)$, where $J(w)$ is defined as follows:

$$J(W) = \sum_{i=1}^{M} w_i \left(S_i^- - S_i^+ + \mu w_i' \right) - \frac{\mu}{2} \sum_{i=1}^{M} w_i^2 \tag{12}$$

where S_i^+, S_i^- are the first and second term in (12), respectively. For the minimization optimization problem $min\, J(w)$, it is a linear constraint function, in which the objective function $J(w)$ is a quadratic function. To our best knowledge, we can get the solution to the quadratic program by utilizing many existing methods. In addition, it is important to note that the regularization parameter μ is a key factor in the optimization problem, so we need assign the appropriate value to it. If the value of μ is set too large or too small, the obtained weights might be not effective enough to distinguish the target from the background.

3.4 Template Update

The template update is also a crucial issue in visual tracking problem since the tracked target generally has a continuous changing appearance during the tracking process. In our work, we employ a simple template update strategy under the particle filter framework. Concretely, let $y_t = \left[y_1^T, y_2^T, \ldots, y_M^T\right]^T$ denote the observation vector with M blocks corresponding the best candidate state of the t - th frame, and $\mathcal{T} = \left[\mathcal{T}_1^T, \mathcal{T}_2^T, \ldots, \mathcal{T}_M^T\right]^T$ denote the template including M blocks as well. When we find the best candidate state of the tracked target in each frame, the template $\mathcal{T}$ will be updated as follows:

$$\left\{ \begin{array}{ll} \mathcal{T}_i = \alpha t p_i + (1 - \alpha) y_i, & \text{if } S(tp_i, y_i) \geq k \\ \mathcal{T}_i = \mathcal{T}_i, & \text{otherwise} \end{array} \right\} \tag{13}$$

where $S(tp_i, y_i)$ expresses the similarity between the current template and observation vector of the i - th block; α, $0 < \alpha \leq 1$ is a update rate which adjust the contribution between the old template and new observations; and k denotes the predefined threshold which determines the template update condition. In our work, α and k are set as 0.9 and 0.8 by trial and error, respectively.

4   Experiments and Results

To evaluate the performance of our proposed person tracker, we conduct experiments on the six challenging person videos listed in Table 1. Partial occlusion, illumination variation, pose change, background clutter and motion blur are the main challenging factors in visual tracking. These selected sequences in our experiments present various challenging situations as mentioned above. We compare our proposed tracker with 13 state-of-the-art trackers: MIL [12], FragT [19], LSHT [20], MTT [10], TLD [21], LSAT [22], VTD [23], APGL1 [24], POLSL [25], IVT [9], LSST [11], ASLSA [26] and WLCS [8].

Table 1. AVERAGE OVERLAP RATES of the different trackers. THE BEST THREE RESULTS are shown IN RED, BLUE, AND GREEN FONTS, respectively.

Sequence	MIL	FragT	LSHT	MTT	TLD	LSAT	VTD	APGL1	POLSL	IVT	LSST	ASLSA	WLCS	Ours
Occlusion1	0.59	0.90	0.93	0.79	0.65	0.90	0.77	0.87	0.90	0.85	0.89	0.83	0.92	0.92
Occlusion2	0.61	0.60	0.70	0.72	0.49	0.33	0.59	0.70	0.69	0.59	0.86	0.81	0.82	0.86
Caviar1	0.25	0.68	0.70	0.45	0.70	0.85	0.83	0.28	0.71	0.28	0.89	0.90	0.90	0.90
Caviar2	0.26	0.56	0.55	0.33	0.66	0.28	0.67	0.32	0.54	0.45	0.80	0.35	0.79	0.79
Singer1	0.34	0.34	0.34	0.32	0.41	0.52	0.79	0.83	0.31	0.66	0.77	0.78	0.85	0.85
Girl	0.52	0.69	0.45	0.63	0.58	0.65	0.51	0.65	0.78	0.43	0.44	0.72	0.64	0.66
Average	0.36	0.43	0.54	0.56	0.53	0.54	0.63	0.62	0.60	0.59	0.73	0.73	0.78	0.79

4.1 Experimental Setup

For our proposed tracker, we sample 600 particles in each frame, and the location of the initial template in the first frame is manually labeled in term of ground truth. Image patch of each particle is resized to $32 * 32$ pixels and divided into $4 * 4$ blocks, so we can achieve a local representation including 16 feature vectors of 64-dimensionality. For the training set, we sample $N_p = 10$ positive samples and $N_n = 50$ negative samples, and then construct $\mathcal{K} = 200$ triplets to learn the parameter matrix A of our similarity metric for every 5 frames. Moreover, the region radius d_α of positive samples is set to 2, and we let the region radius of negative samples range from $d_\beta = 5$ to $d_\gamma = 5$. For the weight update, we empirically set the regularization parameter μ as 0.001. We perform our experiments on a PC with an i5-4210U dual-core CPU and a 8 GB RAM. Our proposed tracker is implemented by MATLAB 2009b, and runs at about 5 fps on the tested sequence on average.

4.2 Quantitative Evaluation

In this paper, two widely-used evaluation metrics are adopted for quantitative evaluation: the average overlap rate (AOR) and the average success rate (ASR), all computed by manually labeled ground truth. We let $area(B_T \cap B_G)/area(B_T \cup B_G)$ denotes the overlap rate, where B_T and B_G are the bounding box of the tracked object and the ground truth, respectively. If the overlap rate is larger than 0.5, we consider the tracking result of the current frame as success. Tables 1 and 2 respectively show the average overlap rate (AOR) and the average success rate (ASR), where a larger AOR or ASR value means a more accurate tracking result. From these tracking results in term of different evaluation metrics, we can conclude that our proposed tracker achieves highly competitive performance to the state-of-the-art trackers.

Table 2. AVERAGE SUCCESS RATES of the different trackers. THE BEST THREE RESULTS are shown IN RED, BLUE, AND GREEN FONTS, respectively.

Sequence	MIL	FragT	LSHT	MTT	TLD	LSAT	VTD	APGL1	POLSL	IVT	LSST	ASLSA	WLCS	Ours
Occlusion1	76	100	100	100	78	100	97	100	100	100	100	97	100	100
Occlusion2	72	65	100	93	52	40	68	93	98	56	100	100	100	100
Caviar1	28	96	98	30	96	99	97	30	98	30	100	99	100	100
Caviar2	34	58	58	43	94	37	76	40	58	43	100	41	100	100
Singer1	25	25	35	25	46	51	95	100	23	94	100	100	100	100
Girl	49	86	37	69	81	84	60	81	99	60	33	99	89	96
Average	36	48	57	67	66	60	79	79	66	71	85	91	97	99

4.3 Qualitative Comparison

We select 6 test sequences for evaluation in our experiment, which involve various kind of challenging factors. We qualitatively evaluate the tracking results of these sequences in the following two aspects.

(1) **Occlusion and Scale Changes:** We evaluate various state-of-the-art trackers on four sequences including Occlusion1, Occlusion2, Caviar1 and Caviar2 with heavy partial occlusion and scale change, as shown in Fig. 1. For the sequences

Occlusion1, Occlusion2 and Caviar1, both our method and ASLAS achieve good performance, and other trackers experience different degree of drifting away from the tracked object due to the partial occlusion and scale changes. In the Caviar2 sequence, the MIL, APGL1 and ASLAS begin to lose the target from the frame #200 because of the occurrence of the object with similar appearance, while our approach correctly tracks the target object and performs slightly better than FragT, IVT and TLD trackers. Obviously, our proposed tracker achieves the best performance on these sequences with heavy occlusion and scale changes, which are attributed to local-based similarity model and the effective update scheme in visual tracking process.

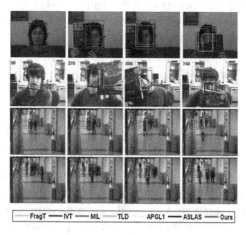

Fig. 1. Tracking results of representative trackers on the sequences with occlusion and scale changes. The sequences are Occlusion1, Occlusion2, Caviar1 and Caviar2 from top to bottom. Frame numbers are shown in the top left of each figure.

(2) **Illumination and Pose Changes:** Figure 2 illustrates the tracking results of different trackers on the sequences Singer1 and Girl with serve illumination, scale change, and pose change. The sequence Singer1 shows significant illumination variation in addition to scale change. The FragT and MIL trackers cannot accurately tracks the object since they lack the ability to deal with the large scale changes (e.g., the frame #180, #300 in Singer1), while the other trackers work well in these two sequences. The girl in the sequence Girl goes through pose change, partial occlusion, and scale change. It can be clearly seen that ASLAS, FragT and our tracker successfully track the target on most of the frames, and ASLAS obtains the more accurate tracking performance, which can be attributed to the use of increment subspace learning. Overall, the proposed tracker can handle the illumination and pose change because of employing discriminative matching during the tracking process.

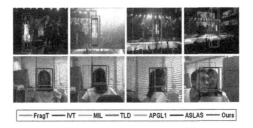

Fig. 2. Tracking results of representative trackers on the sequences with Illumination and Pose Changes. The sequences are Singer and Girl from top to bottom. Frame numbers are shown in the top left of each figure.

5 Conclusions and Future Work

In this paper, we have proposed a robust visual tracker based on local appearance model and online similarity learning. Our basic idea is that each positive pair of objects should have greater similarity than those of negative pairs between objects and backgrounds under our learned distance metric, so that the target objects can be distinguished from the background regions effectively. Experimental evaluations on challenging sequences demonstrated that our method can achieve competitive performance to the state-of-the-art visual tracking methods. In the future, we plan to combine with more effective person representation in the whole tracking process to further improve the tracking performance of our method.

Acknowledgments. This work was partially supported by the National Natural Science Foundation of China under the grant of No. 61601310.

References

1. Mei, X., Ling, H.: Robust visual tracking using $\ell 1$ minimization. In: IEEE International Conference on Computer Vision, pp. 1436–1443 (2009)
2. Hager, G.D., Dewan, M., Stewart, C.V.: Multiple kernel tracking with SSD. In: IEEE Conference on Computer Vision and Pattern Recognition, pp. 790–797 (2004)
3. Comaniciu, D., Ramesh, V., Meer, P.: Kernel-based object tracking. IEEE Trans. Pattern Anal. Mach. Intell. **25**(5), 564–575 (2003)
4. Elgammal, A.M., Duraiswami, R., Davis, L.S.: Probabilistic tracking in joint feature-spatial spaces. In: IEEE Conference on Computer Vision and Pattern Recognition, pp. 781–788 (2003)
5. Jiang, N., Liu, W., Wu, Y.: Order determination and sparsity regularized metric learning adaptive visual tracking. In: IEEE Conference on Computer Vision and Pattern Recognition, pp. 1956–1963 (2012)
6. Li, X., Shen, C., Shi, Q., Dick, A.R., van den Hengel, A.: Nonsparse linear representations for visual tracking with online reservoir metric learning. In: IEEE Conference on Computer Vision and Pattern Recognition, pp. 1760–1767 (2012)
7. Wu, Y., Ma, B., Yang, M., Zhang, J., Jia, Y.: Metric learning based structural appearance model for robust visual tracking. IEEE Trans. Circuits Syst. Video Technol. **24**(5), 865–877 (2014)

8. Wang, D., Lu, H., Bo, C.: Visual tracking via weighted local cosine similarity. IEEE Trans. Cybern. **45**(9), 1838–1850 (2015)

9. Ross, D.A., Lim, J., Lin, R.-S., Yang, M.-H.: Incremental learning for robust visual tracking. Int. J. Comput. Vis. **77**(1–3), 125–141 (2008)

10. Zhang, T., Ghanem, B., Liu, S., Ahuja, N.: Robust visual tracking via multi-task sparse learning. In: IEEE Conference on Computer Vision and Pattern Recognition, pp. 2042–2049 (2012)

11. Wang, D., Lu, H., Yang, M.-H.: Least soft-threshold squares tracking. In: IEEE Conference on Computer Vision and Pattern Recognition, pp. 2371–2378 (2013)

12. Babenko, B., Yang, M.-H., Belongie, S.J.: Visual tracking with online multiple instance learning. In: IEEE Conference on Computer Vision and Pattern Recognition, pp. 983–990 (2009)

13. Zhang, K., Zhang, L., Yang, M.-H.: Real-time compressive tracking. In: European Conference on Computer Vision, pp. 864–877 (2012)

14. Zhang, K., Zhang, L., Yang, M.-H.: Real-time object tracking via online discriminative feature selection. IEEE Trans. Image Process. **22**(12), 4664–4677 (2013)

15. Henriques, J.F., Caseiro, R., Martins, P., Batista, J.: High-speed tracking with kernelized correlation filters. IEEE Trans. Pattern Anal. Mach. Intell. **37**(3), 583–596 (2015)

16. Hare, S., Saffari, A., Torr, P.H.S.: Struck: structured output tracking with kernels. In: IEEE International Conference on Computer Vision, pp. 263–270 (2011)

17. Henriques, J.F., Caseiro, R., Martins, P., Batista, J.: Exploiting the circulant structure of tracking-by-detection with kernels. In: European Conference on Computer Vision, pp. 702–715 (2012)

18. Crammer, K., Dekel, O., Keshet, J., Shalev-Shwartz, S., Singer, Y.: Online passive-aggressive algorithms. J. Mach. Learn. Res. **7**, 551–585 (2006)

19. Adam, A., Rivlin, E., Shimshoni., I.: Robust fragments-based tracking using the integral histogram. In: IEEE Conference on Computer Vision and Pattern Recognition, vol. 1, pp. 798–805 (2006)

20. He, S., Yang, Q., Lau, R., Wang, J., Yang, M.-H.: Visual tracking via locality sensitive histograms. In: IEEE Conference on Computer Vision and Pattern Recognition, pp. 2427–2434 (2013)

21. Kalal, Z., Mikolajczyk, K., Matas, J.: Tracking-learning-detection. IEEE Trans. Pattern Anal. Mach. Intell. **34**(7), 1409–1422 (2012)

22. Liu, B., Huang, J., Yang, L., Kulikowsk, C.A.: Robust tracking using local sparse appearance model and k-selection. In: IEEE Conference on Computer Vision and Pattern Recognition (CVPR), pp. 1313–1320 (2011)

23. Kwon, J., Lee, K.M.: Visual tracking decomposition. In: IEEE Conference on Computer Vision and Pattern Recognition (CVPR), pp. 385–396 (2010)

24. Bao, C., Wu, Y., Ling, H., Ji, H.: Real time robust l1 tracker using accelerated proximal gradient approach. In: IEEE Conference on Computer Vision and Pattern Recognition (CVPR), pp. 1830–1837 (2012)

25. Yao, R., Shi, Q., Shen, C., Zhang, Y., Hengel., A.: Part-based visual tracking with online latent structural learning. In: IEEE Conference on Computer Vision and Pattern Recognition, pp. 2363–2370 (2013)

26. Jia, X., Lu, H., Yang, M.-H.: Visual tracking via adaptive structural local sparse appearance model. In: IEEE Conference on Computer vision and pattern recognition (CVPR), pp. 1822–1829 (2012)

Research on Temporal Structure for Action Recognition

Wengang Feng$^{(\boxtimes)}$, Huawei Tian, and Yanhui Xiao

People's Public Security University of China, Beijing 100038, China
fengwengang@ppsuc.edu.cn

Abstract. Cameras may be employed to facilitate data collection, to serve as a data source for controlling actuators, or to monitor the status of a process which includes tracking. We proposed an algorithm to explore the temporal relations between trajectory groups in videos, and applied it to action recognition and intelligent human-machine interaction systems. The trajectory components are application-independent features, and function well as mid-level descriptors of actions in videos. The experiments demonstrated performance improvements compared with a pure bag-of-features method. The success of this semantics-free recognition method provides the potential to define high-level actions using low-level components and temporal the relationships between them. This is similar to the way humans perceive and recognize actions.

Keywords: Action recognition · Temporal structure · Trajectory component

1 Introduction

The public is becoming accustomed to the ubiquitous presence of camera sensors in private, public, and corporate spaces. Surveillance serves the purposes of security, monitoring, safety, and even provides a natural user interface for human machine interaction. Each video-based action recognition system is constructed from first principles. Signal processing techniques are used to extract mid-level information that is processed to extract entities (e.g., objects) which are then analyzed using deep model semantics to infer the activities in the scene. The major task and challenge for these applications is to recognize action or motion patterns from noisy and redundant visual information. This is partly because actions in a video are the most meaningful and natural expression of its content. The key issues involving action recognition include background modeling, object/human detection and description, object tracking, action description and classification, and others. Depending on specific domains, very different methods can be employed to fulfill each of these aspects.

Existing methods for vision-based action recognition can be classified into two main categories: feature-based bag-of-words and state-based model matching, The latter is distinguished by the use of spatio-temporal relationships. "Bag-of-words" has been successfully extended from text processing to many activity recognition tasks [1, 2]. Features in the bag-of-words are local descriptors which usually capture local orientations. However, the spatio-temporal relations between the descriptors are not used in most bag-of-words-based methods. State-based matching methods establish a

© Springer International Publishing AG 2017
J. Zhou et al. (Eds.): CCBR 2017, LNCS 10568, pp. 625–632, 2017.
https://doi.org/10.1007/978-3-319-69923-3_67

model to describe the temporal ordering of motion segments, which can discriminate between activities, even for those with the same features but different temporal ordering. Methods in this category typically use hidden Markov models (HMMs) [3] or spatio-temporal templates [4] among others. Difficulties with model matching methods include the determination of the model's structure and the parameters.

In this paper, a mixture model of temporal structure between features is proposed to explore the temporal relationships among the features for action recognition in videos. In this study, we further explore the temporal relations between these "visual words" (i.e. trajectory groups). Thus, each video is characterized as a bag-of-words and the temporal relationships among the words. We evaluate our model on public available datasets, and the experiments show that the performance is improved by combining temporal relationships with bag-of-words.

2   Structure of Trajectory Groups

In order to develop an application-independent approach for action recognition, we extract features to express meaningful components based on dense trajectories. For raw trajectory descriptors, we employ the form that Wang et al. proposed [6] but we remove object motion caused by camera movement. In this paper, we therefore cluster these dense trajectories into meaningful mid-level components, and construct a bag-of-components representation to describe them.

2.1   Dense Trajectories

Trajectories based on feature point descriptors such as SIFT are usually insufficient to describe the motion, especially when consistent tracking of the feature points is problematic because of occlusion and noise. This leads to incomplete description of motion. In addition, these sparse trajectories are probably not evenly distributed on the entire moving object but cluttered around some portions of it. We extract dense trajectories from each video to describe the motion of different parts of a moving object. Different from sparse feature-point approaches, the dense trajectories are extracted using the sampled feature points on a grid basis. Figure 1 illustrates the difference between them. To detect scale-invariant feature points, we constructed an image pyramid for each frame of a video, and the feature points are detected at different scales of the frame.

For each pyramid image I of a frame, it is divided into $W \times W$ blocks. We use $W = 5$ as suggested in [6] to assure a dense coverage of the video. For the pixel p at the center of each block, we obtain the covariance matrix of intensity derivatives (a.k.a. structure tensor) over its neighborhood $S(p)$ of size N_s.

Tracking feature points is fulfilled based on optical flow. We use the Gunnar Farneback's implementation in the OpenCV library to compute the dense optical flow. It finds optical flow, $f(y, x)$, of each pixel (y, x) between two frames I_t and I_{t+1} in both y and x directions, so that

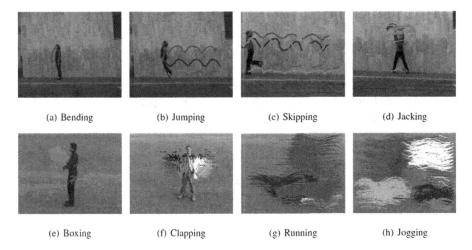

| (a) Bending | (b) Jumping | (c) Skipping | (d) Jacking |

| (e) Boxing | (f) Clapping | (g) Running | (h) Jogging |

Fig. 1. Examples of trajectories from object-based tracking (first row) and dense optical flow-based feature tracking (second row). The dense trajectories are grouped based on their spatio-temporal proximity.

$$I_t(y,x) \approx I_{t+1}(y+f(y,x) \cdot y, x+f(y,x) \cdot x)$$

2.2   Trajectory Descriptors

For each trajectory, we combine three different types of information together with space-time data, i.e. location-independent trajectory shape (S), appearance of the objects being tracked (histograms of oriented gradients, HoG), and motion (histogram of optical flow, HoF, and motion boundary histograms, MBH). Therefore, the feature vector for a single trajectory is in the form of

$$T = \left(t_s, t_e, \bar{x}, \bar{y}, S, HoG, HoF, MBH_x, MBH_y\right)$$

where (t_s, t_e) is the start and end time, and $(\bar{x}, \bar{y})$ is the mean coordinate of the trajectory, respectively.

2.3   Grouping Dense Trajectories

The trajectories are clustered into groups based on their descriptors, and each trajectory group consists of spatio-temporally similar trajectories which characterize the motion of a particular object or its part. The raw dense trajectories encode local motion, and the trajectory groups are mid-level representation of actions, each of which corresponds to a longer term of motion of an object part. To cluster the dense trajectories, we develop a distance metric between trajectories with the consideration of trajectories' spatial and temporal relationships. Given two trajectories Γ^1 and Γ^2, the distance between them is

$$d(\Gamma^1, \Gamma^2) = \frac{1}{L} d_S(\Gamma^1, \Gamma^2) \cdot d_{spatial}(\Gamma^1, \Gamma^2) \cdot d_t(\Gamma^1, \Gamma^2)$$

where d_S is the Euclidean distance between the shape vectors S^1 and S^2, $d_{spatial}(\Gamma^1, \Gamma^2)$ is the spatial distance between corresponding trajectory points, and $d_t(\Gamma^1, \Gamma^2)$ indicates the temporal distance. We choose the following in our experiments. By these definitions, spatio-temporally close trajectories with similar shapes have small distance.

$$d_S(\Gamma^1, \Gamma^2) = \sqrt{\sum_{i=1}^{L} (S_i^1 - S_i^2)^2}$$
$$d_{spatial}(\Gamma^1, \Gamma^2) = \sqrt{(\bar{x}^1 - \bar{x}^2)^2 + (\bar{y}^1 - \bar{y}^2)^2}$$
$$d_t(\Gamma^1, \Gamma^2) = \begin{cases} 1 & |t_s^1 - t_s^2| < L \\ \infty & |t_s^1 - t_s^2| \geq L \end{cases}$$

2.4   Bag of Components

The trajectories and their groups shown in Fig. 1 provide low level description to the action content in a video. Some separated trajectory groups from the previous step can have the same motion characterization. We proposed to use components to represent different types of trajectory groups. A mean feature vector, $\bar{T}$, is obtained for all the trajectories in the same trajectory group. Because of the large motion variation in even the same type of actions, our model constructs a trajectory component codebook, and assigns each trajectory group to its closest component in the codebook. The size of the codebook, D, is determined based on the experiments, and is set to 1000. K-means clustering is used over the $T's(S, HoG, HoF, MBHx, MBHy)$ to generate the components. We use Euclidean distance for each of the descriptors, and combine them using

$$d(\bar{\Gamma}^1, \bar{\Gamma}^2) = e^{\sum_k \frac{d_k(\bar{\Gamma}^1, \bar{\Gamma}^2)}{\pi_k}}$$

where $\bar{\Gamma}^1, \bar{\Gamma}^2$ are two trajectory groups, $k \in (S, HoG, HoF, MBHx, MBHy)$, and $\pi_k = \max\left(d(\bar{\Gamma}^1, \bar{\Gamma}^2)\right)$ is the maximum distance between the descriptors k of two groups in the training datasets. The codebook construction and component assignment is illustrated in Fig. 2. Figure 2(a) shows the results from GANC clustering, and Fig. 2(b) illustrates the assignment of each group Ci to the closest component wi. For instance, both groups $C1$ and $C2$ correspond to the same component $W1$. In the following, $f : g \rightarrow w$ is used to indicate the mapping from a trajectory group to a component.

Given the codebook, the trajectory groups of a video are assigned their closest component, and the video can have a bag-of-components representation as follows, where di is the frequency of component wi in the video.

$$BoC = \{d_1, d_2, \ldots, d_D\}$$

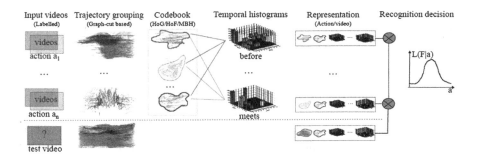

Fig. 2. Flowchart of learning and classification.

2.5   Temporal Structure

To characterize the temporal relationships among actions, our model develops the statistical temporal relationships between the "components", and combines them with bag-of-components representation. According to the conclusions of Allen [6], there exist 13 temporal relations between two actions based on the actions' durance intervals. Before_i means before inversely (i.e. after), and the same for other relations on the right column. As also noticed by Patridis et al. [7], symmetric geometry exists in these relations.

To reduce the redundancy, seven temporal structures are used in our model to represent these temporal relationships, i.e. before(B), meets(M), overlaps(O), starts(S), during(D), finishes(F) and equals(E). Each of them is a two-dimensional matrix, and characterizes one temporal relationship and its inverse. This is achieved by putting each pair of the relationships above and below the diagonal of the matrix respectively.

For each type of action, the temporal relationships between a pair of components are modeled by the seven two-dimensional histograms. Each histogram shows the frequencies with which the relationship is true between a pair of components. That is, for a temporal relation $R_i \in \{B, M, O, S, D, F, \varepsilon\}$ is the frequency of xR_iy between two components x and y. In our model, we construct the temporal relations for each type of action in a supervised manner, i.e. we learn discriminatively $p(R_i \mid \alpha)$ for each action type α.

This process is performed for all pairs of trajectory groups in all the videos of action type α. We obtain the signature for action α by combining the bag-of-components and the temporal relations: $A = \left\{ BoC^\alpha, \{R_i^\alpha\}_{i=1}^7 \right\}$, and this is used as the feature of our model. During recognition a similar process is followed to extract the feature for the target video. Suppose it is $F : \left\{ boc^\alpha, \{R_i^\alpha\}_{i=1}^7 \right\}$. We seek an action α^* which maximizes the likelihood:

$$\alpha^* = \arg \max_\alpha L(F \mid \alpha) = \arg \max_\alpha \prod L(w_j \mid \alpha) \prod L(R_i \mid \alpha)$$

based on the assumption that different groups and temporal relations are independent.

$L(w_j \mid \alpha)$ can be directly retrieved from the signature of action α, denoted as $p(w_j \mid \alpha)$ (see next section), and here we discuss how to obtain the likelihood of $\{R_i^\alpha\}_{i=1}^7$. We make use of the distance between R_i^α and R_i to define the likelihood.

3 Learning and Recognition

To construct the signatures of actions, a supervised discriminative learning approach is applied to obtain the probability of every component given the action $p(w_j \mid \alpha)$ and the seven histograms for temporal relations. We are able to learn the $p(w_j \mid \alpha)$ and the temporal histograms for each type of action.

For a specific dataset, we assume that the labels of the actions, α's, are known, and the codebook of components is first learned from the dataset. To obtain the codebook for the bag-of components representation, we cluster the trajectory groups from all the videos in each training dataset as described in Sect. 2.4. This codebook is also used for the test videos for component assignment.

We apply simple methods to learn the conditional probability and the temporal histograms. Following a Bayesian training procedure, we count the occurrence (T_{wi}) of each component in all the videos of the same action, and then compute the conditional probability $p(w_j \mid \alpha)$ using each component's frequency. The temporal histograms are computed for each video and are then averaged over all videos of an action. For each trajectory component in a video of action α, we compute its temporal distances to all of the other components in that video, determine the Allen temporal relationships between them, and count the frequency of each relationship. The seven temporal histograms are updated correspondingly.

4 Experimental Results

Here we describe experiments to evaluate our approach using the KTH human motion dataset and Weizmann action dataset. The actions in both datasets were recorded in constrained settings.

Figure 2 shows some sample frames from both datasets. Comparison experiments using bag-of components representation were performed for both datasets, and a logic-based action recognition approach with temporal relationships was compared with our approach quantitatively and qualitatively.

4.1 KTH Dataset

The KTH dataset contains six types of human actions (walking, jogging, running, boxing, hand waving and hand clapping) performed several times by 25 subjects in four different scenarios, including outdoors, outdoors with scale variation, outdoors with different clothes, and indoors. All video sequences have static and homogeneous backgrounds at 25 fps frame rate and 160×120 resolution. Altogether there are 2391 sequences.

Long video sequences containing motion clutters were segmented into clips of around 20 s. This pre-processing reduces the number of the trajectories in a video for analysis, and does not affect the application of online action detection. For each category, we have 50 videos for training and 50 videos for testing. Our model achieves 89.7% of accuracy by combining bag-of-components and temporal relations. This verifies the performance improvement compared with the result of bag-of-components. The p-value from F-test is 0.096. Figure 3(a) shows the confusion matrix of recognition results for the KTH dataset.

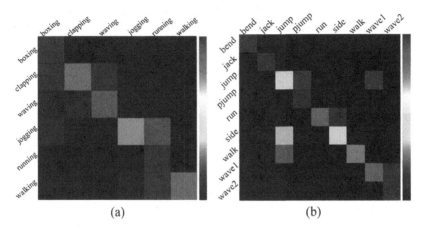

(a)   (b)

Fig. 3. (a) Confusion matrix for KTH dataset. (b) Confusion matrix for Weizmann dataset.

4.2 Weizmann Dataset

The Weizmann dataset consists of 90 low-resolution (144×180 pixels) video sequences showing nine different persons, each performing 10 natural actions: bending, jumping, jumping-in-place (pjump), jacking, running, gallop sideways (side), skipping, walking, waving one hand (wave1) and waving two hands (wave2), as shown in Fig. 1. Nine actions (not including skipping) were also used for experiments. We achieve 94.1% accuracy for 9-class actions, and 87.8% for 10-class actions. Both are better than their pure bag-of-components counterparts. The confusion matrix for 9-action classification results is illustrated in Fig. 3(b). We notice that confusion exists between gallop sideways and jumping. This is probably due to the fact that both have similar movement, and the only difference is that the participants are facing different directions, which our approach has not considered in modeling.

5 Summary

In this study, we used a simple inference/recognition method, the information extracted from the temporal relation between trajectory groups can be input to other inference engines. The extracted components can be used as input for logic-based systems to construct the predicates, which demands semantic assignment to components. Compared to existing logic-based approaches, our approach requires less computationally intensive preprocessing and yet achieves better results. More relationships other than temporal ones can be explored in a similar way to describe more complex actions, as planned for future work.

From the experiments we have done with both approaches, we conclude that our approach can be more easily applied to different scenarios. It is worth mentioning that the trajectory segments in the analysis can be replaced by trajectory components. Aggregation of trajectories into components lead to more robust mid-level representation of actions. While one individual trajectory could be incomplete or erroneous, the collective descriptors of similar trajectories are mostly stable across different scenarios.

Acknowledgement. This paper is supported by the National Natural Science Foundation of China (Grant Nos. 61501467, 61502506, and 61402484).

References

1. Dalal, N., Triggs, B.: Histograms of oriented gradients for human detection, In: IEEE Conference on Computer Vision Pattern Recognition (CVPR), pp. 886–893 (2005)
2. Laptev, I., Caputo, B., Schuldt, C., Lindeberg, T.: Local velocity-adapted motion events for spatio-temporal recognition. Comput. Vis. Image Underst. (CVIU) 108(3), 207–229 (2007)
3. Yu, E., Aggarwal, J.K.: Human action recognition with extremities as semantic posture representation, In: IEEE Conference on Computer Vision and Pattern Recognition Workshops (CVPRW) (2009)
4. Lin, Z., Jiang, Z., Davis, L.: Recognizing actions by shape-motion prototype trees. In: IEEE International Conference on Computer Vision (ICCV), pp. 444–451 (2009)
5. Wang, H., Kläser, A., Schmid, C., Liu, C.-L.: Dense trajectories and motion boundary descriptors for action recognition. Int. J. Comput. Vis. (IJCV) 103(1), 60–79 (2013)
6. Wang, H., Kläser, A., Schmid, C., Liu, C.: Action recognition by dense trajectories, In: IEEE Conference Computer Vision on Pattern Recognition (CVPR), pp. 3169–3176 (2011)
7. Petridis, S., Paliouras, G., Perantonis, S.J.: Allen's hourglass: probabilistic treatment of interval relations, In: International Symposium Temporal Representation and Reasoning, pp. 87–94 (2010)

Real-Time Object Detection Using Efficient Convolutional Networks

Xian Zhou[1,2(✉)], You-Ji Feng[1], and Xi Zhou[1]

[1] Chongqing Institute of Green and Intelligent Technology,
Chinese Academy of Sciences, Beijing, China
1849529790@qq.com
[2] University of Chinese Academy of Sciences, Beijing, China

Abstract. While recent object detection approaches have greatly improved the accuracy and robustness, the detection speed remains a Challenge for the community. In this paper, we propose an efficient fully convolutional network (EFCN) for real time object detection. EFCN employs the lightweight MobileNet [1] as the base network to significantly reduce the computation cost. Meanwhile, it detects objects in feature maps with multiple scales, and deploys a refining module on the top of each of these feature maps to alleviate the accuracy loss brought by the simple base network. We evaluate EFCN on the challenging KITTI [2] dataset and compare it with the state-of-the-art methods. The results show that EFCN keeps a good balance between speed and accuracy, it has 25× fewer parameters and is up to 31× faster than Faster-RCNN [3] while maintaining similar or better accuracy.

Keywords: Real-time · Fully-convolutional network · Refining module

1 Introduction

Deep Convolutional Neural Network (CNN) based methods currently attain top performances on most of the computer vision tasks. State-of-the-art object detection approaches also employ the powerful tool to greatly improve the detection accuracy. R-CNN [4] first samples region proposals at multiple scales, and then classifies these proposals using a CNN. Since CNN is independently computed on each region proposal, R-CNN is time consuming and energy-inefficient. Fast R-CNN [5] addresses this issue by ROI pooling, which only needs to perform the convolutions on the whole image, not the regions. The recently proposed Faster-RCNN further designs a region proposal network (RPN) to quickly predict the candidate regions, which dramatically improves the overall detection speed. Since then, almost all the top-ranked published methods on the KITTI leader board are on the basis of Faster-RCNN. Nevertheless, these approaches are too slow for real-time applications. In YOLO (You Look Only Once) [6], region proposal and object detection are integrated into one single stage. Compared with Faster R-CNN based methods, the single stage detection pipeline of

© Springer International Publishing AG 2017
J. Zhou et al. (Eds.): CCBR 2017, LNCS 10568, pp. 633–641, 2017.
https://doi.org/10.1007/978-3-319-69923-3_68

YOLO is extremely fast. YOLO is the first CNN based object detection model which has real time speed. Yet, its detection accuracy declines rapidly, especially for small objects. Object detection is widely employed in applications such as driving aids and augmented reality. These applications require not only high accuracy but also real time performance. Therefore the development of an effective and computationally efficient object detection approach is highly desirable.

In this paper we propose a new approach which is able to meet the requirements for real time vision applications. We first employ a light-weight deep neural network (MobileNet) in our detection framework to improve the speed. Then, to alleviate the loss of detection accuracy, we detect objects in feature maps with multiple scales and exploit deconvolution and skip connections to refine the feature maps. Experimental results show that our method is able to run in real time with high accuracy.

The rest of the paper is organized as follows. Section 2 gives a brief review of the related works. Section 3 introduces our detection pipeline and the structure of the network. Section 4 demonstrates the training details; Sect. 5 reports our experiment results on the KITTI dataset, and discusses the accuracy, speed, and parameter size of our model. Section 6 draws the conclusion.

2 Related Work

AlexNet [7], VGG16 [8], ResNets [9] are CNN architectures that have been widely used to address various computer vision tasks. However, these networks are too slow during inference because of their large architectures and numerous parameters. SqueezeNet [10] uses a bottleneck approach to devise a very small network, but its accuracy is limited. MobileNet provides an acceptable trade off between the speed and accuracy. It has slightly lower accuracy than VGG16 while being 32 times smaller and having 27 times less computation.

For object detection, it has been shown beneficial to exploit multiple layers within a ConvNet. Some approaches such as Hypercolumns [11], HyperNet [12], ParseNet [13], and ION [14], directly combine multiple feature maps from different layers to predict the class label and object location. While the combined feature is more descriptive, it significantly increases the memory footprint and decreases the speed. SSD [15] and MSCNN [16] use different layers within a ConvNet to predict objects of different scales. Since different layers have different receptive fields, it is natural to predict large objects from deep layers with large receptive fields and use shallow layers with small receptive fields to predict small objects. But directly using information from shallow layers may cause low performance on small objects, because shallow layers have weak semantic abstraction of the image.

3 Method

Our approach adopts a single-pass detection pipeline integrating bounding box localization and classification into a single network. However, unlike YOLO, our model is fully-convolutional. Thus it is highly memory-efficient, computationally effective and not restricted by the resolutions of input images. The key points of our approach are as follows.

3.1   Efficient Convolutional Networks

We choose the MobileNet as the base network to improve the speed. MobileNet is based on depth-wise separable convolutions which factorize a standard convolution into a depth-wise convolution and a 1×1 convolution. The number of times of the arithmetic operations in depth-wise separable convolution is $D_K \cdot D_K \cdot M \cdot D_F \cdot D_F + M \cdot N \cdot D_F \cdot D_F$. While in standard convolution, the number of times of the arithmetic operations is $D_K \cdot D_K \cdot M \cdot N \cdot D_F \cdot D_F$, where M is the number of input channels, N is the number of output channels, $D_K \times D_K$ is the kernel size and $D_F \times D_F$ is the feature map size. The computation cost reduces to $\frac{1}{N} + \frac{1}{D_K^2}$, e.g., when 3×3 depth-wise separable convolutions are used, MobileNet has 8 to 9 times less computation than standard convolutions.

3.2   Multi-scale Detection and Refining Module

The detailed architecture of our network is shown in Fig. 1. The network has a standard CNN trunk and a set of output branches, which derive from different layers of the trunk. In SSD and MS-CNN, these branches only consist of a single prediction layer, and the objective functions are applied on the prediction layer directly. To improve accuracy, we add a refining module to each prediction layer. The refining module combines low-resolution, semantically strong features with high-resolution, semantically weak features by deconvolution and skip connections. As shown in Fig. 2, First, we upsample the low-resolution feature map by a factor of 2. Then, the upsampled map is fused with the corresponding high-resolution map by element-wise sum. Finally, followed by a 1×1 convolution, a 3×3 depth-wise convolution is appended on each fused map to obtain the final feature map. The predictions of each detection branch are combined into the final detection result.

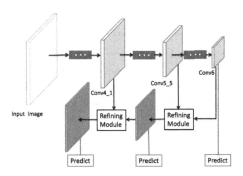

Fig. 1. The pipeline of hierarchical object detection.

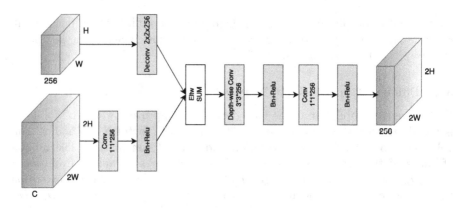

Fig. 2. The refining module.

3.3   Fully Convolutional Predictors for Detection

The last two fully-connected layers of YOLO are replaced by two convolutional layers in our method. The first convolutional layer reduces the number of channels, and the second convolutional layer outputs the detection results. At each spatial grid of the final feature map, the second convolutional layer computes $C + 1 + 4$ values that encodes the bounding box predictions, where $C + 1$ is the number of classes(includes the background), and 4 is the number of the spatial coordinates. Compared with YOLO, our method greatly minimizes the number of the parameters. When the input feature map is of size $7 \times 7 \times 1024$ and the number of classes is 20, the number of the parameters required by the two fully connected layers of YOLO is approximately 212×10^6, while the two convolutional layers in our model has only 0.27×10^6 parameters, $780\times$ fewer than YOLO.

4   Implementation Details

In this section we describe the loss functions we employ as well as other details of our training procedure.

4.1   Scales and Aspect Ratio for Grids

As shown in [13], feature maps from different levels within a network have different empirical receptive field size. In our network, each hierarchical feature layer is designed to detect particular scales of objects. Table 1 lists the scales of grids in each object detection layer. We use the aspect ratio of 1:1 for each scale.

4.2   Loss Functions

We use the sum of two losses for detection. Cross entropy loss is for the classification and L1 loss is for the bounding box localization. The classification loss is defined as follows:

Table 1. The scales and aspect ratio of grids in prediction layers

Layer	$conv4\_1$	$conv5\_5$	$conv6$
Scale	8^2	16^2	32^2
Grid	8×8	16×16	32×32

$$loss_{class}(p, q) = -\frac{1}{|I|} \sum_{i \in I} \sum_{c \in C} q_i(c) \log p_i(c) \tag{1}$$

where p_i is the predicted probability, q_i is the ground-truth label, C is the set of classes and I is the set of examples in the mini batch. Note that the L1 loss is only computed for grids which have been assigned a positive confidence label. The localization loss is computed as:

$$loss_{bbox}(p, q) = \frac{1}{|I|} \sum_{i \in I} \delta_{q_i} (|x_{min}^{p_i} - x_{min}^{q_i}| + |y_{min}^{p_i} - y_{min}^{q_i}| + \\ |x_{max}^{p_i} - x_{max}^{q_i}| + |y_{max}^{p_i} - y_{max}^{q_i}|) \tag{2}$$

where x_{min}, y_{min}, x_{max}, y_{max} are the spatial coordinates of the object, δ_{q_i} is 1 if the grid is positive, and 0 if the grid is negative, p is the prediction, q is the ground truth, C is the set of classes and I is the set of examples in the mini batch.

4.3 Data Augmentation

To make the model more robust to various object sizes and shapes, we perform data augmentation to introduce more diversity into the training data. The data augmentation operations include spatial transformations (rotations, translation, cropping, scaling) and chromatic transformations (color, contrast, brightness), and all these transformations are randomly added to the training images.

5 Experiment

We evaluated our method on the KITTI object detection dataset, which is built for helping to improve the techniques in autonomous driving. Qualitative results are first shown in Fig. 3. And then, we analyzed the average precision (AP), speed, and model size of our method, and gave the comparison with some other state-of-the-art methods.

5.1 Experimental Setup

In KITTI dataset, there are 7481 images for training, and 7518 images for testing. Since no ground truth is available for the test set, we randomly split the training set into a new training set and a validation set. In the experiments, we resized

Fig. 3. Detection results of our method in KITTI dataset.

the input images to 1248 × 384, and used the new training set for learning and the validation set for evaluation. Our results are reported on the validation set. We used ADAM with momentum to optimize the loss function. The first 40k iterations are trained with the learning rete of 1×10^{-5}, then the learning rate is decreased to 5×10^{-6} for the subsequent 30k iterations and further decreased to 2.5×10^{-6} for the last 10k iterations. The batch size is set as 2. At the inference stage, the confidence threshold of 0.6 is used to filter out most of the candidate, then non-maximum suppression (NMS) was applied to obtain the final detection results. We used NVIDIA GTX 1080 GPUs for our experiments.

5.2   Average Precision

In order to qualify the improvement that refining module brings to the detection task, we conducted two contrast experiments (EFCN and EFCN-). EFCN- refers to performing detection on multiple layers of the efficient fully convolutional network without refining modules. What's more, we also trained other detectors (MS-CNN, Faster-RCNN+VGG16, YOLO, RRC [17]) to compare them with our methods. The detection accuracy, measured by average precision is shown in Table 2. From Table 2, we can see that our proposed model achieved much better AP than Faster-RCNN+VGG16 and YOLO in all three difficulty levels of car and pedestrian detection on the KITTI dataset, and achieved similar AP with MS-CNN in car detection. We can also observe that EFCN achieved better AP than EFCN-, especially in moderate difficulty level and hard difficulty level. It proves that refining module is very effective for the small object detection with little time increase.

5.3   Speed

The average precision and inference speed of each method is shown in Table 2 and also in Fig. 4. From Fig. 4, we can see that our method is the only one, which can achieve real-time inference speed with high detection accuracy on KITTI dataset. As we know, YOLO is the fastest open-source algorithm at present. But our proposed model can run faster with much better accuracy than YOLO.

Table 2. Summary of detection accuracy, model size and inference speed of different models on KITTI dataset.

Method	Car			Pedestrian			Model size (MB)	Speed (FPS)
	E	M	H	E	M	H		
MS-CNN	91.4	89.7	78.8	82.2	72.8	68.1	309.6	6.25
Faster-RCNN	88.6	77.2	68.7	68.7	54.4	48.8	546.9	1.9
YOLO	51.3	37.2	31.6	26.8	25.6	17.9	753	33.3
RRC	91.7	91.3	88.1	-	-	-	133.7	2.7
EFCN-	92.3	86.6	75.9	74.1	64.0	60.9	16.7	63.3
EFCN	92.1	88.4	78.1	75.3	66.2	63.8	21.9	58.8

5.4 Model Size

Model size is also of great importance to practical application. While model size is not reported on the KITTI leader board, we still compared our model with other state-of-the-art models. We showed the model size and their average precision in Fig. 5 and summarized them in Table 2. As can be seen in Table 2, our model is 25 smaller than the Faster R-CNN+VGG16 model, and 14 smaller than the MS-CNN model. Compared with YOLO, which has 24 convolutional layers and two fully connected layers, our model is 34 smaller.

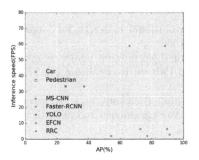

Fig. 4. Inference speed vs AP (moderate)

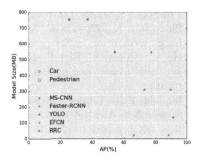

Fig. 5. Model size vs AP (moderate)

6   Conclusion

In this paper, we introduce a fully convolutional neural network for real-time object detection. The key feature of our method is the use of a simple backbone network and detecting object in multi-scale feature maps with the aid of a refining module. This simple backbone network dramatically improves the detection speed, while the refining module prevents the accuracy loss, which makes the proposed method both fast and accurate. Experimental results demonstrate that our method achieves promising performance on the challenging KITTI dataset, and can be implemented in real time.

Acknowledgments. This work was partially supported by the National Natural Science Foundations of China (Grant Nos. 61472386 and 61502444).

References

1. Howard, A.G., Zhu, M., Chen, B., Kalenichenko, D., Wang, W., Weyand, T., Andreetto, M., Adam, H.: Mobilenets: efficient convolutional neural networks for mobile vision applications, arXiv preprint arXiv:1704.04861
2. Geiger, A.: Are we ready for autonomous driving? The Kitti vision benchmark suite. In: IEEE Conference on Computer Vision and Pattern Recognition, pp. 3354–3361 (2012)
3. Ren, S., He, K., Girshick, R., Sun, J.: Faster R-CNN: towards real-time object detection with region proposal networks. In: Advances in Neural Information Processing Systems, pp. 91–99 (2015)
4. Girshick, R., Donahue, J., Darrell, T., Malik, J.: Rich feature hierarchies for accurate object detection and semantic segmentation. In: IEEE Conference on Computer Vision and Pattern Recognition, pp. 580–587 (2014)
5. Girshick, R.: Fast R-CNN, Computer Science
6. Redmon, J., Divvala, S., Girshick, R., Farhadi, A.: You only look once: unified, real-time object detection. In: IEEE Conference on Computer Vision and Pattern Recognition, pp. 779–788 (2016)
7. Krizhevsky, A., Sutskever, I., Hinton, G.E.: Imagenet classification with deep convolutional neural networks. In: International Conference on Neural Information Processing Systems, pp. 1097–1105 (2012)
8. Simonyan, K., Zisserman, A.: Very deep convolutional networks for large-scale image recognition, arXiv preprint arXiv:1409.1556
9. He, K., Zhang, X., Ren, S., Sun, J.: Deep residual learning for image recognition. In: IEEE Conference on Computer Vision and Pattern Recognition, pp. 770–778 (2016)
10. Iandola, F.N., Han, S., Moskewicz, M.W., Ashraf, K., Dally, W.J., Keutzer, K.: SqueezeNet: AlexNet-level accuracy with 50x fewer parameters and ¡0.5 MB model size, arXiv preprint arXiv:1602.07360
11. Hariharan, B., Arbelaez, P., Girshick, R., Malik, J.: Hypercolumns for object segmentation and fine-grained localization. In: IEEE Conference on Computer Vision and Pattern Recognition, pp. 447–456 (2015)
12. Kong, T., Yao, A., Chen, Y., Sun, F.: Hypernet: towards accurate region proposal generation and joint object detection. In: IEEE Conference on Computer Vision and Pattern Recognition, pp. 845–853 (2016)
13. Liu, W., Rabinovich, A., Berg, A.C.: ParseNet: looking wider to see better, arXiv preprint arXiv:1506.04579
14. Bell, S., Zitnick, C.L., Bala, K., Girshick, R.: Inside-outside net: detecting objects in context with skip pooling and recurrent neural networks. In: IEEE Conference on Computer Vision and Pattern Recognition, pp. 2874–2883 (2016)
15. Liu, W., Anguelov, D., Erhan, D., Szegedy, C., Reed, S., Fu, C.-Y., Berg, A.C.: SSD: single shot MultiBox detector. In: Leibe, B., Matas, J., Sebe, N., Welling, M. (eds.) ECCV 2016. LNCS, vol. 9905, pp. 21–37. Springer, Cham (2016). doi:10.1007/978-3-319-46448-0_2

16. Cai, Z., Fan, Q., Feris, R.S., Vasconcelos, N.: A unified multi-scale deep convolutional neural network for fast object detection. In: Leibe, B., Matas, J., Sebe, N., Welling, M. (eds.) ECCV 2016. LNCS, vol. 9908, pp. 354–370. Springer, Cham (2016). doi:10.1007/978-3-319-46493-0_22
17. Ren, J., Chen, X., Liu, J., Sun, W., Pang, J., Yan, Q., Tai, Y.W., Xu, L.: Accurate single stage detector using recurrent rolling convolution

Holistic Crowd Interaction Modelling
for Anomaly Detection

Jiaxing Pan$^{(\boxtimes)}$ and Dong Liang

Collaborative Innovation Center of Novel Software Technology and Industrialization,
College of Computer Science and Technology, Nanjing University of Aeronautics
and Astronautics, Nanjing 211106, People's Republic of China
panjiaxing_happy@163.com, liangdong@nuaa.edu.cn

Abstract. Dense crowd motion analysis in surveillance scenario is a
daunting task that when occlusion and low resolution happen, it is difficult to make effective use of pedestrian detection and tracking algorithms. In this study, we introduce a crowd interaction modelling framework inspired by physical and social science studies. Instead of taking the
pedestrian individual as the unit of analysis, the interaction among individuals could be modeled through the social force model (SFM), and for
robust representation, a modified SFM is proposed. Experiments of the
visualization and anomaly detection tested on UMN and Web dataset
indicate SFM-based interaction modelling outperform optical flow and
particle advection.

Keywords: Dense crowd analysis · Anomaly detection · Social force
model · Optical flow

1   Introduction

Crowd stampede and violence often occur worldwide. The crowd motion analysis
in surveillance scenario is in urgent need for public security. Patch-based models
have been proposed for tracking objects in crowd [16–18]. However, they are time-
consuming. And observing pedestrian individual is difficult for the occlusions,
tiny objects and low resolution in high density surveillance scenes [1]. In such
case, considering macroscopic motion patterns is a wiser choice to exploit the
interaction in the crowd [2], where usually the holistic properties of the scene
are modeled.

High density crowd motion analysis is mainly used in anomaly detection,
where the key problem is robust motion representation. Tal considered the statistics information of the magnitude of flow field vector varies as time goes by,
whereby the proposed ViF descriptor realizes real-time of anomaly detection [3];
Mahadevan proposed a Mixtures of Dynamic Texture method conducting anomaly detection in time and space domain [4]. Meanwhile note that, algorithms
based on deep learning is introduced in crowd scenario analysis [5,6]. However,
this kind of method requires a large scale dataset to train a complex network

© Springer International Publishing AG 2017
J. Zhou et al. (Eds.): CCBR 2017, LNCS 10568, pp. 642–649, 2017.
https://doi.org/10.1007/978-3-319-69923-3_69

containing a large number of parameters. In a recent work [7], the author proposed a method combining acceleration, body compression and aggressive drive attributes extracted from the original video to detect the violence in crowd scenes, and the experimental comparison with a pre-trained convolution neural network [5] gets a better result. Originate in the research of physics, sociology and psychology, Helbing proposed social force model [8] to model the interaction among pedestrian. Mehran et al. apply the model to anomaly detection and localization [9].

This study focuses on the analysis of robustness of social force model and improves it. The comparison of the anomaly detection results with optical flow and particle advection is conducted on UMN [10] and Web [9] benchmark. The paper is organized as follows. In the next section we will introduce related methods and their visual effectiveness. The modified model will be proposed in Sect. 3, then experiments and conclusion come in Sects. 4 and 5 respectively.

2   Crowd Motion Pattren Estimation

Most of the pixel-level motion estimation method is based on optical flow. Also, there are a large number of effective optical flow algorithm used in motion detection and segmentation tasks widely [11,12].

2.1   Particle Advection

Based on the optical flow, [13] computed the particle advection. Firstly, put some particles evenly upon the frame, and then particles move with the optical flow, so as to simulate the motion of individual changes with the people around them. Particle advection can be seen as a smoothing process of optical flow in both spatial and temporal domains. As shown in Fig. 1, the image on the left shows the optical flow field. It can be found that, local random movement happen in the leg or arm part when a person was walking, however, if we carry on the particle advection (right), this problem can be solved well, and which enables a person or area with a relative consistent motion vector.

Fig. 1. Visual effectiveness of *optical flow* (*left two columns*) and *particle advection* (*right two columns*)

In practical experiment, we will uniformly adopt Gaussian kernel with the size of 5×5 as smooth filter in the spatial domain, and in order to obtain smoother, continuous visualization, the video frames used in temporal domain are $T = 10$.

2.2   Social Force Model for Interaction Modeling

Mehran introduces social force model to computer vision field [9]. In this model, each pedestrian i with mass m_i, his/her speed can be defined as the following formula:

$$m_i \frac{dv_i}{dt} = F_a = F_p + F_{int}. \tag{1}$$

F_a is the resultant force of pedestrian, whose value equals to the sum of personal desired force F_p and interaction force F_{int}. Figure 2 is a graphical representation of social force model. Known that pedestrian in the crowd tends reach its destination in a walk. However, due to the obstacle of others and the environment barriers, the actual velocity v_i is different from the expected speed v_i^p. Consequently, one would try to exert a force F_p to achieve the expected speed:

$$F_p = \frac{1}{\tau} \left(v_i^p - v_i \right). \tag{2}$$

τ is a relaxation factor. According to (1) and (2), the key point of the work actually lies in how to represent the actual speed and expectation speed. In [9] Mehran expresses personal expectation speed and the actual speed as:

$$v_i^p = (1 - p_i)O(x_i, y_i) + p_i O_{ave}(x_i, y_i). \tag{3}$$

$$v_i = O_{ave}(x_i, y_i). \tag{4}$$

where p_i is defined as panic weight parameter, for normal scenario $p_i \rightarrow 0$; however, when the herding behavior occurs $p_i \rightarrow 1$. $O(x_i, y_i)$, $O_{ave}(x_i, y_i)$ represent optical flow and the spatio-temporal smooth optical flow in the coordinate (x_i, y_i) respectively. Therefore, we can obtain the interaction force in coordinate (x_i, y_i).

$$F_{int} = m_i \frac{dO_{ave}(x_i, y_i)}{dt} - \frac{1 - p_i}{\tau} (O(x_i, y_i) - O_{ave}(x_i, y_i)). \tag{5}$$

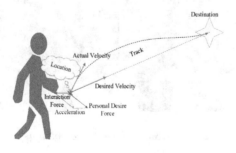

Fig. 2. A graphical representation of social force model

3   Modified Interaction Social Force Model

When solving the problem of anomaly detection using social force model, the key is how to present the particle's desired force. Mehran [9] takes expected speed described as the combination of optical flow and particle advection. However, as we discussed before, since the results of the optical flow field is unstable, a direct subtraction of these two flow field leads local popple. As for desired force, its physical meaning is the force that the individual exerts to achieve the desired speed. We assume that when a person and its surrounding people's movement speed are roughly the same, the force will be small relatively, to be the opposite, the force will shows a large value. We used desired force to measure the effect of surrounding particles put on the current particle movement, also the closer the particles locate, the stronger the force shows. As a result, on the basis of the particle advection field, we use two Gaussian kernel (G_1 and G_2) and the force flow field in convolution processing represent the particle's and its surrounding's motion respectively, so that the interaction force between particles can be expressed as formula (6):

$$F_{int} = (m \frac{dO_{ave}}{dt} - \frac{1-p}{\tau}(O_{ave} * G_1 - O_{ave} * G_2)) \times \Delta. \tag{6}$$

$$\Delta = (cos(O_{ave} * G_1, O_{ave} * G_2) + const)^{-1}. \tag{7}$$

The final results are multiplied by a variable Δ, where we use cosine of two different vector in the same position to measure the consistency of the object and its surroundings and $const = 2$ is added in formula (7) to ensure the denominator is positive and avoid 0.

As shown in Fig. 3, the top image shows social force calculated when a pedestrian is far away from the crowd, and the image below shows the social force calculated when a pedestrian is close to the crowd. With our method, a satisfying visual result can be obtained for retrograde of the pedestrians in the crowd. Besides, if the particles locate in a distance apart from each other, the interaction force would be small, in contrast, the closer the distance, the larger the interaction force could be. The final experiment results confirm our hypothesis.

Fig. 3. Visual effectiveness of *social force* (*green arrows*) calculated by modified model (Color figure online)

4   Experiments

As introduced before, we use BOW (Bag of Words) [14] to extract a set of local patches (visual words) as patterns over the field randomly and the codebook is generated through K-means. Then the LDA (Latent Dirichlet Allocation) model [15] is trained by normal samples. Finally, in test phase the outlier samples will be regarded as anomaly.

4.1   Dataset and Experiments Setting

In this work we mainly use UMN and Web datasets (Fig. 4). UMN contains 3 scenes and 11 fragments in total, including indoor and outdoor scenes. Web dataset is a challenging sequence of videos in open environments collected from websites. There are 20 videos including 12 for normal and the rest for anomaly (bullfight, gang fight, etc.). For each video we divide them into clips (10 frames) without overlap. In the phase of particle advection, the number of particles we put over is 60×60 which are much less than the video resolution for faster calculation. We use BOW to exact the visual words through a fixed window with the size of $5 \times 5 \times 10$. Only normal samples are used to train the LDA model, so $p_i = 0$.

Fig. 4. Some samples of *UMN (left two columns)* and *Web (right two columns)* dataset including *normal (left)* and *anomaly (right)*

4.2   Experiments on UMN

There are 3 scenes in the UMN, and we train and test each scene respectively. C (codebook) contains 10 words; L (latent topic) is 30 and P (patches) extracted from a clip is 30. Figure 5 shows the result of social force model and optical flow. The method based on optical flow has more omission and miscarriage of justice compared with social force model. Also these two methods have some omissions at the end of each anomaly, as there is no person in the last few frames of each abnormal scene, so there are no motion information extracted from these frames. Social force derives from optical flow but it can capture more motion information and more robust compared with the later.

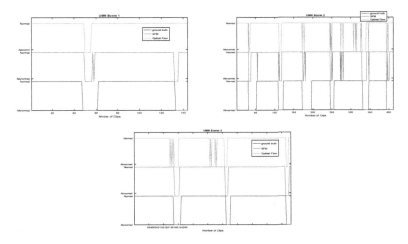

Fig. 5. Results of *SFM* (*red*) and *pure optical flow* (*green*) model (Color figure online)

4.3   Experiments on Web Dataset

Typical evaluating methods such as Accuracy and Precision may lose their efficiency for the number of each class's samples are often skew in anomaly detection problem. So in the following experiments we use the ROC and the AUC to evaluate the relevant methods. At first, we divide the 12 normal videos into 5 groups randomly, and select 4 groups to train the model, then the group left and 8 abnormal videos are chosen as test samples. The 5 groups are used for training and testing in turn and the final result achieved by averaging. Through the Fig. 6 we can find that the AUC is sensitive to the number of patches and the size of codebook, but insensitive to the number of latent topics. As the Fig. 7 (left) shows, with the same parameters setting (C = 50; L = 10; P = 40), social force model is superior to the optical flow and the particle advection based method. Out of our expectation, the particle advection based method give the worst performance. The reason can be got by analyzing the definition of particle advection. It is achieved through smoothing the optical flow field in both spatial and temporal field that it can restrain the local noise of optical flow, but the local

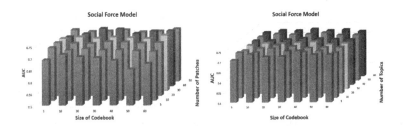

Fig. 6. A comparison of different parameters effecting the AUC

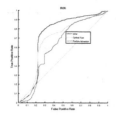 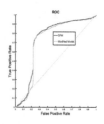

Fig. 7. The ROC curve of *SFM* (*blue*), *optical flow* (*green*), *particle advection* (*red*) and *modified model* (*golden*) (Color figure online)

anomaly is suppressed at the same time. We also apply the social force model and the modified model on the Web dataset, and compare them through AUC and standard deviation in Table 1. According the results, the modified model can achieve equivalent result as original model in average AUC and it is more robust with smaller standard deviation. Also, the reason why the performance doesn't improve is that the modified model is based on particle advection. Through the spatiotemporal smoothing process we get a more robust and successive visual representation, but a set of local information is lost during the procedure that plays an important role in anomaly detection. All of the methods discussed in our experiments can achieve real-time detection using MATLAB with Intel Xeon E5 3.5 GHz CPU and 16 GB RAM.

Table 1. The comparison of 4 methods average AUC on Web dataset and the standard deviation of SFM and the modified model

Model	AUC	Standard deviation
SFM	0.73	0.0196
Modified model	0.71	0.009
Optical flow	0.68	–
Particle advection	0.62	–

5   Discussion and Conclusion

The experiment results on different datasets confirm the superiority of social force model that, it is capable of capturing the interaction between the individual and the surrounding environment without tracking and segmentation, and can effectively deal with the crowded scene. Meanwhile, with its modification, the proposed method could obtain corresponding anomaly detection result in particular dataset, and providing better visual effect.

Our approach is based on optical flow information, there is no doubt that, only movement can produce optical flow. In the process of actual experiments, we found that when the movement speed of crowd is slow or even the moving is stop, our method cannot be used to extract optical flow then to estimate social force in the subsequent process. We will hereafter focus on combining video motion information with static information of video frames, to improve the description of motion pattern.

Acknowledgments. This work is supported by the National Key R&D Program of China under Grant 2017YFB0802300, the National Natural Science Foundation of China 61601223, Natural Science Foundation of Jiangsu Province BK20150756, and Post-doctoral Science Foundation of China 2015M580427.

References

1. Li, T., Chang, H., Wang, M., Ni, B., Hong, R., Yan, S.: Crowded scene analysis: a survey. IEEE Trans. CSVT **25**(3), 367–386 (2015)
2. Solmaz, B., Moore, B.E., Shah, M.: Identifying behaviors in crowd scenes using stability analysis for dynamical systems. IEEE Trans. PAMI **34**(10), 2064–2070 (2012)
3. Hassner, T., Itcher, Y., Klipergross, O.: Violent flows: real-time detection of violent crowd behavior. In: IEEE Conference on CVPR, pp. 1–6 (2012)
4. Mahadevan, V., Li, W., Bhalodia, V., et al.: Anomaly detection in crowded scenes. In: IEEE Conference on CVPR, pp. 1975–1981 (2010)
5. Shao, J., Kang, K., Loy, C.C., Wang, X.: Deeply learned attributes for crowded scene understanding. In: IEEE Conference on CVPR, pp. 4657–4666 (2015)
6. Shao, J., Loy, C., Kang, K., Wang, X.: Slicing convolutional neural network for crowd video understanding. In: IEEE Conference on CVPR, pp. 5620–5628 (2016)
7. Mohammadi, S., Perina, A., Kiani, H., Murino, V.: Angry crowds: detecting violent events in videos. In: Leibe, B., Matas, J., Sebe, N., Welling, M. (eds.) ECCV 2016. LNCS, vol. 9911, pp. 3–18. Springer, Cham (2016). doi:10.1007/978-3-319-46478-7_1
8. Helbing, D., Molnár, P.: Social force model for pedestrian dynamics. Phys. Rev. E **51**, 4282–4286 (1995)
9. Mehran, R., Oyama, A., Shah, M.: Abnormal crowd behavior detection using social force model. In: IEEE Conference on CVPR, pp. 935–942 (2009)
10. A website of UMN. http://mha.cs.umn.edu/movies/crowdactivity-all.avi
11. Hu, M., Ali, S., Shah, M.: Learning motion patterns in crowded scenes using motion flow field. In: ICPR, pp. 1–5 (2008)
12. Yang, Y., Liu, J., Shah, M.: Video scene understanding using multi-scale analysis. In: ICCV, pp. 1669–1676 (2009)
13. Ali, S., Shah, M.: A lagrangian particle dynamics approach for crowd flow segmentation and stability analysis. In: IEEE Conference on CVPR, pp. 1–6 (2007)
14. Feifei, L., Perona, P.: A Bayesian hierarchical model for learning natural scene categories. In: IEEE Conference on CVPR, pp. 524–531 (2005)
15. Blei, D., Ng, A., Jordan, M.: Latent dirichlet allocation. JMLR **3**, 993–1022 (2003)
16. Chen, W., Zhang, K., Liu, Q., et al.: Robust visual tracking via patch based kernel correlation filters with adaptive multiple feature ensemble. Neurocomputing **214**, 607–617 (2016)
17. Zhang, B., et al.: Adaptive local movement modeling for robust object tracking. IEEE Trans. CSVT **27**(7), 1515–1526 (2016)
18. Zhang, B., et al.: Bounding multiple gaussians uncertainty with application to object tracking. IJCV **118**(3), 364–379 (2016)

Robust Partial Person Re-identification Based on Similarity-Guided Sparse Representation

Min Ren[1,2,3], Lingxiao He[1,2,3], Haiqing Li[1,2(✉)], Yunfan Liu[1,2],
Zhenan Sun[1,2], and Tieniu Tan[1,2]

[1] Center for Research on Intelligent Perception and Computing,
CRIPAC, Beijing, China
yunfan.liu@cripac.ia.ac.cn
[2] Institute of Automation, Chinese Academy of Sciences, CASIA, Beijing, China
{renmin2017,tieniu.tan}@ia.ac.cn, {lingxiao.he,hqli,znsun}@nlpr.ia.ac.cn
[3] University of Chinese Academy of Sciences, UCAS,
Beijing 100190, People's Republic of China

Abstract. In this paper, we study the problem of partial person re-identification (re-id). This problem is more difficult than general person re-identification because the body in probe image is not full. We propose a novel method, similarity-guided sparse representation (SG-SR), as a robust solution to improve the discrimination of the sparse coding. There are three main components in our method. In order to include multi-scale information, a dictionary consisting of features extracted from multi-scale patches is established in the first stage. A low rank constraint is then enforced on the dictionary based on the observation that its subspaces of each class should have low dimensions. After that, a classification model is built based on a novel similarity-guided sparse representation which can choose vectors that are more similar to the probe feature vector. The results show that our method outperforms existing partial person re-identification methods significantly and achieves state-of-the-art accuracy.

Keywords: Partial person re-identification · Low rank constraint · Similarity-guided sparse representation

1 Introduction

Person re-identification, which aims to re-identify a specific person in scenes captured by camera after he/she disappears from another disjoint camera view, is particularly an important topic in camera networks study. In recent years, impressive progress has been made in person re-identification techniques [1].

But there are still some challenges for person re-identification techniques in real-world applications, such as view angle, illumination, posture, and occlusion. And situation in which only partial body available is common. This situation can be caused by occlusions of other people, obstacles that are stationary or moving, and the boundary of the camera view. Given a partial probe image, the goal

© Springer International Publishing AG 2017
J. Zhou et al. (Eds.): CCBR 2017, LNCS 10568, pp. 650–659, 2017.
https://doi.org/10.1007/978-3-319-69923-3_70

of re-identification is to find the same individual in a collection of whole body appearance in other views (gallery images). This problem has been addressed by Zheng et al. [2].

Partial person re-identification is more difficult than the general person re-identification problem. First of all, since the amount of information contained by a probe image is less than that in general problem, distinctive features are more likely to be lost, thus increase the chance of mismatching. Secondly, it is hard to normalize and compare the probe images and gallery images due to the scaling issues, as we do not know the proportion of the partial body to the full appearance. The last challenge is that we are unable to know which part of the person is covered by objects and which part of the whole body the partial probe should match with.

To tackle these problems, we propose a new re-identification framework which contains three components. The first component is a multi-scale feature extractor, which extracts feature vectors without normalization of images. The second part of our method is enforcing a low rank constraint on the components of dictionary of each person, so that the features invariant with respect to disturbances could be distilled and the noise could be suppressed. The third component of our framework is a classifier based on similarity-guided sparse representation which is constrained by coefficient of similarity.

The main contributions of this work are: (1) a new partial person re-identification model is proposed in which low rank method is applied, (2) a novel similarity-guided sparse representation is proposed and it is found to be effective, (3) the model proposed achieves state-of-the-art performance.

2   Related Works

Person re-identification has become increasingly popular in computer vision community. To solve this problem, various approaches have been proposed throughout years, including methods based on transferred metric learning [3], post-rank [4], and spatial-temporal [5]. Recently, deep learning [6,7] and video-based modelling [8] were also introduced for person re-identification. However, these algorithms are all based on the assumption that whole body is available in the probe and gallery images. Part-based models are proposed to handle the problem of incomplete body appearance in probe images, offering robust solutions to person re-identification under partial occlusions. In [9], the authors provided a part-based deep hashing model to solve the problem. Sparse representation based method and low-rank attribute embedding model for person re-identification were discussed in [11] and [10], respectively.

The problem of partial person re-identification remains unsolved as much more difficulties will be encountered than in general re-identification problems. As far as we know, partial person re-identification was first addressed in [2], and a matching framework named AMC-SWM was proposed in the work. This framework consists of two parts: a local patch-level matching model and a global part-based matching model. For super-resolution re-identification, an approach which applied low rank regularization and dictionary learning was proposed in [21]. The experiments in [21] shown that low rank regularization could improve the matching rate. Beyond person re-identification, challenge of occlusions has been studied broadly in other computer vision problems, especially in face recognition. A maximum correntropy criterion based sparse algorithm was proposed in [12]. Low-rank matrix recovery [13] and low-rank dictionary learning [14] were also used for robust face recognition. Multi-modal low-rank dictionary learning method for face recognition was proposed in [15]. An alignment free approach for partial face recognition was proposed in [16]. Robust partial face recognition using instance-to-class distance model was proposed in [17]. Sparse representation and collaborative representation were discussed in [18] and a new framework for face recognition was proposed in the same work. Low rank approach and sparse representation were applied to image classification [22]. The methods based on low rank and sparse representation inspired us to employ low rank constraints in partial person re-identification problem and propose a novel sparse representation as a classifier.

3   Methodology

In our work, we consider the partial person re-identification as matching the probe images containing only part of the body with the gallery of whole body images. We manually cropped out the regions of visible body parts from the probe images and then apply the entire algorithm. Our framework consists of three components (Fig. 1): a multi-scale feature extractor, constraint on feature dictionary and similarity-guided sparse representation.

(1) The multi-scale feature extractor computes features from patches sampled from image pyramids. After that, a feature dictionary is established based on the feature vectors extracted from all gallery images.
(2) The second component is to enforce low rank constraint on the dictionary. To be concrete, every part of the dictionary that belongs to the same person could be represented as the summation of a low rank matrix and a sparse matrix. The matrix with low dimensions contains features invariant with respect to disturbances, and the sparse matrix could be considered as noise. Hence, we are able to reduce the influence of the noise by constituting a new dictionary with the low dimension matrix of each class.
(3) A classifier based on similarity-guided sparse representation is then built upon the purified feature dictionary. We measure the similarities between the feature vector of probe image and vectors in the dictionary by a similarity-guided term. And we incorporate this similarity-guided term in the objective function in the sparse representation proposed.

3.1   Multi-scale Feature Extraction

People could appear at various distances that are unknown to the monitoring cameras. Lacking prior knowledge on the location of the target would result

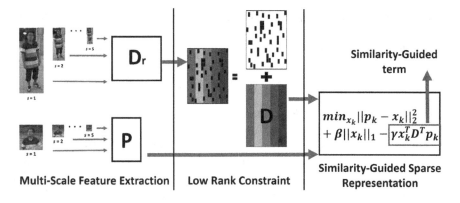

Fig. 1. Framework of our method. Multi-scale feature is extracted in the first portion, low rank constraint is enforced on the feature dictionary in the second portion, and then similarity-guided sparse representation is used to classify the probe images in the third portion

in scaling issue as we do not know how to normalize the probe and gallery images. Besides, in partial person re-identification problem, we are also unaware of the proportion of the partial body to the whole body in another camera view. Therefore, we can not normalize the probe images and gallery images accordingly. To solver this problem, following operations are taken to every gallery image as follows.

(1) If the size of the input image is $W \times H$ and the image pyramid is built with scale S, there will be S images in each image pyramid and the size of the images are $\frac{sW}{S} \times \frac{sH}{S}$, where $s = \{1, 2, \ldots, S\}$.
(2) Segment the images in image pyramid into patches with the same size $L \times L$, where $L = \frac{min(W,H)}{S}$. The sample stride is selected to be L so that there is no overlap between patches.
(3) Resize all the patches to be 20×20 and then extract feature vectors from all the patches.

The feature vector of each patch consists of three components. The first component is the 20-bin histogram of 8 color channels (RGB, YCbCr, HS). The second part is the HOG descriptors (279 dimensions). LBP histogram (256 dimensions) is also included in the feature vector. Concatenating these descriptors gives us a feature vector of 695 dimensions for each patch.

Suppose there are M persons in the gallery, each person has C images and there are $K_{m,c}$ patches in one image. Grouping the feature vectors of the m-th person gives us $D_m = \{D_{m,1}, D_{m,2}, \ldots, D_{m,C}\}$, where $D_{m,c}$ is the collection of feature vectors of the c-th image, every column of $D_{m,c}$ correspond to a patch of the image pyramid and $D_{m,c} \in R^{695 \times K_{m,c}}$. The feature dictionary of the gallery images could be represented as $D_r = \{D_1, D_2, \ldots, D_M\}$, and $D_m \in R^{695 \times \sum\limits_{c} K_{m,c}}$.

Same operations are applied to the probe image as well. The collection of feature vectors extracted from the probe image is: $P = \{p_1, p_2, \ldots, p_K\}$, where p_k is the feature of a patch.

3.2   Low-Rank Constraint on Feature Dictionary

As mentioned in Sect. 3.1, D_m contains information of the m-th person and could be decomposed into two separate parts: (1) the features of the m-th person that are invariant with respect to view angle, posture, lighting conditions and other variations, (2) undesired resultant noise. We assume that the first component A_m is low-rank while the second component E_m is sparse, and A_m is more discriminative than D_m for robust matching. Therefore, we could write the decomposition of D_m as follow:

$$D_m = A_m + E_m \tag{1}$$

With restrictions on rank and sparsity, this problem could be represented as:

$$\min \ rank(A_m) + \lambda ||E_m||_0 \quad s.t. \quad D_m = A_m + E_m \tag{2}$$

This is a NP-hard problem, while remaining convex, it could be relaxed as:

$$\min \ ||A_m||_* + \lambda ||E_m||_1 \quad s.t. \quad D_m = A_m + E_m \tag{3}$$

where $||A_m||_*$ is the trace-norm of A_m. We implement the augmented Lagrange multiplier method mentioned in [14] to solve the decomposition problem and the new feature dictionary could then be written as $D = \{A_1, A_2, \ldots, A_M\}$.

3.3   Similarity-Guided Sparse Representation

We could then transform the matching problem into a sparse representation and classification problem:

$$\min_{x_k} \ ||x_k||_1 \quad s.t. \quad p_k = Dx_k \tag{4}$$

where p_k is the feature of a patch of the probe image, and x_k is the sparse coding of p_k. In order to eliminate the constraint, we relax the optimization problem as follows:

$$\min_{x_k} \ ||p_k - Dx_k||_2^2 + \beta ||x_k||_1 \tag{5}$$

When rebuilding the probe feature vector, we would like to choose vectors which are more similar to the probe feature vector to improve the discrimination of the sparse coding.

The angular similarity between the probe feature vector and vectors in the dictionary could be evaluated using inner product of D^T and p_k. Hence, elements of $D^T p_k$ measure the angular similarity between p_k and corresponding column of D in vector space, in other words, the similarity between patch of probe image and corresponding patch in gallery. And $x_k^T D^T p_k$ is inner product of x_k and $D^T p_k$, it measures the oriented similarity between x_k and $D^T p_k$ in vector space. Hence, the larger $x_k^T D^T p_k$ is, the vectors of D chosen to rebuild p_k is more similar to the probe feature vector. Accordingly, the above equation could be extended to:

$$\min_{x_k} ||p_k - Dx_k||_2^2 + \beta||x_k||_1 - \gamma x_k^T D^T p_k \tag{6}$$

where γ is the coefficient of similarity. Unfolding this equation gives us:

$$\min_{x_k} \frac{1}{2} x_k^T D^T D x_k - (1 + \frac{1}{2}\gamma) x_k^T D^T p_k + \beta||x_k||_1 \tag{7}$$

According to the discussion in [19], this optimization problem could be solved by feature-sign search method. Following this algorithm we could obtain the sparse coding matrix: $X = \{x_1, x_2, \ldots, x_K\}$. The residual error could then be computed as r_m:

$$r_m = ||P - D_m X_m||_F^2 \tag{8}$$

where X_m is the submatrix of X that contains only the columns corresponding to the m-th person. The classifying problem could finally be represented as:

$$m = \arg\min_m \frac{r_m}{K} \tag{9}$$

in which K is the number of the columns of X_m.

4   Experiments

4.1   Datasets and Benchmark Methods

The Partial REID Dataset [2] is the only publicly available partial person re-id dataset. It contains 600 images of 60 people, with 5 full-body images and 5 partial images per person. These images are collected at university campus with different viewpoints as well as background settings, and the partial images contain different types of severe occlusions (Fig. 2).

The QMUL underGround Re-IDentification (GRID) dataset [20] used frequently in re-identification study contains 250 persons and each person is shown by a image pair. Each pair has two images of the same individual seen from different camera views. All images are captured from 8 disjoint camera views installed in a busy underground station. Figure 2 shows a snapshot of camera views in the station and sample images in the GRID dataset. This dataset is challenging due to variations of postures, colours, and illumination conditions; as well as poor image quality caused by low spatial resolution. We randomly crop half of the images of each person to simulate severe occlusions (Fig. 2).

For benchmarking, five existing methods were considered, including AMC-SWM proposed [2], collaborative representation based classification method (CRC-RLS) [18], an alignment-free approach named MTSR proposed [16], discriminative low-rank dictionary learning (DLR) method [14], and method using instance-to-class distance (I2C-Distance) proposed in [17]. We chose some of the partial face recognition methods because they were also designed to solve partial target recognition.

Fig. 2. Examples of partial person images (first row) and the corresponding full images (second row). Columns 1–5 are from Partial REID Dataset, and columns 6–10 are from GRID dataset. (Color figure online)

4.2   Experimental Settings and Evaluations

Both single-shot and multi-shot experiments were conducted. For efficiency of experiments, we randomly selected 100 people from GRID dataset for experiments and all 60 people in Partial REID Dataset were used. In single-shot experiments, only one ($N = 1$) image of each person is included in the gallery set. Multi-shot re-identification indicates that more than one ($N = 2$, $N = 3$) images of each person are used in the gallery. The multi-shot experiments are conducted only on Partial REID Dataset.

There are three parameters in our model, the multi-scale number S, coefficient of low rank (λ in Eq. 3), and coefficient of similarity (γ in Eq. 6). The multi-scale number S was set as 5 in all the experiments. In single-shot experiments, coefficient of low rank was set as 0.4, coefficient of similarity was set as 1.2. In multi-shot experiments, coefficient of low rank was set as 0.7, coefficient of similarity was set as 1.7. Discussions of these parameters can be seen in Sect. 4.4.

We employed cumulative match characteristic (CMC) to measure the matching performance in closed-set setting. To evaluate the performance of our method in open-set setting, we randomly removed 30% (the same percentage with [2]) people and their corresponding images from the gallery and provide the area-under-curve (AUC) values of ROC curves for evaluation.

4.3   Results

Single-Shot Experiments. In single-shot re-identification experiments, we compared SLR-SRM to other existing methods including AMC-SWM, CRC-RLS, MTSR, DLR, and I2C-Distance. The results shown in Table 1 demonstrate clearly that the performance of our method is better than other five methods on both of the two datasets (achieved 55% and 32% matching rate at rank-1). AMC-SWM is the method with minimal gap comparing to our approach (achieved 45% and 20% matching rate at rank-1).

Table 1. Single-shot experiments

Partial REID N = 1				GRID N = 1			
Method	rank-1	rank-5	rank-10	AUC	rank-1	rank-5	rank-10	AUC
SG-SR	**55.0%**	**78.3%**	**86.7%**	**0.925**	**32.0%**	**45.0%**	**54.0%**	**0.860**
AMC-SWM	45.0%	60.0%	70.0%	0.806	20.0%	41.0%	52.0%	0.782
DLR	23.3%	58.3%	66.7%	0.783	14.0%	34.0%	49.0%	0.779
I2C-Distance	15.0%	46.7%	63.3%	0.645	15.0%	31.0%	47.0%	0.734
MTSR	15.0%	30.0%	40.0%	0.668	12.0%	37.0%	50.0%	0.765
CRC-RLS	1.67%	15.0%	28.3%	0.548	2.00%	13.0%	23.0%	0.617

Table 2. Multi-shot experiments

Partial REID N = 2				Partial REID N = 3			
Method	rank-1	rank-5	rank-10	AUC	rank-1	rank-5	rank-10	AUC
SG-SR	**61.7%**	**81.7%**	**86.7%**	**0.934**	**65.0%**	**81.7%**	**88.3%**	**0.956**
AMC-SWM	53.3%	70.0%	76.7%	0.884	55.0%	71.7%	78.3%	0.915
DLR	31.7%	66.7%	75.0%	0.848	31.7%	65.0%	73.3%	0.901
I2C-Distance	26.7%	50.0%	71.7%	0.706	25.0%	51.7%	71.7%	0.733
MTSR	25.0%	46.7%	61.7%	0.808	28.3%	65.0%	75.0%	0.902
CRC-RLS	5.00%	15.0%	38.3%	0.616	20.0%	46.7%	58.3%	0.737

Multi-shot Experiments. In multi-shot re-identification experiments ($N = 2$, $N = 3$), as shown in Table 2, the matching rate at rank-1 increases to 61.7% ($N = 2$), 65.0% ($N = 3$). Again, our approach outperforms all other methods.

4.4 Discussions

The matching rate at rank-1 on Partial REID Dataset under different multi-scale number S was shown in Fig. 3 (left). The results shown that the matching rate

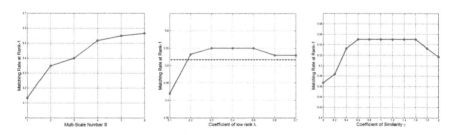

Fig. 3. Evaluation of different multi-scale number S (left), coefficient of low rank λ (middle) and coefficient of similarity γ (right) using matching rate at rank-1 on Partial REID ($N = 1$).

increased as S increased. But the time of recognition was also increased as S increased. So we need to choose an appropriate value of S.

The matching rate under different value of coefficient of low rank was shown in Fig. 3 (middle). The matching rate without low rank constraint was expressed by the imaginary line. The results shown that appropriate value of coefficient of low rank could increase the matching rate by 3.3%.

The matching rate under different value of coefficient of similarity was shown in Fig. 3 (right). The results shown that the matching rate could be increased 8.3% compared with $\gamma = 0$. It demonstrate that similarity-guided sparse representation proposed could improve the discrimination of the sparse coding.

5   Conclusions

In this work, we have proposed a novel framework for partial person re-identification problem. This framework consisted of multi-scale feature extraction, low rank constraint and similarity-guided sparse representation. Our experiments have shown that our approach is more effective than existing methods to solve partial person re-identification. The reasons can be summarized as follow: (1) patches sampled from the image pyramid contain information of different scales, (2) the low rank constraint makes the feature vectors of dictionary more discriminative, (3) the similarity-guided sparse representation makes the vectors of dictionary which are more similar to the probe are more likely to be chosen, thus improves the matching accuracy.

Acknowledgements. This work is supported by the Beijing Municipal Science and Technology Commission (No. Z161100000216144) and the National Natural Science Foundation of China (Grant Nos. 61427811, 61573360).

References

1. Zheng, L., Yang, Y., Hauptmann, A.G.: Person re-identification: past, present and future. CoRR abs/1610.02984 (2016)
2. Zheng, W.S., Li, X., Xiang, T., Liao, S., Lai, J., Gong, S.: Partial person re-identication. In: IEEE International Conference on Computer Vision, pp. 4678–4686 (2015)
3. Li, W., Zhao, R., Wang, X.: Human reidentification with transferred metric learning. In: Lee, K.M., Matsushita, Y., Rehg, J.M., Hu, Z. (eds.) ACCV 2012 Part I. LNCS, vol. 7724, pp. 31–44. Springer, Heidelberg (2013). doi:10.1007/978-3-642-37331-2_3
4. Liu, C., Loy, C.C., Gong, S., Wang, G.: POP: person re-identification post-rank optimisation. In: IEEE International Conference on Computer Vision, pp. 441–448 (2013)
5. Lian, G., Lai, J., Zheng, W.S.: Spatial-temporal consistent labeling of tracked pedestrians across non-overlapping camera views. Pattern Recogn. **44**, 1121–1136 (2011)
6. Wu, L., Shen, C., Hengel, A.V.D.: PersonNet: person re-identification with deep convolutional neural networks. CoRR abs/1601.07255 (2016)

7. Li, D., Chen, X., Zhang, Z., Huang, K.: Learning deep context-aware feature over body and latent parts for person re-identification. In: Proceedings of the IEEE Conference on Computer Vision and Pattern Recognition (2017)
8. You, J., Wu, A., Li, X., Zheng, W.S.: Top-push video-based person re-identification. In: IEEE Conference on Computer Vision and Pattern Recognition, pp. 1345–1353 (2016)
9. Zhu, F., Kong, X., Zheng, L., Fu, H., Tian, Q.: Part-based deep hashing for large-scale person re-identification. IEEE Trans. Image Process. **PP**, 1 (2017)
10. An, L., Chen, X., Yang, S., Bhanu, B.: Sparse representation matching for person re-identification. Inf. Sci. **355–356**, 74–89 (2016)
11. Su, C., Yang, F., Zhang, S., Tian, Q., Davis, L.S., Gao, W.: Multi-task learning with low rank attribute embedding for person re-identification. In: IEEE International Conference on Computer Vision, pp. 3739–3747 (2016)
12. He, R., Zheng, W.S., Hu, B.G.: Maximum correntropy criterion for robust face recognition. IEEE Trans. Pattern Anal. Mach. Intell. **33**, 1561–76 (2011)
13. Chen, C.F., Wei, C.P., Wang, Y.C.F.: Low-rank matrix recovery with structural incoherence for robust face recognition. In: Computer Vision and Pattern Recognition, pp. 2618–2625 (2012)
14. Nguyen, H., Yang, W., Sheng, B., Sun, C.: Discriminative low-rank dictionary learning for face recognition. Neurocomputing **173**, 541–551 (2016)
15. Foroughi, H., Shakeri, M., Ray, N., Zhang, H.: Face recognition using multi-modal low-rank dictionary learning. Computing Research Repository (2017)
16. Liao, S., Jain, A.K., Li, S.Z.: Partial face recognition: alignment-free approach. IEEE Trans. Pattern Anal. Mach. Intell. **35**, 1193 (2013)
17. Hu, J., Lu, J., Tan, Y.P.: Robust partial face recognition using instance-to-class distance. In: Visual Communications and Image Processing, pp. 1–6 (2014)
18. Zhang, L., Yang, M., Feng, X.: Sparse representation or collaborative representation: which helps face recognition? In: International Conference on Computer Vision, pp. 471–478 (2011)
19. Lee, H., Battle, A., Raina, R., Ng, A.Y.: Efficient sparse coding algorithms. In: International Conference on Neural Information Processing Systems, pp. 801–808 (2006)
20. Liu, C., Gong, S., Loy, C.C., Lin, X.: Person re-identification: what features are important? In: Fusiello, A., Murino, V., Cucchiara, R. (eds.) ECCV 2012 Part I. LNCS, vol. 7583, pp. 391–401. Springer, Heidelberg (2012). doi:10.1007/978-3-642-33863-2_39
21. Jing, X.-Y., Zhu, X., Wu, F., Hu, R., You, X., Wang, Y., Feng, H., Yang, J.-Y.: Super-resolution person re-identification with semi-coupled low-rank discriminant dictionary learning. In: 2015 IEEE Conference on Computer Vision and Pattern Recognition (CVPR), pp. 695–704 (2015)
22. Zhu, X., Jing, X.-Y., Wu, F., Wu, D., Cheng, L., Li, S., Hu, R.: Multi-kernel low-rank dictionary pair learning for multiple features based image classification. In: AAAI (2017)

Person Re-identification by Integrating Static Texture and Shape Cues

Canaan Tinotenda Madongo[1], Di Huang[1], and Jiaxin Chen[2(✉)]

[1] Laboratory of Intelligent Recognition and Image Processing,
School of Computer Science and Engineering,
Beihang University, Beijing 100191, China
ctmadongo@yahoo.co.uk, dhuang@buaa.edu.cn
[2] Department of Electrical and Computer Engineering,
New York University Abu Dhabi, Abu Dhabi, UAE
chenjiaxinX@gmail.com

Abstract. Person Re-Identification (Re-ID) is a challenging task with wide ranging applications in various fields. This paper presents a novel hand-crafted method for this issue, enhancing the state of the art ones in literature in two aspects. In contrast to most current studies that analyze texture features, we propose a discriminative and compact shape feature by applying Procrustes shape analysis. It not only retains shape distinctiveness of an individual sample, but also alleviates cross-view impacts. Furthermore, we combine the shape feature with some current popular texture features, namely LOMO and mid-level filters, so that the advantages of multiple clues can be jointly used. A score level fusion strategy is finally adopted to optimally integrate their credits. Evaluated on two public benchmarks, i.e. VIPeR and CUHK03, the proposed method achieves very competitive results, indicating its effectiveness in person Re-ID.

Keywords: Person re-identification · Shape analysis · Feature fusion

1 Introduction

Person Re-IDentification (Re-ID) is one of the major aspects of intelligent surveil-lance systems, especially in cases where more than one camera is used. It compares the identities of visual appearances across cameras and assists human operators so that they can efficiently and reliably fulfill critical security tasks. For example, in con-trolled environments, such as airports, banks, and car parks, it is desirable to quickly detect the threats from the person who is misbehaving. Despite the efforts made in the past several years, person Re-ID is still a very challenging issue, since changes in illumination, viewpoint, occlusion, etc., largely degrade its performance.

Human appearance representation plays a very important role in person Re-ID, and features extracted are expected to be sufficiently discriminative and highly robust to the challenges aforementioned. Many existing approaches focus on this aspect [1–8] and we witness the development from hand-crafted features to deep learning based ones. **The former** are in general artificially designed and recent representatives perform well in distinguishing different subjects. Bazzani *et al.* [3] propose an

© Springer International Publishing AG 2017
J. Zhou et al. (Eds.): CCBR 2017, LNCS 10568, pp. 660–669, 2017.
https://doi.org/10.1007/978-3-319-69923-3_71

approach to characterize the appearance of individuals exploiting body visual clues. The characteristics are extracted using an appearance-based descriptor following symmetry and asymmetry perceptual principles. It allows to segregate meaningful body parts from the background clutter. Liao *et al.* [1] introduce an effective feature, namely Local Maximal Occurrence (LOMO), which analyzes the horizontal occurrence of local features and maximizes the occurrence to achieve a stable representation against viewpoint changes. Zhao *et al.* [9] present a method to learn mid-level filters from automatically discovered patch clusters by pruning hierarchical clustering trees, and the filters are reputed to have good cross-view invariance. **The latter** are hierarchically learnt from a large set of training samples through deep learning models and more recently in end-to-end frameworks. Bak and Carr [10] propose to learn a deep texture representation from intensity images using Convolutional Neural Networks (CNNs) and the embedding produced is color-invariant and shows high performance even on unseen datasets without fine-tuning. In [11], Cheng *et al.* present a multi-channel and part-based CNN model under the triplet framework. The model jointly learns both global full-body and local body-part features and is trained by an improved triplet loss function. This loss pulls the instances of the same person closer and pushes the ones of different persons farther from each other. Chen *et al.* [12] further design a quadruplet loss for the CNN model, leading to the model output with a larger inter-class variation and a smaller intra-class similarity.

The studies mentioned above point out that the difference between viewpoints is the dominant factor which person Re-ID systems suffer from. Although all the hand-crafted features demonstrate their own robustness, due to human cognition limitation, there still exists certain room for performance improvement in single feature spaces. Furthermore, deep features prove more powerful than the hand-crafted ones; however, they generally require a huge amount of training images to feed neutral networks.

In this paper, we present a novel hand-crafted method for person Re-ID, which enhances the state of the art ones in the literature in two aspects. On the one hand, different from most current studies that mainly analyze texture features, we propose a discriminative and compact shape representation by applying Procrustes shape analysis as well as complex vector configurations. It not only retains shape distinctiveness of an individual sample, but also alleviates cross-view influence. On the other hand, we combine the shape feature with some current popular texture features, namely LOMO and mid-level filters, so that the advantages of multiple clues can be jointly used in recognition. A score level fusion strategy is finally adopted to optimally integrate their contributions. Figure 1 illustrates the overview of the proposed method. Evaluated on two public benchmarks, *i.e.*, **VIPeR** and **CUHK03**, our method achieves very competitive results, indicating its effectiveness in person Re-ID.

The remainder of the paper are organized as follows. Section 2 describes the proposed Procrustes shape analysis based appearance representation in detail. Section 3 presents the off-the-shelf features for combination and the fusion scheme. Experimental results are displayed and discussed in Sect. 4. Section 5 concludes the paper.

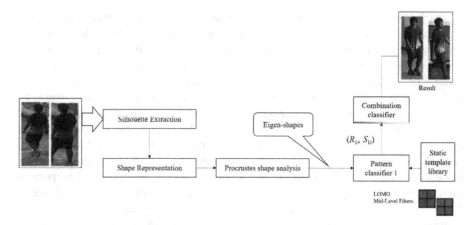

Fig. 1. Overview of the proposed method.

2 Discriminative and Compact Shape Representation

To the best of our knowledge, the majority of existing person Re-ID approaches ex-tract human appearance features to measure similarities between samples, where shape information is almost lost. However, we believe shape clues still capture the distinctiveness of the human body if they are properly described. Therefore, we pro-pose a novel method to represent the human shape, and the feature proves compact and discriminative. It is introduced in detail in the subsequent.

Silhouette Extraction. Before extracting the shape feature, we first segment the person figure from the background image. We adopt the technique proposed in [13], an approach based on optimization by graph-cut. Interactive foreground/background segmentation in still images is of great practical importance. Figure 2 shows an illustration of this procedure.

Fig. 2. Illustration of silhouette extraction.

Shape Vectorization. As the contour of the human body is generated, we compute its shape centroid, de-noted as (x_c, y_c). Let the centroid be the origin of a two-dimensional (2-D) shape space. We can unwrap the boundary as a set of pixel points along the outer contour counter-clockwise in a complex coordinate. That is, each shape can be described as a vector consisting of complex numbers with boundary elements. This process is demonstrated in Fig. 3.

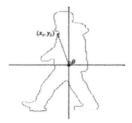

Fig. 3. Illustration of vectorization of human shape.

Specifically, the shape centroid (x_c, y_c) is calculated as:

$$x_c = \frac{1}{k}\sum_{i=1}^{k} x_i, \quad y_c = \frac{1}{k}\sum_{i=1}^{k} y_i \tag{1}$$

where k is the total number of boundary pixels and (x_i, y_i) is a pixel on the boundary. The silhouettes can thus be described as $z = [z_1, z_2, ..., z_k]^T$, where $z_i = x_i + j \cdot y_i$, in a common coordinate system.

Procrustes Shape Analysis. After vectorization, the silhouette is then reconstructed using Eigenshapes according to Procrustes shape analysis. The corresponding coefficients are regarded as its dis-criminative and compact shape representation.

Procrustes analysis [14] is a form of statistical shape analysis that is used to analyze the distribution of a set of shapes, where Procrustes Superimposition (PS) is performed by optimally translating, rotating and uniformly scaling the objects. In other words, both the placements and sizes of the objects are adjusted by minimizing a measure of shape difference, called the Procrustes distance.

A 2-D shape can be described by a vector of k complex numbers, $z = [z_1, z_2, ..., z_k]^T$, namely a configuration. For two shapes, z_1 and z_2, their configurations can be transformed to each other through a combination of translation, scaling, and rotation:

$$z_1 = \alpha 1_k + \beta z_2, \alpha, \beta \in C, \beta = |\beta| e^{j\angle\beta} \tag{2}$$

where $\alpha 1_k$ translates z_2, and $|\beta|$ and $\angle\beta$ scale and rotate z_2. To center shapes, the centered configuration is defined as $u = [u_1, u_2, ..., u_k]^T$, $u_i = z_i - \bar{z}$, $\bar{z} = \sum_{i=1}^{k} z_i/k$. The full Procrustes distance between two configurations u_1 and u_2 can be defined as:

$$d_F(u_1, u_2) = 1 - |u_1^* u_2|^2 / (\|u_1\|^2 \|u_2\|^2) \tag{3}$$

where the superscript * represents the complex conjugation transpose. This Procrustes distance directly measures the similarity between human shapes, where a bigger value indicates a lower similarity and a smaller value indicates a higher one.

3   Texture Feature and Multiple Feature Fusion

In order to comprehensively capture the characteristics of the human body, besides the shape feature, two off-the-shelf features that prove discriminative in texture description, namely Local Maximal Occurrence features (LOMO) and mid-level filters, are adopted. To keep the integrity, in this section, we first briefly review the two local features, and then introduce the fusion strategy.

3.1   Texture Feature Extraction

LOMO analyzes horizontal occurrences of local features and maximizes them to stably represent image patches of human bodies [1], and it reports high performance in person Re-ID. The application of Retinex considers human lightness and color perception and simultaneous application of multi-scale Retinex [6, 15] is implemented to combine small scale Retinex for dynamic feature range compression and large scale Retinex for tonal rendition. After the former, the Scale Invariant Local Ternary Pattern (SILTP) [16] descriptor is applied for lighting invariant texture representation. LOMO hence encodes both color constancy and dynamic range compression, achieving a good approximation to human visual perception. The features are extracted from 16×8 rectangular patches sampled from the image with a grid of 8×4 pixels, *i.e.*, 50% overlap in both directions. Different local features (HSV, Lab and LBP histograms) are extracted from overlapping regions and then concatenated to a single feature vector. We use KISS metric (KISSME) to measure the similarity between the gallery and the probe images. KISSME is one of the Mahalanobis distance learning methods which are obtained from the view of statistical inference.

Mid-level filters [9] are also adopted to capture texture properties. Discriminative and representative local patches are collected to build such filters. Coherent patch clusters are produced by pruning hierarchical clustering trees, and a simple but effective cross-view training strategy is employed to learn filters that are view invariant and discriminative in distinguishing identities. Local patches on a dense grid are extracted. The patch is of the size 10×10 and the grid step is 5 pixels. Color histograms and SIFT features in each LAB channel are computed for a given patch. To quantify the discriminative and generalization power, the pAUC score is calculated based on the distances obtained in constrained patch matching. Patches in a parent node is divided into 4 children nodes and shallow nodes are decomposed into deep nodes in hierarchical clustering. The shallow nodes represent coarse clusters while the deep nodes denote finer clusters. Shallow nodes contain patches with different color and texture patterns while the patch patterns in the deep nodes are more coherent. For integrating the filter responses $\hat{\mathbf{f}}_*^{A,u}$ and $\hat{\mathbf{f}}_*^{B,v}$ with the initial matching scores in (4) into a unified matching model,

$$s_0\left(\mathbf{x}^{A,u}, \mathbf{x}^{B,v}\right) = \mathbf{w}_p^{\mathrm{T}} \mathbf{s}_p\left(\mathbf{x}^{A,u}, \mathbf{x}^{B,v}\right); \tag{4}$$

$$s_{int}\left(\mathbf{x}^{A,u}, \mathbf{x}^{B,v}\right) = \mathbf{w}^{\mathrm{T}} \mathbf{\Phi}\left(\mathbf{x}^{A,u}, \mathbf{x}^{B,v}, \hat{\mathbf{f}}_*^{A,u}, \hat{\mathbf{f}}_*^{B,v}\right); \tag{5}$$

$$\mathbf{\Phi}\left(\mathbf{x}^{A,u}, \mathbf{x}^{B,v}\right)^{\mathrm{T}} = \left[\mathbf{s}_p\left(\mathbf{x}^{A,u}, \mathbf{x}^{B,v}\right)^{\mathrm{T}}, \mathbf{s}_f\left(\mathbf{f}_*^{A,u}, \hat{\mathbf{f}}_*^{B,v}\right)^{\mathrm{T}}\right]; \tag{6}$$

$$\mathbf{s}_f\left(\mathbf{f}_*^{A,u}, \hat{\mathbf{f}}_*^{B,v}\right) = \left[s_{f_1}, \ldots, s_{fNnode}\right]^{\mathrm{T}}; \tag{7}$$

$$s_{fk} = \exp\left(-\left(\mathbf{f}_{k*}^{A,u} - \hat{\mathbf{f}}_{k*}^{B,v}\right)^2 / \sigma_f^2; \tag{8}$$

where $\mathbf{s}_p(\mathbf{x}^{A,u}, \mathbf{x}^{B,v})$ is the patch matching score defined in (4), s_{fk} is the matching score between the k-th filter responses $\mathbf{f}_{k*}^{A,u}$ and $\mathbf{f}_{k*}^{B,v}$, σ_f is a bandwidth parameter, and $\mathbf{w}$ is the unified weighting parameters which are learned by RankSVM training [9].

3.2 Classifiers and Fusion Rules

Similar to [14], we use the Nearest Classifier with class exemplar (ENN) for re-identifying the humans in the shape and texture feature spaces. It assigns a given sample with the label of its nearest-neighbor exemplar. There is no doubt a more sophisticated classifier probably lead to better performance, but the interest here is to evaluate the genuine discriminatory ability of the features extracted. We fuse the Discriminative and Compact Shape Representation, LOMO, and mid-level filters at the matching score level by using different rules. To measure similarity, we make use of the Procrustes mean shape distance defined in (3) for the shape feature. For LOMO and mid-level filters, KISS metric (KISSME) to measure the similarity between the gallery and the probe images.

There exist many fusion schemes in biometric recognition and a few representatives are discussed in [14]. After the score for each feature is available, one generally cannot directly combine these scores in a statistically meaningful way because these scores are usually not direct estimates of the posterior but rather measures of the distances between the test and reference samples. The scores, with quite different ranges and distributions, should be transformed to be comparable before fusion (the logistic function $e^{(\alpha + \beta x)}/\left(1 + e^{(\alpha + \beta x)}\right)$ is used in this paper). Let $r(n, R_i)$ be the rank of the class with name in the ranking; this rule is defined as $\arg\min_n \left(n_k, \sum_{j=1}^R p(n_k, R_j)\right)$ [14]. If the score functions are directly comparable, the simplest way to combine classifiers is to compute the sum of the score functions. Let $s(n, S_i)$ be the score of the class with name n in S_j; this rule is defined as $\arg\min_n \left(n_k, \sum_{j=1}^R p(n_k, S_j)\right)$ [14], *i.e.*, the class with the lowest score sum is the final choice.

4 Experimental Results

To evaluate the performance of our approach, we run experiments on **VIPeR** and **CUHK03**, the standard benchmark databases for single-shot scenarios. A popular measure of performance for Re-ID is Cumulative Match Characteristics (CMC). It indicates the probability that the correct match is included in top-n matches.

The evaluation protocol for VIPeR involves splitting data into a training and test set of equal size. Thus, despite the fact that our system does not require a dedicated training set and can use all samples for testing, we evaluate it only on a subset of 316 randomly selected image pairs. This allows a fair comparison to other methods which also follow the same protocol. The CUHK03 dataset includes 13,164 images of 1,360 pedestrians. We randomly select 1,160 persons for training, 100 persons for validation and 100 persons for testing, following exactly the same setting as [12]. All dataset images are scaled into the same size of 128 × 48 pixels.

Figures 4, 5 and Tables 1, 2 show the performance of the proposed method averaged over three runs on randomly selected subsets of the VIPeR and CHUK03 datasets. We can see that by combining the two texture features, *i.e.*, LOMO and mid-level filters the results achieved are better than the ones of either single feature, which demonstrates that they capture complementary texture properties in representing human appearances. More importantly, when we integrate the shape feature, the accuracies are further ameliorated. Such a fact not only indicates that this shape feature is effective to distinguish different persons, but also suggests that integrating shape and texture features boosts the performance of person Re-ID system.

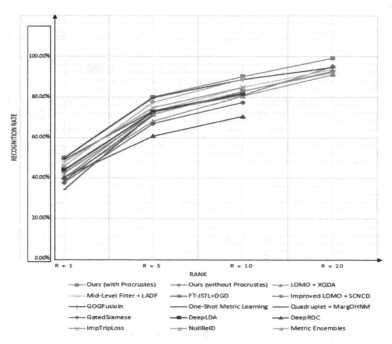

Fig. 4. Average CMC curves on VIPeR.

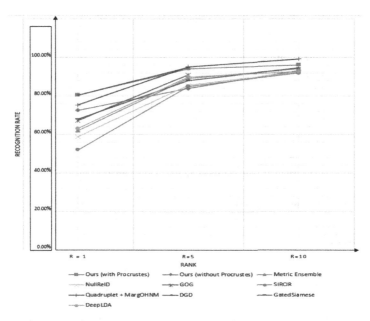

Fig. 5. Average CMC curves on CUHK03.

Table 1. Rank-n matching rates on ViPeR

Method	$n = 1$	$n = 5$	$n = 10$	$n = 20$
Ours (with procrustes)	**50.00%**	**80.00%**	**90.10%**	**99.10%**
Ours (without procrustes)	39.90%	73.00%	81.10%	95.10%
LOMO + XQDA [1]	40.00%	68.10%	80.50%	91.10%
Mid-level filter + LADF [9]	43.40%	73.00%	84.90%	93.70%
Metric ensembles [17]	45.90%	77.50%	88.90%	95.8%
FT-JSTL + DGD [18]	38.60%	–	–	–
Improved LOMO + SCNCD [19]	42.70%	71.50%	83.00%	92.60%
GOG$_{Fusioin}$ [20]	49.70%	79.70%	88.70%	94.50%
One-shot metric learning [10]	34.30%	–	–	–
Quadruplet + MargOHNM [12]	49.10%	73.10%	82.00%	–
GatedSiamese [21]	37.80%	66.90%	77.40%	–
DeepLDA [22]	44.10%	72.60%	81.70%	–
DeepRDC [23]	40.50%	60.80%	70.40%	–
ImpTripLoss [24]	47.80%	74.70%	84.80%	–
NullReID [25]	42.30%	71.50%	82.90%	92.10%

Table 2. Rank-n matching rates on CUHK03

Method	r = 1	r = 5	r = 10
Ours (with procrustes)	**80.5%**	94.3%	96.1%
Ours (without procrustes)	72.6%	83.9%	93.2%
Metric ensemble [17]	62.1%	89.1%	94.3%
NullReID [25]	58.9%	85.6%	92.5%
DeepLDA [22]	63.2%	90.0%	92.7%
GOG [20]	67.3%	91.0%	96.0%
SIRCIR [26]	52.2%	85.0%	92.0%
Quadruplet + MargOHNM [12]	75.3%	**95.2%**	**99.2%**
DGD [18]	**80.5%**	94.9%	97.1%
GatedSiamese [21]	68.1%	88.1%	94.6%

5   Conclusion

In this paper, we present a novel hand-crafted approach to person Re-ID. It enhances the state of the art ones in two aspects. It makes use of a discriminative and compact shape representation by applying Procrustes shape analysis, which not only retains shape distinctiveness of an individual sample, but also alleviates cross-view impacts. Moreover, we combine the shape feature with LOMO and mid-level filters, so that the advantages of multiple clues are jointly used. A score level fusion strategy is finally adopted to optimally integrate their credits. Evaluated on VIPeR and CUHK03, the proposed method reaches very competitive results, proving its effectiveness.

Acknowledgement. This work was supported by the National Key Research and Development Plan (Grant No. 2016YFC0801002).

References

1. Liao, S., Hu, Y., Zhu, X., Li, S.Z.: Person re-identification by local maximal occurrence representation and metric learning. In: IEEE Conference on Computer Vision and Pattern Recognition (2015)
2. Chen, J., Zhang, Z., Wang, Y.: Relevance metric learning for person re-identification by exploiting listwise similarities. IEEE Trans. Image Process. **24**(12), 1657–1662 (2015)
3. Bazzani, L., Cristani, M., Murino, V.: Symmetry-driven accumulation of local features for human characterization and re-identification. Comput. Vis. Image Underst. **117**(2), 130–144 (2013)
4. Chen, J., Wang, Y., Tang, Y.Y.: Person re-identification by exploiting spatio-temporal cues and multi-view metric learning. IEEE Sig. Process. Lett. **23**(7), 998–1002 (2016)
5. Chen, J., Wang, Y., Qin, J., Liu, L., Shao, L.: Fast person re-identification via cross-camera semantic binary transformation. In: IEEE Conference on Computer Vision and Pattern Recognition (2017)
6. Kostinger, M., Hirzer, M., Wohlhart, P., Roth, P.M., Bischof, H.: Large scale metric learning from equivalence constraints. In: IEEE Conference on Computer Vision and Pattern Recognition (2012)
7. Pedagadi, S., Orwell, J., Velastin, S., Boghossian, B.: Local fisher discriminant analysis for pedestrian re-identification. In: IEEE Conference on Computer Vision and Pattern Recognition (2013)

8. Wang, X., Doretto, G., Sebastian, T., Rittscher, J., Tu, P.H.: Shape and appearance context modeling. In: International Conference on Computer Vision (2007)
9. Zhao, R., Ouyang, W., Wang, X.: Learning mid-level filters for person re-identification. In: IEEE Conference on Computer Vision and Pattern Recognition (2014)
10. Bak, S., Carr, K.P.: One-shot metric learning for person re-identification. In: IEEE Conference on Computer Vision and Pattern Recognition (2017)
11. Cheng, D., Gong, Y., Zhou, S., Wang, J., Zheng, N.: Person re-identification by multi-channel parts-based cnn with improved triplet loss function. In: IEEE Conference on Computer Vision and Pattern Recognition (2016)
12. Chen, W., Chen, X., Zhang, J., Huang, K.: Beyond triplet loss: a deep quadruplet network for person re-identification. In: IEEE Conference on Computer Vision and Pattern Recognition (2017)
13. Rother, C., Kolmogorov, V., Blake, A.: GrabCut: interactive foreground extraction using iterated graph cuts. ACM Trans. Graph. 23(3), 309–314 (2004)
14. Wang, L., Ning, H., Tan, T., Hu, W.: Fusion of static and dynamic body biometrics for gait recognition. IEEE Trans. Circ. Syst. Video Technol. 14(2), 149–158 (2004)
15. Jobson, D.J., Rahman, Z.U., Woodell, G.A.: A multiscale retinex for bridging the gap between color images and the human observation of scenes. IEEE Trans. Image Process. 6 (7), 965–976 (1997)
16. Liao, S., Zhao, G., Kellokumpu, V., Pietikainen, M., Li, S.Z.: Modeling pixel process with scale invariant local patterns for background subtraction in complex scenes. In: IEEE Conference on Computer Vision and Pattern Recognition (2010)
17. Paisitkriangkrai, S., Shen, C., van den Hengel, A.: Learning to rank in person re-identification with metric ensembles. In: IEEE Conference on Computer Vision and Pattern Recognition (2015)
18. Xiao, T., Li, H., Ouyang, W., Wang, X.: Learning deep feature representations with domain guided dropout for person re-identification. In: IEEE Conference on Computer Vision and Pattern Recognition (2016)
19. Song, M., Gong, S., Liu, C., Ji, Y., Dong, H.: Person re-identification by improved local maximal occurrence with color names. In: International Congress on Image and Signal Processing (2015)
20. Matsukawa, T., Okabe, T., Suzuki, E., Sato, Y.: Hierarchical Gaussian descriptor for person re-identification. In: IEEE Conference on Computer Vision and Pattern Recognition (2016)
21. Varior, R.R., Haloi, M., Wang, G.: Gated siamese convolutional neural network architecture for human re-identification. In: Leibe, B., Matas, J., Sebe, N., Welling, M. (eds.) ECCV 2016. LNCS, vol. 9912, pp. 791–808. Springer, Cham (2016). doi:10.1007/978-3-319-46484-8_48
22. Wu, L., Shen, C., van den Hengel, A.: Deep linear discriminant analysis on fisher networks: a hybrid architecture for person re-identification. Pattern Recogn. 65, 238–250 (2017)
23. Ding, S., Lin, L., Wang, G., Chao, H.: Deep feature learning with relative distance comparison for person reidentification. Pattern Recogn. 48(10), 2993–3003 (2015)
24. Cheng, D., Gong, Y., Zhou, S., Wang, J., Zheng, N.: Person re-identification by multi-channel parts-based cnn with improved triplet loss function. In: IEEE Conference on Computer Vision and Pattern Recognition (2016)
25. Zhang, L., Xiang, T., Gong, S.: Learning a discriminative null space for person re-identification. In: IEEE Conference on Computer Vision and Pattern Recognition (2016)
26. Wang, F., Zuo, W., Lin, L., Zhang, D., Zhang, L.: Joint learning of single-image and cross-image representations for person re-identification. In: IEEE Conference on Computer Vision and Pattern Recognition (2016)

Feature Extraction and Classification Theory

Decision-Level Fusion Method Based on Deep Learning

Kejun Wang, Meichen Liu, XueSen Hao, and Xianglei Xing[✉]

Harbin Engineering University, Harbin, China
xingxl@hrbeu.edu.cn

Abstract. We present a highly accurate and very efficient approach for personality traits prediction based on video. Unlike the traditional method, we proposed a decision-level information fusion method based on deep learning. We have separated the video modal into two parts, visual modal and audio model. The two models were processed by improved VGG-16 and LSTM network, respectively, and combined with an Extreme Learning Machine (ELM) to architecture decision-level information fusion. Experiments on challenging Youtube-8M dataset show that our proposed approach significantly outperforms traditional decision-level fusion method in terms of both efficiency and accuracy.

Keywords: Deep learning · Decision-level fusion · Convolution neural network

1 Introduction

Information fusion was firstly applied to the military area and got widely developed [1]. For its maximum capability of obtaining information from multi-sensor, as well as the capability of processing redundant information, information fusion has been widely used in other fields, such as sentiment analysis [2], gait recognition [3, 4], industrial robots, natural language understanding, traffic management system, and image processing technology [5], Information fusion technology is mainly divided into data-level fusion (sensor fusion), feature-level fusion [6] and decision-level fusion. Other than pixel-level fusion, decision-level fusion is performed at a higher processing level. In the decision-level approach, each sensor information in classification and decision after the feature extraction, and then the information from each sensor are subsequently combined via a fusion process. However, decision-level fusion is a process accompanied with information loss, and the processing cost is relatively high, which often needs to be used with other fusion method.

Personality is a fundamental component of an individual's affective behavior. Previous work on personality classification has emerged from disparate sources: Varieties of algorithms and feature-selection across spoken and written data have made comparison difficult. Personality traits, which are intimately linked to affect [7], and their detection is of high interest for systems that target users by personalising content (e.g., online stores, recommender systems, social media and search engines; cf. [8]). Direct comparison between these previous personality classification studies is difficult

© Springer International Publishing AG 2017
J. Zhou et al. (Eds.): CCBR 2017, LNCS 10568, pp. 673–682, 2017.
https://doi.org/10.1007/978-3-319-69923-3_72

given inconsistencies in algorithms, feature-selection, and data sources (ranging from speech to essays, emails and blogs).

Recently, deep learning based methods update state-of-the-art constantly of computer vision field from image classification [9], face recognition [10], semantic segmentation [11]. In this paper, we mainly propose a decision-level information fusion method by using deep learning. The contributions of this paper are two folds. Firstly, we propose an improved VGG-16 network that is faster and more accurate in personality traits prediction than the original model. Secondly, we proposed a multi-modal decision-level fusion system based on deep learning.

The rest of the paper is organized as follows: Sect. 2 reviews the necessity of audio modality and visual modality in personality prediction and ELM algorithm. The proposed framework is discussed in detail in Sect. 3. In Sect. 4, many experimental result and comparisons are presented and discussed. Finally, we conclude this work in Sect. 5.

2   Related Work

The common fusion strategies include simple voting method [12], weighted voting method [13], fuzzy membership method [14], maximum probability class method [15], etc. We can directly use traditional feed-forward neural networks to achieve decision-level fusion which is an efficient parallel algorithm, but it drops into local optimum easily. Unlike the other traditional learning algorithms, Extreme learning machine (ELM) [16] stands out from other methods with the following unique characteristics: extremely fast training, good generalization, and universal approximation capability. The parameters of hidden layer in ELM are randomly established and need not be tuned, thus the training of hidden nodes can be established before the inputs are acquired.

For N arbitrary distinct sample $\{x_i, t_i\}_{i=1}^N$, where $x_i = [x_{i1}, x_{i2}, \cdots, x_{in}]^T \in R^n$, t_i is the output tag and activation function $f(x)$ are mathematically modeled as

$$f_L(x) = \sum_{j=1}^L \beta_j\, G(a_j, b_j, x_i) = h(x_i)\beta \tag{1}$$

where a_j is the weight vector connecting the jth hidden neuron; β_j is the weight vector connecting the jth hidden neuron and the output neurons, b_j is the threshold of the ith hidden neuron; $G(a_j, b_j, x_i)$ is the output function of the jth hidden neuron, $h(x_i)$ is called the hidden layer output vector about x_i. In order to improve the generalization of ELM, it is optimized as the optimization problem shown in Eq. (2) [15].

$$
\begin{aligned}
\text{Min}\ :\ & L_{ELM} = \frac{1}{2}\|\beta\|^2 + C\frac{1}{2}\sum_{i=0}^n \|\xi_i\|^2 \\
\text{s.t}\ & h(x_i)\beta = t_i^T - \xi_i^T, \quad i = 1, \ldots, N
\end{aligned}
\tag{2}
$$

Thus, the output equation of ELM can be written as

$$f(x) = h(x)\beta = H^T \left(\frac{I}{C} + HH^T \right)^{-1} T \tag{3}$$

where $\beta = H^T \left(\frac{I}{C} + HH^T \right)^{-1} T$

When using ELM to solve the two classification problem, the decision equation is

$$f(x) = \text{sign} \left(h(x)H^T \left(\frac{I}{C} + HH^T \right)^{-1} T \right) \tag{4}$$

When solving the problem of multiple classification, the decision equation is

$$\text{label}(x) = \arg \max f_i(x) \qquad i \in \{1, \ldots, m\} \tag{5}$$

In personality prediction, it is important to learn the image representations for the visual modality. We use the convolution network to extract the characters, behavior and other features to predictive personality. Speech expression of the pitch variation also represents a different character. Therefore, the representations for audio and visual can independently represent character, but in fact people judge the specific character of an object by fusion presentational integrated information. In this paper, we propose t a decision-level information fusion method based on deep learning (DFDL) framework for personality analysis. As shown in Fig. 1, DFDL treats videos as having with two modalities, i.e., the visual and the audio modality, then by using an Extreme Learning Machine (ELM) to architecture multi-modal information fusion.

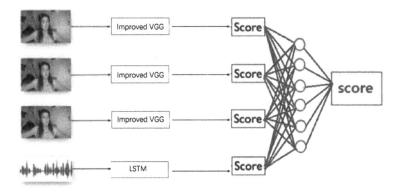

Fig. 1. The structure of our proposed method. The audio model and video model were processed by improved VGG-16 and LSTM network, respectively, and combined with an Extreme Learning Machine (ELM) to architecture decision-level information fusion.

3   Proposed Method

For extract better features for personality traits, in our DFDL framework, we employ and modify multiple VGG-16 to learn the image representations for the visual modality, and then obtain the Big Five Traits predictions by end-to-end training. We extract the feature from the audios of each original video, then by using an Extreme Learning Machine (ELM) to architecture multi-modal information fusion. In this section, we detail these stage, and compare our design choices with other alternatives.

3.1   Visual Modal

In the video, temporal information is important component of recognizing a person's character, but the temporal information is not important as the times become shorter. So we randomly picking a set of frames in the video as original input, by using the improved VGG-16 network for processing. As shown in the Fig. 2. For the original VGG-16 [17] network model, which is through several layers of convolutional and pooling. Finally, the two full connection layers is used as the classification part of the network classified parts.

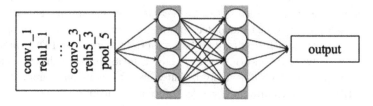

Fig. 2. Original VGG-16 network. Most of the parameters are in the full connection layer.

As shown in the Fig. 3 for improved VGG-16 network. In order to reduce the calculation time, we replace the full connection layer with the pooling layer. In our fusion network, the depth descriptors obtained by the last convolution are performed with maximum pooling and averaging operations, respectively. Each result was normalized to zero mean and unit variance before concatenation. Finally, the concatenation as the final image representation to construct an end-to-end deep learning network.

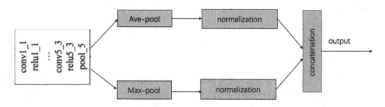

Fig. 3. Architecture of improved VGG-16 network. In our fusion network, the depth descriptors obtained by the last convolution are performed with maximum pooling and averaging operations, respectively. The results are normalized before concatenation.

3.2 Audio Modal

Long Short-Term Memory [18, 19] is a general purpose algorithm for extracting statistical regularities from noisy time series. It learns from scratch, typically with more adjustable parameters (the weights), a larger search space, and less initial bias than HMMs [20], which incorporate prior linguistic knowledge. We use LSTM network to process speech in the video. The original speech is extracted directly from the video as input data. Training data are divided into mini-batches.

3.3 Multi-modal Fusion Method

The two parts of visual and speech are sent into different models for training, and the results were fused. We proposed two approaches to decision-level fusion: In the first, we used by traditional ELM model as shown in Fig. 1. The output is taken as the final character prediction result of the video and audio (DFDL). In the second, we increase the number of hidden layers on ELM, which is called DFDL-1, as shown in Fig. 4. In order to better test the effect, this paper adds a traditional decision-level fusion based on the mean method to compare with DFDL and DFDL-1.

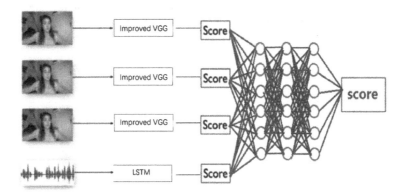

Fig. 4. DFDL-1. We increased two hidden layers on ELM, and the final results are compared with DFDL.

4 Experiments

In this section, we first introduce the databases used in the experiments, then the detail of the experiment setup, and finally analysis the results for our approach. Experiments are performed on a laboratory computer with Intel Xeon E7-8890 v4 CPU at 2.2 GHz and 8.00 GB RAM. All the algorithms have been implemented using DIGITS5 programming.

4.1 Dataset

YouTube-8M [21] is a large video dataset released by Google, which contains 8 million YouTube video URL, representing 500 thousand hours of video with tagging. These notes from a diverse and contains 4800 knowledge mapping entity (Knowledge Graph entity) set. Compared with the existing video datasets, the scale and diversity of YouTube-8M have been significantly improved. The previous largest video dataset contains about 1 million segments of YouTube video and 500 categories of sports domains.

4.2 Dataset Pre-processing

We are given a large newly collected video data set, which contains 10,000 videos of about 15 s each collected from YouTube, and annotated with the Big Five Traits by Amazon Mechanical Turk workers. As shown in Fig. 5, five personality traits in the dataset by manual annotation, in which each character corresponds to a real number between 0 and 1, also bring convenience for the subsequent work to facilitate classification. We use the dataset to predict the five personality traits, including: openness (O), conscientiousness (C), extraversion (E), agreeableness (A) and neuroticism (N). For this dataset, we randomly select about 6000 videos (60%) for training, 2000 videos for validating, and the remaining 2000 videos (20%) for testing.

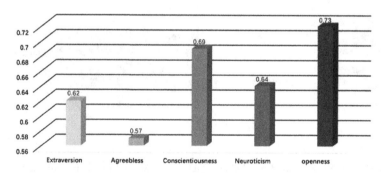

Fig. 5. Character classification data. The x-axis is the index of the "Big five personality" and the y-axis is the value between 0 and 1 of each personality correspond.

4.3 Experimental Results and Analysis

In this experiment, we randomly choose three pictures from the same personality traits in training video samples as input and the corresponding voice samples as input, the results were fused by average method and ELM network, respectively. All experiments were repeated 10 times with different test/train splits and result averaged to ensure stable results. Finally, we add the hidden layers on the ELM network to further verify the fusion effect of the deep network.

In Table 1 we compared the results for our system, trained and tested on the image in the Youtube-8M dataset, with VGG-16 and ResNet-152 system. When we compare our results with the original models, our system shows superior performance against other systems. Table 1 shows that the original VGG-16 to remove the full connection layer so that reducing the number of parameters, the feature dimension also decreases. From that table, we can see that the accuracy based on the improved VGG-16 is 91%, 0.4 point better than that original VGG-16 model, up 0.8 points from ResNet-152. The accuracy of speech training in LSTM network is much better than the conventional method.

Table 1. Comparison of our proposed approach with origin VGG-16, we can see that the accuracy based on the improved VGG-16 is 91%, 0.4 point better than that original VGG-16 model.

	System	Parameter (M)	Dim	Accuracy (%)
Visual model	VGG-16 [17]	138.28	4096	0.9062
	ResNet-152 [22]	58.24	512	0.9016
	Improved VGG-16	14.58	1024	0.9100
Audio model	Linear regression [23]	0.4	79524	0.8940
	LSTM [18]	1.2	80436	0.9501

The finally prediction accuracy of the five personality traits is shown in Table 2. The result of this experiment are presented in Table 3, including Majority voting, Average method, and our proposed system. One can observe that our proposed system always outperformed all the compared methods, but increasing the numbers of the hidden layers on ELM is not obvious improves fusion accuracy.

Table 2. Accuracy of decision level fusion (We use the dataset to predict the five personality traits, including: openness (O), conscientiousness (C), extraversion (E), agreeableness (A) and neuroticism (N)).

personality accuracy personality	E	A	C	N	O
E	0.9129	0.0117	0.0024	0.0190	0.0540
A	0.0434	0.9091	0.0253	0.0204	0.0018
C	0.0121	0.0509	0.9107	0.0208	0.0055
N	0.0242	0.0261	0.0432	0.9064	0.0001
O	0.0074	0.0022	0.0184	0.0334	0.9386

Table 3. The accuracies on fusion information

Method	Majority voting [22]	Mean method [24]	DFDL	DFDL-1
Accuracy (%)	0.8977	0.9019	0.9155	0.9154

At the end of the experiment, we use MatConvnet [25] to visualize the features of the last layer of the model with the deconvolution. The red part indicates the higher energy and the blue color indicates lower energy. The results of the experiment are shown in Fig. 6 (the bright part of the picture is the point of attention), which ResNet-152 and VGG-16 only "attention" on the characters in the video. Our network in the "attention" to the people, while the environment and action information combine to achieve character prediction. On this basis, this paper also tried to face detection preprocessing before the experiment, such as extract the person from the video by OpenCV. But this method has reduced the performance of whole personality prediction. It may be that the video background reflects the character of a person after repeated scrutiny, so we can't directly exclude the background information.

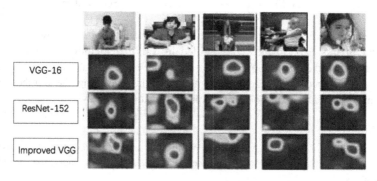

Fig. 6. Pseudo color image - A pseudo color image produced by deconvolution, in which the blue parts represent that background of the original image, and the red parts represent the stronger energy is that the stable feature. (Color figure online)

5   Conclusion

In this paper, we present a framework based on deep learning to achieve decision-level fusion. We use two networks which utilizes different models to deal with different models in the video. We use the convolutional neural network which is extract image feature and the LSTM model based on speech information to process audio. Finally, using the ELM model for decision level fusion. The experimental results have demonstrated that the proposed method achieves high accuracy and performs much better than the traditional decision-level fusion of mean method and majority voting method.

Acknowledgments. This work was supported by the Fundamental Research Funds for the Central Universities of China, Natural Science Foundation of China, and Natural Science Fund of Heilongjiang Province of China under Grand Nos. HEUCFJ170404, 61573114, 61703119, F2015033 and QC2017070.

References

1. Sun, S.L., Deng, Z.L.: Multisensor information fusion with applications. Automatica **40**(6), 1017–1023 (2004)
2. Kapoor, A., Picard, R.W.: Multimodal affect recognition in learning environments. In: ACM International Conference on Multimedia, pp. 677–682. ACM (2005)
3. Xing, X., Wang, K., Yan, T., Lv, Z.: Complete canonical correlation analysis with application to multi-view gait recognition. Pattern Recogn. **50**, 107–117 (2016)
4. Xing, X., Wang, K.: Couple manifold discriminant analysis with bipartite graph embedding for face recognition at a distance. Sig. Process. **125**, 329–335 (2016)
5. Piras, L., Giacinto, G.: Information fusion in content based image retrieval: a comprehensive overview. Inf. Fusion **37**, 50–60 (2017)
6. Xing, X., Wang, K., Lv, Z.: Fusion of gait and facial features using coupled projections for people identification at a distance. IEEE Sig. Process. Lett. **22**(12), 2349–2353 (2015)
7. Eid, M., Diener, E.: Intraindividual variability in affect: reliability, validity, and personality correlates. J. Pers. Soc. Psychol. **76**(4), 662–676 (1999)
8. Reeves, B., Nass, C.: The Media Equation: How People Treat Computers, Television, and New Media Like Real People and Places. Cambridge University Press, New York (1996)
9. Lee, M.J., Choi, S.Y., Jeong, H.J., et al.: A precise image crawling system with image classification based on deep learning. Adv. Sci. Lett. **23**(3), 1623–1626 (2017)
10. Hu, G., Yang, Y., Yi, D., et al.: When face recognition meets with deep learning: an evaluation of convolutional neural networks for face recognition, pp. 384–392 (2015)
11. Noh, H., Hong, S., Han, B.: Learning deconvolution network for semantic segmentation. In: Proceedings of IEEE International Conference of Computer Vision, pp. 1520–1528 (2015)
12. Lin, X.F., Yacou, B., Sherif, B.J., et al.: Performance analysis of pattern classifier combination by plurality voting. Pattern Recogn. Lett. **24**(12), 1959–1969 (2003)
13. Fauvel, M., Chanussot, J., Benediktsson, J.A.: Decision fusion for the classification of urban remote sensing images. IEEE Trans. Geosci. Remote Sens. **44**(10), 2828–2838 (2006)
14. Pan, A., Zhou, J., Zhang, P., et al.: Research on power quality evaluation based on radar chart method and fuzzy membership degree. Energy Power Eng. **09**(4), 725–734 (2017)
15. Liang, L.K., Jing-Bo, L.I.: Discussion on the extraction and standardization of TCM symptom based on maximum probability method. China J. Tradit. Chin. Med. Pharm. **5**, 060 (2017)
16. Huang, G.B., Zhu, Q.Y., Siew, C.K.: Extreme learning machine: a new learning scheme of feed-ward neural networks. In: Proceedings of IEEE International Joint Conference on Neural Networks, vol. 2, pp. 985–990. IEEE (2005)
17. Simonyan, K., Zisserman, A.: Very deep convolutional networks for large-scale image recognition. In: International Conference on Learning Representations (2015)
18. Graves, A.: Long short-term memory. In: Graves, A. (ed.) Supervised Sequence Labelling with Recurrent Neural Networks. Springer, Heidelberg (2012). doi:10.1007/978-3-642-24797-2_4
19. Greff, K., Srivastava, R.K., Koutnik, J., et al.: LSTM: a search space odyssey. IEEE Trans. Neural Netw. Learn. Syst. **PP**(99), 1–11 (2016)

20. Ma, X., Hovy, E.: End-to-end Sequence Labeling via Bi-directional LSTM-CNNs-CRF (2016)
21. Abu-El-Haija, S., Kothari, N., Lee, J., et al.: YouTube-8M: A Large-Scale Video Classification Benchmark (2016)
22. He, K., Zhang, X., Ren, S., et al.: Deep residual learning for image recognition, pp. 770–778 (2015)
23. Naseem, I., Togneri, R., Bennamoun, M.: Linear regression for face recognition. IEEE Trans. Pattern Anal. Mach. Intell. 32(11), 2106–2112 (2010)
24. Tabib Mahmoudi, F., Samadzadegan, F., Reinartz, P.: A decision level fusion method for object recognition using multi-angular imagery. Proc. SPIE **XL1/W3**(1), 62795F-62795F-6 (2013)
25. Vedaldi, A., Lenc, K.: MatConvNet: Convolutional Neural Networks for MATLAB. Eprint Arxiv, pp. 689–692 (2014)

Laplacian Regularized Non-negative Sparse Low-Rank Representation Classification

Jingshan Li, Caikou Chen[(⊠)], Xielian Hou, and Rong Wang

College of Information Engineering, Yangzhou University, Yangzhou, China
lijingshan123@163.com, yzcck@126.com,
1246389084@qq.com, 272270226@qq.com

Abstract. Recently low-rank becomes a popular tool for face representation and classification. None of these existing low-rank based classification methods are in view of the non-linear geometric structures within data, hence the data during the learning process may lose locality and similarity information. Furthermore, Lin et al. propose a Non-negative Sparse Hyper-Laplacian regularized LRR model (NSHLRR) to improve LRR in the above respect and apply it to image clustering. In this paper, we propose a novel classification method, namely NSHLRR-based Classification (NSHLRRC) for face recognition. Experimental results on public face databases clearly show our method has very competitive classification results, which also show that our method outperforms other state-of-the-art methods.

Keywords: Low-rank · Hyper-laplacian · Face recognition · Classification

1 Introduction

Much attention has been attracted to face recognition because of high discrimination and low intrusiveness. Therefore, the scholars in pattern recognition have put forward many classification methods for face recognition.

In recent years, sparse representation-based classification method (SRC) has been presented by Wright et al. [1]. In face recognition SRC has acquired promising experimental results. In SRC method, the training samples are utilized as a dictionary. SRC sparsely encodes a test sample via l_1 norm optimization and obtains the minimal representation residual, which is able to distinguish the category of the test sample. However, its inner classification mechanism remains unclear and it is time-consuming computationally. Recently, Zhang et al. proposed an efficient method in face recognition, called collaborative representation-based classification (CRC) [2]. In CRC method, the l_1 norm is replaced by the l_2 norm and CRC is proved to be timesaving computationally. Collaborative representation for CRC can also achieve similar recognition result as SRC. However, the classification methods do not consider possible corruption of data during training, so the associated performance may be degraded.

To deal with the contamination of training samples, Ref. adopted low-rank matrix recovery to restore a clean, low-rank data matrix [3]. However, low-rank matrix recovery cannot obtain outstanding experimental results when samples are from

© Springer International Publishing AG 2017
J. Zhou et al. (Eds.): CCBR 2017, LNCS 10568, pp. 683–690, 2017.
https://doi.org/10.1007/978-3-319-69923-3_73

multiple subspaces. Thus, Liu et al. proposed a low-rank representation (LRR) method, which can effectively reveal the global structures of data [4]. With the success of low-rank representation, Nguyen et al. proposed a completely new classification method, namely LRR-based Classification (LRRC) [5]. In the classification LRRC has gained quite good experimental results. LRRC method quests for the lowest-rank representation of test samples by utilizing all the training samples as a dictionary.

However, no above low-rank based methods are in view of the non-linear geometric structures within data, hence the data during the learning process may lose locality and similarity information. Thus Lin et al. propose a Non-negative Sparse Hyper-Laplacian regularized LRR model (NSHLRR) to improve LRR in the above respect and apply it to image clustering [6]. Since the NSHLRR method adopts the graph regularizer, it is able to represent the global low-dimensional structures and capture the intrinsic non-linear geometric information in data. Besides, the NSHLRR method can better capture the local structure around each data vector by introducing sparsity criterion.

Based on the recent success of the above model, we propose a novel classification method for robust face recognition, named NSHLRR-based Classification (NSHLRRC). Experimental results on public face databases clearly show our method has very competitive classification results, which also show that our method outperforms other state-of-the-art methods.

2   Related Works

Suppose that we have a collection of training samples' matrix $\mathbf{A} = [\mathbf{A}_1, \mathbf{A}_2, \ldots, \mathbf{A}_m]$, which is composed of m classes' training samples. The matrix $\mathbf{X} = [\mathbf{X}_1, \mathbf{X}_2, \ldots, \mathbf{X}_n]$ is a collection of test samples. By utilizing $\mathbf{A}$ as a dictionary, a linear combination of samples in A is able to represent a test sample $\mathbf{x}_i$ approximately:

$$\mathbf{x}_i = \mathbf{A}\mathbf{z}_i \tag{1}$$

where $\mathbf{z}_i$ is representation coefficient vector of $\mathbf{x}_i$. The formula (1) can be rewritten as:

$$\mathbf{X} = \mathbf{A}\mathbf{Z} \tag{2}$$

where $\mathbf{Z} = [\mathbf{z}_1, \mathbf{z}_2, \ldots, \mathbf{z}_n]$ is the representation matrix of the matrix $\mathbf{X}$.

The LRR method has been put forward to restore subspace structure, aiming at solving the joint minimization problem on lowest-rank representation. Given an appropriate dictionary, LRR represents the data matrix by utilizing the lowest-rank representation and linear combinations of dictionary atoms as follows:

$$\min_{\mathbf{Z}} rank(\mathbf{Z}) + \lambda \|\mathbf{E}\|_1, s.t \ \mathbf{X} = \mathbf{A}\mathbf{Z} + \mathbf{E} \tag{3}$$

where $\mathbf{X}$ is a data matrix, each column of which is a sample. $\mathbf{A}$ is the given dictionary, and $\mathbf{Z}$ is the lowest-rank representation matrix of data matrix $\mathbf{X}$. The rank function is nonconvex and time-consuming computationally, so the form is of no value. However, we can use the nuclear norm instead of the rank function and the nuclear norm is convex.

Therefore, the optimization problem (3) becomes a convex optimization problem:

$$\min_{\mathbf{Z}} \|\mathbf{Z}\|_* + \lambda \|\mathbf{E}\|_1, s.t \ \mathbf{X} = \mathbf{AZ} + \mathbf{E} \tag{4}$$

3   NSHLRRC

We apply a sparse constraint and a non-negative constraint [7] to the representation matrix $\mathbf{Z}$ and make the optimization problem (4) become the follow function:

$$\min_{\mathbf{Z},\mathbf{E}} \|\mathbf{Z}\|_* + \beta \|\mathbf{Z}\|_1 + \lambda \|\mathbf{E}\|_{2,1}$$
$$\text{s.t} \ \mathbf{X} = \mathbf{AZ} + \mathbf{E}, \mathbf{Z} \geq 0 \tag{5}$$

where β is a scalar constant for balancing sparsity and low-rankness. The sparse constraint captures the local structure around each data vector. Besides, the non-negative constraint on $\mathbf{Z}$ guarantees that the coefficients are significant, with which it is better to reflect the dependence between the data points.

Based on the effect of graph based manifold learning [8], we can apply the Laplacian regularization into the function (5) so that similar data points have similar representation coefficients. Since the columns of $\mathbf{Z}$ are new representations of the data under certain dictionary, the distance between $\mathbf{z}_i$ and $\mathbf{z}_j$ is a measure of the difference between the initial data points $\mathbf{x}_i$ and $\mathbf{x}_j$ in actuality. Thus, we can add a regularization term $\sum_{ij} \|\mathbf{z}_i - \mathbf{z}_j\|^2 \mathbf{W}_{ij}$ to the function (5) for similarity matching.

$$\min_{\mathbf{Z},\mathbf{E}} \|\mathbf{Z}\|_* + \beta \|\mathbf{Z}\|_1 + \lambda \|\mathbf{E}\|_{2,1} + \gamma \sum_{ij} \|\mathbf{z}_i - \mathbf{z}_j\|^2 \mathbf{W}_{ij}$$
$$\text{s.t} \ \mathbf{X} = \mathbf{AZ} + \mathbf{E}, \mathbf{Z} \geq 0 \tag{6}$$

After dealing with some algebraic manipulations, the above function have been rewritten as the matrix form of hyper-Laplacian regularized LRR model

$$\min_{\mathbf{Z},\mathbf{E}} \|\mathbf{Z}\|_* + \beta \|\mathbf{Z}\|_1 + \lambda \|\mathbf{E}\|_{2,1} + \gamma \text{tr}(\mathbf{ZLZ}^{\mathrm{T}})$$
$$\text{s.t} \ \mathbf{X} = \mathbf{AZ} + \mathbf{E}, \mathbf{Z} \geq 0 \tag{7}$$

where $\mathbf{L}$ is the Laplacian matrix for the graph constructed on $\mathbf{W}$. Here, we introduce the sum of distance of pairwise LRR coefficients to the function (5), and similarity between the given data points weights the distance.

When introduced an auxiliary variable $\mathbf{H}$, the problem (7) is converted to an equivalent optimization problem as:

$$\min_{\mathbf{Z},\mathbf{E}} \|\mathbf{Z}\|_* + \beta\|\mathbf{H}\|_1 + \lambda\|\mathbf{E}\|_{2,1} + \gamma\mathrm{tr}(\mathbf{ZLZ}^\mathrm{T})$$
$$\text{s.t } \mathbf{X} = \mathbf{AZ} + \mathbf{E}, \mathbf{Z} = \mathbf{H}, \mathbf{H} \geq 0 \tag{8}$$

The solution of optimization problem (8) is linearized alternating direction method with adaptive penalty (LADMAP). The augmented Lagrange function of problem (8) is given as:

$$L = \|\mathbf{Z}\|_* + \beta\|\mathbf{H}\|_1 + \lambda\|\mathbf{E}\|_{2,1} + \gamma\mathrm{tr}(\mathbf{ZLZ}^\mathrm{T}) + \langle\mathbf{Y}_1, \mathbf{X} - \mathbf{AZ} - \mathbf{E}\rangle$$
$$+ \langle\mathbf{Y}_2, \mathbf{Z} - \mathbf{H}\rangle + \frac{\mu}{2}(\|\mathbf{X} - \mathbf{AZ} - \mathbf{E}\|_F^2 + \|\mathbf{Z} - \mathbf{H}\|_F^2) \tag{9}$$

where $\mathbf{Y}_1$ and $\mathbf{Y}_2$ are Lagrangian multipliers, and μ ($\mu > 0$) is the penalty parameter. By simple algebraic manipulation, the above Lagrangian function can be rewritten as:

$$L = \|\mathbf{Z}\|_* + \beta\|\mathbf{H}\|_1 + \lambda\|\mathbf{E}\|_{2,1} - \frac{1}{2\mu}(\|\mathbf{Y}_1\|_F^2 + \|\mathbf{Y}_2\|_F^2) + \mathbf{M}(\mathbf{Z}, \mathbf{H}, \mathbf{E}, \mathbf{Y}_1, \mathbf{Y}_2, \mu)$$
$$where\ \mathbf{M} = \gamma\mathrm{tr}(\mathbf{ZLZ}^\mathrm{T}) + \frac{\mu}{2}(\left\|\mathbf{X} - \mathbf{AZ} - \mathbf{E} + \frac{\mathbf{Y}_1}{\mu}\right\|_F^2 + \left\|\mathbf{Z} - \mathbf{H} + \frac{\mathbf{Y}_2}{\mu}\right\|_F^2) \tag{10}$$

The minimum value of this function L can be easily made optimization by alternately updating the $\mathbf{Z}$, $\mathbf{H}$, $\mathbf{E}$ and other fixed.

(1) Update $\mathbf{Z}$

$$\arg\min\|\mathbf{Z}\|_* + \langle\nabla_\mathbf{Z}\mathbf{M}(\mathbf{Z}_k), \mathbf{Z} - \mathbf{Z}_k\rangle + \frac{\eta_1\mu_k}{2}\|\mathbf{Z} - \mathbf{Z}_k\|_F^2 \tag{11}$$

$$\mathbf{Z}_{k+1} = \Theta_{(\eta_1\mu_k)^{-1}}(\mathbf{Z}_k - \nabla_\mathbf{Z}\mathbf{M}(\mathbf{Z}_k)/\eta_1) \tag{12}$$

where

$$\mathbf{Z}_k - \nabla_\mathbf{Z}q(\mathbf{Z}_k)/\eta_1 = \mathbf{Z}_k + \frac{\mu_k}{\eta_1}\mathbf{A}^\mathrm{T}(\mathbf{X} - \mathbf{AZ}_k - \mathbf{E}_k + \frac{\mathbf{Y}_{1,k}}{\mu_k})$$
$$- \frac{\mu_k}{\eta_1}(\mathbf{Z}_k - \mathbf{H}_k + \frac{\mathbf{Y}_{2,k}}{\mu_k})$$

Θ is the singular value thresholding operator (SVT), $\nabla_\mathbf{Z}\mathbf{M}$ is the partial derivative of function $\mathbf{M}$ with respect to $\mathbf{Z}$.

(2) Fixed $\mathbf{Z}$ and $\mathbf{E}$, update $\mathbf{H}$

$$\min_{\mathbf{H}\geq 0} \beta\|\mathbf{H}\|_1 + \frac{\mu_k}{\eta_1}\left\|\mathbf{H}_k - (\mathbf{Z}_{k+1} + \frac{\mathbf{Y}_{2,k}}{\mu_k})\right\|_F^2 \tag{13}$$

The problem (13) can be solved by:

$$\mathbf{H}_{k+1} = \max\{S_{\frac{\beta}{\mu_k}}(\mathbf{Z}_{k+1} + \frac{\mathbf{Y}_{2,k}}{\mu_k}), 0\} \tag{14}$$

(3) Fixed $\mathbf{Z}$ and $\mathbf{H}$, update $\mathbf{E}$

$$\min_{\mathbf{J}\geq 0} \lambda \|\mathbf{E}\|_{2,1} + \frac{\mu_k}{2} \left\| \mathbf{X} - \mathbf{A}\mathbf{Z}_{k+1} - \mathbf{E}_k + \frac{\mathbf{Y}_{1,k}}{\mu_k} \right\|_F^2 \tag{15}$$

The problem (15) can be solved by:

$$\mathbf{E}_{k+1} = S_{\frac{\lambda}{\mu_k}}(\mathbf{X} - \mathbf{A}\mathbf{Z}_{k+1} + \frac{\mathbf{Y}_{1,k}}{\mu_k}) \tag{16}$$

S represents the soft-thresholding operator in (14) and (16).

Solution to NSHLRRC

Algorithm 1: Solving NSHLRRC by LADMAP

Input: Training sample matrix $\mathbf{A}$, test sample matrix $\mathbf{X}$; **Output:** Matrix $\mathbf{Z}$, $\mathbf{E}$

Initialization:

$\mathbf{Z}_0 = \mathbf{J}_0 = \mathbf{E}_0 = \mathbf{Y}_{1,0} = \mathbf{Y}_{2,0} = 0, \mu_0 = 0.1, \mu_{\max} = 10^{10}$,

$\rho_0 = 1.1, \; \varepsilon_1 = 10^{-6}, \; \varepsilon_2 = 10^{-2}, \eta_1 = \|\mathbf{A}\|_2^2, \; k = 0$

While not converged (k=0, 1, ...) **do**:

1) Update the variables as (16), (18), (20).

2) Update the Lagrange multipliers $\mathbf{Y}_1$ and $\mathbf{Y}_2$:

$\mathbf{Y}_{1,k+1} = \mathbf{Y}_{1,k} + \mu_k(\mathbf{X} - \mathbf{A}\mathbf{Z}_{k+1} - \mathbf{E}_{k+1})$; $\mathbf{Y}_{2,k+1} = \mathbf{Y}_{2,k} + \mu_k(\mathbf{Z}_{k+1} - \mathbf{H}_{k+1})$

3) Update the parameter μ:

$\mu_{k+1} = \min(\rho\mu_k, \mu_{\max})$

$\rho = \begin{cases} \rho_0 & \text{if } \mu_k \max(\sqrt{\eta_1} \|\mathbf{Z}_k - \mathbf{Z}_{k-1}\|_F^2, \|\mathbf{H}_k - \mathbf{H}_{k-1}\|_F^2, \|\mathbf{E}_k - \mathbf{E}_{k-1}\|_F^2)/\|\mathbf{X}\|_F^2 < \varepsilon_2 \\ 1 & \text{otherwise} \end{cases}$

4) Check the convergence conditions:

$\|\mathbf{X} - \mathbf{A}\mathbf{Z}_k - \mathbf{E}_k\|_F^2 / \|\mathbf{X}\|_F^2 \geq \varepsilon_1$ or

$\mu_k \max(\sqrt{\eta_1} \|\mathbf{Z}_k - \mathbf{Z}_{k-1}\|_F^2, \|\mathbf{H}_k - \mathbf{H}_{k-1}\|_F^2, \|\mathbf{E}_k - \mathbf{E}_{k-1}\|_F^2)/\|\mathbf{X}\|_F^2 \geq \varepsilon_2$

End While

Algorithm 2: NSHLRRC-based Classification

Input: Training matrix **A**, test sample matrix **X**;

Output: A class label for each column of **X**.

1. Solve (11) by **Algorithm** 1 and obtain matrix **Z**.

2. for $l = 1, \ldots, p$

3.   for $i = 1, \ldots, k$

4.   Compute the residuals

$$r_i(\mathbf{x}_i) = \left\| \mathbf{x}_i - \mathbf{A}\sigma_i(\mathbf{z}_i) \right\|_2 / \left\| \sigma_i(\mathbf{z}_i) \right\|_2$$

5.   end for

$\text{class}(\mathbf{x}_i) = \arg\min_l r_i(\mathbf{x}_i)$.

6. end for

---

4   Experiments

We will make compare of the proposed NSHLRRC method and some of the most advanced methods in this section. We have conducted extensive experiments on two datasets: CMU PIE database [9] and AR face database [10].

4.1   Experiments on the CMU PIE Database

The CMU PIE database includes more than 40000 face images corresponding to 68 individuals, each of which has about 49 images. Each image is unified into to 32×32 pixels after clipping and scaling. Under different lighting conditions, facial expressions and various angles, the images are recorded and they are all taken under strict control of the conditions. Collection of all samples can be divided into four subsets, subset 1: sample 35–42; subset 2: sample 10, 11, 13, 22, 23, 27, 28, 29, 30, 45; subset 3: sample 8, 9, 12, 14, 15, 16, 17, 18, 21, 24; subset 4: 2, 3, 6, 7, 19, 20, 46, 47, 48, 49. In addition, there are 8 samples in subset 1, and there are 10 samples in subset 2, 3, 4 respectively. Figure 1 shows 8 images of one person in four subsets. From Fig. 1, it can be viewed directly that subset 1, subset 2, subset 3 and subset 4 are gradually affected by the degree of illumination.

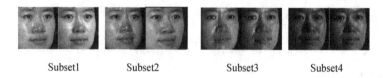

Subset1   Subset2   Subset3   Subset4

Fig. 1. Images of one person in four subsets in AR database

In this session, we take into account 3 scenarios to evaluate the performance of our method. (1) subset 2 as test set: In this scenario, we select 8 samples in subset 1 for training and 10 samples in subset 2 for testing. (2) subset 3 as test set: In this scenario, we select 8 samples in subset 1 for training and 10 samples in subset 3 for testing. (3) subset 4 as test set: In this scenario, we select 8 samples in subset 1 for training and 10 samples in subset 4 for testing. We also compare our method against LRC, and CRC for face recognition, results are shown in Table 1.

Table 1. Comparison of recognition rates on CMU PIE (C05) database.

CMU PIE (C05)	Session 1	Session 2	Session 3
Our method	**0.9206**	**0.8059**	**0.7971**
CRC	0.8926	0.7632	0.7382
SRC	0.9103	0.7706	**0.7971**
LRRC	0.9044	0.7750	0.7912

4.2   Experiments on the AR Database

The AR database includes 3120 face images corresponding to 120 subjects, each of which has 26 images. Each image is unified into to 50×40 pixels after clipping and scaling. Each subject contains 26 images which are separated in two sessions and each session contains 13 images (three images with sunglasses, another three with scarves, and the remaining seven simply with illumination and expressions variations). Figure 2 shows 13 images (including 7 clean faces, 3 faces with sunglasses and 3 faces with scarf) of one person in the Extended Yale B database.

Fig. 2. First session samples of one individual in AR database

In this session, we take into account three occlusion scenarios to evaluate the performance of our method. (1) Mixed: In this scenario, we select samples with sunglasses and samples with scarf for training. That is to say, 7 clean samples, 3 samples with sunglasses and 3 samples with scarf from the first session are chosen for training, the remaining samples are selected for testing. (2) Sunglasses: In this scenario, we select 7 clean samples and 3 samples with sunglasses from the first session for training, the remaining 7 clean samples and 3 samples with sunglasses from the second session for testing. (3) Scarf: In this scenario, we select 7 clean samples and 3 samples with scarf from the first session for training, the remaining 7 clean samples and 3 samples with scarf from the second session for testing. We also compare our method against LRC, SRC, CRC and LRRC for face recognition, results are shown in Table 2.

Table 2. Comparison of recognition rates on AR database.

AR	Session 1	Session 2	Session 3
Our method	**0.7538**	**0.7717**	**0.7450**
CRC	0.7218	0.7525	0.7325
SRC	0.7357	0.7508	0.7192
LRRC	07324	0.7508	0.7292

5 Conclusion

This paper has presented a method, namely NSHLRRC for robust face recognition. Our method has been shown to have superior performance in face recognition. Extensive experimental results on ORL database and Extended Yale B database testify the robustness and effectiveness of our method. Those also show that our method out-performs other state-of-the-art methods. However, our shortcomings lie in the fact that we do not do more validation on different face databases.

References

1. Wright, J., Yang, A.Y., Ganesh, A., Sastry, S., Ma, Y.: Robust face recognition via sparse representation. IEEE Trans. Pattern Anal. Mach. Intell. 31(2), 210–227 (2009)
2. Zhang, L., Yang, M., Feng, X.: Sparse representation or collaborative representation: which helps face recognition: which helps face recognition? In: Proceedings of International Conference on Computer Vision, Barcelona, Spain, pp. 471–478 (2011)
3. Chen, C.F., Wei, C.P., Wang, Y.C.F.: Low-rank matrix recovery with structural incoherence for robust face recognition. In: Proceedings of 2012 IEEE International Conference on Computer Vision and Pattern Recognition (CVPR), pp. 2618–2625 (2012)
4. Liu, G., Lin, Z., Yan, S., Sun, J., Yu, Y., Ma, Y.: Robust recovery of subspace structures by low-rank representation. IEEE Trans. Pattern Anal. Mach. Intell. 35(1), 171–184 (2013)
5. Nguyen, H.V., Huang, R., Yang, W., Sun, C.: Face recognition based on low-rank matrix representation. In: Proceedings of the 33rd Chinese Control Conference (2014)
6. Yin, M., Gao, J., Lin, Z.: Laplacian regularized low-rank representation and its applications. IEEE Trans. Pattern Anal. Mach. Intell. 38(3), 504–517 (2016)
7. Kim, H., Park, H.: Nonnegative matrix factorization based on alternating nonnegativity constrained least squares and active set method. SIAM J. Matrix Anal. Appl. 30(2), 713–730 (2008)
8. Belkin, M., Niyogi, P.: Laplacian eigenmaps and spectral techniques for embedding and clustering. In: Proceedings of Advances in Neural Information Processing Systems, vol. 14, pp. 585–591 (2001)
9. Gross, R., Matthews, I., Cohn, J., Kanade, T., Baker, S.: Multi-PIE. Image Vis. Comput. 28(5), 807–813 (2010)
10. Martinez, A., Benavente, R.: The AR face database. CVC Technical report, vol. 24 (1998)

The Variants of Weber Local Descriptor and Their Applications for Biometrics

Jingting Lu[1,2], Hui Ye[1], Wei Jia[2(✉)], Yang Zhao[2], Hai Min[2],
Wenxiong Kang[3], and Lunke Fei[4]

[1] Institution of Industry and Equipment Technology,
Hefei University of Technology, Hefei, China
[2] School of Computer and Information,
Hefei University of Technology, Hefei, China
China.jiawei@139.com
[3] School of Automation Science and Engineering,
South China University of Technology, Guangzhou, China
[4] School of Computers, Guangdong University of Technology,
Guangzhou, China

Abstract. In computer vision and pattern recognition, handcrafted local features play an important role in many tasks. Many effective handcrafted local features have been proposed. Among them, Weber Local Descriptor (WLD) is a successful one. WLD is a simple but powerful descriptor, and a lot of variants of WLD have also been proposed in recent years, which has been broadly used for texture classification as well as biometrics. In this paper, we make a review for WLD and its variants. Generally, the algorithms of WLD and its variants can be divided into categories such as differential excitation-based, orientation-based and multiple features based. We also summarize their applications for biometrics.

Keywords: Weber local descriptors · Survey · Biometrics

1 Introduction

In computer vision and pattern recognition, image local descriptors play an important role for many recognition tasks. A lot of local descriptors have been proposed in the past decade such as Scale-Invariant Feature Transform (SIFT), Local Binary Pattern (LBP), Histogram of Oriented Gradient (HOG), and Weber Local Descriptor (WLD), etc. Among them, WLD is a new one proposed by Chen et al. [1] in 2010. In WLD, differential excitation and orientation of the input image are firstly calculated, and then the histogram is constructed according to these two components. Generally, WLD descriptor has the following advantages: (1) It utilizes Weber function to detect local salient pattern which make it more robust to noises and illumination changes. (2) It constructs histogram according to salient pattern's gradient orientation, combining two features together make it more discriminatory. After WLD descriptor was proposed, a lot of its variants have been proposed and have achieved very promising performance for different tasks. In this paper, we make a review for WLD and its variants. We firstly

© Springer International Publishing AG 2017
J. Zhou et al. (Eds.): CCBR 2017, LNCS 10568, pp. 691–699, 2017.
https://doi.org/10.1007/978-3-319-69923-3_74

present the basic algorithm of WLD. Secondly, we divide the algorithms of WLD's variants into three categories such as differential excitation-based, orientation-based and multiple features based. Finally, we summarize their applications for biometrics.

2 Basic Algorithm of Weber Local Descriptor

2.1 Weber's Law and Differential Excitation Descriptor

In the fields of psychology, Weber's law holds that the ratio of stimulation increment ΔI to its original intensity I is a constant. It means we have reason to think that the region is background or area containing noises if the region changes after stimulation. Inspired by Weber's Law, Chen et al. [1] proposed differential excitation descriptor to calculate such a change:

$$\xi(x_c) = arctan\left(\frac{v_s^{00}}{v_s^{01}}\right) = arctan\left[\sum_{i=0}^{p-1}\left(\frac{x_i - x_c}{x_c}\right)\right] \quad (1)$$

where p is the number of neighboring pixels, x_c is the central pixel and x_i indicates the ith neighboring pixel, v_s^{00} and v_s^{01} are calculated through two differential excitation masks f_{00} and f_{01} as shown in Fig. 1.

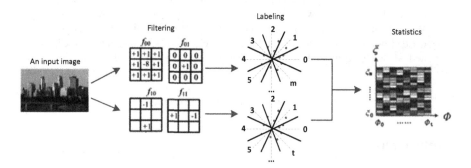

Fig. 1. The construction process of Weber local descriptor.

2.2 Orientation and Histogram

The orientation component of WLD is gradient orientation of current pixel:

$$\theta(x_c) = arctan\left(\frac{x_5 - x_1}{x_7 - x_3}\right) \quad (2)$$

where $x_5 - x_1$ and $x_7 - x_3$ are the intensity differences in vertical and horizontal direction. After calculating these two components, a 2-dimensional histogram $\{WLD(\xi_j, \phi_t)\}$ is constructed for feature representation. For simplicity, this 2D histogram is further encoded into 1D histogram according to each column. Such a WLD feature has been successfully used in texture classification and face recognition [1].

3 The Variants of WLD Descriptor

A lot of variants of WLD have been proposed, which can be classified into three types *i.e.*, differential excitation-based, orientation-based and multiple features-based. Table 1 lists 13 variants of WLD, and these variants will be introduced in our paper one by one.

Table 1. The variants of WLD

Category		Method name	Main changes	Applications	Year
Differential Excitation-based	(1)	MWLD_1 [2]	Template's weights	Space image registration	2010
	(2)	SWLD [3]	Neighboring pixels' numbers	Cross spectral face recognition	2012
	(3)	GWLD [4]	Applying on Gabor magnitude map	Bovine iris recognition	2013
	(4)	IWLD [5]	Considering angles between intensity differences and X direction	Violence detection	2016
Orientation-based	(5)	WLD [6]	Using Sobel operator	Face recognition	2011
	(6)	MWLD_2 [7]	Using orientation component as histogram's weights	Pedestrian detection	2011
	(7)	CHILD [8]	Filtering method modified	Texture classification	2013
	(8)	WOD [9]	Using positive differential excitation and Gabor filters for orientation	Vanishing point detection	2014
	(9)	IWLD [10]	Coding with local binary patterns	Person re-identification	2015
Multiple Features-based	(10)	LBP/WLD [11]	Using LBP for differential excitation	Dynamic texture recognition	2011
	(11)	WLDV [12]	Adding contrast information	Texture classification	2012
	(12)	PWMO [13, 14]	Using p-LBP and local XOR pattern	Face recognition	2012
	(13)	WLBP [15]	Combining LBP with WLD	Face recognition	2013

3.1 Differential Excitation-Based Variants of WLD

The differential excitation component of WLD aims to extract local salient patterns, so it is necessary for this component to be expressive and robust. According to this principle, several variants of WLD have been proposed.

(1) Modified WLD (MWLD)

Jiao and Baojun [2] proposed MWLD for space image registration. The modules of differential excitation and orientation are modified to fit the circle stars' smooth edges and to extract more sharp edge information. Those modules are showed in Fig. 2. Experiments show it is expressive for space images.

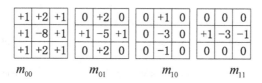

Fig. 2. Modules of differential excitation and orientation in MWLD

(2) Simplified WLD (SWLD)

Zuo *et al.* [3] proposed a methodology for face images called SWLD, which is applied on the magnitude of Gabor filtered image and only computes differential excitation around current pixel's 12 neighbors:

$$SWLD_{l,r,12}(x) = \vartheta_l \left\{ tan^{-1} \left[\sum_{i=0}^{11} \frac{x_i - x}{x} \right] \right\} \tag{3}$$

where x_i are 12 neighbors of x at radius r and ϑ_l is a uniform quantizer with l quantization levels. After calculating SWLD and LBP on magnitude of filtered image and GLBP on phase of filtered image, concatenated histogram is built and successfully used for face recognition.

(3) Gabor WLD (GWLD)

Motivated by WLD and the advantages of Gabor, Sun *et al.* [4] proposed GWLD for bovine iris recognition. The original images are preprocessed with a set of Gabor filters to obtain 40 magnitude maps. Then a modified WLD [16] is applied over each map. It calculates differential excitation with the largest intensity difference in the neighborhood:

$$\xi(x_c) = arctan\left[\frac{f_{00}}{x_c}\right], f_{00} = p * (x_j - x_c) \tag{4}$$

where x_j is the corresponding neighbor pixel of Chebyshev distance:

$$x_j = argmax_{x_i}|x_i - x_c|, i = 0, 1, \ldots, p - 1 \tag{5}$$

Orientation is the same as original WLD's gradient orientation. Finally, GWLD histogram is obtained and experiments show it has encouraging performance, but with high computation cost.

(4) Improved WLD (IWLD)

Since WLD is not good at handling information of flat area, Zhang *et al.* [5] proposed IWLD, which computes the orientation of eight intensity differences separately:

$$\xi_{mx}(x_c) = arctan(\alpha\langle X, J_x\rangle), \xi_{my}(x_c) = arctan(\alpha\langle X, J_y\rangle) \tag{6}$$

where $X = \left(\frac{x_0-x_c}{x_c}, \frac{x_1-x_c}{x_c}, \ldots, \frac{x_{p-1}-x_c}{x_c}\right)^T$ and $\langle,\rangle$ is the inner product operator. $J_x = (cos\theta_0, cos\theta_1, \ldots, cos\theta_{p-1})^T$ and $J_y = (sin\theta_0, sin\theta_1, \ldots, sin\theta_{p-1})^T$ denote the angle between X direction and $x_i - x_c$.

Then, IWLD magnitude and orientation are defined according to those two values:

$$\xi_m(x_c) = \sqrt{(\xi_{mx}(x_c))^2 + (\xi_{my}(x_c))^2}, \xi_o(x_c) = arctan\frac{\xi_{my}(x_c)}{\xi_{mx}(x_c)} \tag{7}$$

Angle information of each neighboring pixel's intensity difference makes contributions to image representation. Experiments on face databases demonstrate the proposed approach's excellent performance.

3.2   Orientation-Based Variants of WLD

Since direction information makes great contributions for some recognition tasks, several orientation-based variants of WLD have also been proposed.

(5) Sobel WLD

Original WLD's gradient orientation considers only vertical and horizontal neighboring pixels, which is susceptible to noises. It has been replaced with Sobel operator [6, 17] and Isotropic Sobel operator [18], which calculates six neighboring pixels instead of four neighboring pixels. Experiments show it can provide more stable feature histograms and enhance the classification rates for face recognition.

(6) Modified WLD (MWLD)

Lian *et al.* [7] proposed MWLD as the pedestrian detector. The novelty is that the histogram is constructed in a new way by voting the gradient magnitude into each bin:

$$MWLD_{2D}(r, t) = \sum_{i=0}^{M-1} \sum_{j=0}^{N-1} \omega(x_{i,j}) \varphi(\xi(x_{i,j}), r) \varphi(\theta(x_{i,j}), t) \tag{8}$$

and

$$\omega(x_{i,j}) = \sqrt{(x_5 - x_1)^2 + (x_7 - x_3)^2}, \varphi(x, y) = \begin{cases} 1, & x = y \\ 0, & otherwise \end{cases} \tag{9}$$

where M*N represents the image size, r and t are the numbers of the differential excitation bins and dominant orientation. Experiments on fast pedestrian detection show MWLD performs better than other descriptors with higher speed.

(7) Computationally-Efficient Histogram-Based Image Local Descriptor (CHILD)

In order to solve the problem of sensitiveness to noise and image rotation, Anamandra and Chandrasekaran [8] proposed a descriptor called CHILD, which uses Laplacian of Gaussian for differential excitation, and the orientation is obtained by convolving with Tiansi fractional derivative filter. CHILD histogram is constructed at last, which seems more robust for texture classification. It has also been used on color texture images in [19].

(8) Weber Orientation Descriptor (WOD)

Weibin et al. [9] designed WOD for vanishing point detection. The differential excitation considers positive value of average differences:

$$\xi_{WOD}(p_c) = \begin{cases} \sqrt{G(p_c)}, & if \ G(p_c) \geq 0 \\ 0, & if \ G(p_c) < 0 \end{cases}, \ G(p_c) = arctan\left(\frac{p_c - \bar{p}_i}{p_c}\right) \tag{10}$$

The orientation is computed as the index of maximum Gabor energy:

$$\theta_{WOD}(p_c) = Argmax_{\varphi_n} E_{\varphi_n}(p_c), E_{\varphi_n}(p_c) = Re\left(\hat{I}_{\varphi_n}(p_c)\right)^2 + Im\left(\hat{I}_{\varphi_n}(p_c)\right)^2 \tag{11}$$

where $\hat{I}_{\varphi_n}(p_c)$ is the convolution of image and Gabor filter g_{φ_n}. Experiments show WOD can achieve favorable performance results.

(9) Improved WLD (IWLD)

After WLD, Chen et al. [10] proposed a new WLD for person re-identification. The orientation component is improved by coding LBP [20] after quantifying gradient orientation into several intervals:

$$LBP_{m,n}(x_c) = \left\lfloor B_{m,n}^p, B_{m,n}^{p-1}, \dots, B_{m,n}^1 \right\rfloor, B_{m,n}^i = q\left(\phi_{m,n}(x_c)\right) \otimes q\left(\phi_{m,n}(x_i)\right) \tag{12}$$

where $\phi_{m,n}(x_c)$ is the value of orientation and q($\cdot$) is the floor function. Then the histogram is constructed according to the bins of differential excitation and orientation. Experimental results proved that the method is robust for image rotation and illumination, it performs well for person re-identification.

3.3   Multiple Features-Combined Variants of WLD

In order to extract richer information for recognition, researchers proposed several variants that combining other descriptors with WLD. In this section, we will briefly introduce these algorithms.

(10) LBP/WLD

Since LBP can capture the orientation of local textures, Yuqing and Yan [11] combined LBP and WLD into dynamic texture representation to achieve better performance.

WLD is computed with the sigmoid function of differential excitation, then the block match information is measured according to their LBP and WLD patterns:

$$(LBP/WLD)_m = \{i|min(Diff(p_0 - p_i))\} \tag{13}$$

where $Diff(\cdot)$ and WLD are defined as:

$$\text{Diff}(p_0 - p_i) = |LBP(p_0) - LBP(p_i)| + |WLD(p_0) - WLD(p_i)| \tag{14}$$

$$\text{WLD}(I_c) = sigmoid\left(\sum_{i=0}^{p-1} \left|\frac{I_i - I_c}{I_c}\right|\right) \tag{15}$$

At last, LBP/WLD histogram is concatenated with dynamic texture histogram. Experiments show it performances better than LBMP for dynamic texture recognition.

(11) WLD Variance (WLDV)

In order to improve texture classification accuracy, Dawood et al. [12] proposed a hybrid approach that combines WLD with contrast information, which is actually image variance calculated with the Probability Weighted Moments:

$$S_p = \frac{\sqrt{\pi}}{n} \sum_{i=0}^{n} \left[X_i - 2\left(1 - \frac{i - 0.5}{n}\right)X_i\right] \tag{16}$$

where X_i indicates ordered observations in a sample of size n. Finally, the joint histogram is represented for texture classification.

(12) Patterns of Weber Magnitude and Orientation (PWMO)

Wang et al. [13, 14] proposed a computationally efficient, discriminative and robust feature descriptor called PWMO for face recognition system. PWMO consist of two parts: patterns of Weber magnitude, which is encoded with patch-based LBP, and patterns of Weber orientation, which is encoded with patch-based local XOR:

$$\text{p\_LBP}(x_c, y_c) = \left[\sum_{n=0}^{7} 2^n D\left(S_1\left(P_{c_n^R}^r\right), S_1(P_c^r)\right), \ldots, \sum_{n=0}^{7} 2^n D\left(S_q\left(P_{c_n^R}^r\right), S_q(P_c^r)\right)\right] \tag{17}$$

where P_c^r is the image patch centered at current pixel with radius r, and c_n^R are the neighboring pixels with radius R. $S(P_c^r)$ is a pre-defined statistic such as the bins of magnitude histogram and the orientation with largest accumulative magnitude.

Finally, the concatenated histogram is constructed and block-based whitened PCA is introduced to select the most discriminative features. Experimental results demonstrate the proposed method is suitable for face recognition.

(13) Weber Local Binary Pattern (WLBP)

Liu et al. [15] proposed a local descriptor called WLBP, which uses Laplacian of Gaussian for differential excitation and uniform pattern of LBP [21] for orientation component. At last, a more discriminative and robust histogram is constructed. Experiments show it is superior to other state-of-the-art methods not only for face recognition, but also for texture classification.

4 Applications for Biometrics

After WLD has been proposed, it has been widely used on many applications. As for biometrics, WLD and its variants have been successfully applied on face detection [1], face recognition [14, 15], fingerprint liveness detection [22], iris recognition [4] and palmprint recognition [23]. WLD feature is robust to variations in facial expression and illumination, which make it performance well for face images. Since WLD is suitable for high-contrast patterns such as the ridges and valleys of fingerprint and palmprint, it achieves greater performance while using for the liveness detection on those two tasks. Besides, WLD also has been extended to bovine iris recognition, which is robust to noise and illumination in the original images, and it indeed has enhanced the representation power.

5 Conclusions

WLD has become one of important local image descriptors. In this paper, it is the first time to make a review of WLD and its variants. We also survey their applications for biometrics. After an analysis, we divide its variants into three categories, *i.e.,* differential excitation-based, orientation-based, and multiple features-based. For differential excitation-based methods, different differential excitation information is added to make the descriptor more robust to noise. For orientation-based methods, direction extraction algorithms are modified to obtain more effective feature representation. For multiple features based methods, WLD is combined with other descriptors to form a new descriptor and can capture richer information. In our future work, we plan to make a performance evaluation of WLD and its variants for different biometrics tasks such as face, iris, palmprint, and vein recognition.

Acknowledgements. This work is partly supported by the grants of the National Science Foundation of China, Nos. 61673157, 61402018, 61702154, 61702110, 61573151, and also partly supported by the fundamental research funds for the Central Universities, Nos. JZ2017HGTA0178, JZ2017HGTB0189.

References

1. Chen, J., Shan, S., He, C., Zhao, G., Pietikainen, M., Chen, X., Gao, W.: WLD: a robust local image descriptor. IEEE Trans. Pattern Anal. Mach. Intell. **32**(9), 1705–1720 (2010)
2. Jiao, J., Baojun, Z.: A new feature descriptor and selection method to space image registration. In: 2010 International Conference on Image Analysis and Signal Processing, 9–11 April 2010, pp. 314–317 (2010)
3. Zuo, J., Nicolo, F., Schmid, N.A., Boothapati, S.: Encoding, matching and score normalization for cross spectral face recognition: matching SWIR versus visible data. In: 2012 IEEE Fifth International Conference on Biometrics: Theory, Applications and Systems (BTAS), 23–27 September 2012, pp. 203–208 (2012)
4. Sun, S., Zhao, L., Yang, S., Sun, S., Zhao, L., Yang, S.: Gabor Weber local descriptor for bovine iris recognition. Math. Prob. Eng. **2013**(2), 1–7 (2013)
5. Zhang, T., Jia, W., He, X., Yang, J.: Discriminative dictionary learning with motion Weber local descriptor for violence detection. IEEE Trans. Circ. Syst. Video Technol. **27**(3), 696–709 (2016)

6. Dayi, G., Shutao, L., Yin, X.: Face recognition using the Weber local descriptor. In: The First Asian Conference on Pattern Recognition, 28 November 2011, pp. 589–592 (2011)
7. Lian, G., Lai, J., Yuan, Y.: Fast pedestrian detection using a modified WLD detector in salient region. In: Proceedings 2011 International Conference on System Science and Engineering, 8–10 June 2011, pp. 564–569 (2011)
8. Anamandra, S.H., Chandrasekaran, V.: CHILD: a robust computationally-efficient histogram-based image local descriptor. In: 2013 Fourth National Conference on Computer Vision, Pattern Recognition, Image Processing and Graphics (NCVPRIPG), 18–21 December 2013, pp. 1–5 (2013)
9. Weibin, Y., Xiaosong, L., Bin, F., Daiming, Z., Yuan Yan, T.: Fast and accurate vanishing point detection in complex scenes. In: 17th International IEEE Conference on Intelligent Transportation Systems (ITSC), 8–11 October 2014, pp. 93–98 (2014)
10. Chen, L., Chen, H., Li, S., Zhu, J.: Person re-identification by Weber local descriptors and color features. In: International Computer Conference on Wavelet Active Media Technology and Information Processing, pp. 273–278 (2015)
11. Yuqing, Q., Yan, T.: Dynamic texture recognition based on multiple statistical features with LBP/WLD. In: Proceedings of 2011 International Conference on Computer Science and Network Technology, 24–26 December 2011, pp. 957–960 (2011)
12. Dawood, H., Dawood, H., Guo, P.: Combining the contrast information with WLD for texture classification. In: 2012 IEEE International Conference on Computer Science and Automation Engineering (CSAE), 25–27 May 2012, pp. 203–207 (2012)
13. Wang, B., Li, W., Li, Z., Liao, Q.: Patterns of Weber magnitude and orientation for face recognition. In: IEEE International Conference on Image Processing, pp. 1441–1444 (2012)
14. Jiang, Y., Wang, B., Zhou, Y., Li, W., Liao, Q.: Patterns of Weber magnitude and orientation for uncontrolled face representation and recognition ★. Neurocomputing 165, 190–201 (2015)
15. Liu, F., Tang, Z., Tang, J.: WLBP: Weber local binary pattern for local image description. Neurocomputing 120(10), 325–335 (2013)
16. Sun, S., Zhao, L.: Efficient modified Weber local descriptor approach to bovine iris recognition. ICIC Exp. Lett. Part B Appl. Int. J. Res. Surv. 3, 1311–1317 (2012)
17. Li, S., Gong, D., Yuan, Y.: Face recognition using Weber local descriptors. Neurocomputing 122, 272–283 (2013)
18. Zhang, X., Yang, J., Dong, S., Wang, C., Chen, Y., Wu, C.: Thermal infrared face recognition based on the modified blood perfusion model and improved Weber local descriptor. In: Sun, Z., Shan, S., Sang, H., Zhou, J., Wang, Y., Yuan, W. (eds.) CCBR 2014. LNCS, vol. 8833, pp. 103–110. Springer, Cham (2014). doi:10.1007/978-3-319-12484-1_11
19. Anamandra, S.H., Chandrasekaran, V.: COLOR CHILD: a novel color image local descriptor for texture classification and segmentation. Pattern Anal. Appl. 19(3), 821–837 (2016)
20. Davarpanah, S.H., Khalid, F., Abdullah, L.N., Golchin, M.: A texture descriptor: BackGround Local Binary Pattern (BGLBP). Multimedia Tools Appl. 75(11), 1–20 (2016)
21. Ojala, T., Pietikäinen, M., Mäenpää, T.: Multiresolution gray-scale and rotation invariant texture classification with local binary patterns. IEEE Trans. Pattern Anal. Mach. Intell. 24(7), 971–987 (2000)
22. Gragnaniello, D., Poggi, G., Sansone, C., Verdoliva, L.: Fingerprint liveness detection based on Weber local image descriptor. In: 2013 IEEE Workshop on Biometric Measurements and Systems for Security and Medical Applications (BIOMS), pp. 46–50 (2013)
23. Aishwarya, D., Gowri, M., Saranya, R.K.: Palm print recognition using liveness detection technique. In: 2016 Second International Conference on Science Technology Engineering and Management (ICONSTEM), 30–31 March 2016, pp. 109–114 (2016)

Generative Multi-region Segmentation by Utilizing Saliency Information

Lei Zhou$^{(\boxtimes)}$ and Yubin Xia

University of Shanghai for Science and Technology,
JunGong Road NO. 516, Shanghai, China
zmbhou@163.com

Abstract. In traditional method, multi-region segmentation is treated as a pre-operation process of semantic method. A method for automatically partitioning an image into multiple regions is presented in this paper. Motivated by the observation that saliency information can exhibit plentiful meaningful cues for segmentation, we propose a semi-supervised multi-region segmentation method in this paper. Saliency features are applied for seeds location together with color information, then the multiregion segmentation problem is solved using a generative semi-supervised framework in which the selected seeds are treated as initializations. The segmentation results are further refined using a segmentation composition strategy. We demonstrate the effectiveness of our algorithm against the state-of-the-art methods on the benchmark Berkley segmentation dataset.

Keywords: Multi-region object segmentation · Semi-supervised learning · Generative model · Segmentation composition

1 Introduction

Object segmentation is a challenging problem in computer vision and it has wide applications in many areas such as object recognition, image classification and image retrieval, etc. Therefore, many methods have been proposed to extract interesting objects automatically. In general, it can be divided into three categories: unsupervised, semi-supervised and fully supervised. The unsupervised methods, such as K-means [1], EM [2], FH segmentation [3], Active contour [4], normalized cut [5] and meanshift clustering [6], are implemented without prior knowledge about the images. In semi-supervised methods [7], users can label pixels as foreground or background with interactive segmentation approaches. User input can locate where the object is (location information), and color and texture information contained in the scribbles provide prior knowledge about what the object is. Fully supervised segmentation methods are mostly designed for detecting and extracting specific object categories in images and an accurately labeled training dataset is required.

In this paper, we explore to design a unified framework for multi-region segmentation. Multi-region segmentation models or boundary detectors are often

© Springer International Publishing AG 2017
J. Zhou et al. (Eds.): CCBR 2017, LNCS 10568, pp. 700–707, 2017.
https://doi.org/10.1007/978-3-319-69923-3_75

taken as a pre-process procedure for semantic segmentation. However the performance will be influenced by the classifier. On the other hand, the traditional segmentation method such as mean-shift or normalized cut are always treated as input for semantic classifiers. In summary, the main contributions of the paper are summarized as follows:

- A simple and effective generative segmentation framework is presented.
- A novel joint multi-region segmentation framework based on seed selection and generative model is proposed by fusing saliency information.

2 Generative Segmentation Model

Our goal is to automatically partition the image into multiple regions. On drawback of the generative model is that it is sensitive to the choice of seeds or initialization for each region. Therefore we propose a simple and efficient method to generate reasonable initial seeds for each region. The segmentation problem is divided into two subproblems. The first one is how to choose the number of regions K and the initial seeds, which will be described in Sect. 2.1. The second one is how to segment the image into k regions for a given number k, which is presented in Sect. 2.2.

2.1 Seeds Selection for Segmentation

The efficiency of the proposed segmentation model depends on the number of labels K and selected seeds (represented as $U^k, k \in \{1, ..., K\}$). In the task of Figure/Ground segmentation, $K = 2$ and the initial seed regions U^1 and U^2 can be obtained by simply separating the image space into two parts. In the task of multiple region segmentation, $K > 2$, we propose an iterative seed selection approach to determine K and the seed sets U. We utilize the saliency information for seeds generation.

Fusion for Seed Generation. The RGB colors are selected as the local features to describe color information for each region $l \in [RS_1, ..., RS_Y]$ and they are modeled using a Gaussian mixture model (GMM). Let the color models be represented by GMM $\{\alpha_c, \mu_c, \Sigma_c\}_{c=1}^C$ in the color space, where $\{\alpha_c, \mu_c, \Sigma_c\}$ contains the weight, the mean color and the covariance matrix of the c-th component. For pixels in each region, a set of GMM parameters are learned. The Gaussian mixture distribution can be written as:

$$V(I_x|l) = \sum_c \alpha_{cl} N(I_x|\mu_{cl}, \Sigma_{cl}), l \in [1, ..., Y], \tag{1}$$

where α_{cl}, μ_{cl} and Σ_{cl} represent the weight, the mean color and the covariance matrix of the c-th component learned from pixels in region l respectively. The parameters of a GMM can be obtained by maximizing the log likelihood function for a GMM using techniques like gradient-based optimization and expectation-maximization algorithm. In our experiments, GMM with one components are used to represent the color statistics in each cluster and the EM algorithm [8] is applied to generate the parameters of GMMs.

Then, the posterior probability $P_{gmm}(l|I_q)$ at each pixel p of the image is:

$$P_{gmm}(l|I_q) = \frac{V(I_q|l)p(l)}{\sum_{l\in[1,...,Y]} V(I_x|l)p(l)}, \quad (2)$$

where the prior probability is set as $p(l) = \frac{1}{Y}, l \in [1, ..., Y]$.

Iterative Initial Seed Generation. At the beginning of *1-st* iteration, the gaussian parameters $(\{\alpha_c, \mu_c, \Sigma_c\}_{c=1}^C)$ of $K(0)$ clusters $RS_1, ..., RS_{K(0)}$ are computed as initialization. $K(0)$ is the cluster number of the *1-st* iteration. Then, the posterior probabilities corresponding to $K(0)$ clusters are defined as $P_{gmm,0}(l|I_q), l \in [1, ..., K(0)]$ (Eq. (2)). The label of pixel p is assigned to the label corresponding to the largest probability:

$$l_p = arg\ max_m\ P_{gmm,0}(l = m|I_p), m \in [1, ..., K(0)] \quad (3)$$

At the end of *1-st* iteration, the image is separated into $K(1)$ regions according the the computed label (Eq. 3). Then, the procedure is repeated. At the beginning of the t-*th* iteration, the Gaussian parameters are computed for the $K(t-1)$ clusters and $K(t-1)$ posterior probabilities $P_{gmm,t}(l|I_i), l \in [1, ..., K(t-1)]$ are obtained. At the end of t-*th* iteration, the image is partitioned into $K(t)$ regions via the maximum posterior probability rule Eq. (3). At the end of T-*th* iteration, $K(T)$ initial regions are obtained.

To reduce the little noise in the selected seeds, we apply some morphological operators such as erosion and dilation and the processed regions are represented as $RSM_1, ..., RSM_{K(T)}$. Finally, the seed set U^k for label $l = k$ is defined as $U^k = \{q|P_{gmm,T}(l = k|I_q) > \varepsilon, q \in RSM_k\}$, where the threshold ε is set as 0.6.

2.2   Generative Segmentation Model

The multiregion image segmentation problem is formulated as a labeling problem based on the extracted seeds $U^z, z \in \{1, ..., T\}$. Each pixel $I_p \in \{I_i, ..., I_N\}$ is assigned one label $l_p \in \{1, ..., T\}$. According to the basic decision theory, we assign I_p the label with the largest posterior probability. Let $U^z = \{U_1^z, ..., U_{N_z}^z\}$ denote the set of the N_z seeds with label l_z. Then, the likelihood for segmentation $P_{seg}(I_i|l)$ is formulated as:

$$P_{seg}(I_i|l = z) = \sum_{m=1}^{N_z} p(I_i|U_m^z, l = z)p(U_m^z|l = z), \quad (4)$$

where the likelihood of each pixel is defined as a mixture of distribution $p(I_i|U_m^z, l = z)$ from each seed U_m^z with seed distribution $p(U_m^z|l = z)$. The distribution $p(I_i|U_m^z, l = z)$ is modeled as the dependency between pixel I_i and label $l = z$. Since the labels are generated automatically, we use the uniform distribution $p(U_m^z | l = z) = \frac{1}{N_z}$ to ensure that our method is less depended on the number of seeds. Based on the affinity scores between pixels defined in Eq. (4), the likelihood at pixel I_i related to labeled pixel U_m^z is represented as $p(I_i | U_m^z, l = z) = Q_{i,U_m^z}$. Then, the likelihood related to label set U^z can be obtained by:

$$P_{seg}(I_i | l = z) = w_1 \Phi(I_i, l = z) + w_2 \Theta(I_i, l = z) + w_3 \Omega(I_i, l = z). \tag{5}$$

where $\Phi(I_i, l = z) = \frac{1}{N_z} \sum_{m=1}^{N_z} Q_{i,U_m^z}$ is the affinity probability and $\Theta(I_i, l = z)$ is the trained classifiers. $\Omega(I_i, l = z)$ is the global classifier.

Similarly, the posterior probability at pixel i is obtained by computing the label prior probability $p_s(l = z)$ and the pixel likelihood: $P_{seg}(I_i | l = z)$ using the Bayesian rules:

$$P_{seg}(l = z | I_i) = \frac{P_{seg}(I_i | l) p_s(l = z)}{\sum_{g=1}^{K} (P_{seg}(I_i | l) p_s(l = g)}, \tag{6}$$

where the label prior probability is defined as a uniform distribution $p_s(l) = \frac{1}{K}, l \in \{1, ..., K\}$.

The label of pixel q is decided according the the maximum posterior probability rule

$$\begin{aligned} l_q = arg\ max_k\ P_{seg}(l = k | I_q) \\ s.t.\quad k \in \{1, ..., K\}. \end{aligned} \tag{7}$$

3   Composition of Segmentations Over Multiple Saliency Models

In this paper, the contrast prior saliency and boundary prior saliency maps are selected to generate segmentation results respectively. Given an image, two segmentations can be generated using the generative models described in Sect. 2. It is observed that the partitioned regions of two categories of segmentations may exhibit complementary segmentation cues. In this section, a spectral clustering algorithm is applied to compose the two kinds of segmentation results.

3.1   Bipartite Graph Construction

To reflect the relationship between regions and regions, regions and pixels, a bipartite graph is constructed firstly. Let SUP represent a set of multi-layer superpixels over an image I, $G = \{X, Y, B\}$ be a bipartite graph and the node set is $X \bigcup Y$, where $X := I \bigcup SUP = \{x_i\}_{i=1}^{N_x}$ and $Y = SUP = \{y_j\}_{j=1}^{N_Y}$. $N_X = |I| + |SUP|$ and $N_Y = |SUP|$. Then, the across affinity matrix defined as $B = (a_{ij})_{N_x \times N_y}$ between X and Y is constructed as follows:

(1) For two nodes x_i and x_j in I, we set

$$w_{ij}^{II} = 0. \tag{8}$$

(2) In the graph, the superpixels in SUP are fully connected. To measure the similarity between superpixels, the RGB/Bhattacharyya descriptor is applied. The RGB color space is used to compute the color histogram and each color channel is divided into 16 levels and the histogram of each region is calculated in the feature space of 4096 bins [9].

$$w_{ij}^{YY} = \rho(Y_i, Y_j), \tag{9}$$

where $\rho(Y_i, Y_j) = \sum_{u=1}^{4096} \sqrt{Hist_{Y_i}^u \cdot Hist_{Y_j}^u}$. $Hist_{Y_i}^u$ and $Hist_{Y_j}^u$ are the normalized histograms of region Y_i and Y_j respectively.

(3) The inter-layer connection reflects the relationship between regions and the corresponding pixels inside.

$$w_{ij}^{IY} = P_{gmm,S_j}(l = j|I_i), \tag{10}$$

where $P_{gmm,S_j}(l = j|I_{xi})$ is the posterior probability learned over the seed set S_j.

3.2 Segmentations Composition

Firstly, a cross-affinity matrix $B = (b_{ij})_{(N_x+N_y) \times N_Y}$ is constructed between pixel and superpixels.

$$b_{ij} = W_{ij}^{IY}, if \quad x_i \in i, x_i \in Y_j, y_j \in SUP.$$
$$b_{ij} = W_{ij}^{YY}, if \quad Y_i \in SUP, Y_j \in SUP. \tag{11}$$
$$b_{ij} = 0, otherwise.$$

Based on the bipartite graph, the fusion of diverse superpixel cues is solved using a principled graph partitioning framework [10]. The approach for bipartite graph partitioning is summarized as follows.

- To form $D_x = diag(B)$, $D_y = diag(B^T)$, $W_Y = B^T D_X^{-1} B$, and $L_Y = D_Y - W_Y$.
- To compute the bottom K_f eigenpairs $\{(\lambda_i, v_i)\}_{i=1}^{K_f}$ satisfying $L_Y v = \lambda D_Y v$. K_f is the cluster number which is set as the $K_f = max(K_{con}, K_{bou})$. K_{con} and K_{bou} are the cluster numbers of contrast prior driven segmentation and boundary prior driven segmentation respectively.
- To obtain γ_i such that $0 \leq \gamma_i \leq 1$ and $\gamma_i(2 - \gamma_i) = \lambda_i$, $i = 1, 2, .., K_f$.
- To compute the engivectors $e_i = (u_i^T, v_i^T)^T$, $i = 1, 2, .., K_f$, with $u_i = \frac{1}{1-\gamma_i} D_X^{-1} B v_i$, $i = 1, 2, .., K_f$.
- To derive the final segmentation results. We apply the k-means to the rows of the matrix $E := (e_1, ..., e_{K_f})$ and the image is separated into K_f clusters.

4   Experimental Results

4.1   Evaluation of Multi-region Segmentation

The segmentation results on Berkley Segmentation Database [11] which consists of 300 natural images are reported. To quantitatively evaluate the segmentation results, four criteria are used: (1) Probabilistic Rand Index (PRI) [12]; (2) Variation of Information (VoI) [13]; (3) Global Consistency Error (GCE) [11]; and (4) Boundary Displacement Error (BDE) [14]. A segmentation is better if PRI is larger and the other three are smaller to the ground truths [10]. We compare the average scores of contrast saliency based segmentation (CBS), boundary saliency based segmentation (BBS) and the segmentation of composition (SOC) with eight benchmark algorithms, Ncut [5], Mean-shift [6], FH [3], JSEG [15], Multi-scale Ncut (MNcut) [16], NTP [17], SDTV [18] and KM [19]. The scores of different methods for comparison are collected from [10,19] and the results are listed in Table 1, with the two best results highlighted in bold for each criterion. We can see that SOC achieves the highest PRI and the lowest BDE scores against the compared methods.

Table 1. Performance evaluation of the proposed method against methods over the Berkley segmentation database.

	PRI	VoI	GCE	BDE
Ncut	0.7242	2.9061	0.2232	17.15
Mean shift	0.7958	1.9725	0.1888	14.41
FH	0.7139	3.3949	0.1746	16.67
JSEG	0.7756	1.8217	0.1989	14.40
MNcut	0.7559	2.4401	0.1925	15.10
NTP	0.7521	2.4954	0.2373	16.30
KM	0.76	2.4	X	X
SDTV	0.7758	1.8165	0.1768	16.24
gPb-Hoiem	0.724	3.149	NA	14.80
SAS(MS)	0.7991	1.9320	0.2222	15.37
BBS	0.7530	4.2460	0.4221	15.98
CBS	0.7852	2.2005	0.2226	12.02
SOC	0.8096	1.9687	0.2175	11.80

In terms of VoI and GCE, mean shift and SDVT outperform SOC. JSEG and MNCut yield better GCE than SOC. The scores of the intermediate results, including the initial K-means segmentation and the generative segmentation results based on the contrast prior and boundary prior saliency models, are listed in Table 1 as well.

It is observed that the generative segmentation model achieves dramatic performance improvement in terms of PRI, VoI and GCE compared with initial K-mean segmentation. In general, the segmentation results generated by contrast prior achieves higher PRI score and lower GCE and BDE scores. We also listed the scores of K-mean clustering and final segmentations based on RGB color space. Saliency based clustering or generative segmentation achieves better performance. This is primarily because that saliency values can reflect rich structural information of images and the saliency values are more discriminative. The pixels can be separated more easily in saliency space than in the RGB color space.

References

1. Kanungo, T., Mount, D.M., Netanyahu, N.S., Piatko, C.D., Silverman, R., Wu, A.Y.: An efficient k-means clustering algorithm: analysis and implementation. IEEE Trans. Pattern Anal. Mach. Intell. **24**(7), 881–892 (2002)
2. Carson, C., Belongie, S., Greenspan, H., Malik, J.: Blobworld: image segmentation using expectation-maximization and its application to image querying. IEEE Trans. Pattern Anal. Mach. Intell. **24**(8), 1026–1038 (2002)
3. Felzenszwalb, P.F., Huttenlocher, D.P.: Efficient graph-based image segmentation. Int. J. Comput. Vis. **59**(2), 167–181 (2004)
4. Caselles, V., Kimmel, R., Sapiro, G.: Geodesic active contours. Int. J. Comput. Vis. **22**(1), 61–79 (1997)
5. Shi, J., Malik, J.: Normalized cuts and image segmentation. IEEE Trans. Pattern Anal. Mach. Intell. **22**(8), 888–905 (2000)
6. Comaniciu, D., Meer, P.: Mean shift: a robust approach toward feature space analysis. IEEE Trans. Pattern Anal. Mach. Intell. **24**(5), 603–619 (2002)
7. Boykov, Y.Y., Jolly, M.-P.: Interactive graph cuts for optimal boundary & region segmentation of objects in ND images. In: 2001 Eighth IEEE International Conference on Computer Vision (ICCV), vol. 1, pp. 105–112. IEEE (2001)
8. Moon, T.K.: The expectation-maximization algorithm. IEEE Sig. Process. Mag. **13**(6), 47–60 (1996)
9. Ning, J., Zhang, L., Zhang, D., Chengke, W.: Interactive image segmentation by maximal similarity based region merging. Pattern Recogn. **43**(2), 445–456 (2010)
10. Li, Z., Wu, X.-M., Chang, S.-F.: Segmentation using superpixels: a bipartite graph partitioning approach. In: 2012 IEEE Conference on Computer Vision and Pattern Recognition (CVPR), pp. 789–796. IEEE (2012)
11. Martin, D., Fowlkes, C., Tal, D., Malik, J.: A database of human segmented natural images and its application to evaluating segmentation algorithms and measuring ecological statistics. In: 2001 Proceedings of the Eighth IEEE International Conference on Computer Vision, ICCV 2001, vol. 2, pp. 416–423. IEEE (2001)
12. Unnikrishnan, R., Pantofaru, C., Hebert, M.: Toward objective evaluation of image segmentation algorithms. IEEE Trans. Pattern Anal. Mach. Intell. **29**(6), 929–944 (2007)
13. Meila, M.: Comparing clusterings: an axiomatic view. In: Proceedings of the 22nd International Conference on Machine Learning, pp. 577–584. ACM (2005)
14. Freixenet, J., Muñoz, X., Raba, D., Martí, J., Cufí, X.: Yet another survey on image segmentation: region and boundary information integration. In: Heyden, A., Sparr, G., Nielsen, M., Johansen, P. (eds.) ECCV 2002. LNCS, vol. 2352, pp. 408–422. Springer, Heidelberg (2002). doi:10.1007/3-540-47977-5_27

15. Deng, Y., Manjunath, B.S.: Unsupervised segmentation of color-texture regions in images and video. IEEE Trans. Pattern Anal. Mach. Intell. **23**(8), 800–810 (2001)
16. Cour, T., Benezit, F., Shi, J.: Spectral segmentation with multiscale graph decomposition. In: 2005 IEEE Computer Society Conference on Computer Vision and Pattern Recognition, CVPR 2005, vol. 2, pp. 1124–1131. IEEE (2005)
17. Wang, J., Jia, Y., Hua, X.-S., Zhang, C., Quan, L.: Normalized tree partitioning for image segmentation. In: 2008 IEEE Conference on Computer Vision and Pattern Recognition, CVPR 2008, pp. 1–8. IEEE (2008)
18. Donoser, M., Urschler, M., Hirzer, M., Bischof, H.: Saliency driven total variation segmentation. In: 2009 IEEE 12th International Conference on Computer Vision, pp. 817–824. IEEE (2009)
19. Salah, M.B., Mitiche, A., Ayed, I.B.: Multiregion image segmentation by parametric kernel graph cuts. IEEE Trans. Image Process. **20**(2), 545–557 (2011)

Truncated Nuclear Norm Based Low Rank Embedding

Fanlong Zhang[1(✉)], Heyou Chang[2], Guowei Yang[1],
Zhangjing Yang[1], and Minghua Wan[1]

[1] School of Technology, Nanjing Audit University, Nanjing 211815, China
csfzhang@126.com, ygw_ustb@163.com, yzj@nau.edu.cn,
wmh36@sina.com
[2] Key Laboratory of Trusted Cloud Computing and Big Data Analysis,
Nanjing Xiaozhuang University, Nanjing 211171, China
cv_hychang@126.com

Abstract. Dimensionality reduction, also called feature extraction, is an important issue in pattern recognition. However, many existing dimensionality reduction methods, such as principal component analysis, fail when there exist noises in data, especially for noise caused by outliers or corruption. Recently, a robust method, named low-rank embedding (LRE) is proposed, which uses the nuclear norm for characterizing the low rank structure hided in the data. However, one major limitation of the nuclear norm is that each singular value is treated equally, since the nuclear norm is defined as the sum of all singular values. Thus the rank function may not be well approximated in practice. To overcome this drawback, this paper presents a truncated nuclear norm based low rank embedding (Truncated-LRE). The truncated nuclear norm can approximate the rank function more accurately than nuclear norm. Experimental results show encouraging results of the proposed methods in comparison with the state-of-the-art matrix dimensionality reduction methods.

Keywords: Dimensionality reduction · Feature extraction · Truncated nuclear norm · Low rank embedding

1 Introduction

Dimensionality reduction, or called feature extraction, is a classical issue in the areas of pattern recognition and computer vision. There exist many methods, such as principal component analysis (PCA) [1], independent component analysis (ICA) [2], Fisher linear discriminate analysis (LDA) [3], and so on. However, they may fail when there exist noises in data, especially for noise caused by outliers or corruption.

Many robust methods have been proposed, such as Euler principal component analysis (EPCA) [4], Locality Preserving Projections (LPP) [5, 6], robust principal component analysis (RPCA) [7], Angle 2DPCA [8], and so on. Recently, Wong et al. [9] proposed a novel robust dimensionality reduction method, named low-rank embedding (LRE). LRE integrates the optimal low rank representation (LRR) [10] and projection learning into one model so as to enhance the robustness of the low rankness

© Springer International Publishing AG 2017
J. Zhou et al. (Eds.): CCBR 2017, LNCS 10568, pp. 708–715, 2017.
https://doi.org/10.1007/978-3-319-69923-3_76

to deal with the occlusive and corrupted image data [9]. In LRE, the nuclear norm is used for characterizing the low rank structure hided in the data.

The nuclear norm is a typical convex approximation of rank function. The nuclear norm is equal to the sum of the singular values of a matrix and is the convex lower bound of the rank function. As shown in [11–13], the low rank matrix can be recovered exactly by minimizing the nuclear norm instead of minimizing the rank function if the subset of elements is sampled uniformly at random and the matrix satisfies a restrictive structural constraint (known as incoherence) on its row and column spaces. The intuition behind this heuristic is that whereas the rank function counts the number of non-vanishing singular values, the nuclear norm sums their amplitude. This is similar to how the l1 norm is used as the surrogate of l0 norm for counting the number of nonzero elements in a vector. Apart from the nuclear norm, another convex approximation of rank function is the max-norm [14].

However, convex approximation often makes the resulting solution deviate from the original matrix [15]. There are many non-convex approximations proposed for addressing this problem, such as truncated nuclear norm [16] and Schatten norm [17]. The truncated nuclear norm is defined as the nuclear norm subtracted by the sum of the largest few singular values. In this way, they can get a more accurate and robust approximation to the rank function.

Motivated by the works [9, 16], this paper proposes a truncated nuclear norm based low rank embedding (Truncated-LRE). Truncated-LRE also integrates the low rank representation and projection learning into one model. Truncated-LRE and LRE differ in characterizing of the low rank structure. In Truncated-LRE, the truncated nuclear norm is employed.

The rest of this paper is organized as follows. Section 2 reviews the related work. Section 3 presents our model and corresponding algorithm. Section 4 reports experimental results. Section 5 offers conclusions.

2 Related Works

Given a data set $\mathbf{X} = [\mathbf{x}_1, \mathbf{x}_2, \ldots, \mathbf{x}_s]$, where each $\mathbf{x}_i$ is a sample. The nuclear norm of the matrix $\mathbf{X}$ is defined by $\|\mathbf{X}\|_* = \sum_i \sigma_i$, which is the sum of the singular values of $\mathbf{X}$. Besides, the $L_{2,1}$ and L_1 norms of a matrix $\mathbf{X}$ are defined by $\|\mathbf{X}\|_{2,1} = \sum_j \sqrt{\sum_i (\mathbf{X}_{ij})^2}$, $\|\mathbf{X}\|_1 = \sum_{i,j} |\mathbf{X}_{ij}|$, respectively, where $\mathbf{X}_{ij}$ means the (i,j)-th entry.

2.1 RPCA and LRR

The data $\mathbf{X}$ is usually corrupted. RPCA tries to decompose $\mathbf{X}$ into two matrices $\mathbf{D}$ and $\mathbf{E}$, where the matrix $\mathbf{D}$ is supposed to have low rank and $\mathbf{E}$ is supposed to be sparse. The decomposition model is given by

$$\min_{\mathbf{D},\mathbf{E}} \|\mathbf{D}\|_* + \lambda \|\mathbf{E}\|_1 \quad \text{s.t.} \quad \mathbf{X} = \mathbf{D} + \mathbf{E}. \tag{1}$$

As an important extension of RPCA, the LRR was presented to segment subspace from a union of multiple linear subspaces, which assumed that the representation coefficient matrix is low-rank. The general formulation of LRR is as follows:

$$\min_{\mathbf{Z},\mathbf{E}} \|\mathbf{Z}\|_* + \lambda \|\mathbf{E}\|_l \quad \text{s.t.} \quad \mathbf{X} = \mathbf{A}\mathbf{Z} + \mathbf{E}. \tag{2}$$

In (2), $\mathbf{A}$ is a dictionary. The $\|\cdot\|_l$ indicates certain regularization strategy, such as the L_1 or $L_{2,1}$ norm. It is shown that the problem of subspace segmentation can be well addressed by solving the following specific LRR problems:

$$\min_{\mathbf{Z},\mathbf{E}} \|\mathbf{Z}\|_* + \lambda \|\mathbf{E}\|_{2,1} \quad \text{s.t.} \quad \mathbf{X} = \mathbf{X}\mathbf{Z} + \mathbf{E}. \tag{3}$$

2.2 LRE

To take full use of LRR's robustness to the noise in dimensionality reduction, the LRE assumes that the data can be approximately reconstructed by a low rank matrix $\mathbf{Z}$ on the orthogonal subspace $\mathbf{P}$. The model is given by (4).

$$\min_{\mathbf{Z},\mathbf{E}} \|\mathbf{Z}\|_* + \lambda \|\mathbf{P}^T\mathbf{X} - \mathbf{P}^T\mathbf{X}\mathbf{Z}\|_{2,1} \quad \text{s.t.} \quad \mathbf{P}^T\mathbf{P} = \mathbf{I}. \tag{4}$$

The experiments in [9] show that LRE is superior to the previous methods of feature extraction.

3   Truncated Nuclear Norm Base Low Rank Embedding

3.1   Model

The truncated nuclear norm $\|\mathbf{X}\|_r$ is defined as the sum of $\min(m,n)$-r minimum singular values, i.e.

$$\|\mathbf{X}\|_r = \sum\nolimits_{i=r+1}^{\min(m,n)} \sigma_i(X). \tag{5}$$

Considering the values of the largest r nonzero singular values will not affect the rank of a matrix, truncated nuclear norm leaves them free and focus on summing the smallest $\min(m,n)$-r singular values. Thus the truncated nuclear norm is a more accurate and robust approximation form to the rank function. Inspirited by this and related work [9], we propose the truncated nuclear norm based low rank embedding (Truncated-LRE), which is modeled by (6).

$$\min_{\mathbf{Z},\mathbf{P}} \|\mathbf{Z}\|_r + \lambda \|\mathbf{P}^T\mathbf{X} - \mathbf{P}^T\mathbf{X}\mathbf{Z}\|_{2,1} \quad \text{s.t.} \quad \mathbf{P}^T\mathbf{P} = \mathbf{I}. \tag{6}$$

3.2   Algorithm

Since truncated nuclear norm $\|\cdot\|_r$ is non-convex operation, it is not easy to solve (6) directly. Fortunately, one has:

$$\|\mathbf{Z}\|_r = \|\mathbf{Z}\|_* - \max_{\mathbf{AA}^T=\mathbf{I},\mathbf{BB}^T=\mathbf{I}} Tr\left(\mathbf{AZB}^T\right). \tag{7}$$

Based on the formulation (7), a two-step iterative scheme for solving (6) can be designed as follows.

(i) Step one: fix $\mathbf{Z}$ and compute $\mathbf{A}$ and $\mathbf{B}$ by solving (8).

$$\max_{\mathbf{AA}^T=\mathbf{I},\mathbf{BB}^T=\mathbf{I}} Tr\left(\mathbf{AZB}^T\right). \tag{8}$$

Denote the singular value decomposition of $\mathbf{Z}$ as:

$$\mathbf{Z} = \mathbf{USV}^T. \tag{9}$$

Then the problem (8) has the closed-form solution [16], which is given by

$$\mathbf{A} = \mathbf{U}_{1:r}, \mathbf{B} = \mathbf{V}_{1:r}^T, \tag{10}$$

where $1:r$ means the first r columns.

(ii) Step two: fix $\mathbf{A}$, $\mathbf{B}$, and update $\mathbf{Z}$ and $\mathbf{P}$ by solving (11).

$$\begin{aligned} \min_{\mathbf{Z},\mathbf{P}} \|\mathbf{Z}\|_* &- Tr\left(\mathbf{AZB}^T\right) + \lambda\left\|\mathbf{P}^T\mathbf{X} - \mathbf{P}^T\mathbf{XZ}\right\|_{2,1} \\ \text{s.t.} \quad \mathbf{P}^T\mathbf{P} &= \mathbf{I} \end{aligned} \tag{11}$$

The problem (11) can be equivalently converted to problem (12).

$$\begin{aligned} \min_{\mathbf{Z},\mathbf{E},\mathbf{P},\mathbf{J}} \|\mathbf{J}\|_* &- Tr\left(\mathbf{AJB}^T\right) + \lambda\|\mathbf{E}\|_{2,1} \\ \text{s.t.} \quad \mathbf{P}^T\mathbf{X} - \mathbf{P}^T\mathbf{XZ} &= \mathbf{E}, \mathbf{P}^T\mathbf{P} = \mathbf{I}, \mathbf{Z} = \mathbf{J} \end{aligned} \tag{12}$$

Then (12) can be solved by alternately updating $\mathbf{P}$ and ($\mathbf{Z}$, $\mathbf{E}$, $\mathbf{J}$). When updating ($\mathbf{Z}$, $\mathbf{E}$, $\mathbf{J}$) the *inexact augmented Lagrange multiplier algorithms* (inexact ALM) [18] can be employed. Note that in the LRR and LRE, the inexact ALM is also used for updating ($\mathbf{Z}$, $\mathbf{E}$, $\mathbf{J}$). The difference is how to update $\mathbf{J}$. So, this paper only focuses on how to update $\mathbf{J}$. Here, the $\mathbf{J}$ can be updated by optimization (13).

$$\min_{\mathbf{J}} \frac{1}{\mu}\|\mathbf{J}\|_* + \frac{4}{2}\left\|\mathbf{J} - \left[\mathbf{Z} + \frac{1}{\mu}\left(\mathbf{Y}_2 + \mathbf{A}^T\mathbf{B}\right)\right]\right\|_F^2, \tag{13}$$

where $\mathbf{Y}_2$ is Lagrangian multiplier and μ is a penalty parameter. Its optimal solutions can be computed via the singular value thresholding operator [19]. Specifically, given a matrix $\mathbf{Q}$ and its singular value decomposition $\mathbf{Q} = \mathbf{USV}^T$, $\mathbf{S} = diag(\sigma_1, \cdots, \sigma_r)$, where $\sigma_1, \cdots, \sigma_r$ are singular values, the singular value shrinkage operator $D_\tau(\cdot)$ at parameter $\tau > 0$ is defined as (14).

$$D_\tau(\mathbf{Q}) = \mathbf{U}\mathrm{diag}\big(\{\max(0, \sigma_j - \tau)\}\big)\mathbf{V}^T. \tag{14}$$

So, the optimal of (13) can be given by (15):

$$\mathbf{J} = D_{\frac{1}{\mu}}\left(\mathbf{Z} + \frac{1}{\mu}(\mathbf{Y}_2 + \mathbf{A}^T\mathbf{B})\right). \tag{15}$$

The algorithms for solving (11) and Truncated-LRE (6) are outlined in Algorithms 1 and 2, respectively.

Algorithm 1. Iterative scheme for solving sub-problem (11).

---

1 Initialize:
  Given iteration number T, and matrices $\mathbf{A}$, $\mathbf{B}$. Let:
    $\mathbf{Z} = \mathbf{M} = 0, \mathbf{E} = 0, \mathbf{Y}_1 = \mathbf{Y}_2 = 0, \quad \mu = 10^{-6}, \rho = 1.1, \varepsilon = 10^{-8}$;
2 Update $\mathbf{J}$ by (15);
3 Update $\mathbf{Z}$ by $\mathbf{Z} = (\mathbf{I} + \mathbf{X}^T\mathbf{P}\mathbf{P}^T\mathbf{X})^{-1}\left[\mathbf{X}^T\mathbf{P}\mathbf{P}^T\mathbf{X} - \mathbf{X}^T\mathbf{P}\mathbf{E} + \mathbf{J} + \frac{1}{\mu}(\mathbf{X}^T\mathbf{P}\mathbf{Y}_1 - \mathbf{Y}_2)\right]$;
4 Update $\mathbf{E}$ by $\min_\mathbf{J} \frac{\lambda}{\mu}\|\mathbf{E}\|_{2,1} + \frac{1}{2}\left\|\mathbf{E} - \left[\mathbf{P}^T\mathbf{X} - \mathbf{P}^T\mathbf{X}\mathbf{Z} + \frac{1}{\mu}\mathbf{Y}_1\right]\right\|_F^2$ [20];
5 Update the multipliers by $\mathbf{Y}_1 = \mathbf{Y}_1 + \mu(\mathbf{P}^T\mathbf{X} - \mathbf{P}^T\mathbf{X}\mathbf{Z} - \mathbf{E}), \mathbf{Y}_2 = \mathbf{Y}_2 + \mu(\mathbf{Z} - \mathbf{J})$;
6 Update μ by $\mu = \min(\rho\mu, 10^6)$;
7 Convergence checking:
  If $\max(\|\mathbf{P}^T\mathbf{X} - \mathbf{P}^T\mathbf{X}\mathbf{Z} - \mathbf{E}\|_\infty, \|\mathbf{Z} - \mathbf{J}\|_\infty) < \varepsilon$,go to 8;otherwise go to 2;
8 Update P by $\min_\mathbf{P} \left\|\mathbf{P}^T\mathbf{X} - \mathbf{P}^T\mathbf{X}\mathbf{Z}\right\|_{2,1}$ s.t. $\mathbf{P}^T\mathbf{P} = \mathbf{I}$ [9];
9 Iteration checking:

Algorithm 2. Two-step iterative scheme for solving Truncated-LRE (6).

---

1 Initialize: Training data $\mathbf{X}$, parameter λ, $\mathbf{P} = \mathbf{I}$, tolerance ε ;
Do
    2 Update $\mathbf{A}$ and $\mathbf{B}$ by (10);
    3 Update $\mathbf{P}$ and $\mathbf{Z}$ by Algorithm 1;
Until $\max(\|\mathbf{P}^{k+1} - \mathbf{P}^k\|_F, \|\mathbf{Z}^{k+1} - \mathbf{Z}^k\|_F) < \varepsilon$;
4 Output: P ,Z.

---

4 Experiments

The proposed algorithm is evaluated and compared with the other feature extraction methods, including PCA, LPP [5], EPCA [4] and LRE [9]. Finally, the nearest neighbor (NN) classifier and support vector machine (SVM) are employed for classification, respectively.

4.1 Experiments on the Extended Yale B Database

In the Extended Yale B database [21], there are 38 subjects. For each subject, there are 64 images under different lighting conditions. For each subject, ten of the images are randomly selected for training, and the rest images for testing. We let the number of features vary from 10 to 100 with an interval 20.

Figure 1 shows recognition rates of all methods with varying features under two classifiers: the NN classifier and SVM. Top recognition rates are in Table 1. It can be seen that Truncated-LRE outperforms other methods in many cases. When SVM is used, the recognition difference among methods is unapparent.

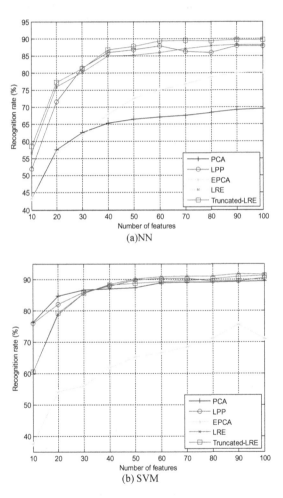

(a)NN

(b) SVM

Fig. 1. Recognition rates with varying feature number on the Extended Yale B database under the NN classifier and SVM.

Table 1. Top recognition rate of each method on the Extended Yale B under the NN classifier and SVM.

	PCA	LPP	EPCA	LRE	Truncated-LRE
NN	69.47	87.81	80.35	88.23	89.63
SVM	89.39	90.44	75.53	90.18	89.65

4.2 Experiments on the USPS Handwritten Digit Database

The USPS handwriting digital image database includes 10 classes from "0" to "9". We used 1000 samples for training and 1000 ones for testing. Each image has size of 16 × 16. Figure 2 shows recognition rates with varying features under NN classifier. Again, the Truncated-LRE outperforms other methods.

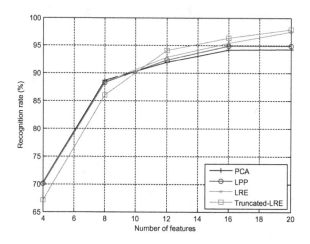

Fig. 2. Recognition rates with varying feature number on the USPS database under the NN classifier.

5   Conclusions

This paper proposes a new dimensionality reduction model and corresponding optimization algorithm. In the new model, the truncated nuclear norm is employed for characterizing the low rank structure hided in the data. The experiments show that the proposed method is efficient in image recognition. In order to speed the algorithm further, we will consider how to deal with the nuclear norm optimization efficiently in our algorithm.

Acknowledgments. This work is supported by the University Natural Science Fund of Jiangsu Province (Grant No. 16KJB520020), the National Key R&D Program (Grant No. 2017YFC0804002), the National Science Fund of China (Grant Nos. 61603192, 61772277, 61462064), and the Natural Science Fund of Jiangsu Province (Grant Nos. BK20161580, BK20171494).

References

1. Jolliffe, I.T.: Principal Component Analysis, 2nd edn. Springer, New York (2002). doi:10.1007/b98835
2. Yang, J., Zhang, D., Yang, J.-Y.: Constructing PCA baseline algorithms to reevaluate ICA-based face-recognition performance. IEEE Trans. Syst. Man Cybern. Part B Cybern. 37 (4), 1015–1021 (2007)
3. Yang, J., Yang, J.-Y.: Why can LDA be performed in PCA transformed space? Pattern Recogn. 36(2), 563–566 (2003)
4. Liwicki, S., Tzimiropoulos, G., Zafeiriou, S., Pantic, M.: Euler principal component analysis. Int. J. Comput. Vis. 101(3), 498–518 (2013)
5. He, X., Yan, S., Hu, Y., Niyogi, P., Zhang, H.-J.: Face recognition using laplacianfaces. IEEE Trans. Pattern Anal. Mach. Intell. 27(3), 328–340 (2005)
6. Wang, R., Nie, F., Hong, R., Chang, X., Yang, X., Yu, W.: Fast and orthogonal locality preserving projections for dimensionality reduction. IEEE Trans. Image Process. 26(10), 5019–5030 (2017)
7. Candès, E., Li, X., Ma, Y., Wright, J.: Robust principal component analysis? J. ACM 58(3), 1–37 (2011)
8. Gao, Q., Ma, L., Liu, Y., Gao, X., Nie, F.: Angle 2DPCA: a new formulation for 2DPCA. IEEE Trans. Cybern. (2017). doi:10.1109/TCYB.2017.2712740
9. Wong, W.K., Lai, Z., Wen, J., Fang, X., Lu, Y.: Low rank embedding for robust image feature extraction. IEEE Trans. Image Process. doi:10.1109/TIP.2017.2691543
10. Liu, G., Lin, Z., Yan, S., Sun, J., Yu, Y., Ma, Y.: Robust recovery of subspace structures by low-rank representation. IEEE Trans. Pattern Anal. Mach. Intell. 35(1), 171–184 (2013)
11. Candès, E., Recht, B.: Exact matrix completion via convex optimization. Found. Comput. Math. 9(6), 717–772 (2009)
12. Candès, E., Tao, T.: The power of convex relaxation: near-optimal matrix completion. IEEE Trans. Inf. Theory 56(5), 2053–2080 (2010)
13. Keshavan, R., Montanari, A., Sewoong, O.: Matrix completion from a few entries. IEEE Trans. Inf. Theory 56(6), 2980–2998 (2010)
14. Srebro, N., Rennie, J., Jaakkola, T.: Maximum-margin matrix factorization. Adv. Neural. Inf. Process. Syst. 17, 1329–1336 (2004)
15. Nie, F., Wang, H., Cai, X., Huang, H., Ding, C.: Robust matrix completion via joint Schatten p-norm and lp-norm minimization. In: IEEE 12th International Conference on Data Mining (ICDM), pp. 566–574 (2012)
16. Hu, Y., Zhang, D., Ye, J., Li, X., He, X.: Fast and accurate matrix completion via truncated nuclear norm regularization. IEEE Trans. Pattern Anal. Mach. Intell. 35(9), 2117–2130 (2013)
17. Wang, Q., Chen, F., Gao, Q., Gao, X., Nie, F.: On the schatten norm for matrix based subspace learning and classification. Neurocomputing 216, 192–199 (2016)
18. Lin, Z., Chen, M., Wu, L., Ma, Y.: The augmented lagrange multiplier method for exact recovery of corrupted low-rank matrices. UIUC Technical report UILU-ENG-09-2215 (2009)
19. Cai, J., Candès, E., Shen, Z.: A singular value thresholding algorithm for matrix completion. SIAM J. Optim. 20(4), 1956–1982 (2008)
20. Yang, J., Yin, W., Zhang, Y., Wang, Y.: A fast algorithm for edge preserving variational multichannel image restoration. SIAM J. Imaging Sci. 2(2), 569–592 (2009)
21. Lee, K.C., Ho, J., Driegman, D.: Acquiring linear subspaces for face recognition under variable lighting. IEEE Trans. Pattern Anal. Mach. Intell. 27(5), 684–698 (2005)

Behavioral Biometrics

Chinese Sign Language Recognition Based on SHS Descriptor and Encoder-Decoder LSTM Model

Xiaoxu Li, Chensi Mao, Shiliang Huang, and Zhongfu Ye[✉]

National Engineering Laboratory for Speech and Language Information
Processing, Department of Electronic Engineering and Information Science,
University of Science and Technology of China, Hefei 230022, China
yezf@ustc.edu.cn

Abstract. This paper presents a novel approach to recognize isolated Chinese sign language. In order to better distinguish different hand shapes, a new Specific Hand Shape (SHS) descriptor is proposed. Based on the SHS descriptor, an encoder-decoder LSTM model is applied to achieve better sign recognition results. A specific hand shape database and an 80 words isolated Chinese sign language database are constructed using Kinect 2.0 to evaluate the proposed methods. Experimental results show the proposed SHS descriptor is more discriminative than the traditional HOG descriptor and the recognition model is more efficient than the HMM based approach.

Keywords: Sign language recognition · SHS descriptor · Encoder-decoder model · Long Short-Term memory · Convolutional Neural Network

1 Introduction

Sign language bridges the communication gap between the normal and the deaf communities. However, since sign language is still inherently arcane for general public, communication difficulty occurs from time to time. The research of sign language recognition (SLR), whose goal is to translate sign language into text or speech, would exploit an effective way to help us get rid of this inconvenience.

Hand shape is an important and meaningful component in sign language. Currently, various SLR research uses the generic descriptors like Histograms of Oriented Gradients (HOG) to describe hand shapes. However, a specially designed hand shape descriptor would be more discriminative than these general descriptors.

The Long Short-Term Memory (LSTM) model has achieved the state of art results in various time-sequential tasks like speech recognition and video description. Since sign language is also a time series action and SLR is very analogous to the above tasks, the LSTM model has high application potential in the field of SLR.

In this paper, we design a Specific Hand Shape (SHS) descriptor and introduce an encoder-decoder LSTM structure to recognize isolated Chinese sign words. The overview of the proposed system is shown in Fig. 1. The Microsoft Kinect 2.0 is used as the data capture device. We establish a specific hand shape database firstly and the

© Springer International Publishing AG 2017
J. Zhou et al. (Eds.): CCBR 2017, LNCS 10568, pp. 719–728, 2017.
https://doi.org/10.1007/978-3-319-69923-3_77

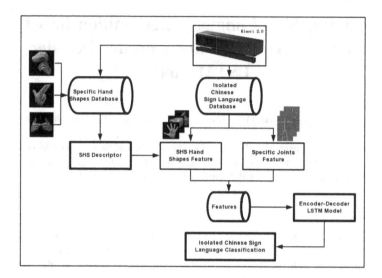

Fig. 1. The overview of the proposed system.

SHS descriptor is designed from this database utilizing Convolutional Neural Network (CNN). In the recognition system, color image, depth map and skeleton information are captured firstly. After a data preprocessing procedure, hand regions and the skeleton joints locations of each sign word are extracted and form the isolated Chinese sign language database. Then, the system extracts both SHS feature and trajectory feature from the database. In the final recognition stage, an encoder-decoder LSTM network is trained using these features and applied for recognizing signs.

The rest of the paper is organized as follows. Section 2 describes the related works. Section 3 explains the proposed method. Section 4 gives the experimental results of the proposed system and Sect. 5 concludes this paper.

2   Related Works

In the early stage, SLR employed data glove [1] and normal video camera [2] to acquire the source data. Yet, most of the consumer data gloves are too expensive or too cumbersome to wear. As for normal video camera, complicated preprocessing procedure is needed to handle the occlusion problem. After year 2010, the somatosensory cameras, Microsoft Kinect [3], has attracted SLR researchers' interest because of its easy acquisition and high precision of human skeletal information.

Zafrulla et al. [3], as pioneers, compared a Kinect-based and data glove-based sign recognition system, and argued that the Kinect could be a workable choice for sign language recognition. Lang et al. [4] extracted hand and elbow coordinates from Kinect and achieved 97% accuracy on a 25 German sign database using HMM model. Jiang et al. [5] proposed a sparse dictionary learning scheme using Kinect and could recognize signs at a rate of 92.36%. Since the Kinect sensor has shown its potential in SLR problem, we choose the Microsoft Kinect 2.0 as the data acquisition device.

Some researchers applied CNN to automatically extract sign features in recent work. Pigou et al. [6] considered CNN as a feature constructor to skip the arduous feature designing work. Huang et al. [7] applied 3D CNN to solve SLR problem. Their system treated color, depth and skeleton stream as the input and achieved 94.2% recognition accuracy which outperformed the traditional GMM-HMM model with HOG feature. These studies reveal that the generic descriptors like HOG may perform no better than the features directly learned from the sign language entity.

Recently, the LSTM model [8] has been used to handle time-sequential problem and shown its potential in SLR research. Venugopalan et al. [9] proposed a LSTM based end-to-end sequence-to-sequence model to generate a description of event for video clips. Pigou et al. [10] applied bidirectional LSTM and temporal convolutions for gesture recognition. To classify isolated Chinese sign language, Liu et al. [11] took trajectories of 4 specific skeleton joints to train an end-to-end LSTM structure and achieved a better recognition accuracy than the traditional HMM method.

3 The Proposed Method

In this section, we introduce the construction of the SHS descriptor and explain its high efficiency in classifying hand shapes of Chinese sign language firstly. Then, the encoder-decoder LSTM recognition architecture will be exhaustively illustrated.

3.1 The Specific Hand Shape (SIIS) Descriptor

The traditional generic image descriptors, like HOG and SIFT, are not specially designed for classifying hand shapes. Although there are more than 5000 entries in Chinese sign language dictionary, only 61 basic hand shapes exist [12]. The specific hand shapes number is still finite even in consideration of hand shape combination. It is possible to design a more discriminative descriptor from these specific hand shapes.

3.1.1 Hand Shape Segmentation

The first step to design SHS descriptor is to segment clean specific hand shape image. Both color image, depth map and hand joints position from Kinect are employed in this stage and the recording environment is indoor. YC_bC_r space has been proved to be effective in skin color detection. A threshold about C_bC_r values is applied to distinguish skin region according to [13].

$$77 \leq C_b \leq 127 \text{ and } 133 \leq C_r \leq 173. \tag{1}$$

Depth value is beneficial to separate face region and hand region. A threshold about depth value $z(x,y)$ is also applied to detect hands.

$$170 < z(x,y) < 340. \tag{2}$$

Then, a square window which centers at the hand position is built to crop the hand region. To ensure hand is at the central of the window, the window is relocated according to the centroid of hand region. What's more, when two palms areas are close or interfere with each other, the two palms compose one meaningful hand shape. Designing a window to crop the two hands together is better than treating them separately. Therefore, we dilate the right and left hand regions for three times. If two palm regions interfere with each other after dilation, a big window will be built to crop the two palms together. These cropped hand images form a hand shape database. Several hand segmentation results are shown in Fig. 2.

Fig. 2. Examples of hand segmentation.

3.1.2 The Specific Hand Shape Database Construction and the SHS Descriptor

A specific hand shape is the meaningful part of a sign word. At the early stage of the SHS database construction, 30 effective samples of each specific hand shape are picked manually as the reference. 6 criteria are designed for defining and picking specific hand shapes. The examples suitable for every criteria are shown in Fig. 3.

1. The selected sample should be a specific hand shape of sign language (Fig. 3a);
2. The selected samples should be as different as possible (Fig. 3b);
3. The selected samples should contain samples from different view angles (Fig. 3c);
4. The set of selected samples should represent the movement states of the specific hand shape (Fig. 3d);
5. For single-hand hand shape, the selected samples should contain samples of both left and right hand (Fig. 3e);
6. Hand shape in the situation of arms naturally sagging should also be considered as a specific hand shape (Fig. 3f);

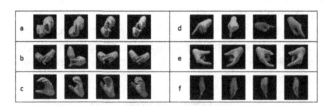

Fig. 3. Examples of each criterion.

After picking 30 samples of each specific hand shape, instead of picking numerous hand shapes by tedious manual work again, an automatic approach is put forward to select the rest specific hand shapes from the hand shape database. Firstly, the HOG features of the 30 samples are extracted. Then the remaining hand shapes are picked using cosine distance in Eq. (3) and a selection threshold in Eq. (4) automatically:

$$distance_i = \frac{<\vec{a}_i, \vec{b}>}{|\vec{a}_i||\vec{b}|} \quad i = 1, 2, \cdots, 30. \tag{3}$$

$$\begin{cases} \min(distance_i) < 0.88 & \text{hand shape is not selected} \\ \min(distance_i) > 0.88 & \text{hand shape is selected} \end{cases} \tag{4}$$

where $\vec{a}_i, \vec{b}$ are the HOG features of the selected samples and the hand shape to be selected respectively, and $distance_i$ is the similarity of the two items. The parameter 0.88 is set for the balance of number of the available hand shape items and the difference between items. For each kind specific hand shape, 1000 samples are then selected randomly from the picked shapes to form the final database. Some samples of the selected specific hand shape of Chinese sign word "house" are shown in Fig. 4.

Fig. 4. Samples of specific hand shapes of Chinese sign language word "house".

Since CNN has achieved outstanding performances in computer vision tasks, we design the SHS descriptor with the help of CNN. In view of the small difference between each class of the specific hand shape and the large difference between classes, we choose the shallow Alexnet [14] model to design the SHS descriptor.

The specific hand shape database is fed into the Alexnet model to train a specific hand shape classification model firstly. After training, features of the output probability layer and features of the last hidden layer in Alexnet are combined as the SHS descriptor. The former one indicates the probability of each specific hand shape and can be seen as the high-level semantic feature (SHS-HF). The later one can be seen as the low-level feature (SHS-LF) like SIFT and HOG. Besides, the previous six selection criteria ensure the SHS descriptor can distinguish the difference between different hand shapes and model the movement states of a specific hand shape. Hence, the SHS descriptor would be more discriminative than the traditional features.

3.2 The Encoder-Decoder LSTM Model for Isolated SLR

We firstly review the theory of the LSTM Recurrent Neural Network (RNN) and then introduce the encoder-decoder LSTM model for isolated SLR in this part.

For an input sequence $X = (x_1, x_2, \ldots, x_i, \ldots, x_T)$, a RNN model can map it to a hidden sequence $H = (h_1, h_2, \ldots, h_i, \ldots, h_T)$ and an output sequence $Y = (y_1, y_2, \ldots, y_i, \ldots, y_T)$:

$$h_t = \sigma(W_{xh}x_t + W_{hh}h_{t-1} + b_h)$$
$$y_t = \sigma(W_{hy}h_t + b_y)$$
$$(5)$$

where all W terms are the weight matrices while b_h and b_y are biases. σ is the sigmoid non-linearity activation function.

As the RNN model suffers from the vanishing gradient problem, the LSTM RNN model provides a solution with introducing a memory cell structure and three gates, input gate i_t, forget gate f_t and output gate o_t [8]. At a time step t, for an input x_t, h_{t-1} and c_{t-1}, the hidden state h_t and the memory cell state c_t of the LSTM model update as follows:

$$i_t = \sigma(W_{xi}x_t + W_{hi}h_{t-1} + b_i)$$
$$f_t = \sigma(W_{xf}x_t + W_{hf}h_{t-1} + b_f)$$
$$o_t = \sigma(W_{xo}x_t + W_{ho}h_{t-1} + b_o)$$
$$g_t = \phi(W_{xg}x_t + W_{hg}h_{t-1} + b_g)$$
$$c_t = f_t \odot c_{t-1} + i_t \odot g_t$$
$$h_t = o_t \odot \phi(c_t)$$
$$(6)$$

where ϕ is the hyperbolic tangent non-linearity activation and $\odot$ is the element-wise operator. The memory cell and gate structure ensure that LSTM has the ability to remember and model the past input information. Since sign language can be seen as a time series action and SLR is a time-sequential task, the LSTM model has the ability in recognizing isolated signs.

Giving a sign with its feature sequence $X = (x_1, x_2, \ldots, x_i, \ldots, x_T)$, where x_i is feature of the i-th frame and T is the length of the sign, the sign's correct class c can be derived from Eq. (7).

$$c = \arg \max_{c_j} p(c = c_j \mid (x_1, x_2, \ldots, x_i, \ldots, x_T)).$$
$$(7)$$

We use an encoder-decoder LSTM model to solve Eq. (7) and the model structure is shown is Fig. 5. In the encoder stage, at time t, the LSTM1 cell encodes both the input features and output of the previous LSTM1 cell. At the last time step T, the encoder module generates an output h_T which is the hidden states of the last LSTM1 cell. In the decoder stage, the LSTM2 cell takes h_T as input and generates the class label of the isolated sign using Eq. (8):

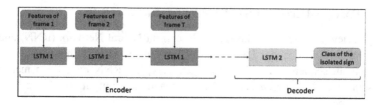

Fig. 5. The structure of the encoder-decoder LSTM model.

$$c = \arg\max_{c_j} p\big(c = c_j \mid h_T\big). \tag{8}$$

where the distribution of $p\big(c = c_j \mid h_T\big)$ is a *softmax* function over all the candidate isolated sign words.

4 Experimental Results and Evaluation

In this section, we first describe the experimental datasets, then give the recognition results and evaluation of the SHS descriptor and the encoder-decoder LSTM model.

4.1 Datasets

We establish two sign language experimental datasets. The first one is the Specific Hand Shape (SHS) database and the second one is the isolated Chinese sign language database. Both datasets are constructed using the Microsoft Kinect 2.0 device and will be released to public in the future.

The SHS database contains 79 different kinds of hand shapes according to the precisely designed six criteria. 32 of them are two hands hand shape and the rest only contain a single hand. Each specific hand shape has 1000 different samples. 800 of them are used for training the Alexnet model and 200 of them are used for testing. Some examples are shown in Fig. 3.

The sign language database consists of 80 commonly used Chinese sign language word. Each word has 100 samples and they are played by 10 signers with 10 times repetitions. 8 signers' samples are selected as the training subsets and the rest are set as the test subsets. We use Kinect 2.0 to capture the color frame, depth map and skeleton joints location. The recording environment is indoor and is the same as [5]. The hand region is segmented using methods in Sect. 3.1. The skeleton joints location is normalized using method in [5]. The final database contains the right and left hand images and the skeleton joints locations of sign word.

4.2 Recognition Results of the SHS Descriptor on SHS Database

The proposed SHS descriptor is learned from the Alexnet. All the 800 samples of each kind specific hand shape are fed into the Alexnet model for training the SHS descriptor. The rest samples are used for testing. The recognition accuracy rate (SHS-NN) is set as the final recognition result of the SHS descriptor on SHS Database.

The SHS descriptor consists of two parts, SHS-HF and SHS-LF. The SHS-HF descriptor indicates the probability of each specific hand shape and the SHS-LF descriptor is a low level feature, similar to HOG. Therefore, we compare the SHS descriptor with the HOG descriptor.

In the contrast experiments, the HOG features of each hand shape in the SHS database are extracted and they are fed into an Artificial Neural Network (ANN) model and a Support Vector Machine (SVM) model separately. The HOG-NN model has two fully connected hidden layer with 4096 and 79 units respectively. The parameters of the

HOG-NN model is the same with the last two layers of the Alexnet model to ensure the reliability of comparison. The HOG-SVM model uses C-SVC and RBF kernel. The HOG-NN experiment is carried out using Caffe. The recognition accuracy rates of the SHS descriptor and the HOG descriptor on the SHS database are shown in Table 1.

Table 1. The recognition accuracy rates of different models on the SHS database.

Approach	Train set accuracy	Test set accuracy
SHS-NN	99.59%	99.41%
HOG-NN	94.35%	90.95%
HOG-SVM	79.32%	77.34%

Since the SHS database is constructed on the basis of the six precisely designed criteria and the SHS descriptor is specially learned from the SHS database, the SHS descriptor is more discriminative than the traditional generic HOG descriptor in recognizing hand shapes. The results also demonstrate that the SHS descriptor performs much better than the compared HOG features.

4.3   Recognition Results of the Encoder-Decoder LSTM Model

The encoder-decoder LSTM model has two LSTM layers and each has 1024 hidden units. During training stage, frame number of each sign is set as a fixed 200 for the balance of memory consumption and information richness. We pad zeros for the shorter signs and discard extra frames for the longer signs. The frame number is not constrained in testing.

The sign database contains the right and left hand images and skeleton joints locations of sign word. We extract the SHS descriptor of the right and left hand images and the trajectory feature of specific skeleton joints as the sign's features. The SHS-LF feature is of 4096 dimensions. In order to increase its generalization ability and speed up the training procedure, we use PCA to reduce its dimensionality to 80. The SHS-HF feature has 79 dimensions. However, since it indicates the probability of each key hand shape, almost all dimensions' value is nearly zero except for the correct hand shape category. The low rank property will slow the convergence rate of the network largely. Therefore, a PCA operation is performed to transform the SHS-HF feature to a more discriminative space and avoid the low rank problem. The new SHS-HF feature has 60 dimensions. The SHS features of the right and left hand are combined together as the visual feature of a sign. The trajectory feature consists of the location of shoulder, elbow, wrist, hand, hand tip and thumb of each hand and is resulting in 36 dimensions.

To evaluate the temporary modeling ability of our model, a HMM model [4] is implemented as comparison. The HOG feature, the SHS-LF feature and the trajectory feature are set as the input features of the HMM model. The HOG feature is also extracted from the hand shapes in the sign database and is of 3600 dimensions. The HOG feature is also fed into the LSTM model as comparison. With the same training consideration of SHS-LF, the HOG feature is also reduced to 80 dimensions using PCA. The recognition accuracy rates of different models on the isolated Chinese sign language database are shown in Table 2.

Table 2. The recognition accuracy rates of different classification models on the isolated Chinese sign language database.

Approach	Train set accuracy	Test set accuracy
SHS-Tra-LSTM	99.49%	98.67%
SHS-LSTM	99.45%	98.35%
SHS-HF-LSTM	99.45%	97.91%
SHS-LF-LSTM	99.35%	98.16%
HOG-LSTM	94.37%	93.23%
Tra-LSTM	82.45%	81.20%
Tra-HMM	73.81%	72.41%
HOG-Tra-HMM	90.76%	88.92%
SHS-LF-Tra-HMM	94.53%	94.18%

The comparison between the results of Tra-LSTM and Tra-HMM means that the encoder-decoder model is more efficient than HMM in modeling temporal information of sign language. The results of HOG-LSTM and SHS-LSTM and the results in the last two rows indicate that no matter what recognition model is, the SHS descriptor performs better than the general features like HOG in SLR. The results also show that using SHS-LF and SHS-HF feature together achieve higher recognizing accuracy than using only SHS-LF or SHS-HF feature. This is because that the SHS-LF and SHS-HF represent different aspect of the hand shape feature and their combination, the SHS descriptor, could depict hand shape feature better.

5 Conclusion and Future Work

This paper proposes a novel approach to recognize isolated Chinese sign language. A specific hand shape database is constructed using six ingenious designed criteria and a SHS descriptor is designed based on the database. The experiments show that the SHS descriptor performs more discriminative than the HOG descriptor in SLR problem. An encoder-decoder LSTM model is developed to recognize the isolated Chinese sign language words. Experimental results show the proposed approach achieves high accuracy and outperforms much better than the compared methods. The future work will focus on applying the proposed methods on large vocabulary database and continues sign language recognition.

Acknowledgments. This work is supported by the Fundamental Research Funds for the Central Universities (Grant No. WK2350000002).

References

1. Lee, C., Xu, Y.S.: Online, interactive learning of gestures for human/robot interfaces. In: Proceedings of 1996 IEEE International Conference on Robotics and Automation, pp. 2982–2987 (1996)
2. Starner, T., Weaver, J., Pentland, A.: Real-time american sign language recognition using desk and wearable computer based video. IEEE Trans. Pattern Anal. Mach. Intell. 20(12), 1371–1375 (1998)
3. Zafrulla, Z., Brashear H., Starner, T., Hamilton, H., Presti, P.: American sign language recognition with the Kinect. In: Proceedings of 13th International Conference on Multimodal Interfaces, pp. 279–286 (2011)
4. Lang, S., Block, M., Rojas, R.: Sign language recognition using Kinect. In: Rutkowski, L., Korytkowski, M., Scherer, R., Tadeusiewicz, R., Zadeh, Lotfi A., Zurada, Jacek M. (eds.) ICAISC 2012. LNCS, vol. 7267, pp. 394–402. Springer, Heidelberg (2012). doi:10.1007/978-3-642-29347-4_46
5. Jiang, Y., Tao, J., Ye, W., Wang, W., Ye, Z.: An isolated sign language recognition system using RGB-D sensor with sparse coding. In: 2014 IEEE 17th International Conference on Computational Science and Engineering (CSE), pp. 21–26 (2014)
6. Pigou, L., Dieleman, S., Kindermans, P., Schrauwen, B.: Sign language recognition using convolutional neural networks. In: Workshop at the European Conference on Computer Vision, pp. 572–578 (2014)
7. Huang, J., Zhou, W., Li, H.: Sign language recognition using 3D convolutional neural networks. In: 2015 IEEE International Conference on Multimedia and Expo (ICME), pp. 1–6 (2015)
8. Hochreiter, S., Schmidhuber, J.: Long short-term memory. Neural Comput. 9(8), 1735–1780 (1997)
9. Venugopalan, S., Rohrbach, M., Donahue, J., Mooney, R., Darrell, T., Saenko, K.: Sequence to sequence-video to text. In: Proceedings of IEEE International Conference on Computer Vision, pp. 4534–4542 (2015)
10. Pigou, L., van den Oord, A., Dieleman, S., Van Herreweghe, M., Damber, J.: Beyond temporal pooling: recurrence and temporal convolutions for gesture recognition in video. Int. J. Comput. Vis. 1–10 (2015)
11. Liu, T., Zhou, W., Li, H.: Sign language recognition with long short-term memory. In: 2016 IEEE International Conference on Image Processing (ICIP), pp. 2871–2875 (2016)
12. Luo, W.: Study on the handshape of Chinese sign language, 《中国手语》手形研究. Beijing Normal University, Beijing (2008)
13. Tang, A., Lu, K., Wang, Y., Huang, J., Li, H.: A real-time hand posture recognition system using deep neural networks. ACM Trans. Intell. Syst. Technol. 6(2), 21 (2015)
14. Krizhevsky, A., Sutskever, I., Hinton, G.E.: ImageNet classification with deep convolutional neural networks. In: Advances in Neural Information Processing Systems, pp. 1097–1105 (2012)

SCUT-MMSIG: A Multimodal Online Signature Database

Xinyi Lu[1], Yuxun Fang[1], Wenxiong Kang[1,2(✉)], Zhiyong Wang[2],
and David Dagan Feng[2]

[1] School of Automation Science and Engineering,
South China University of Technology, Guangzhou 510641, China
auwxkang@scut.edu.cn
[2] School of Information Technologies, The University of Sydney,
Sydney, NSW 2006, Australia

Abstract. In this paper, we present a multimodal online signature database (SCUT-MMSIG). The database was collected on three different devices: mobile phone, pen tablet and monocular camera, consisting of three subcorpora, namely, mobile, tablet and in-air signature subcorpus. In total, 50 subjects are included in each subcorpus, with 20 genuine samples and 20 skilled forgeries per subject. In addition, we explain the signature acquisition process and several verification protocols for further study. The experimental results of a simple DTW-based verification method are also reported under the proposed verification protocols. The database and evaluation codes will be publicly available online.

Keywords: Online signature verification · Multimodal database · Biometrics

1 Introduction

Biometric authentication provides a reliable and convenient mechanism for identity verification. Based on the format of biometric data available, there are two categories of signatures: online and offline. Online (dynamic) signatures are captured by specified hardware (e.g. mobile phone and pen tablet) which is capable of measuring dynamic properties such as location and pressure with a set of time sequences, while signature images are the only information available in offline (static) signatures. Since containing rich information, online signatures are the research focus in this paper.

The first international signature verification competition [1] was organized as a step towards establishing common benchmarking rules and benchmark databases based on pen tablet inputs. This competition promoted the development of signature verification and many outstanding works [2–6] have been put forward since then. To the best of our knowledge, most works on signature verification have been focusing on the pen tablet

---

X. Lu and Y. Fang—These two authors contributed equally to this paper.

© Springer International Publishing AG 2017
J. Zhou et al. (Eds.): CCBR 2017, LNCS 10568, pp. 729–738, 2017.
https://doi.org/10.1007/978-3-319-69923-3_78

mode, which reflect the prevailing social demand. Due to the wide spread use of mobile devices, Sae-Bae and Memon [7] proposed a mobile phone based verification app and experimental results on the self-built database confirmed the effectiveness of the verification system in mobile settings. Similarly, a mobile phone based verification app was developed for practical applications in [8]. Meanwhile, signing in front of a single camera showed promising potential due to its non-contact property and user friendliness. Inspired by these studies, we firstly proposed an in-air signature verification system using a single camera [9] where the signatures captured by camera are defined as in-air signatures. This work pioneered to conduct comprehensive experiments on its self-built in-air signature database and confirmed the promising future of this in-air signature mode.

However, there is a limited number of existing public online signature databases for performance evaluation. Outstanding public signature databases such as MCYT [10], SUSIG [11] and SVC2004 [1] were all collected with pen tablets, placing a restriction on the research of other signature data captured with mobile phones and cameras.

In this paper, the Biometrics and Intelligence Perception Laboratory—BIP Lab, of the South China University of Technology, has established a multimodal online signature database, named as SCUT-MMSIG (Multimodal Signature Database of BIP Lab in SCUT) database, as well as the associated protocols and benchmark results for performance evaluation.

2 SCUT-MMSIG Database

As mentioned above, the SCUT-MMSIG database is a multimodal online signature database and is divided into three subcorpora, namely, mobile, tablet and in-air signature subcorpus. The whole database was collected at South China University of Technology, Guangdong, China, and 50 subjects including both male and female students were recruited in the signature data collecting process. For each subject, we collected 20 genuine samples and 20 skilled forgeries contributed by 4 forgers, 5 samples each. It should be noted that in the three signature subcorpora, each sample contains only one Chinese character considering the regional restrictions in mobile mode. In addition, all skilled forgeries were imitated by 8 well-trained forgers. The detailed introduction of three subcorpora will be presented in the next three subsections.

2.1 The Mobile Signature Subcorpus

Signature verification is an ideal mechanism for security assurance on mobile phones. However, to the best of our knowledge, there are still few large public signature databases based on mobile phone inputs, which probably have limited the studies of signature verification on mobile phones. Therefore, we advanced the work in this paper. We will introduce the carefully designed acquisition process for the mobile subcorpus including signature enrollment and imitation, followed by database description.

Signature Acquisition for Mobile Signature Subcorpus. In this subcorpus, we used an LG-G3 mobile phone and its active area is 5.5 inches with 2560×1440 (2K) resolution. At each sample point the x and y coordinates, time stamp and button status were recorded with the sampling rate of about 120 Hz.

During the enrollment phase, assisted by an Android-based application, trained target contributors were asked to practice several times and then sign 10 genuine samples in the first session, and another 10 in the second session with the interval of one to three months. At the imitation phase, 4 forgers first watched the dynamic signing process of the 10 genuine samples in the first session reproduced by our Android software and then practiced several times to get close to the real samples, both in character shape and signing speed. Figure 1(a) and (b) show how a contributor wrote a Chinese character with mobile phone.

(a)   (b)   (c)

Fig. 1. Illustrations of the mobile signature subcorpus. (Color figure online)

Database Description for Mobile Signature Subcorpus. The mobile signature subcorpus contains $50 \times 20 = 1000$ genuine samples and $50 \times 20 = 1000$ skilled forgeries. Each sample in the subcorpus is saved as a text file, containing the x and y coordinates, time stamps and button status (0 for finger up and 1 for finger down) for each sampling point on the signature trajectory. Some mobile signature samples are shown in Fig. 1(c) where red segmentation representing low speed and green segmentation representing high speed.

2.2   The Tablet Signature Subcorpus

It is apparent that the tablet mode is the most similar to the real signing process and most works on signature verification are based on this mode. Similarly, we first introduce the enrollment and imitation processes and then describe the details of the tablet signature subcorpus.

Signature Acquisition for Tablet Signature Subcorpus. A low-cost UGEE EX05 pen tablet was used as the acquisition device. The tablet resolution is 4000 lines per inch and the precision is ±0.01 mm. The maximum detection height is 15 mm (so also pen-up movements are considered), and the capture area is 85×75 mm. This tablet was set to provide the x and y coordinates and button status with the sampling rate of 60 Hz.

During the enrollment phase, similar to the mobile mode, target contributors were asked to sign 10 genuine samples in the first session, and another 10 genuine samples one to three months later. During the imitation phase, 4 forgers still had the access to the dynamic signing process of the 10 genuine samples in the first session and then tried their best to imitate the target character. Figure 2(a) illustrates the signing process.

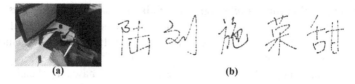

Fig. 2. Illustrations of the tablet signature subcorpus.

Database Description for Tablet Signature Subcorpus. 50×20 = 1000 genuine samples and 50 × 20 = 1000 skilled forgeries which saved as text files compose this subcorpus. Each text file contains the x and y coordinates and the button status (0 for pen-up and 1 for pen-down) of each sampling point on the signature trajectory. Several tablet signature samples are shown in Fig. 2(b).

2.3 The In-Air Signature Subcorpus

The two modes mentioned above are dependent on specific devices like mobile phone and pen tablet. While for the in-air mode, it has no need in touch with devices and all we should do is just signing in front of a single camera. This mode can be applied in the access control systems for security. The introduction of the unique acquisition procedure of the in-air mode and the description of the database will be presented.

Signature Acquisition for the In-Air Signature Subcorpus. In-air signature is a novel signature mode proposed in our latest work [9]. The whole procedure can be divided into two stages: record the signing process and track the fingertip to generate the signature trajectory. The rear camera of iPad Air 2 with the sampling rate of 120 Hz was used to record the process. A real scene of sample acquisition process is shown in Fig. 3(a). Different from the two modes mentioned above, in-air mode has no limitation in signing areas and no visual feedback, which may lead to severe distortion of the signatures. To alleviate this problem, as shown in Fig. 3(a), the monitor will display the mirror image of the iPad screen synchronously to give a rough visual feedback and help contributors adjust the signing areas.

Similarly, target contributors were asked to sign 10 genuine samples in the first session and another 10 genuine samples in the second session with the interval of one to three months during the enrollment phase. For the imitation phase, 4 forgers still had the access to the dynamic signing process of the 10 genuine samples in the first session

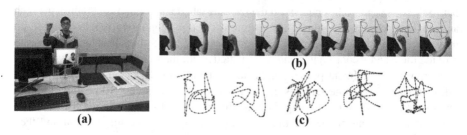

Fig. 3. Illustrations of the in-air signature subcorpus.

and then tried to imitate. Finally, each signature sample was corresponding to one video clip and we tracked the signature trajectory with the aid of a robust tracking algorithm called CSK [12]. Figure 3(b) shows the performance of the CSK tracking algorithm.

Database Description for the In-Air Signature Subcorpus. Due to the unique data acquisition and trajectory generation, each stroke is joined-up, which makes each sample contain more sampling points. In addition, for joined-up characters, it is unnecessary to offer the button status. In total, $50 \times 20 = 1000$ genuine samples and $50 \times 20 = 1000$ skilled forgeries, featured by the x and y coordinates, are offered in the form of text files. Figure 3(c) shows several in-air signature samples.

2.4   Summary of the SCUT-MMSIG Database

A brief summary of SCUT-MMSIG database is given in Table 1. It should be noted that if you want to rebuild a Chinese character using the x and y coordinates in the text file, you should use the $(x, -y)$, $(x, -y)$ and $(-x, -y)$, respectively for the mobile, tablet and in-air subcorpus.

Table 1. A summary of SCUT-MMSIG database

Subcorpus	Size of Subjects	Size of genuine samples*	Size of skilled forgeries	File descriptions**	Sampling rate
Mobile	50	$50 \times (10 + 10) = 1000$	$50 \times 20 = 1000$	[X Y Ts Bs]	$\approx$120 Hz
Tablet	50	$50 \times (10 + 10) = 1000$	$50 \times 20 = 1000$	[X Y Bs]	60 Hz
In-air	50	$50 \times (10 + 10) = 1000$	$50 \times 20 = 1000$	[X Y]	120 Hz

*Each subject contains two sessions and each session contains 10 genuine samples.
**X, Y, Ts, Bs refer to x coordinate, y coordinate, time stamps and button status, respectively.

The differences between other signature databases are also compared in Table 2. It should be emphasized that SCUT-MMSIG database not only contains three different modes, but also has a long time interval between different sessions which is likely to happen in practical applications.

Table 2. The comparison between different databases

Database (subcorpus)	Type	Size of subjects	Size of genuine/ forged samples	Features*	Sessions interval	Sampling rate (Hz)	Number of forgers
MCYT- 100 [10]	Tablet	100	25/25	X, Y, P, Azi, Alt	No interval	100	5
SUSIG-visual [11]	Tablet	100	20/10	X, Y, P, Ts, Azi, Alt	One week	100	2
SVC2004 (task1) [1]	Tablet	100	20/20	X, Y	At least one week	100	At least 4
SVC2004 (task2) [1]	Tablet	100	20/20	X, Y, P, Ts, Bs, Azi, Alt	At least one week	100	At least 4
SCUT-MMSIG	Mobile	50	20/20	X, Y, Ts, Bs	1–3 months	$\approx$120	4
	Tablet	50	20/20	X, Y, Bs	1–3 months	60	4
	In-air	50	20/20	X, Y	1–3 months	120	4

*X, Y, P, Ts, Bs, Azi, Alt refer to x coordinate, y coordinate, pressure, time stamps, button status, Azimuth, and Altitude, respectively.

3 Verification Protocols on SCUT-MMSIG

In order to facilitate researchers to compare algorithm performance under a unified standard, referring to [12], we define five protocols corresponding to different realistic scenarios.

3.1 Protocol Descriptions

In total, we define five protocols, namely, single-session, across-session[5], across-session[10], mixed-session and random forgery protocols. The goal of the single-session protocol is to evaluate the performance of a system under the condition where both reference and test data are collected in the same session. Across-session protocol is used to assess the performance of a system under the more realistic conditions where genuine signatures for reference and test sets are obtained in different sessions. Mixed-session protocol is a mixture of the single and across-session[5] protocols. Since all signatures are used in the verification process and is commonly accepted by most researchers, mixed-session protocol is defined as the base protocol in this paper. While for random forgery protocol, it is used to evaluate a system's performance against a random forgery attack. In this scenario, forgers have no prior information regarding the signature to be forged. The description of reference set and test set is summarized in Table 3.

Table 3. Summary of the protocols

Protocol	Reference	Genuine test	Forgery test
Single-session	GS1[1...5]	GS1[6...10]	SF
Across-session[5]	GS1[1...5]	GS2[1...10]	SF
Across-session[10]	GS1[1...10]	GS2[1...10]	SF
Mixed-session	GS1[1...5]	GS1[6...10] + GS2[1...10]	SF
Random forgery	GS1[1...5]	GS1[6...10] + GS2[1...10]	GS1 [1] of all other subjects

*GS1, GS2 and SF refer to the first session of the genuine signatures, the second session of the genuine signatures and the corresponding skilled forgeries, respectively.

4 Benchmark Results

In order to evaluate the performance of various protocols as a benchmark, we report the results of a simple and executable signature verification system based on the dynamic time warping (DTW) algorithm. Brief introduction of the DTW-based system will be presented in Sect. 4.1 and we will release the code in our website, please contact us for more details. Experimental results including equal error rate (under both user-independent and user-dependent threshold) of each particular protocol are described in Sect. 4.2.

4.1 The Framework of the DTW-Based Verification System

In this paper, we have no intention to present an elaborated algorithm for signature verification, so a simple and common DTW-based system is presented. Empirically, we choose a feature vector including six feature descriptors inspired by [3]. Then we apply the distance normalization to alleviate the negative effects caused by signature length discrepancies between different subjects after calculating the DTW distance. Finally, $\bar{D}_{test} - \bar{D}_{ref}$ (average DTW distance between test sample and reference set and average pairwise DTW distance in the reference set, respectively) is defined as the decision value and the test sample is accepted when the decision value is less than a predetermined threshold, otherwise, it is rejected as a forgery.

4.2 Benchmark Results

In this section, we report the experimental results of two different kinds of thresholds, namely, user-independent and user-dependent threshold. Specifically, user-independent threshold refers to a verification system where all subjects share one common threshold to verify a signature, which is more realistic and valuable for system comparison. While for the user-dependent threshold, each subject has a particular manually selected threshold to verify a signature, which neglects the differences between different subjects. Therefore, the result under the user-dependent threshold is the theoretical optimal result when using the same verification framework, and to some extent, it can measure the verification difficulty of different subcorpus. The experimental results on the three subcorpora using five different protocols are listed in Table 4.

Table 4. Experimental results in three different subcorpora

Protocols	EER (%)					
	The mobile subcorpus		The tablet subcorpus		The in-air subcorpus	
	User-independent	User-dependent	User-independent	User-dependent	User-independent	User-dependent
Single-session	10.28	6.56	8.38	3.06	7.93	3.72
Across-session[5]	22.93	14.20	18.23	10.96	25.25	17.96
Across-session[10]	18.81	13.35	16.08	10.85	24.18	16.10
Mixed-session	20.66	12.19	15.92	9.70	20.92	16.49
Random forgery	0.70	0.12	2.39	0.50	1.44	0.37

Based on the experimental results of different modes, the tablet mode gains relatively better performance under both thresholds, since signing on the tablet is the most similar to the real signing process and users can maintain the natural signing style. In terms of the random forgery protocol, all modes perform well since this protocol is easiest for verification. However, the tablet mode performs worst (2.39%) compared with the mobile mode (0.70%) and in-air mode (1.44%) when attacked by the random forgeries, mainly because the inter-class variance is the major factor under random forgery protocol and the signing style of different Chinese characters are relative similar under the most familiar signing form. But randomness is also an important factor since the EER is very low under this protocol. What's more, when only considering the single-session protocol, the performance of tablet mode (8.38%) is close to the in-air mode (7.93%), while the mobile mode performs worst (10.28%). It can attribute to two aspects: (a) Users may be unskilled when signing with a single finger on the mobile screen; (b) The relative small area of mobile touch screen may affect the natural signing habit of users, which will consequently increase the intra class dissimilarity. In addition, as mentioned above that the results under the user-dependent threshold is the theoretical optimal results compared with the user-independent threshold, the large gap of the experimental results between these two kinds of thresholds indicates that the simple DTW-based system can be further optimized for better performance. It is worth noting that the corresponding result under the user-dependent threshold for three modes and five protocols is similar with that under the user-independent threshold, which further confirms the reliability of our analysis.

To further evaluate the effects of the session interval on the proposed database, we compared the results of single, across-session[5] and mixed-session protocol in Fig. 4. It should be noted that the number of reference samples and forgery test samples are the same under three protocols, and the only difference is that the genuine test samples come from different time sessions.

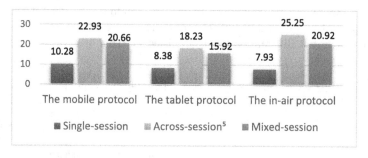

Fig. 4. The EER under user-independent threshold of different protocols

As illustrated in Fig. 4, the result of the mixed-session protocol (base protocol) in each mode is in the middle of the single and across-session[5] protocol, as expected in Sect. 3.1. Interestingly, the EER results of single-session protocol in all three modes are much lower than the across-session[5] and mixed-session (base) protocol. It proves once again that as a learned behavioral biometric, individual signature is different with inherent physiological biometric (e.g. fingerprint), and will change slightly over time, which results in the instability between different time sessions. In addition, compared with other databases whose signatures are relatively complex, the situation that each sample only contains a single Chinese character in SCUT-MMSIG database, which further contributes the instability of signatures between different time sessions. In summary, the large intra-class dissimilarity of different time sessions is a major challenge in the SCUT-MMSIG database.

5 Conclusions

In this work, a multimodal online signature database including three different sub-corpora and associated protocols are presented. Together with this database, we have also established a set of protocols to provide a benchmark for performance evaluation. The database and evaluation codes are publicly available to the research community for further study. Based on the SCUT-MMSIG database, many works related to multi-modal signature verification can be achieved more conveniently. For example, the in-air subcorpus will be firstly available for further researches on this new valuable modes. In addition, since signatures in different modes were collected from the same contributors, the comparison of the signature verification between different modes will be more convincing. Moreover, different from the databases such as SVC2004 [1] and SUSIG [11], the main challenge of SCUT-MMSIG database is the large intra-class dissimilarity between different time sessions, which is likely to happen in practical applications and need to be further studied.

Acknowledgements. This work was supported by the National Natural Science Foundation of China (No. 61573151), the Guangdong Natural Science Foundation (No. 2016A030313468), Science and Technology Planning Project of Guangdong Province (No. 2017A010101026), the Science and Technology Program of Guangzhou (201510010088).

References

1. Yeung, D.-Y., Chang, H., Xiong, Y., George, S., Kashi, R., Matsumoto, T., Rigoll, G.: SVC2004: First international signature verification competition, In: International Conference on Biometric Authentication, pp. 16–22 (2004)
2. Kholmatov, A., Yanikoglu, B.: Identity authentication using improved online signature verification method. Pattern Recogn. Lett. **26**(15), 2400–2408 (2005)
3. Fierrez, J., Ortega-Garcia, J., Ramos, D., Gonzalez-Rodriguez, J.: HMM-based on-line signature verification: feature extraction and signature modeling. Pattern Recogn. Lett. **28** (16), 2325–2334 (2007)
4. Liu, Y., Yang, Z., Yang, L.: Online signature verification based on DCT and sparse representation. IEEE T. Cybern. **45**(11), 2498–2511 (2015)
5. Dash, J.K., Mukhopadhyay, S.: Similarity learning for texture image retrieval using multiple classifier system. Multimed. Tools Appl. 1–25 (2016)
6. Sharma, A., Sundaram, S.: On the exploration of information from the DTW cost matrix for online signature verification. IEEE Trans. Cybern. 1–14 (2017)
7. Sae-Bae, N., Memon, N.: Online signature verification on mobile devices. IEEE Trans. Inf. Forensics Secur. **9**(6), 933–947 (2014)
8. Tang, L., Fang, Y., Wu, Q., Kang, W., Zhao, J.: Online finger-writing signature verification on mobile device for local authentication. In: Chinese Conference on Biometric Recognition, pp. 409–416 (2016)
9. Fang, Y., Kang, W., Wu, Q., Tang, L.: A novel video-based system for in-air signature verification. Comput. Electr. Eng. **57**, 1–14 (2017)
10. Ortega-Garcia, J., Fierrez-Aguilar, J., Simon, D., Gonzalez, J., Faundez-Zanuy, M., Espinosa, V., Satue, A., Hernaez, I., Igarza, J.-J., Vivaracho, C.: MCYT baseline corpus: a bimodal biometric database. IEE Proc.-Vis. Image Sig. **150**(6), 395–401 (2003)

11. Kholmatov, A., Yanikoglu, B.: SUSIG: an on-line signature database, associated protocols and benchmark results. Pattern Anal. Appl. **12**(3), 227–236 (2009)
12. Henriques, J.F., Caseiro, R., Martins, P., Batista, J.: Exploiting the circulant structure of tracking-by-detection with kernels. In: Fitzgibbon, A., Lazebnik, S., Perona, P., Sato, Y., Schmid, C. (eds.) ECCV 2012. LNCS, vol. 7575, pp. 702–715. Springer, Heidelberg (2012). doi:10.1007/978-3-642-33765-9_50

Orientation-Aware Text Proposals Network for Scene Text Detection

Huijuan Huang[1], Zhi Tian[1], Tong He[1], Weilin Huang[1],
and Yu Qiao[1,2(✉)]

[1] Shenzhen Key Laboratory of Virtual Reality and Human Interaction
Technology, Shenzhen Institutes of Advanced Technology,
Chinese Academy of Sciences, Shenzhen, China
huijuan_huang@outlook.com, {zhi.tian,wl.huang,
yu.qiao}@siat.ac.cn, tong.he@whu.edu.cn
[2] The Chinese University of Hong Kong, Hong Kong SAR, China

Abstract. In this paper, we present a novel Orientation-Aware Text Proposals Network (OA-TPN) for detecting text in the wild. The OA-TPN is able to accurately localize arbitrary-oriented text lines in a natural image. Instead of detecting the whole text line at one time, the OA-TPN detects sequences of small-scale orientation-aware text proposals. To handle text lines with different orientations, we utilize deep networks to jointly estimate text proposals with associate directions at the convolutional maps. Final text bounding boxes can be generated from the predicted text proposals by implementing a proposed text-line construction approach. The proposed text detector works reliably on multi-scale and multi-orientation text with single-scale images. Experimental results on the MSRA-TD500 and SWT demonstrate the effectiveness of our methods.

Keywords: Scene text detection · Convolutional maps · Text Proposals Network · Orientation-Aware

1 Introduction

Reading and extracting text information from natural scenes has become increasingly important and popular, due to its numerous potential applications in image retrieval, industrial automation, robot navigation and scene understanding. Although a few commercial OCR systems are sophisticated to understand documental texts and Internet contents, accurate scene text detection in natural images remains a challenging problem. The main difficulty lies in a vast diversity in text scale, orientation, illumination, and font, which often come with a highly complicated background. Generally, scene text reading comprises of two sub-tasks: text localization and recognition. Our work mainly focuses on the localization task, which is usually more challenging than the latter one, where the recognition is carried out on cropped word images with little background interference.

Most of the previous text detection algorithms [5, 10–14, 19, 21] employed a bottom-up pipeline, which required several sequential steps, including text component (character) detection, classification or filtering, text line construction and word splitting.

© Springer International Publishing AG 2017
J. Zhou et al. (Eds.): CCBR 2017, LNCS 10568, pp. 739–749, 2017.
https://doi.org/10.1007/978-3-319-69923-3_79

Such complicated pipeline will result in error accumulation in later steps. More importantly, these approaches mostly explore hand-crafted features to capture the properties of scene text, which are not efficient and less powerful.

Thanks to deep learning, strong features can be learned automatically from training data with deep networks, which greatly boosts the performance of text detection in the past few years. Recent deep learning based approaches [4, 5, 10, 15–18, 20] have shown promising performance, but most of them are limited to work on horizontal or near-horizontal text region detection. For example, recent Connectionist Text Proposal Network (CTPN) developed in [4] casts the problem of text detection into localizing a sequence of fine-scale text proposals. Nonetheless, CTPN is limited to detect near-horizontal text line due to the property of the designed text proposals. In real-world applications, a number of the text regions are not horizontal, usually presented in an unnatural shape with different orientations, thus the horizontal-specific methods are difficult to be widely applied for these complicated real-world cases.

In this paper, we come up with an improved framework Orientation-Aware Text Proposals Network (OATPN) for multi-orientation text detection. Particularly, orientation information is encoded by the redesigned text proposals. Comparison between the previous horizontal-based approach and ours are illustrated in Fig. 1. The main contributions are summarized as follows,

(1) We design novel text proposals that represent text regions with a line segment. This new design makes it more flexible to cover text lines of arbitrary orientation or even curved text and it requires less anchors to detect a wider range of aspect ratio than other RPN-based approaches [1, 20].
(2) We proposed a simple yet efficient text-line construction method that accurately group the detected oriented text proposals, making the entire system lightweight and fast.
(3) We evaluated our model on two standard benchmarks, MSTD-RA500 and SWT, and obtained state-of-the-art performance with fast speeds.

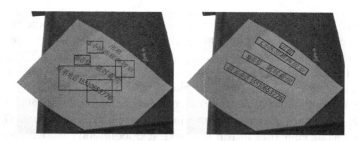

Fig. 1. Evaluations of CTPN [4] (left) and the proposed OATPN (right).

1.1   Related Works

Past work on text detection mainly focus on the design of hand-crafted features [5, 10, 13, 19], such as gradient, stroke width, and covariance descriptor. These features were used subsequently for classifying text and non-text in pixel level. Then multiple bottom-up steps were designed to group pixels into characters, which further formed character pairs, and text lines. These bottom-up approaches are time-consuming and error-prone, especially when dealing with challenging scenarios.

Recently, deep-learning based algorithms [3–5, 8] have become the mainstream in the area of scene text detection, with impressive results achieved. Huang et al. [5] first used optimized MSER to find text candidates and then used character-based horizontal text CNN classifier to filter false positives. Zhang et al. [8] utilized Fully Convolutional Network (FCN) [9] to efficiently generate a pixel-wise text/non-text salient map, which is then combined with character components to estimate text line hypotheses. More recently, EAST [3] directly produces word level predictions by using FCN to generate score and geometry maps. Liu and Jin [6] come up with DMPNet to predict text with compact quadrangle.

Our work is also related to several recent RPN-based text detectors. Ma et al. [1] adopted RPN to solve the multi-oriented text detection problem by using rotation anchors. They introduce 54 anchors (k = 54) with different scales, aspect ratios and angles, while we only use eight anchors that are able to cover text lines of all angles and shapes, even the curved text regions. Shi et al. [2] extended the idea of detecting sequences of small text pieces by adding rotation angle to each default box, and a segment-and-link mechanism was developed to link the text pieces. In this work, we propose a simple proposal grouping method with little influence on the final results.

2 Methodology

We describe the details of the proposed Orientation-Aware Text Proposals Network (OATPN), which is extended from previous CTPN [4] for multi-orientation text detection. The network design is illustrated in Fig. 3, and details of each key technical component will be described in the following parts.

2.1 Orientation-Aware Text Proposals

CTPN detects a text line in a sequence of fine-scale text proposals with fixed width of 16 pixels. The text proposals it used are small horizontal bounding boxes with 16-pixel width. Such axis-aligned text proposal is limited to detect horizontal text lines.

To address this limitation, we develop new text proposals able to handle text line in multiple orientations and shapes. Similarly our OATPN considers a text line as a sequence of text proposals, and employs anchor regression mechanism to jointly predict text/non-text scores, position and size of each proposal. The main difference is that our text proposals are more flexible to indicate orientation of the detected text. As shown in Fig. 2(a), they are defined as a sequence of line segments that cover the whole text line and each can be represented by tuple (x, y, h, θ), indicating coordinates of the center, height, and rotation angle.

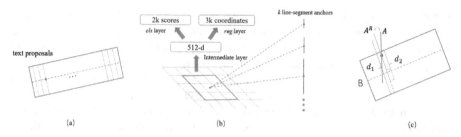

Fig. 2. (a) The blue box denotes the text line bounding box while orange line segments represent text proposals. (b) Design of line-segment anchors. (c) Method to calculate the IOU given an anchor and a GT box. (Color figure online)

2.2   Line-Segment Anchors

Different from CTPN which uses a small bounding box to circle a small text region, we use a line segment to identify a text region, which allows our design to incorporate the rotation information into the text proposals. A line-segment anchor can be represented with three variables (x^a, y^a, h^a), where x^a and y^a are the coordinates of the anchor center, and h^a is anchor height. For each spatial location on the convolutional feature maps, k anchors with different heights are generated. Three relative parameterized coordinates with respect to an anchor will be predicted to obtain a text proposal. For text proposal regression, we adopt the parameterizations of the three coordinates as following,

$$t_x = (x - x^a)/h^a, \quad t_x^* = (x^* - x^a)/h^a,$$
$$t_y = (y - y^a)/h^a, \quad t_y^* = (y^* - y^a)/h^a, \tag{1}$$
$$t_h = \log(h/h^a), \quad t_h^* = (h^*/h^a),$$

variables x^a, y^a, h^a can be precomputed from an input image. x^*, y^*, h^* are the GT coordinates. The predicted text proposal can be computed as follow,

$$x = x^a - t_x h^a, \quad y = y^a - t_y h^a, \quad h = e^{t_h} h^a, \quad \theta = \arctan(t_y/t_x) \tag{2}$$

where the rotation angle θ is measured by t_x and t_y. By implicitly calculating the rotation angle, we avoid regressing the angle separately which is incompatible with distance regression and often involves a different loss.

2.3   Network Design

The overall architecture is shown in Fig. 3. We take the very deep VGG16 [7] as baseline, and make a few modifications that tailor it toward our task. We set the total stride to 8 pixels, instead of 16 pixels, to make dense prediction that improves the accuracy. This can be achieved by simply removing the pool4 layer, but would result in a reduction of receptive filed (RF). In the case of text detection, we need contextual information from relatively large regions to accurately distinguish text and non-text

Fig. 3. Architecture of the Orientation-Aware Text Proposal Network (OATPN).

objects, and to make precise prediction of the orientation of text lines. Imagine that if we can only see a small part of a text line, it is difficult to estimate its height and orientation reliably. Therefore we employ dilated convolution proposed in [22], which can quickly expand the RF without losing resolution or adding extra parameters. As a result, the total RF of the top layer of our model is 492 pixels.

The detection process can be summarized as follows. Given an input image, we have conv6 feature maps with size of $W \times H \times C$, where C is the number of feature maps or channels, and $W \times H$ is the spatial arrangement. Then we use a 3×3 window to slide every spatial location of conv6 feature maps, and takes a convolutional feature of $3 \times 3 \times C$ to produce the prediction for each anchor correspondingly. The location of k anchors can be pre-computed by mapping the spatial window location in the conv6 onto the input image. The regressors, composed of three FC layers, simultaneously outputs the text/non-text scores, and the three parameterized coordinates t_x, t_y, t_h. Each regressor is responsible for one scale. The detected text proposals are generated from the anchors having a text/non-text score of >0.7. By the designed line-segment anchor mechanism, our detector is able to handle text lines in a wide range of scales, aspect ratios and orientation with a single-scale input image.

CTPN incorporated a layer-wise RNN into a convolutional layer for encoding the sequential context information through the whole line. However, this horizontal based RNN design is difficult to function on multi-orientation text.

2.4 Loss Function

We employ multi-task learning to jointly optimize model parameters. We introduce two loss functions, L_{cls}, and L_{reg}, for classification and regression tasks respectively. With these considerations, we follow the multi-task loss applied in [23, 24], and minimize an overall objective function L for an image as,

$$L(\{s_i\}, \{t_j\}) = \frac{1}{N_s} \sum_i L_{cls}(s_i, s_i^*) + \lambda \frac{1}{N_t} \sum_j L_{reg}(t_j, t_j^*). \tag{3}$$

Here, i is the index of an anchor in a mini batch, and N_s denotes the size of the mini batch that used by L_{cls}. s_i is the predicted probability of i-th anchor being a true text. $s_i^* = \{0, 1\}$ is the ground truth (GT). j is the index of an anchor in the set of valid anchors for parameterized coordinate regression, and N_t denotes the size of the valid anchor set that used by L_{reg}. The definition of valid anchor for regression is defined in Sect. 3.1. t_j and t_j^* are the prediction and GT parameterized coordinates associated with the j-th anchor. By following [23, 24], we use a softmax loss and the smooth L1 function for the classification task and regression task respectively. λ is the loss weight that balances different tasks, which is empirically set to 1.0.

2.5   Text-Line Construction

The output of OATPN is a number of sequential text proposals. We develop an efficient text proposal grouping approach that connects these small-scale text proposals into text-lines. Those proposals which are not connected, should be clustered into different groups, according to predefined criteria related to position, orientation, shape etc. Each group of the proposals forms a single text line bounding box. We observe that neighboring text proposals can be connected by expanding them to a small rotated rectangle, whose width is fixed to 8 pixels, and height is set to 0.2 times of the initial height. We assign a short height for the generated rectangle to avoid adhesion of closely-positioned text lines. By filling the generated rectangles on the mask, we get connected regions corresponding to different text lines (Fig. 4(b)). However, they cannot precisely indicate the position of a text line, instead we use the connected regions to classify text proposals. Text proposals whose centers fall in the same connected region are grouped together.

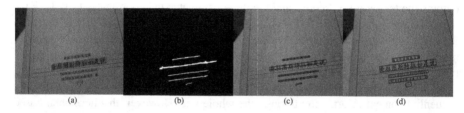

Fig. 4. Text-line construction method. (a) Text proposals generated by our model. (b) Convert text proposals into tiny rotated boxes which further form the connected regions. (c) Find the minimum bounding boxes for each connected region, and then find corresponding text proposals whose centers are located into the bounding boxes. (d) Calculate text-line bonding boxes by merging a group of text proposals.

The next step is to utilize proposals in the same group to generate the corresponding text line bounding box, which is denoted by tuple $\{\{x_c, y_c, w, h, \theta\}\}$. Here, x_c, y_c are the coordinates of the box center, w, h, θ are the width, height and rotation angle respectively. x_c is computed as, $x_c = (\min\{x_i\} + \max\{x_i\})/2$, where x_i denotes the x-coordinate of the center for the i-th text proposal. Then we find a line that fits all centers of the text proposals with the minimum error, the angle of line is the box orientation θ. Now, we get y_c by fitting x_c into the line function. Height $h = \sum_i h_i/N$, where h_i denotes the height of i-th proposal, and N is the total number of proposals. Width $w = 2\max\left\{\sqrt{(x_i - x_c)^2 + (y_i - y_c)^2}\right\}$, which is calculated by measuring the max distance between the box's center and proposals. It depends on the positions of the marginal proposals.

In fact, other text-line construction methods can be readily applied to our framework, such as constructing a directed graph and finding a reached path in this graph. However, such approach is time costly due to the large amount of text proposals. Moreover, it needs NMS to filter out the overlapped boxes, which further increases the processing time. Thus, the proposed method is more efficient, and results in higher performance in comparisons. An example is demonstrated in Fig. 4.

3   Training Details

The proposed OATPN can be trained end-to-end by using standard back-propagation and stochastic gradient descent (SGD). Similar to RPN [12], the training samples are the anchors. The training labels of each anchor can be computed from the corresponding word or text line GT bounding box, by following [4, 12].

3.1   Label Generation for Rotated Anchor

The process of computing the GTs is summarized as follows. For each anchor, we compute the perpendicular foot from the anchor center to the center line of a text bounding box. We consider a valid anchor when the perpendicular foot falls exactly on the center line with an IOU > 0.5. The valid anchor can be regressed to a text proposal, where the regression target of the anchor center (x^*, y^*) is the computed perpendicular foot, and the regression target of the anchor height (h^*) is the height of the text bounding box. Subsequently, GT values of the three parameterized coordinates t_x^*, t_y^*, t_h^* can be computed. For each anchor with an IOU > 0.7, it is referred as a positive anchor, while those with an IOU < 0.5 are considered as negative ones, and the rest is referred as Not Care which are not used for training.

Figure 2(c) describes our method to calculate the IOU. First, we rotate the anchor A to make it perpendicular to the center line, and denote the rotated anchor as A^R. Then the IOU is computed as the height overlap ratio between A^R and the bounding box B, $IOU = d_2/d_1$, where $d_1 = A_h^R \cup B_h$, $d_2 = A_h^R \cap B_h$ and A_h^R, B_h denote the height of A^R and B respectively.

3.2   Training Data

Our model was trained on images we collected and training set of MSTD-RA 500, ICDAR 2013, ICDAR 2015. The training data contains both Chinese and English. All training images are not overlapped with any test image in all three benchmarks. We also applied data augmentation strategy to generate more training data, by simply rotating each image in several randomly selected angles. This results in nearly 25,000 images in total.

With 1:1 ratio, the positive and negative anchors are randomly selected to form a mini-batch with $N_s = 128$. A mini-batch is pad with negative anchors when the positive ones is < 64. The anchors with IOU > 0.5 are used to compute regression loss.

3.3 Implementation Details

We use images of a single scale for both training and testing. Images are resized to a shorter side of 600 pixels. We use 8 anchors with 8 heights {4, 8, 16, 32, 64, 128, 256, 512}. Our model was implemented on Caffe. We follow the standard practice by exploring the VGG16 [3] pre-trained on ImageNet. The model was trained end-to-end by fixing the parameters in the first two convolutional layers. We initialize the new layers (e.g., conv6 and fc layers) by using random weights with Gaussian distribution. We used 0.9 momentum and 0.0005 weight decay. The learning rate is set to 0.001, while the iteration size is set to 10. In the first 10K iterations, a min-batch is formed by randomly selecting positive and negative samples. Then Online Hard Example Mining (OHEM) [27] was applied in the next 14K iterations.

4 Experimental Results and Comparisons

The proposed model is evaluated on two public benchmarks: MSRA-TD500 and SWT. The **MSTD-RA500** contains 500 natural images taken from both indoor and outdoor, including 300 training images and 200 test images. It contains arbitrary-oriented text in different languages (Chinese, English or mixture of both). We follow the evaluation protocol in [19]. The **SWT** dataset [15] consists of 307 color images with varied sizes, and is very challenging due to some extremely small-scale text.

We demonstrated our detector on a number of challenging images. As shown in Fig. 5 (left), our detector is able to correctly localize text regions of various languages, scales and orientation, even in highly challenging scenarios.

Fig. 5. Left: Correct detection samples; **Right**: Failure cases.

Performance Comparisons. The full results on both benchmarks are reported in Tables 1 and 2. We compared our performance against recently published results in [4, 8, 12, 13, 15, 19, 25, 26]. As shown in Table 1, our detector achieves promising results which are tied with state-of-the-art. It achieved the highest recall of 0.68 among the

Table 1. Comparisons on the MSRA-TD500 database.

Algorithm	Year	Recall	Precision	F-score	Time (s)
Epshtein et al. [15]	2010	0.25	0.25	0.25	6
TD-ICDAR [19]	2012	0.52	0.53	0.50	7.2
TD-Mixture [19]	2012	0.63	0.63	0.60	7.2
Yao et al. [28]	2014	0.62	0.64	0.61	7.2
Yin et al. [13]	2014	0.61	0.71	0.65	0.8
Kang et al. [25]	2014	0.62	0.71	0.66	–
Yin et al. [12]	2015	0.63	0.81	0.71	1.4
Zhang et al. [8]	2016	0.67	**0.83**	**0.74**	2.1
Ours	–	**0.68**	0.74	0.71	0.39

Table 2. Comparisons on the SWT database.

Algorithm	Year	Recall	Precision	F-score
Epshtein et al. [15]	2010	0.42	0.54	0.47
Mao et al. [26]	2013	0.41	0.58	0.48
Zhang et al. [8]	2015	0.53	**0.68**	0.60
CTPN [4]	2016	**0.65**	**0.68**	**0.66**
Ours	–	0.63	0.61	0.62

compared algorithms. On the SWT only including horizontal text, it is outperformed slightly by CTPN, which is particularly powerful to detect near-horizontal text, while our detector generalizes better to multi-orientation text.

Speed Comparison. As shown in Table 1, we investigate the running time of various methods. The average running time of our detector is 0.39 s/image GPU time (with the shorter side of 600 pixels), which is the fastest among all compared detectors.

Error Analysis. Figure 5 (right) shows a number of failure cases. Our detector is prone to fail in the following situations: (i) it is hard to predict the orientation of isolated text regions in square shape; (ii) closely placed text region with even character spaces and line spaces; (iii) characters with large margin tend to be separated; (iv) stroke-like background patterns.

5 Conclusion

We have introduced an end-to-end trainable framework, Orientation-Aware Text Proposals Network (OA-TPN), to detect arbitrary-oriented text lines in natural images. The OATPN detects a text line in a sequence of text proposals by using the anchor regression mechanism. We develop novel orientation-aware text proposal for efficiently encoding the rotation information. Furthermore, we propose a simple yet efficient text-line construction approach that clusters and groups text proposals into text lines. These key technical improvements result in a powerful text detector which is able to detect highly challenging text reliably with fewer false detections. Experimental results on the MSRA-TD500 and SWT demonstrate the effectiveness and efficiency of the proposed methods in comparisons with state-of-the-arts.

Acknowledgments. This work was supported in part by National Natural Science Foundation of China (U1613211, 61503367), Shenzhen basic research program (JCYJ20160229193541167, JCYJ20150401145529049), and Guangdong Research Program (2015B010129013, 2015A030310289).

References

1. Ma, J., Shao, W., Ye, H., Wang, L., Wang, H., Zheng, Y., Xue, X.: Arbitrary-oriented scene text detection via rotation proposals. arXiv preprint arXiv:1703.01086 (2017)
2. Shi, B., Bai, X., Belongie, S.: Detecting oriented text in natural images by linking segments. In: CVPR (2017)
3. Zhou, X., Yao, C., Wen, H., Wang, Y., Zhou, S., He, W., Liang, J.: EAST: an efficient and accurate scene text detector. In: CVPR (2017)
4. Tian, Z., Huang, W., He, T., He, P., Qiao, Y.: Detecting text in natural image with connectionist text proposal network. In: Leibe, B., Matas, J., Sebe, N., Welling, M. (eds.) ECCV 2016. LNCS, vol. 9912, pp. 56–72. Springer, Cham (2016). doi:10.1007/978-3-319-46484-8_4
5. Huang, W., Qiao, Y., Tang, X.: Robust scene text detection with convolution neural network induced MSER trees. In: Fleet, D., Pajdla, T., Schiele, B., Tuytelaars, T. (eds.) ECCV 2014. LNCS, vol. 8692, pp. 497–511. Springer, Cham (2014). doi:10.1007/978-3-319-10593-2_33
6. Liu, Y., Jin, L.: Deep matching prior network: toward tighter multi-oriented text detection. In: CVPR (2017)
7. Simonyan, K., Zisserman, A.: Very deep convolutional networks for large-scale image recognition. In: ICLR (2015)
8. Zhang, Z., Zhang, C., Shen, W., Yao, C., Liu, W., Bai, X.: Multi-oriented text detection with fully convolutional networks. In: CVPR (2016)
9. Long, J., Shelhamer, E., Darrell, T.: Fully convolutional networks for semantic segmentation. In: CVPR (2015)
10. Tian, S., Pan, Y., Huang, C., Lu, S., Yu, K., Tan, C.L.: Text flow: a unified text detection system in natural scene images. In: ICCV (2015)
11. Busta, M., Neumann, L., Matas, J.: Fastext: efficient unconstrained scene text detector. In: ICCV (2015)
12. Yin, X.C., Pei, W.Y., Zhang, J., Hao, H.W.: Multi-orientation scene text detection with adaptive clustering. PAMI 37(9), 1930–1937 (2015)
13. Yin, X.C., Yin, X., Huang, K., Hao, H.W.: Robust text detection in natural scene images. PAMI 36(5), 970–983 (2014)
14. Li, Y., Jia, W., Shen, C., van den Hengel, A.: Characterness: an indicator of text in the wild. IEEE Trans. Image Process. 23(4), 1666–1677 (2014)
15. Epshtein, B., Ofek, E., Wexler, Y.: Detecting text in natural scenes with stroke width transform. In: CVPR (2010)
16. Wang, K., Belongie, S.: Word spotting in the wild. In: Daniilidis, K., Maragos, P., Paragios, N. (eds.) ECCV 2010. LNCS, vol. 6311, pp. 591–604. Springer, Heidelberg (2010). doi:10.1007/978-3-642-15549-9_43

17. Bissacco, A., Cummins, M., Netzer, Y., Neven, H.: PhotoOCR: reading text in uncontrolled conditions. In: ICCV (2013)
18. Jaderberg, M., Vedaldi, A., Zisserman, A.: Deep features for text spotting. In: Fleet, D., Pajdla, T., Schiele, B., Tuytelaars, T. (eds.) ECCV 2014. LNCS, vol. 8692, pp. 512–528. Springer, Cham (2014). doi:10.1007/978-3-319-10593-2_34
19. Yao, C., Bai, X., Liu, W., Ma, Y., Tu, Z.: Detecting texts of arbitrary orientations in natural images. In: CVPR (2012)
20. Liao, M., Shi, B., Bai, X., Wang, X., Liu, W.: TextBoxes: a fast text detector with a single deep neural network. In: AAAI (2017)
21. Zhu, S., Zanibbi, R.: A text detection system for natural scenes with convolutional feature learning and cascaded classification. In: CVPR, pp. 625–632 (2016)
22. Yu, F., Koltun, V.: Multi-scale context aggregation by dilated convolutions. In: ICLR (2015)
23. Ren, S., He, K., Girshick, R., Sun, J.: Faster R-CNN: towards real-time object detection with region proposal networks. In: NIPS (2015)
24. Girshick, R.: Fast R-CNN. In: ICCV (2015)
25. Kang, L., Li, Y., Doermann, D.: Orientation robust text line detection in natural images. In: CVPR (2014)
26. Mao, J., Li, H., Zhou, W., Yan, S., Tian, Q.: Scale based region growing for scene text detection. In: Proceedings of ACM International Conference on Multimedia (ACM MM) (2013)
27. Shrivastava, A., Gupta, A., Girshick, R.: Training region-based object detectors with online hard example mining. In: CVPR (2016)
28. Yao, C., Bai, X., Liu, W.: A unified framework for multioriented text detection and recognition. IEEE Trans. Image Process. **23**, 4737–4749 (2014)

Uyghur Off-Line Signature Recognition Based on Local Central Line Features

Kurban Ubul[1], Ya-li Zhu[1], Mutallip Mamut[2], Nurbiya Yadikar[1], and Tuergen Yibulayin[1(✉)]

[1] School of Information Science and Engineering,
Xinjiang University, Shengli Road No. 666, Urumqi 830046, China
{kurbanu, turgun}@xju.edu.cn
[2] Library of Xinjiang University,
Shengli Road No. 666, Urumqi 830046, China

Abstract. In this paper, a local central line features based off-line signature recognition method proposed for Uyghur handwritten signature. The signature images were pre-processed based on the nature of Uyghur signature firstly. Then global central line features (GCLF-16, GCLF-24, and GCLF-32), local central line features from two horizontally centers (2LCLF-16H, 2LCLF-24H, and 2LCLF-32H) and local central line features from two vertically centers (2LCLF-16V, 2LCLF-24V, and 2LCLF-32V) were extracted respectively. Experiments were performed using Euclidean distance based similarity measuring method and non-linear SVM classifier for Uyghur signature samples from 75 different people with 1500 signatures, two kinds of experiments were performed for and variations in the number of training and testing datasets, and a high recognition rate of 96.8% was achieved with 2LCLF-32H. The experimental results indicated that modified corner curve features in this paper can efficiently capture the writing style of Uyghur signature.

Keywords: Uyghur · Off-line · Handwritten signature · Local central line features · Recognition

1 Introduction

Handwritten signature is one of the commonly used behavioural characteristics in biometric based human identity identification [1]. The aim of the recognition is to identify the signer of a given sample, and the purpose of verification is to confirm or reject the sample.

Survey papers [1–4] summarized many techniques appeared in the area of automatic signature recognition and verification in recent 20 years. An off-line Arabic signature recognition and verification system was proposed in [5] that a combination of global and local based features and the multi-stage classifier was used in recognition step, and a fuzzy concept was used in its verification step. Yilmaz and Yanıkoğlu [6] were presented a system which is used different local features such as histogram of oriented gradients (HOG), local binary patterns (LBP) and scale invariant feature transform (SIFT) descriptors, and a score-level fusion of complementary classifiers.

© Springer International Publishing AG 2017
J. Zhou et al. (Eds.): CCBR 2017, LNCS 10568, pp. 750–758, 2017.
https://doi.org/10.1007/978-3-319-69923-3_80

Porwik et al. [7] used k-NN classifier and self-adaptive hotelling data reduction technique in handwritten signatures recognition. Kudłacik and Porwik [8] presented characteristic feature extraction based a new fuzzy approach for off-line handwritten signature recognition. Ghandali and Moghaddam [9] proposed an off-line Persian signature identification and verification scheme based on image registration, discrete wavelet transform and image fusion. These reports about signature recognition and verifications were mostly based on Latin signatures, Chinese signatures, Arabic signatures, Persian signatures, and so on. However, only a few reports that are our previous research were published for off-line Uyghur signature recognition. For Uyghur handwritten signature recognition, modified grid information features [10], combining of directional features and local central features [11] and density features [12] was proposed respectively, and thinning effects on the recognition rate was studied in [13]. So there is enough research room for studying Uyghur handwritten signatures by realizing existed algorithms creatively or developing new algorithms based on the nature of Uyghur signature.

2   Feature Extraction

The common steps for signature recognition include data acquisition, pre-processing, feature extraction and classification. Since pre-processing is not key point in here and it was adapted to the nature of Uyghur signature in our previous work [13], so it is omitted to describe them again. It was extracted global central line features (GCLF) described in [5], and the local central line features from two centres (abbreviated as 2LCLF) were extracted respectively in this work here.

Global Central Line Features (GCLF). The GCLF composed of the crossed point's coordinates which lines crossed with black pixels of signatures. Assume that, there are 16 lines started from the point O which is also called centre point of lines, and they are crossed with a signature. The central lines and crossed points were illustrated as the follo GCLF is:g Fig. 1:

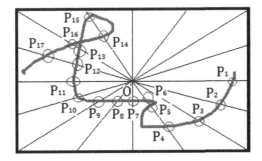

Fig. 1. The central lines and crossed points

In Fig. 1, these 16 lines are crossed with the signature in 17 points, such as $P_1(x_1, y_1)$, $P_2(x_2, y_2)$, ..., and $P_{17}(x_{17}, y_{17})$ respectively. Thus, the GCLF composed coordinates of n crossed points $P_1(x_1, y_1)$, $P2(x_2, y_2)$, ..., $P_n(x_n, y_n)$, and the GCLF is:

$$F = [P_1, P_2, \ldots, P_n] = [x_1, y_1, x_2, y_2, \ldots, x_n, y_n] \qquad (1)$$

where, the coordinate of central point is $O(0, 0)$, and coordinates of points xi, yi ($i = 1$, 2, ..., n) are distributed on the four quadrant of rectangular coordinate system.

Since the size of Uyghur signature image is normalized to 384×96 based on the nature of Uyghur signature, and the angles between the two neighbour lines was to be selected as equal for quantifying the feature and it is selected as 16 lines, 24 lines and 32 lines separately in this paper. They are abbreviated as GCLF-16, GCLF-24 and GCLF-32 separately. Because the variety of Uyghur handwritten signature, there are several crossed points in some lines and there is no crossed point in some lines, such as illustrated as the following Fig. 2:

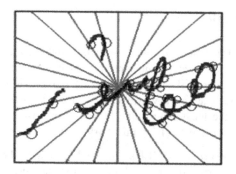

Fig. 2. Crossed points in a Uyghur handwritten signature

It can be seen from Fig. 2 that the numbers of crossed points are different in lines to lines. It is pointed out that, only one word is illustrated in Fig. 2, and common Uyghur signature is composed of two words, first name and surname, and first name comes first. It is complicated if the crossed points are concerned in the two words in a Uyghur signature. This phenomenon was became much more complex if different kinds of Uyghur signatures are concerned when feature extraction.

For quantifying the feature extraction and feature matching, only one (first) point in a line is selected, and its coordinates is set zero if there is no crossed point in a line in this paper. If there is no crossed points in i th ($1 < i < n$) lines, this kind of point is called blank point, and the coordinate of related point $Pi(0, 0)$. Thus GCLF is:

$$F = [P_1, P_2, \ldots, P_i, \ldots, P_n] = [x_1, y_1, x_2, y_2, \ldots, 0, 0, \ldots, x_n, y_n] \qquad (2)$$

where, $1 < i < n$, and there is only one blank point among selected points. The related coordinates are taken zero is if there are many blank points. For GCLF-24 here, the angles between the two lines is $\theta_i = 360°/24$, and it include 24 central lines, and 24 crossed points were selected from these 24 lines in Uyghur signature, thus 48 dimensional GCLF is extracted. Similarity, it is extracted 32 and 64 dimensional GCLF features were extracted with GCLF-16 and GCLF-32 respectively.

The Local Central Line Features from Two Centres (2LCLF). The local central line features from two centres (2LCLF) is composed of coordinates of crossed points which are selected from different lines from two original (central) points at the same time. The two local central points are located the centre of each subarea of signature after dividing 2 parts horizontally or vertically. Then, several lines are originated from each of the central point. The points crossed with central line and signatures in the 2 kinds of situation are illustrated as the following Fig. 3.

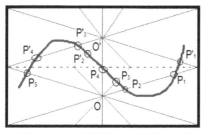 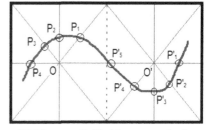

(a) The area divided 2 parts horizontally   (b) The area divided 2 parts vertically

Fig. 3. The points of 2LCLF with different division

It is indicated the area divided in 2 parts horizontally and vertically in Fig. 3(a) and (b) respectively. O and O′ is the central points of the lines, and they are located vertically and horizontally in the two circumstances. There are 10 lines originated from each centre in Fig. 3(a), similarly, 8 lines originated from each centre in Fig. 3(b), and there are 9 crossed points each of them. The LCLF indicated in Fig. 3(a) abbreviated as 2LCLF-10H in this paper, where 10 refers to the lines from each centre, and H is refers to the area divided horizontally. Assume that, there are 2 centres O and O′, the number of lines centred from them are n and m respectively. Thus the 2LCLF include crossed n points P1(x1, y1), P2(x2, y2), ..., Pn(xn, yn) from the centre O, and crossed m points $P'_1(x'_1, y'_1), P'_2(x'_2, y'_2), \ldots P'_m(x'_m, y'_m)$ from the centre O′, the feature vector is:

$$F = [p_1, p_2, \ldots, p_n; \ p'_1, p'_2, \ldots, p'_m]$$
$$= [x_1, y_1, x_2, y_2, \ldots, x_n, y_n; \ x'_1, y'_1, x'_2, y'_2, \ldots, x'_m, y'_m] \tag{3}$$

where n, m is the number of point selected from lines originated from the two central pointes O and O′ respectively. All the lines are distributed on the four quadrant of rectangular coordinate system. All the feature extraction rules of 2LCLF are same as the GCLF except the number originated central points. Thus, the numbers of features are doubled in 2LCLF compared with GCLF. So, it is extracted 128, 96 and 64 dimensional features were extracted with 2LCLF-32, 2LCLF-24 and 2LCLF-16 separately.

3   Classification

The Euclidean distance based similarity measuring method and Support Vector Machine (SVM) classifier are used in classification.

Euclidean Distance. The Euclidean distance between X_1 and X_2 is just the Euclidean length of this distance (or displacement) vector:

$$d_{12} = \sqrt{\sum_{k=1}^{n} (x_{1k} - x_{2k})^2} \tag{4}$$

where x_{1k} and x_{2k} are the elements of two different eigenvectors X_1 and X_2 respectively.

SVM Classifier. The SVM classifier is to be selected here since it has more accuracy than liner one and other. If the weight vector can be expressed as a linear combination of the training examples, i.e. $w = \sum_{i=1}^{n} a_i x_i$, then:

$$f(x) = \sum_{i=1}^{n} a_i x_i^T x + b \tag{5}$$

In the feature space F, this expression takes the form:

$$f(x) = \sum_{i=1}^{n} a_i \phi(x_i)^T \phi(x) + b \tag{6}$$

The representation in terms of the variables α_i is known as the dual representation of the decision boundary. The feature space F may be high dimensional as indicated Eq. (10), making this trick impractical unless the Gaussian kernel function $k\,(x, x_i)$ can be computed efficiently denoted as:

$$k(x, x') = \exp\{-\frac{\|x - x_i\|}{\sigma^2}\} \tag{7}$$

In terms of the kernel function the discriminate function is:

$$f(x) = \sum_{i=1}^{n} a_i k(x, x_i) + b \tag{8}$$

4   Experimental Results

Euclidean distance based similarity measuring method and non-linear SVM classifier were used in classification. To the experiment, 1500 samples collected from 75 Uyghur people (20 samples per person) were selected from in our database [12]. Three types

CCF and MCCF features were extracted respectively after pre-processing. Two kinds of experiments were performed based on the training data set with 1200 and 750 images from the database separately. The rest of the signature images of the data set were separately used as the testing data set. For the distribution of the training and test set, take 1200 samples for training as an example, 16 samples of each class was used for the training, and rest of them are used for the testing.

Signature Recognition Results with Euclidean Distance. The experimental results using Euclidean distance based similarity measuring method when 750 and 1200 signatures were trained respectively are indicated in Table 1 as below.

Table 1. Signature recognition results with Euclidean distance

Features	Trial	
	Training 750 samples	Training 1200 samples
GCLF-16	70.1%	74.5%
GCLF-24	74.3%	77.8%
GCLF-32	79.2%	83.2%
2LCLF-16V	74.9%	80.9%
2LCLF-24V	79.4%	84.4%
2LCLF-32V	81.8%	85.3%
2LCLF-16H	78.5%	82.9%
2LCLF-24H	81.4%	85.0%
2LCLF-32H	82.3%	86.3%

It can be seen from the Table 1 that the 86.3% of highest recognition rate was achieved when 2LCLF-32H were extracted during Euclidean distance based similarity measuring method of training 1200 dataset. While the other features were indicated lower recognition rate than 2LCLF-32. Similarity, 2LCLF-xH is more efficient than GCLF and 2LCLF-xV with the same number of features. The average identification rates decreased if the number of training samples was reduced to 750 samples, and the 82.3% of highest accuracy was obtained in this kind of experiment. The accuracy of signature recognition using non-liner SVM classifier based trial of training 800 and 500 signature image dataset indicated as in the following Table 2.

Signature Recognition Results with SVM Classifier. The experimental results using SVM classifier when 750 and 1200 genuine signatures were trained respectively were illustrated as the following Table 2.

It was clear from the Table 2 that the 96.8% of highest recognition rate in this paper was obtained when 2LCLF-32H was extracted using non-linear SVM classifier based trial of training 1200 dataset. While the other features were indicated lower recognition rate than 2LCLF-32 in this kind of experiment. Similarity, 2LCLF-xH is more efficient than GCLF and 2LCLF-xV with the same number of features. The average identification rates decreased if the number of training samples was reduced to 750 samples, and the 93.9% of highest accuracy was obtained in this experiment.

Table 2. Signature recognition results with SVM classifier

Features	Trial	
	Training 750 samples	Training 1200 samples
GCLF-16	78.6%	81.2%
GCLF-24	81.8%	84.6%
GCLF-32	88.5%	90.9%
2LCLF-16V	88.2%	90.7%
2LCLF-24V	90.0%	92.5%
2LCLF-32V	92.3%	94.6%
2LCLF-16H	88.7%	91.3%
2LCLF-24H	91.4%	94.1%
2LCLF-32H	93.9%	96.8%

It can be seen from the two tables (Tables 1 and 2) that non-linear SVM classifier indicates higher accuracy than Euclidean distance based similarity measuring method with GCLF and 2LCLF, that is, its identification rates is at least 7.5% higher than Euclidean distances' both the two kinds of experiments. 2LCLF-32 was indicates higher identification rates than 2LCLF-16, and 2LCLF-24 during the same kind of experiment; similarity, 2LCLF-xH is more efficient than GCLF and 2LCLF-xV. The accuracy of 2LCLF-32H was about 3.5% higher than accuracy of 2LCLF-32V.

5   Discussion

For validating the efficiency of the proposed method, its related parameters of the system and datasets are compared with related reports [10–13]. The comparison of Uyghur signature recognition methods, which is including techniques, size of datasets in the experiments and experimental results are indicated as the following Table 3.

Table 3. Comparison of Uyghur signature recognition methods

References	Features	Classifier	Dataset size	Training data	Accuracy
Ubul et al. [10]	Modified grid information features	KNN classifier	1000 samples	800 samples	93.53%
Ubul et al. [13]	Directional features using thinned samples	Chi-square distance	1000 samples	800 samples	96.0%
Abliz et al. [11]	Directional and local central point features	Chi-square distance	1000 samples	800 samples	98.5%
Ubul et al. [12]	Density feature	Vector distance	1500 samples	1200 samples	96.0%
This paper	2LCLF-32H	SVM classifier	1500 samples	1200 samples	96.8%

Table 3 presents the experimental results lower than report [11], but the size of dataset used in here is larger than that report. So, the contrast experiments using same dataset with [11] were conducted. It was obtained 99.0% of accuracy during the experiment using SVM with 2LCLF-32H. So the proposed method indicated higher accuracy than the report [11].

6 Conclusion

In this paper, a local central line features based off-line signature recognition method proposed for Uyghur handwritten signature in this paper. The signature images were pre-processed based on the nature of Uyghur signature. Then global central line features (GCLF-16, GCLF-24, and GCLF-32), local central line features from two horizontally centers (2LCLF-16H, 2LCLF-24H, and 2LCLF-32H) and local central line features from two vertically centers (2LCLF-16V, 2LCLF-24V, and 2LCLF-32V) were extracted respectively. Experiments were performed using Euclidean distance based similarity measuring method and non-linear SVM classifier for Uyghur signature samples from 75 different people with 1500 signatures, two kinds of experiments were performed for and variations in the number of training and testing datasets, and a high recognition rate of 96.8% was achieved with 2LCLF-32H. It can be pointed out from the experimental results that this kind of local centre line features based recognition method can capture the nature of Uyghur signature more efficiently.

In future work, this methods proposed in this paper will upgraded by including more signatures in the database, exploring more efficient features, and performing more experiments with other efficient methods and algorithms.

Acknowledgements. This work is supported by the National Natural Science Foundation of China (Nos. 61163028, 61563052, 61363064).

References

1. Plamondon, R., Srihari, S.N.: On-line and off-line handwriting recognition: a comprehensive survey. IEEE Trans. PAMI **22**(1), 63–84 (2000)
2. Impedovo, D., Pirlo, G.: Automatic signature verification: the state of the art. IEEE Trans. Syst. Man Cybern. Part C **38**(5), 60–75 (2008)
3. Bhosale, V., Karwankar, A.: Automatic static signature verification systems: a review. Int. J. Comput. Eng. Res. **3**(2), 8–12 (2013)
4. Ubul, K., Ablikim, R., Yadikar, N., Zunun, M.: Non-Western script based off-line handwritten signature technology: a survey. Appl. Mech. Mater. **519**, 606–610 (2014)
5. Ismail, M.A., Gad, S.: Off-line Arabic signature recognition and verification. Pattern Recogn. **33**(10), 1727–1740 (2000)
6. Yılmaz, M.B., Yanıkoğlu, B.: Score level fusion of classifiers in off-line signature verification. Inf. Fus. **32**, 109–119 (2016)
7. Porwik, P., Doroz, R., Orczyk, T.: The k-NN classifier and self-adaptive Hotelling data reduction technique in handwritten signatures recognition. Pattern Anal. Appl. **18**, 983–1001 (2015)
8. Kudłacik, P., Porwik, P.: A new approach to signature recognition using the fuzzy method. Pattern Anal. Appl. **17**, 451–463 (2014)

9. Ghandali, S., Moghaddam, M.E.: Off-line Persian signature identification and verification based on image registration and fusion. J. Multimedia **4**, 137–144 (2009)

10. Ubul, K., Adler, A., Abliz, G., Yasin, M., Hamdulla, A.: Off-line Uyghur signature recognition based on modified grid information features. In: Proceedings of 11th International Conference on Information Sciences, Signal Processing and Their Applications (ISSPA 2012), Montreal, Canada, pp. 182–188 (2012)

11. Abliz, G., Ubul, K., Moyidin, K., Hamdulla, A.: Research on off-line Uyghur signature recognition technology based on multi resolution geometric features. Comput. Eng. Appl. **49** (16), 168–171 (2013). (in Chinese)

12. Ubul, K., Ablikim, R., Yadikar, N., Aysa, A., Yibulayin, T.: Off-line Uyghur signature recognition technology based on density feature. Comput. Eng. Des. **37**(8), 2200–2205 (2016). (in Chinese)

13. Ubul, K., Adler, A., Yadikar, N.: Effects on accuracy of Uyghur handwritten signature recognition. Commun. Comput. Inf. Sci. **321**(6), 548–555 (2012)

Author Index